WHAT THE BIBLE TEACHES

R.A. TORREY

W Whitaker House

WHAT THE BIBLE TEACHES

ISBN: 0-88368-400-4
Printed in the United States of America
Copyright © 1996 by Whitaker House

Whitaker House
580 Pittsburgh Street
Springdale, PA 15144

1 2 3 4 5 6 7 8 9 10 11 12 13 / 06 05 04 03 02 01 00 99 98 97 96

PREFACE.

This book represents years of study. Its contents have been tested again and again in the classroom—in classes composed, in some instances, of representatives of thirty-six denominations. However, it is not supposed for a moment that it exhausts all the Bible has to say on the topics treated, much less that it takes up and exhausts every topic dealt with in the Bible. The Bible is the one inexhaustible book. This work is simply an attempt at a careful, unbiased, systematic, thorough-going, *inductive* study and statement of Bible truth. The method of the book is rigidly inductive. The material contained in the Bible is brought together, carefully scrutinized, and then what is seen to be contained in it stated in the most exact terms possible. Exactness of statement is first aimed at in every instance, then clearness of statement. Beauty and impressiveness must always yield to precision and clearness. The scripture from which a proposition is deduced is always given before the proposition. The methods of modern science are applied to Bible study—thorough analysis followed by careful synthesis. Though no Hebrew nor Greek words appear in the work, it is based upon a careful study of the original text as decided by the best textual critics (especially Tischendorf and Westcott and Hort in the New Testament, though other editors, and the manuscripts themselves, have been considered in some instances). Wherever possible the text of the Authorized Version has been given. In many instances this was impossible, as the Revised Version is manifestly much more exact. Had it appeared that the Revised Version would soon obtain that general acceptance and use which it seems to

so richly deserve, the author would have adopted it through
out; except in those rare instances where it is manifestly in
error.   In very few instances, indeed, has it been necessary to
adopt renderings differing from both the Authorized Version
and the Revised Version, and from the American Appendix
to the Revised Version.

Some of the propositions in this book may appear new
and even startling to many, but it is believed that they fairly
and exactly state the contents of the passages upon which
they are based.

It is hoped that the book will prove of interest and help,
both to those who believe in the Divine origin of the Bible
and to those who do not.   One of the most satisfactory ways
of determining whether the Bible is of Divine origin or not, is
by finding out precisely what it teaches and whether there is
one deep philosophy running through the book composed
by such a multiplicity and variety of human authors.   The
writer must confess that his own conviction that there was
one Author back of the many writers, and that that one
Author was God, has ever deepened as he studied.

Just the suggestion of a few ways in which this book can
be used with profit:

Its most apparent use is as a classbook in Bible Theology,
its arrangement by sections and propositions having had
such use in mind.   The book can also be used in family
devotions by those who desire something more orderly, systematic and thorough than the methods usually employed
in this important, but neglected, department of Christian
culture.

It is hoped that it may be helpful also in private devotional study of the Bible.   While the book aims to be
scientific, it is not cold.   Too much devotional study of the
Bible is haphazard.   By the use of this book it can be made
orderly, thorough and progressive.

The author has received numerous letters from groups of
believers where there were no churches, and from other

groups in various churches, asking for a definite outline of Bible study, and trusts that this book may be helpful in many such cases. Why, for example, could not groups of Christians who are shut out from ordinary church privileges gather together and study the Bible itself with the help of this book?

In all study of the book the scriptures given should first be pondered carefully; the reader should then put his own understanding of the contents of those scriptures, in respect of the subject in hand, into his own language before considering the author's statement in the proposition. In many instances the reader will thus be able to improve upon the author's statement; if not, he will understand it and appreciate it all the more for having done a little thinking for himself.

TABLE OF CONTENTS.

ment of the sinner—The holiness of God manifested in an infinite sacrifice to save others from sin to holiness—Practical inferences from the holiness of God: Must draw nigh to God with awe, the blackness of our sin as seen in the white light of His holiness, the wonderfulness of the love of a holy God to sinful men.

God is love—What does "love" mean—Whom does God love—His love to sinners and to saints compared—How the love of God is manifested.

God is righteous—What does righteous mean—The ordinary conception of the righteousness of God unbiblical—How the righteousness of God is manifested—The righteousness of God in its relation to the protection of His people more prominent in the Bible than His righteousness in relation to the punishment of sinners.

"Mercy" and "loving-kindness" different translations of the same word—Primary meaning of the word—God is plenteous in mercy—Toward whom the mercy of God is manifested—How the mercy of God is manifested.

God is faithful—What faithful means; etymology and usage of the Hebrew and Greek words translated "faithful"—The extent of God's faithfulness—How the faithfulness of God is manifested.

BOOK II.—WHAT THE BIBLE TEACHES ABOUT JESUS CHRIST.

Sixteen names clearly implying Deity used of Christ—Five or more distinctively Divine attributes ascribed to Jesus Christ—Seven distinctively Divine offices predicated of Jesus Christ—Very many statements, which in the O. T. are distinctively made of Jehovah God, taken in the N. T. to refer to Jesus Christ—The name of Jesus Christ coupled again and again with that of God the Father in a way in which it would be impossible to couple the name of any finite being with that of the Deity—Divine worship to be rendered to Jesus Christ by angels and men—The awful guilt of rejecting the Divine Christ.

The Father greater than Jesus Christ the Son—The Father begat Jesus Christ the Son—The Son can do nothing independently of the Father—The Son sent by and receiving all His authority from the Father—Jesus Christ shall ultimately deliver up His kingdom to the Father—God the Father, not Jesus Christ the Son, the ultimate goal—God the Father is Jesus Christ's God—Jesus Christ is, and eternally shall be, subordinated to God the Father.

CHAPTER III.—THE HUMAN NATURE OF JESUS CHRIST, 89

Human names, Son of Man, etc.—Human physical nature—Human parentage—Human limitations, physical, intellectual and moral—Subject to all the intellectual and moral limitations essential to human nature—Limitations of power—Human relation to God—Human in all things; in every respect a real man--How reconcile the Bible doctrine of the true Deity of Jesus Christ with the Bible doctrine of the real human nature of Christ.

CHAPTER IV.—THE CHARACTER OF JESUS CHRIST, 97

Section I. The Holiness of Jesus Christ: Jesus Christ is holy, absolutely holy, the Holy One—How the holiness of Jesus Christ manifests itself—Witnesses to the holiness of Jesus Christ.
Section II. The Love of Jesus Christ to God the Father: The one thing that Jesus Christ desired the world to know about Himself was that He loved the Father—How the love of Jesus Christ to the Father manifested itself.
Section III. The Love of Jesus Christ to Men: Whom among men did Jesus Christ love—His general love and His special love—How the love of Jesus Christ to men has manifested itself, is manifesting itself, and will manifest itself " in the ages to come."
Section IV. Jesus Christ's Love for Souls: The purpose of His coming into the world—His watch for and pursuit of the lost—His joy over souls saved—His grief over lost souls that refused to be saved—His sacrifice to save souls.
Section V. The Compassion of Christ: The objects of Christ's compassion—The way in which the compassion of Christ was manifested.
Section VI. The Prayerfulness of Jesus Christ: Jesus Christ was a man of prayer—When Christ prayed—Where Christ prayed—With whom Christ prayed—In whose behalf Christ prayed—How Christ prayed—The effect of Christ's prayers.
Section VII. The Meekness and Gentleness of Jesus Christ: What is meekness—How the meekness of Christ was manifested.
Section VIII. The Humility of Jesus Christ: Ten ways in which the humility of Christ manifested itself.

CHAPTER V.—THE DEATH OF JESUS CHRIST, - - - 144

The importance of His death—The purpose of His death—For whom Christ died—The results of Christ's death: (1) In relation to men in general, (2) In relation to believers, (3) In relation to the Devil and his angels, (4) In relation to the material universe—The purging of the heavenly things by the atoning blood of Christ—The immense sweep of the atonement.

CHAPTER VI.—THE RESURRECTION OF JESUS CHRIST, - 166

The Resurrection of Christ the Gibraltar of Christian evidences and Waterloo of Rationalism and Infidelity—The conclusive and unanswerable proof that Jesus was raised from the dead—Admissions of Strauss, Baur, Schenkel and Renan—The doctrinal importance of the Resurrection of Christ—The manner of the Resurrection—The results of the Resurrection.

CHAPTER VII.—THE ASCENSION OR EXALTATION OF JESUS CHRIST, - - - - - - - - - 187

The fact of the Ascension—The manner of the Ascension and Exaltation—The purpose of the Exaltation of Jesus Christ—The results of the Exaltation.

BOOK IV.—WHAT THE BIBLE TEACHES ABOUT MAN.

BOOK V.—WHAT THE BIBLE TEACHES ABOUT ANGELS.

BOOK VI.—WHAT THE BIBLE TEACHES ABOUT THE DEVIL, OR SATAN.

BOOK I.

—

WHAT THE BIBLE TEACHES ABOUT GOD.

BOOK I.

WHAT THE BIBLE TEACHES ABOUT GOD

CHAPTER I.

GOD AS SPIRIT.

As the aim of this book is to ascertain and state in system-atic form what the Bible teaches, the method pursued will be to first give the Scripture statements, and then sum up their contents in a proposition, following the proposition by such comments as may appear necessary.

I. The fact that God is Spirit.

Jno. 4: 24—" *God is (a) Spirit:* and they that worship him must worship him in spirit and in truth."

FIRST PROPOSITION: God is Spirit.

QUESTION: What is spirit?

ANSWER: Luke 24: 39—"Behold my hands and my feet, that it is I myself: handle me and see; for a spirit hath not flesh and bones, as ye see me have." A spirit is incorporeal, invisible reality. To say God is spirit is to say God is incorporeal and invisible. (Compare Deut., 4: 15-18.)

QUESTION: What does it mean, then, when it says in Gen. 1: 27: "God created man *in his own image?*"

The answer to this question is plainly given in the following passages:

Col. 3: 10—"And have put on the new man, which is renewed *in knowledge after the image* of him that created him."

Eph. 4: 23, 24—"And be renewed in the spirit of your mind; and that ye put on the new man, which, *after God*, is created *in righteousness and true holiness.*"

Col. 1: 15—"Who is *the image of* the *invisible* God, the first-born of every creature." (Compare 1 Tim. 1: 17.)

The words "image" and "likeness" evidently do not refer to visible or bodily likeness, but to intellectual and moral likeness—likeness "in knowledge," "righteousness" and "holiness of truth."

II. The manifestation of Spirit in visible form.

> Jno. 1:32—"And John bare record, saying, I saw the Spirit descending from heaven *like a dove*, and it abode upon him."
> Heb. 1:7—"And of the angels he saith, who maketh his angels spirits and his ministers a flame of fire."

SECOND PROPOSITION: <u>*That which is spirit may manifest itself in visible form.*</u>

III. God manifested in visible form.

> Ex. 24:9, 10—"Then went up Moses, and Aaron, Nadab and Abihu: and seventy of the elders of Israel; <u>and *they saw* the God of Israel</u>, and there was under his feet as it were a paved work of sapphire stone, and as it were the body of heaven in his clearness."

THIRD PROPOSITION: *God has in times past manifested Himself in visible form.*

V. What was seen in these manifestations of God.

> Jno. 1:18—"*No man hath seen God at any time;* the only begotten Son, which is in the bosom of the Father, he hath declared Him."
> Ex. 33:18-23—"And he said, I beseech thee, show me thy glory. And he said, I will make all my goodness pass before thee, and I will proclaim the name of the Lord before thee; and will be gracious to whom I will be gracious, and will show mercy on whom I will show mercy. And he said, Thou *canst not see my face*, for there shall no man *see me* and live. And the Lord said, Behold, there is a place by me, and thou shalt stand upon a rock. And it shall come to pass, while my glory passeth by, that I will put thee in a cleft of the rock, and I will cover thee with my hand while I pass by. And I will take away my hand, and *thou shalt see my back parts*, but *my face shall not be seen.*"

FOURTH PROPOSITION: *That which was seen in these manifestations of God was not God Himself—God in His invisible essence—but a manifestation of God.*

QUESTION: Is there any contradiction between Ex. 24:9, 10 ("Then went up Moses, and Aaron, Nadab and Abihu, and seventy of the elders of Israel; and *they saw the God of Israel*"), Is. 6:1 ("In the year that king Uzziah died <u>I saw also the Lord</u> sitting upon a throne, high and lifted up, and his train filled the temple"), and

Jno. 1:18 ("No man hath seen God at any time; the only begotten Son, which is in the bosom of the Father, he hath declared Him")?

ANSWER: None whatever. To illustrate: A man may see the reflection of his face in a glass. It would be true for the man to say "I saw my face," and also true to say "I never saw my face." So men have seen a manifestation of God, and it is perfectly true to say those men saw God. No man ever saw God as He is in His invisible essence, and so it is perfectly true to say: "No man hath seen God at any time."

Under this head of manifestations of God belongs "The angel of the LORD" in O. T. Clear distinction is drawn in the Bible in the original languages between " An angel of the Lord " and "The angel of the Lord." The R.V. always preserves this distinction; the A.V. does not.

Gen. 16: 7-10, 13—" And the angel of the LORD found her by a fountain of water in the wilderness, by the fountain in the way to Shur. And he said, Hagar, Sarai's maid, whence comest thou and whither wilt thou go? And she said, I flee from the face of my mistress Sarai. And the angel of the LORD said unto her, return to thy mistress, and submit thyself unto her hands. And *the angel of the* LORD said unto her, *I will multiply* thy seed exceedingly, that it shall not be numbered for multitude. And she called *the name of the Lord that spake unto her*, Thou God seest me: for she said, Have I also here looked after him that seeth me ? "

Here " the angel of the LORD " in verse 10 is clearly identified with the Lord (Jehovah) in verse 13.

Gen. 21: 17, 18—"And God heard the voice of the lad: and *the angel of God* called to Hagar out of heaven, and said unto her, What aileth thee, Hagar? fear not; for *God hath heard* the voice of the lad where he is Arise, lift up the lad, and hold him in thy hand; for *I will make him a great nation.*"

Gen. 22: 11, 12—" And the angel of the LORD called unto him out of heaven and said, Abraham, Abraham: and he said, Here am I. And he said, Lay not thine hand upon the lad, neither do thou anything unto him; for now I know that thou fearest God, seeing thou hast not withheld thy son, thine only son, *from me.*"

Here " the angel of the LORD " in verse 11 is identified with God in verse 12.

Judges 2: 1, 2, R.V.—" And the angel of the LORD came up from Gilgal to Bochim, and he said, *I* made you to go up out of Egypt, and have brought you unto the land which *I* sware unto your fathers: and *I said, I* will never break my covenant with you: And ye shall make no covenant with the inhabitants of this land; ye shall throw down their altars: but ye have not hearkened to MY voice; why have ye done this? "

Here " the angel of the LORD " distinctly says " *I* " did what Jehovah did.   (See also Judges 6:11-14, 19-24, R.V., especially verse 14.)

A very noteworthy passage is:

Gen. 18: 1, 2, 9, 10, 13, 14, 16—"And *the* LORD appeared unto him in the plains of Mamre, and he sat in the tent door in the heat of the day. And he lifted up his eyes and looked, and, lo, *three* men stood by him: and when he saw them he ran to meet them from the tent door, and bowed himself toward the ground.   And they said unto him, Where is Sarah, thy wife?   And he said, Behold in the tent.   And *he said*, *I* will certainly return unto thee according to the time of life, and, lo, Sarah, thy wife, shall have a son.   And Sarah heard it in the tent door, which was behind him.   And *the* LORD said unto Abraham, wherefore did Sarah laugh, saying, Shall I of a surety bear a child, which am old ?   Is anything too hard for the LORD ?   At the time appointed I will return unto thee, according to the time of life, and Sarah shall have a son.   And the men rose up from thence, and looked toward Sodom; and Abraham wènt with them to bring them on the way."

In these verses one of the three clearly identifies himself with the LORD or Jehovah.   In the nineteenth chapter (v. 1) only two come to Sodom.   One has remained behind, two have gone on.   Who the one was, appears as we read on.

Gen. 18: 17, 20—And *the* LORD *said*, Shall *I* hide from Abraham that thing which *I* do.   Seeing that Abraham shall surely become a great and mighty nation, and all the nations of the earth shall be blessed in him·?   For *I* know him, that he will command his children and his household after him, and they shall keep the way of the LORD, to do justice and judgment; that the LORD may bring upon Abraham that which he hath spoken of him.   And *the* LORD *said*, because the cry of Sodom and Gomorrah is great, and because their sin is very grievous."

Then in verse 22 we read: "Abraham stood yet before the LORD (Jehovah)."   Clearly the one of the three who remained behind was Jehovah manifested in the form of a man.   In verse 33 the story continues: "The' LORD (Jehovah) went his way as soon as he had left communing with Abraham."   (See also chapter 19: 27.)

FIFTH PROPOSITION: The angel of the Lord is clearly identified with Jehovah—a visible manifestation of Jehovah.

QUESTION: Just who was this "The angel of the LORD ? "

Judges 13: 18, R.V.—"And the angel of the LORD said unto him, Wherefore asketh thou after my name, seeing it is *wonderful?*"

Compare Isaiah 9: 6—"For unto us a child is born unto us a son is given; and the government shall be upon his shoulder; and his name shall be called *Wonderful*, Counsellor, The mighty God, The everlasting Father, The Prince of Peace."

(In the Hebrew, the word for " wonderful " in the passage in which " the angel of the LORD " gives it as his name, is practically the same as the word in Isaiah, where it is given as the name of the coming Christ.)

Mal. 3:1—" Behold, I will send *my messenger*, and he shall prepare the way before me; and the Lord, whom ye seek, shall suddenly come to his temple, *even the messenger of the covenant*, whom ye delight in: behold he shall come, saith the Lord of hosts."

ANSWER: The angel of the Lord was the Son of God before His permanent incarnation. (See also Jno. 8:56—" Your father Abraham rejoiced to see *my* day: and he saw it, and was glad.")

" The angel of the Lord " does not appear after birth of Christ. The expression occurs in A.V., but is always a mistranslation, as the R.V. shows. (See Matt. 1:20, 28:2; Luke 2:9; Acts 8:26; 12:7, 23.)

CHAPTER II.

THE UNITY OF GOD.

I. The Fact of the Unity of God.

Deut. 4:35—"Unto thee it was showed that thou mightest know that the Lord he is God: there is *none else beside him.*"

Deut. 6:4—"Hear, O Israel: The Lord our God is ONE Lord."

Is. 43:10—"Ye are my witnesses, saith the Lord, and my servants whom I have chosen; that ye may know and believe me, and understand that I am he: before me there was no God formed, neither shall there be after me."

Is. 44:6—"Thus saith the Lord the King of Israel, and his Redeemer the Lord of hosts; I am the first, and I am the last; and *besides me there is no God.*"

Is. 45:5—"I am the Lord, and there is none else; there is no God beside me: I girded thee, though thou hast not known me." (See, also, vv. 14, 18.)

1 Tim. 2:5—"For there is one God and one mediator between God and men, the man Christ Jesus."

Mark 10:18—"And Jesus said unto him, Why callest thou me good? There is none good but one, that is God."

Mark 12:29—"And Jesus answered him, the first of all the commandments is, Hear, O Israel; the Lord our God is ONE Lord."

FIRST PROPOSITION: The Lord our God is one Lord, and there is no God besides Him.

II. The Nature of the Divine Unity.

QUESTION: Is there a multiplicity of persons in this one God?

ANSWER: (1) <u>The Hebrew word translated "one" in these passages denotes a compound unity—not a simple unity.</u>

Illu's See Gen. 2:24—"Therefore shall a man leave his father and his mother, and shall cleave unto his wife: and they shall be *one* flesh."

Gen. 11:6—"And the Lord said, Behold <u>the people is *one*</u>, and they have all one language; and this they begin to do: and now nothing will be restrained from them, which they have imagined to do."

We find a similar use of the Greek word for "one" in the New Testament.

1 Cor. 3: 6–8—"I have planted, Apollos watered, but God gave the increase. So then neither is he that planteth anything, neither he that watereth; but God, that giveth the increase. Now he that planteth and he that watereth are one; and every man shall receive his own reward according to his labor."

1 Cor. 12: 13—"For by one Spirit are we all baptized into one body, whether we be Jews or Gentiles, whether we be bond or free: and have been all made to drink into one Spirit."

Compare Jno. 17: 22, 23—"And the glory which thou gavest me, I have given them; that they may be one, even as we are one: I in them, and thou in me, that they may be made perfect in one; and that the world may know that thou hast sent me, and hast loved them, as thou hast loved me."

Gal. 3: 28—"There is neither Jew or Greek, there is neither bond or free, there is neither male or female: for ye are all one in Christ Jesus."

(2)   The Old Testament word most frequently used for God is plural in form.

(3)   God uses plural pronouns in speaking of Himself.

Gen. 1: 26—"And God said, Let us make man in our image, after our likeness: and let them have dominion over the fish of the sea, and over the fowl of the air, and over the cattle, and over all the earth, and over every creeping thing that creepeth upon the earth."

Gen. 11: 7—"Go to, let us go down, and there confound their language, that they may not understand one another's speech."

Gen. 3: 22—"—And the Lord God said, Behold, the man is become as one of us, to know good and evil."

Is. 6: 8—"Also I heard the voice of the Lord, saying, Whom shall I send, and who will go forth for us? Then said I, Here am I; send me."

(4)   Zech. 2: 10, 11—"Sing and rejoice, O daughter of Zion: for lo, I come, and I will dwell in the midst of thee, saith the Lord. And many nations shall be joined to the Lord in that day, and shall be my people, and I will dwell in the midst of thee, and thou shalt know that the Lord of hosts hath sent me unto thee."

Here the Lord (Jehovah) speaks of Himself as sent by the Lord (Jehovah) of Hosts.

(5)   "The Angel of the Lord" is at the same time distinguished from and identified with the Lord.   (See preceding chapter.)

(6)   Jno. 1: 1—"In the beginning was the Word, and the Word was with God, and the Word was God."

(7) We shall see later that the Father, the Son and the Holy Spirit are all clearly designated as Divine Beings and as clearly distinguished from one another (*e. g.*, Matt. 3:16, 17; 28:19; 2 Cor. 13:14.)

QUESTION: How can God be three and one at the same time ?

ANSWER: He can not be three and one in the same sense. In what sense can He be one and three ? A perfectly satisfactory answer to this question is manifestly impossible from the very nature of the case: (1) Because God is Spirit, and numbers belong primarily to the physical world, and difficulty must arise when we attempt to conceive spiritual being in the forms of physical thought (2) God is infinite, we are finite. He "dwells in the light no man can approach unto." Our attempts at a philosophical explanation of the tri-unity of God is an attempt to put the facts of infinite being into the forms of finite thought, and of necessity can be, at the best, only partially successful. This much we know—that God is essentially one, and that He also is three. There is but one God: but this one God makes Himself known to man as Father, Son and Holy Spirit, and they are separate personalities.

Jno. 14:16—"And *I* will pray *the Father*, and he shall give you *another comforter*, that he may abide with you forever."

Mark 1:10, 11—"And straightway coming up out of the water, HE saw the heavens opened, and *the Spirit*, like a dove, descending upon him. And there came a voice from heaven, saying, Thou art my beloved Son, in whom *I* am well pleased."

SUMMARY OF DOCTRINE CONTAINED IN THESE SCRIPTURES.

There is one God eternally existing and manifesting Himself to us in three persons—Father, Son and Holy Spirit.

CHAPTER III.

THE ETERNITY OF GOD,

I. God eternal.

Gen. 21: 33—"And Abraham planted a grove in Beer-sheba, and called there on the name of the LORD, *the everlasting God.*"

Is. 40: 28—"Hast thou not known? hast thou not heard that *the everlasting God*, the LORD, the Creator of the ends of the earth, fainteth not, neither is weary? there is no searching of his understanding."

Hab. 1: 12—"Art thou not *from everlasting*, O LORD my God, mine Holy One? We shall not die. O LORD, thou hast ordained them for judgment; and, O mighty God, thou hast established them for correction."

Ps. 90: 2, 4—"Before the mountains were brought forth, or ever thou hadst formed the earth and the world, even from everlasting to everlasting, thou art God. For a thousand years in thy sight are but as yesterday when it is past, and as a watch in the night."

Ps. 102: 24-27—"I said, O my God, take me not away in the midst of my days: Thy years are throughout all generations. Of old hast thou laid the foundations of the earth: and the heavens are the work of thy hands. They shall perish, but thou shalt endure: yea, all of them shall wax old like a garment; as a vesture shalt thou change them, and they shall be changed. But thou art the same, and thy years shall have no end." (See also Is. 57: 15; Rom. 1: 20, Greek; Gen. 1: 1; John 1: 1.)

FIRST PROPOSITION: God is eternal. His existence had no beginning and will have no ending. He always was, always is and always will be. (Compare Ex. 3: 14.) He is the I Am— Jehovah.

II. God immutable.

Mal. 3: 6, f. h.—"For I am the LORD, I change not."

Jas. 1: 17—"Every good gift and every perfect gift is from above, and cometh down from the Father of lights, with whom is *no variableness*, neither shadow of turning."

1 Sam. 15: 29—"And also the Strength of Israel will not lie nor repent: for he is not a man, that he should repent." (See also Heb. 6: 17; Num. 23: 19.)

SECOND PROPOSITION: God is <u>unchangeable</u>. His counsel, purpose and character are always the same.

OBJECTION: Jonah 3: 10—"And God saw their works, that they turned from their evil way; and God repented of the evil, that he had said that he would do unto them; and he did it not." It is here said God repented.

ANSWER: God remained the same in character, infinitely hating sin, and in His purpose to visit sin with judgment; but as Nineveh changed in its attitude toward sin, God necessarily changed in His attitude toward Nineveh.   If God remains the same, if His attitude toward sin and righteousness are unchanging, then must His dealings with men change as they turn from sin to repentance.   His character remains ever the same; but His dealings with men change, as they change from a position that is hateful to His unchangeable hatred of sin, to one that is pleasing to his unchangeable love of righteousness.

OBJECTION: Gen. 6: 6—"And it repented the LORD that He had made man on the earth, and it grieved Him at His heart." Here it not only says that God repented of what He had done in creating man, but "it grieved Him at His heart."

ANSWER: (1) Man's wickedness was so great and so abhorrent that his very creation was an object of great grief to God.   This does not necessarily imply that God wished, all things considered, that He had not created man, but only just as is said, that He grieved that He had.   Many things that we do are a grief to us, and yet, everything considered, we do not wish that we had not done them.   (2) By God's repenting that He had made man is meant (as the context, v. 7, clearly shows) that He turned from His creative dealings with man to His destroying dealings (v. 7).   This was necessitated by man's sin.   The unchangeably holy God must destroy man who has become so sunken in sin.

III. God self-existent.

John 5: 26, f. h.—"For as the Father hath life in Himself.

THIRD PROPOSITION: God has life in Himself. He is self-existent. God not only exists from eternity, but also exists from Himself. (See also Acts 17: 24–28.)

CHAPTER IV.

THE OMNIPRESENCE OF GOD.

I. God everywhere.

Ps. 139: 7–10—"Whither shall I go from thy spirit? or whither shall I flee from thy presence? If I ascend up into heaven, thou art there: if I make my bed in hell, behold, thou art there. If I take the wings of the morning, and dwell in the uttermost parts of the sea; even there shall thy hand lead me, and thy right hand shall hold me."

Jer. 23: 23, 24—"Am I a God at hand, saith the Lord, and not a God afar off? Can any hide himself in secret places that I shall not see him? saith the Lord. Do not I fill Heaven and earth? saith the Lord."

Acts 17: 24–28—"God that made the world and all things therein, seeing that he is Lord of Heaven and earth, dwelleth not in temples made with hands. Neither is worshiped with men's hands, as though he ·needed anything, seeing he giveth to all life, and breath, and all things; and hath made of one blood all nations of men for to dwell on all the face of the earth, and hath determined the times before appointed, and the bounds of their habitation: that they should seek the Lord, if haply they might feel after him, and find him, though he be not far from every one of us: for in him we live, and move, and have our being; as certain also of your own poets have said, for we are also of his offspring." (See also Is. 57: 15.)

FIRST PROPOSITION: God is everywhere. He is in all parts of the universe and near each individual. In Him each individual lives and moves and has his being.

II. God not everywhere in the same sense.

John 14: 28—"Ye have heard how I said unto you, I go away and come again unto you. If ye loved me, ye would rejoice, because I said, *I go unto* the Father: for my Father is greater than I."

John 20: 17—"Jesus saith unto her, touch me not; for I am not yet ascended to my Father: but go to my brethren, and say unto them, I *ascend unto my Father*, and your Father, and to my God, and your God.'

Eph. 1: 20--"Which he wrought in Christ, when he raised him

from the dead, and set him *at his own right hand in the heavenly places.*"

Rev. 21: 2, 3, 10, 22, 23—"And I, John, saw the holy city, new Jerusalem, coming *down from God out of Heaven,* prepared as a bride adorned for her husband. And I heard a great voice out of heaven saying, behold, the tabernacle of God is with men, and he will dwell with them, and they shall be his people, and God himself shall be with them, and be their God. And he carried me away in the spirit to a great and high mountain, and showed me that great city, the holy Jerusalem, descending out of heaven from God. And I saw no temple therein: for the Lord God Almighty and the Lamb are the temple of it. And the city had no need of the sun, neither of the moon, to shine in it: for the glory of God did lighten it, and the Lamb is the light thereof."

Rev. 22: 1, 3—"And he showed me a pure river of water of life, clear as crystal, proceeding out of the throne of God and of the Lamb. And there shall be no more curse: but the throne of God and of the Lamb shall be in it, and his servants shall serve him "

SECOND PROPOSITION: *God is in some places in a way that He is not in other places.* (Is. 66:1—"Thus saith the Lord, the heaven is my throne, and the earth is my footstool: where is the house that ye build unto me, and where is the place of my rest ?) *There is a fullness and manifestation of His presence in some places that there is not in others.* *" Heaven " is the place where at the present time, the presence and glory of God is especially and visibly manifested.*

Note.—Mark 1:9-11—"And it came to pass in those days, that Jesus came from Nazareth of Galilee, and was baptized of John in Jordan. And straightway coming up out of the water, he saw the heavens opened, and the spirit, like a dove, descending upon him. And there came a voice from heaven, saying, thou art my beloved son, in whom I am well pleased."

God the Father is especially manifested in heaven. God the Son has been especially manifested on earth. (See also John 3:13, the entire gospels and " the Angel of the Lord " in O. T.) God the Son is now in heaven. (Acts 7: 56; Eph. 1: 20 and many other passages.) God the Holy Spirit is manifested everywhere. (*a*) In nature (Gen. 1: 2; Ps. 104: 30); (*b*) In all believers (John 14: 16, 17; Rom. 8: 9); (*c*) With unbelievers (John 16: 7–11). Through the Spirit, the Father and the Son dwell in the believer (John 14: 17, 19, 20, 23.) (See also Matt. 28: 19, 20.)

CHAPTER V.

THE PERSONALITY OF GOD.

We have seen that God is omnipresent. This conception of God must be balanced by the conception of God as a person or we run into Pantheism, *i. e.*, the conception that God is not only everywhere and *in* everything, but that God is everything and everything is God; that God has no existence separate from His creatures.

I. God a living God.

Jer. 10: 10-16—"But the LORD is the true God, he is the *living* God, and an everlasting King: at his wrath the earth shall tremble, and the nations shall not be able to abide his indignation. Thus shall ye say unto them, The gods that have not made the heavens and the earth, even they shall perish from the earth, and from under these heavens. He hath made the earth by his power, he hath established the world by his wisdom, and hath stretched out the heavens by his discretion. When he uttereth his voice, there is a multitude of waters in the heavens, and he causes the vapors to ascend from the ends of the earth. He maketh lightnings with rain, and bringeth forth the wind out of his treasures. Every man is brutish in his knowledge: every founder is confounded by the graven image: for his molten image is falsehood, and there is no breath in them. They are vanity, and the work of errors: in the time of their visitation they shall perish. The portion of Jacob is not like them: for he is the former of all things; and Israel is the rod of his inheritance: the LORD of Hosts is his name."

(Note the context vv. 3-9, especially 5, 8, 9.) God is here distinguished from idols, which are things, not persons, "speak not" "cannot go," "cannot do good, neither is it in them to do evil;" but Jehovah is wiser than "all the wise men," is "the living God," "an everlasting King" a being who hath "wrath and indignation" separate from His creatures—"at His wrath the earth trembleth and the nations are not able to abide his indignation."

Acts 14: 15—"And saying, Sirs, why do ye these things? We

also are men of like passions with you, and preach unto you that ye should turn from these vanities unto the *living* God, *which made* heaven, and earth, and the sea, and all things that are therein."

1 Thess. 1:9—"For they themselves shew of us what manner of entering in we had unto you, and how ye turned to God from idols to serve *the living* and true God."

2 Chron. 16:9—"For the eyes of the LORD run to and fro throughout the whole earth, to show himself strong in the behalf of them whose heart is perfect toward him."

Ps. 94:9, 10—"He that planted the ear, shall he not hear? He that formed the eye, shall he not see? He that chastiseth the heathen, shall not he correct? He that teacheth man knowledge, shall not he know?" (and numerous other passages).

FIRST PROPOSITION: God is a living God. He hears, sees, knows, feels, wills, acts, is a person. He is to be distinguished from idols, which are things, not persons. He is to be distinguished from the works of His hands which he formed.

NOTE.—Personality is characterized by knowledge, feeling and will. Some confuse personality with corporeity.

II. God's relation to the affairs of men.

Josh. 3:10—"And Joshua said, Hereby ye shall know that the living God is among you, and that he will without fail drive out from before you the Canaanites, and the Hittites, and the Hivites, and the Perizzites, and the Girgashites, and the Amorites, and the Jebusites."

Daniel 6:20-22, 26, 27—"And when he came to the den he cried with a lamentable voice unto Daniel: and the king spake and said to Daniel, O Daniel, servant of the living God, is thy God, whom thou servest continually, able to deliver thee from the lions? Then said Daniel unto the king, O king, live forever. My God hath sent His angel, and hath shut the lions' mouths, that they have not hurt me: forasmuch as before him innocency was found in me; and also before thee, O king, have I done no hurt. * * * I make a decree that in every dominion of my kingdom men tremble and fear before the God of Daniel: for he is the living God, and steadfast forever, and his kingdom that which shall not be destroyed, and his dominion shall be even unto the end. He delivereth and rescueth, and he speaketh signs and wonders in heaven and in earth, who hath delivered Daniel from the power of the lions."

1 Tim. 4:10—"For therefore we both labor and suffer reproach, because we trust in the living God, who is the Savior of all men, specially of those that believe."

Heb. 10:28-31—"He that despised Moses' law died without mercy under two or three witnesses. Of how much sorer punishment, suppose ye, shall he be thought worthy, who hath trodden under foot the Son of God, and hath counted the blood of the covenant, wherewith he was sanctified, an unholy thing, and hath done despite unto the Spirit of grace? For we know him that hath said, Vengeance belongeth unto me, I will recompense saith the Lord. And again, the Lord shall judge his people. It is a fearful thing to fall into the hands of the living God."

SECOND PROPOSITION: *God has a present, personal interest and an active hand in the affairs of men. He makes a path for His people and leads them. He delivers, saves and punishes.*

The God of the Bible is not only to be distinguished from the God of the Pantheist, who has no existence separate from His creation, but also from the God of the Deist, who has created the world and put into it all the necessary powers of self-action and development, and set it going, and left it to go of itself. God is personally and actively present in the affairs of the universe.

III. God as Creator.

Gen. 1: 1—"In the beginning God created the heaven and the earth."
Jno. 1: 1–3—"In the beginning was the Word, and the Word was with God, and the Word was God. The same was in the beginning with God. All things were made by him; and without him was not anything made that was made."

THIRD PROPOSITION: God is the Creator of all existing things.

IV. God's present relation to the world He has created.

Ps. 104: 27–30—"These wait all upon thee; that thou mayest give them their meat in due season. That thou givest them they gather: thou openest thine hand, they are filled with good. Thou hidest thy face, they are troubled: thou takest away their breath, they die, and return to the dust. Thou sendest forth thy spirit, they are created: and thou renewest the face of the earth."
Is. 45: 5–7—"I am the LORD, and there is none else, there is no God beside me: I girded thee, though thou hast not known me. That they may know from the rising of the sun, and from the west, that there is none beside me, I am the LORD, and there is none else. I form the light, and create darkness: I make peace, and create evil: I the LORD do all these things."
Ps. 75: 6, 7—"For promotion cometh neither from the east, nor from the west, nor from the south. But God is the Judge: he putteth down one, and setteth up another."

FOURTH PROPOSITION: <u>*God sustains, governs and cares for*</u> <u>*the world He has created.*</u> *He shapes the whole present history of the world.*

V. The extent of God's care and government.

(1) Matt. 6: 26, 28–30—"Behold the fowls of the air: for they sow not, neither do they reap, nor gather into barns; yet your Heavenly Father feedeth them. Are ye not much better than they ? And why take ye thought for raiment ? Consider the lilies of the field, how they grow; they toil not neither do they spin. And yet I say unto you, that even Solomon in all his glory was not arrayed like one of these. Wherefore, if God so clothe the grass of the field, which to-day is, and to-morrow is cast into the oven, shall he not much more clothe you, O ye of little faith ?"

Matt. 10: 29, 30—"Are not two sparrows sold for a farthing ? and one of them shall not fall on the ground without your Father. But the very hairs of your head are all numbered."

FIFTH PROPOSITION: <u>*God s care and government extend to*</u> <u>*all His creatures.*</u>

(2) Gen. 39: 21—"But the Lord was with Joseph, and showed him mercy, and gave him favor in the sight of the keeper of the prison."

Dan. 1: 9—"Now God had brought Daniel into favor and tender love with the prince of the eunuchs."

1 Kings, 19 : 5–7—"And as he lay and slept under a juniper tree, behold, then an angel touched him, and said unto him, Arise and eat. And he looked, and behold, there was a cake baken on the coals, and a cruse of water at his head. And he did eat and drink and laid him down again. And the angel of the LORD came again the second time, and touched him, and said, Arise and eat ; because the journey is too great for thee."

SIXTH PROPOSITION: <u>*God's care and ministry and govern-*</u> <u>*ment extend to the individual.*</u>

(3) Matt. 10 : 29, 30—"Are not two sparrows sold for a farthing ? and one of them shall not fall on the ground without your Father. But the very hairs of your head are all numbered."

SEVENTH PROPOSITION: <u>*God's care and ministry and gov-*</u> <u>*ernment extend to the minutest matters.*</u>

(4) Ps. 76 : 10—"Surely *the wrath of man* shall praise thee : the remainder of wrath shalt thou restrain."

Gen. 50 : 20—"But as for you, *ye thought evil* against me; *but*

God meant it unto good, to bring to pass, as it is this day, to save much people alive." (And Rom. 9: 17, 19.)

Acts 2 : 22, 23—"Ye men of Israel, hear these words; Jesus of Nazareth, a man approved of God among you by miracles and wonders and signs, which God did by him in the midst of you, as ye yourselves also know. Him, being delivered by the *determinate counsel and fore-knowledge of God*, ye have taken and *by wicked hands* have crucified and slain."

Job. 1 : 12—"And the Lord said unto Satan, Behold all that he hath is in thy power ; only upon himself put not forth thine hand. So Satan went forth from the presence of the Lord."

Job 2: 6—"And the Lord said unto Satan, behold, he is in thy hand; but save his life."

Luke 22: 3—"And Satan entered into Judas who was called Iscariot, being one of the number of the twelve."

EIGHTH PROPOSITION: <u>*God's control and government extend to the wicked devices and doings of evil men, and of Satan, and He makes even these work out His own glory and His people's good.*</u>

(Compare Rom. 8: 28—"And we know that all things work together for good to them that love God, to them who are the called according to His purpose.")

CHAPTER VI.

OMNIPOTENCE.

I. The fact that God is omnipotent.

Job 42:2—"I know that Thou *canst do everything*, and that no thought can be withholden from Thee."

Gen. 18:14—"*Is anything too hard* for the Lord?"

Matt. 19:26—"But Jesus beheld them, and said unto them, With men this is impossible; but with God *all things are possible.*"

FIRST PROPOSITION: God can do all things, nothing is too hard for him, all things are possible with Him. God is omnipotent.

(1) Gen. 1:3—"And ·God said, Let there be light: and there was light.

Ps. 33:6-9—"By the word of the Lord were the Heavens made; and all the host of them by the breath of his mouth. He gathereth the waters of the sea together as an heap: he layeth up the depth in storehouses. Let all the earth fear the Lord; let all the inhabitants of the world stand in awe of him. For he spake, and it was done; he commanded, and it stood fast."

Ps. 107:25-29—"For he commandeth, and raiseth the stormy wind, which lifteth up the waves thereof. They mount up to the heaven, they go down again to the depths: their soul is melted because of trouble. They reel to and fro, and stagger like a drunken man, and are at their wit's end. Then they cry unto the Lord in their trouble, and he bringeth them out of their distresses. He maketh the storm a calm, so that the waves thereof are still."

Nah. 1:3-6—"The LORD is slow to anger, and great in power, and will not at all acquit the wicked: the Lord hath his way in the whirlwind and in the storm, and the clouds are the dust of his feet. He rebuketh the sea and maketh it dry, and drieth up all the rivers: Bashan languisheth, and Carmel, and the flower of Lebanon languisheth. The mountains quake at him, and the hills melt, and the earth is burned at his presence, yea, the world, and all that dwell therein. Who can stand before his indignation? And who can abide in the fierceness of his anger? His fury is poured out like fire, and the rocks are thrown down by him."

All nature is absolutely subject to God's will and word.

(2) Jas. 4: 12-15—"There is one lawgiver, who is able to save and to destroy: who art thou that judgest another ? Go to now, ye that say, To-day or to-morrow we will go into such a city and continue there a year, and buy and sell, and get gain. Whereas ye know not what shall be on the morrow. For what is your life ? It is even a vapour, that appeareth for a little time, and then vanisheth away. For that ye ought to say, If the Lord will, we shall live, and do this, or that."

All men are absolutely subject to His will and word.

NOTE.—Happy is the man who voluntarily subjects himself to God's will and word.

(3) Heb. 1: 13, 14—"But to which of the angels said he at any time, Sit on my right hand, until I make thine enemies thy footstool ? Are they not all ministering spirits, sent forth to minister for them who shall be heirs of salvation ?"

Angels are subject to His will and word.

(4) Job. 1: 12—"And the Lord said unto Satan, Behold all that he hath is in thy power; only upon himself put not forth thine hand. So Satan went forth from the presence of the Lord."

Job 2: 6 —"And the Lord said unto Satan, Behold, he is in thine hand; but save his life."

Satan is absolutely subject to His will and word.

II.   The exercise of God's omnipotence limited by His will.

Is. 59: 1, 2—"Behold, the Lord's hand is not shortened, that it cannot save; neither his ear heavy, that it cannot hear. But your iniquities have separated between you and your God, and your sins have hid his face from you, that he will not hear."

SECOND PROPOSITION: The exercise of God's omnipotence is limited by His own wise and holy and loving will. God can do anything, but will do only what infinite wisdom and holiness and love dictate.

QUESTION: Why doesn't God destroy Satan ?

ANSWER: It would not be wise to destroy him yet. By his malevolence he is working out part of God's benevolent plans.

CHAPTER VII

OMNISCIENCE.

I. The fact that God is omniscient.

1 Jno. 3: 20—"For if our heart condemn us, God is greater than our heart, and *knoweth all things.*"

Job 37: 16—"Dost thou know the balancings of the clouds, the wondrous works of him which is *perfect in knowledge ?*"

Ps. 147: 5—"Great is the Lord, and of great power: his *understanding is infinite.*"

FIRST PROPOSITION: God " knoweth all things." He is " perfect in knowledge." " His understanding is infinite."

Literally, "of his understanding there is no number" (See Marg.)

II. What God knows.

(1) Prov. 15: 3, R.V.—"The eyes of the Lord are in every place, keeping watch upon the evil and the good."

FIRST PROPOSITION: He sees all that occurs in every place and keeps watch upon the evil and the good.

(2) Ps. 147: 4—"He telleth the number of the stars; he calleth them all by their names."

Matt. 10: 29—"Are not two sparrows sold for a farthing ? and one of them shall not fall on the ground without your Father."

SECOND PROPOSITION: He knows everything in nature, every star and every sparrow."

(3) Ps. 33: 13-15—"The Lord looketh from heaven; he beholdeth all the sons of men. From the place of his habitation he looketh upon all the inhabitants of the earth. He fashioneth their hearts alike; he considereth all their works."

Prov. 5: 21—"For the ways of man are before the eyes of the Lord, and he pondereth all his goings."

THIRD PROPOSITION: " *He beholdeth all the sons of men* " *and* " *considereth all their works.*" " *The ways of men are before*" *His eyes, and* " *He pondereth* (or maketh level) *all his goings.*"

(4)   Ps. 139: 2, 3—"Thou knowest my downsitting and mine up-rising, thou understandest my thought afar off.   Thou compassest my path and my lying down, and art acquainted with all my ways."

FOURTH PROPOSITION: He knows all man's deeds and ex-periences.

(5)   Ps. 139: 4—"For there is not a word in my tongue, but lo, O Lord, thou knowest it altogether."

FIFTH PROPOSITION: He knoweth altogether all man's words.

(6)   Ex. 3: 7—"And the Lord said, I have surely seen the affliction of my people which are in Egypt, and have heard their cry by reason of their task-masters; for I know their sorrows."

SIXTH PROPOSITION: He knows all man's sorrows.

It seems sometimes as if He did not.   It must have seemed so sometimes to Israel in Egypt, but He did, and in time proved it.

(7)   Ps. 139: 1, 2—"O Lord, thou hast searched me and known me. Thou knowest my downsitting and mine uprising, thou understandest my thought afar off."

I Chron. 28: 9—"And thou Solomon my son, know thou the God of thy father, and serve him with a perfect heart and with a willing mind: for the Lord searcheth all hearts, and understandeth all the imaginations of the thoughts: if thou seek him, he will be found of thee; but if thou forsake him, he will cast thee off forever."

SEVENTH PROPOSITION: He " *understandeth all the imagi-nations of the thoughts.*"   *He understands our thoughts afar off.*

(8)   Matt. 10: 29, 30—"Are not two sparrows sold for a farthing? and one of them shall not fall on the ground without your Father. But the very hairs of your head are all numbered."

EIGHTH PROPOSITION: God's knowledge extends to minutest particulars.

(9)   Acts 15: 18—"Known unto God are all his works from the begin-ning of the world."   (See R.V.)

Is. 46:9, 10—"Remember the former things of old: for I am God, and there is none else; I am God, and there is none like me. Declaring the end from the beginning, and from ancient times the things that are not yet done, saying, My counsel shall stand, and I will do all my pleasure."

NINTH PROPOSITION: God knows from all eternity what shall be to all eternity.

(Compare 1 Pet. 1: 20, R.V.—"Christ: who was foreknown indeed before the foundation of the world, but was manifested at the end of the times." Mark 13:32.)

(10) Matt. 20: 17-19—"And Jesus going up to Jerusalem took the twelve disciples apart in the way, and said unto them: Behold we go up to Jerusalem; and the Son of man shall be betrayed unto the chief priests and unto the scribes, and they shall condemn him to death. And shall deliver him to the Gentiles to mock, and to scourge, and to crucify him; and the third day he shall rise again."

Ex. 3: 19, R.V.—"And I know that the king of Egypt will not give you leave to go, no, not by a mighty hand."

Acts 3: 17, 18—"And now, brethren, I wot that through ignorance ye did it as did also your rulers. But those things, which God before had showed by the mouth of all his prophets, that Christ should suffer, he hath so fulfilled."

2 Kings 7: 1, 2—"Then Elisha said, Hear ye the word of the Lord. Thus saith the Lord, To-morrow about this time shall a measure of fine flour be sold for a shekel, and two measures of barley for a shekel, in the gate of Samaria. Then a lord on whom the king leaned answered the man of God, and said, Behold, if the Lord would make windows in heaven, might this thing be? And he said, Behold, thou shalt see it with thine eyes, but shalt not eat thereof."

Ps. 41:9—"Yea, mine own familiar friend, in whom I trusted, which did eat of my bread, hath lifted up his heel against me."

Gal. 1: 15, 16—"But when it pleased God, who separated me from my mother's womb, and called me by his grace to reveal his Son in me, that I might preach him among the heathen; immediately I conferred not with flesh and blood."

1 Pet. 1: 2—"Elect *according to the foreknowledge of God* the Father, through sanctification of the Spirit, unto obedience and sprinkling of the blood of Jesus Christ: Grace unto you and peace be multiplied "

TENTH PROPOSITION: God knows from the beginning what each individual man will do.

(11) Eph. 1: 9, 12—" Having made known unto us the mystery of his will, according to his good pleasure which he hath purposed in himself. That in the dispensation of the fullness of times he might gather

together in one all things in Christ, both which are in heaven, and which are on earth ; even in him. In whom also we have obtained an inheritance, being predestinated according to the purpose of him who worketh all things after the counsel of his own will. That we should be to the praise of his glory, who first trusted in Christ."

Eph. 3: 4-9, R. V.—"Whereby, when ye read, ye can perceive my understanding in the mystery of Christ ; which in other generations was not made known unto the sons of men, as it hath now been revealed unto his holy apostles and prophets in the Spirit; to-wit, that the Gentiles are fellow-heirs, and fellow-members of the body, and fellow-partakers of the promise in Christ Jesus through the gospel, whereof I was made a minister, according to the gift of that grace of God which was given me according to the working of his power. Unto me, who am less than the least of all saints, was his grace given, to preach unto the Gentiles the unsearchable riches of Christ: and to make all men see what is the dispensation of the mystery which from all ages hath been hid in God, who created all things."

Col. 1: 25, 26—"Whereof I was made a minister, according to the dispensation of God, which was given to me for you, to fulfill the word of God. Even the mystery which hath been hid from all ages and generations."

ELEVENTH PROPOSITION: The whole plan of the ages and each man's part in it has been known to God from all eternity.

There are no afterthoughts with God. Well may we exclaim: "O, the depth of the riches both of the wisdom and knowledge of God ! how unsearchable are his judgments and his ways past finding out ! " (Rom, 11: 33.)

CHAPTER VIII.

THE HOLINESS OF GOD.

I. The fact of God's Holiness.

Is. 6: 3—" And one cried unto another, and said, Holy, holy, holy, is the LORD of hosts: the whole earth is full of his glory."

Josh. 24: 19—"And Joshua said unto the people, Ye cannot serve the LORD: for he is an holy God; he is a jealous God; he will not forgive your transgressions nor your sins."

Ps. 22: 3—" But thou art holy, O thou that inhabitest the praises of Israel."

Ps. 99: 5, 9—" Exalt ye the LORD our God, and worship at his footstool; for he is holy. Exalt the LORD our God, and worship at his holy hill; for the LORD our God is holy."

Is. 5: 16—" But the LORD of hosts shall be exalted in judgment, and God that is holy shall be sanctified in righteousness."

Jno. 17: 11—"And now I am no more in the world, but these are in the world, and I come to thee. *Holy* Father, keep through thine own name those whom thou hast given me that they may be one, as **we** are."

1 Pet. 1: 15, 16—" But as he which hath called you is holy, so be ye holy in all manner of conversation. Because it is written, be ye holy; for I am holy."

FIRST PROPOSITION: God is holy. Absolutely holy.

God is called the Holy One of Israel about thirty times in Isaiah, and is so called also in Jeremiah and Ezekiel, and elsewhere. In the New Testament God the Son is spoken of as *the holy* one. (1 Jno. 2: 20.) The third person of the Trinity is constantly spoken of as the Holy Spirit. Holiness is the essential moral nature of God.

Is. 57: 15—" For thus saith the high and lofty one that inhabiteth eternity, *whose name is Holy;* I dwell in the high and holy place, with him also that is of a contrite and humble spirit, to revive the spirit of the humble, and to revive the heart of the contrite ones." (The name stands for the character and being.)

II. What does Holy mean ?

Lev. 11:43-45—"Ye shall not make yourselves abominable with any creeping thing that creepeth, neither shall ye make yourselves *unclean* with them, that ye should be *defiled* thereby. For I am the Lord your God: ye shall therefore sanctify yourselves, and ye shall be holy; for I am holy: *neither shall ye defile yourselves* with any manner of creeping thing that creepeth upon the earth. For I am the Lord that bringeth you up out of the land of Egypt, to be your God: ye shall therefore be holy, for I am holy."

Deut. 23: 14—"For the Lord thy God walketh in the midst of thy camp, to deliver thee, and to give up thine enemies before thee; therefore shall thy camp be holy: that he *see no unclean thing* in thee, and turn away from thee." (Note the context of this verse.)

SECOND PROPOSITION: Holy means free from all defilement, pure. " God is holy," means, " God is absolutely pure."

1 Jno. 1:5—"This then is the message which we have heard of him, and declare unto you, that *God is light*, and *in him is no darkness at all.*"

NOTE.—The entire Mosaic system of washings; divisions of the tabernacle; divisions of the people into ordinary Israelites, Levites, Priests and High Priests, who were permitted different degrees of approach to God, under strictly defined conditions; the insisting upon sacrifice as a necessary medium of approach to God; God's directions to Moses in Ex. 3: 5, to Joshua in Josh. 5: 15, the punishment of Uzziah in 2 Chron. 26: 16–26; the strict orders to Israel in regard to approaching Sinai when Jehovah came down upon it; the doom of Korah, Dathan and Abiram in Num. 16: 1–33; and the destruction of Nadab and Abihu in Lev. 10: 1–3: all these were intended to teach, emphasize and burn into the minds and hearts of the Israelites the fundamental truth that God is Holy, unapproachably holy. The truth that God is Holy is the fundamental truth of the Bible, of the Old Testament and the New Testament, of the Jewish Religion and the Christian Religion.

III. How the Holiness of God is manifested.

(1) Hab. 1: 13—"Thou art of purer eyes than to behold evil, and canst not look upon iniquity: wherefore lookest thou upon them that deal treacherously, and holdest thy tongue when the wicked devoureth the man that is more righteous than he ?"

Gen. 6: 5, 6—"And God saw that the wickedness of man was great in the earth and that every imagination of the thoughts of the heart was only evil continually. And it repented the Lord that he had made man on the earth, and it grieved him at his heart."

Deut. 25: 16—"For all that do such things, and all that do unright-
eously, are an abomination unto the Lord thy God."

Prov. 15: 9, 26 ———"The way of the wicked is an abomination
unto the Lord. The thoughts of the wicked are an abomination to the
Lord."

THIRD PROPOSITION: The Holiness of God manifests itself in a hatred of sin.

(2)   Prov. 15: 9 ———" But he loveth him that followeth after righteousness."

×   Lev. 19: 2—"Speak unto all the congregation of the children of
Israel, and say unto them, Ye shall be holy: for I the Lord your God
am holy."

Lev. 20: 26—"And ye shall be holy unto me: for I the Lord am
holy, and I have severed you from other people, that ye should be
mine."

FOURTH PROPOSITION: The holiness of God manifests itself in delight in righteousness and holiness.

(3)   Job. 34: 10—"Therefore hearken unto me, ye men of understanding: far be it from God, that he should do wickedness; and from
the Almighty, that he should commit iniquity."

FIFTH PROPOSITION: The Holiness of God manifests itself in His never doing wickedness or iniquity.

(4)   Is. 59: 1, 2—" Behold the Lord's hand is not shortened, that it
cannot save; neither his ear heavy, that it cannot hear. But your iniquities have separated between you and your God, and your sins have
hid his face from you, that he will not hear."

SIXTH PROPOSITION: The Holiness of God is manifested in the separation of the sinner from Himself.

Herein lieth the need of atonement before the sinner can approach God.   This appears in the following passages:

Eph. 2: 13—" But now in Christ Jesus ye who sometimes were far
off are made nigh by the blood of Christ."

Heb. 10: 9—"Then said he, Lo, I come to do thy will, O God. He
taketh away the first that he may establish the second. By the which
will we are sanctified through the offering of the body of Jesus Christ
once for all."

Jno. 14: 6—"Jesus saith unto him, I am the way, the truth and the
life: no man cometh unto the Father but by me."

All approach to God is on the ground of shed blood. The atonement has its deepest demand in the holiness of God. Any doctrine of the atonement that sees its need only in the necessity that man be influenced by a mighty motive, or in the necessities of governmental expediency, does not go to the root of things. The first and fundamental reason why "without shedding of blood there is no remission " is because God is Holy and sin must be covered before there can be fellowship between God and the sinner.

(5) Ex. 34: 6, 7—"And the LORD passed by before him, and proclaimed, The LORD, The LORD God, merciful and gracious, long-suffering, and abundant in goodness and truth. Keeping mercy for thousands, forgiving iniquity and transgression and sin, and that will by no means clear the guilty; visiting the iniquity of the fathers upon the children, and upon the children's children, unto the third and fourth generation."

Gen. 6: 5-7—" And God saw that the wickedness of man was great in the earth, and that every imagination of the thoughts of his heart was only evil continually. And it repented the LORD that he had made man on the earth, and it grieved him at his heart. And the LORD said, I will destroy man whom I have created from the face of the earth; both man, and beast, and the creeping things, and the fowls of the air; for it repenteth me that I have made them."

Ps. 5: 4-6—" For thou art not a God that hath pleasure in wickedness: neither shall evil dwell with thee. The foolish shall not stand in thy sight: thou hatest all workers of iniquity. Thou shalt destroy them that speak leasing: the LORD will abhor the bloody and deceitful man."

SEVENTH PROPOSITION: The holiness of God manifests itself in the punishment of the sinner.

God does not punish the sinner merely because the sinner's good makes it necessary. God is Holy. God hates sin. His holiness and hatred of sin, like every attribute of His, is living and active and must manifest itself. His holy wrath at sin must strike. (See Is. 53: 6—" All we like sheep have gone astray; we have turned every one to his own way; and the Lord hath laid on him the iniquity of us all. " See also R. V. Marg. The literal translation of the Hebrew for "hath laid upon " is "caused to strike upon.")

Any view of the punishment of sin that leaves out the thought of its being an expression of God's holy hatred of sin, is not only unbiblical, but shallow and dishonoring to God. God is holy, infinitely holy, and infinitely hates sin. We get glimpses at times of what God's hatred of sin must be, in our own burning indignation at some enormous iniquity, but God is infinitely holy and God's wrath at the smallest sin is infi‧ nitely greater than ours at the greatest enormity. God is love, it is true, but this love is not of the sentimental sort that sends costly bouquets and tender missives to moral monsters, as some of our Universalist theologians would have us think. "Our God is a consuming fire." (Heb. 12:29.) God's love to sinners will never be appreciated until seen in the light of His blazing wrath at sin.

(6) Jno. 3:16—"For God *so* loved the world, that he gave his only begotten son, that whosoever believeth in him should not perish, but have everlasting life."

1 Pet. 3:18—"For Christ also hath once suffered for sins, the just for the uujust, that he might bring us to God, being put to death in the flesh, but quickened by the Spirit."

EIGHTH PROPOSITION: The holiness of God manifests itself in His making an infinite sacrifice to save others from sin unto holiness.   The death of Christ is not merely a manifestation of the love of God but of His holiness as well.

IV. Practical inferences from the doctrine that God is Holy.

(1) Heb. 12:28, 29—"Wherefore we receiving a kingdom which can not be moved, let us have grace whereby we may serve God acceptably with reverence and godly fear. For our God is a consuming fire."

Ex. 3:4, 5—"And when the LORD saw that he turned aside to see, God called to him out of the midst of the bush, and said, Moses, Moses. And he said, Here am I. And he said, Draw not nigh hither: put off thy shoes from off thy feet, for the place whereon thou standest is holy ground."

Is. 6:1-3—"In the year that King Uzziah died I saw also the LORD sitting upon a throne, high and lifted up, and his train filled the temple. Above it stood the seraphim: each one had six wings; with twain he covered his face, and with twain he covered his feet, and with twain he did fly. And one cried unto another, and said, Holy, holy, holy is the LORD of hosts: the whole earth is full of his glory."

We must draw nigh to God with awe. Even the holy seraphim covered their faces and their feet in His presence. They have four wings for worship and but two for service

(2) Is. 6: 5, 6—"Then said I, Woe is me! for I am undone be-cause I am a man of unclean lips, and I dwell in the midst of a people of unclean lips: for mine eyes have seen the King, the Lord of hosts. Then flew one of the seraphim unto me, having a live coal in his hand, which he had taken with the tongs from off the altar."

The pure light of God's holiness reveals the blackness of our sin.

(Compare Job 42: 5, 6—" I have heard of thee by the hearing of the ear: but now mine eye seeth thee. Wherefore I abhor myself, and repent in dust and ashes.")

If any man think well of himself, he has never met God. Nothing will demolish self-righteousness like one real sight of God. In dealing with self-righteous persons get them into the holy presence of God if you can.

(3) Heb. 9: 22—"And almost all things are by the law purged with blood; and without shedding of blood there is no remission."

There is no forgiveness without atonement. Sin must be covered from the holy gaze of God, and nothing will cover it but blood.

(4) Rom. 5: 8—"But God commendeth his love toward us, in that, while we were yet sinners, Christ died for us."

The wonderfulness of God's love! It would be no wonder if an unholy God could love unholy men; but that the God whose name is Holy, the Infinitely Holy God, could love be-ings so utterly sinful as we are, that is the wonder of the eter-nities. There are many deep mysteries in the Bible, but no other so profound as this.

CHAPTER IX.

THE LOVE OF GOD

I. The fact that God is Love.

1 Jno. 4: 8, 16—"He that loveth not knoweth not God; for *God is love*. And we have known and believed the love that God hath to us. *God is love;* and he that dwelleth in love dwelleth in God, and God in him."

FIRST PROPOSITION: *God is love. Not merely God loves, but God is love. Love is the very essence of His moral nature. He is the source of all love.*

1 Jno. 4: 7—"Beloved, let us love one another; for love is of God; and every one that loveth is born of God, and knoweth God."

QUESTION: What is love?

ANSWER:

1 Jno. 3: 16, 17, R.V.—"Hereby know we love, because he laid down his life for us; and we ought to lay down our lives for the brethren. But whoso has this world's goods and beholdeth his brother in need, and shutteth up his compassion from him, how doth the love of God abide in him?"

Matt. 5: 44, 45—"But I say unto you, Love your enemies, bless them that curse you, do good to them that hate you, and pray for them which despitefully use you, and persecute you. That ye may be the children of your Father which is in heaven: for He maketh the sun to rise on the evil and on the good, and sendeth rain on the just and on the unjust."

Love is a desire for and delight in the welfare of the one loved.

II. Whom does God Love?

(1) Matt. 3: 17—"And lo a voice from heaven saying, This is my beloved Son, in whom I am well pleased."

Matt. 17: 5—"While he yet spake, behold, a bright cloud overshadowed them: and behold a voice out of the cloud, which said, This is my beloved Son, in whom I am well pleased; hear ye him."

Luke 20: 13—"Then said the Lord of the vineyard, What shall I do? I will send my beloved Son: it may be they will reverence him when they see him."

SECOND PROPOSITION: God loves <u>His Son.</u> God's Son is the original and eternal Object of His love.

Jno. 17: 24—"Father, I will that they also, whom thou hast given me, be with me where I am; that they may behold my glory which thou hast given me; for thou lovedst me before the foundation of the world."

If God is eternal love, that love must have an eternal object. There must, then, because of a necessity in the Divine Being Himself, be a multiplicity of persons in the Godhead. The eternal object of the Divine Love is the Eternal Son.

(2) Jno. 16: 27—"For the Father himself *loveth you, because ye have loved me,* and *have believed* that I came out from God."

Jno. 14: 21, 23—"He that hath my commandments, and keepeth them, he it is that loveth me: and *he that loveth me* shall be loved of my Father, and I will love him, and will manifest myself to him. Jesus answered and said unto him, *If a man love me,* he will keep my words: and my Father will love him, and we will come unto him, and make our abode with him."

THIRD PROPOSITION: God loves those who are <u>united to the</u> <u>Son by faith and love.</u>

God loves, as we shall shortly see, all men, but He has an altogether peculiar love for those who are in Christ.

Jno. 17: 23—"I in them, and thou in me, that they may be made perfect in one; and that the world may know that thou hast sent me, and *hast loved them, as thou hast loved me.*"

<u>God has precisely the same love to those who are in Christ that He has to Christ Himself.</u> Of course there is a love of God to those who are now in Christ which is antecedent to their love to Christ. (1 Jno. 4:19—"We love Him, because He first loved us.")

(3) Jno. 3: 16—"For God so loved *the world* that he gave his only begotten Son, that whosoever believeth in him should not perish, but have everlasting life."

1 Tim. 2: 4—"Who will have *all men* to be saved, and to come unto the knowledge of the truth."

2 Pet. 3: 9—"The Lord is not slack concerning his promise, as some men count slackness; but is long suffering to us-ward, *not willing that any should perish,* but that all should come to repentance."

FOURTH PROPOSITION: God loves <u>the world</u>—the whole human race and each individual in it.

(4)   Rom. 5:6–8—"For when we were yet without strength, in due time Christ died *for the ungodly.* For scarcely for a righteous man will one die: yet peradventure for a good man some would even dare to die. But God commendeth his love toward us, in that, *while we were yet sinners*, Christ died for us."

Eph. 2:4, 5—"But God, who is rich in mercy, for his great love wherewith he loved us, *even when we were dead in sins*, hath quickened us together with Christ (by grace ye are saved)."

Ez. 33:11—"Say unto them, As I live, saith the Lord God, I have no pleasure in the death of the wicked; but that the wicked turn from his way and live: turn ye, turn ye from your evil ways; for why will ye die, O house of Israel?"

FIFTH PROPOSITION: God loves the <u>sinner</u>, the ungodly, those dead in sins.

<u>God has not the same love for the unregenerate sinner that He has for the one in Christ</u>. (Jno. 14:21, ·23; Jno. 17:23; Rom. 8:30–39.) But God has a peculiar interest in lost ones. (Luke 15:7–10—"I say unto you, that likewise joy shall be in Heaven over one sinner that repenteth, more than over ninety and nine just persons which need no repentance. Likewise, I say unto you, there is joy in the presence of the angels of God over one sinner that repenteth.") This can be understood by a father's love for a true son and a wayward son.

III. How does the Love of God manifest itself?

(1)   Is. 48:14, 20, 21—"All ye assemble yourselves, and hear; which among them hath declared these things? The Lord hath loved him: he will do his pleasure on Babylon, and his arm shall be on the Chaldeans. Go ye forth of Babylon, flee ye from the Chaldeans, with a voice of singing declare ye, tell this, utter it even to the end of the earth; say ye, The Lord hath redeemed his servant Jacob. And they thirsted not when he led them through the deserts: he caused the waters to flow out of the rock for them: he clave the rock also, and the waters gushed out."

Deut, 32:9–12—"For the Lord's portion is his people; Jacob is the lot of his inheritance. He found him in a desert land, and in the waste howling wilderness; he led him about, he instructed him, he kept him as the apple of his eye. As an eagle stirreth up her nest, fluttereth over her young, spreadeth abroad her wings, taketh them, beareth them on her wings: So the LORD alone did lead him, and there was no strange God with him."

Deut. 33: 3, 12—"Yea, he loved the people; all his saints are in thy hand: and they sat down at thy feet; every one shall receive of thy words. And of Benjamin he said, the beloved of the LORD shall dwell in safety by him; and the LORD shall cover him all the day long, and he shall dwell between his shoulders."

FIRST PROPOSITION: God's love manifests itself in minister-ing to the need and joy *of those He loves, and protecting them from all evil.*

(2) Heb. 12:6-11—"For whom the Lord loveth he *chasteneth*, and *scourgeth* every son whom he receiveth. If ye endure chastening, God dealeth with you as with sons: for what son is he whom the father chasteneth not ? But if ye be without chastening, whereof all are par-takers, then are ye bastards, and not sons. Furthermore we have had fathers of our flesh which corrected us, and we gave them reverence: shall we not much rather be in subjection unto the Father of Spirits, and live ? For they verily for a few days chastened us after their own pleasure; but he for our profit, that we might be partakers of his holiness. Now no chastening for the present seemeth to be joyous, but grievous: nevertheless afterward it yieldeth the peaceable fruit of righteousness unto them which are exercised thereby."

SECOND PROPOSITION: God's love manifests itself in chasten-ing and scourging His loved ones *for their profit, that out of this chastening the peaceable fruit of righteousness may come.*

(3) Is. 63:9—"In all their affliction he was afflicted, and the angel of his presence saved them: in his love and in his pity he redeemed them; and he bare them, and carried them all the days of old."

THIRD PROPOSITION: God's love manifests itself in His being Himself afflicted when His loved ones are afflicted, *even when that affliction comes from His own hand.*

(4) Is. 49: 15, 16—"Can a woman forget her sucking child, that she should not have compassion on the son of her womb ? Yea, they may forget, yet will I not forget thee. Behold, I have graven thee on the palms of my hands; thy walls are continually before me."

FOURTH PROPOSITION: God's love is manifested in His never forgetting those He loves. *He seems to forget, but He never does.*

(5) 1 Jno. 4:9, 10—"In this was manifested the love of God toward us, because that God *sent his only begotten Son into the world*, that

we might live through him.   Herein is love, not that we loved God, but
that he loved us, and sent his Son to be the propitiation for our
sins."

Jno. 3: 16—"For God so loved the world that he *gave his only begotten Son*, that whosoever believeth in him should not perish, but
have everlasting life."

FIFTH PROPOSITION: *God s love has manifested itself by
His making the greatest sacrifice in His power for those He loves
—the sacrifice of His Son to be the propitiation for our sins.*

Sacrifice is the measure of love.   The sacrifice of Christ is
the measure of God's love.   (Compare Gen. 22: 12—"And he
said, Lay not thine hand upon the lad, neither do thou anything
unto him: for now I know that thou fearest God, *seeing thou
hast not withheld thy son, thine only son, from me.*")

(6) Is. 38: 17—"Behold, for peace I have great bitterness: but thou
hast in love to my soul delivered it from the pit of corruption: for thou
hast cast all my sins behind thy back."

Is. 55: 7—"Let the wicked forsake his ways, and the unrighteous
man his thoughts: and let him return unto the Lord, and he will have
mercy upon him ; and to our God, for he will abundantly pardon."

SIXTH PROPOSITION: *God's love manifests itself in His forgiving sins.*

(7) Eph. 2: 4, R.V.—"But God, being rich in mercy, for his great
love wherewith he loved us, even when we were dead through our trespasses, quickened us together with Christ (by grace have ye been
saved), and raised us up with him, and made us to sit with him in the
heavenly places, in Christ Jesus: that in the ages to come he might
show the exceeding riches of his grace in kindness toward us in Christ
Jesus: for by grace have ye been saved through faith ; and that not
of yourselves: it is the gift of God."

SEVENTH PROPOSITION: *God's love manifests itself.   (1)   In
His imparting life to those dead in trespasses and sins.   (2)   In
His raising them up with Christ.   (3)   In His making them sit
with Christ in the heavenly places.   (4)   In His showing to us
in the ages to come the exceeding riches of His grace in kindness
toward us through Christ Jesus.*

God has only begun to do for us.   The fullness of His love
is not yet manifested.   It is just beginning to unfold itself.
"Beloved, now are we the sons of God, and it doth not yet appeal

what we shall be: but we know that when he shall appear, we shall be like him ; for we shall see him as he is." (1 Jno. 3: 2.)

(8) 1 Jno. 3: 1, R.V.—"Behold what manner of love the Father hath bestowed upon us, that we should be called children of God: and such we are. For this cause the world knoweth us not, because it knew him not."

EIGHTH PROPOSITION: God s love manifests itself in His granting us that "we should be called children of God."

(9) Zep. 3: 17—" The Lord thy God in the midst of thee is mighty; he will save, he will rejoice over thee with joy; he will rest in his love, he will joy over thee with singing."

NINTH PROPOSITION : God's love manifests itself in His rejoicing over His saved people with joy and singing.

Compare Luke 15: 23, 24—"And bring hither the fatted calf, and kill it; and let us eat and be merry. For this, my son, was dead, and is alive again; he was lost, and is found. And they began to be merry."

CHAPTER X.

THE RIGHTEOUSNESS, OR JUSTICE OF GOD.

PRELIMINARY NOTE: The words "Righteous" and "Just," also "Righteousness" and "Justice," in the English Bible represent the same Hebrew and Greek words in the Old and New Testaments.

I. The Fact that God is Righteous.

Ezr. 9: 15—"O LORD God of Israel, thou art righteous."

Ps. 116: 5—"Gracious is the LORD, and righteous; yea, our God is merciful."

Ps. 145: 17—"The LORD is righteous in all his ways, and holy in all his works."

Jer. 12: 1—"Righteous art thou, O LORD, when I plead with thee."

Jno. 17: 25—"O righteous Father, the world hath not known thee, but I have known thee, and these have known that thou hast sent me."

FIRST PROPOSITION: God is righteous, or just.

II. What is it to be righteous, or just?

Ez. 18: 5—"But if a man be just, and do that which is lawful and right."

Zeph. 3: 5—"The just Lord is in the midst thereof; *he will not do iniquity:* every morning doth he bring his judgment to light, he faileth not; but the unjust knoweth no shame."

To be just, or righteous, is to have that character that leads one to always do that which is right.

The Hebrew word, according to its etymology, means "right" or "straight." The etymology of the English word "righteous" is the same. The etymology of the Greek word is "custom" or "usage"—that which conforms to custom.

The Righteousness or Justice of God is that attribute that leads Him always to do right. It is not to be limited, as it so often is in modern theological usage, to His punitive justice. This, as we shall shortly see, is only one manifestation of the

Justice, or Righteousness of God, and not the one that is most prominent in Biblical usage.

Holiness seems to have more reference to God's character as He is in Himself; Righteousness to His character as manifested in his dealings with others.

III.   How the Righteousness, or Justice of God is manifested.

(1) Ps. 11: 4-7— "The Lord is in his holy temple, the Lord's throne is in heaven: his eyes behold, his eyelids try, the children of men. The Lord trieth the righteous: but the wicked and him that loveth violence his soul hateth.   Upon the wicked he shall rain snares, fire and brimstone, and an horrible tempest: this shall be the portion of their cup.   For the righteous Lord loveth righteousness; his countenance doth behold the upright."

FIRST PROPOSITION: The Righteousness of God is manifested in His loving righteousness and hating iniquity.

(2) Ex. 9: 23-27—"And Moses stretched forth his rod toward heaven: and the Lord sent thunder and hail, and the fire ran along upon the ground; and the Lord rained hail upon the land of Egypt. So there was hail, and fire mingled with the hail, very grievous, such as there was none like it in all the land of Egypt since it became a nation.   And the hail smote throughout all the land of Egypt all that was in the field, both man and beast; and the hail smote every herb of the field, and brake every tree of the field.   Only in the land of Goshen, where the children of Israel were, was there no hail.   And Pharaoh sent, and called for Moses and Aaron, and said unto them, I have sinned this time: the Lord is righteous, and I and my people are wicked."

2 Chron. 12: 5, 6—"Then came Shemaiah the prophet of Rehoboam, and to the princes of Judah, that were gathered together to Jerusalem because of Shishak, and said unto them, Thus saith the Lord, Ye have forsaken me, and therefore have I also left you in the hand of Shishak.   Whereupon the princes of Israel and the king humbled themselves; and they said, The Lord is righteous."

Dan. 9: 12, 14—"And he hath confirmed his words, which he spake against us, and against our judges that judged us, by bringing upon us a great evil: for under the whole heaven hath not been done as hath been done upon Jerusalem.   Therefore hath the Lord watched upon the evil, and brought it upon us: for the Lord our God is righteous in all his works which he doeth: for we obeyed not his voice."

Rev. 16: 5, 6—"And I heard the angel of the waters say, Thou art righteous, O Lord, which art and wast, and shall be, because thou hast judged thus.   For they have shed the blood of saints and prophets, and thou hast given them blood to drink; for they are worthy."

SECOND PROPOSITION: The Righteousness of God is mani-
fested in his visiting upon sinners the punishment due to their
sins.

(3) 2 Tim. 4: 8—"Henceforth there is laid up for me a crown of
righteousness, which the Lord, the righteous judge, shall give me at
that day: and not to me only, but unto all them also that love his appearing."

1 Kings 8: 32—"Then hear thou in heaven, and do, and judge thy
servants, condemning the wicked, to bring his way upon his head;
and justifying the righteous, to give him according to his righteousness."

Ps. 7: 9-11—"O, let the wickedness of the wicked come to an end;
but establish the just: for the righteous God trieth the hearts and
reins. My defense is of God, which saveth the upright in heart.
God judgeth the righteous, and God is angry with the wicked every
day."

Heb. 6: 10—" For God is not unrighteous to forget your work and
labor of love, which ye have shewed toward his name, in that ye have
ministered to the saints, and do minister."

THIRD PROPOSITION: The Righteousness of God is mani-
fested in His bestowing upon the righteous the reward due their
faithfulness.

(4) Ps. 98: 1-3—"O, sing unto the LORD a new song; for he hath
done marvelous things: his right hand, and his holy arm, hath gotten him the victory. The LORD hath made known his salvation:
his righteousness hath he openly showed in the sight of the heathen.
He hath remembered his mercy and his truth toward the house of
Israel: all the ends of the earth have seen the salvation of our God."

Ps. 103: 6—" The LORD executeth righteousness and judgment for
all that are oppressed."

Ps. 129: 1-4—"Many times have they afflicted me from my
youth, may Israel now say: Many a time have they afflicted me
from my youth: yet they have not prevailed against me. The
plowers plowed upon my back: they made long their furrows. The
LORD is righteous: he hath cut asunder the cords of the wicked."

2 Thess. 1: 6, 7—"Seeing it is a righteous thing with God to recompense tribulation to them that trouble you. And to you who are
troubled rest with us, when the Lord Jesus shall be revealed from
heaven with his mighty angels."

FOURTH PROPOSITION: The Righteousness of God is mani-fested in His protecting and delivering His people from all their adversaries.

In modern theological discussions we hear more of the Jus-tice, or Righteousness of God in its relation to the punishment of sinners, but in the Bible we read of it more in relation to the protection of His people. In modern usage it is more frequently held up as an attribute of God at which sinners should tremble; in the Bible it is constantly dwelt upon as an attribute of God at which His people should rejoice and be confident. See, for ex-ample:

Ps. 96: 11-13—" Let the heavens *rejoice*, and let the earth be glad; let the sea roar, and the fulness thereof. Let the field *be joyful*, and all that is therein: then shall all the trees of the wood *rejoice*, before the LORD: for he cometh, *for he cometh to judge* the earth: he shall judge the world *with righteousness*, and the people with his truth." Jer. 9:24—" But let him that glorieth glory in this, that he under-standeth and knoweth me, that I am the LORD which exercise loving-kindness, judgment and righteousness in the earth: for in these things I delight, saith the LORD." Ps. 116: 5, 6—" Gracious is the LORD, and righteous; yea, our God is merciful. The LORD preserveth the simple: I was brought low, and he helped me." Ps. 145: 5, 15-19—" The LORD upholdeth all that fall, and raiseth up all those that are bowed down. The eyes of all wait upon thee; and thou givest them their meat in due season. Thou openest thine hand, and satisfiest the desire of every living thing. *The* LORD *is righteous* in all his ways, and holy in all his works. The LORD is nigh unto all them that call upon him, to all that call upon him in truth. He will fulfill the desire of them that fear him: he also will hear their cry, and will save them." Rev. 15: 3—" And they sing the song of Moses, the servant of God, and the song of the Lamb, saying, Great and marvelous are thy works, Lord God Almighty; just and true are thy ways, thou King of Saints."

Even the righteousness of God in the punishment of the sin-her is sometimes spoken of in relation to its connection with the deliverance or avenging of His people. As in:

2 Thess. 1: 6, 7—" Seeing it is a righteous thing with God to recom-pense tribulation to them that trouble you. And to you who are troubled rest with us, when the Lord Jesus shall be revealed from heaven with his mighty angels."

Rev. 19: 1, 2—" And after these things I heard a great voice of much people in heaven, saying, Alleluia; Salvation and glory, and honor, and power, unto the Lord our God: For true and righteous

are his judgments: for he hath judged the great whore, which did cor·
rupt the earth with her fornication, and hath avenged the blood of his
servants at her hand."

Rev. 16: 4-6—"And the third angel poured out his vial upon the
rivers and fountains of water; and they became blood. And I heard
the angel of the waters say, Thou art righteous, O Lord, which art,
and wast, and shalt be, because thou hast judged thus. For they have
shed the blood of saints and prophets, and thou hast given them
blood to drink; for they are worthy."

Here it is the vindication and avenging of His people, rather
than the suffering of the wicked, that is the prominent thought.

(5) Neh. 9: 7, 8—"Thou art the LORD the God, who didst choose
Abram, and broughtest him forth out of Ur of the Chaldees, and
gavest him the name of Abraham, and foundest his heart faithful before thee, and madest a covenant with him to give the land of
the Canaanites, the Hittites, the Amorites, and the Perizzites, and
the Jebusites, and the Girgashites, to give it, I say, to his seed, and
hast performed thy words; for thou art righteous."

*FIFTH PROPOSITION: The Righteousness of God is man·
ifested in His keeping His promises.*

(6) Rom. 3: 25—"Whom God hath set forth to be a propitiation,
through faith, in his blood, to declare his righteousness, because of
the passing over of the sins done aforetime, in the forbearance of
God; for the showing, I say, of his righteousness at the present
season: that he might himself be just, and the justifier of him that
hath faith in Jesus."

*SIXTH PROPOSITION: The Righteousness of God is man·
ifested.   (1)   In His providing a propitiation when sin was forgiven.   (2)   In His justifying him that hath faith in the substitute.*

(7) 1 Jno. 1: 9—"If we confess our sins, he is faithful and just to
forgive us our sins, and to cleanse us from all unrighteousness."

*SEVENTH PROPOSITION: The Righteousness of God is
manifested in the forgiveness of the sins of the believer when they
are confessed.*

CHAPTER XI.

THE MERCY, OR LOVING KINDNESS OF GOD.

PRELIMINARY NOTE: The same Hebrew word is translated sometimes "mercy" and sometimes "loving-kindness." These two words, therefore, mean precisely the same thing. The Hebrew word should have been translated uniformly the one or the other. The word "mercy" in our English translation of the Old Testament is in a few instances a translation of another Hebrew word. This latter word corresponds to the Greek word always translated "compassion" in the New Testament. It covers essentially the same thought as the other word; in fact, in the quotation in Rom. 9: 15—"For he saith to Moses, I will have mercy on whom I will have mercy, and I will have compassion on whom I will have compassion," it is translated by the Greek word for mercy. The primary meaning of the word most frequently used is "kindness," especially kindness exercised toward the suffering or sinning. It is so translated thirty-nine times in the Authorized Version. In thirty-one of these instances it is used of the kindness of man toward man, in the remaining eight of the kindness of God toward man.

I. The fact that God is Merciful.

Ps. 103: 8—"The LORD is merciful and gracious, slow to anger, and plenteous in mercy."

Deut. 4: 31—"(For the LORD thy God is a merciful God); he will not forsake thee, neither destroy thee, nor forget the covenant of thy fathers which he sware unto them."

Ps. 62: 12—"Also unto thee, O LORD, belongeth mercy."

Ps. 145: 8—"The LORD is gracious and full of compassion; slow to anger, and of great mercy."

Ps. 86: 15—"But thou, O LORD, art a God full of compassion, and gracious, long-suffering, and plenteous in mercy and truth."

PROPOSITION: God is merciful, plenteous in mercy.

II.   Toward whom is the mercy of God manifested ?

(1)   Rom. 9: 15, 18—"For he saith to Moses, I will have mercy on whom I will have mercy, and I will have compassion on whom I will have compassion.   Therefore hath he mercy on whom he will have mercy, and whom he will he hardeneth."

FIRST PROPOSITION: God's mercy is manifested toward whom He will.   He is absolutely sovereign in the exercise of His mercy.

But it should be remembered that while God is absolutely sovereign in the exercise of His mercy, while no one can dictate upon whom He shall have mercy, in point of fact He wills to have mercy on all upon whom He can have mercy.   (See 2 Pet. 3: 9— "The Lord is not slack concerning His promise, as some men count slackness; but is long-suffering to us-ward, not willing that any should perish, but that all should come to repentance.")

(2)   Deut. 7: 9—"Know therefore that the Lord thy God, he is God, the faithful God, which keepeth covenant and mercy with them that love him and keep his commandments to a thousand generations."

Ex. 20: 6—"And showing mercy unto thousands of them that love me, and keep my commandments."

Ps. 103: 11, 17—"For as the heaven is high above the earth, so great is his mercy toward them that fear him.   But the mercy of the Lord is from everlasting to everlasting upon them that fear him, and his righteousness unto children's children."

2 Chron. 6: 14—"And said, O Lord God of Israel, there is no God like Thee in the heaven, nor in the earth; which keepest covenant, and showest mercy unto thy servants, that walk before Thee with all their hearts."

SECOND PROPOSITION: God's mercy is manifested toward those who fear or love Him: His servants, who walk before Him with all their hearts.

"The fear of the Lord" and "the love of God" as used in the Bible are nearly synonymous.   (Compare Prov. 8: 13; 16: 6 with 1 Jno. 5: 3.)   They look at the same practical attitude toward God from different points of view.

(3)   Prov. 28: 13—"He that covereth his sins shall not prosper but whoso confesseth and forsaketh them shall have mercy."

THIRD PROPOSITION: The mercy of God is manifested toward every one who confesses and forsakes his sins.

(4) Ps. 32: 10—"Many sorrows shall be to the wicked; but he that trusteth in the LORD, mercy shall compass him about."

FOURTH PROPOSITION: The mercy of God is manifested toward the one who trusteth in the Lord—"Mercy shall compass him about."

(5) Ps. 86: 5—"For Thou, LORD, art good, and ready to forgive; and plenteous in mercy unto all them that call upon Thee."

FIFTH PROPOSITION: The mercy of God is manifested toward all them that call upon Him. (See also Rom. 10: 12, 13—"For there is no difference between the Jew and the Greek; for the same Lord over all is rich unto all that call upon Him. For whosoever shall call upon the name of the LORD shall be saved."

(6) Is. 49: 13—"Sing, O Heavens; and be joyful, O earth; and break forth in singing, O mountains: for the LORD hath comforted His people, and will have mercy upon his afflicted."

SIXTH PROPOSITION: The mercy of God is manifested toward His afflicted people.

III. How is the mercy of God manifested ?

(1) Ex. 34: 7—"Keeping mercy for thousands, forgiving iniquity and transgression and sin, and that will by no means clear the guilty; visiting the iniquities of the fathers upon the children, and upon the children's children, unto the third and fourth generation."

Is. 55: 7—"Let the wicked forsake his way, and the unrighteous man his thoughts; and let him return unto the LORD, and He will have mercy upon him; and to our God, for He will abundantly pardon."

Jonah 4: 2—"And he prayed unto the LORD, and said, I pray Thee, O LORD, was not this my saying, when I was yet in my country ? therefore I fled before unto Tarshish: for I knew that Thou art a gracious God, and merciful, slow to anger, and of great kindness, and repentest Thee of the evil."

Jer. 3: 12—"Go and proclaim these words toward the north, and say, Return, thou backsliding Israel, saith the LORD; and I will not cause mine anger to fall upon you: for I am merciful, saith the LORD, and I will not keep anger forever."

Mic. 7: 18—"Who is a God like unto thee, that pardoneth iniquity,

and passeth by the transgression of the remnant of his heritage ? He
retaineth not His anger forever because He delighteth in mercy."

Ps. 51: 1—"Have mercy upon me, O God, according to thy loving·
kindness: according unto the multitude of thy tender mercies blot out
my transgressions."

Num. 14:18, 19, 20—"The LORD is longsuffering, and of great
mercy, forgiving iniquity and transgression, and by no means clearing
the guilty, visiting the iniquity of the fathers upon the children unto
the third and fourth generation. Pardon, I beseech thee, the iniquity
of this people according unto the greatness of thy mercy, and as thou
hast forgiven this people, from Egypt even until now. And the LORD
said, I have·pardoned according to thy word."

*FIRST PROPOSITION: The mercy of God is manifested in his
pardoning sin when confessed and forsaken.*

This manifestation of God's mercy lies at the basis of many
other manifestations. Nevertheless, it is not true, according to
Biblical usage, that "mercy is exercised only when there is
guilt."

(2) Neh. 9: 16-18, 26, 27, 30, 31—"But they and our fathers dealt
proudly, and hardened their necks and hearkened not to thy command·
ments. And refused to obey, neither were mindful of thy wonders
that thou didst among them; but hardened their necks, and in their
rebellion appointed a captain to return to their bondage: but thou art
a God ready to pardon, gracious and merciful, slow to anger, and of
great kindness and forsookest them not. Yea, when they had made
them a molten calf, and said, this is thy God that brought thee up
out of Egypt, and had wrought great provocations." (See also inter-
vening verses.) "Nevertheless, they were disobedient and rebelled
against thee, and cast thy law behind their backs and slew thy prophets
which testified against them to turn them to thee, and they wrought
great provocations. Therefore, thou deliverest them into the hand
of their enemies, who vexed them: and in the time of their trouble,
when they cried unto thee, thou heardest them from heaven; and according to thy manifold mercies thou gavest them saviours, who saved
them out of the hand of the enemies. Yet many years didst thou for-
bear them, and testifiedst against them by thy spirit in thy prophets:
yet would they not give ear: therefore gavest thou them into the hand
of the people of the lands. Nevertheless for thy great mercies' sake
thou didst not utterly consume them nor forsake them; for thou art a
gracious and merciful God."

*SECOND PROPOSITION: The mercy of God is manifested in
his bearing long with sinners even when they harden their necks*

and persist in sin.—(Cf. 2 Pet., 3:9.—"The Lord is not slack concerning his promise, as some men count slackness; but is longsuffering to us-ward, not willing that any should perish, but that all should come to repentance.")

(3) Ps. 6:1-4—"O LORD, rebuke me not in thine anger, neither chasten me in thy hot displeasure. Have mercy upon me, O LORD, for I am weak: O LORD, heal me, for my bones are vexed. My soul is also sore vexed: but thou, O LORD, how long? Return, O LORD, deliver my soul: oh save me for thy mercies' sake."

Phil. 2:27—"For indeed he was sick nigh unto death: but God had mercy on him; and not on him only, but on me also, lest I should have sorrow upon sorrow."

Ex. 15:13—"Thou in thy mercy hast led forth the people which thou hast redeemed: thou hast guided them in thy strength unto thy holy habitation."

THIRD PROPOSITION: The mercy of God is manifested in His delivering from sickness, sorrow and oppression.

(4) Ps. 21:7 "For the king trusteth in the LORD, and through the mercy of the most high he shall not be moved."

FOURTH PROPOSITION: The mercy of God is manifested in His maintaining the security of those who trust Him.

(5) Ps. 59:16—"But I will sing of thy power; yea, I will sing aloud of thy mercy in the morning: for thou hast been my defense and refuge in the day of my trouble."

FIFTH PROPOSITION: The mercy of God is manifested in His acting as a defense and refuge in the day of trouble.

CHAPTER XII.

THE FAITHFULNESS OF GOD.

I. The fact that God is faithful.

Deut. 7: 9—"Know therefore that the LORD thy God, he is God, *the faithful God* which keepeth covenant and mercy with them that love and keep his commandments to a thousand generations."

Deut. 32: 4, R.V.—"The rock, his work is perfect;
For all his ways are judgment:
A God of faithfulness and without iniquity,
Just and right is he."

Is. 49: 7—"Thus saith the LORD, the Redeemer of Israel, and his Holy One to him whom man despiseth, to him whom the nation abhorreth, to a servant of rulers, kings shall see and arise, princes also shall worship, because of *the* LORD *that is faithful* and the Holy One of Israel, and he shall choose thee."

1 Cor. 1: 9—"*God is faithful*, by whom ye were called unto the fellowship of his son, Jesus Christ, our Lord."

1 Cor. 10: 13—"There hath no temptation taken you but such as is common to man: but *God is faithful*, who will not suffer you to be tempted above that ye are able; but will with the temptation also make a way to escape, that ye may be able to bear it."

1 Thess. 5: 24—"*Faithful* is he that calleth you, who also will do it."

2 Thess. 3: 3—"But *the Lord is faithful*, who shall establish you and keep you from evil."

1 Jno. 1: 9—"If we confess our sins, *he is faithful* and just to forgive us our sins, and to cleanse us from all unrighteousness."

FIRST PROPOSITION: God is faithful.

II. What does "faithful" mean ?

(1) THE ETYMOLOGY.—The Hebrew root from which the words translated "faithful" and "faithfulness" in the Old Testament are <u>derived means to prop or stay or support</u>. The intransitive use of the word signifies to stay oneself or be supported: hence the word "faithful," as applied to a person, <u>means such an one as</u>

one may safely lean upon.   The Greek word used in the New
Testament means trustworthy or to be relied upon, but this
Greek word is the same used in the LXX for the Hebrew word
mentioned above, and of course gets its meaning from this usage.

(2)   USAGE.—Ps. 119 : 86.   "All thy commandments are faithful."   Prov. 14 : 5.—"A faithful witness will not lie: but a
false witness will utter lies."

Matt. 24 : 45, 46— "Who then is a faithful and wise servant,
whom his Lord hath made ruler over his household, to give
them meat in due season ?   Blessed is that servant, whom his
Lord when he cometh shall find so doing."   Matt. 25 : 21, 23—
"His Lord said unto him, Well done, thou good and faithful
servant: thou hast been faithful over a few things, I will make
thee ruler over many things: enter thou into the joy of thy
Lord.   His Lord said unto him, Well done, good and faithful
servant; thou hast been faithful over a few things, I will make
thee ruler over many things: enter thou into the joy of thy
Lord."

1 Tim. 1 : 15—"This is a faithful saying, and worthy of all acceptation, that Christ Jesus came into the world to save sinners;
of whom I am chief."   Rev. 21 : 5—"And he that sat upon
the throne said, Behold I make all things new.   And he said
unto me, Write, for these words are true and faithful."

The Biblical usage of the word conforms to its etymology.
The thought will come out more fully and definitely as we come
to see how the faithfulness of God is manifested.   Therefore,
the proposition God is faithful means *God is a being upon whom
we can absolutely rely or stay ourselves.*

III.   The extent of God's faithfulness.

(1)   Lam. 3 : 23—"They are new every morning: great is thy faithfulness."

FIRST PROPOSITION: God's faithfulness is great.

(2)   Ps. 36 : 5, R.V.—"Thy loving kindness, O LORD, is in the heavens; thy faithfulness reacheth unto the skies."

SECOND PROPOSITION: God's faithfulness reacheth unto the skies. (Note context, v. 6. Compare Ps. 89: 2—"For I have said, Mercy shall be built up forever: thy faithfulness shalt thou establish in the very heavens.")

(3) Ps. 33: 4, R.V.—"For the word of the LORD is right; and all His work is done in faithfulness."

THIRD PROPOSITION: All God's work is done in faithfulness.

IV.   How the faithfulness of God is manifested.

(1) Heb. 10: 23, 36, 37—"Let us hold fast the profession of our faith without wavering (for he is faithful that promised). For we have need of patience, that after ye have done the will of God, ye might receive the promise. For yet a little while, and he that shall come will come, and will not tarry."

Deut. 7: 9—"Know therefore that the LORD thy God, he is God, the faithful God, which keepeth covenant and mercy with them that love him and keep his commandments to a thousand generations."

Cf. 1 Kg: 8, 23, 24, 56—"And he said, LORD God of Israel, there is no God like thee, in heaven above, or on earth beneath, who keepest covenant and mercy with thy servants that walk before thee with all their heart: Who hast kept with thy servant David my father that thou promisedst him: thou speakest also with thy mouth, and hast fulfilled it with thine hand, as it is this day. Blessed be the LORD, that hath given rest unto his people Israel, according to all that he promised: there hath not failed one word of all his good promise, which he promised by the hand of Moses, his servant."

Ps. 89: 33, 34—"Nevertheless my loving kindness will I not utterly take from him, nor suffer my faithfulness to fail. My covenant will I not break, nor alter the thing that is gone out of my lips."

Ps. 119: 89, 90—"Forever, O LORD, thy word is settled in Heaven. Thy faithfulness is unto all generations: thou hast established the earth, and it abideth."

FIRST PROPOSITION: God's faithfulness is manifested in His keeping His promise and covenant.   His fulfilling every word that goes out of His mouth regardless of what man does.

(2) 1 Pet. 4: 19—"Wherefore let them that suffer according to the will of God commit the keeping of their souls to him in well doing, as unto a faithful Creator."

Ps. 89; 20-26—"I have found David my servant; with my holy oil have I anointed him: with whom my hand shall be established: mine arm also shall strengthen him. The enemy shall not exact upon him: nor the son of wickedness afflict him. And I will beat down his foes before his face and plague them that hate him. But my faithfulness and my mercy shall be with him: and in my name shall his horn be exalted. I will set his hand also in the sea, and his right hand in the rivers. He shall cry unto me, Thou art my father, my God, and the rock of my salvation."

This might well be called "The Faithfulness Psalm." (See v. 1, etc.)

SECOND PROPOSITION: *God's faithfulness is manifested in the* unfailing defense and deliverance of His servants in times of trial, testing and conflict.

(3) Lam. 3:22-23—"It is of the LORD's mercies that we are not consumed, because his compassion fail not. They are new every morning; great is thy faithfulness."

(Cf. Jer. 51:5—"For Israel hath not been forsaken, nor Judah of his God, of the LORD of hosts; though their land was filled with sin against the Holy One of Israel.")

THIRD PROPOSITION: *God's faithfulness is manifested in His standing by His people and saving them even when they are unfaithful to him.*

Cf. 2 Tim. 2: 13, R. V.—"If we are faithless, he abideth faithful: for he cannot deny himself."

1 Sam., 12, 20-22—"And Samuel said unto the people, Fear not: ye have done all this wickedness: yet turn not aside from following the LORD, but serve the LORD with all your heart; And turn ye not aside: for then should ye go after vain things, which cannot profit nor deliver; for they are vain. For the LORD will not forsake his people for his great name's sake: because it has pleased the LORD to make you his people."

Our security is in His faithfulness, not in our own.

(4) 1 Cor. 10: 13—"God is faithful, who will not suffer you to be tempted above that ye are able; but will with the temptation make a way to escape, that ye may be able to bear it."

FOURTH PROPOSITION: *God's faithfulness is manifested in His* not suffering His children to be tempted above that which they are able, *but with the temptation making also a way to escape, that they may be able to bear it.*

(5) 2 Thess. 3: 3, R.V.—"But the Lord is faithful, who shall establish you, and guard you from the evil one."

1 Cor. 1: 8, 9—"Who shall also confirm you unto the end, that ye
may be blameless in the day of our Lord Jesus Christ. God is faithful, by whom ye are called unto the fellowship of his Son Jesus Christ
our Lord."

1 Thess. 5: 23, 24, R.V.—"And the God of peace himself sanctify you
wholly; and may your spirit and soul and body be preserved entire,
without blame at the coming of our Lord Jesus Christ. Faithful is
he that calleth you, who will also do it."

*FIFTH PROPOSITION: The faithfulness of God is manifested
in confirming and establishing those whom He has called, guarding them from the evil one, sanctifying them wholly and preserving
them entire—spirit, soul and body—without blame at the coming
of our Lord Jesus Christ. The confidence of God's children in
regard to their future is not in their faithfulness, but in His.*

Cf. Jno. 10: 28, 29—"And I give unto them eternal life; and they
shall never perish, neither shall any man pluck them out of my hand.
My Father, which gave them me, is greater than all ; and no man is
able to pluck them out of my Father's hand."

(6) Ps. 119: 75—"I know, O LORD, that thy judgments are right,
and that Thou in faithfulness hast afflicted me."

*SIXTH PROPOSITION: God's faithfulness is manifested in
His chastening His children when they go astray.*

Cf. Heb. 12: 6—"For whom the LORD loveth he chasteneth, and
scourgeth every son whom he receiveth."

(7) 1 Jno. 1: 9—"If we confess our sins, He is faithful and just to
forgive us our sins, and to cleanse us from all unrighteousness."

*SEVENTH PROPOSITION: God's faithfulness is manifested
in His forgiving His children when they confess their sins.*

Our confidence that God will forgive our sins when confessed
rests upon two known facts about God, viz: God is righteous and
God is faithful. To doubt that your sin is forgiven when you
have confessed it is to question His righteousness and His faithfulness as well as His veracity. It is not humility, but presumption.

(8) Ps. 143: 1, 2—"Hear my prayer, O LORD, give ear to my supplications; in thy faithfulness answer me, and in thy righteousness.
And enter not into judgment with thy servant : for in thy sight shall
no man living be justified."

EIGHTH PROPOSITION: God's Faithfulness is manifested in His answering the prayers of His children.

The Righteousness, Mercy and Faithfulness of God run along nearly parallel lines, and they are all pledged to the deliverance, defense and complete and eternal salvation of God's people.

BOOK II.

—

WHAT THE BIBLE TEACHES ABOUT JESUS CHRIST.

CHAPTER I.

HIS DIVINITY.

I. Divine Names.

(1) Luke 22:70—"Then said they all, Art thou then the Son of God? And he said unto them, Ye say that I am."

"The Son of God." This name is given to Christ forty times. Besides this the synonymous expressions, "His Son," "My Son," are of frequent occurrence. That this name, as used of Christ, is a distinctly divine name appears from Jno. 5:18— "Therefore the Jews sought the more to kill him, because He not only had broken the Sabbath, but said also that God was His Father, *making himself equal with God.*"

(2) Jno. 1:18—"No man hath seen God at any time; the only begotten Son, which is in the bosom of the Father, he hath declared him."

"The Only Begotten Son." This occurs five times. It is evident that the statement that Jesus Christ is the Son of God only in the same sense that all men are sons of God is not true. Compare Mark 12:6—"Having yet therefore *one son*, his well-beloved, he sent him also last unto them, saying, They will reverence my son." Here Jesus Himself, having spoken of all the prophets as servants of God, speaks of Himself as "one," a beloved "Son."

(3) Rev. 1:17—"And when I saw him, I fell at his feet as dead. And he laid his right hand upon me, saying unto me, Fear not; I am the first and the last."

"The First and the Last." Compare Is. 41:4—"Who hath wrought and done it, calling the generations from the beginning? I the Lord, the first, and with the last; I am he." Is. 44:6—"Thus saith the Lord the King of Israel, and his redeemer the Lord of Hosts; I am the first, and I am the last; and beside me there is no God." In these latter passages it is "Jehovah" "Jehovah of hosts" who is "the first and the last."

(4) Rev. 22:12, 13, 16—"And, behold, I come quickly; and my reward is with me, to give every man according as his work shall be.

I am Alpha and Omega, the beginning and the end, the first and the last.   I, Jesus, have sent mine angel to testify unto you these things in the churches.   I am the root and the offspring of David, and the bright and morning star."

First.—"THE ALPHA AND OMEGA."

Second.—"THE BEGINNING AND THE ENDING."

Cf. Rev. 1: 8, R. V.—"I am the Alpha and the Omega *saith the Lord God,* which is and which was and which is to come, the Almighty."   Here it is the Lord God who is the Alpha and Omega.

(5) Acts 3: 14—"But he denied the Holy One and the just, and desired a murderer to be granted unto you."

"THE HOLY ONE."—In Hosea 11: 9—("I will not execute the fierceness of mine anger, I will not return to destroy Eph-raim: for I am God and not man; the Holy One in the midst of thee: and I will not enter into the city"), and many other pas-sages; it is God who is "the Holy One."

(6) Mal. 3: 1—"Behold I will send my messenger, and he shall pre-pare the way before me: and the Lord, whom ye seek, shall suddenly come to his temple, even the messenger of the covenant, whom ye de-light in: behold he shall come, saith the LORD of Hosts."

Luke 2: 11—"For unto you is born this day in the city of David a Saviour, which is Christ the Lord."

Acts 9: 17—"And Ananias went his way, and entered into the house; and putting his hands on him said, Brother Saul, the Lord, even Jesus, that appeared unto thee in the way as thou camest, hath sent me, that thou mightest receive thy sight, and be filled with the Holy Ghost." (Cf. Jno. 20: 28; Heb. 1: 10.)

"THE LORD."   This name or title is used of JESUS several hundred times.   The word translated "Lord" is used in the New Testament in speaking of men nine times; *e. g.,* Acts 16: 30; Eph. 4: 1; Jno. 12: 21, but not at all in the way in which it is used of CHRIST.   He is spoken of as "*the* Lord" just as God is.   Cf. Acts 4: 26—"The kings of the earth stood up, and the rulers were gathered together against the Lord, and against his Christ," with 4: 33—"And with great power gave the apostles witness of the resurrection of the Lord Jesus: and great grace was given them all."

Note also Matt. 22: 43-45,—"He saith unto them, H ow, then, doth David in spirit call him Lord, saying, The Lord said unto my Lord, sit thou on my right hand, until I make thine enemies thy footstool. If David called him Lord, how is he his son?" Phil. 2: 11—"And that every tongue should confess that Jesus Christ is Lord to the glory of God the Father." Eph. 4:5—"One Lord, one faith, one baptism."

If any one doubts the attitude of the apostles of JESUS toward Him as divine they would do well to read one after another the passages which speak of him as Lord.

(7) Acts 10: 36—"The word which God sent unto the children of Israel, preaching peace by Jesus Christ (he is *Lord of all*)."

"LORD OF ALL."

(8) 1 Cor. 2: 8—"Which none of the princes of this world knew: for had they known it, they would not have crucified the Lord of glory."

"THE LORD OF GLORY."

In Ps. 24: 8-10—"Who is this King of Glory? The LORD strong and mighty, the LORD mighty in battle. Lift up your heads, O ye gates: even lift them up, ye everlasting doors: and the king of glory shall come in. Who is this King of Glory? *The* LORD *of hosts*, he is the King of Glory." It is the LORD of Hosts who is the King of Glory.

(9) Is. 9:6—(*a*) "WONDERFUL." (Cf, Judges 13: 18, R.V. "And the angel of the Lord said unto him, Wherefore askest thou after my name, seeing it is wonderful?") (*b*) "MIGHTY GOD." (*c*) "FATHER OF ETERNITY." (See R.V., Marg.)

(10) Heb. 1: 8—"But unto the son he saith, Thy throne, *O God*, is forever and ever: a sceptre of righteousness is the sceptre of Thy kingdom."

"GOD."

In Jno. 20: 28—"And Thomas answered and said unto him, My Lord and my God." Thomas calls Jesus "my God," and is gently rebuked for not believing it before.

(11) Matt. 1:23—"Behold, a virgin shall be with child, and shall bring forth a son, and they shall call his name Emmanuel, which being interpreted is, God with us."

"GOD WITH US."

(12) Tit. 2: 13, R.V.—"Looking for the blessed hope and appearing of the glory of our great God and Savior JESUS CHRIST."

"OUR GREAT GOD."

(13) Rom. 9: 5—"Whose are the fathers, and of whom as concerning the flesh Christ came, who is over all, God blessed forever. Amen."

"GOD BLESSED FOREVER."

PROPOSITION: Sixteen names clearly implying Deity are used of Christ in the Bible, some of them over and over again, the total number of passages reaching far into the hundreds.

II. Divine attributes.

(1) OMNIPOTENCE.

(*a*) Luke 4: 39—"And he stood over her, and rebuked the fever: and it left her: and immediately she arose and ministered unto them."

JESUS has power over disease, it is subject to his word.

(*b*) Luke 7: 14, 15—"And he came and touched the bier: and they that bare him stood still. And he said, Young man, I say unto thee, Arise. And he that was dead sat up, and began to speak. And he delivered him to his mother."

Luke 8: 54, 55—"And he put them all out, and took her by the hand, and called, saying, Maid, arise. And her spirit came again, and she arose straightway: and he commanded to give her meat."

Jno. 5: 25—"Verily, verily, I say unto you, the hour is coming, and now is, when the dead shall hear the voice of the Son of God: and they that hear shall live."

The Son of God has power over death; it is subject to His word.

(*c*) Matt. 8: 26, 27—"And he saith unto them, Why are ye fearful, O ye of little faith ? Then he arose, and rebuked the winds and the sea; and there was a great calm. But the men marvelled, saying, What manner of man is this, that even the winds and the sea obey him ?"

JESUS has power over the winds and sea; they are subject to His word.

(*d*) Matt. 8: 16—"When the even was come, they brought unto him many that were possessed with devils: and he cast out the spirits with his word, and healed all that were sick."

Luke 4: 35, 36, 41—"And Jesus rebuked him, saying, Hold thy peace, and come out of him. And when the devil had thrown him in the midst, he came out of him, and hurt him not. And they were all amazed, and spake among themselves, saying, What a word is this! for with authority and power he commandeth the unclean spirits, and they come out. And devils also came out of many, crying out, and saying, Thou art Christ the Son of God. And he rebuking them, suffered them not to speak: for they knew that he was Christ."

JESUS the CHRIST, the Son of God, has power over demons; they are subject to His word.

(*e*) Eph. 1: 20-23—"Which he wrought in Christ, when he raised him from the dead, and set him at his own right hand in the heavenly places. Far above all principality, and power, and might, and dominion, and every name that is named, not only in this world, but also in that which is to come. And hath put all things under his feet, and gave him to be the head over all things to the church. Which is his body, the fulness of him that filleth all in all."

CHRIST is far above all principality, and power, and might, and dominion, and every name that is named, not only in this world, but also in that which is to come; all things are in subjection (R. V.) under His feet. All the hierarchies of the angelic world are under Him.

(f) Heb. 1:3—"Who being the brightness of his glory, and the express image of His person, and upholding all things by the word of his power, when he had by himself purged our sins, sat down on the right hand of the majesty on high."

The Son of God upholds all things by the word of His power.

FIRST PROPOSITION: Jesus Christ, the Son of God, is omnipotent.

(2) OMNISCIENCE.

(a) Jno. 4:16-19— "Jesus saith unto her, Go, call thy husband, and come hither. The woman answered and said, I have no husband. Jesus said unto her, Thou hast well said, I have no husband: For thou hast had five husbands; and he whom thou now hast is not thy husband; in that saidst thou truly. The woman saith unto him, Sir, I perceive that thou art a prophet."

JESUS knew men's lives, even their secret history.

(b) Mark 2:8—"And immediately when Jesus perceived in his spirit that they so reasoned within themselves, he said unto them, Why reason ye these things in your hearts?"

Luke 5:22—"But when Jesus perceived their thoughts, he answering said unto them, What reason ye in your hearts?"

Jno. 2:24, 25—"But Jesus did not commit himself unto them, because he knew all men. And needed not that any should testify of man: for he knew what was in man." (See also Acts 1:24.)

JESUS knew the secret thoughts of men; He knew all men; He knew what was in man.

In 2 Chron. 6:30—["Then hear thou from heaven, thy dwelling-place, and forgive, and render unto every man according unto all his ways whose heart thou knowest (for thou only knowest the hearts of the children of men). Jer. 17:9, 10—"The heart is deceitful above all things, and desperately wicked: who can know it? I, the LORD search the heart, I try the reins, even to give every man according to his ways, and according to the fruit of his doings"] we are told that God "only knoweth the hearts of the children of men."

(c) Jno. 6:64—"But there are some of you that believe not. For Jesus knew from the beginning who they were that believed not, and who should betray him."

JESUS knew from the beginning that Judas would betray Him. Not only men's present thoughts but their future choices were known to Him.

(d) Jno. 1:48—"Nathanael saith unto him, Whence knowest thou me? Jesus answered and said unto him, Before that Philip called thee, when thou wast under the fig tree, I saw thee."

JESUS knew what men were doing at a distance.

(e) Luke 22:10-12—"And he said unto them, Behold when ye are entered into the city, there shall a man meet you, bearing a pitcher of water; follow him into the house where he entereth in. And ye shall say unto the good man of the house, The Master saith unto thee, Where is the guest chamber, where I shall eat the Passover with my disciples? And he shall show you a large upper room furnished: there make ready."

Jno. 13:1—"Now before the feast of the passover, when Jesus knew that his hour was come that he should depart out of this world unto the Father, having loved his own which were in the world, he loved them unto the end."

Luke 5:4-6—"Now when he had left speaking, he said unto Simon, Launch out into the deep, and let down your nets for a draught. And Simon answering said unto him, Master, we have toiled all night and have taken nothing: nevertheless at Thy word I will let down the net. And when they had this done, they enclosed a great multitude of fishes: and their net brake."

JESUS knew the future regarding not only God's acts, but regarding the minute specific acts of men, and even regarding the fishes of the sea.

NOTE.—Many, if not all, of these items of knowledge up to this point could, if they stood alone, be accounted for by saying that the Omniscient God revealed these specific things to JESUS.

(f) Jno. 21:17—"He saith unto him the third time, Simon, son of Jonas, lovest thou me? Peter was grieved because he said unto him the third time, Lovest thou me? And he said unto Him, Lord, thou knowest all things; Thou knowest that I love thee. Jesus saith unto him, Feed my sheep."

16:30—"Now are we sure that thou knowest all things, and needest not that any man should ask thee : by this we believe that thou camest forth from God."

Col. 2: 3—"In whom are hid all the treasures of wisdom and knowledge."

Jesus knew all things; in Him are hid all the treasures of wisdom and knowledge.

SECOND PROPOSITION: Jesus Christ is omniscient.

Note.—There was, as we shall see when we come to study the humanity of CHRIST, a voluntary veiling and abnegation of the exercise of His inherent Divine Omniscience. (Compare Mark 11: 12-14: Phil. 2: 7.)

(3) OMNIPRESENCE.

(*a*) Matt. 18: 20—"For where two or three are gathered together in my name, there am I in the midst of them."

JESUS CHRIST is present in every place where two or three are gathered together in His name.

(*b*) Matt. 28: 20—"Teaching them to observe all things whatsoever I have commanded you : and, lo, I am with you alway, even unto the end of the world. Amen."

JESUS CHRIST is present with every one who goes forth into any part of the world to make disciples, etc.

(*c*) Jno. 3: 13—"And no man hath ascended up to heaven, but he that came down from heaven, even the son of man which is in heaven."

The Son of Man was in heaven while He was here on earth.

Note.—The reading here is doubtful. It is found in this way in the Alexandrian MS., and almost all versions. The closing words are omitted in the Sinaitic and other important MSS. It is accepted by most of the best editors; *e. g.*, Tischendorf and Tregelles, but it is rejected by Westcott and Hort.

(*d*) Jno. 14: 20—"At that day ye shall know that I am in my Father, and ye in me, and I in you."

2 Cor. 13: 5—"Examine yourselves, whether ye be in the faith ; prove your own selves. Know ye not your own selves, how that JESUS CHRIST is in you, except ye be reprobates ?"

JESUS CHRIST is in each believer.

(*e*) Eph. 1: 23—"Which is his body, the fulness of him that filleth all in all."

JESUS CHRIST filleth all in all.

THIRD PROPOSITION: Jesus Christ is Omnipresent.

(4) ETERNITY.

Jno. 1: 1—"In the beginning was the Word, and the Word was with God, and the Word was God."

Mic. 5:2—"But thou, Beth-lehem Ephratah, though thou be little among the thousands of Judah, yet out of thee shall he come forth unto me that is to be ruler in Israel ; whose goings forth have been from of old, *from everlasting.*"

Col. 1:17—"And he is before all things, and by him all things consist."

Is. 9:6—"For unto us a child is born, unto us a son is given : and the government shall be upon his shoulder : and his name shall be called Wonderful, Counsellor, The Mighty God, *The Everlasting Father*, the Prince of Peace."

Jno. 17:5—"And now, O Father, glorify thou me with thine own self with the glory which I had with thee before the world was." (See also Jno. 6:62.)

Jno. 8:58—"Jesus said unto them, Verily, verily, I say unto you, Before Abraham was, I am."

1 Jno. 1:1—"That which was from the beginning, which we have heard, which we have seen with our eyes, which we have looked upon, and our hands have handled, of the Word of life."

Heb. 13:8—"Jesus Christ the same yesterday, and to-day, and forever."

FOURTH PROPOSITION : The Son of God was from all eternity.

(5) IMMUTABILITY,

Heb. 13:8—"Jesus Christ the same yesterday, and to-day, and forever."

Heb. 1:12—"And as a vesture shalt thou fold them up, and they shall be changed: but thou art the same, and thy years shall not fail."

FIFTH PROPOSITION : Jesus Christ is unchangeable. He not only always is but always is the same.

(6.) Phil. 2:6—"Who being in the form of God, thought it not robbery to be equal with God."

SIXTH PROPOSITION : Jesus Christ before His incarnation was in the form of God.

NOTE.—The Greek word translated "form," means "the form by which a person or thing strikes the vision; the external appearance." (Thayer, Greek-Eng. Lexicon of the N. T.)

(7) Col. 2:9.—"For in him dwelleth all the fulness of the God-head bodily."

SEVENTH PROPOSITION : In Christ dwelleth all the fulness of the God-head in a bodily way.

GENERAL PROPOSITION: Five or more distinctively Divine Attributes are ascribed to Jesus Christ and all the fulness of the God-head is said to dwell in Him.

III. Divine Offices.

(1) CREATION.

Heb. 1: 10—"And thou, Lord, in the beginning hast laid the foundation of the earth; and the heavens are the works of thy hands."

Jno. 1: 3. "All things were made by him; and without him was not anything made that was made."

Col. 1: 16—"For by him were all things created that are in heaven, and that are in earth, visible and invisible, whether they be thrones, or dominions, or principalities, or powers: all things were created by him, and for him."

FIRST PROPOSITION: The Son of God, the Eternal Word, the Lord, is Creator of all created things.

(2) PRESERVATION.

Heb. 1: 3—"Who, being the brightness of his glory, and the express image of his person, and upholding all things by the word of his power, when he had by himself purged our sins, sat down on the right hand of the Majesty on high."

SECOND PROPOSITION: The Son of God is the Preserver of all things.

(3) THE FORGIVENESS OF SIN.

Mark 2: 5-10—"When Jesus saw their faith, he said unto the sick of the palsy, Son, *thy sins be forgiven thee.* But there were certain of the scribes sitting there, and reasoning in their hearts, Why doth this man thus speak blasphemies? *Who can forgive sins but God only?* And immediately when JESUS perceived in his spirit that they so reasoned within themselves, he said unto them, Why reason ye these things in your hearts? Whether is it easier to say to the sick of the palsy, Thy sins be forgiven thee; or to say, Arise, and take up thy bed, and walk? But that ye may know that the Son of man hath power on earth to forgive sins (he saith to the sick of the palsy)."

Luke 7: 48—"And he said unto her, *Thy sins are forgiven.*"

THIRD PROPOSITION: Jesus Christ had power on earth to forgive sins.

NOTE.—He taught that sins were sins against Himself. (See Luke 7:

40-47—"And Jesus answering said unto him, Simon, I have somewhat to say unto thee. And he saith, Master, say on. There was a certain credit-or which had two debtors: the one owed five hundred pence, and the other fifty. And when they had nothing to pay, he frankly forgave them both. Tell me, therefore, which of them will love him most? Simon an-swered and said, I suppose that he, to whom he forgave most. And he said unto him, Thou hast rightly judged. And he turned unto the wom-an, and said unto Simon, Seest thou this woman? I entered into thine house, thou gavest me no water for my feet: but she has washed my feet with tears, and wiped them with the hairs of her head. Thou gavest me no kiss: but this woman since the time I came in hath not ceased to kiss my feet. My head with oil thou didst not anoint: but this woman hath anointed my feet with ointment. Wherefore, I say unto thee, Her sins, which are many, are forgiven; for she loved much: but to whom little is forgiven, the same loveth little."

He speaks of both Simon and the woman, as sinners, being debtors to himself.

(Compare Ps. 51:4—"Against thee, thee only, have I sinned, and done this evil in thy sight: that thou mightest be justified when thou speakest, and be clear when thou judgest.")

(4)   RAISING OF THE DEAD.

Jno. 6: 39, 44—"And this is the Father's will which hath sent me, that of all which he hath given me I should lose nothing, but should raise it up at the last day. No man can come to me, except the Father which hath sent me draw him: and I will raise him up at the last day."

FOURTH PROPOSITION: It is Jesus Christ who raises the dead.

QUESTION: Did not Elijah and Elisha raise the dead? No. God raised the dead in answer to their prayer, but JESUS CHRIST will raise the dead by his own word. During his humilia-tion it was by prayer that CHRIST raised the dead. (Jno. 11:41—"Then they took away the stone from the place where the dead was laid. And Jesus lifted up his eyes, and said, Father, I thank thee that thou hast heard me.")

(5)   TRANSFORMATION OF BODIES.

Phil. 3:21, R.V.—"Who shall fashion anew the body of our humil-iation that it may be conformed to the body of his glory, according to the working whereby he is able to subject all things unto himself."

FIFTH PROPOSITION: Jesus Christ shall fashion anew the body of our humiliation into the likeness of His glorious body.

(6) JUDGMENT.

2 Tim. 4: 1, R.V.—"I charge thee in the sight of God, and of Christ Jesus, who shall judge the quick and the dead, and by his appearing and his kingdom."

SIXTH PROPOSITION: Christ Jesus shall judge the quick and the dead.

NOTE.—JESUS Himself emphasized the Divine character of this office. John 5: 22, 23—"For the Father judgeth no man, but hath committed all judgment unto the Son: *That all men should honor the Son even as they honor the Father.* He that honoreth not the Son honoreth not the Father which hath sent Him."

(7) THE BESTOWAL OF ETERNAL LIFE.

Jno. 10: 28—"And I give unto them eternal life; and they shall never perish, neither shall any man pluck them out of my hand."

Jno. 17: 2—"As thou hast given him power over all flesh, that he should give eternal life to as many as thou hast given him."

SEVENTH PROPOSITION : Jesus Christ is the giver of Eternal Life.

GENERAL PROPOSITION : Seven distinctly Divine Offices are predicated of Jesus Christ.

IV. Statements which in the Old Testament are made distinctly of Jehovah, God, taken in the New Testament to refer to Jesus Christ.

(1) Ps. 102: 24-27—"I said, O my God, take me not away in the midst of my days: thy years are throughout all generations. Of old hast thou laid the foundation of the earth: and the heavens are the work of thy hands. They shall perish, but thou shalt endure: yea, all of them shall wax old like a garment; as vesture shalt thou change them, and they shall be changed: But thou art the same, and thy years shall have no end."

In Heb. 1: 10-12—"And thou, Lord, in the beginning hast laid the foundation of the earth; and the heavens are the works of Thy hands. They shall perish; but thou remainest; and they all shall wax old as doth a garment. And as a vesture shalt thou fold them up, and they shall be changed: but thou art the same, and thy years shall not fail"—this statement is interpreted as referring to JESUS CHRIST.

(2) Is. 40: 3, 4—"The voice of him that crieth in the wilderness, Prepare ye the way of the LORD (Jehovah), make straight in the desert the highway for our God. Every valley shall be exalted, and every mountain and hill shall be made low: and the crooked shall be made straight, and the rough places plain."

In Matt. 3:3; Luke 1: 68, 69, 76—"Blessed be the Lord God of Israel; for he hath visited and redeemed his people. And hath raised up an horn of salvation for us in the house of his servant David. And thou, child shall be called the prophet of the highest: for thou shalt go before the face of the Lord to prepare his ways"—JESUS is the Lord before whose face the messenger goes.

(3) Jer. 11:20—"But, O LORD of hosts, that judgest righteously, that triest the reins and the heart, let me see thy vengeance on them: for unto thee have I revealed my cause."

Jer. 17:10—"I, the LORD, search the heart, I try the reins, even to give every man according to his ways, and according to the fruit of his doings."

In Rev. 2: 23—"And I will kill her children with death; and all the churches shall know that I am he which searcheth the reins and hearts: and I will give unto every one of you according to your works"—it is JESUS who does what is distinctly said of Jehovah in the Old Testament passage.

(4) Is. 60: 19—"The sun shall be no more thy light by day; neither for brightness shall the moon give light unto thee: but the LORD shall be unto thee an everlasting light, and thy God thy glory." (See also Zech. 2: 5.)

This is said of Jesus in Luke 2: 32—"A light to lighten the Gentiles, and the glory of thy people Israel."

(5) Is. 6: 1, 3, 10—"In the year that king Uzziah died I saw also the LORD sitting upon a throne high and lifted up, and his train filled the temple. And one cried unto another and said, Holy, holy, holy is the LORD of hosts: the whole earth is full of his glory. Make the heart of this people fat, and make their ears heavy and shut their eyes; lest they see with their eyes, and hear with their ears, and understand with their heart, and convert and be healed." (Compare Jno. 12: 37-41—"But though he had done so many miracles before them, yet they believed not on him. That the saying of Esaias the prophet might be fulfilled which he spake, Lord, who hath believed our report?

and to whom hath the arm of the Lord been revealed? Therefore they could not believe, because that Esaias said again, He hath blinded their eyes and hardened their hearts; that they should not see with their eyes, nor understand with their hearts and be converted, and I should heal them. These things said Esaias *when he saw his glory*, and spake *of him*.")

In the Old Testament passage it was when he saw the glory of Jehovah of hosts that Isaiah spoke these things, but in the New Testament John says it was when Isaiah saw the glory of JESUS CHRIST that he said this. The inference is simple.

(6) Is. 8: 13, 14—"Sanctify the LORD of hosts himself: and let him be your fear, and let him be your dread. And he shall be for a sanctuary; but for a stone of stumbling and for a rock of offense to both the houses of Israel, for a gin and for a snare to the inhabitants of Jerusalem." (Compare 1 Pet. 2: 7, 8—"Unto you therefore which believe he is precious: but unto them which be disobedient, the stone which the builders disallowed, the same is made the head of the corner, and a stone of stumbling and a rock of offence, even to them which stumble at the word, being disobedient: whereunto also they were appointed.")

In the Old Testament Jehovah is the stone of stumbling, etc. In the New Testament it is JESUS CHRIST.

(7) Is. 8: 12, 13--"Say ye not, a confederacy, to all them to whom this people shall say, a confederacy; neither fear ye their fear, nor be afraid. Sanctify the LORD of hosts Himself; and let him be your fear, and let him be your dread." (Compare 1 Pet. 3: 14—"But and if ye should suffer for righteousness' sake, blessed are ye: and fear not their fear neither be troubled; but sanctify in your hearts *Christ as Lord:* being ready always to give answer to every man that asketh you a reason concerning the hope that is in you, yet with meekness and fear.")

(8) Num. 21: 6, 7—"And the LORD sent fiery serpents among the people, and they bit the people; and much people of Israel died. Therefore the people came to Moses, and said, We have sinned, for we have spoken *against the* LORD, and against thee; pray unto the LORD, that he take away the serpents from us, and Moses prayed for the people."

(Compare 1 Cor. 10: 9—"Neither let us *tempt Christ*, as some of them also tempted, and were destroyed of serpents.")

(9) Ps. 23: 1—"The LORD is my shepherd; I shall not want."

Is. 40: 10, 11—"Behold, the Lord GOD will come with strong hand, and his arm shall rule for him: behold his reward is with him, and his work before him. He shall feed his flock like a shepherd: he shall gather the lambs with his arm, and carry them in his bosom, and shall gently lead those that are with young." (Compare Jno. 10: 11—"I am the good shepherd: the good shepherd giveth his life for the sheep.")

In the Old Testament Jehovah is the good shepherd; in the New Testament Jesus.

(10) Ezek. 34: 11, 12, 18—"For thus saith the Lord God: Behold, I, even I, will both search my sheep, and seek them out. As a shepherd seeketh out his flock in the day that he is among his sheep that are scattered; so will I seek out my sheep, and will deliver them out of all places where they have been scattered in the cloudy and dark day. Seemeth it a small thing unto you to have eaten up the good pasture, but ye must tread down with your feet the residue of your pasture? and to have drunk of the deep waters, but ye must foul the residue with your feet?" (Compare Luke 19:10—"For *the Son of Man* is come to seek and to save that which was lost."

In the O. T. Jehovah, in the N. T. Jesus "seeks and saves the lost."

(11) Lord in the Old Testament always refers to God except where the context clearly indicates otherwise: Lord in the New Testament always refers to Jesus Christ except where the context clearly indicates otherwise.

PROPOSITION: Very many statements which in the Old Testament are made distinctly of Jehovah, God, are taken in the New Testament to refer to Jesus Christ; i. e., in New Testament thought and doctrine Jesus Christ occupies the place that Jehovah occupies in Old Testament thought and doctrine.

V. The way in which the name of God the Father and Jesus Christ the Son are coupled together.

2 Cor. 13: 14—"The grace of the Lord Jesus Christ, and the love of God, and the communion of the Holy Ghost, be with you all. Amen."

Matt. 28: 19—"Go ye, therefore, and teach all nations, baptizing them in the name of the Father, and of the Son, and of the Holy Ghost."

1 Thess. 3: 11—"Now God himself and our Father, and our Lord Jesus Christ, direct our way unto you."

1 Cor. 12: 4–6—"Now there are diversities of gifts, but of the same spirit. And there are differences of administrations, but the same Lord. And there are diversities of operations, but it is the same God, which worketh all in all."

Tit. 3: 4, 5—"But after that the kindness and love of God our Saviour toward man appeared. Not by works of righteousness which we have done, but according to his mercy he saved us, by the washing of regeneration, and renewing of the Holy Ghost." (Compare Tit. 2: 13—" Looking for the blessed hope, and the glorious appearing of the great God and our Saviour Jesus Christ.")

Rom. 1: 7—" To all that be in Rome, beloved of God, called to be saints: grace to you and peace from God our Father and the Lord Jesus Christ." (Many instances of this sort in all the Pauline Epistles.)

Jas. 1: 1—" James, a servant of God *and of the Lord Jesus Christ,* to the twelve tribes which are scattered abroad, greeting."

Jno. 14: 23—" Jesus answered and said unto him, if a man love me, he will keep my words: and my Father will love him, and We will come unto him, and make our abode with him."

" WE," GOD AND I.

2 Pet. 1: 1—" Simon Peter, a servant and an apostle of Jesus Christ, to them that have obtained like precious faith with us through the righteousness of God and our Saviour Jesus Christ." (Compare R. V.)

Col. 2: 2—" That their hearts might be comforted, being knit together in love, and unto all riches of the full assurance of understanding, to the acknowledgment of the mystery of God, and of the Father, and of Christ." (See R.V.)

Jno. 17: 3—" And this is life eternal, that they might know thee the only true God, and Jesus Christ, whom thou hast sent."

Jno. 14: 1—" Let not your heart be troubled: ye believe in God, *believe also in me.*" (Compare Jer. 17: 5-7—" Thus saith the LORD; cursed be the man that trusteth in man, and maketh flesh his arm, and whose heart departeth from the LORD. Blessed is the man that trusteth in the LORD, and whose hope the LORD is.")

Rev. 7: 10—" And cried with a loud voice, saying, Salvation to our God which sitteth upon the throne, *and unto the Lamb.*"

Rev. 5: 13—" And every creature which is in heaven, and on the earth, and under the earth, and such as are in the sea, and all that are in them, heard I saying, Blessing, and honor, and glory, and power, be unto him that sitteth upon the throne, *and unto the Lamb* for ever and ever." (Compare Jno. 5: 23—" That all men should honor the Son, even as they honor the Father. He that honoreth not the Son honoreth not the Father which hath sent him.")

PROPOSITION: The name of Jesus Christ is coupled with that of God the Father in numerous passages in a way in which it would be impossible to couple the name of any finite being with that of the Deity.

VI. Divine Worship to be given to Jesus Christ.

(1) Matt 28:9—" And as they went to tell his disciples, behold

Jesus met them, saying, All hail. And they came and held him by the feet, and *worshipped him.*"

Luke 24: 52—" And they *worshipped him* and returned to Jerusalem with great joy."

Matt. 14: 33—" Then they that were in the ship came and *worshipped him*, saying, Of a truth thou art the Son of God." (Compare Acts. 10: 25, 26—" And as Peter was coming in, Cornelius met him and fell down at his feet and *worshipped him.* But Peter took him up, saying, *Stand up; I myself also am a man.*")

Rev. 22: 8, 9—"And I John saw these things and heard them. And when I had heard and seen I fell down to *worship* before the feet of the angel which showed me these things. Then saith he unto me, *See thou do it not:* for I am thy fellow servant, and of thy brethren, the prophets, and of them which keep the sayings of this book: *worship God.*"

Matt. 4: 9, 10—" And saith unto him, All these things will I give thee if thou wilt fall down and worship me. Then saith Jesus unto him, Get thee hence, Satan: for it is written thou shalt *worship the Lord thy God, and him only* shalt thou serve."

FIRST PROPOSITION: Jesus Christ accepted without hesitation a worship which good men and angels declined with fear (horror).

QUESTION: Is not the verb translated "worship" in tnese passages, sometimes used of reverence paid to men in high position?

ANSWER: Yes, but not in this way by worshipers of Jehovah, as is seen by the way in which both Peter and the angel drew back when such worship was offered to them.

(2) 1 Cor. 1: 2—" Unto the church of God which is at Corinth, to them that are sanctified in Christ Jesus, called to be saints, with all that in every place *call upon the name of Jesus Christ our Lord*, both theirs and ours."

2 Cor. 12: 8, 9—"For this thing *I besought the* LORD thrice, that it might depart from me. And he said unto me, My grace is sufficient for thee: for *my strength* is made perfect in weakness. Most gladly, therefore, will I rather glory in my infirmities, that *the power of Christ* may rest upon me."

Acts. 7: 59—"And they stoned Stephen, *calling upon the Lord*, and saying, *Lord Jesus* receive my spirit."

SECOND PROPOSITION: Prayer is to be made to Christ.

(3) Ps. 45: 11—"So shall the king greatly desire thy beauty: for he is thy LORD; and *worship thou him.*"

Jno. 5: 23—"That all men should honor the son, *even as they honor the father*. He that honoreth not the son honoreth not the father which hath sent him." (Compare Rev. 5: 8, 9, 12, 13—"And when he had taken the book, the four beasts and four and twenty elders fell down *before the lamb*, having every one of them harps, and golden vials full of odors, which are the prayers of saints. And they sung a new song, saying, Thou art worthy to take the book and to open the seals thereof: for thou wast slain, and hast redeemed us to God by thy blood out of every kindred, and tongue, and people, and nation. Saying, with a loud voice, Worthy is the lamb that was slain to receive power, and riches, and wisdom, and strength, and honor, and glory, and blessing. And every creature which is in heaven and on the earth, and under the earth, and such as are in the sea and all that are in them, heard I saying, Blessing, and honor, and glory, and power, be unto him that sitteth upon the throne, and *unto the Lamb* for ever and ever.")

THIRD PROPOSITION: It is God the Father's will that all men pay the same divine honor to the son as to himself.

(4) Heb. 1: 6—"And again, when he bringeth in the first begotten into the world, he saith, And *let all the angels of God worship him.*"

Phil. 2 :10, 11—"That at the name of Jesus every knee should bow, of things in heaven, and things in earth, and things under the earth: And that every tongue should confess that JESUS CHRIST is LORD to the glory of God the Father." (Compare Is. 45; 21-23. Where it is unto Jehovah that every knee is to bow, etc.")

FOURTH PROPOSITION: The Son of God, Jesus, is to be worshipped as God by angels and men.

GENERAL PROPOSITION: Jesus Christ is a person to be worshipped by angels and men, even as God the Father is worshipped,

SUMMARY: By the use of numerous Divine names, by the ascription of all the distinctively Divine attributes, by the predication of several Divine offices, by referring statements which in the Old Testament distinctly name Jehovah God as their subject to JESUS CHRIST in the New Testament, by coupling the name of JESUS CHRIST with that of God the Father in a way in which it would be impossible to couple that of any finite being with that of the Deity, and by the clear teaching that · JESUS CHRIST should be worshipped, even as God the Father is worshipped—in all these unmistakable ways, God in His word distinctly proclaims that Jesus Christ is a Divine Being, is God.

NOTE: Whoever refuses to accept JESUS as his Divine Savior and LORD is guilty of the enormous sin of rejecting God. A man often thinks he is good because he never stole or never murdered or never cheated. "Of what great sin am I guilty?" he complacently asks. "You are guilty of the awful, damning sin of rejecting God," we reply. But suppose one questions or denies His divinity. That does not change the fact nor lessen his guilt. Questioning or denying a fact never changes it. Suppose that one denies the goodness of a man who is in fact the soul of honor. It would not alter the fact but simply make the questioner guilty of awful slander. So denying the fact of the Deity of JESUS CHRIST does not make it any less a fact, but it does make the denier guilty of awful blasphemous slander.

CHAPTER II.

THE SUBORDINATION OF THE SON TO THE FATHER.

I. Jno. 14: 28—" Ye have heard how I said unto you, I go away, and come again unto you. If ye loved me, ye would rejoice, because I said, I go unto the Father: for my Father is greater than I."

FIRST PROPOSITION : God the Father is greater than Jesus Christ the Son.

II. Heb. 1: 5—" For unto which of the angels said he at any time, Thou art my Son, this day have I begotten thee ? And again, I will be to him a Father, and he shall be to me a Son ?

Jno. 3: 16—" For God so loved the world, that he gave his only begotten Son that whosoever believeth in him should not perish, but have everlasting life."

SECOND PROPOSITION : God the Father begat Jesus Christ the Son.

QUESTION: Does this begetting refer to the origin of the Eternal Word or to the origin of the incarnate JESUS ?

ANSWER: Ps. 2:7—"I will declare the decree: the Lord hath said unto me, Thou art my Son; this day have I begotten Thee." (See context vv. 1, 2, 6, 8.) Luke 1:35—"And the angel answered and said unto her, The Holy Ghost shall come upon thee, and the power of the Highest shall overshadow thee: therefore also that holy thing which shall be born of thee shall be called the Son of God."

III. Jno. 6: 57, R.V.—" As the living Father sent me, and I live because of the Father; so he that eateth me, he also shall live because of me."

THIRD PROPOSITION: Jesus Christ lives because of the Father.

IV. Jno. 5: 19—"Then answered Jesus and said unto them, Verily,

verily, I say unto you, The Son can do nothing of himself, but what he seeth the Father do: for what things soever he doeth, these also doeth the Son likewise."

FOURTH PROPOSITION: *The Son can do nothing independently of the Father.*

V. Jno. 6: 29—"Jesus answered and said unto them, This is the work of God, that ye believe on him whom he hath sent."

Jno. 8: 29, 42—" And he that sent me is with me: the Father hath not left me alone; for I do always those things that please him. * * * Jesus said unto them: If God were your Father, ye would love me, for I proceeded forth and came from God; neither came I of my-self, but he sent me."

FIFTH PROPOSITION: *Jesus Christ was sent by the Father.*

VI. Jno. 10: 18—"No man taketh it from me, but I lay it down of myself. I have power to lay it down, and I have power to take it again. This commandment have I received of my Father."

SIXTH PROPOSITION: *Jesus Christ received commandment from the Father, was under his authority and directions.*

VII. Jno. 13: 3—"Jesus knowing that the Father had given all things into his hands, and that he was come from God, and went to God."

SEVENTH PROPOSITION: *Jesus Christ received His own authority from the Father.*

VIII. Jno. 8: 26, 40—" I have many things to say and to judge of you: but he that sent me is true; and I speak to the world those things which I have heard of him. But now ye seek to kill me, a man that hath told you the truth, which I have heard of God: this did not Abraham."

EIGHTH PROPOSITION: *Jesus Christ received His message from the Father.*

IX. Jno. 5: 36, R.V.—" But the witness which I have is greater than that of John: for the works which the Father hath given me to accomplish, the very works that I do, bear witness of me, that the Father hath sent me."

Jno. 14: 10—" Believest thou not that I am in the Father, and the

Father in me: the words that I speak unto you I speak not of myself;
but the Father that dwelleth in me, he doeth the works."

*NINTH PROPOSITION: The Father gave to Jesus Christ His
works to accomplish, and it was the indwelling Father who did the
works.*

X.   Luke 22: 29—"And I appoint unto you a kingdom, as my Father hath appointed unto me."

*TENTH PROPOSITION: Jesus   Christ's   kingdom   was   ap-
pointed unto Him by the Father.*

XI.   1 Cor. 15: 24—"Then cometh the end, when he shall have delivered up the kingdom to God, even the Father," etc.

*ELEVENTH PROPOSITION: Jesus   Christ   shall   ultimately
deliver up the kingdom to the Father.*

XII.   1 Cor. 15: 27, 28, R.V.—"For, he put all things in subjection under his feet.   But when he saith, All things are put in subjection, it is evident that he excepted who did subject all things unto
him.   And when all things have been subjected to him, then shall
the son also himself be subjected to him that did subject all things
unto him, that God may be all in all."

*TWELFTH PROPOSITION: Jesus   Christ   Himself   shall   be
subjected unto the Father that God may be all in all.*

XIII.   1 Cor. 11: 3—"But I would have you know, that the head
of every man is Christ; and the head of the woman is the man; and
the head of Christ is God."

*THIRTEENTH PROPOSITION: God the Father is head of
Christ as Christ is the head of every man, and as the man is
head of the woman.*

XIV.   Heb. 7: 25, R.V.—"Wherefore also he is able to save to
the uttermost them that draw near unto God through him, seeing he
ever liveth to make intercession for them."

*FOURTEENTH PROPOSITION: Men draw near unto God
through Christ.   God, not Christ, is the ultimate goal.   He is
the way unto the Father.   (Jno. 14: 6—"Jesus saith unto him,
I am the way, the truth and the life: no man cometh unto the
Father but by me.")*

XV.   Jno. 20: 17—"Jesus saith unto her, I ascend unto . . . . my God."

FIFTEENTH PROPOSITION: *God the Father is Jesus Christ's God.*

GENERAL PROPOSITION: Jesus Christ is, and eternally shall be, subordinate to God the Father. In God the Father we have the source of Deity; in Jesus Christ, Deity in its outflow. But in the stream is all the perfection of the fountain. (See Col. 2 :9). God the Father is the source of glory; Jesus Christ the Son is the effulgence (shining forth or off-flash) of His glory. (Heb. 1: 3, R. V.— "Who being the effulgence of His glory.")

All the passages quoted have reference to the incarnate CHRIST and not to the pre-existent Word.

CHAPTER III.

THE HUMAN NATURE OF JESUS CHRIST.

1. Human names.

(1) 1 Tim. 2: 5—"For there is one God, and one mediator between God and man, *the man* Christ Jesus."

FIRST PROPOSITION: Christ Jesus is called man even after His ascension.

(2) Luke 19: 10—"For the Son of man is come to seek and to save that which was lost."

SECOND PROPOSITION: Jesus is called the Son of Man (77 times). Stephen spoke of Him as the Son of Man even when he saw Him in the glory standing on the right hand of God. (Acts 7: 55.)

II. Human physical nature.

(1) Jno. 1: 14—"And the word was made flesh, and dwelt among us (and we beheld his glory, the glory of the only begotten of the Father), full of grace and truth."

Heb. 2: 14—"Forasmuch, then, as the children are partakers of flesh and blood, he also himself likewise took part of the same; that through death he might destroy him that had the power of death, that is, the devil."

FIRST PROPOSITION: The Eternal Word was made flesh, partook of flesh and blood. Jesus Christ had a true human body.

Note 1.—The denial of the reality of Christ's body is the mark of the spirit of anti-Christ.

1 Jno. 4: 2, 3—"Hereby know ye the spirit of God: every spirit that confesseth that Jesus Christ is come in the flesh is of God. And every spirit that confesseth not that Jesus Christ is come in

the flesh is not of God : and this is that spirit of anti-Christ, whereof ye have heard that it should come and even now already is it in the world."

NOTE 2.—The indwelling divine glory sometimes shone through and transfigured the veil of flesh. (Matt. 17: 2.)

(2) Luke 24: 39—"Behold my hands and my feet, that it is I myself: handle me and see; for a spirit hath not flesh and bones, as ye see me have."

Jno. 20: 27—"Then sayeth he to Thomas, reach hither thy finger, and behold my hands ; and reach hither thy hand, and thrust it into my side : and be not faithless, but believing."

SECOND PROPOSITION: Jesus Christ had a true human body after his resurrection.

(3) Acts 7: 55, 56—"But he, being full of the Holy Ghost, looked up steadfastly into heaven, and saw the glory of God, and Jesus standing on the right hand of God, and said, behold, I see the heavens opened, and the Son of man standing on the right hand of God."

Rev. 5:6—"And I beheld, and lo ! in the midst of the throne and of the four beasts, and in the midst of the elders, stood a lamb as it had been slain, having seven horns and seven eyes, which are the seven spirits of God sent forth into all the earth."

Matt. 26: 64—"Jesus saith unto him, Thou hast said : nevertheless I say unto you, Hereafter shall ye see the Son of man sitting on the right hand of power, and coming in the clouds of heaven."

THIRD PROPOSITION: Jesus Christ still has a human body in the glory.   He shall come again on the clouds of heaven as "the Son of Man."

NOTE.—Our bodies at His coming shall be transformed into the likeness of His own. (Phil. 3; 21.)

III. Human parentage.

(1) Luke 2: 7—"And she brought forth *her* firstborn son, and wrapped him in swaddling clothes, and laid him in a manger; because there was no room for them in the inn."

Acts 2: 30—"Therefore, being a prophet, and knowing that God had sworn with an oath to him, that of *the fruit of his loins*, according to the flesh, he would raise up Christ to sit on his throne."

Acts 13: 23—"*Of this man's seed* hath God according to his promise raised unto Israel a saviour, Jesus."

Rom. 1: 3—"Concerning his Son Jesus Christ our Lord, which was made *of the seed of David according to the flesh.*"

Gal. 4:4—"But when the fulness of the time was come, God sent forth his Son, *made of a woman*, made under the law."

Heb. 7:14—"For it is evident that our Lord *sprang out of Juda;* of which tribe Moses spake nothing concerning priesthood."

FIRST PROPOSITION: Jesus Christ had a human parentage and human ancestry. He was Mary's son and David s seed.

Mary was as truly the mother of JESUS CHRIST as God was His Father.

IV. Human limitations.

(1) PHYSICAL LIMITATIONS.

(*a*) Jno. 4:6—"Now Jacob's well was there. Jesus, therefore, being wearied with his journey, sat thus on the well: and it was about the sixth hour."

JESUS CHRIST *was weary.* Compare Is. 40:28—"Hast thou not known? hast thou not heard, that the everlasting God, the LORD, the Creator of the ends of the earth, fainteth not, *neither is weary?* there is no searching of his understanding."

(*b*) Matt. 8:24—"And behold there arose a great tempest in the sea, insomuch that the ship was covered with the waves: but he was asleep."

JESUS CHRIST *slept.* Compare Ps. 121:4, 5—"Behold he that keepeth Israel shall neither *slumber nor sleep.* The LORD is thy keeper; the Lord is thy shade upon thy right hand."

(*c*) Matt. 21:18—"Now in the morning as he returned into the city, he hungered."

JESUS CHRIST *hungered.*

(*d*) Jno. 19:28—"After this, Jesus knowing that all things were now accomplished, that the scripture might be fulfilled, saith, I thirst."

JESUS CHRIST *thirsted.*

(*e*) Luke 22:44—"And being in an agony he prayed more earnestly: and his sweat was as it were great drops of blood falling down to the ground."

JESUS CHRIST *suffered physical agony.*

(*f*) 1 Cor. 15:3—"For I delivered unto you first of all that which I also received, how that Christ died for our sins according to the scriptures."

JESUS CHRIST *died.*

FIRST PROPOSITION: Jesus Christ was subject to weariness, hunger, thirst, agony and death—to the physical limitations of human nature.

(2) INTELLECTUAL AND MORAL LIMITATIONS.

(*a*) Luke 2: 52, R.V.—"And Jesus advanced in wisdom and stature, and in favor with God and man."

JESUS CHRIST advanced in wisdom and stature and in favor with God and man.   He was subject to human conditions of physical, mental and moral growth.

(*b*) Mark 11: 13—"And seeing a fig tree afar off having leaves, he came, if haply he might find anything thereon: and when he came to it, he found nothing but leaves; for the time of figs was not yet."

13: 32—"But of that day and that hour knoweth no man; no, not the angels which are in Heaven, neither the Son, but the Father."

SECOND PROPOSITION: The knowledge of Jesus Christ was subject to limitations. (Compare Luke 2:52.)

NOTE 1.—His knowledge was self-limited.   (Phil. 2: 5, R.V. "*Emptied* himself."   Must not press this verse too far.   The context shows an emptying of glory rather than of attributes.)

NOTE 2.—Jno. 3: 34—"For he whom God hath sent speaketh the words of God: for God giveth not the Spirit by measure unto him."   As a teacher JESUS was divinely and fully inspired so that he spoke "the words of God."

NOTE 3.—The indwelling Divine Nature often burst through the veil of flesh (see passages under Chapter I), but *as a man* he was a real man in his mental make-up.

(*b*) Heb. 4: 15—"For we have not an high priest which cannot be touched with the feeling of our infirmities; but was in all points *tempted* like as we are, yet without sin."

Heb. 2: 18—"For in that he himself hath suffered *being tempted*, he is able to succor them that are tempted."

(Comp. Jas. 1: 13—"Let no man say when he is tempted, I am tempted of God: for *God can not be tempted* with evil, neither tempteth he any man. ")

THIRD PROPOSITION: Jesus Christ was tempted. He was subject to the essential moral limitations of human nature.

NOTE 1.—A carnal nature is not an essential part of human nature.   It does not belong to human nature as God made it.   It is what has become part of human nature by sin.

NOTE 2.—Heb. 2:14—"Forasmuch then as the children are partakers of flesh and blood, he also himself likewise *took part of the same:* that through death he might destroy him that had the power of death, that is, the devil."

Phil. 2:5-8—"Let this mind be in you, which was also in Christ Jesus: Who being in the form of God, thought it not robbery to be equal with God. But *made himself* of no reputation, and took upon him the form of a servant, and was made in the likeness of men: And being found in fashion as a man, he humbled himself, and became obedient unto death, even the death of the cross."

JESUS CHRIST in His moral limitations was self-limited. He voluntarily placed himself underneath the essential moral limitations that man is under in order to redeem man. Wondrous love !

NOTE 3.—He was tempted "without sin."

GENERAL PROPOSITION: Jesus Christ was subject to the intellectual and moral limitations essential to human nature.

(3) LIMITATIONS OF POWER.

(a) Mark 1:35—"And in the morning, rising up a great while before day, he went out, and departed into a solitary place, and there *prayed.*"

John 6:15—"When Jesus therefore perceived that they would come and take him by force, to make him a king, he departed again into a mountain himself alone." (Comp. Matt. 14:23—"And when he had sent the multitudes away, he went up into a mountain apart to *pray:* and when the evening was come, he was there alone.")

Luke 22:41-45—"And he was withdrawn from them about a stone's cast, and kneeled down, and *prayed,* saying, Father, if thou be willing, remove this cup from me: nevertheless, not my will, but thine, be done. And there appeared an angel unto him from heaven, strengthening him. And being in an agony he prayed more earnestly: and his sweat was as it were great drops of blood falling down to the ground. And when he rose up from prayer, and was come to his disciples, he found them sleeping for sorrow."

Heb. 5:7—"Who in the days of his flesh, when he had *offered up prayers and supplications* with strong crying and tears unto him that was able to save him from death, and was heard in that he feared."

FIRST PROPOSITION: Jesus Christ prayed (25 times mentioned). He obtained power for work and for moral victory as other men do, by prayer. He was subject to human conditions for obtaining what He desired.

(*b*) Acts 10: 38—" How *God anointed Jesus of Nazareth with the Holy Ghost and with power:* who went about doing good, and healing all that were oppressed of the devil; for God was with him."

SECOND PROPOSITION: Jesus Christ obtained power for His divine works not by His inherent Divinity but by the anointing of the Holy Spirit. He was subject to the same conditions of power as other men.

(*c*) Jno. 14: 12—" Verily, verily, I say unto you, he that believeth on me, the works that I do shall he do also; and *greater works than these shall he do;* because I go unto my Father."

THIRD PROPOSITION: Jesus Christ was subject to limitations in the exercise of power during the days of His humiliation.

GENERAL PROPOSITION: Jesus Christ was subject to human conditions for the obtaining of power and human limitations in its exercise. This was during the days of His humiliation.

IV.   Human Relation to God.

Jno. 20: 17—" Jesus saith unto her, touch me not; for I am not yet ascended to my Father: but go to my brethren, and say unto them, I ascend unto my Father and your Father; and to my God and your God."

FIRST PROPOSITION: Jesus Christ called the Father " My God."

JESUS CHRIST bore the relation of man to God the Father.

V.   Human in all things.

Heb. 2: 17, R.V.—" Wherefore it behooved him *in all things* to be made like unto his brethren, that he might be a merciful and faithful high priest in things pertaining to God, to make propitiation for the sins of the people."

FIRST PROPOSITION: Jesus Christ was made "in all things" like unto His brethren, subject to all the physical, mental and moral conditions of existence essential to human nature.

GENERAL PROPOSITION: <u>*Jesus Christ was in every respect a*</u>
<u>*real man. He became so voluntarily to redeem man.*</u> (Phil. 2: 5-8;
2 Cor. 8: 9.) *He partook of human nature that we might be-*
come partakers of the Divine nature. 2 Pet. 1: 4—"Whereby
are given unto us exceeding great and precious promises; that
by these ye might be partakers of the Divine nature, having
escaped the corruption that is in the world through lust."

QUESTION: How shall we reconcile the Bible doctrine of
the true Deity of JESUS CHRIST with the Bible doctrine of the real
human nature of CHRIST?

ANSWER: That is not our main business. Our first business
is to find out what the various passages mean in their natural
grammatical interpretation. Then if we can reconcile them,
well; if not, believe them both and leave the reconciliation to increasing knowledge. It is a thoroughly vicious principle of interpretation that we must interpret every passage in the Bible so
that we can readily reconcile it with every other passage. This
gives rise to a one-sided theology. One man becomes a one-sided
Calvinist and another a one-sided Arminian, and so on through
the whole gamut of doctrine. Our business is to find out the
plainly intended sense of the passage in hand as determined by
usage of words, grammatical construction and context. Remember that in many cases two truths that seemed utterly irrec-
oncilable or perfectly contradictory to us once are now, with increased knowledge, seen to beautifully harmonize. Truths that
still seem to us to be contradictory perfectly harmonize in the infinite wisdom of God, and will some day, when we approach more
nearly to God's omniscience, perfectly harmonize in our minds.
How fearlessly the Bible puts the Deity and manhood of JESUS
CHRIST in closest juxtaposition.

Matt. 8: 24-26—"And, behold, there arose a great tempest in the
sea, insomuch that the ship was covered with the waves: *but he was*
asleep. And he saith unto them, Why are ye fearful, O ye of little
faith? Then he arose, and *rebuked the winds and the sea; and there*
was a great calm."

Luke 3: 21, 22—"Now when all the people were baptized, it came to
pass that *Jesus also being baptized,* and *praying,* the heaven was
opened. And the Holy Ghost descended in a bodily shape like a dove
upon him, and a voice came from heaven, which said, *Thou art my*
beloved Son; in thee I am well pleased."

Jno. 11:38, 43, 44—"Jesus, therefore, again *groaning in himself cometh* to the grave. It was a cave, and a stone lay upon it. And when he had thus spoken, he cried with a loud voice, Lazarus, come forth. And *he that was dead came forth*, bound hand and foot with grave-clothes; and his face was bound about with a napkin. Jesus saith unto them, Loose him, and let him go."

Luke 9:28, 29, 35—"And it came to pass about an eight days after these sayings, he took Peter and John and James, and went up into a mountain *to pray*. And as he prayed, the fashion of his countenance was altered, and his raiment was white and glistening. And there came a voice out of the cloud, saying, *This is my beloved Son:* hear him."

Matt. 16:16, 17, 21—"And Simon Peter answered and said, Thou art ·the Christ, the Son of the living God. And Jesus answered and said unto him, Blessed art thou, Simon Bar-jona: for flesh and blood hath not revealed it unto thee, but my Father which is in heaven. From that time forth began JESUS to show unto his disciples, how that he must go unto Jerusalem, and *suffer* many things of the elders and chief priests and scribes, and *be killed*, and be raised again the third day."

Heb. 1:6—"And again, when he bringeth in the first-begotten into the world, he saith, And let all the angels of God worship him." (Compare Heb. 2:18—"For in that he himself hath suffered *being tempted*, he is able to succor them that are tempted.")

Heb. 4:14, 15—"Seeing then that we have a great high priest, that is passed into the heavens, *Jesus, the Son of God*, let us hold fast our profession. For we have not a high priest which cannot be touched with the feeling of our infirmities: but was *in all points tempted* like as we are, yet without sin."

CHAPTER IV.

THE CHARACTER OF JESUS CHRIST.

I. The Holiness of Jesus Christ.

(1) THE FACT OF CHRIST'S HOLINESS.

Acts 4: 27, 30—"For of a truth against thy _holy_ child Jesus, whom thou hast anointed, both Herod and Pontius Pilate, with the Gentiles, and the people of Israel, were gathered together. By stretching forth thine hand to heal; and what signs and wonders may be done by the name of the _holy_ child Jesus."

Mark 1: 24—"Saying, Let us alone; what have we to do with thee, thou Jesus of Nazareth? Art thou come to destroy us? I know thee who thou art, the _Holy One of God_."

Luke 4: 34—"Saying. Let us alone; what have we to do with thee, thou Jesus of Nazareth? Art thou come to destroy us? I know thee who thou art; the _Holy One of God_."

Acts 3: 14—"But ye denied the _Holy One_ and the Just, and desired a murderer to be granted unto you."

1 Jno. 2: 20—"For ye have an unction from the _Holy One_, and ye know all things."

FIRST PROPOSITION: _Jesus Christ is Holy, absolutely Holy. He is "The Holy One."_

NOTE.—In the Old Testament it is Jehovah God who is called the Holy One. Jehovah is called "The Holy One of Israel" about thirty times in Isaiah. (Compare Lecture on the Holiness of God.)

(2) WHAT DOES HOLY MEAN?

Lev. 11: 43-45—"Ye shall not make yourselves abominable with any creeping thing that creepeth, neither shall ye make yourselves unclean with them, _that ye should be defiled_ thereby. For I am the LORD your God: ye shall therefore sanctify yourselves and ye shall be holy; for I am holy; _neither shall ye defile yourselves_ with any manner of creeping thing that creepeth upon the earth. For I am the LORD that bringeth you up out of the land of Egypt to be your God: ye shall therefore _be holy_, for I am holy."

Deut. 23: 14—"For the LORD thy God walketh in the midst of thy camp, to deliver thee, and to give up thine enemies before thee; therefore shall thy camp be *holy: that he see no unclean thing* in thee, and turn away from thee." (Study context.)

Holy means free from defilement. To say that CHRIST is absolutely holy, is to say that He is absolutely pure. (Compare 1 Jno. 3:3—"Every man that hath this hope in him purifieth himself, even as he is pure.")

Note the many ways in which the Bible brings out this absolute purity of CHRIST:

Heb. 7:26, R. V.—"For such a high priest became us *holy, guileless, undefiled, separated from sinners*, and made higher than the heavens."

Heb. 9:14, R. V.—"How much more shall the blood of Christ, who through the Eternal Spirit offered himself *without blemish* unto God, cleanse your conscience from dead works to serve the living God?"

1 Pet. 1:19—"But with the precious blood of Christ, as of a lamb *without blemish* and *without spot*."

1 Jno. 3:5—"And ye know that he was manifested to take away our sins; and *in him is no sin*."

2 Cor. 5:21—"For he hath made him to be sin for us, who *knew no sin;* that we might be made the righteousness of God in him."

Heb. 4:15—"For we have not a high priest which cannot be touched with the feeling of our infirmities; but was in all points tempted like as we are, yet *without sin*."

1 Jno. 3:3—"And every man that hath this hope in him purifieth himself, even as *he is pure*."

SECOND PROPOSITION: The Bible multiplies expressions and figures to produce an adequate conception of the absolute holiness or moral purity of Christ. Nothing in nature with which to compare it except light.

1 Jno. 1:5—"This then is the message which we have heard of him, and declare unto you, that God is light, and in him is no darkness at all." (Compare Jno. 8:12—"Then spake Jesus again unto them, saying, I am the light of the world: he that followeth me shall not walk in darkness, but shall have the light of life.")

The dazzling white light that glorified the face and garments of JESUS on the Mount of Transfiguration (Matt. 17:2; Luke 9:29) was the outshining of the moral purity within.

(3)   HOW THE HOLINESS OF JESUS CHRIST MANIFESTED ITSELF.

(*a*)   Heb. 1:9—"Thou hast loved righteousness, and hated iniquity;

therefore God, even thy God, hath anointed thee with the oil of gladness above thy fellows."

FIRST PROPOSITION: *The Holiness of Jesus Christ manifested itself in a love of righteousness and hatred of iniquity.*

It is not enough to love righteousness; iniquity must be hated
as well.   On the other hand it is not enough to hate iniquity;
righteousness must be loved as well.   There are those who profess to love righteousness, but they do not seem to hate iniquity.
They are strong in applauding right, but not equally strong in
denouncing evil.   There are also those who profess to hate sin,
but they do not seem to love righteousness.   They are strong in
denouncing evil, but not equally strong in applauding right.
Jesus Christ's holiness was full-orbed as well as spotless; he loved
righteousness and hated iniquity.

(*b*)   1 Pet. 2: 22—"Who did no sin, neither was guile found in his
mouth."
Jno. 8: 29—"And he that sent me is with me: the Father hath not
left me alone; for I do always those things that please him."
Matt. 17: 5—"While he yet spake, behold, a bright cloud over-
shadowed them: and behold a voice out of the cloud, which said,
This is my beloved Son, in whom I am well pleased; hear ye him."
(Compare Jno. 12: 49—"For I have not spoken of myself; but the
Father which sent me, he gave me a commandment, what I should say,
and what I should speak.")

SECOND PROPOSITION: *The Holiness of Jesus Christ manifested itself in deed and word;* NEGATIVELY, *in His never doing sin
or speaking falsehood;* POSITIVELY, *in His always doing what
was pleasing to God and always speaking the things which pleased
God.*

The holiness of Jesus manifested itself not merely negatively
in not doing nor speaking wrong, but positively also in speaking
all that God desired, all that was right to do or speak.   A full
manifestation of holiness does not consist merely in doing nothing
wrong, but in doing all that is right.

(*c*)   Heb. 4: 15—"For we have not a high priest which cannot be
touched with the feeling of our infirmities; but was in all points tempted
like as we are, yet without sin."

THIRD PROPOSITION: The Holiness of Jesus manifested itself in constant and never-failing victory over temptation. It was not merely the negative innocence that results from being shielded from contact with evil, but the positive holiness that meets evil and overcomes it.

(*d*) The entire Sermon on the Mount (Matt. 5-7), especially Matt. 5: 48—"Be ye therefore perfect, even as your Father which is in heaven is perfect."

FOURTH PROPOSITION: The Holiness of Jesus Christ manifested itself in demanding absolute perfection of His disciples and refusing any compromise with evil.

(*e*)   Matt. 23: 13—"But woe unto you Scribes and Pharisees, hypocrites ! for ye shut up the kingdom of heaven against men: for ye neither go in yourselves, neither suffer ye them that are entering to go in."

Matt. 16: 23—"But he turned, and said unto Peter, Get thee behind me, Satan: thou art an offense unto me: for thou savorest not the things that be of God, but those that be of men."

Jno. 4: 17, 18—"The woman answered and said, I have no husband. Jesus said unto her, Thou hast well said, I have no husband: For thou hast had five husbands; and he who thou now hast is not thy husband: in that saidst thou truly."

Matt. 23: 33—"Ye serpents, ye generation of vipers, how can ye escape the damnation of hell ?"

FIFTH PROPOSITION: The Holiness of Jesus Christ manifested itself in the stern and scathing rebuke of sinners.

(*f*) 1 Pet. 2: 24—"Who in his own self bare our sins in his own body on the tree, that we, being dead to sins, should live unto righteousness: by whose stripes ye were healed."

1 Pet. 3: 18—"For Christ also hath once suffered for sins, the just for the unjust, that he might bring us to God, being put to death in the flesh, but quickened by the Spirit."

2 Cor. 5: 21—"For he hath made him to be sin for us, who knew no sin; that we might be made the righteousness of God in him." (Cf. Jno. 10: 17, 18—"Therefore doth my Father love me, because I lay down my life, that I might take it again. No man taketh it from me, but I lay it down of myself. I have power to lay it down and I have power to take it again. This commandment have I received of my Father.")

Phil. 2: 6-8—"Who, being in the form of God, thought it not rob-bery to be equal with God: But made himself of no reputation, and took upon him the form of a servant, and was made in the likeness of men: And being found in fashion as a man, he humbled himself and became obedient unto death, even the death of the cross."

Gal. 3: 13—"Christ hath redeemed us from the curse of the law, being made a curse for us: For it is written, cursed is every one that hangeth on a tree."

SIXTH PROPOSITION: The Holiness of Jesus Christ mani-fested itself in His making the greatest sacrifice in His power to save others from the sin He hated and to the righteousness He loved.

This was the crowning manifestation of His holiness. He so hated sin and loved righteousness that He was not only willing to die rather than sin Himself, but even to give up His Divine glory, and be made in fashion as a man, and die the death of a malefactor, and be rejected of man and separated from God, *that others might not sin.* He was willing to make any sacrifice to do away with sin.

(*g*) Matt. 25: 31, 32, 41—"When the Son of man shall come in his glory, and all the holy angels with him, then shall he sit upon the throne of his glory: And before him shall be gathered all nations: and he shall separate them one from another, as a shepherd divideth his sheep from the goats: Then shall he say also unto them on the left hand, De-part from me, ye cursed, into everlasting fire, prepared for the devil and his angels."

2 Thess. 1: 7-9—"And to you who are troubled rest with us, when the Lord Jesus shall be revealed from heaven with his mighty angels, in flaming fire taking vengeance on them that know now God, and they that obey not the gospel of our Lord Jesus Christ: Who shall be punished with everlasting destruction from the presence of the Lord, and from the glory of his power."

SEVENTH PROPOSITION: The Holiness of Jesus Christ will manifest itself in the awful, irrevocable punishment of those who refuse to be separated from their sin.

He died to separate men whom He loves from sin which He hates. If men refuse this separation, He leaves them to their self-chosen partnership and the doom which it involves. Men talk much of the holiness of God and love of JESUS, but JESUS is just as holy as God, and God is just as loving as JESUS. (Jno. 3: 16; Eph. 2: 4, 5.) In this as in all else JESUS and the Father are one. (Jno. 10: 30.)

Let us remember that first of all our Saviour is Holy. Until we have an adequate conception of His Holiness we can have no adequate conception of His love.

(4) WITNESSES TO THE HOLINESS OF JESUS CHRIST.

(*a*) Acts 3: 14—"But ye denied the Holy One and the Just, and desired a murderer to be granted unto you."—*Peter*.

(*b*) 1 Jno. 3:5—"And ye know that he was manifested to take away our sins; and in him is no sin."—*John*.

(*c*) 2 Cor. 5:21—"For he hath made him to be sin for us, who knew no sin; that we might he made the righteousness of God in him."—*Paul*.

(*d*) Acts 4: 27—"For of a truth against thy holy child Jesus, whom thou hast anointed, both Herod, and Pontius Pilate, with the Gentiles, and the People of Israel, were gathered together."—*The whole Apostolic Company in Concert*.

(*e*) Acts 22:14—"And he said, the God of our Fathers hath chosen thee, that thou shouldst know his will, and see that Just One, and shouldst hear the voice of his mouth."—*Ananias*.

(*f*) Luke 23:41—"And we indeed justly; for we receive the due reward of our deeds: but this man hath done nothing amiss."—*The Dying Thief*.

(*g*) Luke 23: 47—"Now when the centurion saw what was done, he glorified God, saying, Certainly this was a righteous man."—*The Roman Centurion*.

(*h*) Matt. 27: 19—"When he was set down on the judgment seat, his wife sent unto him, saying, Have thou nothing to do with that just man: for I have suffered many things this day in a dream because of him."—*Pilate's Wife*.

(*i*) Jno. 18: 38—"Pilate saith unto him, What is truth? And when he had said this, he went out again unto the Jews, and saith unto them, I find no fault in him at all."

Jno. 19:4, 6—"Pilate therefore went forth again, and saith unto them, Behold, I bring him forth to you, that ye may know that I find no fault in him. When the chief priests therefore and officers saw ʰim, they cried out, saying, Crucify him, crucify him. Pilate saith unto them, Take ye him, and crucify him: for I find no fault in him."—*Pilate, himself, three times*.

(*j*) Matt. 27:3, 4—"Then Judas, which had betrayed him, when he saw that he was condemned repented himself, and brought again the thirty pieces of silver to the chief priests and elders, saying, I have sinned in that I have betrayed the innocent blood."—*Judas Iscariot*.

(*k*) Mark 1: 23, 24—"And there was in their synagogue a man with an unclean spirit; and he cried out, saying, Let us alone; what have we to do with thee, thou Jesus of Nazareth ? Art thou come to destroy us ? I know thee who thou art, the Holy One of God."—*The Unclean Spirit.*

(*l*) Jno. 8: 46—"Which of you convinceth me of sin ? And if I say the truth, why do ye not believe me ? "

Jno. 14: 30—"Hereafter I will not talk much with you: for the prince of this world cometh, and hath nothing in me."—*Jesus himself.*

(*m*) Jno. 16: 8, 10—"And when he; is come, he will reprove the world of sin, and of righteousness, and of judgment: Of righteousness, because I go to my Father, and ye see me no more."—*The Holy Spirit.*

(*n*) Heb. 1: 8, 9—"But unto the Son he saith, Thy throne, O God, is for ever and ever: a sceptre of righteousness is the sceptre of thy kingdom. Thou hast loved righteousness, and hated iniquity; therefore God, even thy God, hath anointed thee with the oil of gladness above thy fellows."

Matt. 17: 5—"While he yet spake, behold, a bright cloud overshadowed them: and behold a voice out of the cloud, which said, This is my beloved Son, in whom I am well pleased; hear ye him."—*God the Father.*

II. The Love of Jesus Christ to God the Father.

(1) THE FACT OF HIS LOVE.

Jno. 14: 31—" But that the world may know that I love the **Father;** and as the Father giveth me commandment, even so I do. Arise, let us go hence."

FIRST PROPOSITION: Jesus Christ loved the Father.

The one thing that JESUS desired the world to know about Him was that He loved the Father. If the secret of His life **was** asked, it was this: "I love the Father." If we wish to know what love to God means in its purity and its fulness we have to look at JESUS CHRIST.

(2) HOW THE LOVE OF JESUS CHRIST TO THE FATHER MANIFESTED ITSELF.

(*a*) Jno. 14: 21—" But that the world may know that I love the Father; and as the Father gave me commandment, even so I do."

Jno. 15: 10—" If ye keep my commandments, ye shall abide in **my** love, even as I have kept my Father's commandments, and abide **in** his love."

FIRST PROPOSITION: The Love of Jesus Christ to the Father manifested itself in His doing as the Father gave Him commandment. (Compare 1 Jno. v: 3 f 1-2.)

NOTE 1.—Jno. 6: 38—"For I came down from heaven, not to do my own will, but the will of him that sent me."

His obedience to the Father's will faltered not at forsaking the glory of heaven 'for the shame of earth.

NOTE 2.—Phil. 2: 8—"And being found in fashion as a man, he humbled himself, and became obedient unto death, even the death of the cross."

His obedience to his Father's will faltered not at death, even the death of the cross.

Comp. Jno. 10: 15, 17, 18—"As the Father knoweth me, even so know I the Father; and I lay down my life for the sheep. Therefore doth my Father love me, because I lay down my life, that I might take it again. No man taketh it from me, but I lay it down of myself. I have power to lay it down, and I have power to take it again. This commandment have I received of my Father."

His death was in the highest sense voluntary. It was the goal toward which JESUS deliberately walked.

Luke 9: 51—"And it came to pass, when the time was come that he should be received up, he steadfastly set his face to go to Jerusalem."

But it was not only on that last journey that "He steadfastly set His face to go to Jerusalem;" but when He first took upon Him the nature of man, He had steadfastly set His face to go to Calvary. The Jews stood beside the tomb of Lazarus and saw JESUS weeping and said "Behold how He loved Him" (Jno. 11: 36)—loved Lazarus. We stand beside the cross and behold JESUS bleeding and we cry "Behold how He loved Him"—loved God.

(b) Jno. 8: 55, R.V.—"And ye have not known him: but I know him; and if I should say, I know him not, I shall be like unto you, a liar: but I know him, *and keep his word.*"

SECOND PROPOSITION: The Love of Jesus Christ to the Father manifested itself in His keeping; i. e., attending to carefully, or guarding, the Father's word.

To keep God's word means more than to obey His commandments. A man may obey commandments without hearty love to them, but we guard that which we regard as a precious treasure. This JESUS did. The Father's word was His most precious treasure. He guarded it as other men do their gold and jewels. This esteem for His Father's word was a peculiar mark of His love to the Father. The Destructive Critics profess to love God. How little of it they show in this way They are ready to give away God's word to the first plausible sophist that advances a high-sounding argument for surrendering some precious portion of the Word of God.

(c) Matt. 26:39, 42—"And he went a little further, and fell on his face, and prayed, saying, O my Father, if it be possible, let this cup pass from me: nevertheless, not as I will, but as thou wilt. He went away again the second time, and prayed, saying, O my Father, if this cup may not pass away from me, except I drink it, thy will be done."

THIRD PROPOSITION: The Love of Jesus Christ to the Father manifested itself in unwavering submission to the Father's will, even when that will might require that from which the soul shrank in heart-breaking anguish.

(d) Ps. 40:8—"I delight to do thy will, O my God: yea, thy law is within my heart."

FOURTH PROPOSITION: The Love of Jesus Christ to the Father manifested itself in positive delight in doing the Father's will. The connection shows that the Father's will here was His own sacrificial death.

NOTE 1.—Luke 2:49—"And he said unto them, How is it that ye sought me? Wist ye not that I must be about my Father's business?" This delight in the Father's will manifested itself even in the boyhood of JESUS.

NOTE 2.—Jno. 4:34, R. V.—"Jesus saith unto them, My meat is to do the will of him who sent me, and to accomplish his work." The doing of the Father's will, and accomplishing his work was JESUS CHRIST's meat, it was more to him than His necessary food. (See context.)

(e) Jno. 8:29, R. V.—"And he that sent me is with me; he hath not left me alone; for I do always the things that are pleasing to him."

FIFTH PROPOSITION: The love of Jesus Christ to the Father manifested itself in His always doing the things which were pleasing to the Father.

This is more than obedience to express commandments. A son may do whatever a father bids him, but a more loyal and loving son will not wait to be bidden, but study to find out what is pleasing to his father and anticipate the expression of his will. To know what was pleasing to the Father was JESUS CHRIST'S constant study; to do these things was his unvarying practice.

(*f*) Jno. 5: 30—"I can of ·mine own self do nothing: as I hear, I judge: and my judgment is just; because I seek not mine own will, but the will of the Father which hath sent me."

SIXTH PROPOSITION: *The Love of Jesus Christ to the Father manifested itself in His seeking the Father's will.*

The accomplishment of His Father's will was the one object of His pursuit. As other men hunt for gold, or pleasure, or honor, or the accomplishment of their own will, He sought for the accomplishment of His Father's will.

(*g*) Jno. 5: 34, 41, R.V.—"But the witness which I receive is not from man: howbeit I say these things, that ye may be saved. I receive not glory from men." (Compare v. 44.)

SEVENTH PROPOSITION: *The Love of Jesus Christ to the Father manifested itself in His seeking and accepting testimony and glory from the Father alone.*

(*h*) Jno. 17: 4—"I have finished the work which thou gavest me to do."

EIGHTH PROPOSITION: *The Love of Jesus Christ to the Father manifested itself in His finishing the work the Father gave Him to do.*

NOTE.—When was that work finished? (Jno. 19: 30—"When Jesus therefore had received the vinegar, he said, It is finished: and he bowed his head and gave up the ghost.") On the cross. It was love to God before love to man that brought Jesus to Calvary. We speak of God the Father loving men in Christ, which is true, but it is also true that Christ's sacrifice for men finds its final reason and original source in obedience to the will of the Father, who was the object of His Supreme love.

(*i*) Jno. 7: 18—"He that speaketh of himself seeketh his own glory: but he that seeketh his glory that sent him, the same is true, and no unrighteousness is in him."

Jno. 17:4—"I have glorified thee on the earth: I have finished the work which thou gavest me to do."

Jno. 17:1—"These words spake Jesus, and lifted up his eyes to heaven, and said, Father, the hour is come; glorify thy Son, that thy Son also may glorify thee."

NINTH PROPOSITION: *The Love of Jesus Christ to the Father manifested itself in His seeking the glory of the Father alone.*

The Father's glory was JESUS CHRIST's first and great ambition, the consuming passion of His life. It was for the Father's glory He planned, prayed, acted, suffered and died. JESUS taught that the first and great commandment is "Thou shalt love the Lord thy God, with all thy heart, and with all thy soul, and with all thy mind." (Matt. 22:37, 38.) His own life is the supreme manifestation of this law which He taught.

III. The Love of Jesus Christ to men.

(1) WHOM AMONG MEN DID JESUS LOVE?

(a) Eph. 5:25—"Husbands, love your wives, even as Christ also *loved the church*, and gave himself for it."

FIRST PROPOSITION: *Jesus Christ loved the Church.*

The Church is loved by CHRIST in a particular sense and a peculiar way. While a philanthropist may love all mankind and yet, if he is a true man, will in a peculiar way love his own wife as he loves no other woman, so CHRIST has a peculiar love for the Church, His bride. We must be on our guard, in studying the various passages in the Bible which speak about the love of CHRIST, to note whether they refer to His love in general, *i. e.,* His love to all mankind, or His love in particular; *i. e.,* His love to the Church, which is His body and His bride.

(b) Eph. 5:2—"And walk in love, as Christ also hath *loved us*, and hath given himself for us as offering and a sacrifice to God for a sweet smelling savour."

Gal. 2:20—"I am crucified with Christ: nevertheless, I live; yet not I, but Christ liveth in me: and the life which I now live in the flesh, I live by the faith of the Son of God, who *loved me*, and gave himself for me."

SECOND PROPOSITION: *Jesus Christ loves individual be-* *lievers.*   *Jesus Christ not only loves His church as a whole, but* *He loves each individual who believes in Him.*

(c) Jno. 13:1—"Now before the feast of the passover, when Jesus knew that his hour was come that he should depart out of this world unto the Father, having *loved his own* which were in the world, he loved them unto the end."

THIRD PROPOSITION: *Jesus Christ "loved His own" which* *were in the world.*   *Not all men were " His own " when He was* *here upon earth, neither are all His own to-day.*

QUESTION: Who are His own?

Jno. 17:2, 9, 12—"As thou hast given him power over all flesh, that he should give eternal life to *as many as thou hast given him.* I pray for them: I pray not for the world, but for *them which thou hast given me;* for they are thine. While I was with them in the world, I kept them in thy name: *those that thou gavest me* I have kept, and none of them is lost, but the son of perdition; that the scripture might be fulfilled."

JESUS CHRIST's own are those whom God the Father has given unto Him. The proof that anyone belongs to this elect company is that he comes to CHRIST. Jno. 6:37—"All that the Father giveth me shall come to me; and him that cometh to me I will in no wise cast out."

This highly favored company given unto CHRIST by the Father, and who come to CHRIST, are objects of CHRIST's special love. To them He ministers in a special way (see context Jno. 13:1), and them He guards so that not one of them perishes. (Jno. 17:12, R.V.—"While I was with them, I kept them in thy name which thou hast given me: and I guarded them, and not one of them perished, but the son of perdition; that the scriptures might be fulfilled;" 18:9—"That the word might be fulfilled which he spake. Of those whom thou hast given me *I lost not one.*")

(d) Jno. 14:21—"He that hath my commandments, and keepeth them, he it is that loveth me; and he that loveth me shall be loved of my Father, and I will love him, and will manifest myself to him."

FOURTH PROPOSITION: *Jesus Christ loves him that hath* *His commandments and keepeth them.*

CHRIST has an altogether special love for His obedient disciples; to them He manifests Himself as not unto the world.

NOTE 1.—Jno. 15: 10—"If ye keep my commandments, ye shall abide in my love; even as I have kept my Father's commandments and abide in his love." Those who keep his commandments abide in his love. This does not mean, as sometimes interpreted, "abide in the consciousness of his love." It means rather what it says. There is a love of CHRIST out of which one steps by disobedience.

NOTE 2.—Mark 3: 35—"For whosoever shall do the will of God, the same is my brother, and my sister, and mother." Whosoever does the will of God stands in the relation of closest kinship to Christ. Such an one is to Him his brother and sister and mother. A man may love all men and yet he has a peculiar love to his own brother and his own sister, and above all, to his own mother. Toward whosoever does the will of God, JESUS CHRIST has that love which combines all three in one.

NOTE 3.—Jno. 15: 9—"As the Father hath loved me, so have I loved you: continue ye in my love." (See also v. 10.) JESUS CHRIST'S love to those who keep His commandments is just the same as His Father's love to Him.

(e) Matt. 9: 13—"But go ye and learn what that meaneth, I will have mercy; and not sacrifice: for I am not come to call the righteous, but *sinners* to repentance."

Luke 19: 10—"For the Son of man is come to seek and to save that which was *lost*."

Rom. 5:6, 8—"For when we were yet without strength, in due time Christ died for the *ungodly*. But God commendeth his love toward us, in that, *while we were yet sinners*, Christ died for us."

FIFTH PROPOSITION: *Jesus Christ loves sinners, the lost, the ungodly.*

JESUS CHRIST loves the vilest sinner as truly as He loves the purest saint, but He does not love the vilest sinner in the same way that He loves the purest saint. His love to the sinner is one thing; His love to the obedient disciple quite another. Toward the one He has pity, in the other He takes pleasure. There is an attraction in both cases. In the one case it is the attraction of need appealing to compassion; in the other case it is the attraction of beauty appealing to appreciation and delight. CHRIST pities the sinner, He delights in the saint. He loves them both. In the parable of the lost sheep we see that the attraction of need is the greater.

(f) Luke 23: 34—"Then said Jesus, Father, forgive them; for they know not what they do."

SIXTH PROPOSITION: Jesus Christ <u>loved His enemies</u>.

(*g*)   Jno. 19 : 25–27—" Now there stood by the cross of Jesus his mother, and his mother's sister, Mary the wife of Cleophas, and Mary Magdalene.   When Jesus therefore saw his mother, and the disciple standing by, whom he loved, he saith unto his mother, Woman, behold thy son !   Then saith he to the disciple, Behold thy mother !   And from that hour that disciple took her unto his own home."

1 Cor. 15: 7—"After that he was seen of James."   (Comp. Jno. 7 : 5 —" For neither did his brethren believe in him.")

Jesus seems to have shown himself to no unsaved man after his resurrection, except his brother.

SEVENTH PROPOSITION: Jesus Christ loved His own kin-dred.   Jesus Christ had a peculiar interest in and love for those who were His kindred according to the flesh.   Christianity does not ignore but sanctifies natural ties.

(*h*)   Mark 10: 13–16—" And they brought *young children* to him, that he should touch them; and his disciples rebuked those that brought them.   But when Jesus saw it, he was much displeased, and said unto them, Suffer the little children to come unto me, and forbid them not; for of such is the kingdom of God.   Verily, I say unto you, Whosoever shall not receive the kingdom of God as a little child he shall not enter therein.   And he took them up in his arms, put his hands upon them, and blessed them."

EIGHTH PROPOSITION: Jesus Christ <u>loved children</u>.   Children had an especial attraction for Jesus Christ, and were the objects of his especial solicitude and care.

Matt. 18: 3, 6, 10—" And said, Verily, I say unto you, except ye be converted and become as little children, ye shall not enter into the kingdom of heaven.   But whoso shall offend one of these little ones which believe in me, it were better for him that a millstone were hanged about his neck, and that he were drowned in the depth of the sea.   Take heed that ye despise not one of these little ones; for I say unto you, that in heaven their angels do always behold the face of my Father which is in heaven."

The man or woman who has not an especial love for children is not Christlike.

(*i*)   Jno. 11: 5—" Now Jesus loved Martha, and her sister, and Lazarus."   (Mark 10: 21).

Jno. 19: 26—" When Jesus therefore saw his mother, and *the disciple* standing by, *whom he loved*, he saith unto his mother, Woman, behold thy son ! "

NINTH PROPOSITION: Jesus Christ loved especial individuals in an especial way.

While JESUS CHRIST loves all men with infinite love, while he has a peculiar love to His Church as His bride and His body, while He has an individual love to each member of His body, while He has a still more especial love to all those who have His commandments and keep them and do His Father's will, yet, the more open any heart is to Him by faith and love, the more is that person the object of His especial delight.

(2) HOW THE LOVE OF JESUS CHRIST TO MEN MANIFESTS ITSELF.

(*a*) 2 Cor. 8: 9, R.V.—"For ye know the grace of our Lord Jesus Christ, that, though he was rich, yet *for your sakes he became poor*, that ye through his poverty might become rich."

FIRST PROPOSITION: The love of Jesus Christ to men manifested itself in His becoming poor that we might become rich.

How great the riches He renounced and how great the poverty He assumed is seen in Phil. 2: 6–8—"Who *being in the form of God*, thought it not robbery to be equal with God: But *made Himself of no reputation*, and took upon him the form of a servant, and was made in the likeness of men: And being found in fashion as a man, he humbled himself, and *became obedient unto death, even the death of the cross.*" How great the riches we obtain through His becoming poor we see in Rom. 8: 16, 17: "The Spirit itself beareth witness with our spirit, that we are the children of God: And if children, then heirs; *heirs of God, and joint heirs with Christ;* if so be that we suffer with him, that we may be also glorified together."

(*b*) Eph. 5: 2—"And walk in love, as Christ also hath loved us, and hath given himself for us an offering and a sacrifice to God for a sweet smelling savour."

Gal. 2: 20—"I am crucified with Christ: nevertheless I live; yet not I, but Christ liveth in me: and the life which I now live in the flesh I live by the faith of the Son of God, who loved me, and gave himself for me."

1 Jno. 3: 16—"Hereby perceive we the love of God, because he laid down his life for us: and we ought to lay down our lives for the brethren."

Jno. 15: 13—" Greater love hath no man than this, that a man lay down his life for his friends."

SECOND PROPOSITION: The love of Jesus Christ for us manifested itself in His giving Himself, laying down His life for us.

His was a self-sacrificing love. The death of CHRIST was not the only sacrifice He made, but the crowning one. His whole life was a sacrifice, from the manger to the cross. His becoming man at all was a sacrifice of immeasurable greatness and meaning. (Phil. 2: 6, 7.)

(*c*) Luke 7: 48—" And he said unto her, Thy sins are forgiven."

THIRD PROPOSITION: The Love of Jesus to the vilest sinner was manifested in His forgiving them when they repented and believed on Him.

(*d*) Rev. 1: 5—" And from Jesus Christ, who is the faithful witness, and the first begotten of the dead, and the prince of the kings of the earth. Unto him that loved us, and washed us from our sins in his own blood."

FOURTH PROPOSITION: The Love of Jesus Christ to us manifests itself in His washing (or loosing, R. V.) us from our sins in His own blood.

(*e*) Luke 15: 4, 5, 6, 7—" What man of you, having a hundred sheep, if he lose one of them, doth not leave the ninety and nine in the wilderness and go after that which is lost, until he find it ? And when he hath found it he layeth it on his shoulders, rejoicing. And when he cometh home, he calleth together his friends and neighbors, saying unto them, Rejoice with me; for I have found my sheep which was lost. I say unto you, that likewise joy shall be in heaven over one sinner that repenteth more than over ninety and nine just persons, which need no repentance."

FIFTH PROPOSITION: The Love of Jesus Christ to His lost sheep manifests itself (a) *in His going after them until He finds them;* (b) *in His rejoicing over the lost one found;* (c) *in His laying the lost one found on His own shoulders;* (d) *in His bringing it safely home.*

(*f*) Jno. 10:4—"When he hath put forth all his own, he goeth before them, and the sheep follow him: for they know his voice."

Is. 40. 11—"He shall feed his flock like a shepherd: he shall gather the lambs with his arm, and carry them in his bosom, and shall gently lead those that are with young."

SIXTH PROPOSITION: The Love of Jesus Christ to His flock manifests itself in His tender care for each member of the flock.

(*g*) Matt. 8:17—"That it might be fulfilled which was spoken by Esaias the prophet, saying, Himself took our infirmities, and bare our sicknesses."

SEVENTH PROPOSITION: The Love of Jesus Christ for men was manifested in Himself taking our infirmities and bearing our sicknesses

(*h*) Matt. 14:14—"And Jesus went forth, and saw a great multitude, and was moved with compassion toward them, and he healed their sick."

EIGHTH PROPOSITION: The Love of Jesus Christ for men was manifested in His having compassion upon them and delivering them from their sicknesses.

(*i*) Matt. 15:32—"Then Jesus called his disciples unto him, and said, I have compassion on the multitude because they continue with me now three days, and have nothing to eat: and I will not send them away fasting, lest they faint in the way."

NINTH PROPOSITION: The Love of Jesus Christ to men was manifested in His having compassion upon them and supplying their physical needs.

(Compare Heb. 13:8, R. V.—"Jesus Christ is the same yesterday and to-day, yea and forever.")

(*j*) Rev. 3:19, R. V.—"As many as I love, I reprove and chasten: be zealous therefore, and repent."

TENTH PROPOSITION: The Love of Jesus Christ to men is manifested in His reproving them in order to bring them to repentance.

(*k*) Jno. 14:18, R. V—"I will not leave you desolate: I come unto you."

*ELEVENTH PROPOSITION: The Love of Jesus Christ to His
disciples is manifested in His not leaving them desolate.   He
Himself comes to them.*

(*l*) Jno. 11: 33–36: "When Jesus therefore saw her weeping, and
the Jews also weeping which came with her, he groaned in the spirit,
and was troubled, and said, Where have ye laid him ?   They say unto
him, Lord, come and see.   Jesus wept.   Then said the Jews, Behold
how he loved him !"

*TWELFTH PROPOSITION: The Love of Jesus Christ was man-
ifested in weeping over the sorrow of His loved ones.*

NOTE.—He knew that this sorrow was but for a moment, that it
was founded upon a misapprehension, that in a few moments it would
be changed for exceeding joy; but it was real, and as it was theirs it
was His also.

(*m*) Jno. 14: 1—"Let not your heart be troubled: ye believe in God,
believe also in me."

*THIRTEENTH PROPOSITION: The Love of Jesus Christ to
His disciples was manifested in his comforting them in their
sorrow and anxiety.*

This is the purpose of the entire fourteenth chapter.   Note
vv. 1 and 27—"Let not your heart be troubled: ye believe in
God, believe also in me;"   27—"Peace I leave with you, my
peace I give unto you: not as the world giveth, give I unto you.
Let not your heart be troubled, neither let it be afraid."

(*n*) Jno. 14: 27—"Peace I leave with you, my peace I give unto
you: not as the world giveth, give I unto you," etc.
Jno. 15: 11—"These things have I spoken unto you, that my joy
might remain in you and that your joy might be full."

*FOURTEENTH PROPOSITION: The love of Jesus Christ to
His disciples was manifested in His leaving them His own peace
and His own joy.*

(*o*) Mark 3: 5, R.V.—"And when he had looked round about on
them with anger, being grieved at the hardening of their heart, he
saith unto the man, Stretch forth thy hand.   And he stretched it forth:
and his hand was restored."

FIFTEENTH PROPOSITION: The Love of Jesus Christ to men was manifested in His grieving over the hardening of their hearts.

The hardening of their hearts, as shown by the context, was shameful and outrageous. It aroused Christ's anger. But it also moved Him to grief. Would that we had that feeling toward even the most outrageous sin that our anger would be mixed with tears.

(*p*) Luke 22: 32—"But I have prayed for thee, that thy faith fail not: and when thou art converted strengthen thy brethren."

Jno. 17: 15—"I pray not that thou shouldest take them out of the world, but that thou shouldest keep them from the evil."

Luke 23: 34—"Then said Jesus, Father, forgive them; for they know not what they do. And they parted his raiment, and cast lots."

SIXTEENTH PROPOSITION: The love of Jesus Christ toward His disciples and toward His enemies was manifested in His praying for them.

This is a most important manifestation of love.

(*q*) Luke 24: 38, 39, 40—"And he said unto them, Why are ye troubled? and why do thoughts arise in your hearts? Behold my hands and my feet, that it is I myself: handle me and see; for a spirit hath not flesh and bones, as ye see me have. And when he had thus spoken, he showed them his hands and his feet."

Jno. 20: 24-29—"But Thomas, one of the twelve, called Didymus, was not with them when Jesus came, the other disciples therefore said unto him, We have seen the Lord. But he said unto them, Except I shall see in his hands the prints of the nails, and put my finger into the print of the nails, and thrust my hand into his side, I will not believe. And after eight days again his disciples were within, and Thomas with them: then came Jesus, the doors being shut, and stood in the midst, and said, Peace be unto you. *Then saith he to Thomas, Reach hither thy finger*, and behold my hands; and *reach hither thy hand*, and thrust it into my side; and be not faithless, but believing. And Thomas answered and said unto him, My Lord and my God. Jesus saith unto him, Thomas, because thou hast seen me, thou hast believed: blessed are they that have not seen, and yet have believed."

SEVENTEENTH PROPOSITION: The Love of Jesus Christ toward skeptics was manifested in patient dealing with unreasonable, inexcusable and stubborn doubts.

(*r*) Mark 16: 7—"But go your way, tell his disciples *and Peter* that he goeth before you into Galilee: there shall ye see him, as he said unto you."

EIGHTEENTH PROPOSITION: The Love of Jesus Christ toward a weak disciple was manifested by patient and tender dealing with his lapse into grievous sin and apostacy.

(*s*) Rom. 8: 37—"Nay, in all these things we are more than conquerors through him that loved us."

NINETEENTH PROPOSITION: The Love of Jesus Christ to those who believe in Him is manifested in His giving them overwhelming victory in all their conflicts.

(*t*) Jno. 19: 26, 27—"When JESUS therefore saw his mother, and the disciple standing by, whom he loved, he saith unto his mother, Woman, Behold thy son! Then saith he to the disciple, Behold thy mother! And from that hour that disciple took her unto his own home."

TWENTIETH PROPOSITION: The Love of Jesus Christ was manifested (a) *in His forgetting His own awful agony in His sympathy for the sorrows of others;* (b) *by intrusting His own work to the one He loved. It was to the disciple He loved that He intrusted His own most sacred charge.*

(*u*) Jno. 13: 1-5, R.V.—"Now, before the feast of the passover, Jesus knowing that his hour was come that he should depart out of this world unto the Father, having loved his own which were in the world, he loved them unto the end. And during supper, the devil having already put into the heart of Judas Iscariot, Simon's son, to betray him, Jesus, knowing that the Father had given all things into his hands, and that he came forth from God, and goeth unto God, riseth from supper, and laying aside his garments; and he took a towel, and girded himself. Then he poured water into the basin, and began to wash the disciples' feet, and wipe them with the towel wherewith he was girded."

TWENTY-FIRST PROPOSITION: The Love of Jesus Christ to men manifested itself in His performing the lowliest and most menial service for them.

It is easy to perform the most menial services for those we love. A mother can perform the most humiliating and repulsive service for the babe she loves. (Yet wealthy mothers usually employ a hireling to do it.) What but love, wondrous love, could enable the only begotten of God, in the full consciousness "that the Father had given all things into His hands, and that He came forth from God, and goeth unto God," to arise from the table and with His own hands do this menial service for His disciples? And Judas was there, too, and the devil had already put it into his heart to betray Jesus. (Vv. 2, 10, 11, R.V.)

(v) Jno. 15:15—"Henceforth I call you not servants; for the servant knoweth not what his Lord doeth; but I have called you friends; for all things that I have heard of my Father I have made known unto you."

TWENTY-SECOND PROPOSITION: Jesus Christ's love to His friends manifests itself by His making known unto them all things that the Father makes known unto Him.

When you discover some great truth, what do you wish to do with it? Do you not wish to hurry away to your most-loved ones and make it known to them? So Jesus, in the fulness of His love to us, hastens to make known unto us all that the Father makes known unto Him.

(w) Jno. 10:3—"To him the porter openeth; and the sheep hear his voice: and he calleth his own sheep by name, and leadeth them out."

TWENTY-THIRD PROPOSITION: Jesus' love to His own sheep is manifested in His calling them by name.

This looks like a very small matter, but in that fact lies part of its significance. It is a tender illustration of the Savior's love for His own. There was also something peculiar in the way in which He called His own by name. (Compare Jno. 20:16.)

(x) Jno. 17:12—"While I was with them in the world, I kept them in thy name: those that thou gavest me, I have kept and none of them is lost, but the son of perdition; that the scriptures might be fulfilled."

Jno. 18:8, 9, R.V.—"Jesus answered, I told you that I am he: if therefore ye seek me, let these go their way: that the word might be fulfilled which he spake. Of those whom thou hast given me I lost not one."

Rom. 8: 35-39—"Who shall separate us from the love of Christ?
Shall tribulation, or distress, or persecution, or famine, or nakedness,
or peril, or sword ? As it is written, For thy sake we are killed all the
day long; we are accounted as sheep for the slaughter. Nay, in all
these things we are more than conquerors through him that loved us.
For I am persuaded that neither death, nor life, nor angels, nor principalities, nor powers, nor things present, nor things to come, nor
height, nor depth, nor any other creature, shall be able to separate us
from the love of God, which is in Christ Jesus our LORD."

*TWENTY-FOURTH PROPOSITION: The love of Jesus Christ
to His own manifests itself in His keeping them so that not one
of them is lost.*

(*y*) Acts 9: 5—"And he said, Who art thou, Lord? And the Lord
said, I am Jesus *whom thou persecutest:* it is hard for thee to kick
against the pricks."

Matt. 25: 37-40, 41-45—"Then shall the righteous answer him,
Lord, when saw we thee a hungered, and fed thee? or thirsty, and gave
thee drink? When saw we thee a stranger, and took thee in? or naked,
and clothed thee? Or when saw we thee sick, or in prison, and came
unto thee? And the king shall answer and say unto them, Verily I
say unto you, *Inasmuch as ye have done it unto one of the least of these
my brethren,* ye have done it unto me. Then shall he say also unto
them on the left hand, Depart from me, ye cursed, into everlasting
fire, prepared for the devil and his angels: for I was a hungered, and ye
gave me no meat: I was thirsty, and ye gave me no drink: I was a
stranger, and ye took me not in: naked, and ye clothed me not: sick,
and in prison, and ye visited me not. Then shall they also answer
him, saying, Lord, when saw we thee a hungered, or athirst, or a
stranger, or naked, or sick, or in prison, and did not minister unto
thee? Then shall he answer them, saying, Verily I say unto you,
Inasmuch as ye did it not unto one of the least of these, ye did it not
to me."

*TWENTY-FIFTH PROPOSITION: The love of Jesus Christ to
His disciples manifests itself in His so thoroughly identifying
Himself with them that He regards all that is done unto the least
of them as done unto Himself.*

(*z*) Eph. 5: 31, 32—"For this cause shall a man leave his father and
mother, and shall be joined unto his wife, and they two shall be one
flesh. This is a great mystery: but I speak concerning Christ and the
church."

TWENTY-SIXTH PROPOSITION: The love of Jesus Christ to the church was manifested in His leaving the Father to cleave unto the church, so that they two shall be one flesh. This is, indeed, a great mystery.

(*aa*) Jno. 14: 21-23—"He that hath my commandments, and keepeth them, he it is that loveth me: and he that loveth me shall be loved of my Father, and I will love him, and will manifest myself to him. Judas saith unto him, not Iscariot, Lord, how is it that thou wilt manifest thyself unto us, and not unto the world? Jesus answered and said unto him, If a man love me, he will keep my words: and my Father will love him, and we will come unto him, and make our abode with him."

TWENTY-SEVENTH PROPOSITION: The love of Jesus Christ to those who keep His commandments is manifested in His manifesting Himself unto them and making His abode with them.

(*bb*) Jno. 14: 2—"In my Father's house are many mansions: if it were not so, I would have told you. I go to prepare a place for you."

TWENTY-EIGHTH PROPOSITION: The love of Jesus Christ to His disciples has been manifested in His going to prepare a place for us.

(*cc*) Jno. 14: 3—"And if I go and prepare a place for you, I will come again, and receive you unto myself: that where I am, there ye may be also."

TWENTY-NINTH PROPOSITION: The love of Jesus Christ to His disciples will manifest itself in His coming again for us to receive us unto Himself, that we may be no more separated one from the other.

(Compare 1 Thess. 4: 16, 17—"For the Lord himself shall descend from heaven with a shout, with the voice of the archangel, and with the trump of God: and the dead in Christ shall rise first: Then we which are alive and remain shall be caught up together with them in the clouds, to meet the Lord in the air: and so shall we ever be with the Lord.")

NOTE 1.—He comes Himself: "I come again." He sends no mere messenger.

NOTE 2.—It is to receive us "unto *Himself.*" Not merely into heaven. It is as if He longed for us, longed to press us to His very soul, His very self "unto himself." We long for Him, but not as He longs for us. Heaven is a lonely place to Him without us. Earth ought to be a lonely place to us without Him. Godet's comment on these words is worth repeating. "He presses him to His heart, so to speak, while bearing him away. There is an infinite tenderness in these last words. It is for Himself that He seems to rejoice in and look to this moment which will put an end to all separation." (Godet's John, Vol. 2, p. 270, Am. Ed.)

(*dd*) Eph. 5: 25–27—"Husbands, love your wives, even as Christ also loved the church, and gave himself for it: That he might sanctify and cleanse it with the washing of water by the word, that he might present it to himself a glorious church, not having spot or wrinkle, or any such thing; but that it should be holy and without blemish."

THIRTIETH PROPOSITION: The love of Jesus Christ to the church manifested itself in the past by His giving Himself for it; manifests itself in the present in His sanctifying and cleansing it with the washing of water by the word; will manifest itself in the future by His presenting it to Himself "a glorious church not having spot, or wrinkle, or any such thing," but "holy and without blemish."

IV.—Jesus Christ's Love for Souls.

(1) Luke 19: 10—"For the Son of man is come to seek and to save that which was lost."

FIRST PROPOSITION: The Son of man came to seek and to save the lost.

This was the great object of His earthly mission. Not to receive honor nor to accumulate wealth nor to gain a kingdom. He left behind greater glories than the world contained. To save the lost. Lost men were of more value and preciousness in His sight than all earth's wealth and glory. A single soul was of priceless value. The whole material universe had not the value in His sight of a single soul. Each soul had this value in His sight. Not only the soul of the philosopher and the saint, but the soul of the savage and of the outcast.

(2) Jno. 4: 6, 7, 10—"Now Jacob's well was there. Jesus therefore being wearied with his journey, sat thus on the well: and it was about the sixth hour. There cometh a woman of Samaria to draw

water: Jesus saith unto her, Give me to drink. . . . Jesus answered and said unto her, If thou knewest the gift of God, and who it is that saith to thee, Give me to drink, thou wouldst have asked him, and he would have given thee living water."

SECOND PROPOSITION: Jesus Christ was ever on the watch for opportunities to save perishing souls.

We see this again in Jno. 9:35—"Jesus heard that they had cast him out; and when he had found him he said unto him, *Dost thou believe on the Son of God?*" And in Mark, 2:4, 5— "And when they could not come nigh unto him for the press, they uncovered the roof where he was: and when they had broken it up, they let down the bed wherein the sick of the palsy lay. When Jesus saw their faith, he said unto the sick of the palsy, Son, *thy sins be forgiven thee.*" "He made use of His miracles as stepping-stones to reach the soul." (Stalker: "Imago Christi"; p. 231.) So ought we to use every act of kindness which we are able to perform for men.

(3) Luke 15:4—"What man of you, having a hundred sheep, if he lose one of them, doth not leave the ninety and nine in the wilder-ness, and go after that which is lost, until he find it?"

THIRD PROPOSITION: Jesus Christ went after lost souls.

He not only watched for and welcomed opportunities when they came in His way, He sought opportunities. He not only re-ceived the lost when they came to Him, He went after them. A true love for souls will always reveal itself in a going out in search of them.

(4) Jno. 4:32-34—"But he said unto them, I have meat to eat that ye know not of. Therefore said the disciples one to another, Hath any man brought him aught to eat? Jesus saith unto them, My meat is to do the will of him that sent me, and to finish his work."

FOURTH PROPOSITION: Jesus Christ found His joy and satisfaction in saving lost souls.

In this work He forgot weariness, hunger, thirst. In it He found joy and refreshment for His body. Mark 3:20, 21—"And the multitude cometh together again, so that they could not so much as eat bread, and when his friends heard of it they went out to lay hold on him: for they said, He is beside himself." Jesus so lost himself in His work that He neglected the ordinary needs of his body in its prosecution and His friends said, "He is beside himself."

(5) Luke 15: 5-7—"And when he hath found it, he layeth it on his shoulders, rejoicing. And when he cometh home, he calleth together his friends and neighbors, saying unto them, Rejoice with me; for I have found my sheep which was lost. I say unto you that likewise joy shall be in heaven over one sinner that repenteth, more than over ninety and nine just persons, which need no repentance."

FIFTH PROPOSITION: Jesus Christ rejoiced with great joy over lost souls found.

As a shepherd rejoices over the sheep that had gone astray when he finds it; as the woman rejoices over the coin lost from her marriage necklace when it is found again; as the gold-hunter rejoices over the great nugget of gold that he digs from the rock; as the merchantman seeking goodly pearls rejoices over the one pearl of great price—so and infinitely more Jesus rejoices over a lost soul found.

(6) Jno. 5: 40—"And ye will not come to me, that ye might have life."

Luke 19: 41, 42—"And when he was come near, he beheld the city, and wept over it, saying, If thou hadst known, even thou, at least in this thy day, the things which belong unto thy peace! but now they are hid from thine eyes."

Matt. 23: 37—"O Jerusalem, Jerusalem, thou that killest the prophets, and stonest them which are sent unto thee, how often would I have gathered thy children together, even as a hen gathereth her chickens under her wings, and ye would not!"

SIXTH PROPOSITION: Jesus Christ grieved with great grief over lost souls that refused to be saved.

No woman ever grieved over her stolen jewels, no mother over a lost child, as Jesus over lost men who refused to be saved. No words can picture the agony that shot through the heart of Jesus Christ when men refused to come to him that they might have life.

(7) Jno. 10: 11—"I am the good shepherd: the good shepherd giveth his life for the sheep."

Matt. 20: 28—"Even as the Son of man came not to be ministered unto, but to minister, and to give his life a ransom for many."

SEVENTH PROPOSITION: *Jesus Christ gladly laid down His life to save souls.*

V. The Compassion of Jesus Christ.

(1) THE OBJECTS OF CHRIST'S COMPASSION.

(*a*) Mark 6: 34—"And Jesus, when he came out, saw much people, and was moved with compassion toward them, because they were as sheep not having a shepherd: and he began to teach them many things."

Matt. 9: 36, R.V—"But when he saw the multitudes, he was moved with compassion for them, because they were distressed and scattered, as sheep not having a shepherd."

FIRST PROPOSITION: *Jesus Christ had compassion on the multitude who were distressed and scattered abroad as sheep not having a shepherd.*

What if Jesus were in Chicago? How does He feel toward the hundreds of millions in China? Contrast the Pharisees: Jno. 7: 48, 49—"Hath any of the rulers believed on him, or of the Pharisees? But this multitude which knoweth not the law are accursed." Which are we more like, Christ or the Pharisees?

(*b*) Mark 8: 2—"I have compassion on the multitude, because they have now been with me three days, and have nothing to eat."

SECOND PROPOSITION: *Jesus Christ had compassion on the hungry multitude.*

Not only the spiritual destitution of men, but their physical need as well appealed to the compassion of Jesus Christ.

(*c*) Matt. 14: 14—"And Jesus went forth, and saw a great multitude, and was moved with compassion toward them, and he healed their sick."

THIRD PROPOSITION: *Jesus Christ had compassion on the multitude in general.*

Whenever Jesus saw a crowd of men He was moved with compassion. His compassion on the multitude is mentioned five times. A crowd of men is a pitiful sight. It represents so much of sorrow, so much of pain, so much of sin. What is your feeling when you look out upon a crowd? Judging by the context of this passage, the sick seem to have especially drawn out His compassion.

(*d*) Matt. 20: 34—"So Jesus had compassion on them, and touched their eyes: and immediately their eyes received sight, and they followed him."

FOURTH PROPOSITION: *Jesus Christ had compassion on the blind.*

(*e*) Mark. 9: 22, 25—"And ofttimes it hath cast him into the fire, and into the waters, to destroy him: but if thou canst do anything, have compassion on us, and help us. When Jesus saw that the people came running together, he rebuked the foul spirit, saying unto him, Thou dumb and deaf spirit, I charge thee, come out of him, and enter no more into him."

FIFTH PROPOSITION: *Jesus Christ had compassion on the demonized, the victims of the power of unclean spirits.*

In the last case mentioned there was much in the man that was repulsive and hateful, but Jesus beheld him with compassion.

(*f*) Mark. 1: 40, 41—"And there came a leper to him, beseeching him, and kneeling down to him, and saying unto him, if thou wilt, thou canst make me clean. And Jesus moved with compassion, put forth his hand, and touched him, and saith unto him, I will; be thou clean."

SIXTH PROPOSITION: *Jesus Christ had compassion on the leper.*

The world, even the religious world of that day, met the leper with repulsion and disgust and scorn. Christ met him with compassion. The world drew away from him, Christ drew toward him.

(*g*) Luke 7: 12, 13—"Now when he came nigh to the gate of the city, behold there was a dead man carried out, the only son of his mother, and she was a widow, and much people of the city was with her. And when the Lord saw her, he had compassion on her, and said unto her, Weep not."

SEVENTH PROPOSITION: *Jesus Christ had compassion upon the one bereaved of a loved one.*

This is the only recorded case in which Jesus met a funeral procession, and we see what His feeling was toward the mourner. What is your feeling toward mourners? What is your feeling when you meet a funeral procession ?

(*h*) Luke 15:20—"And he arose and came to his father. But when he was yet a great way off, his father saw him, and had compassion, and ran, and fell on his neck, and kissed him." (Compare vv. 1, 2—"Then drew near unto him all the publicans and sinners for to hear him, and the Pharisees and scribes murmured, saying, This man receiveth sinners, and eateth with them.")

EIGHTH PROPOSITION: Jesus Christ had compassion on the sinful, the lost, the spiritually dead.

(*i*) Mark 3:5—"And when he had looked round about on them with anger, being grieved for the hardness of their hearts, he saith unto the man, Stretch forth thine hand. And he stretched it out: and his hand was restored whole as the other."

NINTH PROPOSITION: Jesus Christ had compassion on all men afflicted by any form of misfortune, or wretchedness, or degradation.

Jesus Christ did not go about his work from a cold sense of duty, but His own heart drew Him out towards those He helped and saved. His deeds of mercy cost Him something more than the sacrifice of leisure and the expenditure of effort and power. They cost him heartaches. He made other men's sorrows His own sorrows, other men's agony His own agony, other men's sin and shame His own sin and shame. He could not look upon misery, pain, death or sin without heart pangs. (Jno. 11:33— "When Jesus therefore saw her weeping, and the Jews also weeping which came with her, he groaned in the spirit and was troubled.") Herein lay one great secret of His power. It is the misery that we make our own that we can comfort; it is the want that we make our own that we can fully satisfy; it is the sin we make our own that we can save another from. (2 Cor. 5:21— "For he hath made him to be sin for us, who knew no sin; that we might be made the righteousness of God in him.") Real power to help men is a very expensive thing, but anyone can have it who is willing to pay the price. But the one who is **not** willing to give up lightness of heart, and take instead burden of heart over the world's sin and sorrow and shame, may as well give up the thought of being a helper, much less a savior of men. Men can not be saved by burning words. No! only by bleeding hearts.

(2.) THE WAY IN WHICH THE COMPASSION OF CHRIST WAS MANIFESTED.

(*a*) Luke 10: 33, 34, 35, 36—"But a certain Samaritan, as he journeyed, came where he was; and when he saw him he had compassion on him, and went to him, and bound up his wounds, pouring in oil and wine, and set him on his own beast, and brought him to an inn, and took care of him. And on the morrow when he departed, he took out two pence, and gave them to the host, and said unto him, Take care of him: and whatsoever thou spendeth more, when I come again, I will repay thee. Which now of these three, thinkest thou was neighbor unto him that fell among the thieves ?"

The good Samaritan in the last analysis is a picture of Jesus Christ.

FIRST PROPOSITION: The compassion of Jesus Christ was not manifested in mere feelings or words, but in action, in self-sacrificing and persistent and thoroughgoing ministration to the needs of the one upon whom He had compassion.

(*b*) Mark 6: 34—"And Jesus, when he came out, saw much people, and was moved with compassion toward them, because they were as sheep not having a shepherd: and he began to teach them many things."

SECOND PROPOSITION: The compassion of Jesus Christ toward the unshepherded was manifested in His patiently teaching them when He himself was weary and sore at heart.

He taught before he fed. Why ? This manifestation of compassion there is abundant opportunity for us all to imitate. Get an unshepherded child of the street, if you can do no more.

(*c*) Matt. 14: 14—"And Jesus went forth, and saw a great multitude, and was moved with compassion toward them, and he healed their sick."

THIRD PROPOSITION: The compassion of Jesus Christ toward the unshepherded was manifested in His healing the sick.

(*d*) Matt. 15: 32—"Then Jesus called his disciples unto him and said, I have compassion, because they continue with me now three days, and have nothing to eat." (See following verses.)

FOURTH PROPOSITION: The compassion of Jesus Christ was manifested in feeding the hungry.

(*e*) Matt. 20: 32-34—"And Jesus stood still, and called them, and said, What will ye that I shall do unto you? They say unto him, Lord, that our eyes may be opened. So Jesus had compassion on them, and touched their eyes; and immediately their eyes received sight, and they followed him."

FIFTH PROPOSITION: The compassion of Jesus Christ was manifested: (a) In standing still when on most important and urgent business to listen to the cry of two blind beggars. (b) In opening the eyes of the blind.

(*f*) Mark 5: 8—"For he said unto him, Come out of the man, thou unclean spirit."
Mark 9: 25—"When Jesus saw that the people came running together, he rebuked the foul spirit, saying unto him, Thou dumb and deaf spirit, I charge thee, come out of him, and enter no more into him."

SIXTH PROPOSITION: The compassion of Jesus Christ was manifested in casting unclean spirits out of men.

(*g*) Mark 1: 41—"And Jesus, moved with compassion, put forth his hand, and touched him, and saith unto him, I will: be thou clean."

SEVENTH PROPOSITION: The compassion of Jesus Christ was manifested: (a) In putting forth His hand and touching the leper. (For years that leper had not felt the touch of a clean and loving hand. That is what many a moral leper needs to-day, the touch of a clean and loving hand.) (b) *In healing the leper.*

(*h*) Luke 7: 12, 13, 14—"Now when he came nigh to the gate of the city, behold there was a dead man carried out, the only son of his mother, and she was a widow: and much people of the city were with her. And when the Lord saw her, he had compassion on her, and said unto her, Weep not. And he came and touched the bier: and they that bare him stood still. And he said, Young man, I say unto thee, Arise."

EIGHTH PROPOSITION: The compassion of Jesus Christ was manifest: (a) *In bidding the sorrowing to no longer weep.* (b) *In restoring the departed to the one bereft.*

(*i*) Luke 7: 48, 50—"And he said unto her, Thy sins are forgiven. And he said to the woman, Thy faith hath saved thee; go in peace." Jno. 6: 37—"All that the father giveth me shall come to me; and him that cometh to me I will in no wise cast out."

NINTH PROPOSITION: The compassion of Jesus Christ was manifest in welcoming and pardoning the sinner and bidding her go in peace.

In all this let us remember, Heb. 13: 8—"Jesus Christ the same yesterday, and to-day and forever," and 1 Jno. 2: 6—"He that saith he abideth in him ought himself also so to walk, even as he walked."

VI. The Prayerfulness of Jesus Christ.

(1) THE FACT OF HIS PRAYERFULNESS.

Heb. 5: 7—"Who in the days of his flesh, when he had offered up prayers and supplications with strong crying and tears unto him that was able to save him from death, and was heard in that he feared."

FIRST PROPOSITION: Jesus Christ in the days of His flesh offered up prayers and supplications. He was a man of prayer.

The words "prayer" and "pray" are used at least twenty-five times in connection with Him, and there are many instances in which the fact of His praying is mentioned where the words do not occur. His praying is mentioned by each of the four evangelists. The life of Christ had many marked characteristics, but nothing is more marked than His prayerfulness. The extent to which He was a man of prayer will appear more clearly when we consider the next point.

(2) WHEN CHRIST PRAYED.

(*a*) Luke 6: 12—"And it came to pass in those days, that he went out into a mountain to pray, and continued all night in prayer to God."

FIRST PROPOSITION: Jesus Christ prayed in the night—in some instances continuing all night in prayer.

Why in the night ?   That he might be alone and have un·disturbed communion with God.

(*b*)   Mark 1: 35: "And in the morning, rising up a great while before day, he went out, and departed into a solitary place, and there prayed."

SECOND PROPOSITION: Jesus Christ rose very early in the morning, a great while before day, to pray.

This was apparently partly that he might have solitude for communion with God and partly as a preparation for the day's work.

(*c*)   Luke 3: 21, 22:   "Now when all the people were baptized, it came to pass, that Jesus also being baptized, and praying, the heaven was opened.   And the Holy Ghost descended in a bodily shape like a dove upon him, and a voice came from heaven, which said, Thou art my beloved Son: in thee I am well pleased."

Mark 1: 35, 38:   " And in the morning, rising up a great while before day, he went out, and departed into a solitary place, and there prayed.   And he said unto them, let us go into the next towns, that I may preach there also: for therefore came I forth."

Luke 6: 12, 13—"And it came to pass in those days, that he went out into a mountain to pray, and continued all night in prayer to God. And when it was day, he called unto him his disciples: and of them he chose twelve, whom also he named apostles."

Luke 9: 18, 21, 22—" And it came to pass, as he was alone praying, his disciples were with him; and he asked them saying, Whom say the people that I am ?   And he straightly charged them, and commanded them to tell no man that thing; saying, The Son of man must suffer many things, and be rejected of the elders and chief priests and scribes, and be slain and be raised the third day."

THIRD PROPOSITION: Jesus Christ prayed before His baptism with the Holy Spirit and entrance upon His public ministry; before entering upon an evangelistic tour, before choosing the twelve, before announcing to the twelve His approaching death: i. e., before important steps in His life.   He prepared for the important events of life by especial seasons of prayer.

(*d*)   Matt. 14: 23—"And when he had sent the multitudes away, he went up into a mountain apart to pray: and when the evening was come, he was there alone."

Jno. 6: 15—"When Jesus therefore perceived that they would come and take him by force, to make him a king, he departed again into a mountain himself alone."

FOURTH PROPOSITION: *Jesus Christ prayed after the great achievements and important crises of His life.*

Why? (*a*) To recruit His strength. Christ's miracles cost Him something, an expenditure and loss of power. (Cf. Mark 5: 30.) (*b*) To guard against temptations to pride, or satisfaction, or contentment, with the work already achieved. Jesus Christ was truly human, subject to the same temptations we are, and He met them with the same weapons we must—the Word of God and prayer. It is more common for most of us to pray before the great events of life than after them, but the latter is as important as the former. If we would pray after the great achievements of life we might go on to greater. As it is we are often either puffed up or exhausted by them, and we proceed no further.

(*e*) Matt. 14: 19—" And he commanded the multitude to sit down on the grass, and took the five loaves, and the two fishes, and looking up to heaven, he blessed, and brake, and gave the loaves to his disciples, and the disciples to the multitude."
Luke 24: 30—"And it came to pass, as he sat at meat with them, he took bread, and blessed it, and brake, and gave to them."

FIFTH PROPOSITION: *Jesus Christ prayed before He ate.*

He prayed in connection with the simplest, commonest event of every-day life. So characteristic was Christ's manner of praying in connection with His meals that He was known by this act to the disciples who had failed to discover who He was up to that point. (Luke 24: 30, 31) It is in connection with little things that many of us most forget to pray. Every step of Christ's life seems to have been accompanied with prayer.

(*f*) Luke 5: 15, 16—" But so much the more went there a fame abroad of him: and great multitudes came together to hear, and to be healed by him of their infirmities. And he withdrew himself into the wilderness, and prayed."

SIXTH PROPOSITION: *Jesus Christ, when life was unusually busy, withdrew into a solitary place to pray.*

Some men are so busy, that they can find no time to pray Apparently, the busier Christ's life was the more he prayed. Sometimes He had no time to eat (Mark 3:20). Sometimes He had not time for needed rest and sleep (Mark 6:31, 33, 46), but He always took time to pray, and the more the work crowded the more He prayed. Martin Luther, Adam Clarke and many another mighty man of God has learned this secret from Christ. Many another mighty man of God has lost his power because he did not learn this secret, and he has allowed increasing work to crowd out prayer.

(g) Mark 6:31, 33, 34, 35, 46—"And he said unto them, Come ye yourselves apart into a desert place, and rest awhile: for there were many coming and going, and they had no leisure so much as to eat. And the people saw them departing, and many knew him, and ran afoot thither out of all cities, and outwent them, and came together unto him. And Jesus, when he came out, saw much people, and was moved with compassion toward them, because they were as sheep not having a shepherd: and he began to teach them many things. And when the day was now far spent, his disciples came unto him, and said, This is a desert place, and now the time is far passed. . . And when he had sent them away, he departed into a mountain to pray."

SEVENTH PROPOSITION: Jesus Christ prayed when weary.

The night vigil in Mark 6:46, was after a day when he had been so busy he could not eat and when he had taken the disciples aside to rest awhile. But the needed and desired rest had been immediately broken in upon by the multitude who outran Him, and the entire day had been spent in teaching and healing the sick and feeding the multitude. That weary day was followed, not by sleep, but by a night of prayer.' There is a better way to recuperate exhausted energies than by sleep. Ofttimes when we are so tired we cannot sleep, and waste time tossing to and fro upon our beds, if we would arise and pour out our hearts to God we would get far more rest and go back to bed to sleep.

h) Matt. 26:36—"Then cometh Jesus with them unto a place called Gethsemane, and saith unto the disciples, Sit ye here, while I go and pray yonder."

Luke 22:39-41—"And he came out, and went, as he was wont, to the mount of Olives; and his disciples also followed him. And when he was at the place, he said unto them, Pray that ye enter not into temptation. And he was withdrawn from them about a stone's cast, and kneeled down and prayed."

EIGHTH PROPOSITION: Jesus Christ prayed before great temptations.

He prepared for the temptations He saw drawing near by prayer, so He always came off victorious. The disciples, despite His warning, slept while He prayed; so He stood and they fell. The calm majesty of His bearing amid the awful onslaughts of Pilate's judgment hall and of Calvary was the outcome of the struggle, agony and victory of Gethsemane.

(*i*) Luke 23: 34, 46—"Then said Jesus, Father forgive them; for they know not what they do. And they parted his raiment, and cast lots. And when Jesus had cried with a loud voice, he said, Father, into thy hands I commend my spirit: and having said thus, he gave up the ghost."

NINTH PROPOSITION: Jesus Christ prayed in the last moments of His life.

His last utterance was a prayer. His life had been a life of prayer, and with prayer it came to a fitting close.

(3)   WHERE JESUS CHRIST PRAYED.

(*a*)   Matt. 14: 23—"And when he had sent the multitudes away, he went up into a mountain apart to pray: and when the evening was come, he was there alone."
Mark 6: 46—"And when he had sent them away, he departed into the mountain to pray."
Luke 6: 12—"And it came to pass in those days, that he went into a mountain to pray, and continued all night in prayer to God."
Jno. 6: 15—"When Jesus therefore perceived that they would come and take him by force, to make him a king, he departed again into a mountain himself alone."

FIRST PROPOSITION: Jesus Christ went out into a mountain apart to pray.

Each of the four evangelists makes mention of His going into the mountain to pray, and it is said in Luke 22:39, "as his custom was." Stalker says: "When he arrived in a town, His first thought was which was the shortest way to the mountain, just as ordinary travelers inquire where are the most noted sights and which is the best hotel." ("Imago Christi," p. 131.) He went to the mountain because of its solitude, and because it brought Him near to God.

(*b*) Mark 1: 35—" And in the morning, rising up a great while before day, he went out, and departed into a solitary place, and there prayed."

SECOND PROPOSITION: Jesus Christ went out into solitary places to pray.

There is doubtless a sense in which we can find a solitary place in our crowded streets, but it is well to follow Christ's example literally, and get away from the sight and sound of men, and get alone with God. If you have never known what it is to kneel down in the woods where no human voice could be heard, or beneath a tree in the silent starlight or moonlight, and look up with open eyes toward the face of God and talk to Him, you have missed a blessing that cannot be described, but that every child of God should know.

(4) WITH WHOM CHRIST PRAYED.

(*a*) Matt. 14: 23—" And when he had sent the multitudes away, he went up into a mountain apart to pray: and when the evening was come he was there alone."

FIRST PROPOSITION: Jesus Christ prayed alone—by Himself.

(*b*) Luke 9: 28—" And it came to pass an eight days after these sayings, he took Peter and John and James, and went up into a mountain to pray."

SECOND PROPOSITION: Jesus Christ prayed with a chosen few.

(*c*) Luke 9: 18—" And it came to pass, as he was alone praying, his disciples were with him; and he asked them saying, Whom say the people that I am ? "

THIRD PROPOSITION: Jesus Christ prayed with the whole apostolic company. They were his family and this was family prayer.

(*d*) Matt. 14: 19—" And he commanded the multitude to sit down on the grass, and took the five loaves, and the two fishes, and looking up to heaven, he blessed, and brake, and gave the loaves to his disciples, and the disciples to the multitude."

FOURTH PROPOSITION: *Jesus Christ prayed in the midst of a great multitude.*

Those who would contend from Matt. 6:6—"But thou, when thou prayest, enter into thy closet, and when thou hast shut thy door, pray to thy Father which is in secret; and thy Father which seeth in secret shall reward thee openly," that we must confine our prayers to our closets can find no support in Christ's example. He Himself prayed in public.

(5) IN WHOSE BEHALF JESUS CHRIST PRAYED.

(*a*) Jno. 12: 28—"Father, glorify thy name. Then came there a voice from heaven, saying, I have both glorified it and will glorify it again."

FIRST PROPOSITION: *Jesus Christ prayed in God's behalf, for God's glory.*

He had a supreme regard for God's interest in His prayers. In the prayer He taught His disciples the first petition was that God's name might be hallowed. (Matt. 6:9.)

(*b*) Jno. 17: 1—"These words spake Jesus, and lifted up his eyes to heaven, and said, Father, the hour is come: glorify thy Son, that thy Son also may glorify thee."
Heb. 5: 7—"Who in the days of his flesh, when he had offered up prayers and supplications with strong crying and tears unto him that was able to save him from death, and was heard in that he feared."

SECOND PROPOSITION: *Jesus Christ prayed in His own behalf.*

It was not in any sense a selfish prayer, though it was for self. He prayed the Father to glorify Him in order that He in turn might glorify the Father. He prayed for deliverance from premature death that He might finish the work the Father had given Him to do. There is nothing more unselfish in the world than a true prayer for oneself.

(*c*) Jno. 14: 16, 17—"And I will pray the Father, and he shall give you another comforter, that he may abide with you for ever; even the spirit of truth; whom the world cannot receive, because it seeth him not, neither knoweth him: but ye know him; for he dwelleth with you, and shall be in you."

Jno. 17: 9, 20—"I pray for them: I pray not for the world, but for them which thou hast given me; for they are thine. Neither pray I for these alone, but for them also which shall believe on me through their word."

THIRD PROPOSITION: Jesus Christ prayed in behalf of all His own. Christ's own, those given to Him by the Father are the objects of His prayer in a sense no others are. It is for them He now intercedes as High Priest and Advocate.

Heb. 7: 25—"Wherefore he is able also to save them to the uttermost *that come unto God by him,* seeing he ever liveth to make intercession for them."

Rom. 8: 34—"Who is he that condemneth? It is Christ that died, yea rather, that is risen again, who is even at the right hand of God, who also maketh intercession *for us.*"

1 Jno. 2: 1—' My little children, these things write I unto you, that ye sin not. And if any man sin, *we* have an advocate with the Father, Jesus Christ the righteous."

(*d*) Luke 22: 31, 32—"And the Lord said, Simon, Simon, behold, Satan hath desired to have you, that he might sift you as wheat: but I have prayed for thee, that thy faith fail not: and when thou art converted, strengthen thy brethren."

FOURTH PROPOSITION: Jesus Christ prayed for Peter, for an individual disciple.

Christ does not merely pray for believers in a mass, he **prays** for individual believers.

1 Jno. 2: 1—"My little children, these things write I unto you, that ye sin not. And if any man sin, we have an advocate with the Father, Jesus Christ the righteous."

(*e*) Luke 23: 34—"Then said Jesus, Father forgive them; for they know not what they do. And they parted his raiment and cast lots."

FIFTH PROPOSITION: Jesus Christ prayed for His enemies.

(6) How Jesus Christ Prayed.

(*a*) Jno. 17: 1—"These words spake Jesus, and lifted up his eyes to heaven, and said, Father, the hour is come: glorify thy Son, *that thy Son may glorify thee.*"

FIRST PROPOSITION: Jesus Christ prayed with God's glory first in view. (Compare Jas. 4: 3, R.V.; Matt. 6: 9.)

(*b*) Matt. 26: 42—" He went away again the second time and prayed, saying, O my Father, if this cup may not pass away from me, except I drink it, thy will be done."

SECOND PROPOSITION: Jesus Christ prayed in perfect submission to the Father's will.

This did not introduce any element of uncertainty into his prayers when the will of God was clearly revealed and known. Compare Jno. 11: 41, 42—"Then they took away the stone from the place where the dead was laid. And Jesus lifted up his eyes and said, Father, I thank thee that thou hast heard me. And I know that thou hearest me always: but because of the people which stand by I said it, that they may believe that thou hast sent me."

(*c*) Luke 22:41—"And he was withdrawn from them about a stone's cast, and kneeled down and prayed."

THIRD PROPOSITION: Jesus Christ prayed on His knees.

(*d*) Matt. 26: 39—"And he went a little further, and fell on his face, and prayed, saying, O my Father, if it be possible, let this cup pass from me: nevertheless, not as I will, but as thou wilt."

FOURTH PROPOSITION: Jesus Christ prayed on His face before God.

If the sinless Son of God got upon his knees and upon his face before the Father, what shall we do?

(*e*) Matt. 14: 19—"And he commanded the multitude to sit down on the grass, and took the five loaves, and the two fishes, and looking up to heaven, he blessed, and brake, and gave the loaves to his disciples, and the disciples to the multitude."

Jno. 17: 1—"These words spake Jesus, and lifted up his eyes to heaven, and said, Father, the hour is come; glorify thy Son, that thy Son also may glorify thee."

FIFTH PROPOSITION: Jesus Christ prayed with open, upturned eyes.

We do well often to close our eyes that we may shut the world out, but there are times when it is well to look right up with open eyes into the face of God as Jesus did.

(*f*) Luke 22: 44—"And being in agony he prayed more earnestly: and his sweat was as it were great drops of blood falling down to the ground."

SIXTH PROPOSITION :   Jesus Christ prayed earnestly.

The literal force of the world translated "earnestly" is "stretched-out-ly." The thought is of the soul stretched out in intensity of desire.

(*g*) Heb. 5: 7—"Who in the days of his flesh, when he had offered up prayers and supplications with strong crying and tears unto him that was able to save him from death, and was heard in that he feared."

SEVENTH PROPOSITION: Jesus Christ prayed " with strong crying and tears."

The word translated "crying" is a very strong word, meaning "outcry" or "clamor." The force of it is increased by the qualifying adjective "strong." He prayed "with mighty outcry." There are some who speak of it as an attainment of superior faith to always be very calm in prayer, and "just take" in childlike confidence what they ask. They have either gotten beyond their Master, or else do not know what Holy Ghost earnestness means. It is to be suspected that sometimes their calm comes not from the Holy Ghost, but from indifference. The Holy Ghost makes intercession "with groanings which cannot be uttered." (Rom. 8: 26.) Be careful not to confuse the laziness of indifference with "the rest of faith." Any rest of faith that does not leave room for mighty conflicts in prayer and deed is not Christlike. A "groaning" and "tears" and "outcry" that are simulated, or the product of fleshly working of oneself up, are worse yet.

(*h*) Luke 6: 12—"And it came to pass in those days, that he went into a mountain to pray, and continued all night in prayer to God."

EIGHTH PROPOSITION: Jesus Christ prayed with a large outlay of time—" all night."

The time element in prayer is of vast importance. By the use of modern machinery a man can do more in a minute than he could once do in hours.   No machinery has ever been invented by which the work of prayer can be expedited.

(*i*)   Matt. 26: 44—"And he left them, and went away again, and prayed the third time, saying the same words."

NINTH PROPOSITION: Jesus Christ prayed importunately— three times for the same thing.

In the face of what is recorded of Christ it will not do to say that the failure to take what you ask the first time you pray necessarily indicates a weakness of faith.

(*j*)   Jno. 11: 41, 42—"Then they took away the stone from the place where the dead was laid.   And Jesus lifted up his eyes, and said, Father, I thank thee that thou hast heard me.   And I know that thou hearest me always: but because of the people which stand by I said it, that they may believe that thou hast sent me."

TENTH PROPOSITION: Jesus Christ prayed: (a)   *With thanksgiving.*   (Compare Phil. 4: 6.)   In this case the thanksgiving was for an answer yet to be and that only faith could see.   (b)   *Believingly.*   He believed that He had received the petition, He asked of the Father though there was as yet no visible proof of it.

(Compare 1 Jno. 5: 14, 15—"And this is the confidence that we have in him, that if we ask anything according to his will, he heareth us: And if we know that he hear us, whatsoever we ask, we know that we have the petitions that we desired of Him."   And Mark 11: 24, R.V.—"All things whatsoever ye pray and ask for, *believe that ye have received them,*" etc.).

(7)   THE EFFECT OF CHRIST'S PRAYERS.

(*a*)   Jno. 11: 41, 42—"Then they took away the stone from the place where the dead was laid.   And Jesus lifted up his eyes, and said, Father, I thank thee that thou hast heard me.   And I know that thou hearest me always: but because of the people which stand by I said it, that they may believe that thou hast sent me."   (Compare 1 Jno. 5: 15—"And if we know that he hear us, whatsoever we ask, we know that we have the petitions that we desired of him.")

FIRST PROPOSITION: The Father always heard Christ's prayers and therefore He always received what He asked.

Jesus Christ accomplished things by prayer which even He could accomplish in no other way. Thus He saved Peter when warnings and teachings failed. Thus He overcame temptation, wrought miracles, escaped death and glorified God, finishing the work the Father gave Him to do.

VII. The meekness of Jesus Christ.

(1) THE FACT OF HIS MEEKNESS.

Matt. 11: 29—"Take my yoke upon you, and learn of me; for I am meek and lowly in heart: and ye shall find rest unto your souls."

2 Cor. 10: 1—"Now I Paul myself beseech you by the meekness and gentleness of Christ, who in presence am base among you, but being absent am bold toward you."

Matt. 21: 5—"Tell ye the daughter of Zion, Behold thy king cometh unto thee, meek, and sitting upon an ass, and a colt the foal of an ass."

FIRST PROPOSITION: Jesus Christ was meek.

QUESTION: What is meekness ?

1 Cor. 4: 21—"What will ye ? shall I come unto you with a rod, or in love, and in the spirit of meekness ?"

2 Cor 10: 1—"Now I Paul myself beseech you by the meekness and gentleness of Christ, who in presence am base among you, but being absent am bold toward you."

Gal. 6: 1—"Brethren, if a man be overtaken in a fault, ye which are spiritual, restore such a one in the spirit of meekness; considering thyself, lest thou also be tempted."

2 Tim. 2: 24, 25—"And the servant of the Lord must not strive; but be gentle unto all men, apt to teach, patient; In meekness instructing those that oppose themselves; if God peradventure will give them repentance to the acknowledging of the truth."

Tit. 3: 2—"To speak evil of no man, to be no brawlers, but gentle, showing all meekness unto all men."

ANSWER: Meekness is that attitude of mind that is opposed to harshness and contentiousness, and that shows itself in gentleness and tenderness in dealing with others. The thought of "meekness" as "patient submissiveness under injustice and injury," does not seem to be the prominent thought in the Bible usage of the word. The thought rather of gentleness in dealing with and correcting the errors of others seems to be the predominant thought.

(2) How the Meekness of Christ was manifested.

(*a*) Matt. 12: 20—"A bruised reed shall he not break, and smoking flax shall he not quench, till he send forth judgment unto victory."

FIRST PROPOSITION: The meekness of Jesus Christ was manifested in his not breaking the bruised reed or quenching the smoking flax.

He dealt tenderly with the broken, and cherished the fire that was well-nigh gone out.

(*b*) Luke 7: 38, 48, 50—"And stood at his feet behind him weeping, and began to wash his feet with tears, and did wipe them with the hairs of her head, and kissed his feet, and anointed them with the ointment. And he said unto her, Thy sins are forgiven. And he said to the woman, Thy faith hath saved thee; go in peace."

SECOND PROPOSITION: The meekness of Jesus Christ was manifested in His gently telling the outrageous but penitent sinner that her sins were forgiven and to go in peace.

(*c*) Mark 5: 33, 34—"But the woman fearing and trembling, knowing what was done in her, came and fell down before him, and told him all the truth. And he said unto her, Daughter, thy faith hath made thee whole; go in peace, and be whole of thy plague."

THIRD PROPOSITION: The meekness of Jesus was manifested in His tenderly saying to the poor afflicted one who had tried to steal the blessing unseen by any: "Daughter, thy faith hath made thee whole; go in peace and be whole of thy plague."

(*d*) Jno. 20: 29—"Jesus saith unto him, Thomas, because thou hast seen me, thou hast believed: blessed are they that have not seen, and yet have believed."

FOURTH PROPOSITION: The meekness of Jesus was manifested in the gentleness with which He rebuked the stubborn unbelief of doubting Thomas.

(*e*) Jno. 21: 15-17—"So when they had dined, Jesus saith to Simon Peter, Simon, son of Jonas, lovest thou me more than these? He saith unto him, Yea, Lord: thou knowest that I love thee. He saith unto him, Feed my lambs. He saith to him again the second time, Simon; son of Jonas, lovest thou me? He saith unto him, Yea,

Lord: thou knowest that I love thee. He saith unto him, Feed my sheep. He saith unto him the third time, Simon, son of Jonas, lovest thou me? Peter was grieved because he said unto him the third time, Lovest thou me? And he said unto him, thou knowest all things; thou knowest that I love thee. Jesus saith unto him, Feed my sheep."

FIFTH PROPOSITION: The meekness of Jesus Christ was manifested in the tenderness with which He rebuked Peter's self-confidence and subsequent unfaithfulness and thrice-repeated and flagrant denial of his Lord.

(*f*) Jno. 13: 21, 27—" When Jesus had thus said, he was troubled in spirit, and testified and said, Verily, verily, I say unto you, that one of you shall betray me. And after the sop Satan entered into him. Then Jesus said unto him, That thou doest, do quickly."

SIXTH PROPOSITION: The meeekness of Jesus Christ was manifested in His gentle, tender and pleading reproof of Judas Iscariot, His betrayer.

(*g*) Luke 23: 34—" Then said Jesus, Father, forgive them; for they know not what they do. And they parted his raiment, and cast lots."

SEVENTH PROPOSITION: The meekness of Jesus Christ was manifested in His praying for His murderers.

VIII.—The Humility of Jesus Christ.

(1) THE FACT OF HIS HUMILITY.

Matt. 11: 29—" Take my yoke upon you, and learn of me; for I am meek and lowly in heart: and ye shall find rest unto your souls."

FIRST PROPOSITION: Jesus Christ was lowly in heart.

(2) HOW THE HUMILITY OF JESUS CHRIST WAS MANIFESTED.

(*a*) Jno. 8: 50—" And I seek not mine own glory."

FIRST PROPOSITION: The humility of Jesus Christ was manifested in His not seeking His own glory.

(*b*) Is. 42: 2—" He shall not cry, nor lift up, nor cause his voice to be heard in the street."

SECOND PROPOSITION: The humility of Jesus Christ was manifested in His avoiding notoriety and praise.

Many professed followers of Jesus Christ court notoriety. He shunned it. He strictly charged those whom He had bene-fitted not to make it known. He kept no advertising bureau.

(c) Matt. 9: 10—"And it came to pass, as Jesus sat at meat in the house, behold, many publicans and sinners came and sat down with him and his disciples."

Luke 15: 1, 2—"Then drew near unto him all the publicans and sinners for to hear him. And the Pharisees and scribes murmured, saying, This man receiveth sinners, and eateth with them."

THIRD PROPOSITION: The humility of Jesus Christ was manifested in His associating with the despised and outcast.

(d) Is. 50: 5, 6—"The Lord God hath opened mine ear, and I was not rebellious, neither turned away back. I gave my back to the smiters, and my cheeks to them that plucked off the hair: I hid not my face from shame and spitting."

Heb. 12: 3—"For consider him that endured such contradiction of sinners against himself, lest ye be weary and faint in your minds."

FOURTH PROPOSITION: The humility of Jesus Christ was manifested in patient submission to outrageous injury and in-justice.

(e) Is. 53: 7, R.V.—"He was oppressed, yet he humbled himself and opened not his mouth; as a lamb that is led to the slaughter, and as a sheep that before her shearers is dumb; yet, he opened not his mouth."

FIFTH PROPOSITION: The humility of Jesus Christ was manifested in silence under outrageous injury and injustice.

(f) 1 Pet. 2: 23—"Who, when he was reviled, reviled not again; when he suffered, he threatened not; but committed himself to him that judgeth righteously."

Matt. 26: 60–63—"But found none: yea, though many false wit-nesses came, yet found they none. At the last came two false wit-nesses. And said, This fellow said, I am able to destroy the temple of God, and to build it in three days. And the high priest arose, and said unto him, Answerest thou nothing? What is it which these wit-ness against thee? But Jesus held his peace. And the high priest answered and said unto him, I adjure thee by the living God that thou tell us whether thou be the Christ, the son of God."

Luke 23: 8–10—"And when Herod saw Jesus, he was exceeding glad: for he was desirous to see him of a long season, because he had heard many things of him; and he hoped to have seen some miracle done by him. Then he questioned with him in many words; but he answered him nothing. And the chief priests and scribes stood and vehemently accused him."

SIXTH PROPOSITION: The humility of Jesus Christ manifested itself in silence under false accusations.

Jesus did not defend His own good name. He left that to God. He "committed Himself to Him that judgeth righteously," and He hath given Him "the name that is above every name." (Phil. 2: 9.)

(*g*) Matt. 20: 28—"Even as the Son of man came not to be ministered unto, but to minister, and to give his life a ransom for many."

SEVENTH PROPOSITION: The humility of Jesus Christ was manifested in His coming to minister and not to be ministered unto.

(*h*) Jno. 13: 4, 5—"He riseth from supper, and laid aside his garments; and took a towel, and girded himself. After that he poured water into a basin, and began to wash the disciples' feet and to wipe them with the towel wherewith he was girded."

EIGHTH PROPOSITION: The humility of Jesus Christ was manifested in His performing the most humble and menial and repulsive services for others.

(*i*) Phil. 2: 6, 7—"Who, being in the form of God, thought it not robbery to be equal with God: But made himself of no reputation, and took upon himself the form of a servant, and was made in the likeness of men."

NINTH PROPOSITION: The humility of Jesus Christ was manifested in His choosing the lowliest place of service as a slave, instead of the loftiest place of glory as God.

(*j*) Phil. 2: 8—"And being found in fashion as a man, he humbled himself, and became obedient unto death, even the death of the cross."

TENTH PROPOSITION: The humility of Jesus Christ was manifested in His being "obedient unto death, even the death of the cross."

(It is in this connection that Paul charges us: "Have this mind in you which was also in Christ Jesus.")

CHAPTER V.

THE DEATH OF JESUS CHRIST.

I. The Importance of Christ's Death.

*FIRST PROPOSITION: The death of Jesus Christ is mentioned
directly more than one hundred and seventy-five times in the New
Testament.   Besides this there are very many prophetic and typ-
ical references to the death of Jesus Christ in the Old Testament.*

(2)   Heb. 2:14—"Forasmuch then as the children are partakers of
flesh and blood, he also himself likewise took part of the same; *that
through death* he might destroy him that had the power of death, that
is, the devil."

*SECOND PROPOSITION: Jesus Christ became a partaker of
flesh and blood in order that He might die.*

The incarnation was for the purpose of the death.   Jesus
Christ's death was not a mere incident of His human life, it was
the supreme purpose of it.   He became man in order that He
might die as man and for man.

(3)   Matt. 20:28—"Even as the Son of man came not to be
ministered unto, but to minister, and to give his life a ransom for
many."

*THIRD PROPOSITION: Jesus Christ came into the world that
He might die as a ransom.*

(4)   Luke 9: 30, 31—"And behold there talked with him two men,
which were Moses and Elias: Who appeared in glory, and spake of
his decease which he should accomplish at Jerusalem."

*FOURTH PROPOSITION. The death of Jesus Christ was the
subject that Moses and Elias talked with Him about when they
appeared in glory.*

(5)   1 Pet. 1:11—"Searching what, or what manner of time the
Spirit of Christ which was in them did signify, when it testified
beforehand the sufferings of Christ, and the glory that should
follow."

FIFTH PROPOSITION: *The prophesied death of Christ was a subject of deep interest and earnest inquiry to the Old Testament prophets.*

(6) 1 Pet. 1: 12—"Unto whom it was revealed, that not unto them-selves, but unto us they did minister the things, which are now reported unto you by them that have preached the gospel unto you with the Holy Ghost sent down from heaven; which things the angels desire to look into."

SIXTH PROPOSITION: *The death of Jesus Christ was a subject of deep interest and earnest inquiry to the angels.*

(7) Rev. 5: 8-12—"And when he had taken the book, the four beasts and four and twenty elders fell down before the Lamb, having every one of them harps, and golden vials full of odours, which are the prayers of saints. And they sung a new song, saying, Thou art worthy to take the book, and to open the seals thereof: *for thou wast slain,* and hast redeemed us to God *by thy blood* out of every kindred, and tongue, and people, and nation; And hast made us unto our God kings and priests: and we shall reign on the earth. And I beheld, and I heard the voice of many angels round about the throne, and the beasts, and the elders: and the number of them was ten thousand times ten thousand, and thousands of thousands; Saying with a loud voice, Worthy is *the Lamb that was slain* to receive power, and riches, and wisdom, and strength, and honour, and glory, and blessing."

SEVENTH PROPOSITION: *The death of Jesus Christ is the central theme of heaven's song.*

(8) 1 Cor. 15: 1, 3, 4—"Moreover, brethren, I declare unto you *the gospel which I preached* unto you, which also ye have received, and wherein ye stand; *For I delivered unto you first of all* that which I also received, *how that Christ died* for our sins according to the Scriptures; and that he was buried, and that he rose again the third day according to the Scriptures."

EIGHTH PROPOSITION: *The death of Jesus Christ is one of the two fundamental truths of the Gospel.*

(Compare 1 Cor. 11: 26—"For as often as ye eat this bread, and drink this cup, ye do show *the Lord's death* till he come." 1 Cor. 2: 2—"For I determined not to know anything among you, save Jesus Christ, *and him crucified.*")

The importance of Jesus Christ's death will come out further as we consider the purpose and results of His death. The modern preaching that lays the principal emphasis upon the life and example of Jesus Christ is thoroughly unscriptural.

II. The purpose of Jesus Christ's death, or Why did Jesus Christ die ?

(1) Is. 53: 5—"But he was wounded (Hebrew 'pierced'; same Hebrew word is so translated in R.V. of Is. 51: 9) for our transgressions, he was bruised for our iniquities: the chastisement of our peace was upon him; and with his stripes we are healed."

Is. 53: 8, 11, 12:—"·He was taken from prison and from judgment: and who shall declare his generation ? for he was cut off out of the land of the living: *for the transgression of my people was he stricken.* He shall see of the travail of his soul, and shall be satisfied: by his knowledge shall my righteous servant justify many; for he shall bear their iniquities. Therefore will I divide him a portion with the great, and he shall divide the spoil with the strong; because he hath poured out his soul unto death: and he was numbered with the transgressors; and he *bare the sin of many*, and made intercession for the transgressors."

1 Pet. 3: 18—"For Christ also hath once suffered for sins, *the just for the unjust*, that he might bring us to God, being put to death in the flesh, but quickened by the Spirit."

Rom. 4: 25—"Who was delivered *for our offenses*, and was raised again for our justification."

1 Cor. 15: 3—"For I delivered unto you first of all that which I also received, how that Christ died *for our sins* according to the Scriptures."

1 Pet. 2: 24—"Who his own self *bare our sins* in his own body on the tree, that we, being dead to sins, should live unto righteousness: by whose stripes ye are healed."

FIRST PROPOSITION: Jesus Christ died because of the sins of others—i. e., (a) *It was sin that made His death necessary.* (b) *It was not His own sin, but that of others that He bore in His death. His death was vicarious*—i. e., *A just one who deserved to live, dying in the place of unjust men who deserved to die.*

(2) Matt. 20: 28—"Even as the Son of man came not to be ministered unto, but to minister, and *to give his life a ransom* for many."

SECOND PROPOSITION: Jesus Christ gave His life as a ransom—i. e., *His death was the price paid to redeem others from death.*

(3) Is. 53: 10, R.V.—"Yet it pleased the LORD to bruise him; he hath put him to grief when thou shalt make his soul an offering for sin (Heb. 'a guilt-offering'), he shall see his seed, he shall prolong his days, and the pleasure of the LORD shall prosper in his hand."

THIRD PROPOSITION: Jesus Christ's soul was made a guilt-offering for sin—i. e., *It was on the ground of His death that pardon is granted to sinners.* (See Lev. 6: 6, 7, R.V.)

Compare Heb. 9: 22—"And almost all things are by the law purged with blood: and without shedding of blood is no remission." And Heb. 9: 28—"So Christ was once offered to bear the sins of many; and unto them that look for him shall he appear the second time without sin unto salvation." (Cf. Is. 53: 12.)

(4) 1 Jno. 4: 10—"Herein is love, not that we loved God, but that he loved us, and sent his Son to be the propitiation for our sins." (The definition in Thayer's Greek-English Lexicon of the New Testament of the word translated "propitiation" is, a "means of appeasing.")

Rom. 3: 25—"Whom God set forth to be a propitiation, through faith, by his blood, to show his righteousness, because of the passing over of the sins done aforetime, in the forbearance of God." (The word here translated "propitiation" means practically the same as that used above—"an expiatory sacrifice.")

FOURTH PROPOSITION: Jesus Christ is the propitiation for our sins. God set Him forth to be a propitiation by His blood—i. e., *He, through the shedding of His blood, or death, is that by which the wrath of God against us as sinners is appeased.*

God is holy and must hate sin. His holiness and hatred of sin must manifest itself. His wrath at sin must strike somewhere, on the sinner himself or upon a lawful substitute. Is. 53: 6—"All we like sheep have gone astray; we have turned every one to his own way; and the LORD hath laid on him the iniquity of us all." (See R.V. Marg. The Hebrew literally translated, "made to strike upon.") And Is. 53: 8, R.V. Am. App.—"By oppression and judgment he was taken away; and as for his generation, who among them considered that he was cut off out of the land of the living, for the transgression of my people to whom the stroke was due." "The stroke due" to others fell upon Him and He was consequently "cut off out of the land of the living." The death of Christ has its first cause in the demands of God's holiness.

(5) Gal. 3: 10, 13—"For as many as are of the works of the law are under the curse: for it is written, Cursed is every one that continueth not in all things which are written in the book of the law to do them. Christ hath redeemed us from the curse of the law, being made a curse for us: for it is written, Cursed is every one that hangeth on a tree."

FIFTH PROPOSITION: Jesus Christ died to redeem us from the curse of the law by bearing that curse Himself.

(6) 1 Cor. 5: 7—"For even Christ our passover is sacrificed for us." (Compare Ex. 12: 13, 23—"And the blood shall be to you for a token upon the houses where ye are: and *when I see the blood*, I will pass over you, and the plague shall not be upon you to destroy you, when I smite the land of Egypt. For the LORD will pass through to smite the Egyptians; and *when he seeth the blood* upon the lintel, and on the two side posts, the LORD will pass over the door, and will not suffer the destroyer to come in unto your houses to smite you.")

SIXTH PROPOSITION: Jesus Christ died as our passover sacrifice—i. e., that His shed blood might serve as a ground upon which God would pass over and spare us.

(7) Gal. 4: 4, 5—"But when the fulness of the time was come, God sent forth his Son, made of a woman, made under the law, to redeem them that were under the law, that we might receive the adoption of sons."

SEVENTH PROPOSITION: Jesus Christ died to redeem them that were under the law that we might receive the adoption of sons—i. e., that the death of Christ might serve as a ground upon which men might be delivered from the claims of the law and be made sons.

(8) Gal. 1: 4—"Who gave himself for our sins, that he might deliver us from this present evil world, according to the will of God and our Father."

EIGHTH PROPOSITION: Jesus Christ died to deliver us from this present evil world or age.

We were in bondage to this age by sin and the law. By the death of Jesus Christ we were delivered from this age to become citizens of heaven and sons of God. (Phil. 3: 20.) (Compare Gal. 4: 3–5, 7, 8, 9: 5, 1.)

(9) 1 Pet. 3: 18—"For Christ also hath once suffered for sins, the just for the unjust, that he might bring us to God, being put to death in the flesh, but quickened by the Spirit."

NINTH PROPOSITION: Jesus Christ died to bring us to God.

His death puts out of the way the impassable gulf that yawns between a holy God and sinful man.

(10) Jno. 12: 24—"Verily, verily, I say unto you, Except a corn of wheat fall into the ground and die, it abideth alone: but if it die, it bringeth forth much fruit."

TENTH PROPOSITION: Jesus Christ died that He might bring forth much fruit. From His death sprang up the new race of Sons of God.

(11) Rom. 14: 9, R.V.—"For to this end Christ died, and lived again, that he might be the Lord of both the dead and the living."

ELEVENTH PROPOSITION: Jesus Christ died and lived again that He might be the Lord of both the dead and living.

III. For whom Christ died.

(1) Rom. 8: 32—"He that spared not his own Son, but delivered him up *for us all*, how shall he not with him also freely give us all things?"

Eph. 5: 2—"And walk in love, as Christ also hath loved us, and hath *given himself for us* an offering and a sacrifice to God for a sweet-smelling savour."

Tit. 2: 14—"Who *gave himself for us*, that he might redeem us from all iniquity, and purify unto himself a peculiar people, zealous of good works."

1 Cor. 5: 7—"Purge out therefore the old leaven, that ye may be a new lump, as ye are unleavened. For even Christ *our passover* is sacrificed for us."

2 Cor. 5: 21—"For he hath made him to be sin *for us*, who knew no sin; that we might be made the righteousness of God in him."

FIRST PROPOSITION: Jesus Christ died "for us"—i. e., for believers in Jesus Christ.

We shall see that Jesus Christ died for all men, but His death was especially for those who should appropriate to themselves by faith the blessings which that death secured. (1 Tim. 4: 10—"For therefore we both labor and suffer reproach, because we trust in the living God, who is the Saviour of all men, *specially of those that believe.*" This is the truth contained in the old doctrine of a limited atonement.

(2) Eph. 5: 25-7—"Husbands, love your wives, even as Christ also loved the church, and gave himself for it; that he might sanctify and cleanse it with the washing of water by the word, that he might present it to himself a glorious church, not having spot, or wrinkle, or any such thing; but that it should be holy and without blemish."

SECOND PROPOSITION: Jesus Christ gave himself for the church.

While Christ died for all, He had His bride, whom He would redeem for Himself, especially in view, and His death avails especially for Her.

(3) Gal. 2:20—"I am crucified with Christ: nevertheless I live; yet not I, but Christ liveth in me: and the life which I now live in the flesh I live by the faith of the Son of God, who loved me, and gave himself *for me.*"

THIRD PROPOSITION: Jesus Christ gave Himself for individual believers; not merely for the church as a body, but for each individual in the body, so that each believer can say, "He loved me and gave himself for me."

(4) Rom. 14:15—"But if thy brother be grieved with thy meat, now walkest thou not charitably. Destroy not him with thy meat, for whom Christ died."

1 Cor. 8:11—"And through thy knowledge shall the weak brother perish, for whom Christ died?"

FOURTH PROPOSITION: Jesus Christ died for the weak brother.

Not only for the strong, enlightened, mature Christian, but for the weakest member of the household of faith as well. If we would bear this in mind would we not be more patient with and considerate toward the weak Christian who does not come on as rapidly as we wish? He is a weak brother, it is true, but he is "the weak brother for whom Christ died"

(5) Matt. 20:28—"Even as the Son of man came not to be ministered unto, but to minister, and to give his life a ransom for many."

FIFTH PROPOSITION: Jesus Christ died for many. It was no small company for whom Christ died.

(6) Rev. 5:9, R.V.—"Worthy art thou to take the book, and to open the seals thereof: for thou wast slain, and didst purchase unto God with thy blood men of every tribe, and tongue, and people, and nation."

SIXTH PROPOSITION: Jesus Christ died for men of every tribe, and tongue, and people, and nation.

Here is the foundation warrant for world-wide missions, and here is the urgent call to press the work. "Let me go and find in the heart of Africa the men of that tribe for whom Christ died."

(7) Jno. 1: 29—"The next day John seeth Jesus coming unto him, and saith, Behold the Lamb of God, which taketh away the sin of the world ! "

SEVENTH PROPOSITION: Jesus Christ died for the whole world.

On the ground of Christ's death God can deal with the whole world in mercy. The death of Christ is sufficient for the whole world; it is fully efficient only for believers. We shall see that it is in part efficient for all mankind. (1 Jno. 2: 2; 1 Cor. 15: 22.) Jesus Christ was in an especial sense the head of the church (Eph. 1: 22) and died as its head and for it. But He is also in another sense the head of the race—the second Adam—and died as the head of the race and for all men. (1 Cor. 15: 22, 45.)

(8) 1 Tim. 2: 6—"Who gave himself a ransom for all, to be testified in due time."

EIGHTH PROPOSITION: Jesus Christ gave Himself a ransom for all.

He died for all. The ransom price is paid for all. Provision is made for all. Mercy can be preached to all. The sin accounts of all men are all settled. All men are potentially forgiven; all they need to do is to accept by faith and thus make their own the pardon purchased.

(9) Heb. 2: 9—"But we see Jesus, who was made a little lower than the angels for the suffering of death, crowned with glory and honor; that he by the grace of God should taste death for every man."

NINTH PROPOSITION: Jesus Christ tasted death for every man.

He died for every man. Not only for all men as a race, but for each individual man in the race. On the ground of Christ's death God can deal in mercy with each individual and offer him salvation on the ground of Christ's death.

(10) 1 Pet. 3:18—" For Christ also hath once suffered for sins, the just for the unjust, that he might bring us to God, being put to death in the flesh, but quickened by the Spirit."

TENTH PROPOSITION: Jesus Christ died for the unjust.

(11) Rom. 5:8—" But God commendeth his love toward us, in that, while we were yet sinners, Christ died for us."

ELEVENTH PROPOSITION: Jesus Christ died for sinners.

(12) Rom. 5:6—" For when we were yet without strength, in due time Christ died for the ungodly."

TWELFTH PROPOSITION: Jesus Christ died for the ungodly.

IV. The Results of Christ's Death.

(1) IN RELATION TO MEN IN GENERAL.

(a) Jno. 12:32, 33: " And I, if I be lifted up from the earth, will draw all men unto me. This he said, signifying what death he should die."

FIRST PROPOSITION: Through the death of Jesus Christ all men are drawn unto Him.

The death of Christ is the world's great magnet drawing all men unto Him. There are many who will resist that drawing to their own ruin. (Jno. 5: 40.) But the crucified Christ draws all men.

(b) 1 Jno. 2:2—" And he is the propitiation for our sins; and not for ours only, but also for the sins of the *whole world.*"

SECOND PROPOSITION: By the death of Jesus Christ a propitiation is provided for the world.

A basis is provided upon which God can deal in mercy with the world. All God's dealings in mercy with any man are on the ground of Christ's death. Only on the ground of Christ's death could God deal in mercy with any man.

QUESTION: How, then, did God deal in mercy with those before Christ's time ?

ANSWER: Rev. 13: 8—" And all that dwell upon the earth shall worship Him, whose names are not written in the Book of Life of the Lamb *slain from the foundation of the world.*" The death of Christ was in God's sight an eternal fact. He planned it from the beginning.

NOTE.—The propitiation of Christ bears a different relation to the believer from that which it bears to the world in general. 1 Jno. 2:2, R.V—"He is the propitiation *for* OUR SINS; and not for ours only, but also for the whole world" (but not "the sins of" the whole world). The propitiation avails for all, but it fully avails only for us. (Compare 1 Tim 4:10—"For therefore we both labor and suffer reproach, because we trust in the living God, who is the Saviour of all men, specially of those that believe." Rom. 3:25—"Whom God hath set forth to be a propitiation *through faith* in his blood, to declare his righteousness for the remission of sins that are past, through the forbearance of God.")

(c) Jno. 1:29—"The next day John seeth Jesus coming unto him, and saith, Behold the Lamb of God, which taketh away the sin of the world!"

THIRD PROPOSITITON: *Jesus Christ by His death took away the sin of the world.*

His death took the sin of the world out of the way so that a clear way to God and pardon and life was opened for all.

(d) Rom. 5:18, R.V—"So then as through one trespass the judgment came unto all men to condemnation; even so through one act of righteousness the free gift came unto all men to justification of life."

1 Cor. 15:21, 22—"For since by man came death, by man came also the resurrection of the dead. For as in Adam all die, even so in Christ shall all be made alive."

FOURTH PROPOSITION: *Through the death of Jesus Christ all men obtain resurrection from the dead.*

To what it shall be a resurrection, whether unto life or unto condemnation, shame and everlasting contempt (Jno. 5:28, 29; Dan. 12:2), depends entirely upon what attitude the individual takes towards Christ.

(2) THE RESULTS OF CHRIST'S DEATH IN RELATION TO THE BELIEVER.

(a) Is. 53:10, R.V.—"Yet it pleased the LORD to bruise him; he hath put him to grief; when thou shalt make his soul an offering for sin, *he shall see his seed*, he shall prolong his days, and the pleasure of the LORD shall prosper in his hand."

FIRST PROPOSITION: Through Christ's soul being made a guilt-offering for sin—i. e., through His death, He sees His seed, He begets a spiritual progeny.

The new race of sons of God springs from Christ's death. (Compare Jno. 12:24.) (In this spiritual progeny that springs from His death Jesus sees of the travail of His soul and is satisfied. Is. 53:11.)

(*b*) Heb. 9:26—"For then must he often have suffered since the foundation of the world: but now once in the end of the world hath he appeared to put away sin by the sacrifice of himself."

SECOND PROPOSITION: By the sacrifice of Himself Jesus Christ has put away sin, or rather rendered sin void, or nullified sin. (The context shows it is the sin of the believer that is in question.)

(*c*) Gal. 3:13—"Christ hath redeemed us from the curse of the law, being made a curse for us: for it is written, Cursed is every one that hangeth on a tree."

THIRD PROPOSITION: By the death of Jesus Christ the believer is redeemed from the curse of the law.

The penalty of the broken law has been paid by Jesus Christ, and the broken law has no longer any claim for satisfaction upon the believer.

(*d*) Col. 2:14, R.V.—"Having blotted out the bond written in ordinances that was against us, which was contrary to us: and he hath taken it out of the way, nailing it to the cross."

FOURTH PROPOSITION: By His death upon the cross Jesus Christ has "blotted out," and "taken out of the way," and "nailed to the cross," "the bond written in ordinances that was against us," (i. e., the law).

Not only has the curse which the law imposes upon the breaker of it been settled, but the law itself has been done away with by the death of Christ. (Compare 2 Cor. 3:7, 11, R.V.)

Christ has settled all the claims of the law, fulfilled it, and done away with it.

(Compare Rom. 7:1-4, 6, R.V.) "Or are ye ignorant, brethren (for I speak to men that know the law), how that the law hath dominion over a man for so long time as he liveth? For the woman that hath a husband is bound by law while he liveth; but if the husband die, she is discharged from the law of the husband. So then if, while the husband liveth, she be joined to another man, she shall be called an adulteress: but if the husband die, she is free from the law, so that she is no adulteress, though she be joined to another man. Wherefore, my brethren, ye also *were made dead to the law* through the body of Christ; that ye should be joined to another, even to him who was raised from the dead, that ye might bring forth fruit unto God. But now *we have been discharged from law,* having died to that wherein we were holden; so that we serve in newness of the spirit, and not in the oldness of the letter."

(e) Eph. 2: 14-16—"For he is our peace, who hath made both one, and hath broken down the middle wall of partition between us; having abolished in his flesh the enmity, even the law of command-ments contained in ordinances; for to make in himself of twain one new man, so making peace; And that he might reconcile both unto God in one body by the cross, having slain the enmity thereby."

FIFTH PROPOSITION: By the death of Jesus Christ the separation between Jew and Gentile is done away.

It is the law that separates Jew and Gentile. This Jesus abolished in his flesh, and now in Christ Jesus there is neither Jew nor Greek, &c., but all are one man in Christ Jesus. (Gal. 3: 28, R.V.) The blood of Christ is the cement of all nations making them one.

(f) Gal. 4: 3-5—"Even so we, when we were children, were in bondage under the elements of the world: But when the fulness of the time was come, God sent forth his Son, made of a woman, made under the law, to redeem them that were under the law, that we might receive the adoption of sons." (Compare Ch. 3: 13—"Christ hath redeemed us from the curse of the law, being made a curse for us: for it is written, Cursed is every one that hangeth on a tree.")

SIXTH PROPOSITION: By the death of Christ Jewish be-lievers are redeemed from subjection to the law to receive the adoption of sons.

(g) Eph. 2: 11-13, 19—"Wherefore remember, that ye being in time past Gentiles in the flesh, who are called Uncircumcision by that which is called the Circumcision in the flesh made by hands; that at that time ye were without Christ, being aliens from the commonwealth of Israel, and strangers from the covenants of promise, having no hope, and without God in the world: But now, in Christ Jesus, ye who some time were afar off are made nigh by the blood of Christ. Now therefore ye are no more strangers and foreigners, but fellow citizens with the saints, and of the household of God."

SEVENTH PROPOSITION: By the death of Christ Gentile believers, who were afar off, aliens from the commonwealth of Israel, strangers from the covenants of promise, having no hope and without God in the world, are made nigh, fellow-citizens with the saints and of the household of God.

(*h*) Rom. 5: 10—"For if, when we were enemies, we were reconciled to God by the death of his Son; much more, being reconciled, we shall be saved by his life."

EIGHTH PROPOSITION: By the death of God s Son believers who were once sinners are reconciled to God.

That is, the enmity between God and the sinner is done away. It is already done away. Christ *has* made peace through the blood of the cross. He *hath* reconciled believers in the body of His flesh through death.

(Col. 1: 20-22—"And *having made peace* through the blood of his cross, by him to reconcile all things unto himself; by him, I say, whether they be things in earth, or things in heaven. And you that were sometimes alienated and enemies in your mind by wicked works, yet now *hath* he reconciled in the body of his flesh through death, to present you holy and unblameable and unreproveable in his sight.")

(*i*) Eph. 1: 7—"In whom *we have redemption* through his blood, the forgiveness of si , according to the riches of his grace.")

NINTH PROPOSITION: Through the blood of Jesus Christ believers HAVE *redemption, the forgiveness of their sins.*

Forgiveness is not something which believers are to secure, it is something the blood has secured and which our faith has appropriated.

(*j*) 1 Jno. 1: 7—"But if we walk in the light, as he is in the light we have fellowship one with another, and the blood of Jesus Christ his Son cleanseth us from all sin."

TENTH PROPOSITION: The blood of Jesus Christ cleanseth (is continually cleansing) those who walk in the light, from all sin.

QUESTION: Does this mean cleanseth from the guilt that sin brings upon the sinner, or does it mean cleanseth from the very presence of sin itself?

Lev. 16: 30—"For on that day shall the priest *make an atonement* for you, to cleanse you, that ye may be clean from all your sins before the Lord."

Lev. 17: 11—"For the life of the flesh is in the blood; and I have given it to you upon the altar *to make an atonement* for your souls: for it is the blood that maketh an atonement for the soul."

Lev. 14: 19, 31—"And the priest shall offer the sin offering, and *make an atonement* for him that is to be cleansed from his uncleanness; and afterward he shall kill the burnt offering: Even such as he is able to get, the one for a sin offering, and the other for a burnt offering, with the meat offering: and the priest shall *make an atonement* for him that is to be cleansed before the Lord."

Jer. 33: 8—"And I will cleanse them from all their iniquities, whereby they have sinned against me; *and I will pardon* all their iniquities, whereby they have sinned, and whereby they have transgressed against me."

Ps. 51: 7—"Purge me with hyssop, and I shall be clean: wash me and I shall be whiter than snow."

Rev. 1: 5—"And from Jesus Christ, who is the faithful witness, and the first-begotten of the dead, and the prince of the kings of the earth. Unto him that loved us, and washed us from our sins in his own blood."

Rev. 7: 14—"And I said unto him, Sir, thou knowest. And he said to me, These are they which came out of great tribulation, and have washed their robes, and made them white in the blood of the Lamb."

Heb. 9: 22, 23—"And almost all things are by the law purged with blood; and without shedding of blood there is *no remission*. It was therefore necessary that the patterns of things in the heavens should be purified with these; but the heavenly things themselves with better sacrifices than these."

Eph. 1: 7—"In whom we have redemption through his blood, *the forgiveness of sins*, according to the riches of his grace."

Rom. 3: 25—"Whom God hath set forth to be a *propitiation* through faith in his blood, to declare his righteousness for the remission of sins that are past, through the forbearance of God."

Rom. 5: 9—"Much more then, being now *justified by his blood*, we shall be saved from wrath through him."

Matt. 26: 28—"For this is my blood of the new testament, which is shed for many *for the remission of sins*."

ANSWER: From these passages it is evident, that in Bible usage, cleansing by blood is cleansing from guilt. Through the shed blood of Christ, all who walk in the light are cleansed continuously—every hour and minute—from all the guilt of sin. There is absolutely no sin *upon them;* there may still be sin *in them.* It is not the blood, but the living Christ, and the Holy Spirit, who deal with that.

(*k*)   Rom. 5: 9—"Much more then, being now *justified by his blood*, we shall be saved from wrath through him."

ELEVENTH PROPOSITION: By (or in) the blood of Christ believers are justified.

QUESTION: What is the difference between forgiveness and justification ?

ANSWER: Forgiveness is negative—the putting away of sin: Justification is positive—the reckoning positively righteous. By reason of Christ's death there is an interchange of positions between Christ and the believer. In death Christ takes our place of condemnation before God, and we take His place of acceptance before God. (2 Cor. 5: 21—" For he hath made him to be sin for us, who knew no sin, that we might be made the righteousness of God in him.")

(*l*)   Rom. 8: 33, 34—" Who shall lay anything to the charge of God's elect ? It is God that justifieth. Who is he that condemneth ? It is Christ that died, yea rather, that is risen again, who is even at the right hand of God, who also maketh intercession for us."

TWELFTH PROPOSITION: Because of Christ's death none can lay anything to the charge of, or condemn, the elect (or the believer in Christ).

There is absolutely no condemnation to them who are in Christ Jesus—the death of Christ has settled that forever.

Rom. 8: 1, 3, R.V.—" There is now no condemnation to them which are in Christ Jesus. For that the law could not do, in that it was weak through the flesh, God sending his own Son in the likeness of sinful flesh, and as an offering for sin, condemned sin in the flesh."

(*m*)   Acts 20: 28—" Take heed therefore unto yourselves, and to all the flock, over the which the Holy Ghost hath made you overseers, to feed the church of God, which he hath *purchased with his own blood.*"

1 Cor. 6: 20—" For ye are *bought* with a price: therefore glorify God in your body, and in your spirit, which are God's."

Rev. 5: 9, 10, R.V.—"And they sang a new song, saying, Worthy art thou to take the book, and to open the seals thereof: for thou wast slain, and *didst purchase unto God* with thy blood men of every tribe, and tongue, and people, and nation, and madest them to be unto God a kingdom and priests; and they reign upon the earth."

THIRTEENTH PROPOSITION: By the death of Jesus Christ the whole church, and each believer, were purchased unto God and are now His own property.

We belong to God. Neither the Devil, nor the world, nor ourselves have any claims upon us. God will take care of His own property.

> (Compare 1 Pet. 2: 9, R.V—"But ye are an elect race, a royal priesthood, a holy nation, a *people for God's own possession*, that ye may shew forth the excellencies of him who called you out of darkness into his marvellous light.")
>
> (*n*) Heb. 10: 10—"By the which will we are sanctified through the offering of the body of Jesus Christ once for all."

FOURTEENTH PROPOSITION: Through the offering of the body of Christ believers in Him are sanctified.

Every believer in Christ is sanctified. The sacrifice of Christ sets Him apart for God. The blood of Christ separates the believer from the world. (Compare Ex. 11: 7 with Ex. 12: 13.) We are to live out in our walk this separation between us and the world, which already exists by virtue of Christ's death.

> (*o*) Heb. 10:14—"For by one offering he hath perfected for ever them that are sanctified."

FIFTEENTH PROPOSITION: By one offering—i. e., the offering of His own life—Jesus Christ has perfected us forever. Believers have been made forever perfect by the death of Christ.

QUESTION: In what sense have believers been made forever perfect?

ANSWER: Verses 1, 2—"For the law having a shadow of good things to come, and not the very image of the things, can never with those sacrifices, which they offered year by year continually, *make the comers thereunto perfect.* For then would they not have ceased to be offered, Because that the worshippers once purged should have had no more conscience of sins?" Perfect in their standing before God, not perfect in their state. By the death of Christ the believer is forever cleansed from guilt. He need have no more conscience of sins. The blood removes all sense of guilt. His sins are put away by the one all-sufficient sacrifice.

> (*p*) Heb. 9: 14—"How much more shall the blood of Christ, who through the eternal spirit offered himself without spot to God, purge your conscience from dead works to serve the living God? '

SIXTEENTH PROPOSITION: The blood of Christ cleanses the conscience of the believer from dead works to serve the living God.

Not only does the blood of Christ relieve the conscience of the believer from the burden of guilt, but also from the burden of his self-efforts to atone for sin and please God—"dead works." Sin is seen entirely settled by the perfect sacrifice, and now the believer, with a conscience free from guilt, and also from the burden of his own imperfect works, enters into the service of the living God in the liberty and power of sonship.

(Compare Rom. 8: 15—"For ye have not received the spirit of bondage again to fear; but ye have received the spirit of adoption, whereby we cry, Abba, Father.")

There are many to-day who call themselves Christians who have not permitted the blood of Christ to cleanse their conscience from "dead works." They are constantly under the burden of *doing something* to atone for sin and to commend them to God. We have nothing to do, it is all done, the blood of Christ has forever commended us to God.

(2 Cor. 5: 21—"For he hath made him to be sin for us, who knew no sin; that we might be made the righteousness of God in him." Rom. 3: 21, 22—"But now the righteousness of God *without the law* is manifest, being witnessed by the law and the prophets; Even the righteousness of God which is by faith of Jesus Christ unto all and upon all them that believe; for there is no difference.")

There are three classes of men.   (1.)   Those who are not burdened by sin, but love it.   (2.)   Those who are burdened by sin, and seek to get rid of the burden by self-efforts, by doing something to atone for it and commend them to God—"dead works."   No peace can be found along this line, nor real love to and service of God.   (3.)   Those who believe in Christ and His atoning blood, and see their sin settled forever by his death, and so have a conscience cleansed from both guilt and "dead works." Their hearts are filled with love to God, and they serve the living God in the freedom of the love born of a faith in the cleansing and perfecting blood.

(*q*)   Heb. 10: 19, 20—"Having, therefore, brethren, boldness to enter into the holiest by the blood of Jesus, by a new and living way, which he hath consecrated for us, through the veil, that is to say, his flesh."

SEVENTEENTH PROPOSITION: By the blood of Christ—because of His death—the believer has boldness to enter into the holy place, into the very presence of God.

God is holy ? Yes. And I am a sinner ? Yes; but by the wondrous offering of Christ, "once for all," I am perfected; and on the ground of that blood, so precious to God, I can march boldly into the very presence of God. Oh, wondrous blood !

(*r*) Rev. 22: 14, R.V.—"Blessed are they that wash their robes, that they may have the right to come to the tree of life, and may enter in by the gates into the city." (Compare 7: 14—"And I say unto him, my Lord, thou knowest. And he said to me, These are they which come out of the great tribulation, and they washed their robes, and made them white in the blood of the Lamb."

EIGHTEENTH PROPOSITION: Because of the cleansing power of the shed blood those who have washed their robes in it have the right to come to the tree of life and to enter in by the portals into the city.

(Compare Gen. 3: 22–24—"And the LORD God said, Behold, the man is become as one of us, to know good and evil: and now, lest he put forth his hand and take also of the tree of life, and eat, and live forever: Therefore the LORD God sent him forth from the garden of Eden, to till the ground from whence he was taken. So he drove out the man: and he placed at the east of the garden of Eden cherubim, and a flaming sword which turned every way, to keep the way of the tree of life."

(*s*) 1 Thess. 5: 10—"Who died for us, that, whether we wake or sleep, we should live together with him."

NINETEENTH PROPOSITION: Because of the death of Christ believers shall live together with Him.

(*t*) Rev. 7: 14, 15—"And I said unto him, Sir, thou knowest, And he said to me, These are they which came out of great tribulation, and have washed their robes, and made them white in the blood of the Lamb. Therefore are they before the throne of God, and serve him day and night in his temple: and he that sitteth on the throne shall dwell among them."

TWENTIETH PROPOSITION: Because of the cleansing power of His blood those who wash their robes and make them white in it shall be before the throne of God.

Christ on the cross opens the way for others before the throne.

NOTE.—These seem to be the tribulation believers. (See R.V.) We shall be on the throne, not before it. Rev. 3: 21—"To him that overcometh will I grant to sit with me in my throne, even as I also overcome, and am set down with my Father in his throne."

(*u*) Heb. 9: 15, R.V.—"And for this cause he is the mediator of a new covenant, that a death having taken place for the redemption of the transgressions that were under the first covenant, they that have been called may receive the promise of the eternal inheritance."

TWENTY-FIRST PROPOSITION: Because of Christ's death for the redemption of the transgressions that were under the first covenant, they that have been called receive the promise of the eternal inheritance.

(*v*) Rom. 6: 3, 6, 8, R.V.—"Or are ye ignorant that all who were baptized into Christ Jesus were baptized into his death? Knowing this, that our old man was crucified with him, that the body of sin might be done away, that so we should no longer be in bondage to sin; But if *we died with Christ*, we believe that we shall also live with him."

Gal. 2: 20, R.V.—"*I have been crucified with Christ;* yet I live; and yet no longer I, but Christ liveth in me: and that life which I now live in the flesh I live in faith, the faith which is in the Son of God, who loved me, and gave himself up for me."

Gal. 6: 14—"But God forbid that I should glory, save in the cross of our Lord Jesus Christ, by whom the world is crucified unto me, and *I unto the world.*"

2 Cor. 5: 14, R.V.—"For the love of Christ constraineth us; because we thus judge, that one died for all, therefore *all died.*"

TWENTY-SECOND PROPOSITION: In the death of Christ we died; in His crucifixion we were crucified; when He was nailed to the cross "the old man" was nailed to the cross. This is our real position because of His death.

Christian living consists in living this out in life. As I was crucified I should see self on the cross in the place of the curse (as a cursed thing) and no longer try to live, but let Christ live in me. As the old man was crucified I should reckon myself dead unto sin but alive unto God in Christ Jesus. (Rom. 6: 11, R.V.) How few of us see ourselves where the death of Christ put us. This is the great reason why the risen Christ cannot live the fulness of His resurrection life in us. We must be dead with Christ before we can live with Him.

(*w*) 1 Pet. 2: 21—" For even hereunto were ye called: because Christ also suffered for us, leaving us an example, that we should follow his steps."

Matt. 16: 24—" Then said Jesus unto his disciples, If any man will come after me, let him deny himself, and take up his cross and follow me."

TWENTY-THIRD PROPOSITION: By the death of Christ an example is left us that we should follow His steps.

This was evidently not the main purpose of His death, as so many make it to-day, but an incidental result.

(See also 1 Pet. 1: 18, 19—" Forasmuch as ye know that ye were not redeemed with corruptible things, as silver and gold, from your vain conversation received by tradition from your fathers; But with the precious blood of Christ, as of a lamb without blemish and without spot.")

(*x*) Rom. 8: 32—" He that spared not his own Son, but delivered him up for us all, how shall he not with him also freely give us all things ? "

TWENTY-FOURTH PROPOSITION: In the death of His Son God has given to the believer a guarantee that He will freely give us all things.

(*y*) Heb. 2: 14, 15, R.V.—" Since then the children are sharers in flesh and blood, he also himself in like manner partook of the same; that through death he might bring to naught him that had the power of death, that is, the devil; and might deliver all them who through fear of death were all their lifetime subject to bondage."

TWENTY-FIFTH PROPOSITION: By His death Jesus Christ has delivered all them who through fear of death were all their lifetime subject to bondage.

(This might come under the Purpose of Christ's death.)

(3) THE RESULTS OF CHRIST'S DEATH IN RELATION TO THE DEVIL AND THE POWERS OF DARKNESS.

(*a*) Jno. 12: 31—" Now is the judgment of this world: now shall the prince of this world be cast out." (See context vv. 27, 28, 32, 33.)

FIRST PROPOSITION: Through Christ's death the casting out of the prince of this world is secured.

Since Christ's death Satan is a usurper whose ultimate dethronement is secured.

(*b*)   Heb. 2:14, R.V.—"Since then the children are sharers in flesh and blood, he also himself in like manner partook of the same; that through death he might bring to naught him that had the power of death, that is, the devil."

SECOND PROPOSITION: Through the death of Christ, the Devil is brought to naught or rendered ineffective.

The death of Christ was death to Satan's power. He could no longer wield the power of death over those who appropriated to themselves the virtue of Christ's death.

(*c*)   Col. 2:14, 15—"Blotting out the handwriting of ordinances that was against us, which was contrary to us, and took it out of the way, nailing it to his cross; and having spoiled principalities and powers, he made a show of them openly, triumphing over them in it."

THIRD PROPOSITION: In the death of Christ on the cross God triumphed over the principalities and the powers, and exposed them to open disgrace.

As to what these principalities and powers are, see Eph. 6: 12, R.V.—"For our wrestling is not against flesh and blood, but against the principalities, against the powers, against the world-rulers of this darkness, against the spiritual hosts of wickedness in the heavenly places." It was in the cross of Christ that God fought the decisive battle, and won the decisive victory over the Devil. The moment of Satan's seeming victory was the moment of his overwhelming defeat. He is now a conquered foe. In the cross God celebrated a triumph over him. The whole meaning of this conflict and this victory at the cross will be, I believe, a subject for contemplation and wonder at the manifold wisdom of God in the eternal world.

(4) THE RESULTS OF CHRIST'S DEATH IN RELATION TO THE MATERIAL UNIVERSE.

Col. 1:19, 20—"For it pleased the Father that in him should all fulness dwell; and, having made peace through the blood of his cross, by him to reconcile all things unto himself; by him, I say, whether they be things in earth, or things in heaven."

FIRST PROPOSITION: Through the death of Christ the whole Material Universe—"all things, whether they be things in earth, or things in heaven"—is reconciled unto God.

The Material Universe has fallen away from God in connection with sin (Rom. 8: 20, R. V.; Gen. 3: 18). Not earth only, but heaven has been invaded and polluted by sin. (Eph. 6: 12, R. V.; Heb. 9: 23, 24.) Through the death of Christ this pollution is put away. Just as the blood of the Old Testament sacrifice was taken into the most holy place, the type of heaven, Christ has taken the blood of the better sacrifice into heaven itself and cleansed it. "All things * * * whether they be things in earth or things in heaven" are now reconciled to God. "The creation itself also shall be delivered from the bondage of corruption into the liberty of the glory of the children of God." (Rom. 8: 21.) "We look for new heavens and a new earth, wherein dwelleth righteousness." (2 Pet. 3: 13.) The atonement of Christ has an immense sweep—far beyond the reach of our human philosophies. We have just begun to understand what that blood that was spilled on Calvary means. Sin is a far more awful, ruinous and far-reaching evil than we have been wont to think, but the blood of Christ has a power and efficiency, the fulness of which only eternity will disclose.

CHAPTER VI.

THE RESURRECTION OF JESUS CHRIST.

I. The Fact of the Resurrection.

(1) 2 Tim. 2:8—"Remember that Jesus Christ of the seed of David was raised from the dead, according to my gospel."

1 Cor. 15:4—"And that he was buried, and that he rose again the third day according to the scriptures." (Many other passages.)

FIRST PROPOSITION: Jesus Christ was raised from the dead.

The Resurrection of Christ is in many respects the most important fact of Christian history. It is the Gibraltar of Christian Evidences, the Waterloo of Infidelity and Rationalism. If the scriptural assertions of Christ's Resurrection can be established as historic certainties, the claims and doctrines of Christianity rest upon an impregnable foundation.

There are three lines of argument for the truthfulness of the Biblical statements:

First.—THE EXTERNAL PROOFS OF THE AUTHENTICITY AND TRUTHFULNESS OF THE GOSPEL NARRATIVES.

Into this argument we need not enter at this time. The others are perfectly sufficient without it.

Second.—THE INTERNAL PROOFS OF TRUTHFULNESS.

We have four accounts of the Resurrection. Suppose we had no external means of knowing by whom they were written; that we had nothing but the accounts themselves from which to decide as to their truthfulness or untruthfulness.

(a) By a careful comparison of the four accounts we see that they are four separate and independent accounts. This is evident from the apparent discrepancies in the four accounts. There is a real harmony between the accounts, but it can be discovered only by minute and careful study. On the surface there is discrepancy and apparent contradiction. It is just such a harmony as would not exist in four accounts prepared in collusion. In that case, on the surface there would appear agreement. Whatever contradiction there might be would be discovered only by careful study. But the fact is that the discrepancy is on the surface; the real harmony has only been discovered by careful and prolonged study. It is just such a harmony as would exist between four independent, honest witnesses, each relating the events from his own point of view. The four accounts supplement one another, a third account sometimes reconciling apparent discrepancies of two. These four accounts must be either true or fabrications. If fabrications they must have been made up either independently or in collusion. They cannot have been made up independently; the agreements are too marked and too many. They cannot have been made up in collusion; the apparent discrepancies are too numerous and too noticeable. They were, therefore, not made up at all. They are a true relation of facts.

(b) The next thing we notice about these accounts is that they bear striking indications of having been written or spoken by eye-witnesses. The account of an eye-witness is readily distinguished from that of one who is merely retailing what others have told him. Any careful student of the Gospel records of the Resurrection will readily detect many marks of the eye-witness.

(c) The third thing we note is their artlessness, straightforwardness and simplicity. It sometimes happens, when a witness is on the stand, that the story he tells is so artless, straightforward, simple and natural; there is such an utter absence of any attempt at coloring or effect; that it carries conviction independently of any knowledge we may have of the witness. As we listen to this witness we say at once, "This man is telling the truth." The weight of this kind of evidence is greatly increased, and reaches practical certainty, if we have several independent witnesses of this sort, all bearing testimony to the same essential facts, but with varieties of detail, one omitting what another tells. This is the exact case with the four Gospel narrators of the Resurrection. While the stories have to do with the supernatural, the stories themselves are most natural. The Gospel authors do not seem to have reflected at all upon the meaning or bearing of many of the facts they relate. They simply tell right out what they saw in all simplicity and straightforwardness, leaving the philosophizing to others. Furness, the Unitarian scholar (quoted in Abbot on Matt., p. 331, and also Furness, "The Power of the Spirit"), says: "Nothing can exceed in artlessness and simplicity the four accounts of the first appearance of Jesus after his crucifixion. If these qualities are not discernible here we must despair of ever being able to discern them anywhere." Suppose we had four accounts of the battle of Monmouth, and upon examination we found that they were manifestly independent accounts—we found striking indications that they were from eye-witnesses; we found them all marked by that artlessness, simplicity and. straightforwardness that carry conviction; we found that they agreed substantially in their account of the battle— even though we had no knowledge of the authorship or date of these accounts, would we not, in the absence of any other account, say, "Here is a true account of the battle of Monmouth?"

(*d*) The unintentional evidence of words, phrases and accidental details. It often happens when a witness is on the stand that the unintentional evidence he bears by words, phrases and accidental details is more effective than his direct testimony, because it is not the testimony of the witness, but the testimony of the truth to itself. The Gospel stories abound in this sort of evidence.

(2) Luke 24: 16—"But their eyes were holden that they should not know him."

Here and elsewhere we are told that Jesus was not recognized at once by His disciples when He appeared to them after His resurrection. There was no point to be gained by their telling the story in this way. They give no satisfactory explanation of the fact. We are left to study it out for ourselves. Why, then, do they tell it this way? Because this is the way it occurred and they are not making up a story, but telling what occurred. If they had been making up a story, they would never have made it up this way.

(3) 1 Cor. 15: 5-8—"And that he was seen of Cephas, then of the twelve: After that he was seen of above five hundred brethren at once; of whom the greater part remain unto this present, but some are fallen asleep. After this he was seen of James; then of all the apostles. And last of all he was seen of me also, as of one born out of due time."

Here, as everywhere else, Jesus is represented as appearing only to His disciples, with the single exception of His brother. Why is it so represented? Because it so happened. If a story had been made up years after, Jesus would certainly have been represented as appearing to and confounding some, at least, of His enemies.

(4) Represented as appearing only occasionally.

(5) Jno. 20:17—"Jesus said unto her, Touch me not; for I am not yet ascended to my Father: but go to my brethren, and say unto them, I ascend to my Father, and your Father; and to my God, and your God."

There is no explanation of these words "touch me not." It has been the puzzle of centuries for the commentators to explain them. Why is it told this way? Because this is the way it occurred.

(6) Jno. 19:34—"But one of the soldiers with a spear pierced his side, and forthwith came there out blood and water."

Why is this told? Modern physiologists tell us that the physical explanation of this is that Jesus suffered from extravasation of the blood, or, in popular language, "a broken heart," and that other facts recorded (as *e. g.*, the dying cry) prove the same thing. But John knew nothing of modern physiology. Why does he insert a detail that it takes centuries to explain? Because he is recording events as they occurred and as he saw them.

(7) Jno. 20:24, 25—"But Thomas, one of the twelve, called Didymus, was not with them when Jesus came. The other disciples therefore said unto him, We have seen the Lord. But he said unto them, Except I shall see in his hands the print of the nails, and put my finger into the print of the nails, and thrust my hand into his side, I will not believe."

This is most true to life. It is in perfect harmony with what is told of Thomas elsewhere, but to make it up would require a literary art that immeasurably exceeded the possibilities of the author.

(8) Jno. 20:4–6—"So they ran both together: and the other disciple did outrun Peter, and came first to the sepulchre. And he stooping down, and looking in, saw the linen clothes lying; yet went he not in. Then cometh Simon Peter following him, and went into the sepulchre, and seeth the linen clothes lie."

This is again in striking keeping with what we know of the men. John, the younger, outruns Peter, but hesitatingly, reverently, stops outside and first looks in. But impetuous, older Peter, lumbers on as best he can behind, but when once he reaches the tomb, never waits a moment outside, but plunges in. Who was the literary artist who had the skill to make this up, if it did not happen just so?

(9) Jno. 21:7—"Therefore that disciple whom Jesus loved saith unto Peter, It is the Lord. Now when Simon Peter heard that it was the Lord, he girt his fisher's coat unto him, (for he was naked,) and did cast himself into the sea."

Here, again, we have the unmistakable marks of truth. John, the man of quick perception, is the first to recognize his Lord. Peter, the man of impetuous and unthinking devotion, so soon as he is told who it is, tumbles into the water and swims ashore to meet him. Was this made up?

(10) Jno. 20 : 15—"Jesus saith unto her, Woman, why weepest thou? whom seekest thou? She supposing him to be the gardener, saith unto him, Sir, if thou have borne him hence, tell me where thou hast laid him, and I will take him away."

Here is surely a touch that surpasses the art of any man of that day or any day. Mary, with a woman's love, forgets a woman's weakness and cries, "Tell me where thou hast laid him, and *I* will take him away." Of course she lacked the strength to do it, but woman's love never stops at impossibilities. Was this made up?

(11) Mark 16:7—"But go your way, tell his disciples *and Peter* that he goeth before you into Galilee: there shall ye see him, as he said unto you."

"And Peter." Why "And Peter"? No explanation is vouchsafed, but reflection shows it was the utterance of love toward a despondent and despairing disciple who had thrice denied his Lord and would not think himself included in a general invitation. Was this made up?

(12) Jno. 20: 27–29—"Then saith he to Thomas, Reach hither thy finger, and behold my hands; and reach hither thy hand, and thrust it into my side, and be not faithless, but believing. And Thomas said unto him, My Lord and my God. Jesus saith unto him, Thomas, because thou hast seen me, thou hast believed: blessed are they that have not seen and yet have believed."

The action of Thomas here is too natural and the rebuke of Jesus too characteristic to be attributed to the art of some master of fiction.

(13) Jno. 21: 21, 22—"Peter seeing him saith to Jesus, Lord, and what shall this man do? Jesus saith unto him, If I will that he tarry till I come, what is that to thee? follow thou me."

This, too, is a characteristic rebuke on Jesus' part.

(Compare Luke 13: 23, 24—"Then said one unto him, Lord, are there few that be saved? And he said unto them, *Strive* to enter in at the strait gate: for many, I say unto you, will seek to enter in, and shall not be able.")

Jesus never answered questions of speculative curiosity but always pointed the questioner to his own immediate duty.

(14) Jno. 21: 15-17—"So when they had dined, Jesus saith to Simon Peter, Simon, son of Jonas, lovest thou me more than these? He saith unto him, Yea, Lord, thou knowest that I love thee. He saith unto him, Feed my lambs. He saith unto him again the second time, Simon, son of Jonas, lovest thou me? He saith unto him, Yea, Lord: thou knowest that I love thee. He saith unto him, Feed my sheep. He saith unto him the third time, Simon, son of Jonas, lovest thou me? *Peter was grieved because he said unto him the third time,* Lovest thou me? And he said unto him, Lord, thou knowest all things; thou knowest that I love thee. Jesus saith unto him, Feed my sheep."

There is no explanation of why Jesus asked three times or why Peter was grieved because Jesus did ask three times. We must read this in the light of the thrice-repeated, threefold denial to understand it. But the author does not tell us so. He surely would if he had been making this up with this fact in view. He is simply reporting what actually occurred.

(15) *Appropriateness of the way in which Jesus revealed Himself to different persons after His resurrection—*

To Mary:

Jno. 20: 16—"Jesus saith unto her, Mary. She turned herself, and saith unto him, Rabboni; which is to say, Master."

What a delicate touch of nature! Up to this point Mary had not recognized her Lord, but in that one word, "Mary," uttered as no other but He had ever uttered it, she knew Him and fell at His feet and tried to clasp them, crying "Rabboni." Was that made up?

To the Two:

Luke 24: 30, 31—"And it came to pass, as he sat at meat with them, he took bread, and blessed it, and brake, and gave to them. And their eyes were opened, and they knew him; and he vanished out of their sight."

Knew Him in the breaking of bread. Why? The evangelist ventures no explanation. But we easily read between the lines that there was a something so characteristic in the way he re- turned thanks at meals, so real and so different from the way in which they had ever seen any other do it, that they knew Him at once by that. Is that made up?

To Thomas:

Jno. 20: 25-28—"The other disciples therefore said unto him, We have seen the Lord. But he said unto them, Except I shall see in his hands the print of the nails, and put my finger into the print of the nails, and thrust my hand into his side, I will not believe. And after eight days again his disciples were within, and Thomas with them: then came Jesus, the doors being shut, and stood in the midst, and said, Peace be unto you. Then said he to Thomas, Reach hither thy finger and behold my hands; and reach hither thy hand, and thrust it into my side; and be not faithless, but believing."

To John and Peter:

Jno. 21: 5-7—"Then Jesus saith unto them, Children, have ye any meat? They answered him, No. And he said unto them, Cast the net on the right side of the ship, and ye shall find. They cast there- fore and now they were not able to draw it for the multitude of fishes. Therefore that disciple whom Jesus loved saith unto Peter, It is the Lord. Now when Simon Peter heard that it was the Lord, he girt his fisher's coat unto him (for he was naked), and did cast himself into the sea."

To Thomas, the man of sense, He makes Himself known by sensible proof. To John and Peter as at the first by a mirac- ulous draught of fishes.

(16) Jno. 20: 7—"And the napkin that was about his head, not lying with the linen clothes, but wrapped together in a place by itself."

How strange that this little detail is added to the story with absolutely no attempt of saying why. But how deeply signifi- cant this little unexplained detail is. In that supreme moment when the breath of God passes over and through that cold and silent clay, and Jesus rises triumphant over death and Satan, there is no excitement upon His part, but with that same majestic self-composure and serenity that marked His whole life, absolutely without human haste or flurry or disorder, He even rolls up the napkin that was about His head and lays it away in an orderly manner by itself. Was that made up ?

These are little things, but it is from that very fact that they gain much of their significance. It is in just such little things that a fiction would disclose itself. Fiction betrays its difference from fact in the minute. But the more microscopically we examine the Gospel Narrative the more we become impressed with its truthfulness. The artlessness and naturalness of the narrative surpass all art.

Third.—THE CIRCUMSTANTIAL EVIDENCE.

There are certain unquestionable facts of history that demand the Resurrection of Christ to account for them.

(1) Beyond a question the foundation truth preached in the early years of the Church's history was the Resurrection.

(*a*) Why should the Apostles use this as the corner-stone of their creed if not well attested and firmly believed ?

(*b*) If Jesus had not risen there would have been some evidence He had not. But the Apostles went up and down the very city where He had been crucified, and proclaimed right to the face of His slayers that He had been raised and no one could produce evidence to the contrary. The best they could do was to say that the guards went to sleep and the disciples stole the body. But if they had stolen the body they would have known it, and the great moral transformation in the disciples would remain unaccounted for.

(2) The change in the day of rest. Changed by no express decree but by general consent. In the Bible days we find the disciples meeting on the first day.

Acts 20: 7—"And upon the first day of the week, when the disciples came together to break bread, Paul preached unto them, ready to depart on the morrow; and continued his speech until midnight."

1 Cor. 16: 2—"Now the first day of the week let every one of you lay by him in store, as God hath prospered him, that there be no gatherings when I come."

(3) The change in the disciples. From blank and utter despair to a courage nothing could shake. (*e. g.*, Peter. Acts 4: 19, 20; 5: 29. James the Lord's brother.) Such a sudden and radical change demands an explanation. Nothing short of the fact of the Resurrection will explain it.

These unquestionable facts are so impressive and so conclusive that infidel and Jewish scholars admit that the Apostles BELIEVED that Jesus rose from the dead. Baur admits this. Even Strauss says: "Only this much need be acknowledged—that the Apostles firmly believed that Jesus had arisen." Schenkel says: "It is an indisputable fact that in the early morning of the first day of the week following the crucifixion, the grave of Jesus was found empty. * * * It is a second fact that the disciples and other members of the apostolic communion were convinced that Jesus was seen after the crucifixion." These admissions are fatal to the rationalists who make them.

The question at once arises, Whence this conviction and belief? Renan attempts an answer by saying: "The passion of a hallucinated woman (Mary) gives to the world a resurrected God." (Renan, "Life of Jesus," p. 357.) But we answer: "The passion of a hallucinated woman" is not equal to this task. There was a Matthew and Thomas in the apostolic company to be convinced, and a Paul outside to be converted. It takes more than the passionate hallucination of a woman to convince a Jew taxgatherer, a stubborn unbeliever, and a fierce and conscientious enemy.

Strauss tries to account for it by inquiring whether the appearances may not have been visionary. We answer: "There was no subjective starting-point for such visions in the Apostles, and furthermore eleven men do not have the same visions at the same time, much less five hundred." (1 Cor. 15: 6.)

A third attempt at an explanation is that Jesus was not really dead. To sustain this view appeal is made to the short time He hung on the cross, and that history tells of one in the time of Josephus taken down from the cross and nursed back to life. In reply, we say: *First*—Remember the events that preceded the crucifixion and the physical condition in which they left Jesus. Remember, too, the water and the blood—the broken heart. *Second*—His enemies would and did take all necessary precautions.   (Jno. 19: 34.)   *Third*—If Jesus had been merely resuscitated he would have been so weak, such an utter physical wreck—as was the man cited in proof—that His reappearance would have been measured at its real value.   *Fourth*—The Apostles would have known how they brought Him back to life, and the main fact to account for, the change in them, would remain unaccounted for.   *Fifth*—Still, the moral difficulty is greatest of all.   If it was merely a case of resuscitation, then Jesus tried to palm himself off as one risen from the dead when He knew He was nothing of the sort.   He was an arch impostor, and the whole Christian system rests on a fraud.   It is impossible to believe that such a system of religion as that of Jesus Christ, embodying such exalted precepts and principles of truth, purity and love "originated in a deliberately planned fraud."   No one whose own heart is not cankered by fraud and trickery can believe Jesus an impostor and His religion founded upon fraud.

We have eliminated all other possible suppositions; we have but one left: Jesus really was raised from the dead the third day.   The desperate straits to which those who attempt to deny it are driven are in themselves proof of the fact.   Furthermore, if the Apostles really, firmly believed, as is admitted, that Jesus arose from the dead, they had some facts upon which they founded their belief.   These are the facts they would have related in recounting the story and not have made up a story out of imaginary incidents.   But, if the facts were as recounted in the Gospels, there is no possible escaping the conclusion that Jesus actually arose.

We have, then, several independent lines of argument pointing to the resurrection of Christ from the dead.   Taken separately they satisfactorily prove the fact.   Taken together they constitute an argument that makes doubt of the resurrection of Christ impossible to a candid man.

There is really but one weighty objection to the doctrine that Christ arose from the dead—*i. e.*, *"That there is no conclusive evidence that any other ever arose."*   To this a sufficient answer would be: Even if it were certain that no other ever arose, the life of Jesus was unique, His nature was unique, His mission was unique, His history was unique, and it is not to be wondered at, but to be expected, that the issue of His life should also be unique.

II. The Importance of the Resurrection of Jesus Christ.

FIRST PROPOSITION: The Resurrection of Jesus Christ is mentioned directly 104 or more times in the New Testament (Under word " raised," 37; "raise,"1; "rise," 10; "risen," 21; " rose," 6; "rising," 1; "life," 1; "alive," 2; "liveth," 6; "brought again," 1; "quickened," 3; "begotten," 1; "resurrection," 11.)

(2) Acts 1: 21, 22—"Wherefore of these men which have companied with us all the time that the Lord Jesus went in and out among us, beginning from the baptism of John, unto the same day that he was taken up from us, must one be ordained *to be a witness with us of his resurrection.*"

Acts 2: 24, 29-32—"Whom God hath raised up, having loosed the pains of death: because it was not possible that he should be holden of it. Men and brethren, let me freely speak unto you of the Patriarch David, that he is both dead and buried, and his sepulchre is with us unto this day. Therefore being a prophet, and knowing that God had sworn with an oath to him, that of the fruit of his loins, according to the flesh, he would raise up Christ to sit on his throne: He seeing this before, spake of *the resurrection of Christ*, that his soul was not left in hell, neither his flesh did see corruption. *This Jesus hath God raised up, whereof we all are witnesses.*"

Acts 4: 33—"And with great power gave the apostles *witness of the resurrection* of the Lord Jesus: and great grace was upon them all."

Acts 17: 18—"Then certain philosophers of the Epicureans, and of the Stoics, encountered him. And some said, What will this babbler say? other some, He seemeth to be a setter forth of strange gods: because he *preached unto them Jesus, and the resurrection.*"

Acts 23: 6—"But when Paul perceived that the one part were Sadducees, and the other Pharisees, he cried out in the council, Men and brethren, I am a Pharisee, the son of a Pharisee: *of the hope and resurrection of the dead I am called in question.*"

1 Cor. 15: 15—"Yea, and we are found false witnesses of God; because *we have testified of God that he raised up Christ:* whom he raised not up, if so be that the dead rise not."

SECOND PROPOSITION: The Resurrection of Jesus Christ was the most prominent and cardinal point in the apostolic testimony.

The Resurrection of Jesus Christ had a prominence in the apostolic teaching that it has not in modern preaching.

(3) 1 Cor. 15: 1, 3, 4—"Moreover, brethren, I declare unto you the gospel which I preached unto you, which also ye have received, and

wherein ye stand: For I delivered unto you first of all that which I also received, how that Christ died for our sins according to the scriptures; and that he was buried, and *that he rose again* the third day according to the scriptures."

THIRD PROPOSITION: The Resurrection of Jesus Christ is one of the two fundamental truths of the Gospel.

Gospel preachers nowadays preach the gospel of the Crucifixion, the Apostles preached the gospel of the Resurrection as well. (2 Tim. 2: 8—" Remember that Jesus Christ of the seed of David was raised from the dead, according to my gospel.") The Crucifixion loses its meaning without the Resurrection. Without the Resurrection the death of Christ was only the heroic death of a noble martyr; with the Resurrection it is the atoning death of the Son of God. It shows that death to be of sufficient value to cover all our sins, for it was the sacrifice of the Son of God. In it we have an all-sufficient ground for knowing that the blackest sin is atoned for. My sin may be as high as the highest mountain, but the sacrifice that covers it is as high as the highest heaven; my guilt may be as deep as the ocean, but the atonement that swallows it up is as deep as eternity.

(4) 1 Cor. 15:14, 17—"And if Christ be not risen, then is our preaching vain, and your faith is also vain. And if Christ be not raised, your faith is vain; ye are yet in your sins."

FOURTH PROPOSITION: Disprove the Resurrection of Jesus Christ and Christian faith is vain.

(The two Greek words used in passages quoted above mean " empty " and " forceless.")

On the other hand, as we shall shortly see (under " Results of the Resurrection"), if Jesus Christ did rise, Christian preaching and Christian faith rest upon a solid and unassailable foundation of fact.

(5) Rom. 10:9, 10—" That if thou shalt confess with thy mouth the Lord Jesus, and shalt believe in thine heart that God hath raised him from the dead, thou shalt be saved. For with the heart man believeth unto righteousness; and with the mouth confession is made unto salvation."

FIFTH PROPOSITION: The doctrine of the Resurrection of Jesus Christ has power to save anyone who believes it with the heart.

(6) Phil. 3:8-10—"Yea doubtless, and I count all things but loss for the excellency of the knowledge of Christ Jesus my Lord: for whom I have suffered the loss of all things, and do count them but dung, that I may win Christ, and be found in him not having mine own righteousness, which is of the law, but that which is through the faith of Christ, the righteousness which is of God by faith: That I may know him, and the power of his resurrection, and the fellowship of his sufferings, being made conformable unto his death."

SIXTH PROPOSITION: To know the power of Christ's Resurrection is one of the highest ambitions of the intelligent believer, to attain which he sacrifices all things and counts them but refuse.

The importance of the Resurrection of Jesus Christ will come out still further when we come to study the "Results of His Resurrection."

III. The Manner of the Resurrection of Jesus Christ.

(1) Acts 2:24, 32—"Whom God hath raised up, having loosed the pains of death: because it was not possible that he should be holden of it. This Jesus hath God raised up, whereof we all are witnesses

Acts 10:40—"Him God raised up the third day, and showed him openly."

Acts 13:30—"But God raised him from the dead."

Rom. 10:9—"That if thou shalt confess with thy mouth the Lord Jesus, and shalt believe in thine heart that God raised him from the dead, thou shalt be saved."

Col. 2:12—"Buried with him in baptism, wherein also ye are raised with him through the faith of the operation of God, who hath raised him from the dead."

Eph. 1:19, 20—"And what is the exceeding greatness of his power to us-ward who believe, according to the working of his mighty power, which he wrought in Christ, when he raised him from the dead, and set him at his own right hand in the heavenly places."

FIRST PROPOSITION: God raised up Jesus Christ from the dead by the working of the strength of His might.

It was not so much that Jesus Christ arose as that God raised Him. It was God who put forth the might, it was God who loosed the pains of death. He was raised by an act of power from without and not by the fulness of life within. He laid down His life to the fullest extent, He was in the fullest sense dead, and it took the strength of God's might to raise Him.

(2) Jno. 20: 27—"Then saith he to Thomas, Reach hither thy fin-ger, and behold my hands; and reach hither thy hand, and thrust it into my side; and be not faithless, but believing."

Acts 10: 40, 41—"Him God raised up the third day, and showed him openly; Not to all the people, but unto witnesses chosen before of God, even to us, who did eat and drink with him after he rose from the dead."

Luke 24: 39—"Behold my hands and my feet, that it is I myself; handle me, and see; for a spirit hath not flesh and bones, as ye see me have."

Luke 24: 15, 18—"And it came to pass, that, while they communed together and reasoned, Jesus himself drew near, and went with them. And one of them, whose name was Cleopas, answering said unto him, Art thou only a stranger in Jerusalem, and hast not known the things which are come to pass there in these days ?"

Jno. 20: 14, 15—"And when she had thus said, she turned herself back, and saw Jesus standing, and knew not that it was Jesus. Jesus saith unto her, Woman, why weepest thou? whom seekest thou? She, supposing him to be the gardener, saith unto him, Sir, if thou have borne him hence, tell me where thou hast laid him, and I will take him away."

SECOND PROPOSITION: Jesus Christ, after His resurrection, ate and drank, had hands, feet, flesh and bones, and all the appearance of a man.

(3) Jno. 21: 4, 12—"But when the morning was now come, Jesus stood on the shore; but the disciples knew not that it was Jesus. Jesus saith unto them, Come and dine. And none of the disciples durst ask him, Who art thou? knowing that it was the Lord."

THIRD PROPOSITION: Jesus Christ's resurrection appearance was so different from His earthly appearance as not to be clearly recognizable by His intimate friends.

(4) Jno. 20: 19, 26—"Then the same day at evening, being the first day of the week, when the doors were shut where the disciples were assembled for fear of the Jews, came Jesus and stood in the midst, and saith unto them, Peace be unto you."

Luke 24: 31—"And their eyes were opened, and they knew him; and he vanished out of their sight."

FOURTH PROPOSITION: Jesus Christ's resurrection body was of such a character that He could appear in a room where the doors were shut and could vanish from the sight of men. It was not subject to some of the limitations under which ordinary earthly bodies exist and act.

(5) Phil. 3: 21—" Who shall change our vile body, that it may be fashioned *like unto his glorious body*, according to the working whereby he is able even to subdue all things unto himself." (Compare 1 Cor: 15, 42–49, 50:—"So also is the resurrection of the dead. It is sown in corruption, it is raised in incorruption: It is sown in dishonor, it is raised in glory: it is sown in weakness, it is raised in power: It is sown a natural body, it is raised a spiritual body. There is a natural body, and there is a spiritual body. And so it is written: The first man Adam was made a living soul; the last Adam was made a quickening spirit. Howbeit that was not first which is spiritual, but that which is natural; and afterward that which is spiritual. The first man is of the earth, earthy: the second man is the Lord from heaven. As is the earthy, such are they also that are earthy: and as is the heavenly, such are they also that are heavenly. And as we have borne the image of the earthy, we shall also bear the image of the heavenly. Now this I say, brethren, that flesh and blood cannot inherit the kingdom of God; neither doth corruption inherit incorruption.")

FIFTH PROPOSITION: Jesus Christ had a transformed body, incorruptible, glorious, mighty, spiritual, heavenly, not FLESH AND BLOOD *("flesh and bones" is not "flesh and blood").*

IV. The Results of the Resurrection of Jesus Christ.

(1) 1 Pet. 1: 21, R.V—"Who through him are believers in God who raised him from the dead, and gave him glory; so that your faith and hope might be in God."

FIRST PROPOSITION: Through Jesus Christ men became believers in God who raised Him from the dead. By the resurrection of Jesus Christ a solid foundation is laid for our faith in God.

Men have been looking constantly for proofs of the existence and character of God. There is the argument from the marks of creative intelligence and design in the material universe, the argument from the evidence of an intelligent guiding hand in human history, the ontological argument, etc., but the resurrection of Jesus Christ points with unerring certainty to the existence, power and holiness of the God who raised Him. On the other hand, if Christ be not raised our faith is vain. (1 Cor. 15: 17—"And if Christ be not raised, your faith is vain; ye are yet in your sins.") My belief in the God of the Bible is not a felicitous fancy, it is a fixed faith resting upon an incontrovertibly firm fact.

(2) 1 Pet. 1: 3, 4, R.V.—" Blessed be the God and Father of our Lord Jesus Christ, who according to his great mercy begat us again *unto a living hope by the resurrection of Jesus Christ* from the dead, unto an inheritance incorruptible, and undefiled, and that fadeth not away, reserved in heaven for you."

SECOND PROPOSITION: By the Resurrection of Jesus Christ. believers are begotten again unto a living hope, unto an inheritance incorruptible, and undefiled, and that fadeth not away, reserved in heaven.

The Resurrection of Jesus Christ is the truth which, made living in our hearts by the Holy Spirit, results in the "new birth unto a living hope, and an incorruptible, etc., inheritance." (Compare Rom. 10: 9.) Through our believing in a Risen and Living Christ, Christ begins to live in us. The Resurrection of Christ also forms a firm foundation of fact upon which to build our hope for the future.

(3) Rom. 1: 4—"And declared to be the Son of God with power, according to the spirit of holiness, by the resurrection from the dead."

THIRD PROPOSITION: By His Resurrection Jesus Christ is declared (or openly appointed or designated) to be the Son of God with power.

The claim that Jesus made was that, while even the greatest and best of the prophets were only servants, He was a Son, a beloved and only one of the Father. That while other faithful messengers were only servants in the kingdom of God, it belonged to Himself as His own inheritance. (Mark 12: 6, 7.) That He was one with the Father, and that men should honor Him "even as they honor the Father." (Jno. 10: 30; Jno. 5: 23, R.V.) By raising Christ from the dead God set His seal to this claim. Others, it is true, have been raised from the dead by God's power, but they made no such claim as this prior to their death. But Jesus made this extraordinary claim; was put to death for making it; previous to His death claimed that God would raise Him again the third day. God did so, and thus affirmed the claim of Jesus Christ, and announced to all ages in a way more convincing and satisfying than an audible voice from heaven, "Jesus Christ is my Son and all men must honor the Son even as they honor me." The admission of the Resurrection of Jesus Christ leads logically to the admission of His deity.

(4) Acts 17: 31—"Because he hath appointed a day, in the which he will judge the world in righteousness by that man whom he hath ordained; whereof he hath given assurance unto all men in that he hath raised him from the dead."

FOURTH PROPOSITION: By the Resurrection of Jesus Christ God " has given assurance unto all men," that " He will judge the world in righteousness by " Jesus Christ."

Jesus Christ claimed that God would judge the world by Him.   (Jno. 5: 22, 27–29.)   By raising Christ from the dead God has set His seal to that claim.   If men ask me how I know there is a judgment day coming when Christ shall judge the world in righteousness, I reply because I know Jesus Christ arose.   The sure fact of the Resurrection of Jesus Christ in the past, points unerringly forward to the sure coming of judgment in the future. Belief in a judgment day is no guess of theologians, it is a positive faith founded upon a proved fact.

(5) Rom. 4: 25—"Who was delivered for our offenses, and was raised again for our justification."

FIFTH PROPOSITION: By the Resurrection of Jesus Christ believers in Him are justified—i. e., declared righteous.

(*a*) Christ gave His life a propitiation for believers. He "was delivered up for our transgressions." The Resurrection settles it beyond a peradventure that God has accepted the propitiation.   The Resurrection is God's declaration of His acceptance of the propitiation, and is, therefore, the declaration of our justification.   When another agrees to settle for my responsibilities, I always wish to know whether the settlement is accepted.   By the Resurrection, God declares that He has accepted and is satisfied with the settlement Christ has made.   I am thus declared righteous in God's sight.   If we are ever troubled with doubts as to whether God has accepted the offering Christ made, we have only to look at the empty tomb and the Risen Lord.

(*b*) When Christ arose He arose as our representative: He died as our representative, He arose as our representative, He ascended as our representative, He is seated as our representative. (Eph. 2: 5, 6.)   As one risen, ascended, seated, He is declared to be God's chosen and accepted one, and we are declared chosen, accepted, righteous in Him.

(6) Rom. 7: 4, R.V.—"Wherefore, my brethren, ye also were made dead to the law through the body of Christ; that ye should be joined to another, even to him who was raised from the dead, that we might bring forth fruit unto God."

SIXTH PROPOSITION: It is through being joined to the Risen Christ that the believer brings forth fruit unto God.

The only living or doing or accomplishing in the Christian life that is acceptable to God is through union with the Risen Christ. Through union with the crucified Christ we get our pardon, our cleansing from guilt, our justification, our perfect standing before God. Through union with the Risen Christ we get power for life and fruit. One reason why there is so little of life and fruit in many professedly Christian lives is because there is so little knowledge of the Risen and Living Christ. Paul tells us that we were raised with Christ through faith in the working of God, who raised Him from the dead. (Col. 2: 12.) We are raised with Him to walk in newness of life. (Rom. 6: 4.) This is the truth which baptism symbolizes. (Rom. 6: 3, 4.) The full power of Christ's resurrection we shall not know until we attain unto the resurrection from the dead. (Phil. 3: 10, 11.) "He that raised up Jesus from the dead shall also quicken our mortal bodies by His spirit which dwelleth in you." (Rom. 8: 11.) But "the power of this resurrection" in our moral and spiritual lives, begetting "newness of life," and "fruit unto God," we may know even now, through being "joined to him who was raised from the dead." Are you "joined to another, even to him who was raised from the dead?" Here lies the secret of holy living, "newness of life," victory over sin, fruit unto God.

(7) Rom. 5: 9, 10—"Much more then, being justified by his blood, we shall be saved from wrath through him. For if, when we were enemies, we were reconciled to God by the death of his Son; much more, being reconciled, we shall be saved by his life."

SEVENTH PROPOSITION: Through the life of Jesus Christ believers shall be saved.

NOTE I.—The life here spoken of evidently does not refer to the example of Christ, but to His life, which is the outcome of His Resurrection. (Compare Jno. 14: 19—"Yet a little while, and the world seeth me no more; but ye see me: because I live, ye shall live also.")

NOTE 2.—The salvation here spoken of evidently does not refer to salvation from the guilt of sin—*i. e.*, pardon and justification. That has been spoken of in the preceding verse as already secured "by his blood." It is a salvation in the future—"*shall be* saved by his life." By a comparison with the previous verse it is evidently salvation from the coming wrath. The life of Christ that is the outcome of the Resurrection secures this for us. This life will have its perfect manifestation in the coming of the Lord. (Col. 3:4, R.V.; 2 Thess. 1:9, 10.)

(8) Rom. 8:34—"Who is he that condemneth? It is Christ that died, yea rather, that is risen again, who is even at the right hand of God, who also maketh intercession for us."

Heb. 7:25—"Wherefore he is able also to save them to the uttermost that come unto God by him, seeing he ever liveth to make intercession for them."

EIGHTH PROPOSITION: Through the Resurrection of Jesus Christ we have an ever-living high priest at the right hand of God to continually make intercession for us, and who is therefore able to save to the uttermost (or " unto all-completeness").

Salvation is begun by the atoning death of Jesus Christ; it is continued by the Resurrection and Intercession of Christ. We have not only a Saviour who died and so made atonement for sin, but also a Saviour who rose and carried the blood into the holy of holies—God's own presence—and presents it there, and who ever lives and pleads our case in every new failure.

1 Jno. 2:1—"My little children, these things write I unto you, that ye sin not. And if any man sin, we have an advocate with the Father, Jesus Christ the righteous." (Compare Luke 22:31, 32—"And the Lord said, Simon, Simon, behold Satan hath desired to have you, that he may sift you as wheat: But I have prayed for thee, that thy faith fail not: and when thou art converted, strengthen thy brethren.")

Jno. 11:42—"And I know that thou hearest me always."

Herein lie our abiding security and our assurance of the ultimate perfect completeness of Christ's work for us and in us.

Note the believer's triumphant challenge in Rom. 8:33, 34: "Who shall lay anything to the charge of God's elect? It is God that justifieth. Who is he that condemneth? It is Christ that died, yea rather, that is risen again, who is even at the right hand of God, who also maketh intercession for us."

(9) Eph. 1:18-20—"The eyes of your understanding being enlightened; that ye may know what is the hope of his calling, and what the riches of the glory of his inheritance in the saints, and what is the

exceeding greatness of his power to us-ward who believe, according to the working of his mighty power, which he wrought in Christ, when he raised him from the dead, and set him at his own right hand in the heavenly places."

NINTH PROPOSITION: In the Resurrection of Jesus Christ we have an illustration and proof of the exceeding greatness of God's power to us-ward.

If we would understand and know what God can do in and for us, we have simply to look at and meditate upon the Resurrection of Jesus Christ, looking unto God to give us "a spirit of wisdom and revelation in the knowledge of Him." (Eph. 1: 17.)

(10) 1 Thess. 4: 14—"For if we believe that Jesus died and rose again, even so them also which sleep in Jesus will God bring with him."

2 Cor. 4: 14—"Knowing that he which raised up the Lord Jesus shall raise up us also by Jesus, and shall present us with you."

TENTH PROPOSITION: The Resurrection of Jesus Christ is the guarantee of our own resurrection.

We know that God will raise us up because He raised Him up. We are so united to Christ by faith that if He rose we must. If the spirit of Him who raised up Christ from the dead dwell in us also, He that raised up Christ from the dead will also quicken our mortal bodies by His spirit that dwelleth in us. (Rom. 8: 11.) The Resurrection of Jesus Christ has robbed death of its terrors for the believer. (1 Cor. 15: 55–57.)

(11) Acts 13: 32, 33—"And we declare unto you glad tidings, how that the promise which was made unto the fathers, God hath fulfilled the same unto us their children, in that he hath raised up Jesus again; as it is also written in the second Psalm, Thou art my Son, this day have I begotten thee."

ELEVENTH PROPOSITION: The Resurrection of Jesus Christ is the fulfillment of the promise made to the Fathers.

QUESTION: What was the promise made to the Fathers of which the Resurrection of Christ is the fulfillment?

ANSWER: Acts 3: 25—"Ye are the children of the prophets and of the covenant which God made with our fathers, saying unto Abraham, And in thy seed shall all the kindreds of the earth be blessed." (Compare Gen. 22: 18; 26: 4; 12: 3; Gal, 3: 16; Gen.

3: 15.)   The Risen Jesus Christ is the seed in which all nations shall be blessed in His turning them away from their iniquities.

> Acts 3: 26—"Unto you first God, *having raised up* his son Jesus, sent him to bless you, in turning away every one of you from his iniquities."

Furthermore, "Resurrection" is the substance of the promise made to the Fathers. (Acts 26: 6–8.   Compare 23: 6.)   And Jesus the resurrected one, and first fruits of them that sleep, is the fulfillment of this promise.   The Resurrection of Jesus Christ is the guarantee of the fulfillment of all the promises of God: *First*, because it declares Him to be the Son of God with power, and thus that the promises of the Bible all of which He endorses (Luke 24: 44) are the sure words of God.   *Second*, because it reveals God's ability to keep His word and also His mighty power to us-ward.   He that keeps His word in raising the dead can surely fulfill all His promises.   (Compare Acts 13: 38, 39,—" therefore.")   If we wish to know that all the promises of God are yea and amen in Christ Jesus, we have only to look to that most marvelous fulfillment of God's word and promise that has already taken place—the Resurrection—and see in that the guarantee of the fulfillment of all.   If you are ever tempted to think any promise of the Word too large and that you must discount it, remember that Christ is risen and that therein you have a proof and illustration of the "exceeding greatness of his power to us-ward who believe."

CHAPTER VII.

THE ASCENSION OR EXALTATION OF JESUS CHRIST.

I. The Fact of the Ascension or Exaltation of Jesus Christ.

(1) Eph. 4: 8—"Wherefore he saith, When he ascended up on high he led captivity captive, and gave gifts unto men."

Acts 1: 9—"And when he had spoken these things, while they beheld, he was taken up; and a cloud received him out of their sight."

Luke 24: 51—"And it came to pass, while he blessed them, he was parted from them, and carried up into heaven."

Heb. 10: 12—"But this man, after he had offered one sacrifice for sins for ever, sat down on the right hand of God."

FIRST PROPOSITION: Jesus Christ has ascended up on high, been received into Heaven, has sat down at the right hand of God.

The Ascension or Exaltation of Jesus Christ is definitely spoken of thirty-three or more times in the New Testament.

II. The Manner of the Ascension or Exaltation of Jesus Christ.

(1) Luke 24: 51—"And it came to pass, while he blessed them, he was parted from them, and carried up into heaven."

Acts 1: 9—"And when he had spoken these things, while they beheld, he was taken up; and a cloud received him out of their sight."

FIRST PROPOSITION: Jesus Christ was carried up into Heaven while the disciples were looking and received out of their sight.

(2) Jno. 17: 5—"And now, O Father, glorify thou me with thine own self with the glory which I had with thee before the world was."

SECOND PROPOSITION: Jesus Christ has been glorified with the Father Himself with the glory which He had with Him before the world was.

(3) Heb. 7: 26—"For such a high priest became us, who is holy, harmless, undefiled, separate from sinners, and made higher than the heavens."

THIRD PROPOSITION: Jesus Christ has been made higher than the heavens. (Compare Heb. 4: 14, R. V., "passed through the heavens." Eph. 4: 10, R. V.)

(4) Eph. 1: 20—"Which he wrought in Christ, when he raised him from the dead, and set him at his own right hand in the heavenly places."

Col. 3: 1—"If ye then be raised with Christ, seek those things which are above, where Christ sitteth on the right hand of God."

FOURTH PROPOSITION: Jesus Christ is now seated on the right hand of God.

QUESTION: Is this to be taken literally of location, or figuratively of power?

ANSWER: Acts 7: 55, 56—"But he, being full of the Holy Ghost, looked up steadfastly into heaven, and saw the glory of God, and Jesus standing on the right hand of God, and said, Behold, I see the heavens opened, and the Son of man standing on the right hand of God." Though God is in a sense everywhere, there is a place where He peculiarly manifests Himself and His glory—a place where He can be said to dwell in a sense in which He dwells nowhere else. Jesus Christ is at His right hand in that place.

(5) Eph. 1: 21—"Far above all principalities, and power, and might, and dominion, and every name that is named, not only in this world, but also in that which is to come."

FIFTH PROPOSITION: Jesus Christ has been exalted far above all principalities (R.V. "rule") *and power* (R.V. "authority") *and might* (R.V. "power") *and dominion, and every name that is named, not only in this world, but also in that which is to come.* (Compare Eph. 6: 12, A.V. and R.V. and Greek. The R.V. is not consistent in its translation of words in these two passages.)

(6) Acts 5: 31—"Him hath God exalted with his right hand to be a Prince and a Saviour, for to give repentance to Israel, and forgiveness of sins."

SIXTH PROPOSITION: God the Father exalted Jesus Christ with His right hand. (Compare Eph. 1: 19, 20.)

III. The Purpose of the Exaltation of Jesus Christ.

(1) Jno. 17: 1—"These words spake Jesus, and lifted up his eyes to heaven, and said, Father, the hour is come; glorify thy Son, that thy Son also may glorify thee."

FIRST PROPOSITION. Jesus Christ was glorified in order that He might glorify the Father.

(2) Acts 5: 31—"Him hath God exalted with his right hand to be a Prince and a Saviour for to give repentance to Israel, and forgiveness of sins."

SECOND PROPOSITION: Jesus Christ was exalted that He might be a Prince and a Saviour, to give repentance to Israel and forgiveness of sins.

It is the "Ascended" or "Exalted" Christ that now rules the believer and saves him and gives repentance and forgiveness of sins.

(3) Heb. 6: 20—"Whither the forerunner is for us entered, even Jesus, made a high priest forever after the order of Melchisedec."

THIRD PROPOSITION: Jesus Christ was exalted to enter heaven as a forerunner for us.

He has gone ahead to prepare the way and open the gates by His atoning blood and priestly intercession.

(4) Jno. 14 2—"In my father's house are many mansions: if it were not so, I would have told you. I go to prepare a place for you."

FOURTH PROPOSITION: Jesus Christ has ascended into heaven to prepare heaven itself as an abode for us.

QUESTION: How?

ANSWER: Heb. 9: 21–24—"Moreover he sprinkled with blood both the tabernacle, and all the vessels of the ministry. And almost all things are by the law purged with blood; and without shedding of blood is no remission. It was therefore necessary that the patterns of things in the heavens should be purified with these; *but the heavenly things themselves with better sacrifices* than these. For Christ is not entered into the holy places made with hands, which are the figures of the true; but into heaven itself, now to appear in the presence of God for us." Heaven itself must be sprinkled with blood to be fitted to be the abode of blood-sprinkled sinners.

(5) Heb. 9: 24—"For Christ is not entered into the holy places made with hands, which are the figures of the true; but into heaven itself, now to appear in the presence of God for us."

FIFTH PROPOSITION: *Jesus Christ ascended and entered heaven now to appear before the face of God for us*—i. e., *to act as high priest on our behalf; to present the blood of atonement and make intercession for us.*

This is illustrated by the Old Testament high priest who was only the type of Him that was to come.

(6)   Heb. 10: 12, 13—"But this man, after he had offered one sacrifice for sins forever, sat down on the right hand of God; from henceforth expecting till his enemies be made his footstool."

Acts 2: 34, 35—"For David is not ascended into the heavens: but he saith himself, the Lord said unto my Lord, Sit thou on my right hand, until I make thy foes thy footstool."

Acts 3: 20, 21—"And he shall send Jesus Christ, which before was preached unto you: whom the heaven must receive until the times of restitution of all things, which God hath spoken by the mouth of all his holy prophets since the world began."

SIXTH PROPOSITION: *Jesus Christ ascended into heaven and sat down on the right hand of God to await the complete subjection of His enemies and the restitution of all things. When that time comes He will come forth and His enemies be quickly subdued before him.* (See Chapter on the "Second Coming of Christ.")

(7)   Eph. 4: 10, R.V.—"He that descended is the same also that ascended far above all the heavens, that he might fill all things."

SEVENTH PROPOSITION: *Jesus Christ ascended far above all the heavens that He might fill all things.*

IV.   The Results of the Exaltation of Jesus Christ.

(1)   Eph. 1: 18-20—"The eyes of your understanding being enlightened; that ye may know what is the hope of his calling, and what the riches of the glory of his inheritance in the saints. And what is the exceeding greatness of his power to us-ward who believe, according to the working of his mighty power, which he wrought in Christ, when he raised him from the dead, and set him at his own right hand in the heavenly places."

FIRST PROPOSITION: *In the Exaltation of Jesus Christ, as in His Resurrection, the exceeding greatness of God's power to us-ward is seen.*

(2)   Heb. 4: 14-16, R.V.—"Having then a great high priest, who hath passed through the heavens, Jesus the Son of God, let us hold

fast our confession. For we have not a high priest that cannot be touched with the feeling of our infirmities; but one that hath been in all points, tempted like as we are, yet without sin. Let us therefore draw near with boldness unto the throne of grace, that we may receive mercy, and may find grace to help us in time of need."

SECOND PROPOSITION: Through the Exaltation of Jesus Christ we have a great high priest who has passed through the heavens and we can hold fast our confession and draw near with boldness unto the throne of grace.

If we have any hesitation or fear in our approach to God, all we need to do is to remember our ascended Saviour, our great high priest in the presence of God, at the very "right hand of the throne, the Majesty in the heavens." (Heb. 8: 1.)

(3) Acts 2: 33—"Therefore being by the right hand of God exalted, and having received of the Father the promise of the Holy Ghost, he hath shed forth this, which ye now see and hear."

THIRD PROPOSITION: Because of His Exaltation Jesus Christ has received of the Father the promise of the Holy Spirit and poured Him forth upon His believing and obedient disciples.

It is the ascended Christ who baptizeth with the Holy Spirit   (Jno. 7: 39; 16: 7; Acts 1: 5.)

(4) Jno. 14: 12—"Verily, verily, I say unto you, He that believeth on me, the works that I do shall he do also; and greater works than these shall he do; because I go unto my Father."

FOURTH PROPOSITION: Because of the Exaltation of Jesus Christ those who believe on Him will do greater works than He Himself wrought during the days of His humiliation.

(5) Heb. 2: 9—"But we see Jesus, who was made a little lower than the angels for the suffering of death, crowned with glory and honor; that he by the grace of God should taste death for every man."

FIFTH PROPOSITION: Because of His Exaltation Jesus Christ is seen clothed with glory and honor.

(6) Heb. 1: 3, 4—"Who being the brightness of his glory, and the express image of his person, and upholding all things by the word of his power, when he had by himself purged our sins, sat down on the right hand of the Majesty on high; Being made so much better than the angels, as he hath by inheritance obtained a more excellent name than they."

SIXTH PROPOSITION: By His Exaltation Jesus Christ is made better than (exalted above) the angels.

(7) Phil. 2: 9, R.V—"Wherefore also God highly exalted him, and gave unto him the name which is above every name."

SEVENTH PROPOSITION: By His Exaltation Jesus Christ has been given the name which is above every name.

(8) 1 Pet. 3: 22—"Who is gone into heaven, and is on the right hand of God; angels and authorities and powers being made subject unto him."

EIGHTH PROPOSITION: By the Exaltation of Jesus Christ angels and authorities and powers have been made subject unto Him.

(9) Eph. 1: 22, R.V.—"And he put all things in subjection under his feet, and gave him to be head over all things to the church."

NINTH PROPOSITION: By the Exaltation of Jesus Christ: (a) *All things have been put in subjection under His feet.* (b) *He has been made head over all things to the church.*

(10) Phil. 2: 9–11—"Wherefore God also hath highly exalted him, and given him a name which is above every name: That at the name of Jesus every knee should bow, of things in heaven, and things in earth, and things under the earth; And that every tongue should confess that Jesus Christ is Lord, to the glory of God the Father." (See R.V.)

TENTH PROPOSITION: Because of the Exaltation of Jesus Christ, in the name of Jesus every knee shall ultimately bow and every tongue confess that Jesus Christ is Lord to the glory of God the Father.

CHAPTER VIII.

THE COMING AGAIN OF JESUS CHRIST.

I. The Fact of His Coming Again.

Jno. 14: 3—"And if I go and prepare a place for you, *I will come again*, and receive you unto myself; that where I am, there ye may be also."

Heb. 9: 28—"So Christ was once offered to bear the sins of many; and unto them that look for him *shall he appear the second time without sin* unto salvation."

Phil. 3: 20, 21—"For our conversation is in heaven; *from whence also we look for the Saviour*, the Lord Jesus Christ: Who shall change our vile body, that it may be fashioned like unto his glorious body, according to the working whereby he is able even to subdue all things unto himself."

1 Thess. 4: 16, 17—"For *the Lord himself shall descend* from heaven with a shout, with the voice of the archangel, and with the trump of God: and the dead in Christ shall rise first: Then we which are alive and remain shall be caught up together with them in the clouds, to meet the Lord in the air: and so shall we ever be with the Lord."

Acts 3: 19, 20 R.V.—"Repent ye therefore, and turn again, that your sins may be blotted out, that so there may come seasons of refreshing from the presence of the Lord; *and that he may send the Christ* who hath been appointed for you, even Jesus: whom the heaven must receive until the times of restoration of all things whereof God spake by the mouth of his holy prophets which have been since the world began."

FIRST PROPOSITION: Jesus Christ is coming again.

NOTE 1.—This coming again of Christ is not at the death of the believer. (*a*) He does not come again at death "with a shout," etc. (*b*) Those who are alive and remain are not caught up, etc., at the death of individual believers. (Jno. 14: 3, and 1 Thess. 4: 16, 17, manifestly refer to the same event. They are exactly parallel in the three facts stated: 1. The "I will come again" of Jesus, equals "The Lord Himself shall descend from heaven" of Paul. 2. The "Receive you unto myself" of Jesus, equals the "Shall be caught up in the clouds to meet the Lord" of Paul. 3. The "That where I am, there ye may be also" of Jesus, equals the "So shall we ever be with the Lord" of Paul. Paul's words are manifestly an inspired commentary on those of Jesus, and the refer-

ence of the words of Jesus to His coming at death is thus made impossible.) (c) Jno. 21: 22—"Jesus saith unto him, If I will that he tarry till I
come, what is that to thee? Follow thou me," shows how utterly impossible it is to make Christ's coming refer to death. "If I will that he
tarry," evidently means, "If I will that he remain alive." Now put
Christ's coming at the believer's death and you get this nonsense: "If I
will that he remain alive until he die, what is that to thee?"

NOTE 2.—The "coming again" in the verses given above is not the
coming of Christ at the coming of the Holy Spirit. That is, in a very
real and important sense, a coming of Christ. This appears from Jno. 14:
15-18, 21-23—"If ye love me keep my commandments. And I will pray
the Father, and he shall give you another Comforter, that he may abide
with you forever; Even the Spirit of truth; whom the world cannot receive, because it seeth him not, neither knoweth him: but ye know him;
for he dwelleth with you, and shall be in you. I will not leave you com-
fortless: *I will come to you.* He that hath my commandments, and keepeth
them, he it is that loveth me; and he that loveth me shall be loved of my
Father, and I will love him, and will manifest myself to him. Judas saith
unto him, not Iscariot, Lord how is it that thou wilt manifest thyself unto
us, and not unto the world? Jesus answered and said unto him, If a man
love me, he will keep my words: and my Father will love him, and we
will come unto him, and make our abode with him." But this coming
of Christ is not that which is referred to in the passages under considera-
tion. (a.) All of these promises but one (Jno. 14: 3) were made after the
coming of the Holy Spirit and pointed to a coming still future. (b.)
Jesus does not receive us unto Himself to be with Him at the coming
of the Holy Spirit. At the coming of the Holy Spirit He comes to be
with us (Jno. 14: 18, 21, 23), at His coming again mentioned in Jno. 14: 3;
1 Thess. 4: 16, 17, etc., He takes us to be with Him. (c.) He does not
at His coming in the Spirit "fashion anew the body of our humiliation,
that it may be conformed to the body of His glory." (Phil. 3: 20, 21.)
(d.) There is no trump of the archangel, no shout, no resurrection, no
rapture in the clouds, at this coming of the Christ. In other words, this
coming in scarcely any particular conforms to the plain and explicit statements of Christ and the Apostles concerning His coming again.

NOTE 3.—The "coming again" mentioned in the verses above was not
at the Destruction of Jerusalem. The Destruction of Jerusalem was in a
sense the precursor, prophecy and type of the Judgment at the end of the
Age, and therefore in Matt. 24 and Mark 13 the two events are described
in connection with each other. But God's judgment on Jerusalem is
manifestly not the event referred to in the texts given above. (a.) On
that occasion those who sleep in Jesus were not raised, living believers
were not caught up to meet the Lord in the air, the bodies of believers
were not transformed. (b.) Years after the Destruction of Jerusalem we
find John still looking forward to the Lord's coming. (Rev. 22: 20.) See
also, Jno. 21: 22, 23—"Jesus saith unto him, If I will that he tarry till I

come, what is that to thee? follow thou me. Then went this saying abroad among the brethren that that disciple should not die: yet Jesus said not unto him, He shall not die; but if I will that he tarry till I come, what is that to thee?" These words were written years after the Destruction of Jerusalem. Not any one of these events, nor all of them together, nor any other event that has yet occurred fulfills the very plain, explicit and definite predictions of Christ and the Apostles regarding Christ's coming again. *The Coming Again of Jesus Christ, so frequently mentioned in the New Testament as the great hope of the Church, is still in the future.*

II.   The Importance of the Doctrine of the Coming Again of Jesus Christ.

FIRST PROPOSITION: The Second Coming of Christ is said to be mentioned 318 times in the 260 chapters of the New Testament and "it occupies one in every twenty-five verses" from Matthew to Revelation.

SECOND PROPOSITION: By far the greater number of the predictions concerning Christ in the Old Testament are connected with His Second Coming.

(3) 1 Thess. 4: 18—"Wherefore comfort one another with these words." (See context.)

THIRD PROPOSITION: The Coming Again of Jesus Christ is the doctrine with which God bids us to comfort sorrowing saints.

This is true also of the Old Testament.   (Compare Is. 40: 1, 9, 10—"Comfort ye, comfort ye my people, saith your God.   O Zion, that bringest good tidings, get thee up into the high mountain; O Jerusalem, that bringest good tidings, lift up thy voice with strength; lift it up, be not afraid; say unto the cities of Judah, Behold your God! *Behold, the Lord* God *will come* with strong hand, and his arm shall rule for him; behold, his reward is with him, and his work before him."

(4) Tit. 2: 13—"Looking for that blessed hope and the glorious appearing of the great God and our Saviour Jesus Christ."

2 Pet. 3: 11, 13, R.V.—"Seeing that these things are thus all to be dissolved what manner of persons ought ye to be in all holy living and godliness, *looking for and earnestly desiring* the coming of the day of God, by reason of which the heavens being on fire shall be dissolved, and the elements shall melt with fervent heat?"

FOURTH PROPOSITION: The Coming Again of Jesus Christ and the events connected therewith are the blessed hope and eager desire of the true believer.

The last prayer in the Bible is "Even so, come Lord Jesus."
(Rev. 22: 20.)

(5) 2 Pet. 3: 3, 4, R. V.—"Knowing this first, that in the last days
mockers shall come with mockery, walking after their own lusts, and
saying, Where is the promise of his coming? for, from the day that
the fathers fell asleep, all things continue as they were from the beginning of the creation."

*FIFTH PROPOSITION: The Coming Again of Jesus Christ is
a doctrine which is the particular object of the hatred and ridi-
cule of mockers who walk after their own lusts.*

A worldly church and worldly Christians also hate this
doctrine.

(6) Matt. 24: 44-46—"Therefore be ye also ready; for in such an
hour as ye think not the Son of man cometh. Who then is a faithful
and wise servant, whom his Lord hath made ruler over his household,
to give them meat in due season ? Blessed is that servant, whom his
Lord when he cometh shall find so doing."

Luke 21: 34-36—"And take heed to yourselves, lest at any time
your hearts be overcharged with surfeiting, and drunkenness and
cares of this life, and so that day come upon you unawares. For as a
snare shall it come on all them that dwell on the face of the whole
earth. Watch ye therefore, and pray always, that ye may be accounted worthy to escape all these things that shall come to pass, and
to stand before the Son of man."

1 Jno. 2 : 28—"And now, little children, abide in him; that, when
he shall appear, ye may have confidence, and not be ashamed before
him at his coming."

*SIXTH PROPOSITION: The fact of the Coming Again of
Jesus Christ is the great Bible argument for a life of watch-
fulness, fidelity, wisdom, activity, simplicity, self-restraint,
prayer and abiding in Christ. (See also Matt. 25.   Entire
Chapter.)*

(7) Luke 12: 35, 36—"Let your loins be girded about, and your
lamps burning; and be ye yourselves like unto men looking for their
Lord, when he shall return from the marriage feast, that when he
cometh and knocketh, they may straightway open unto him."

*SEVENTH PROPOSITION: The Coming Again of Jesus
Christ is the one event for which the disciples of Christ should
be looking.*

ın verse 37 an especial blessing is promised upon those whom the Lord when He cometh shall find watching. (Compare Heb. 9: 28—"So Christ was once offered to bear the sins of many; and *unto them that look for Him* shall He appear the second time without sin unto salvation.")

III. The Manner of Christ's Coming Again.

(1) 1 Thess. 4: 16, 17—"For the Lord himself shall descend from heaven with a shout, with the voice of the archangel, and with the trump of God: and the dead in Christ shall rise first: Then we which are alive and remain shall be caught up together with them in the clouds, to meet the Lord in the air: and so shall we ever be with the Lord."

Matt. 25: 31, 32—"When the Son of man shall come in his glory, and all the holy angels with him, then shall he sit upon the throne of his glory: And before him shall be gathered all nations: and he shall separate them one from another, as a shepherd divideth his sheep from the goats."

2 Thess. 2: 7, 8—"For the mystery in iniquity doth already work: only he who now letteth will let, until he be taken out of the way. And then shall that wicked be revealed, whom the Lord shall consume with the spirit of his mouth, and shall destroy with the brightness of his coming."

Zech. 14: 4, 5—"And his feet shall stand in that day upon the mount of Olives, which is before Jerusalem on the east, and the mount of Olives shall cleave in the midst thereof toward the east and toward the west, and there shall be a very great valley; and half of the mountain shall remove toward the north, and half of it toward the south. And ye shall flee to the valley of the mountains; for the valley of the mountains shall reach unto Azal: yea, ye shall flee, like as ye fled from before the earthquake in the days of Uzziah king of Judah: and the LORD my God shall come, and all the saints with thee."

It is evident from a comparison of the above passages that the Coming Again of Jesus Christ has various steps or stages:

(*a*) FIRST STAGE: In the air whither His believing people are caught up to meet Him.

(*b*) SECOND STAGE: To the earth.   In this latter stage His saints come with Him.

1 Thess. 3: 13—"To the end he may establish your hearts unblamable in holiness before God, even our Father, at the coming of our Lord Jesus Christ with all his saints."

Col. 3: 4, R.V.—"When Christ, who is our life, shall be manifested, then shall ye also with him be manifested in glory."

I Thess. 4: 14—"For if we believe that Jesus died and rose again, even so them also which sleep in Jesus will God bring with him."

In the air Christ comes for His own; to the earth He comes with them. For anything we know a considerable interval may take place between these two stages of the Lord's coming. Luke 21: 36—("Watch ye therefore, and pray always, that ye may be accounted worthy to escape all these things that shall come to pass, and to stand before the Son of man.") and 2 Thess. 2: 7, 8— ("For the mystery of iniquity doth already work: only he who now letteth will let, until he be taken out of the way")—seem to hint that the whole period of the great tribulation intervenes between the coming of Jesus in the air for His earthly saints and His coming to the earth with His saints. There are not, however, two comings, but two stages in the one coming. Bearing in mind the distinction between these two will help to solve many of the seeming discrepancies between different texts of the Bible on this subject.

(c) THIRD STAGE: A succession of events follows His coming to the earth.

(2) Acts 1: 11—"Which also said, Ye men of Galilee, why stand ye gazing up into heaven? this same Jesus, which is taken up from you into heaven, shall so come in like manner as ye have seen him go into heaven."

Heb. 9: 28—"So Christ was once offered to bear the sins of many; and unto them that look for him shall he appear the second time without sin unto salvation." ("Shall appear," literally "*shall be seen.*")

Rev. 1: 7—"Behold, he cometh with clouds; and *every eye shall see him*, and they also which pierced him: and all kindreds of the earth shall wail because of him. Even so, Amen."

SECOND PROPOSITION: Jesus Christ shall come again bodily and visibly.

(3) Matt. 24: 26, 27—"Wherefore if they shall say unto you, Behold, he is in the desert; go not forth: behold, he is in the secret chambers; believe it not. For as the lightning cometh out of the east, and shineth even unto the west; so shall also the coming of the Son of man be."

THIRD PROPOSITION: Jesus Christ is coming again with great publicity.

(Compare Rev. 1: 7—"Behold, he cometh with clouds; and every eye shall see him, and they also which pierced him: and all kindreds of the earth shall wail because of him. Even so, Amen.")

These "inner chamber" Christs and "obscure corner" Christs are a humbug long since predicted and exploded. Even at His coming for His saints there seems to be a large measure of publicity about it. (1 Thess. 4: 16, 17—"For the Lord himself shall descend from heaven with a shout, with the voice of the archangel, and with the trump of God: and the dead in Christ shall rise first.") The doctrine of a secret rapture of believers does not seem to have much support in Scripture.

(4) Matt. 24: 30—"And then shall appear the sign of the Son of man in heaven: and then shall all the tribes of the earth mourn, and they shall see the Son of man coming in the clouds of heaven with power and great glory."

FOURTH PROPOSITION: The Son of man is coming in the clouds of heaven with power and great glory.

"In the clouds."

Compare Ex. 19: 9—"And the LORD said unto Moses, *Lo, I come unto thee in a thick cloud,* that the people may hear when I speak with thee, and believe thee for ever. And Moses told the words of the people unto the LORD."

Ex. 34: 5—"And *the* LORD *descended in the cloud,* and stood with him there, and proclaimed the name of the LORD."

Ps. 97: 1, 2—"The LORD reigneth; let the earth rejoice; let the multitude of isles be glad thereof. *Clouds and darkness are round about him;* righteousness and judgment are the habitation of his throne."

Matt. 17: 5—"While he yet spake, *behold a bright cloud* overshadowed them: and behold a voice out of the cloud, which said, This is my beloved Son, in whom I am well pleased; hear ye him."

Ps. 104: 3—"Who layeth the beams of his chambers in the waters; who maketh *the clouds* HIS *chariot:* who walketh upon the wings of the wind."

Is. 19: 1—"The burden of Egypt. Behold, *the* LORD *rideth upon a swift cloud,* and shall come into Egypt: and the idols of Egypt shall be moved at his presence, and the heart of Egypt shall melt in the midst of it."

From these passages it appears that it was Jehovah who came in the clouds; therefore, to say that Jesus is coming in the clouds is to say that He is coming as a Divine one or in Divine glory.

(5) Matt. 16: 27—"For the Son of man shall come in the glory of his Father with his angels; and then he shall reward every man according to his works."

Mark 8: 38—"Whosoever therefore shall be ashamed of me and of my words, in this adulterous and sinful generation, of him also shall the Son of man be ashamed, when he cometh in the glory of his Father with the holy angels."

2 Thess. 1: 7, R.V.—"And to you that are afflicted rest with us, at the revelation of the Lord Jesus from heaven with the angels of his power in flaming fire."

FIFTH PROPOSITION: Jesus Christ is coming in the glory of His Father with the holy angels.

(6) Rev. 16: 15—"Behold, I come as a thief. Blessed is he that watcheth, and keepeth his garments, lest he walk naked, and they see his shame."

1 Thess. 5: 2, 3—"But of the times and the seasons, brethren, ye have no need that I write unto you. For yourselves know perfectly that the day of the Lord so cometh as a thief in the night."

SIXTH PROPOSITION: Jesus Christ shall come as a thief— unannounced, without warning, unexpectedly, suddenly.

The world will be taken up with its usual occupations.

Matt. 24: 37-39—"But as the days of Noe were, so shall also the coming of the Son of man be. For as in the days that were before the flood they were eating and drinking, marrying and giving in marriage, until the day that Noe entered into the ark, and knew not until the flood came, and took them all away; so shall also the coming of the Son of man be."

The attempt to lay out a complete and fully defined chart of events leading up to the Lord's coming, loses sight of this clearly revealed fact about His coming. Our part is to see to it that that day does not come upon us as a snare.

Luke 21: 34, 35—"And take heed to yourselves, lest at any time your hearts be overcharged with surfeiting, and drunkenness, and cares of this life, and so that day come upon you unawares. For as a snare shall it come on all them that dwell on the face of the whole earth."

IV. The Purposes of Christ's Coming Again.

(1) Jno. 14: 3—"And if I go and prepare a place for you, I will come again, and *receive you unto myself;* that where I am, there ye may be also."

1 Thess. 4: 16, 17—"For the Lord himself· shall descend from heaven with a shout, with the voice of the archangel, and with the trump of God: and the dead in Christ shall rise first: *Then we who,*

are alive and remain shall be caught up together with them in the clouds, to meet the Lord in the air; and so shall we ever be with the Lord."

FIRST PROPOSITION: *Jesus Christ is coming again to receive His own unto Himself; that where He is, there they may be also.*

It is primarily love to His own that draws Jesus Christ to this earth again.   He so loves us that He cannot get on without us.

(Compare Jno. 17: 24—"Father, I will that they also, whom thou hast given me, be where I am; that they may behold my glory, which thou hast given me: for thou lovedst me before the foundation of the world.")

(2)   Phil. 3: 20, 21, R.V.—"For our citizenship is in heaven; from whence also we wait for a Saviour, the Lord Jesus Christ: *who shall fashion anew the body of our humiliation*, that it may be conformed to the body of his glory, according to the working whereby he is able even to subject all things unto himself."

SECOND PROPOSITION: *Jesus Christ is coming again to fashion anew the body of our humiliation, that it may be conformed to the body of His glory.*

(3)   Matt. 25: 19—"After a long time the Lord of those servants cometh, and reckoneth with them."

THIRD PROPOSITION: *Jesus Christ is coming again to reckon with His servants.*

(4)   Matt. 16: 27, R.V.—"For the Son of man shall come in the glory of his Father with his angels; and then shall he render unto every man according to his deeds."

FOURTH PROPOSITION: *Jesus Christ is coming again to render unto every man according to his deeds.*

It is not at death, but at the coming of the Lord that we receive our full reward.

2 Tim. 4: 8—"Henceforth there is laid up for me a crown of righteousness, which the Lord, the righteous judge, shall give me *at that day:* and not to me only, but unto all them also that love his appearing."

1 Pet. 5: 4, R.V.—"And *when the chief Shepherd shall be manifested*, ye shall receive the crown of glory that fadeth not away."

(5)   2 Thess. 1: 10, R.V.—"When he shall come to be glorified in his saints, and to be marveled at in all them that believed (because our testimony unto you was believed) in that day."

FIFTH PROPOSITION: Jesus Christ is coming again to be glorified in His saints and to be marveled at in all them that believe.

(6) Matt. 25: 10—"And while they went to buy, the bridegroom came; and they that were ready went in with him to the marriage: and the door was shut."

Rev. 19: 7–9—"Let us be glad and rejoice, and give honour to him: for the marriage of the Lamb is come, and his wife hath made herself ready.   And to her was granted that she should be arrayed in fine linen, clean and white: for the fine linen is the righteousness of saints. And he saith unto me, Write, Blessed are they which are called unto the marriage supper of the Lamb.   And he saith unto me, these are the true sayings of God."

SIXTH PROPOSITION: Jesus Christ is coming again to be united in marriage with His betrothed bride, the Church (Compare Eph. 5: 23–32), *and to celebrate the marriage supper.*

(7) Luke 19: 12, 15—" He said therefore, A certain nobleman went into a far country to receive for himself a kingdom, and to return. And it came to pass, that when he was returned, having received the kingdom, then he commanded these servants to be called unto him, to whom he had given the money, that he might know how much every man had gained by trading."

Matt. 25: 31—"When the Son of man shall come in his glory, and all the holy angels with him, *then shall he sit upon the throne of his glory.*"

Jer. 23: 5, 6—"Behold, the days come, saith the LORD, that I will raise unto David a righteous Branch, and *a King shall reign and prosper*, and shall execute judgment and justice in the earth.   In his days Judah shall be saved, and Israel shall dwell safely: and this is his name whereby he shall be called, THE LORD OUR RIGHTEOUSNESS."

Ps. 2: 6—"Yet have I set my king upon my holy hill of Zion."

Zech. 14: 9—"And the LORD *shall be king* over all the earth: in that day shall there be one LORD, and his name one."

Rev. 19: 12, 15, 16—" His eyes were as a flame of fire, and on his head were many crowns; and he had a name written, that no man knew, but he himself.   And out of his mouth goeth a sharp sword, that with it he should smite the nations; and he shall rule them with a rod of iron: and he treadeth the winepress of the fierceness and wrath of Almighty God.   And he hath on his vesture and on his thigh a name written, KING OF KINGS, AND LORD OF LORDS."

Rev. 20: 4—"And I saw thrones, and they sat upon them, and judgment was given unto them: and I saw the souls of them that were beheaded for the witness of Jesus, and for the word of God, and which had not worshipped the beast, neither his image, neither had received his mark upon their foreheads, or in their hands; and *they lived and reigned with Christ* a thousand years."

Rev. 11: 15—"And the seventh angel sounded; and there were great voices in heaven, saying, The kingdoms of this world are become the kingdoms of our Lord, and of his Christ; and *he shall reign* for ever and ever."

SEVENTH PROPOSITION: Jesus Christ is coming again to reign as a king.

(8) Zech. 14: 1-4—"Behold the day of the LORD cometh, and thy spoil shall be divided in the midst of thee. For I will gather all nations against Jerusalem to battle; and the city shall be taken, and the houses rifled, and the women ravished; and half of the city shall go forth into captivity, and the residue of the people shall not be cut off from the city. Then shall the LORD go forth, and fight against those nations, as when he fought in the day of battle. And his feet shall stand in that day upon the mount of Olives, which is before Jerusalem on the east, and the mount of Olives shall cleave in the midst thereof toward the east and toward the west and there shall be a very great valley; and half of the mountain shall remove toward the north, and half of it toward the south."

EIGHTH PROPOSITION: Jesus Christ is coming again to deliver Israel in the day when his trials and sufferings shall culminate.

(9) Zech. 8: 3, 7, 8—"Then saith the LORD, I am returned unto Zion, and will dwell in the midst of Jerusalem: and Jerusalem shall be called a city of truth; and the mountain of the LORD of hosts, The holy mountain. Thus saith the LORD of hosts; Behold I will save my people from the east country, and from the west country; and I will bring them, and they shall dwell in the midst of Jerusalem: and they shall be my people, and I will be their God, in truth and in righteousness."

NINTH PROPOSITION: Jesus Christ is coming again to gather together the outcasts of Israel from the East country and the West country into Jerusalem.

(10) Rom. 11: 26—"And so all Israel shall be saved: as it is written, There shall come out of Sion the Deliverer, and shall turn away ungodliness from Jacob."

TENTH PROPOSITION: Jesus Christ is coming again to deliver Israel and turn away ungodliness from Jacob.

(11)   Mal. 3: 1–3—"Behold I will send my messenger, and he shall prepare the way before me: and the LORD, whom ye seek, shall suddenly come to his temple, even the messenger of the covenant, whom ye delight in: behold, he shall come, saith the LORD of hosts. But who may abide the day of his coming? and who shall stand when he appeareth? for he is like a refiner's fire, and like fullers' soap: And he shall sit as a refiner and purifier of silver: and he shall purify the sons of Levi, and purge them as gold and silver, that they may offer unto the LORD an offering in righteousness."

ELEVENTH PROPOSITION: Jesus Christ is coming again as a refiner and purifier of silver.

(12)   2 Tim. 4: 1—"I charge thee therefore before God, and the Lord Jesus Christ, who shall judge the quick and the dead at his appearing and his kingdom."

TWELFTH PROPOSITION: Jesus Christ is coming again to judge the living and the dead.

(*a*)   Matt. 25: 31, 32—"But when the Son of man shall come in his glory, and all the angels with him, then shall he sit on the throne of his glory: and before him shall be gathered all the nations."

Jesus Christ is coming again to judge all the nations. The nations here spoken of are the nations living on the earth at the coming of the Lord.

(*b*)   Rev. 20: 11, 12—"And I saw a great white throne, and him that sat on it, from whose face the earth and the heaven fled away; and there was found no place for them. And I saw the dead, small and great, stand before God; and the books were opened; and another book was opened, which is the book of life: and *the dead* were judged out of those things which were written in the books, according to their works."

Jesus Christ is coming again to judge the dead. One thousand years separate these two judgments. (Rev. 20: 7–11.)

(13)   Jude 14, 15, R.V.—"And to these also Enoch, the seventh from Adam, prophesied, saying, Behold, the Lord came with ten thousands of his holy ones, to execute judgment upon all, and to convict all the ungodly of all their works of ungodliness which they have ungodly wrought, and of all the hard things which ungodly sinners have spoken against him."

THIRTEENTH PROPOSITION: Jesus Christ is coming again to execute judgment upon all, and to convict all the ungodly of all their works of ungodliness which they have ungodly wrought, and of all the hard things which ungodly sinners have spoken against Him.

(14)   Is. 26: 21—" For, behold, the LORD cometh out of his place to punish the inhabitants of the earth for their iniquity: the earth also shall disclose her blood, and shall no more cover her slain."

FOURTEENTH PROPOSITION: Jesus Christ is coming to punish the inhabitants of the earth for their iniquity.

(15)   2 Thess. 1: 7–9, R.V.—"And to you who are afflicted rest with us, at the revelation of the Lord Jesus from heaven with the angels of his power in flaming fire, rendering vengeance to them that know not God, and to them that obey not the gospel of our Lord Jesus."

FIFTEENTH PROPOSITION: Jesus Christ is coming again to render vengeance to them that know not God, and to them that obey not the gospel of our Lord Jesus Christ.

(16)   2 Thess. 2: 8, R.V.—"And then shall be revealed the lawless one, whom the Lord Jesus shall slay with the breath of his mouth, and bring to naught by the manifestation of his coming."

SIXTEENTH PROPOSITION: Jesus Christ is coming again to slay the lawless one with the breath of his mouth and to bring him to naught by the manifestation of His coming.

(17)   Is. 11: 1, 2, 4, 5, 9—" And there shall come forth a rod out of the stem of Jesse, and a Branch shall grow out of his roots; And the Spirit of the LORD shall rest upon him, the spirit of wisdom and understanding, the spirit of counsel and might, the spirit of knowledge and of the fear of the LORD; But with righteousness shall he judge the poor, and reprove with equity for the meek of the earth; and he shall smite the earth with the rod of his mouth, and with the breath of his lips shall he slay the wicked. And righteousness shall be the girdle of his loins, and faithfulness the girdle of his reins. They shall not hurt nor destroy in all my holy mountain: for the earth shall be full of the knowledge of the LORD, as the waters cover the sea."

SEVENTEENTH PROPOSITION: Jesus Christ is coming again to establish a universal reign of righteousness and godliness upon earth.

The coming of Christ is the true solution of all social problems.

V. The Results of Christ's Coming Again.

NOTE.—The Results of Christ's coming again naturally run parallel to the purpose of His coming again. But some passages are better classified under the Purpose and others under the Results.

(1) As regards God.

(a) Is. 40:5—"And the glory of God shall be revealed, and all flesh shall see it together: for the mouth of the LORD hath spoken it." (Note context vv. 3, 9-11.)

FIRST PROPOSITION: In the Coming Again of Jesus Christ the glory of the Lord shall be revealed, and all flesh shall see it together.

(2) As regards the Church.

(a) 1 Thess. 4:16—"For the Lord himself shall descend from heaven with a shout, with the voice of the archangel, and with the trump of God: and the dead in Christ shall rise first."

FIRST PROPOSITION: At the coming of Jesus Christ the dead in Christ shall rise.

(b) Phil. 3:20, 21—"For our conversation is in heaven; from whence also we look for the Savior, the Lord Jesus Christ: who shall change our vile body, that it may be fashioned like unto his glorious body, according to the working whereby he is able even to subdue all things unto himself."

SECOND PROPOSITION: At the Coming Again of Jesus Christ the bodies of believers shall be transformed into the likeness of the body of His glory.

(Compare Rom. 8:23—"And not only they, but ourselves also, which have the first fruits of the Spirit, even we ourselves, groan within ourselves, waiting for the adoption, to wit, the redemption of our body." Then the work of regeneration is completed.)

(c) 1 Thess. 4:17—"Then we which are alive and remain shall be caught up together with them in the clouds, to meet the Lord in the air: and so shall we ever be with the Lord."

THIRD PROPOSITION: At the Coming Again of Jesus Christ all believers—those still living and those who had fallen asleep but are now raised—shall be caught up together to meet the Lord in the air to be forever with Him. (Compare Jno. 14:3.)

(d) 1 Jno. 3:2—"Beloved, now are we the sons of God, and it doth not yet appear what we shall be: but we know that, when he shall appear, we shall be like him; for we shall see him as he is."

FOURTH PROPOSITION: At the Coming Again of Jesus Christ believers shall be made like Him because they shall see Him as He is.

Beholding Christ transforms into the image of Christ. (2 Cor. 3: 18, R. V.) But now we see through a glass darkly and the reflection is imperfect. Then we shall see Him face to face in His undimmed glory and shall perfectly reflect it.

(e) Col. 3: 4, R.V.—"When Christ, who is our life, shall be manifested, then shall ye also with him be manifested in glory."

FIFTH PROPOSITION: When Christ comes again and is manifested, then shall believers be manifested with Him in glory.

(f) 2 Tim. 4: 8—"Henceforth there is laid up for me a crown of righteousness, which the Lord, the righteous judge, shall give me at that day: and not to me only, but unto all them also that love his appearing."

SIXTH PROPOSITION: At the Coming Again of the Lord those who love His appearing shall receive a crown of righteousness.

(g) 1 Pet. 5: 4, R.V.—"And when the chief shepherd shall be manifested, ye shall receive the crown of glory that fadeth not away."

SEVENTH PROPOSITION: At the Coming Again of Jesus Christ faithful shepherds of the flock (see context as to what constitutes faithfulness) *shall receive a crown of glory that fadeth not away.*

(h) Rev. 20: 4—"And I saw thrones, and they sat upon them, and judgment was given unto them: and I saw the souls of them that were beheaded for the witness of Jesus, and for the word of God, and which had not worshipped the beast, neither his image, neither had received his mark upon their foreheads, or in their hands; and they lived and reigned with Christ a thousand years."

EIGHTH PROPOSITION: At the Coming Again of Jesus Christ His people shall live and reign with Him.

NOTE.—This verse seems to refer primarily to the tribulation saints, but by implication to all believers. Certainly the bride must reign with her husband.

(3) As REGARDS ISRAEL.

(a) Is. 25: 9—"And it shall be said in that day, Lo, this is our God; we have waited for him, and he will save us: this is the LORD; we have waited for him, we will be glad and rejoice in his salvation."

FIRST PROPOSITION: Because of the Coming Again of Jesus Christ there shall be great joy among His people.

This can hardly be limited to Israel, but the context seems to imply that the primary reference is to them.

(*b*) Is. 11: 11, 12—"And it shall come to pass in that day, that the Lord shall set his hand again the second time to recover the remnant of his people, which shall be left, from Assyria, and from Egypt, and from Pathros, and from Cush, and from Elam, and from Shinar, and from Hamath, and from the islands of the sea. And he shall set up an ensign for the nations, and shall assemble the outcasts of Israel, and gather together the dispersed of Judah from the four corners of the earth."

Ezek. 36: 24, R.V.—"For I will take you from among the nations, and gather you out of all the countries, and will bring you into your own land."

Ezek. 37: 21—"And say unto them, Thus saith the Lord God: Behold, I will take the children of Israel from among the nations, whither they be gone, and will gather them on every side, and bring them into their own land."

Zeph. 3: 19, 20—"Behold, at that time I will undo all that afflict thee: and I will save her that halteth, and gather her that was driven out; and will get them praise and fame in every land where they have been put to shame. At that time I will bring you again, even at the time that I gather you: for I will make you a name and a praise among all people of the earth, when I turn back your captivity before your eyes, saith the Lord."

SECOND PROPOSITION: Because of the Coming Again of Jesus Christ the children of Israel shall be gathered together from among the nations, from the four corners of the earth, and brought into their own land.

(*c*) Ezek. 37: 19, 22, 24 (See context)—"Say unto them, Thus saith the Lord God; Behold, I will take the stick of Joseph, which is in the hand of Ephraim, and the tribes of Israel his fellows, and will put them with him, even with the stick of Judah, and make them one stick, and they shall be one in my hand. And I will make them one nation in the land upon the mountains of Israel; and one king shall be king to them all: and they shall be no more two nations, neither shall they be divided into two kingdoms any more at all. And David my servant shall be king over them; and they all shall have one shepherd: they shall also walk in my judgments, and observe my statutes, and do them."

THIRD PROPOSITION: At the Coming Again of Jesus Christ divided Israel—Ephraim and Judah—shall be reunited into one nation under the one king David—Jesus.

(*d*) Jer. 23: 5, 6—"Behold the days come, saith the LORD, that I will raise unto David a righteous Branch, and a king shall reign and prosper, and shall execute judgment and justice in the earth. In his days Judah shall be saved, and Israel shall dwell safely: and this is his name whereby he shall be called, THE LORD OUR RIGHTEOUSNESS."

FOURTH PROPOSITION: Because of the Coming Again of Jesus Christ Judah shall be saved and Israel shall dwell safely.

(Compare Rom. 11: 26—"And so all Israel shall be saved: as it is written, There shall come out of Sion the Deliverer, and shall turn away ungodliness from Jacob.")

(*e*) Ezek. 37: 23—"Neither shall they defile themselves any more with their idols, nor with their detestable things, nor with any of their transgressions: but I will save them out of all their dwelling places, wherein they have sinned, and will cleanse them: so shall they be my people, and I will be their God."

Ezek. 36: 25-27, 29 (Note context)—"Then will I sprinkle clean water upon you, and ye shall be clean: from all your filthiness, and from all your idols, will I cleanse you. A new heart also will I give you, and a new spirit will I put within you: and I will take away the stony heart out of your flesh, and I will give you a heart of flesh. And I will put my spirit within you, and cause you to walk in my statutes, and ye shall keep my judgments, and do them. I will also save you from all your uncleannesses: and I will call for the corn, and will increase it, and lay no famine upon you."

FIFTH PROPOSITION: Because of the Coming Again of Jesus Christ Israel shall be cleansed from all their filthiness and from all their idols, a new heart will be given them and a new spirit put within them, the stony heart shall be taken away from them and they given a heart of flesh. God will put His Spirit within them and cause them to walk in his statutes and they shall keep His judgments and do them.

(Compare Jer. 31: 31-34—"Behold, the days come, saith the LORD, that I will make a new covenant with the house of Israel, and with the house of Judah: Not according to the covenant that I made with their fathers, in the day that I took them by the hand to bring them out of the land of Egypt; which my covenant they brake, although I was a husband unto them, saith the LORD: But this shall be the covenant that I will make with the house of Israel; After those days, saith the LORD, I will put my law in their inward parts, and write it in their hearts; and will be their God and they shall be my people. And they shall teach no more every man his neighbor, and every man his brother, saying, Know the LORD: for they shall all know me, from the

least of them unto the greatest of them, saith the Lord: for I will forgive their iniquity, and I will remember their sin no more.")

(*f*) Ezek. 36: 37, 38—"Thus saith the Lord God; I will yet for this
be inquired of by the house of Israel, to do it for them; I will increase
them with men like a flock. As the holy flock, as the flock of Jerusalem
in her solemn feasts; so shall the waste cities be filled with flocks of
men: and they shall know that I am the Lord."

Jer. 31: 27—"Behold the days come, saith the Lord, that I will
sow the house of Israel and the house of Judah with the seed of man,
and with the seed of beast."

Ezek. 36: 33-37—"Thus saith the Lord God; in the day that I shall
have cleansed you from all your iniquities I will also cause you to dwell
in the cities, and the wastes shall be builded. And the desolate land
shall be tilled, whereas it lay desolate in the sight of all that passed by.
And they shall say, this land that was desolate is become like the
garden of Eden; and the waste and desolate and ruined cities are
become fenced, and are inhabited. Then the heathen that are left
round about you shall know that I the Lord build the ruined places
and plant that that was desolate: I the Lord have spoken it, and I will
do it. Thus saith the Lord God; I will yet for this be inquired of by
the house of Israel, to do it for them; I will increase them with men like
a flock. As the holy flock, as the flock of Jerusalem in her solemn
feasts; so shall the waste cities be filled with flocks of men: and they
shall know that I am the Lord."

Zech. 8: 3-5—"Thus saith the Lord; I am returned unto Zion, and
will dwell in the midst of Jerusalem: and Jerusalem shall be called a
city of truth; and the mountain of the Lord of hosts, The holy mountain. Thus saith the Lord of hosts: There shall yet old men and old
women dwell in the streets of Jerusalem, every man with his staff in
his hand for very age. And the streets of the city shall be full of boys
and girls playing in the streets thereof."

*SIXTH PROPOSITION: Because of the Coming Again of Jesus
Christ and the events that grow out of that coming Israel shall
be wondrously multiplied, and the waste, desolate and ruined cities
shall be rebuilt, and the desolate land made like the garden of
Eden. Jerusalem shall be called " the City of Truth," and shall
be filled with peace, prosperity and gladness.*

(*g*) Zech. 8: 23—"Thus saith the Lord of hosts; In those days it
shall come to pass, that ten men shall take hold out of all languages of
the nations, even shall take hold of the skirt of him that is a Jew, saying, We will go with you: for we have heard that God is with you."

Is. 49: 22, 23—"Thus saith the Lord God, Behold, I will lift up my
hand to the Gentiles, and set up my standard to the people: and they
shall bring thy sons in their arms, and thy daughters shall be carried

upou their shoulders. And kings shall be thy nursing fathers, and their queens thy nursing mothers: they shall bow down to thee with their face toward the earth, and lick up the dust of thy feet; and thou shalt know that I am the LORD: for they shall not be ashamed that wait for me."

SEVENTH PROPOSITION: Because of the Coming Again of Jesus Christ Israel shall be greatly exalted above the nations.

(*h*) Is. 66: 19 (Note context)—"And I will set a sign among them, and I will send those that escape of them unto the nations, to Tarshish, Pul, and Lud, that draw the bow, to Tubal and Javan, to the isles afar off, that have not heard my fame, neither have seen my glory; and they shall declare my glory among the Gentiles."

EIGHTH PROPOSITION: At the Coming Again of Jesus Christ Israel shall go forth as preachers of the glory of Jehovah to the nations.

(4) As Regards the Nations and Unregenerate Individuals.

(*a*) Matt. 24: 30—"And then shall appear the sign of the Son of man in heaven: and then shall all the tribes of the earth mourn, and they shall see the Son of man coming in the clouds of heaven with power and great glory."

Rev. 1: 7, R.V.—"Behold he cometh with the clouds; and every eye shall see him, and they which pierced him; and all the tribes of the earth shall mourn over him. Even so, Amen."

FIRST PROPOSITION: At the Coming Again of Jesus Christ all the tribes of the earth shall mourn over Him.

The gladdest day of all for His people, the saddest day of all for those who are not His people

(*b*) Matt. 25: 31, 32—"When the Son of man shall come in his glory, and all the holy angels with him, then shall he sit upon the throne of his glory: And before him shall be gathered all nations."

SECOND PROPOSITION: At the Coming Again of Jesus Christ all the nations shall be gathered before Him for judgment, and He shall separate them one from another, as a shepherd divideth his sheep from his goats, &c.

(*c*) Acts 15: 16, 17—"After this I will return, and will build again the tabernacle of David, which is fallen down; and I will build again the ruins thereof, and I will set it up: That the residue of men might seek after the Lord, and all the Gentiles, upon whom my name is called, saith the Lord, who doeth all these things."

Zech. 8: 20–23, R.V.—"Thus saith the LORD of hosts: It shall yet come to pass, that there shall come peoples, and the inhabitants of many cities: and the inhabitants of one city shall go to another, say-ing, let us go speedily to intreat the favor of the LORD, and to seek the LORD of hosts: I will go also. Yea, many peoples and strong nations shall come to seek the LORD of hosts in Jerusalem, and to intreat the favor of the LORD. Thus saith the LORD of hosts: In those days it shall come to pass, that ten men shall take hold, out of all the lan-guages of the nations, shall even take hold of the skirt of him that is a Jew, saying, We will go with you, for we have heard that God is with you."

Is. 2: 2, 3—"And it shall come to pass in the last days, that the mountain of the LORD's house shall be established in the top of the mountains, and shall be exalted above the hills; and all nations shall flow unto it. And many people shall go and say, Come ye, and let us go up to the mountain of the LORD, to the house of the God of Jacob; and he will teach us of his ways, and we will walk in his paths: for out of Zion shall go forth the law, and the word of the LORD from Jerusalem."

THIRD PROPOSITION: At the Coming Again of Jesus Christ the residue of men and all the Gentiles (nations) upon whom His name is called will seek after the Lord. Peoples shall come and the inhabitants of many cities. Yea, many peoples and strong nations shall come to seek the Lord of Hosts in Jerusalem, and to intreat the favor of the Lord.

QUESTION: How can this be if immediately upon His coming the nations are gathered before Him, judged, separated and as-signed to their eternal destiny?

ANSWER.—It is not said that *immediately upon* His coming the nations will be gathered, etc. Our difficulties arise from the fact that we assume what the Bible never asserts nor implies; viz., that these things are all crowded into a day or a few days or a year. These events are connected with and result from His coming, but they take time for their development. I doubt if the prophecies are intended to give us a definite and detailed history in their order of all the events connected with the Lord's coming. The great important facts necessary to keep us watching and to cheer our hearts and fire us for our work are given in outline. But always remember that, while prophecy is exactly and literally true in every word, prophecy is not history.

(*d*) Ps. 2:9 (See context vv. 6, 8.)—"Thou shalt break them with a rod of iron: thou shalt dash them in pieces like a potter's vessel."

FOURTH PROPOSITION: At the Coming Again of Jesus Christ and His glorious reign, rebels against Him will be shattered.

(*e*) 2 Thess. 1: 7–9, R.V.—"And to you that are afflicted rest with us, at the revelation of the Lord Jesus from heaven with the angels of his power in flaming fire, rendering vengeance to them that know not God, and to them that obey not the gospel of our Lord Jesus: who shall suffer punishment, even eternal destruction from the face of the Lord and from the glory of his might."

FIFTH PROPOSITION: At the Coming Again of Jesus Christ those who know not God and those who obey not the Gospel of our Lord Jesus Christ shall suffer punishment, even eternal destruction from the face of the Lord and from the Glory of His might.

(As to what "destruction" means, compare Rev. 17: 11, with 20: 10, and Rev. 19: 20. See also, chapter on the future destiny of those who reject the redemption that is in Jesus Christ.)

(*f*) Zech. 14: 16—"And it shall come to pass, that every one that is left of all the nations which come against Jerusalem, shall even go up from year to year to worship the king, the LORD of hosts, and to keep the feast of tabernacles."

Is. 49: 7—"Thus saith the LORD, the Redeemer of Israel, and his Holy One, to him whom man despiseth, to him whom the nations abhorreth, to a servant of rulers, Kings shall see and arise, princes also shall worship, because of the LORD that is faithful, and the Holy One of Israel, and he shall choose thee."

Rev. 15: 4—"Who shall not fear thee, O Lord, and glorify thy name ? for thou only art holy: for all nations shall come and worship before thee; for thy judgments are made manifest."

Ps. 2: 8—"Ask of me and I shall give thee the heathen for thine inheritance, and the uttermost parts of the earth for thy possession."

Ps. 72: 8–11—"He shall have dominion also from sea to sea, and from the river unto the ends of the earth. They that dwell in the wilderness shall bow before him; and his enemies shall lick the dust. The kings of Tarshish and of the isles shall bring presents: the kings of Sheba and Seba shall offer gifts. Yea, all kings shall fall down before him: all nations shall serve him."

SIXTH PROPOSITION. At the Coming Again of Jesus Christ every one that is left of the nations, and kings and princes shall worship and serve Jesus Christ.

(*g*) Zech. 9: 10—"And I will cut off the chariot from Ephraim, and the horse from Jerusalem, and the battle bow shall be cut off: and he shall speak peace unto the heathen: and his dominion shall be from sea even to sea, and from the river even unto the ends of the earth."

Rev. 11: 15, R.V.—"And the seventh angel sounded; and there followed great voices in heaven, and they said, The kingdom of the world is become the kingdom of our Lord, and of his Christ: and he shall reign for ever and ever."

SEVENTH PROPOSITION: At the Coming Again of Jesus Christ the kingdom of this world shall become the kingdom of our Lord and of His Christ: and He shall reign forever and ever.

(*h*) Is. 2: 4 (See context v. 2)—"And he shall judge among the nations, and shall rebuke many people: and they shall beat their swords into ploughshares, and their spears into pruning-hooks: nation shall not lift up sword against nation, neither shall they learn war any more."

Mic. 4: 3, 4—"And he shall judge among many people and rebuke strong nations afar off; and they shall beat their swords into ploughshares, and their spears into pruning hooks: nation shall not lift up a sword against nation, neither shall they learn war any more. But they shall sit every man under his vine and under his fig tree; and none shall make them afraid: for the mouth of the LORD of hosts hath spoken it."

Ps. 72: 7, 16—"In his days shall the righteous flourish; and abundance of peace so long as the moon endureth. There shall be a handful of corn in the earth upon the top of the mountains; the fruit thereof shall shake like Lebanon: and they of the city shall flourish like grass of the earth."

EIGHTH PROPOSITION: At the Coming Again of Jesus Christ war shall cease, peace and plenty shall reign, and the righteous shall flourish.

(5) THE RESULTS OF CHRIST'S COMING AS REGARDS HUMAN SOCIETY AS A WHOLE.

(*a*) Is. 11:9—"They shall not hurt nor destroy in all my holy mountain: for the earth shall be full of the knowledge of the LORD, as the waters cover the sea."

FIRST PROPOSITION. The earth shall be full of the knowledge of the Lord, as the waters cover the sea.

The day of Christ's Coming Again and reign will indeed be the golden age and well may we cry, "Amen; come Lord Jesus."

(6) THE RESULTS OF CHRIST'S COMING AGAIN AS REGARDS THE ANTI-CHRIST AND THE DEVIL.

(a) 2 Thess. 2: 8, R.V.—"And then shall be revealed the lawless one, whom the Lord Jesus shall slay with the breath of his mouth, and bring to nought by the manifestation of his coming."

FIRST PROPOSITION: The Anti-Christ shall be slain (or put out of the way.   Compare Rev. 19 20.) *by the breath of His mouth and brought to naught by the manifestation of His coming.*

(b)   Rev. 20: 1–3, R.V.—"And I saw an angel coming down out of heaven, having the key of the abyss and a great chain in his hand. And he laid hold on the dragon, the old serpent, which is the Devil and Satan, and bound him for a thousand years, and cast him into the abyss, and shut it, and sealed it over him, that he should deceive the nations no more, until the thousand years should be finished: after this he must be loosed for a little time."

Rev. 20: 10, R.V.—"And the devil that deceived them was cast into the lake of fire and brimstone, where are also the beast and the false prophet; and they shall be tormented day and night forever and ever."

SECOND PROPOSITION: The Devil shall be chained and cast into the abyss for a thousand years, and then after a little space of liberty be cast into the lake of fire where he shall be tormented day and night forever and ever.

(7) THE RESULTS OF CHRIST'S COMING AGAIN AS REGARDS THE PHYSICAL UNIVERSE.

(a)   Rom. 8: 19–21, R.V.—"For the earnest expectation of the creation waiteth for the revealing of the sons of God. For the creation was subjected to vanity, not of its own will, but by reason of him who subjected it, in hope that the creation itself also shall be delivered from the bondage of corruption into the liberty of the glory of the children of God."

Is. 55: 13   (See context).—" Instead of the thorn shall come up the fir tree, and instead of the brier shall come up the myrtle tree: and it shall be to the LORD for a name, for an everlasting sign that shall not be cut off."

Is. 65: 25—"The wolf and the lamb shall feed together, and the lion shall eat straw like the bullock: and dust shall be the serpent's meat.   They shall not hurt nor destroy in all my holy mountain, saith the LORD."

Is. 32: 15—"Until the Spirit be poured upon us from on high, and the wilderness be a fruitful field, and the fruitful field be counted for a forest."

Is. 35: 1, R.V.—"The wilderness and the solitary place shall be glad; and the desert shall rejoice, and blossom as the rose." (Context vv. 2, 4.)

FIRST PROPOSITION: In connection with Christ's Coming Again—the creation itself shall be delivered from the corruption to which it is now subject into the liberty of the glory of the children of God. Thorns, briers and carnage shall be no more. The wilderness and the solitary place shall be glad, and the desert shall rejoice and blossom as the rose.

(*b*) 2 Pet. 3: 12, 13—"Looking for and hasting unto the coming of the day of God, wherein the heavens being on fire shall be dissolved, and the elements shall melt with fervent heat? Nevertheless we, according to his promise, looking for new heavens and a new earth, wherein dwelleth righteousness."

Rev. 21: 1—"And I saw a new heaven and a new earth: for the first heaven and the first earth were passed away; and there was no more sea."

SECOND PROPOSITION: There shall be a new heaven and a new earth. (Compare Rev. 21: 2–27.)

As the result of Christ's coming there will be a new and glorious man, in a new and glorious body, in a new and glorious society, in a new and glorious universe.

"Amen Come Lord Jesus."

VI. The time of the Coming Again of Jesus Christ.

(1) Matt. 24: 36, 42—"But of that day and hour knoweth no man, no, not the angels of heaven, but my Father only. Watch therefore; for ye know not what hour your Lord doth come."

Mark 13: 32—"But of that day and that hour knoweth no man, no, not the angels which are in heaven, neither the son, but the Father."

FIRST PROPOSITION: The exact time of the Coming Again of Jesus Christ is not revealed to us.

NOTE.—Calculations from the data given in Daniel by which some try to fix the exact date of Christ's return are utterly unreliable. They attempt the impossible. The statements were not intended to give us a clue to the exact date of Christ's return. It is a part of God's purpose and method in dealing with men to keep them in uncertainty on this point. The prophecies of Daniel were extant in the day when Christ uttered Mark 13: 32—"But of that day and that hour knoweth no man, no, not the angels which are in heaven, neither the Son, but the Father." And He doubtless understood the lessons those prophecies were intended to teach, but He distinctly declares that even He did not know the day or the hour of His coming again. Any teacher who attempts to fix the date of Christ's return is at once discredited, and it is entirely unnecessary to wade through his calculations. God does not desire us to know just when His Son shall return. Acts 1: 7—"And he said unto them, It is not for you to know the times or the seasons, *which the Father hath put in his own power.*" Let us leave the times where God has put them, "in his own power." He does desire that we shall be always ready for that return.

(2) Matt. 24: 44:—"Therefore be ye also ready: for in such an hour as ye think not the Son of man cometh."

SECOND PROPOSITION: The Coming Again of Jesus Christ will be at such a time as even His disciples think not. Even the faithful and wise servant will be taken unawares, but he will be found doing His Master's will. (vv. 45, 46.)

(3) Luke 17: 26-30—"And as it was in the days of Noe, so shall it be also in the days of the Son of man. They did eat, they drank, they married wives, they were given in marriage, until the day that Noe entered into the ark, and the flood came, and destroyed them all. Likewise also as it was in the days of Lot; they did eat, they drank, they bought, they sold, they planted, they builded; But the same day that Lot went out of Sodom it rained fire and brimstone from heaven, and destroyed them all. Even so shall it be in the day when the Son of man is revealed."

THIRD PROPOSITION: The time when the Son of man is revealed will be a time when the world is absorbed in its usual occupations.

(4) 2 Thess. 2: 2-4—"That ye be not soon shaken in mind, or be troubled, neither by spirit, nor by word, nor by letter as from us, as that the day of Christ is at hand. Let no man deceive you by any means: for that day shall not come, except there come a falling away first, and that man of sin be revealed, the son of perdition; Who opposeth and exalted himself above all that is called God, or that is worshipped; so that he as God sitteth in the temple of God, shewing himself that he is God."

FOURTH PROPOSITION: The day of the Lord will not come until after the revelation of the man of sin.

Of course the day of the Lord is the time of the Lord's coming to the earth. This is preceded by His coming in the air to receive His bride, the Church, unto Himself. (1 Thess. 4: 16, 17.) There is nothing to show that quite an interim may not occur between this coming of Christ for His saints in the air and His coming with His saints to the earth. There are indications that there must be such an interval. (*a*) Christ has much to do with His people before He comes to deal with the world. (*b*) It is distinctly taught that there is now a restraining power that hinders the manifestation of the man of sin. (2 Thess. 2, vv. 6, 7, R. V.) It is natural to presume that this restraining power has something to do with the Church.

(5) 1 Tim. 4: 1—"Now the Spirit speaketh expressly, that in the latter times some shall depart from the faith, giving heed to seducing spirits, and doctrines of devils."

2 Ti. 3: 1–5, R.V.—"But know this, that in the last days *grievous times shall come*. For men shall be lovers of self, lovers of money, boastful, haughty, railers, disobedient to parents, unthankful, unholy, without natural affection, implacable, slanderers, without self-control, fierce, no lovers of good, traitors, headstrong, puffed up, lovers of pleasure rather than lovers of God; holding a form of godliness, but having denied the power thereof: from these also turn away."

Luke 18: 8—"I tell you that he will avenge them speedily. Never-theless, when the Son of man cometh, shall he find faith on the earth ?"

FIFTH PROPOSITION: *The last days, and the time of the Coming Again of the Son of man, will be a time of apostasy, grievous times, and faith will be hard to find.*

2 Tim. 3: 1–5, gives a very accurate picture of our own time. But we should bear in mind that earnest men of God and students of the Bible have often thought in times past that the coming of the Lord was very near. So it was and they were not mistaken, as were those who thought it was so far away that they let it have no effect over their lives. The multiplying iniquities of our day, the apostasy of many professed Christians, preachers and professors of theology into damning error and unbelief, the increase of lawlessness on the part of great corporations on the one hand and the oppressed poor on the other—these are all signs of His coming, which may be very near at hand. Men's hearts are "fainting for fear, and for expectation of the things which are coming on the world." (Luke 21: 26, R. V.) But when we see these things begin to come to pass we should then look up and lift up our heads because our redemption draweth nigh. (Luke 21: 28.)

(6) Mark 13: 34, 35, 36—"For the Son of man is as a man taking a far journey, who left his house, and gave authority to his servants,

and to every man his work, and commanded the porter to watch. Watch ye therefore: for we know not when the master of the house cometh, at even, or at midnight, or at the cockcrowing, or in the morning: lest coming suddenly he find you sleeping."

Luke 12: 35, 36—" Let your loins be girded about, and your lights burning; and ye yourselves like unto men that wait for their Lord, when he will return from the wedding: that when he cometh and knocketh, they may open unto him immediately."

Matt. 25: 13—"Watch therefore; for ye know neither the day nor the hour wherein the Son of man cometh."

Matt. 24: 42, 44—"Watch therefore; for ye know not what hour your Lord doth come. Therefore be ye also ready: for in such an hour as ye think not the Son of man cometh."

SIXTH PROPOSITION: We are repeatedly exhorted to be watching, looking and ready for our Lord's return. It must, therefore, be an event that, as far as we know, may occur at any moment.

There is no event predicted in Scripture, or series of events, that must occur before Jesus comes to receive His own unto Himself. There are events that must occur before He comes to the earth with His saints. (2 Thess. 2.) He may come for us *as far as we know* at any moment, and it stands us in hand to be always ready, for in such an hour as we think not the Son of man cometh. (Matt. 24: 44.)

QUESTIONS: *First.* Is not the world to be converted before Jesus Christ comes ?

ANSWER:—

Rev. 1: 7—"Behold, he cometh with clouds; and every eye shall see him, and they also which pierced him: and all kindreds of the earth shall wail because of him. Even so, Amen."

Matt. 25: 31, 32—"When the Son of man shall come in his glory, and all the holy angels with him, then shall he sit upon the throne of his glory: And before him shall be gathered all nations: and he shall separate them one from another, as a shepherd divideth his sheep from the goats."

2 Thess. 2: 2-4, 8—"That ye be not soon shaken in mind, or be troubled, neither by spirit, nor by word, nor by letter as from us, as that the day of Christ is at hand. Let no man deceive you by any means: for that day shall not come, except there come a falling away first, and that man of sin be revealed, the son of perdition; who opposeth and exalteth himself above all that is called God, or that is worshipped; so that he as God sitteth in the temple of God, shewing himself that he is God. And then shall that Wicked one be revealed, whom the Lord shall consume with the spirit of his mouth, and shall destroy with the brightness of his coming."

Luke 18: 8—" I tell you that he will avenge them speedily. Nevertheless, when the Son of man cometh, shall he find faith on the earth ?"

Luke 21: 35—"For as a snare shall it come on all them that dwell on the face of the whole earth."

2 Tim. 3: 1-5—"This know also, that in the last days perilous times shall come. For men shall be lovers of their own selves, covetous, boasters, proud, blasphemers, disobedient to parents, unthankful, unholy, without natural affection, trucebreakers, false accusers, incontinent, fierce, despisers of those that are good, traitors, heady, high-minded, lovers of pleasures more than lovers of God; having a form of godliness, but denying the power thereof: from such turn away."

These passages show us a world anything but converted at the coming of Christ. 2 Thess. 1: 7-10—["And to you who are troubled rest with us, when the Lord Jesus shall be revealed from heaven with his mighty angels, in flaming fire taking vengeance on them that know not God, and that obey not the gospel of our Lord Jesus Christ: Who shall be punished with everlasting destruction from the presence of the Lord, and from the glory of his power; When he shall come to be glorified in his saints, and to be admired in all them that believe (because our testimony among you was believed) in that day,"] shows us two classes—converted and unconverted—at the revelation 'of Jesus Christ from heaven.

Second. How shall we explain Matt. 24: 14—"And this gospel of the kingdom shall be preached in all the world for a witness unto all nations; and then shall the end come?"

ANSWER: (1) This verse tells us that the gospel is to be preached "*for a testimony*" (R. V.) unto all the nations, not that all the nations will be converted. (2) In a sense, in a scriptural sense too, this has already been done. (Rom. 10: 18—"But I say, Have they not heard? Yes verily, their sound went into all the earth, and their works unto the ends of the world." Col. 1: 23, (R. V.)—"If so be that ye continue in the faith, grounded and stedfast, and not moved away from the hope of the gospel which ye heard, which was preached in all creation under heaven; whereof I Paul was made a minister.") (3) It shall be preached before *the end* come," but the coming of Jesus Christ to receive His own is not the end but the beginning of the end.

Third. How shall we explain 2 Thess. 2: 1-4—"Now we beseech you, brethren, by the coming of our Lord Jesus Christ, and by our gathering together unto him, that ye be not soon shaken in mind, or be troubled, neither by spirit, nor by word, nor by letter as from us, as that the day of Christ is at hand

Let no man deceive you by any means: for that day shall not come, except there come a falling away first, and that man of sin be revealed, the son of perdition; who opposeth and exalteth himself above all that is called God, or that is worshipped; so that he as God sitteth in the temple of God, shewing himself that he is God."

ANSWER: It is true that the man of sin must be revealed before "*the day of the Lord* is present." (R.V.) But the day of the Lord is not the coming of Christ to receive His Church but that which follows it. How closely it follows it, it is difficult to say. The Thessalonians were troubled by the doctrine that the Day of the Lord was, not at hand, as Authorized Version reads, but already begun. This Paul shows them could not be, for "the man of sin," who was to be especially dealt with in the Day of the Lord, had not yet been revealed. There is reason to think, as already said, that the taking away of the Church must precede this revelation of the man of sin.

NOTE.—There is a quite widely accepted theory that "the man of sin" has already been revealed in the Pope. But he does not fill out the picture. In the Pope there is a preparing for the man of sin.

Fourth. Will the Church pass through the great tribulation?

ANSWER: It is clear from the Bible that the Church will pass through *tribulation* (Acts 14: 22; and other passages), but that does not prove at all that the Church will pass through "*the great tribulation*," when God deals with a Christ-rejecting world. There is much to indicate that the Church will be sheltered during this period. (Luke 21: 36. See also the whole book of Revelation where all after Ch. 4: 1, has to do with the time after "the Rapture of the Church.")

Fifth. Is the world getting better?

ANSWER: 1 Jno. 5: 19, R. V.—"We know that we are of God, and the whole world lieth in the evil one." In Biblical usage "the world" is the body of men and women that rejects Christ and lies in the wicked one. The Devil is its God (2 Cor. 4: 4.), and of course it is necessarily growing worse. But if we mean by "the world"—as men usually mean when they ask this question—the entire mass of men, Christians and non-Christians, then it is to be said that there are two developments going on side by side, the development of the kingdom of God and the development of the kingdom of Satan, to be brought to a crisis when the Anti-Christ is developed at the head of the one and the Christ appears at the head of the other. This crisis will end in the complete victory of Christ and the kingdom of God. In the meantime, on the one hand God is gathering out of the world a people for His name (Acts 15: 14), and His people are growing in the knowledge and likeness of himself, and the world is of necessity to a certain extent influenced by them. On the other hand, there is a development of "the mystery of lawlessness" (2 Thess. 2: 7, R. V.), resulting in increasing error and apostasy in the professing Church as well as out of it, and in growing immorality, and especially the development of anarchy or "lawlessness" among all classes of society.

BOOK III.

—

WHAT THE BIBLE TEACHES ABOUT THE HOLY SPIRIT.

CHAPTER I.

THE PERSONALITY OF THE HOLY SPIRIT.

I. The Importance of the Doctrine.

1. It is of the highest importance from the standpoint of worship that we decide whether the Holy Spirit is a divine person worthy to receive our adoration, our faith and our love, or simply an influence emanating from God, or a power that God imparts to us. If the Holy Spirit is a Divine Person and we know it not, we are robbing a Divine Being of the love and adoration which are his due.

2. It is of the highest practical importance that we decide whether the Holy Spirit is a power that we in our weakness and ignorance are somehow to get hold of and use, or whether the Holy Spirit is a personal being infinitely wise, infinitely holy, infinitely tender, who is to get hold of and use us. The one conception is heathenish, the other Christian. The one conception leads to self-humiliation, self-emptying and self-renunciation; the other conception leads to self-exaltation.

3. It is of the highest experimental importance that we know the Holy Spirit as a person. Many can testify to the blessing that came into their lives when they came to know the Holy Spirit not merely as a gracious influence (emanating, it is true, from God), but as an ever-present loving-friend and helper.

II. The Fact of the Personality of the Holy Spirit.

1. THE USE OF PERSONAL PRONOUNS.

Jno. 15: 26—"But when the Comforter is come, whom I will send unto you from the Father, even the Spirit of truth, which proceedeth from the Father, He shall testify of me."

Jno. 16: 7, 8, 13, 14—"Nevertheless I tell you the truth; It is expedient for you that I go away: for if I go not away, the Comforter will not come unto you; but if I depart, I will send Him unto you. And when he is come, He will reprove the world of sin, and of righteousness, and of judgment."

"Howbeit when He, the spirit of truth, is come, he will guide you into all truth: for he will not speak of Himself; but whatsoever he shall hear, that shall he speak: and he will show you things to come. He shall glorify me: for he shall receive of mine, and shall show it unto you."

FIRST PROPOSITION: Various pronouns that clearly imply personality are repeatedly used of the Holy Spirit.

The use of these pronouns is the more remarkable from the fact that in the Greek language the word for Spirit is a neuter noun, and, according to Greek usage, the pronouns that refer to it should be neuter, and yet in numerous instances a masculine pronoun is used, thus bringing out very strikingly how the Bible idea of the personality of the Holy Spirit dominates grammatical construction. There are instances, of course, where the natural grammatical usage is followed and a neuter pronoun used. (Rom· 8: 16, 26.) But in many instances this construction is set aside and the masculine personal pronoun used to refer to the neuter noun.

2. Personal Characteristics Ascribed to the Holy Spirit.

(1) 1 Cor. 2: 10, 11—"For God hath revealed them unto us by his Spirit: for the Spirit searcheth all things, yea, the deep things of God. For what man knoweth the things of a man, save the spirit of man which is in him? even so the things of God knoweth no man, but the Spirit of God."

Knowledge is ascribed to the Holy Spirit.

(2) 1 Cor. 12: 11—"But all these worketh that one and the self-same Spirit, dividing to every man severally as he will."

Will is ascribed to the Spirit.

(3) Rom. 8: 27—"And he that searcheth the hearts knoweth what is in the mind of the Spirit, because he maketh intercession for the saints according to the will of God."

Mind is ascribed to the Holy Spirit. The word here translated mind is a comprehensive word including the ideas of thought, feeling and purpose. (Compare Rom. 8: 7—"Because the carnal mind is enmity against God; for it is not subject to the law of God, neither indeed can be.")

(4) Rom. 15: 30—"Now I beseech you, brethren, for the Lord Jesus Christ's sake, and for the love of the Spirit, that ye strive together with me in your prayers to God for me."

Love is ascribed to the Holy Spirit.

(5) Neh. 9: 20—"Thou gavest also thy good Spirit to instruct them, and withheldest not thy manna from their mouth, and gavest them water for their thirst."

Intelligence and goodness are ascribed to the Holy Spirit. Note that this passage is from the Old Testament, where the truth of the personality of the Holy Spirit is not as fully developed as in the New Testament.

(6) Eph. 4: 30—"And grieve not the Holy Spirit of God, whereby ye are sealed unto the day of redemption."

Grief is ascribed to the Holy Spirit. The Holy Spirit thinks, feels, purposes, knows, wills, loves, grieves.

SECOND PROPOSITION: Many characteristics that only a person can possess are ascribed to the Holy Spirit.

3. PERSONAL ACTS ASCRIBED TO THE HOLY SPIRIT.

(1) 1 Cor. 2: 10—"But God hath revealed them unto us by his Spirit: for the Spirit searcheth all things, yea, the deep things of God."

The Holy Spirit searcheth the deep things of God.

(2) Rev. 2: 7—"He that hath an ear, let him hear what the Spirit saith unto the churches: To him that overcometh will I give to eat of the tree of life, which is in the midst of the paradise of God."

The Holy Spirit speaks.

(3) Gal. 4: 6—"And because ye are sons, God hath sent forth the Spirit of his Son into your hearts, crying, Abba, Father."

The Holy Spirit crieth out.

(4) Rom. 8: 26, R.V.—"And in like manner the Spirit also helpeth our infirmity: for we know not how to pray as we ought; but the Spirit himself maketh intercession for us with groanings which can not be uttered."

The Holy Spirit maketh intercession.

(5) Jno. 15:26—"But when the Comforter is come, whom I will send unto you from the Father, even the Spirit of truth, which proceedeth from the Father, he shall testify of me."

The Holy Spirit gives testimony.

(6) Jno. 14: 26—"But the Comforter, which is the Holy Ghost, whom the Father will send in my name, he shall teach you all things, and bring all things to your remembrance, whatsoever I have said unto you." (Compare Jno. 16: 12-14:—"I have yet many things to say unto you, but ye cannot bear them now. Howbeit when he, the Spirit

of truth is come, he will guide you into all truth: for he shall not speak of himself; but whatsoever he shall hear, that shall he speak: and he will show you things to come. He shall glorify me: for he shall receive of mine, and shall show it unto you." Neh. 9: 20—"Thou gavest also thy good Spirit to instruct them, and withheldest not thy manna from their mouth, and gavest them water for their thirst.")

The Holy Spirit teaches all the truth.

(7) Rom. 8: 14—"For as many as are led by the Spirit of God, they are the sons of God."

The Holy Spirit leads or directs men what to do.

(8) Acts 16: 6, 7—"Now when they had gone throughout Phrygia and the region of Galatia, and were forbidden of the Holy Ghost to preach the word in Asia, After they were come to Mysia, they assayed to go into Bithynia: but the Spirit suffered them not."

The Holy Spirit commands men.

(9) Acts 13: 2—"As they ministered to the Lord, and fasted, the Holy Ghost said, Separate me Barnabas and Saul for the work whereunto I have called them."

Acts 20: 28—"Take heed therefore unto yourselves, and to all the flock, over the which the Holy Ghost hath made you overseers, to feed the church of God, which he hath purchased with his own blood."

The Holy Spirit calls men to work and appoints them to office.

(10) Jno. 15: 26—"But when the Comforter is come, whom I will send unto you from the Father, even the Spirit of truth, which proceedeth from the Father, he shall testify of me."

The Holy Spirit goes forth upon the mission to which He is sent.

THIRD PROPOSITION: Many acts that only a person can perform are ascribed to the Holy Spirit.

4. PERSONAL OFFICE.

(1) Jno. 14: 16, 17—"And I will pray the Father, and he shall give you another Comforter, that he may abide with you forever; Even the Spirit of truth; whom the world cannot receive, because it seeth him not, neither knoweth him: but ye know him; for he dwelleth with you, and shall be in you."

It is the office of the Holy Spirit to be "another Comforter" (or paraclete) to take the place of the absent Saviour. Is it possible that Jesus Christ could use such language in speaking of an impersonal influence or power? (Of Jno. 16: 7.)

FOURTH PROPOSITION: An Office is predicated of the Holy Spirit that could only be predicated of a person.

5.   PERSONAL TREATMENT.

(1) Is. 63: 10, R.V.—"But they rebelled, and grieved his holy spirit: therefore he was turned to be their enemy, and himself fought against them."

The Holy Spirit is rebelled against and grieved.   (Compare Eph. 4: 30.)

(2) Heb. 10: 29—"Of how much sorer punishment, suppose ye, shall he be thought worthy, who hath trodden under foot the Son of God, and hath counted the blood of the covenant wherewith he is sanctified, an unholy thing, and hath done despite unto the Spirit of grace."

The Holy Spirit is "done despite unto" ("treated with contumely"—"Thayer's Greek-Eng. Lex. of the N. T.")

(3) Acts 5: 3—"But Peter said, Ananias, why hath Satan filled thine heart to lie to the Holy Ghost, and to keep back part of the price of the land?"

The Holy Spirit is lied to.

(4) Matt. 12: 31, 32—"Wherefore I say unto you, All manner of sin and blasphemy shall be forgiven unto men: but the blasphemy against the Holy Ghost shall not be forgiven unto men.   And whoso ever speaketh a word against the Son of man, it shall be forgiven him: but whosoever speaketh against the Holy Ghost, it shall not be forgiven him, neither in this world, neither in the world to come."

The Holy Spirit is blasphemed against.

FIFTH PROPOSITION: A treatment is predicated of the Holy Spirit that could only be predicated of a person.

GENERAL PROPOSITION: The Holy Spirit is a person.

Theoretically we may believe this.   Do we in our real thought of Him, or in our practical attitude toward Him, treat Him as a person?   Do we regard Him as indeed as real a person as Jesus Christ—as loving, wise and strong, as worthy of our confidence and love and surrender, as He?   He came to be to the disciples, and to us, what Christ had been to them during the days of His personal companionship with them. (Jno. 14: 16, 17.)   Do we know "the communion or fellowship" of the Holy Ghost?"   (2 Cor. 13: 14.)

CHAPTER II.

THE DEITY OF THE HOLY SPIRIT.

I. Divine Attributes.

(1) Heb. 9: 14—"How much more shall the blood of Christ, who through the *eternal* Spirit offered himself without spot to God, purge your conscience from dead works to serve the living God?"

FIRST PROPOSITION: The Holy Spirit is eternal.

(2) Ps. 139: 7-10—"Whither shall I go from thy Spirit? or whither shall I flee from thy presence? If I ascend up into heaven, thou art there: if I make my bed in hell, behold, thou art there. If I take the wings of the morning, and dwell in the uttermost parts of the sea; even there shall thy hand lead me, and thy right hand shall hold me."

SECOND PROPOSITION: The Holy Spirit is omnipresent.

(3) Luke 1: 35—"And the angel answered and said unto her, *The Holy Ghost* shall come upon thee, and the *power of the highest* shall overshadow thee: therefore also that holy thing which shall be born of thee shall be called the Son of God."

THIRD PROPOSITION: The Holy Spirit is omnipotent.

(4) 1 Cor. 2: 10, 11—"For God hath revealed them unto us by his Spirit: for the Spirit *searcheth all things*, yea, the deep things of God. For what man knoweth the things of a man, save the spirit of man which is in him? even so the things of God knoweth no man, but the Spirit of God."

Jno. 14: 26—"But the Comforter, which is the Holy Ghost, whom the Father will send in my name, he shall *teach you all things*, and bring all things to your remembrance, whatsoever I have said unto you."

Jno. 16: 12, 13—"I have yet many things to say unto you, but ye can not bear them now.   Howbeit when he, the Spirit of truth, is come, he will *guide you into all truth:* for he shall not speak of himself; but whatsoever he shall hear, that shall he speak: and he will show you things to come."

FOURTH PROPOSITION: The Holy Spirit is Omniscient.

GENERAL PROPOSITION: Each of the four distinctly Divine Attributes is ascribed to the Holy Spirit

II. Divine Works.

(1) Job. 33: 4—"The Spirit of God *hath made me*, and the breath of the Almighty hath given me life."

Ps. 104: 30—"Thou sendest forth thy spirit, *they are created*: and thou renewest the face of the earth."

FIRST PROPOSITION: Creation is ascribed to the Holy Spirit.

(2) Jno. 6: 63—"It is the Spirit that quickeneth; the flesh profiteth nothing: the words that I speak unto you, they are spirit, and they are life."

Rom. 8: 11—"But if the Spirit of him that raised up Jesus from the dead dwell in you, he that raised up Christ from the dead shall also quicken your mortal bodies by his Spirit that dwelleth in you."

Gen. 2: 7—"And the LORD God formed man of the dust of the ground, and breathed into his nostrils the breath of life; and man became a living soul.

SECOND PROPOSITION: The impartation of life is ascribed to the Holy Spirit.

(3) 2 Pet. 1: 21, R.V.—"For no prophecy ever came by the will of man: but men spake from God, being moved by the Holy Ghost."

2 Sam 23: 2, 3—"*The Spirit of the* LORD *spake* by me, and his word was in my tongue. The God of Israel said, The Rock of Israel spake to me, He that ruleth over men must be just, ruling in the fear of God."

THIRD PROPOSITION: The authorship of Divine prophecies is ascribed to the Holy Spirit.

GENERAL PROPOSITION: Three distinctively divine works are ascribed to the Holy Spirit.

III. Statements which refer to the Lord or Jehovah in the Old Testament applied to the Holy Spirit in the New Testament.

(1) Is. 6: 8–10—"Also I heard the voice of the LORD, saying, whom shall I send, and who will go for us? Then said I, Here am I; send me. And he said, Go, and tell this people, hear ye indeed, but understand not; and see ye indeed, but perceive not. Make the heart of this people fat, and make their ears heavy, and shut their eyes; lest they see with their eyes and hear with their ears, and understand with their heart, and convert, and be healed." (Compare Acts 28: 25-27: "And when they agreed not

among themselves, they departed, after that Paul had spoken one word. *Well spake the Holy Ghost* by Esaias the prophet unto our fathers, saying, Go unto this people, and say, Hearing ye shall hear, and shall not understand; and seeing ye shall see, and not perceive: For the heart of this people is waxed gross, and their ears are dull of hearing, and their eyes have they closed; lest they should see with their eyes, and hear with their ears, and understand with their hearts and should be converted, and I should heal them."

This same passage is applied to Jesus Christ. May it be that in the threefold "Holy" of the seraphic cry in Is. 6: 3, ("And one cried unto another, and said, Holy, holy, holy, is the LORD of hosts: the whole earth is full of his glory,") we have a hint of the tri-personality of the Jehovah of Hosts and hence the propriety of the threefold application of the vision ?

(2) Ex. 16: 7—"And in the morning, then ye shall see the glory of the LORD; for that he heareth your murmurings against the LORD; and what are we, that ye murmur against us ?" Compare Heb. 3: 7-9— "Wherefore as the Holy Ghost saith, To-day if ye will hear his voice, harden not your hearts, as in the provocation, in the day of temptation in the wilderness: When your fathers tempted *me*, proved *me*, and saw my works forty years." (Compare Ps. 95: 8-11.)

GENERAL PROPOSITION: Statements which in the Old Testament distinctly name the Lord, God, or Jehovah, as their subject are applied to the Holy Spirit in the New Testament. That is, the Holy Spirit occupies the position of Deity in the New Testament thought.

IV. The way in which the Name of the Holy Spirit is coupled with that of God.

(1) 1 Cor. 12: 4-6—"Now there are diversities of gifts, but *the same Spirit*. And there are differences of administrations, but *the same Lord*. And there are diversities of operations, but it is *the same God* which worketh all in all."

(2) Matt. 28: 19—"Go ye therefore, and teach all nations, baptizing them in the name of *the Father*, and of *the Son*, and of *the Holy Ghost*."

(3) 2 Cor. 13, 14—"The grace of *the Lord Jesus Christ*, and the love of *God*, and the communion of *the Holy Ghost*, be with you all. Amen."

GENERAL PROPOSITION: The name of the Holy Spirit is coupled with that of God in a way that it would be impossible for a reverent and thoughtful mind to couple the name of any finite being with that of the Deity.

V. The Divine Name.

1. Acts 5: 3, 4—"But Peter said, Ananias, why hath Satan filled thine heart to lie to *the Holy Ghost*, and to keep back part of the price of the land? While it remained, was it not thine own? and after it was sold, was it not in thine own power? why hast thou conceived this thing in thine heart? *thou hast not lied unto men, but unto God.*"

GENERAL PROPOSITION: The Holy Spirit is called God.

SUMMARY. By the ascription of all the distinctively Divine attributes, and several distinctively Divine operations, by referring statements which in the Old Testament distinctly name Jehovah, the Lord, or God, as their subject to the Holy Spirit in the New Testament, by coupling the name of the Holy Spirit with that of God in a way that it would be impossible to couple that of any finite being with that of the Deity, by calling the Holy Spirit "God," in all these unmistakable ways, God in His word distinctly proclaims that the Holy Spirit is a Divine Person.

CHAPTER III.

THE DISTINCTION OF THE HOLY SPIRIT FROM THE FATHER AND FROM HIS SON, JESUS CHRIST.

(1) Luke 3: 21, 22—"Now when all the people were baptized, it came to pass, that Jesus also being baptized, and praying, the heaven was opened, and the Holy Ghost descended in a bodily shape like a dove upon him, and a voice came from heaven, which said, Thou art my beloved Son; in thee I am well pleased."

FIRST PROPOSITION: A clear distinction is drawn between Jesus Christ, who was on the earth, the Father who spoke to him from heaven, and the Holy Spirit who descended in a bodily form as a Dove, upon Him.

(2) Matt. 28:19—"Go ye therefore, and teach all nations, baptizing them in the name of the Father, and of the Son, and of the Holy Ghost."

SECOND PROPOSITION: A clear distinction is drawn between "the name of the Father" and "of the Son" and "of the Holy Ghost."

(3) Jno. 14: 16—"And I will pray the Father, and he shall give you another Comforter, that he may abide with you forever."

THIRD PROPOSITION: A clear distinction is drawn between the Son who prays and the Father to whom He prays, and the "Another Comforter" who is given in answer to the prayer.

(4) Jno. 16: 7—"Nevertheless I tell you the truth: it is expedient for you that I go away: for if I go not away, the Comforter will not come unto you; but if I depart, I will send him unto you."

FOURTH PROPOSITION: A clear distinction is drawn between Jesus who goes away and the Holy Spirit, who comes to take His place.

(5) Acts 2: 33—"Therefore being by the right hand of God exalted, and having received of the Father the promise of the Holy Ghost, he hath shed forth this, which ye now see and hear."

FIFTH PROPOSITION.   A clear distinction is drawn between the Son exalted to the right hand of the Father, and the Father Himself, and the Holy Ghost, whom the Son receives from the Father and sheds upon the church.

GENERAL PROPOSITION: Again and again the Bible draws the clearest possible distinction between the Holy Spirit and the Father and the Son.   They are separate personalities, having mutual relations to one another, acting upon one another, speaking of or to one another, applying the pronouns of the second and third persons to one another.

It has been said that the doctrine of the Trinity is not taught in the Bible, and it is true that it is not directly taught; but the doctrine of the Trinity is the putting together of truths that are taught.   It is clearly taught in the Bible that there is but one God.   It is also clearly taught that there are three Divine Persons—the Father, the Son, and the Holy Ghost.

CHAPTER IV.

THE SUBORDINATION OF THE SPIRIT TO THE FATHER AND THE SON.

(1) Jno. 14: 26—"But the Comforter, which is the Holy Ghost, *whom the Father will send* in my name, he shall teach you all things, and bring all things to your remembrance, whatsoever I have said unto you."

Jno. 15: 26—"But when the Comforter is come, *whom I will send* unto you from the Father, even the Spirit of truth, which proceedeth from the Father, he shall testify of me."

FIRST PROPOSITION: The Holy Spirit is sent by the Father and also by the Son.

Elsewhere we are taught that Jesus Christ was sent by the Father. (Jno. 6: 29; 8: 29, 42.)

(2) Rom. 8: 9—"But ye are not in the flesh, but in the Spirit, if so be that the Spirit of God dwell in you. Now if any man have not the Spirit of Christ, he is none of his."

SECOND PROPOSITION: The Holy Spirit is called "the Spirit of God" and "the Spirit of Christ."

(Compare Acts 16: 7, R.V.—"And when they were come over against Mysia, they assayed to go into Bithynia; and *the spirit of Jesus* suffered them not.")

(3) Jno. 16: 13, R.V.—"Howbeit when he, the Spirit of truth, is come, he shall guide you into all the truth: for he shall not speak from himself; but *what things soever he shall hear*, these shall he speak: and he shall declare unto you the things that are to come."

THIRD PROPOSITION: The Holy Spirit speaks not from Himself but speaks the things which He hears.

In a similar way Jesus said of Himself "my teaching is not mine, but His that sent Me." (Jno. 7: 16; 8: 26, 40.)

(4) Jno. 16: 14—"He shall glorify me: for he shall receive of mine, and shall show it unto you."

FOURTH PROPOSITION: <u>*It is the work of the Holy Spirit to glorify Christ.*</u>

In a similar way Christ sought not His own glory but the glory of Him that sent Him. (Jno. 7: 18.)

GENERAL PROPOSITION: *The Holy Spirit in His present work is subordinated to the Father and to the Son.*

NOTE.—We shall see later that in his earthly life Jesus lived and taught and worked in the power of the Holy Spirit.

CHAPTER V.

THE NAMES OF THE HOLY SPIRIT.

(1) 1 Cor. 2: 10, R.V.—"But unto us God revealed them through *the Spirit:* for *the Spirit* searcheth all things, yea, the deep things of God."

"THE SPIRIT."

The word means "breath," or "wind." Both thoughts are in the word as applied to the Holy Spirit. In Jno. 20:22 ("And when he had said this, *he breathed on them*, and saith unto them, Receive ye the Holy Ghost,") and Gen. 2:7 ("And the LORD God formed man of the dust of the ground, and *breathed* into his nostrils the breath of life; and man became a living soul." Com pare Ps. 104: 30—"Thou sendest forth *thy spirit*, they are created: and thou renewest the face of the earth,") and Job 33: 4 (" *The Spirit of God hath made me*, and the breath of the Almighty hath given me life,") we have the idea of the Spirit as the breath of Christ and of God.

In Jno. 3: 6–8 ("That which is born of the flesh is flesh; and that which is born of the Spirit is spirit. Marvel not that I said unto thee, Ye must be born again. The wind bloweth where it listeth, and thou hearest the sound thereof, but canst not tell whence it cometh, and whither it goeth: so is every one that is born of the Spirit,") we have the idea of the Spirit as the wind. The full significance of this name as applied to the Holy Spirit it may be beyond us to fathom, but this much seems clear:

1.   That the Spirit is the outbreathing of God, His life going forth to quicken. Possibly we should notice the fact that the breath is itself the vital principle, and some have thought that the Spirit is therefore the inmost life of God.

2.   The Spirit, like the wind, is (*a*) *Sovereign.* "Bloweth where it listeth." (Jno. 3: 8.) (Compare 1 Cor. 12: 11—"But all these worketh that one and the selfsame Spirit, dividing to every man severally as he will.") (*b*) *Invisible.* "Thou hearest the

sound thereof." (Jno. 3:8.) (c) _Inscrutable._ "Thou knowest not whence it cometh and whither it goeth." (Jno. 3:8.) (d) _Indispensable._ Without air in motion there is no life. (Jno. 3:5—"Jesus answered, Verily, verily, I say unto you, _Except a man be born of water and of the Spirit_, he cannot enter into the kingdom of God.") (e) _Lifegiving._ Ezek. 37:8, 9, 10—"And when I beheld, lo, the sinews and the flesh came up upon them, and the skin covered them above: but there was no breath in them. Then said he unto me, Prophesy unto _the wind,_ prophesy, son of man, and say to the wind, Thus saith the Lord God; Come from the four winds, O breath, and breathe upon these slain, that they may live. So I prophesied as he commanded me, and _the breath came into them, and they lived_, and stood up upon their feet, an exceeding great army." (Compare Jno. 3:5.)

NOTE.—Much at least of the difficulty in Jno. 3:5 would disappear if we would remember that "spirit" means "wind" and translate literally "Except a man be born of water and wind, he cannot enter into the Kingdom of God" (_i. e._, except a man be born of the cleansing and quickening power of the Spirit or of the cleansing word—Compare Jno. 15:3, Eph. 5:26, Jas. 1:18, 1 Pet. 1:23—and the quickening power of the Holy Spirit).

(_f._) _Irresistible._ (Compare Acts 1:8—"But _ye shall receive power_, after that the Holy Ghost is come upon you: and ye shall be witnesses unto me both in Jerusalem, and in all Judea, and in Samaria, and unto the uttermost part of the earth," and Acts 6:10—"And they were not able to resist the wisdom and the spirit by which he spake.") A man filled with the Holy Ghost is transformed into a cyclone.

(2) 1 Cor. 3:16—"Know ye not that ye are the temple of God, and that the Spirit of God dwelleth in you?"

"THE SPIRIT OF GOD."

The same essential thought as the former, but His Divine origin, character and power emphasized.

(3) Is. 11:2—"And _the Spirit of the_ LORD shall rest upon him, the spirit of wisdom and understanding, the spirit of counsel and might, the spirit of knowledge and of the fear of the LORD." (Compare Is. 63:14.)

"THE SPIRIT OF JEHOVAH."

(4) Is. 61:1—"_The Spirit of the Lord_ GOD is upon me; because the LORD hath anointed me to preach good tidings unto the meek; he hath sent me to bind up the brokenhearted, to proclaim liberty to the captives, and the opening of the prison to them that are bound."

"The Spirit of the Lord God," or rather "Lord Jehovah."
This is still more emphatic.

(5) 2 Cor. 3: 3—"Forasmuch as ye are manifestly declared to be
the epistle of Christ ministered by us, written not with ink, but with
the Spirit of the living God; not in tables of stone, but in fleshly tables
of the heart."

"THE SPIRIT OF THE LIVING GOD."

(6) Rom. 8: 9—"But ye are not in the flesh, but in the Spirit if so
be that the Spirit of God dwell in you. Now if any man have not *the
Spirit of Christ*, he is none of his."

"THE SPIRIT OF CHRIST."

This name brings out the relation of the Spirit to Christ as
well as to the Father. (Compare Acts. 2: 33—"Therefore being by
the right hand of God exalted, and having received of the Father
the promise of the Holy Ghost, he hath shed forth this, which ye
now see and hear.")

(7) Gal. 4: 6—"And because ye are sons, God hath sent forth *the
Spirit of his Son* into your hearts, crying, Abba, Father."

"THE SPIRIT OF HIS SON."

This name is given to the Holy Spirit in especial connection
with His testifying to the sonship of the believer. It is "the
Spirit of His Son" who testifies to our sonship.

(8) Phil. 1: 19—"For I know that this shall turn to my salvation
through your prayer, and the supply of *the Spirit of Jesus Christ.*"

"THE SPIRIT OF JESUS CHRIST."

The Spirit is not merely the spirit of the eternal word, but
the spirit of the word incarnate, Jesus Christ. It is the man
Jesus exalted to the right hand of the Father who receives and
sends the Spirit.

(Acts 2: 32, 33—"This Jesus hath God raised up, whereof we all
are witnesses. Therefore, being by the right hand of God exalted,
and having received of the Father the promise of the Holy Ghost, he
hath shed forth this, which ye now see and hear."

(9) Acts. 16: 7, R.V.—"And when they were come over against
Mysia, they assayed to go into Bithynia: and *the Spirit of Jesus* suffered them not." (Compare v. 6—"And they went through the
region of Phrygia and Galatia, having been forbidden of the Holy
Ghost to speak the word in Asia.")

"THE SPIRIT OF JESUS."

The thought of the relation of the Spirit to the man Jesus is still more clear here.

(10) Luke 11: 13—"If ye then, being evil, know how to give good gifts unto your children; how much more shall your heavenly Father give *the Holy Spirit* to them that ask him?" (and many places).

"THE HOLY SPIRIT."

This name emphasizes <u>the essential moral character of the Spirit.</u> He is Holy in Himself. <u>He imparts holiness to others.</u> (Compare 1 Pet. 1: 2.) Oh, if we only realized more deeply and constantly that He is the HOLY Spirit. Well may we, as the seraphim, bow in His presence and cry, "Holy, Holy, Holy." Yet how thoughtlessly many talk about Him and pray for Him. We pray for Him to come into our churches and our hearts, but what will He find there?

(11) Is. 4: 4—"When the LORD shall have washed away the filth of the daughters of Zion, and shall have purged the blood of Jerusalem from the midst thereof by the spirit of judgment, and by *the spirit of burning.*"

"THE SPIRIT OF BURNING."

This name emphasizes His searching, refining, dross-consuming, illuminating, energizing work.

(12) Rom. 1: 4—"And declared to be the Son of God with power, according to *the Spirit of holiness*, by the resurrection from the dead."

"THE SPIRIT OF HOLINESS."

This possibly emphasizes the Holiness of the Spirit even more than "the Holy Spirit."

(13) Eph. 1: 13, R.V.—"In whom ye also, having heard the word of truth, the gospel of your salvation, in whom, having also believed, ye were sealed with *the Holy Spirit of promise.*"

"THE HOLY SPIRIT OF PROMISE."

This refers to His being the great promise of the Father and the Son. (Compare Acts 1: 4, 5—"And, being assembled together with them, commanded them that they should not depart from Jerusalem, but wait for *the promise of the Father*, which, saith he, ye have heard of me. For John truly baptized with water; but ye shall be baptized with the Holy Ghost not many days hence."

(Acts 2: 33—" Therefore being by the right hand of God exalted, and having received of the Father *the promise of the Holy Ghost*, he hath shed forth this, which ye now see and hear.")

(14) Jno. 14: 17—" Even *the Spirit of truth;* whom the world cannot receive, because it seeth him not, neither knoweth him: but ye know him; for he dwelleth with you, and shall be in you."

Jno. 15: 26—" But when the Comforter is come, whom I will send unto you from the Father, even *the Spirit of truth*, which proceedeth from the Father, he shall testify of me."

Jno. 16: 13—" Howbeit when he, *the Spirit of truth*, is come, he will guide you into all truth: for he shall not speak of himself; but whatso-ever he shall hear, that shall he speak: and he will show you things to come."

" THE SPIRIT OF TRUTH."

(1) His essence is truth (Compare 1 Jno. 5: 7, R.V.— " And it is the Spirit that beareth witness, because the Spirit is the truth ") and (2) It is His work to communicate truth. (Compare Jno. 14: 26; 16: 13.) All truth is from Him.

(15) Rom. 8: 2—" For the law of *the Spirit of life* in Christ Jesus hath made me free from the law of sin and death."

" THE SPIRIT OF LIFE."

(16) Is. 11: 2—" And the Spirit of the LORD shall rest upon him, the Spirit of wisdom and understanding, the Spirit of counsel and might, the Spirit of knowledge and of the fear of the LORD. "

(1)　" THE SPIRIT OF WISDOM AND UNDERSTANDING."

(2)　" THE SPIRIT OF COUNSEL AND MIGHT."

(3)　" THE SPIRIT OF KNOWLEDGE AND OF THE FEAR OF THE LORD."

All these suggestive names refer to the gracious work of the Spirit in " the servant of the Lord." (See context.)

(17) Heb. 1: 9—" Thou hast loved righteousness, and hated iniquity; therefore God, even thy God, hath anointed thee with *the oil of gladness* above thy fellows."

" THE OIL OF GLADNESS."

A most beautiful and suggestive name of Him whose fruit is first " love, ' then " joy." (Gal. 5: 22.)

(18) Heb. 10: 29—" Of how much sorer punishment, suppose ye, shall he be thought worthy, who hath trodden under foot the Son of God, and hath counted the blood of the covenant, wherewith he was sanctified, an unholy thing, and hath done despite unto *the Spirit of grace ?* "

"THE SPIRIT OF GRACE."

This name brings out the fact that it is the Holy Spirit's work to administer and to apply the grace of God. Not only is He gracious, but He is making ours, experimentally, the multifold grace of God.

(19) 1 Pet. 4: 14—"If ye be reproached for the name of Christ, happy are ye; for the Spirit of glory and of God resteth upon you: on their part he is evil spoken of, but on your part he is glorified."

"THE SPIRIT OF GLORY."

This name is intended to teach not only that He is glorious Himself, but that He imparts the glory of God to us.

(Compare v. 13—"But rejoice, inasmuch as ye are partakers of Christ's sufferings; that, when his glory shall be revealed, ye may be glad also with exceeding joy," and Rom. 8: 16, 17—"The Spirit himself beareth witness with our spirits, that we are the children of God: and if children, then heirs; heirs of God, and joint heirs with Christ; if so be that we suffer with him, that we may be also glorified together.")

The Holy Spirit is the administrator of glory as well as grace, or rather of a grace that culminates in glory.

(Compare Eph. 3: 16-19—"That he would grant you, according to the riches of his glory, to be strengthened with might by his Spirit in the inner man; that Christ may dwell in your hearts by faith; that ye, being rooted and grounded in love, may be able to comprehend with all saints what is the breadth, and length, and depth, and height; and to know the love of Christ, which passeth knowledge, that ye might be filled with all the fulness of God.")

(20) Heb. 9: 14—"How much more shall the blood of Christ, who through *the eternal Spirit* offered himself without spot to God, purge your conscience from dead works to serve the living God?"

"THE ETERNAL SPIRIT."

(21) Jno. 14: 26—"But *the Comforter*, which is the Holy Ghost, whom the Father will send in my name, he shall teach you all things, and bring all things to your remembrance, whatsoever I have said unto you."

Jno. 15: 26—"But when *the Comforter* is come, whom I will send unto you from the Father, even the Spirit of truth, which proceedeth from the Father, he shall testify of me." (See also Jno. 16: 7.)

"THE COMFORTER."

The word translated "Comforter" means far more than that. It means literally "one called to another's side," the idea being one at hand to take another's part. It is the same word translated "advocate" in 1 Jno. 2: 1. (" My little children, these things write I unto you, that ye sin not. And if any man sin, we have an *advocate* with the Father, Jesus Christ the righteous.") The thought is that the Holy Spirit is one who is called to our side, one who is ever ready "to stand by us," to take our part. It is a wonderfully tender name for this Holy One. When we think of the Holy Spirit He seems so far away, but when we think of the Paracletos, or in plain English, our "standbyer," or our "part-taker," how near He is! In what numerous ways He stands by us will appear when we come to consider His work. But let us get this thought firmly fixed now, that the Holy Spirit is one called to our side to take our part.

> " Ever present, truest friend,
> Ever near thine aid to lend."

CHAPTER VI

THE WORK OF THE HOLY SPIRIT.

I. The Work of the Spirit in the Universe.

(1) Ps. 33: 6—"By the word of the LORD were the heavens made, and all the host of them *by the breath of his mouth.*"

Job 33: 4—"*The Spirit of God hath made* me, and the breath of the Almighty hath given me life."

FIRST PROPOSITION: The Creation of the material universe and man is effected through the agency of the Holy Spirit.

NOTE.—In Col. 1: 16, R.V. ("For *in him* were all things created, in the heavens and upon the earth, things visible and things invisible, whether thrones or dominions or principalities or powers; all things have been created through him and unto him;") all things are said to have been created in the Son, and in Heb. 1: 2 ("Hath in those last days spoken unto us by his Son, whom he hath appointed heir of all things, by whom also he made the worlds") God is said to have made the worlds (or ages) through Him.   In the first passage given above the word as well as the Spirit is mentioned in connection with creation. (Compare Gen. 1: 2, 3.) The Father, Son and Holy Spirit are all active in the creative work. The Father works through His Word and His Spirit.

(2) Ps. 104: 29, 30—"Thou hidest thy face, they are troubled: thou takest away their breath, they die, and return to their dust. *Thou sendest forth thy spirit,* they are created: and thou renewest the face of the earth."

SECOND PROPOSITION: The maintenance of living creatures is through the agency of the Holy Spirit.

(3) Gen. 1: 2, 3—"And the earth was without form and void; and darkness was upon the face of the deep. And *the Spirit of God moved* upon the face of the waters. And God said, Let there be light: and there was light."

Gen. 2: 7—"And the LORD God formed man of the dust of the ground, *and breathed* into his nostrils the breath of life; and man became a living soul."

THIRD PROPOSITION: The development of the present order of things from the early chaotic, undeveloped state, is effected through the agency of the Holy Spirit.

NOTE 1.—Seemingly, each new and higher impartation of the Spirit of God brings forth a higher order of being—inert matter, motion, light, vegetable life, animal life, man (the new man), Jesus Christ. This is Biblical development, as distinguished from the godless evolution so popular to-day. This, however, is only hinted at in the Bible.

NOTE 2.—The *Word of God* is even more plainly active in each stage of progress in creation. " God *said* " occurs ten times in Gen. 1.

II   The Work of the Spirit in Man in general.

1. Jno. 15:26, 27— " But when the Comforter is come, whom I will send unto you from the Father, even the Spirit of truth, which proceedeth from the Father, he *shall testify of me:* And ye also shall bear witness, because ye have been with me from the beginning."

Acts 5: 30-32—" The God of our fathers raised up Jesus, whom ye slew and hanged on a tree. Him hath God exalted with his right hand to be a Prince and a Saviour, for to give repentance to Israel, and forgiveness of sins. And we are his witnesses of these things; and *so is also the Holy Ghost*, whom God hath given to them that obey him."

FIRST PROPOSITION: The Holy Spirit bears witness to the truth regarding Jesus Christ.

NOTE 1.—At first sight this testimony would seem to be confined to the believer, for Jno. 15: 26 ("But when the Comforter is come, whom I will send unto you from the Father, even the Spirit of truth, which proceedeth from the Father, he shall testify of me ") says, '*Whom I will send unto you* ' (*i. e.*, of course, believers), but in the next chapter, verses 7, 8 (" Nevertheless I tell you the truth; it is expedient for you that I go away: for if I go not away, the Comforter will not come unto you; but if I depart, I will send him unto you. And when he is come, he will reprove the world of sin, and of righteousness, and of judgment "), where the Holy Spirit's work in *the world* is distinctly described, it says, " I will send him unto *you*." The truth seems clearly to be that the Spirit works on the world through the believers to whom He is sent. If we as believers realized the utter dependence of the world upon us for the Spirit's gracious work, would we not be more careful to see that the Spirit found in us an unobstructed channel? How slowly the world comes to know Jesus because of the unfaithfulness of the church.

NOTE 2.—Jno. 14: 17—" Even the Spirit of truth; whom the world cannot receive, because it seeth him not, neither knoweth him: but ye know him; for he dwelleth with you, and shall be in you." All truth is from the Spirit—He is " the Spirit of truth " but it is His especial work to bear witness to Him who is the truth—Jesus Christ. (Jno. 14: 6.)

NOTE 3.—It is only through the testimony of the Holy Spirit that men ever come to a true knowledge of Christ. (Cf. 1 Cor. 12: 3.) If you wish men to get a true view of Jesus Christ—such a view of Him that they may believe and be saved—you must seek for them the testimony of the Holy Spirit. Neither your testimony, nor even that of the Word alone, will effect this—though it is your testimony or that of the word which the Holy Spirit uses. But unless your testimony and that of the word is taken up by the Holy Spirit and He Himself testifies, they will not believe. This explains why it is that one who has been long in darkness concerning Jesus Christ so quickly comes to see the truth when he surrenders his will to God and seeks light from Him. (Compare Jno. 7: 17, and Acts 5: 32.) It explains also why it is that when you have shown a man the truth about Christ over and over again and he has seen nothing, suddenly it all bursts upon him, and he sees and believes. The Spirit has borne His witness to Christ. It was not merely Peter's words about Christ that convinced the Jews of the truth concerning Christ on the Day of Pentecost. It was the Spirit Himself bearing witness. If you wish men to see the truth about Christ, do not depend upon your own powers of expression and persuasion, but cast yourself upon the Holy Spirit and seek for them His testimony and see to it that they put themselves in a place where the Spirit can testify. This is the cure for both ignorance and skepticism concerning Christ. (Cf. Jno. 7: 17.)

NOTE 4.—The testimony of the Holy Spirit to Christ is different from His testimony to our sonship. That we will consider later.

(2) Jno. 16: 8-11, R.V.—"And he, when he is come, will convict the world in respect of sin, and of righteousness, and of judgment: of sin, because they believe not on me; of righteousness, because I go to the Father, and ye behold me no more; of judgment, because the prince of this world hath been judged."

SECOND PROPOSITION: The Holy Spirit convicts the world of sin and of righteousness and of judgment.

He convicts the world of its sin in not believing on **Christ.**

(Compare Acts 2: 36, 37—"Therefore let all the house of Israel know assuredly that God hath made that same Jesus, whom ye have crucified, both Lord and Christ. Now when they heard this, they were pricked in their hearts, and said unto Peter and to the rest of the apostles, Men and brethren, what shall we do?")

He convicts (that is convinces with a convincing that is self-condemning) the world of Christ's righteousness attested by His going to the Father, the coming of the Spirit being in itself a proof that Christ has gone to the Father.

(Compare Acts 2: 33—"Therefore being by the right hand of God exalted, and having received of the Father the promise of the Holy Ghost, he hath shed forth this, which ye now see and hear.")

He convicts the world of judgment, because the ruler of this world has been judged. He was judged at the cross.

(Compare Col. 2: 15—"And having spoiled principalities and powers, he made a shew of them openly, triumphing over them in it." Jno. 12: 31—"Now is the judgment of this world: now shall the prince of this world be cast out." Heb. 2:14—"Forasmuch then as the children are partakers of flesh and blood, he also himself likewise took part of the same; that through death he might destroy him that had the power of death, that is, the devil."

It is ours to preach the word and look to the Holy Spirit to produce conviction. (Acts 2: 4, 37.) Ofttimes the reason why we fail to produce conviction is because we are trying to do it ourselves. Let us not forget on the other hand that it is *through us* the Spirit produces conviction. (Jno. 16: 7, 8.)

III. The Work of the Holy Spirit in the Believer.

(1) Tit. 3: 5, R. V.—"Not by works done in righteousness, which we did ourselves, but according to his mercy he saved us, through the washing of regeneration and *renewing of the Holy Ghost.*"

Jno. 3: 3–5—"Jesus answered and said unto him, Verily, verily, I say unto thee, Except a man be born again, he can not see the kingdom of God. Nicodemus saith unto him, How can a man be born again when he is old? Can he enter the second time into his mother's womb, and be born? Jesus answered, Verily, verily, I say unto thee, Except a man be *born* of water and *of the Spirit*, he can not enter into the kingdom of God."

FIRST PROPOSITION: The Holy Spirit makes anew or regenerates the believer. (Compare Rom. 12: 2; 2 Cor. 5: 17.)

Regeneration is the Holy Spirit's work. Regeneration is the impartation of life, spiritual life, to the one "dead in trespasses and sins." (Eph. 2: 1.) It is the Holy Spirit who imparts this life.

(Jno. 6: 63—"It is the spirit that quickeneth; the flesh profiteth nothing: the words that I speak unto you, they are spirit, and they are life.")

Note 1.—In 2 Cor. 3: 6, we are told that the letter killeth, but the Spirit giveth life. This is sometimes interpreted to mean that the literal interpretation of the Scripture killeth, but that the interpretation that gives the spirit of the passage giveth life. It means nothing of the kind, as the context shows. This is a favorite perversion of Scripture with those who do not like to take the Bible as meaning just what it says. Still another false interpretation is that the letter means the old covenant, the law; the spirit, the new covenant, the Gospel. But this is not the thought. The contrast, as is seen from v. 3, is between the mere written word written with ink, and the living word written in the heart "with the Spirit of the living God." This much is true in the second interpretation, that the law was "the ministration of death" (v. 7), because unaccompanied by the Spirit's power, and the gospel is a ministration of life, because it is a ministration of the Spirit. But the Gospel is a ministration of the Spirit and of life only when the Gospel is preached " not in persuasive words of wisdom, but in demonstration of the Spirit and of power" (1 Cor. 2: 4); or as Paul puts it in another place (1 Thess. 1: 5) when the Gospel comes " not in word only, but also in power, and in the Holy Ghost." The mere letter of the Gospel will merely condemn and kill unless accompanied by the Spirit's power. The ministry of many an orthodox preacher and teacher is a ministry of death. It is true the word of the Gospel is the instrument God uses in regeneration (Compare Jas. 1: 18; 1 Pet. 1:23; 1 Cor. 4: 15), but it is not the bare word, but the word made a living thing in the heart by the power of the Holy Spirit. No amount of preaching, no matter how orthodox it may be, no amount of mere study of the Word, will regenerate unless the Holy Spirit works. It is He and He alone that makes a man a new creature. This He is ever ready to do when the conditions are supplied. But we are utterly dependent upon Him. Just as we are utterly dependent upon the work of Christ for us in justification, so we are utterly dependent upon the work of the Holy Spirit in us for regeneration. Regeneration is the impartation of a new nature—God's nature. (2 Pet. 1: 4.) It is the Holy Spirit who imparts this to us, makes us partakers of the divine nature. (Compare Luke 1: 35.) It is done through the Word. (2 Pet. 1: 4, and 1 Cor. 4: 15.) To put it in a word: The human heart is the soil, the preacher or teacher is the sower, the word of God is the seed, the Spirit of God quickens the seed, and the Divine nature is the result.

NOTE 2.—The Spirit of God dwells in the one thus born of the Spirit. (1 Cor. 3: 16—" Know ye not that ye are the temple of God, and that the Spirit of God dwelleth in you?") Some say that it is not the individual believer, but the church who is thus indwelt by the Spirit of God. But 1 Cor. 6: 19 ("What! know ye not that your body is the temple of the Holy Ghost which is in you, which ye have of God, and ye are not your own?") shows that Paul conceives of the individual believer as the temple of the indwelling Spirit. In the indwelling of the Spirit we have an advance upon the work of regeneration. That is a momentary act, the impartation of life, the implantation of a new nature. But in the indwelling Spirit is an abiding presence. (Jno. 14: 17.) The Holy Spirit dwells in every one who belongs to Christ. (Rom. 8: 9—" But ye are not in the flesh, but in the Spirit, if so be that the Spirit of God dwell in you. Now, if any man have not the Spirit of Christ, he is none of his.") The Corinthian believers were very imperfect believers, but Paul told them that they were temples of the Holy Spirit even when dealing with them concerning gross immorality. (See 1 Cor. 6: 15-19.) The Holy Spirit dwells in every child of God. In some, however, He dwells way back in the hidden sanctuary of their spirit and is not allowed to take possession as He desires of the whole man—spirit, soul and body. Some, therefore, are not distinctly conscious of His indwelling, but He is there. What a solemn but glorious thought. If we are children of God we are not so much to pray that the Spirit may come and dwell in us; for He does that already. We are rather to recognize His presence, His gracious and glorious indwelling, and give Him complete control of the house He already inhabits, and strive to so live as not to grieve this Holy one, this Divine guest. We shall see later that it is right to pray for "the filling" or "baptism" with the Spirit. What a thought it gives of the hallowedness of life and of the sacredness of the body, to think of the Holy Spirit dwelling within us. How carefully we ought to walk so as not to grieve Him. How considerately we ought to treat these bodies, and how sensitively we ought to shun everything that will defile them.

NOTE 3.—This indwelling Spirit is a source of everlasting satisfaction and life. Jno. 4: 14—"But whosoever drinketh of the water that I shall give him shall never thirst; but the water that I shall give him shall be in him a well of water springing up into everlasting life." (From a comparison with Jno. 7: 37-39, it is plain that the water here spoken of is the Holy Spirit.) The one who drinks of this water "shall never thirst" or literally shall not thirst unto eternity. He has a fountain within. No need now to go outside for satisfaction. He is independent of environment for life and joy. Why then do so many professed Christians feel compelled to run into the world for their satisfaction?

(2) Rom. 8: 2—"For the law of the Spirit of life in Christ Jesus hath made me free from the law of sin and death."

SECOND PROPOSITION: The Holy Spirit sets the believer in Christ free from the law of sin and death.

What the law of sin and death is we see in the preceding chapter. (Rom. 7: 9-24.) Paul had been aroused by the law of God to see what was holy and just and good. He delighted in this law after the inward man (Rom. 7: 22) and strove to keep it. But he found that there was not only this "holy and just and good" law without him, but he found there was another law in his members warring against the law of his mind. This law of sin and death was, that when he would do good evil was present. (7: 21.) "To will is present to me, but to do that which is good is not." (V. 18, R. V.) In this wretched position of approving of the law in his mind, but in servitude to the law of sin and death in his actions, Paul found himself until he discovered in Christ Jesus a third law, "the law of the Spirit of life." This law set him free from the law of sin and death so that now he not only could "will" but also "do," and the righteousness of the law was fulfilled in him who walked not after the flesh, but after the Spirit. (Rom. 8: 3.) It is the work of the Holy Spirit when we give up trying to live right in our own strength—*i. e.*, in the energy of the flesh—and surrender to the Holy Spirit to live after Him and walk in his blessed power, to set us free from this awful law of sin and death.

There are many professed Christians to-day living in Rom. 7: 9–24. Some even go so far as to reason that this is the normal Christian life. But Paul tells us distinctly in v. 9 that this was "when the commandment came," and again in v. 14 that this was his experience as "carnal, sold under sin," but in Rom. 8: 9 he tells us how not to be in the flesh but in the Spirit. In the eighth chapter of Romans we have the picture of the true Christian life, the life that is possible to and that God expects from every one of His children—the life where not merely the commandment comes, but the Spirit comes and works obedience and victory. Life not in the flesh but in the Spirit, where we not only see the beauty of the law, but where the Spirit imparts power to keep it. (Rom. 8: 4.) We still have "the flesh," but we do not live after it; we "through the Spirit do mortify the deeds of the body." (Rom. 8: 13.) We walk after the Spirit and do not fulfill the lusts of the flesh. (Gal. 5: 16.) We "have crucified the flesh with the passions and lusts thereof." (Gal. 5: 24, R. V.) It is thus our privilege in the Spirit's power to get daily, hourly, constant victory over the flesh and over sin. But this victory is not in ourselves, not in any strength of our own. Left to ourselves, deserted of the Spirit of God, we would be as helpless as ever. It is still true that in us, that is, in our flesh, dwelleth no good thing. (Rom. 7: 18.) It is all in the Spirit's power. The Spirit's power may be in such fulness, that one is not conscious even of the presence of the flesh—it seems dead and gone—but it is only kept in the place of death by the Holy Spirit's power. If we try to take one step in our own strength we fail. We must live in the Spirit and walk in the Spirit if we would have victory. (Gal. 5: 16, 25.)

NOTE.—In Jno. 8: 32, it is the truth that sets us free and gives victory over sin, and in Ps. 119: 11, the indwelling word. In this, as in everything else, what in one place is attributed to the Spirit is elsewhere attributed to the word.

(3) Eph. 3: 16, R.V.—" That he would grant you, according to the riches of his glory, that ye may be strengthened with power through his Spirit in the inward man."

THIRD PROPOSITION: The Holy Spirit strengthens the believer with power in the inward man.

The result of this strengthening is seen in vv. 17–19: "That Christ may dwell in your hearts through faith; to the end that ye, being rooted and grounded in love, may be strong to apprehend with all the saints what is the breadth and length and height and depth, and to know the love of Christ which passeth knowledge, that ye may be filled unto all the fulness of God." This work of the Holy Spirit is very closely akin to that mentioned in the preceding section.   It is a carrying out of the former work to completion.   Here the power of the Spirit manifests itself not merely in giving us victory over sin, but *(a)* in Christ's dwelling (a strong word meaning permanently settling) in our hearts, and *(b)* in our being rooted and grounded in love and *(c)* in our being made strong to apprehend with all the saints what is the breadth and length and height and depth and to know the love of Christ which passeth knowledge.   It all ultimates in our being *(d)* " filled unto all the fulness of God."

(4) Rom. 8: 14—" For as many as are led by the Spirit of God, they are the sons of God."

FOURTH PROPOSITION: The Holy Spirit leads us into a holy life—a life as sons of God, a godlike life.

Not merely does the Holy Spirit give us power to live a holy life, a life well pleasing to God when we have discovered what that life is; He takes us as it were by the hand and leads us into that life. Our whole part is simply to surrender ourselves utterly to Him to lead and mold us.   Those who do this are not merely God's offspring which all men are (Acts 17: 28), neither are we merely God's children.   "These are *sons* of God."

(5) Rom. 8: 16, R.V.—"The Spirit himself beareth witness with our spirit, that we are children of God."

FIFTH PROPOSITION: The Holy Spirit bears witness together with the spirit of the believer that he is a child of God.

Note that Paul does not say that the Spirit bears witness *to* our spirit but *with* it—" *together with our spirit,*" is the exact force of the words used. That is, there are two who bear witness to our sonship; first our spirit bears witness that we are children of God; second, the Holy Spirit bears witness together with our spirit that we are children of God.

How does the Holy Spirit bear His testimony to this fact? Gal. 4: 6—"And because ye are sons, God has sent forth the Spirit of his Son into your hearts. crying, Abba, Father."

It is only when "the law of the Spirit of life in Christ Jesus has made me free from the law of sin and death (v. 2), and so "the righteousness of the law is fulfilled" in me "who walk not after the flesh but after the Spirit" (v. 4), and I "through the Spirit of God do mortify the deeds of the body" (v. 13), and when I am surrendered to the Spirit's leading (v. 14)—it is then and only then that I can expect (v. 16) to be realized in my experience, and to have the clear assurance of sonship that comes from the Spirit of God testifying together with my spirit that I am a child of God. There are many seeking this testimony of the Holy Spirit in the wrong place—*i. e.*, as a condition of their surrendering wholly to God and confessing the crucified and risen one as their Saviour and Lord.

(6) Gal. 5: 22, 23—"But the fruit of the Spirit is love, joy, peace, longsuffering, gentleness, goodness, faith, meekness, temperance: against such there is not law."

SIXTH PROPOSITION: The Holy Spirit brings forth fruit in the believer in Christlike graces of character.

(Compare Rom. 14: 17—"For the kingdom of God is not meat and drink; but righteousness and peace, and joy in the Holy Ghost." Rom. 15: 13—"Now the God of hope fill you with all joy and peace in believing, that ye may abound in hope, through the power of the Holy Ghost." Rom. 5: 5—"And hope maketh not ashamed; because the love of God is shed abroad in our hearts by the Holy Ghost which is given unto us.")

All real beauty of character, all real Christlikeness in us, is the Holy Spirit's work, it is His fruit. He bears it, not we. Notice these graces are not said to be the fruits of the Spirit, they are the fruit. There is a unity of origin running through all the multiplicity of manifestation. It is a beautiful life that is set forth in these verses. Every word is worthy of earnest study and profound meditation. "Love," "joy," "peace," "long-suffering," "kindness," "goodness," "faith," "meekness," "self control." Is not this the life we all long for, the Christ-life? It is not natural to us, and it is not attainable by any effort of the flesh or nature. The life that is natural to us is set forth in the three preceding verses (19–21). But when the indwelling Spirit is given full control in the one He inhabits, when we are brought to realize the utter badness of the flesh and give up in hopeless despair of ever attaining to anything in its power—when, in other words, we come to the end of self and just give over the whole work of making us what we ought to be to the indwelling Holy Spirit, then, and only then, holy graces of character are His fruit. Do you wish these graces in your character and life? Renounce self utterly and all its striving after holiness, and let the Holy Spirit, who dwells in you, take full control and bear His own glorious fruit. (We get the same essential truth from another point of view in Gal. 2: 20, R. V., Am. App.)

Settle it clearly and forever that the flesh can never bear this fruit, that you can never attain these things by your own effort, that they are "the fruit of the Spirit." We hear a good deal in these days about "ethical culture," which usually means a cultivation of the flesh, until it bears the fruit of the Spirit. It can not be done until thorns can be made to bear figs, and a bramble bush grapes. (Luke 6: 44; Matt. 12: 33.)

We hear also a good deal about "character-building." That is all very well if you let the Holy Spirit do the building, and then it is not so much building as fruit-bearing. (See, however, 2 Pet. 1: 5–7.)

We hear also about cultivating graces of character, but we must always bear in mind that the way to cultivate true graces of character is by submitting ourselves utterly to the Spirit to do His work. "This is sanctification of the Spirit." (1 Pet. 1: 2; 2 Thess. 2: 13.)

There is a sense, however, in which cultivating graces of character is right. We look at Jesus Christ to see what we ought to be, then we look to the Holy Spirit to make us this that we ought to be.

(7) Jno. 16:13, R.V.—"Howbeit when he, the Spirit of truth, is come, *he shall guide you into all the truth:* for he shall not speak from himself: but what things soever he shall hear, these shall he speak: and <u>he shall declare unto you the things that are to come.</u>"

SEVENTH PROPOSITION: The Holy Spirit guides the be-liever into all the truth.

This promise was made in the first instance to the Apostles, but the Apostles themselves applied it to all believers. (1 Jno. 2: 20, 27.) It is the privilege of each of us to be "taught of God." Each believer is independent of human teachers—"ye need not that any man teach you." This does not mean, of course, that we may not learn much from others who are taught of the Holy Spirit. If John had thought that he would never have written this epistle to teach others. The man who is most fully taught of God, is the very one who will be most ready to listen to what God has taught others. Much less does it mean that when we are taught of the Spirit we are independent of the Word of God. For the Word is the very place to which the Spirit leads His pupils and the instrument through which He instructs them. (Eph. 6:17; Jno. 6:63; Eph. 5:18, 19; Compare Col. 3:16.) But while we may learn much from men we are not dependent upon them. We have a Divine teacher, the Holy Spirit.

We shall never truly know the truth until we are thus taught. No amount of mere human teaching, no matter who our teachers may be, will give us a correct apprehension of the truth, not even a diligent study of the Word either in the English or original languages will give us a real understanding of the truth. We must be taught of the Holy Spirit. And we may be thus taught, each of us. The one who is thus taught will understand the truth of God better, even if he does not know a word of Greek or Hebrew, than the one who knows Greek and Hebrew and all the cognate languages, and is not taught of the Spirit.

The Spirit will guide the one He teaches into *all* the truth. Not in a day, nor in a week, nor in a year, but step by step. There are two especial lines of the Spirit's teaching mentioned. (*a*) "He shall declare unto you the things that are to come." Many say we can know nothing of the future, that all our thoughts on that subject are guesswork. Anyone taught by the Spirit knows better than that. (*b*) "He shall glorify me (*i. e.*, Christ), for he shall take of mine, and shall declare it unto you." This is the Holy Spirit's especial line with the believer as with the unbeliever, to declare unto them the things of Christ and glorify Him.

Many fear to emphasize the truth about the Holy Spirit lest Christ be disparaged, but no one magnifies Christ as the Holy Spirit does. We shall never understand Christ nor see His glory until the Holy Spirit interprets Him to us. The mere listening to sermons and lectures, the mere study of the Word even, will never give you to see "the things of Christ." The Holy Spirit must show you, and He is willing to do it. He is longing to do it. I suppose the Holy Spirit's most intense desire is to reveal Jesus Christ to men. Let Him do it. Christ is so different when the Spirit glorifies Him by taking of the things of Christ and showing them unto us.

(8) Jno. 14:26—" But the Comforter, which is the Holy Ghost, whom the Father will send in my name, he will teach you all things, *and bring all things to your remembrance*, whatsoever I have said unto you."

Here again we have the teaching of the Holy Spirit, but we have something besides.

EIGHTH PROPOSITION: The Holy Spirit brings to remembrance the words of Christ.

This promise was made primarily to the Apostles, and is the guarantee of the accuracy of their report of what Jesus said; but the Holy Spirit does a similar work with each believer who expects it of Him, and looks to Him to do it. He brings to mind the teachings of Christ and the Word, just when we need them for either the necessities of our life or of our service. How many of us could tell of occasions when we were in great distress of soul, or great questioning as to duty, or great extremity as to what to say to one whom we were trying to lead to Christ or to help, and just the Scripture we needed—some passage we had not thought of for a long time and perhaps never in this connection—was brought to mind. It was the Holy Spirit who did this, and He is ready to do it even more when we expect it from Him. Is it without significance that in the verse following this blessed promise, Jesus says: "Peace I leave with you, my peace I give unto you?" If we will just look to the Holy Spirit to bring to mind Scripture just when we need it and just the Scripture we need, we will indeed have Christ's peace.

(9) 1 Cor. 2:9–14—"But as it is writtten, Eye hath not seen, nor ear heard, neither have entered into the heart of man, the things which God hath prepared for them that love him. But God hath revealed them unto us by his Spirit: for the Spirit searcheth all things, yea, the deep things of God. For what man knoweth the things of a man, save the spirit of man which is in him? even so the things of God knoweth no man, but the Spirit of God. Now we have received, not the spirit of the world, but the Spirit which is of God; that we might know the things that are freely given to us of God. Which things also we speak, not in the words which man's wisdom teacheth, but which the Holy Ghost teacheth; comparing spiritual things with spiritual. But the natural man receiveth not the things of the Spirit of God: for they are foolishness unto him: neither can he know them, because they are spiritually discerned."

NINTH PROPOSITION: In these verses we have a twofold work of the Spirit. (a) *The Holy Spirit reveals to us the deep things of God which are hidden from and foolishness to the natural man.* (It is primarily to the Apostles, that He does this, but we cannot limit this work of the Spirit to them.) (b) *The Holy Spirit imparts power to discern, know and appreciate what he has taught.*

Not only is the Holy Spirit the Author of Revelation—the written word of God—He is also the interpreter of what He has revealed. How much more interesting and helpful any deep book becomes when we have the author of the book right at hand to interpret it to us. This is what we always may have when we study the Bible. The author, the Holy Spirit, is right at hand to interpret. To understand the book we must look to Him and the darkest places become clear. We need to pray often with the Psalmist: "Open thou mine eyes, that I may behold wondrous things out of thy law." (Ps. 119:18.) It is not enough that we have the objective revelation in the written word, we must have the (subjective) inward illumination of the Holy Spirit to enable us to comprehend it. It is a great mistake to try to comprehend a spiritual revelation with the natural understanding. It is the foolish attempt to do this that has landed so many in the bog of "the higher criticism." A man with no aesthetic sense might as well expect to appreciate the Sistine Madonna because he is not color-blind, as an unspiritual man to understand the Bible simply because he understands the laws of grammar and the vocabulary of the languages in which the Bible was written. I would as soon think of setting a man to teach art because he understood paints, as to set him to teach the Bible because he understood Greek and Hebrew. We all need not only to recognize the utter insufficiency and worthlessness before God of our own righteousness, which is the lesson of opening chapters of the Epistle to the Romans, but also the utter insufficiency and worthlessness in the things of God of our own wisdom, which is the lesson of the first Epistle to the Corinthians, especially the first to the third chapters. (See, e. g., 1 Cor. 1: 19–21, 26, 27.)

The Jews had a revelation by the Spirit but they failed to depend upon Him to interpret it to them, so they went astray. The whole evangelical church recognizes the utter insufficiency of man's righteousness, theoretically at least. Now it needs to be taught and made to feel the utter insufficiency of man's wisdom. That is perhaps the lesson that this nineteenth century of overweening intellectual conceit needs most of any.

To understand God's word we must empty ourselves utterly of our own wisdom, and rest in utter dependence upon the Spirit of God to interpret it to us. (Matt. 11: 25—" At that time Jesus answered and said, I thank thee, O Father, Lord of heaven and earth, because thou hast hid these things from the wise and prudent, and hast revealed them unto babes.")

When we have put away our own righteousness, then, and only then, we get the righteousness of God. (Phil. 3:4–7, 9— "Though I might also have confidence in the flesh. If any other man thinketh that he hath whereof he might trust in the flesh, I more: Circumcised the eighth day, of the stock of Israel, of the tribe of Benjamin, a Hebrew of the Hebrews; as touching the law, a Pharisee; concerning zeal, persecuting the church; touching the righteousness which is in the law, blameless. But what things were gain to me, those I counted loss for Christ. * * * And be found in him, not having mine own righteousness, which is of the law, but that which is through the faith of Christ, the righteousness which is of God by faith." Rom. 10: 3—" For they, being ignorant of God's righteousness, and going about to establish their own righteousness, have not submitted themselves unto the righteousness of God.")

When we put away our own wisdom—then, and only then, we get the wisdom of God. (1 Cor. 3: 18—"Let no man deceive himself. If any man among you seemeth to be wise in this world, *let him become a fool,* that he may be wise." Matt. 11: 25—"At that time Jesus answered and said, I thank thee, O Father, Lord of heaven and earth, because thou hast hid these things from the wise and prudent, and hast revealed them unto babes." See also 1 Cor. 1: 25–28.)

When we put away our own strength, then, and then only, we get the strength of God. (Is. 40: 29—"He giveth power *to the faint;* and *to them that have no might* he increaseth strength." 2 Cor. 12: 9—"And he said unto me, My grace is sufficient for thee: for my strength is made perfect in weakness. Most gladly therefore will I rather glory in my infirmities, that the power of Christ may rest upon me." 1 Cor. 1: 27. 28—"But God hath chosen the foolish things of the world to confound the wise; and God hath chosen the weak things of the world to confound the things which are mighty; and base things of the world, and things which are despised, hath God chosen, yea, and things which are not, to bring to nought things that are.")

Emptying must precede filling. Self-poured-out that God may be poured in.

We must *daily* be taught by the Spirit to understand the word. I cannot depend to-day on the fact that the Spirit taught me yesterday. Each new contact with the Word must be in the power of the Spirit. That the Holy Spirit once illumined our mind to grasp a certain passage is not enough. He must do so each time we confront that passage. Andrew Murray has put this truth well. He says: "Each time you come to the Word in study, in hearing a sermon or reading a religious book, there ought to be, as distinct as your intercourse with the external means, a definite act of self-abnegation, denying your own wisdom and yielding yourself in faith to the Divine teacher." ("The Spirit of Christ," p. 221.)

(10) 1 Cor. 2: 1–5—"And I, brethren, when I came to you, came not with excellence of speech or of wisdom, declaring unto you the testimony of God. For I determined not to know anything among you,

save Jesus Christ and him crucified. And I was with you in weakness, and in fear, and in much trembling. And my speech and preaching was not with enticing words of man's wisdom, but in demonstration of the Spirit and of power: that your faith should not stand in the wisdom of men, but in the power of God."

1 Thess. 1: 5—"For our Gospel came not unto you in word only, but also in power, and in the Holy Ghost, and in much assurance: as ye know what manner of men we were among you for your sake."

Acts 1: 8—"But ye shall receive power, after that the Holy Ghost is come upon you: and ye shall be witnesses unto me both in Jerusalem, and in all Judea, and in Samaria, and unto the uttermost part of the earth."

TENTH PROPOSITION: The Holy Spirit enables the believer to communicate to others in power the truth He Himself has been taught.

We not only need the Holy Spirit to reveal the truth in the first place, and the Holy Spirit in the second place to interpret to us as individuals the truth He has revealed, but, in the third place also we need the Holy Spirit to enable us to effectually communicate to others the truth He Himself has interpreted to us. We need Him all along the line. One great cause of real failure in the ministry even when there is seeming success, and not only in the ministry, but in all forms of service by Christian men and women, is from the attempt to teach by "enticing words of man's wisdom"—*i. e.,* by the arts of human logic, rhetoric and eloquence—what the Holy Spirit has taught us. What is needed is Holy Ghost power "demonstration of the Spirit and of power"

There are three causes of failure in preaching:

First. Some other message is taught than the message which the Holy Spirit has revealed in the Word—men preach science, art, philosophy, sociology, history, experience, etc., and not the simple word of God as found in the Holy Spirit's Book, the Bible.

Second. The Spirit-taught message, the Bible, is studied and sought to be comprehended by the natural understanding—*i. e.,* without the Spirit's illumination. That, alas! is too common even in institutions where men are being trained for the ministry.

Third. The Spirit-given message, the Word, the Bible, studied and comprehended under the Holy Ghost illumination, is

given out to others with "enticing words of man's wisdom," and
not "in demonstration of the Spirit and of power."

We need, we are absolutely dependent upon, the Spirit all
along the line. He must teach us how to speak as well as what
to speak. His must be the power as well as the message.

(11) Jude 20:—"But ye, beloved, building up yourselves on your
most holy faith, *praying in the Holy Ghost.*"

Eph. 6: 18—"Praying always *with all prayer and supplication in
the Spirit*, and watching thereunto with all perseverance and supplication
for all saints."

Rom. 8: 26, 27, R. V.

*ELEVENTH PROPOSITION: The Holy Spirit helps, guides
and gives power to the believer in prayer.*

The disciples did not know how to pray as they ought, so
they came to Jesus and said: "Lord, teach us to pray." (Luke
11: 1.) "We know not how to pray as we ought," but we have
another paraclete right at hand to help. (Jno. 14: 16, 17.)—"The
Spirit helpeth our infirmity." (Rom. 8: 26, R. V.) He teaches
us to pray. True prayer is prayer in the Spirit—*i. e.*, the prayer
the Spirit inspires and directs. When we come into God's presence we should recognize our infirmity, our ignorance of what we
should pray for, or how we should do it, and in the consciousness
of our utter inability to pray aright, look up to the Holy Spirit,
and cast ourselves utterly upon Him, to direct our prayers, to
lead out our desires and guide our utterance of them. Rushing
heedlessly into God's presence and asking the first thing that
comes into our mind, or that some thoughtless one asks us to pray
for, is not praying "in the Holy Spirit," and is not true prayer.
We must wait for the Holy Spirit, and surrender ourselves to the
Holy Spirit. The prayer that God the Holy Spirit inspires is the
prayer that God the Father answers.

NOTE I.—Rom. 8: 26, 27, R. V.—"And in like manner the Spirit also
helpeth our infirmity: for we know not how to pray as we ought; but
the Spirit himself maketh intercession for us with groanings which cannot be uttered. And he that searcheth the hearts knoweth what is the
mind of the Spirit, because he maketh intercession for the saints according to the will of God." The longings which the Holy Spirit begets in
our hearts are often too deep for utterance, too deep apparently for clear
and definite comprehension on the part of the believer himself in whom
the Holy Spirit is working. God Himself must "search the heart" to
know "what is the mind of the Spirit" in these unuttered and unutter-

able longings. But God does know what is the mind of the Spirit, He does know what those Spirit-given longings mean, even if we do not, and these longings are "according (to the will of) God," and He grants them, so it comes to pass that "He is able to do exceedingly above all that we ask or think, according to the power that worketh in us." (Eph. 3: 20.)

NOTE 2.—1 Cor. 14: 15—"What is it then? I will pray with the Spirit, and I will pray with the understanding also: I will sing with the Spirit, and I will sing with the understanding also." There are other times when the Spirit's leadings are so clear that we "pray with the Spirit . . . and with the understanding also."

(12) Eph. 5: 18–20, R.V—"And be not drunken with wine, wherein is riot, but be filled with the Spirit; speaking one to another in psalms and hymns and spiritual songs, singing and making melody with your heart to the Lord; giving thanks always for all things in the name of our Lord Jesus Christ to God, even the Father."

TWELFTH PROPOSITION: The Holy Spirit inspires the believer to and guides him in praise and thanksgiving.

Not only does He teach us to pray, He also teaches us to render thanks. One of the most prominent characteristics of "the spirit-filled life" is thanksgiving. (Compare Acts 2: 4, 11.) True thanksgiving is "to God, even the Father," through or "in the name of our Lord Jesus Christ," in the Holy Spirit. The same is true of prayer. (Compare Eph. 2: 18, R.V.)

(13) Phil. 3: 3, R.V.—"For we are the circumcision, who *worship by the Spirit of God*, and glory in Christ Jesus, and have no confidence in the flesh."

THIRTEENTH PROPOSITION: The Holy Spirit inspires worship on the part of the believer.

Prayer is not worship, thanksgiving is not worship. Worship is a definite act of the creature in relation to God. Worship is bowing before God in adoring acknowledgment and contemplation of Himself. Someone has said: "In our prayers we are taken up with our needs, in our thanksgiving we are taken up with our blessings, in our worship we are taken up with Himself."

There is no true and acceptable worship except that which the Holy Spirit prompts and directs. "Such doth the Father seek to be His worshippers." (Jno. 4: 23, R.V.) The Flesh seeks to enter every sphere of life. It has its worship as well as its lusts. The worship which the flesh worships is an abomination unto God. (Herein we see the folly of any attempt at a Parliament of Religions, where the representatives of different religions attempt to *worship* together.)

Not all earnest and honest worship is worship in the Spirit. A man may be very honest and very earnest in his worship, and still not have submitted himself to the guidance of the Holy Spirit in the matter, and so his worship is in the flesh. Even when there is great loyalty to the letter of the Word, worship may not be "in the Spirit"—*i. e.*, inspired and directed by Him. To worship aright we must "have no confidence in the flesh," we must recognize the utter inability of the flesh—*i. e.*, our natural self, as contrasted to the Divine Spirit that dwells in and should mold everything in the believer—to worship acceptably; we must realize also the danger there is that the flesh, self, intrude itself into our worship. In utter self-distrust and self-abnegation we must cast ourselves upon the Holy Spirit to lead us aright in our worship.

Just as we must renounce any merit in ourselves and cast ourselves utterly upon Christ and His work for us for justification, just so must we renounce any capacity for good in ourselves, and cast ourselves utterly upon the Holy Spirit and His work in us, in holy living. knowing, praying, thanking and worshipping, and all else that we are to do.

(14) Acts 13:2, 4—"As they ministered to the Lord, and fasted, the Holy Ghost said, Separate me Barnabas and Saul for the work *whereunto I have called them.* So they, being sent forth by the Holy Ghost, departed unto Seleucia; and from thence they sailed to Cyprus."

FOURTEENTH PROPOSITION: The Holy Spirit calls men and sends them forth to definite lines of work.

The Holy Spirit not only calls men in a general way into Christian work, but selects the specific work and points it out.

"Shall I go to China, to Africa, to India?" many a one is asking, and many another ought to ask. You cannot rightly settle that question for yourselves, neither can any other man settle it rightly for you. Not every Christian man is called to China or Africa, or any other foreign field, or to the foreign field at all. God alone knows whether He wishes you in any of these places. He is willing to show you.

How does the Holy Spirit call?   The passage before us does not tell us.   It is presumably purposely silent on this point, lest, perhaps, we think that He must always call in precisely the same way.   There is nothing to indicate that He spoke by an audible voice, much less that He made His will known in any of the fantastic ways in which some profess to discern His leading—as *e. g.*, by twitchings of the body, opening of the Bible at random and putting the finger on a passage that may be construed into some entirely different meaning than that the inspired writer intended by it   But the important point is, He made His will clearly known and He is willing to make His will clearly known to us to-day.

The great need in Christian work to-day is men and women whom the Holy Spirit calls and sends forth.   We have plenty of men and women whom men have called and sent forth, or who have called themselves.   (There are many to-day who object strenuously to being sent forth by men, by any organization of any kind, who are, what is immeasurably worse than that, sent forth by self, not by God.)

How shall we receive the Holy Spirit's call?   By desiring it, seeking it, waiting upon the Lord for it, and expecting it.   " As they *ministered to the Lord* and *fasted*," the record reads.   Many a man is saying in self-justification for staying out of the ministry, and staying at home from the foreign field, " I have never had a call."   How do you know that?   Have you been listening for it? God speaks often in a " still small voice."   Only the listening ear can catch it.   Have you definitely offered yourself to God to send you where He will?   While no man ought to go to China or Africa unless he is clearly and definitely called, he ought to definitely offer himself to God for this work, to be ready for a call and to be listening sharply that he may hear it when it comes.   No educated Christian man or woman has a right to rest easy out of the foreign field unless he has definitely offered himself to God for that work, and is clear no call from God has come.   A man needs no more definite call to Africa than to Boston, or New York, or Chicago.

(15)   Acts 8: 27-29—" And he arose and went: and, behold, a man of Ethiopia, a eunuch of great authority under Candace queen of the Ethiopians, who had the charge of all her treasure, and had come

to Jerusalem for to worship, was returning, and sitting in his chariot read Esaias the prophet. Then the Spirit said unto Philip, Go near, and join thyself to this chariot."

Acts 16: 6, 7—"Now when they had gone throughout Phrygia and the region of Galatia, and were *forbidden of the Holy Ghost* to preach the word in Asia, after they were come to Mysia, they assayed to go into Bithynia: but *the Spirit suffered them not.*"

FIFTEENTH PROPOSITION: The Holy Spirit guides in the details of daily life and service, as to where to go and where not to go; what to do and what not to do.

It is possible for us to have the unerring guidance of the Holy Spirit at every turn of life. For example, in personal work it is manifestly not God's intention that we speak to every one we meet. There are some to whom we ought not to speak. Time spent on them would be taken from work more to God's glory. Doubtless Philip met many as he journeyed toward Gaza before he met the one of whom the Spirit said: "Go near, and join thyself to this chariot." So is He ready to guide us also. So also in all the affairs of life, business, study, everything, we can have God's wisdom. There is no promise more plain and explicit than Jas. 1:5—"If any of you lack wisdom, let him ask of God, that giveth to all men liberally, and upbraideth not; and it shall be given him."

How shall we gain this wisdom?

Jas. 1:5-7—"If any of you *lack* wisdom, let him *ask* of God, that giveth to all men liberally and upbraideth not; and it shall be given him. But let him *ask in faith*, nothing wavering: for he that wavereth is like a wave of the sea driven with the wind and tossed. For let not that man think that he shall receive anything of the Lord."

Here are really five steps:

First. That we "lack wisdom." We must be conscious of and fully admit our own inability to decide wisely. Not only the sinfulness, but the wisdom of the flesh must be renounced.

Second. We must really desire to know God's way, and be willing to do God's will. That is implied in the asking if the asking is sincere. This is a point of fundamental importance. Here we find the reason why men ofttimes do not know God's will and have the Spirit's guidance. They are not really willing to do whatever the Spirit leads. It is "the meek" whom He guides in judgment and "the meek " to whom "He will teach his way." (Ps. 25: 9.) *It is he that "willeth* to do his will" who shall know, etc. (Jno. 7: 17, R. V.)

Third. We must "ask," definitely ask guidance.

Fourth. We must confidently expect guidance. "Let him ask in faith, nothing doubting." (Vv. 6, 7, R. V.)

Fifth. We must follow step by step as the guidance comes. Just how it will come no one can tell, but it will come. It may come with only a step made clear at a time. That is all we need to know—the next step. Many are in darkness about guidance because they do not know what God will have them do next week, or next month, or next year. Do you know the next step? That is enough. Take it and He will show you the next. (Num. 9: 17–23—" And when the cloud was taken up from the tabernacle, then after that the children of Israel journeyed: and in the place where the cloud abode, there the children of Israel pitched their tents. At the commandment of the LORD the children of Israel journeyed, and at the commandment of the LORD they pitched; as long as the cloud abode upon the tabernacle they rested in their tents. And when the cloud tarried long upon the tabernacle many days, then the children of Israel kept the charge of the LORD, and journeyed not. And so it was, when the cloud was a few days upon the tabernacle; according to the commandment of the LORD they abode in their tents, and according to the commandment of the LORD they journeyed. And so it was, when the cloud abode from even unto the morning, and that the cloud was taken up in the morning, then they journeyed: whether it was by day or by night that the cloud was taken up, they journeyed. At the commandment of the LORD they rested in their tents, and at the commandment of the LORD they journeyed: they kept the charge of the LORD, at the commandment of the LORD by the hand of Moses.")

GOD'S GUIDANCE IS CLEAR GUIDANCE. (1 Jno. 1: 5—"God is light, and in him is no darkness at all.")

Many are tortured by leadings they fear may be from God, but of which they are not sure. You have a right, as God's children, to be sure. Go to God. Say, " Here I am, heavenly Father, I am willing to do thy will, but make it clear. If this is thy will I will do it, but make it clear if it is so." He will do so, if it is His will, and you are willing to do it; and you need not, and ought not to do that thing until He does make it clear. We have no right to dictate to God *how* He shall give His guidance: by shutting up every other way, or by a sign, or by letting us put our finger on a text. It is ours to seek and expect wisdom, but it is not ours to dictate how it shall be given. (1 Cor. 12:11—"But all these worketh that one and the selfsame Spirit, dividing to every man severally *as he will*.")

Two things are evident from what has been said thus far about the work of the Holy Spirit in the believer:

First. How utterly dependent we are upon the Holy Spirit at every turn of Christian life and service.

Second. How perfect is the provision for life and service that God has made and what the fulness of privilege that is open to the humblest believer through the Holy Spirit's work. It is not so much what we are by nature, either intellectually, morally, spiritually, or even physically, that is important, but what the Holy Spirit can do for us, and what we will let Him do. The Holy Spirit often takes the one who gives the least natural promise and uses him beyond those who give the greatest natural promise. Christian life is not to be lived in the realm of natural temperament, and Christian work is not to be done in the power of natural endowment, but Christian life is to be lived in the realm of the Spirit, and Christian work is to be done in the power of the Spirit. The Holy Spirit is willing and eagerly desirous to do for each of us His whole work. He will do for each of us all that we let Him do.

(16) Rom. 8:11—"But if the Spirit of Him that raised up Jesus from the dead dwell in you, he that raised up Christ from the dead shall also *quicken your mortal bodies by his Spirit* that dwelleth in you."

SIXTEENTH PROPOSITION: The Holy Spirit quickens the mortal body of the believer.

This, as the context shows, refers to the future Resurrection of the body. This is the Spirit's work. The glorified body is from Him. It is a spiritual body. We now have the first fruits of the Spirit, but are waiting for the full harvest, the redemption of the body. (Rom. 8:23—"And not only they, but ourselves also, which have the first fruits of the Spirit, even we ourselves groan within ourselves, waiting for the adoption, to wit, the redemption of our body.")

NOTE.—There is a sense in which the Holy Spirit even now quickens our bodies. Matt. 12: 28—"But if I cast out devils by the Spirit of God, then the kingdom of God is come unto you." Acts 10: 38—"How God anointed Jesus of Nazareth with the Holy Ghost and with power: who went about doing good, *and healing* all that were oppressed of the devil: for God was with him." James 5: 14—"Is any sick among you: let him call for the elders of the church; and let them pray over him, anointing him with oil in the name of the Lord." God by His Holy Spirit does impart new health and vigor to these mortal bodies in the present life. Compare Ps. 104: 29, 30—"Thou hidest thy face, they are troubled: thou takest away their breath, they die, and are returned to the dust. Thou sendest forth thy spirit, they are created: and thou renewest the face of the earth."

CHAPTER VII.

THE BAPTISM WITH THE HOLY SPIRIT.

I. What the Baptism with the Holy Spirit is.

(1) Acts 1: 5—"For John truly baptized with water; but ye shall be *baptized with the Holy Ghost* not many days hence." Compare 2: 4, 38 —"And they were all *filled with the Holy Ghost*, and began to speak with other tongues, as the Spirit gave them utterance. Then Peter said unto them, Repent, and be baptized every one of you in the name of Jesus Christ for the remission of sins, and ye shall *receive the gift of the Holy Ghost.*"

4: 8—"Then Peter, *filled with the Holy Ghost*, said unto them, Ye rulers of the people, and leaders of Israel."

10: 44-46—"While Peter yet spake these words, *the Holy Ghost fell on* all them which heard the word. And they of the circumcision which believed were astonished, as many as came with Peter, because that on the Gentiles also was *poured out the gift of the Holy Ghost.* For they heard them speak with tongues, and magnify God."

Compare 11: 15-17—"And as I began to speak, *the Holy Ghost fell on them*, as on us at the beginning. Then remembered I the word of the Lord, how that he said, John indeed baptized with water; but *ye shall be baptized with the Holy Ghost.* Forasmuch then as God gave them the like gift as he did unto us, who believed on the Lord Jesus Christ, what was I, that I could withstand God ?"

19: 2-6—"He said unto them, *Have ye received the Holy Ghost* since ye believed ? And they said unto him, We have not so much as heard whether there be any Holy Ghost. And he said unto them, Unto what then were ye baptized ? And they said, Unto John's baptism. Then said Paul, John verily baptized with the baptism of repentance, saying unto the people, that they should believe on him which should come after him, that is, on Christ Jesus. When they heard this, they were baptized in the name of the Lord Jesus. And when Paul had laid his hands upon them, *the Holy Ghost came on them;* and they spake with tongues, and prophesied."

Heb. 2: 4—"God also bearing them witness, both with signs and wonders, and with divers miracles, and *gifts of the Holy Ghost*, according to his own will."

I Cor. 12: 4, 11, 13—"Now there are diversities of gifts, but the same Spirit. . . . But all these worketh that one and the selfsame Spirit, dividing to every man severally as he will. . . . For *by one Spirit* are we all *baptized* into one body, whether we be Jews or gentiles, whether we be bond or free; and have been all made to drink into one Spirit."

Luke 24: 49—"And behold I send *the promise of my Father* upon you: but tarry ye in the city of Jerusalem, until ye be *endued with power from on high.*"

FIRST PROPOSITION: A number of suggestive phrases— "Baptized with the Holy Spirit," "Filled with the Holy Ghost," "The Holy Ghost fell on them," "The gift of the Holy Ghost was poured out," "Receive the Holy Ghost," "The Holy Ghost came on them," "Gifts of the Holy Ghost," "I send the promise of my Father upon you," "Endued with power from on high," are used in the New Testament to describe one and the same experience.

(2) Acts 19: 2, R.V.—"And he said unto them, Did ye receive the Holy Ghost when ye believed? And they said unto him, Nay, we did not so much as hear whether the Holy Ghost was given."

SECOND PROPOSITION: The baptism with the Holy Spirit is a definite experience of which one may and ought to know whether he has received it or not.

(Compare Acts 8: 15, 16—"Who, when they were come down, prayed for them, that they might receive the Holy Ghost: *For as yet he was fallen upon none of them:* only they were baptized in the name of the Lord Jesus." Gal. 3: 2—"This only would I learn of you, *Received ye the Spirit* by the works of the law, or by the hearing of faith?")

(3) Acts 1: 5—"For John truly baptized with water; but ye shall be baptized with the Holy Ghost *not many days hence.*"

Here was a company of regenerated men pronounced so by Christ Himself. (Compare Jno. 15: 3—"*Now are ye clean through the word* which I have spoken unto you," and Jno. 13: 10—"Jesus saith to him, He that is washed needeth not save to wash his feet, but is clean every whit: and ye are *clean*, but not all.") And yet the baptism with the Spirit lay for them some days in the future.

Acts 8: 12—"But when they believed Philip preaching the things concerning the kingdom of God, and the name of Jesus Christ, they were baptized, both men and women."

In this company of baptized believers there were certainly same regenerated people, but we read in vv. 15: 16:

"Who, when they were come down, prayed for them, that they might receive the Holy Ghost: (For *as yet he was fallen upon none of them:* only they were baptized in the name of the Lord Jesus.")

Regenerated but not baptized with the Holy Ghost. We see the same thing in Acts 19: 1, 2:

"And it came to pass, that while Apollos was at Corinth, Paul having passed through the upper coasts, came to Ephesus; and finding certain disciples, He said unto them, *Have ye received the Holy Ghost* since ye believed? and they said unto him, we have not so much as heard whether there be any Holy Ghost." Compare v. 6—"And when Paul had laid his hands upon them, the Holy Ghost came on them; and they spake with tongues, and prophesied."

THIRD PROPOSITION: The Baptism with the Holy Spirit is an operation of the Holy Spirit distinct from and subsequent and additional to His regenerating work.

A man may be regenerated by the Holy Spirit and still not be baptized with the Holy Spirit. In regeneration there is an impartation of life, and the one who receives it is saved; in the Baptism with the Holy Spirit there is an impartation of power and the one who receives it is fitted for service.

EVERY TRUE BELIEVER HAS THE HOLY SPIRIT.

Rom. 8: 9—"But ye are not in the flesh, but in the Spirit, if so be that the Spirit of God dwell in you. Now, if any man have not the Spirit of Christ, he is none of his." (See also, 1 Cor. 6: 19.)

But not every believer has the Baptism with the Holy Spirit, though every believer, as we shall see, may have. The Baptism with the Holy Spirit may be received immediately after the new birth—as *e. g.*, in the household of Cornelius. In a normal state of the church every believer would have the Baptism with the Holy Spirit, as in the Church at Corinth. (1 Cor. 12: 13—"For by one Spirit *are we all baptized into one body*, whether we be Jews or Gentiles, whether we be bond or free; and have been all made to drink into one Spirit.")

In such a normal state of the church the Baptism with the Holy Spirit would be received immediately upon repentance and baptism into the name of Jesus Christ for the remission of sins. (Acts 2: 38.) But the doctrine of the Baptism with the Holy Spirit has been so allowed to drop out of sight, and the church has had so little expectancy along this line for its young children, that a large portion of the church is in the position of the churches in Samaria and Ephesus, where someone has to come and call the attention of the mass of believers to their privilege in the Risen Christ and claim it for them.

(4) Acts 1: 5, 8—"For John truly baptized with water; but ye shall be baptized with the Holy Ghost not many days hence. But *ye shall receive power*, after that the Holy Ghost is come upon you: and *ye shall be witnesses* unto me both in Jerusalem and in all Judea, and in Samaria, and unto the uttermost parts of the earth."

Luke 24: 49—"And behold I send the promise of my Father upon you: but tarry ye in the city of Jerusalem, until ye be *endued with power from on high*."

Acts. 2: 4—"And they were all filled with the Holy Ghost, and began *to speak with other tongues*, as the spirit gave them utterance."

Acts. 9: 17, 20—"And Ananias went his way, and entered into the house; and putting his hands on him said, Brother Saul, the Lord, even Jesus, that appeared unto thee in the way as thou camest, hath sent me, that thou mightest receive thy sight, and be filled with the Holy Ghost. *And straightway he preached Christ* in the synagogues, that he is the Son of God."

1 Cor. 12: 4–14—"Now there are *diversities of gifts*, but the same Spirit. And there are differences of administrations, but the same Lord. And there are diversities of operations, but it is the same God which worketh all in all. But the manifestation of the Spirit is given to every man to profit withal. For to one is given by the Spirit *the word of wisdom;* to another *the word of knowledge by the same Spirit:* To another *faith by the same Spirit:* to another the *gifts of healing* by the same Spirit: to another *the working of miracles;* to another *prophecy*, to another *discerning of Spirits;* to another *divers kinds of tongues;* to another *the interpretation of tongues:* But all these worketh out that one and the selfsame Spirit, dividing to every man severally as he will. For as the body is one, and hath many members, and all the members of that one body, being many, are one body: so also is Christ. For by one Spirit are we all baptized into one body, whether we be Jews or Gentiles, whether we be bond or free; and have been all made to drink into one Spirit."

FOURTH PROPOSITION: The Baptism with the Holy Spirit is an experience connected with and primarily for the purpose of service.

The Baptism with the Spirit is not primarily intended to make believers happy nor holy, but to make them useful. In every passage in the Bible in which the results of the Baptism with the Holy Spirit are mentioned they are related to testimony and service. The Baptism with the Holy Spirit has no direct reference to cleansing from sin. It has to do with gifts for service rather than with graces of character. The steps by which one ordinarily receives the Baptism with the Holy Spirit are of such a character, and the Baptism with the Holy Spirit makes God so real that this Baptism is in most cases accompanied by a great moral uplift, or even a radical transformation, but the Baptism with the Holy Spirit is not in itself either an eradication of the carnal nature or cleansing from an impure heart. It is the impartation of supernatural power or gifts in service, and sometimes one may have rare gifts by the Spirit's power and few graces. (Compare 1 Cor. 13: 1-3—"Though I speak with the tongues of men and of angels, and have not charity, I am become as sounding brass, or a tinkling cymbal. And though I have the gift of prophecy, and understand all mysteries, and all knowledge; and though I have all faith, so that I could remove mountains, and have not charity, I am nothing. And though I bestow all my goods to feed the poor, and though I give my body to be burned, and have not charity, it profiteth me nothing." And Matt. 7: 22, 23—"Many will say to me in that day, Lord, Lord, have we not *prophesied in Thy name*, and in Thy name have *cast out devils*, and in Thy name *done many wonderful works?* And then will I profess unto them, I never knew you; depart from me, ye that work iniquity.")

It is indeed the work of the Holy Spirit to cleanse from sin, and to empower one for and lead one into a life of victory over the world, the flesh and the Devil, but this is not the Baptism with the Holy Spirit. It is, however, more fundamental and important. It is well to remember also that Jesus promised a twofold baptism, "with the Holy Ghost *and with fire*." This can not be interpreted to mean two contrasted baptisms, one of blessing and the other of judgment. The Greek does not permit of this interpretation. It is one twofold baptism. Many seem to get only part of it, "the Holy Wind," but the "fire" is for us too, if we claim it. And fire searches, refines, consumes, illuminates, makes to glow, energizes, spreads. "Fire" is what many need to-day, and it is for us.

II. Results of the Baptism with the Holy Spirit.

(1) 1 Cor. 12: 4-10—"Now there are *diversities* of gifts, but the same Spirit. And there are *differences* of administrations, but the

same Lord. And there are *diversities* of operations, but it is the same God which worketh all in all. But the manifestation of the Spirit is given to every man to profit withal. For *to one* is given by the Spirit the word of wisdom; *to another* the word of knowledge by the same Spirit; *to another* faith by the same Spirit; *to another* the gifts of healing by the same Spirit; *to another* the working of miracles; *to another* prophecy; *to another* discerning of spirits; *to another* divers kinds of tongues: *to another* the interpretation of tongues.''

FIRST PROPOSITION: The specific manifestations of the Baptism with the Holy Spirit are not precisely the same in all persons.

''There are diversities of gifts, but the same Spirit.'' The gifts vary with the different lines of service to which God has called different persons. The church is a body, and different parts of the body have different functions, and the Spirit imparts to the one who is baptized with the Spirit those gifts which fit him for the work to which the Spirit has called him. For examample, many in the early church who were baptized with the Holy Spirit spake with tongues (Acts 10: 46; 19: 6), but not all. (1. Cor. 12: 27–30.) So to-day the Holy Spirit imparts to some gifts as an evangelist, to others as pastors and teachers. To others as ''helps, governments,'' etc.

(2) 1 Cor. 12: 7—''For the manifestation of the Spirit is given to every man to profit withal.''

SECOND PROPOSITION: There will be some gift to every one baptized with the Holy Spirit.

(3) 1 Cor. 12: 11, R.V.—''But all these worketh the one and the same Spirit, dividing to each one severally even as he will.''

THIRD PROPOSITION: The Holy Spirit divides to each one severally as He will. The Holy Spirit is absolutely sovereign in deciding how—in what special gift, operation or power—the Baptism with the Holy Spirit shall manifest itself.

It is not for us to pick out some place of service and then ask the Holy Spirit to qualify us for that service; it is not for us to select some gift and then ask the Holy Spirit to impart to us that gift. It is for us to simply put ourselves entirely at the disposal of the Holy Spirit to send us where He will, to select for us what kind of service He will, and to impart what gift He will.

He is absolutely sovereign, and our position is that of unconditional surrender to Him. I am glad that this is so: that He, in His infinite wisdom and love, is to select the field, service and gifts and not I, in my shortsightedness and folly. It is because of a failure to recognize this absolute sovereignty of the Spirit that many fail of the blessing and meet with disappointment. They are trying to select the gift and so get none. Of course, it is scriptural, while recognizing and rejoicing in the sovereignty of the Holy Spirit, to "covet earnestly the best gifts." (1 Cor. 12: 31.)

(4) Acts 1: 5, 8—" For John truly baptized with water; but ye shall be baptized with the Holy Ghost not many days hence. For *ye shall receive power*, after that the Holy Ghost is come upon you; and ye shall be witnesses unto me both in Jerusalem, and in all Judea, and in Samaria, and unto the uttermost part of the earth."

FOURTH PROPOSITION: The Baptism with the Holy Spirit always imparts power in service.

The power may be of one kind in one person and of another kind in another person, but there will always be power—and the very power of God at that. As sure as anyone who reads these pages, who has not already received the Baptism with the Holy Spirit, seeks it in God's way, there will come into his service a power that was never there before—power for the very work God has for you to do. The results of that power may not be manifest at once in conversions. (Acts 7: 55–60.)

(5) Acts. 4: 29, 31—"And now, Lord, behold their threatenings: and grant unto thy servants, that with all boldness they may speak thy word. . . . And when they had prayed, the place was shaken where they were assembled together; and they were all filled with the Holy Ghost, and they *spake the word of God with boldness.*

FIFTH PROPOSITION: The Baptism with the Holy Spirit imparts boldness in testimony and service.

The Baptism with the Spirit converts cowards into heroes. (Compare Acts 4: 8–12.)

(6) Acts 2: 4, 7, 8, 11—"And they were all filled with the Holy Ghost, and began to speak with other tongues, as the Spirit gave them utterance. And they were all amazed and marvelled, saying one to another, Behold, are not all these which speak Galileans? And how

hear we every man in our own tongue, wherein we were born? Cretes and Arabians, we do hear them *speak* in our tongues *the wonderful works of* God."

Acts 4: 31, 33, 8–10—"And when they had prayed, the place was shaken where they were assembled together; and they were all filled with the Holy Ghost, and they spake the word of God with boldness. And with great power gave the apostles *witness of the resurrection of the Lord Jesus:* and great grace was upon them all. . . . Then Peter, *filled with the Holy Ghost,* said unto them, Ye rulers of the people, and elders of Israel, if we this day be examined of the good deed done to the impotent man, by what means he is made whole; be it known unto you all, and to all the people of Israel, that by *the name of Jesus Christ of Nazareth*, whom ye crucified, whom God raised from the dead, even by him doth this man stand here before you whole."

Acts 9: 17, 20—"And Ananias went his way, and entered into the house; and putting his hands on him said, Brother Saul, the Lord, even Jesus, that appeared unto thee in the way as thou camest, hath sent me, that thou mightest receive thy sight, and be *filled with the Holy Ghost.* . . . And *straightway he preached Christ* in the synagogues, that he is the Son of God."

Acts 10: 44–46—"While Peter yet spake these words, the Holy Ghost fell on all them which heard the word. And they of the circumcision which believed were astonished, as many as came with Peter, because that on the Gentiles also was poured out the gift of the Holy Ghost, for they heard them speak with tongues, *and magnify God.*"

Eph. 5: 18, 19—"And be not drunk with wine, wherein is excess; but be filled with the Spirit; speaking to yourselves in psalms and hymns and spiritual songs, singing and *making melody in your heart to the Lord.*"

SIXTH PROPOSITION: The Baptism with the Holy Spirit causes one to be occupied with God and Christ and spiritual things.

The man who is filled with the Holy Ghost will not be singing sentimental ballads, nor comic ditties, nor operatic airs while the power of the Holy Ghost is upon him. If the Holy Ghost should come upon one while listening to the most innocent of the world's songs he would not enjoy it. He would long to hear something about Christ.

GENERAL PROPOSITION: The Baptism with the Holy Spirit is the Spirit of God coming upon the believer, filling his mind with a real apprehension of truth, and taking possession of his faculties, imparting to him gifts not otherwise his, but which qualify him for the service to which God has called him.

III. The Necessity of the Baptism with the Holy Spirit.

(1) Luke 24: 48, 49—"And ye are witnesses of these things. And behold, I send the promise of my Father upon you: but *tarry ye* (sit ye down) in the city of Jerusalem, until ye be endued with power from on high."

Acts 1: 4, 5, 8—"And, being assembled together with them, commanded them that they should not depart from Jerusalem, *but wait* for the promise of the Father, which, saith he, ye have heard of me. . . . But ye shall receive power, *after that* the Holy Ghost is come upon you: and ye shall be witnesses unto me both in Jerusalem, and in all Judea, and in Samaria, and unto the uttermost part of the earth."

FIRST PROPOSITION: Jesus Christ commanded the disciples not to enter upon the work to which He had Himself called them until baptized with the Holy Ghost.

NOTE 1.—They were rarely fitted for the work by experience, and by association with Himself, and by long training at His own hands, but the further preparation of the Baptism with the Holy Spirit was so all essential that they must not move without it.

NOTE 2.—There was apparently imperative need that something be done *at once*. The whole world was perishing and they alone knew the saving truth. Nevertheless Jesus strictly charged them "wait." What a testimony to the all importance of "the Baptism with the Holy Spirit" as a preparation for work that shall be acceptable to Christ.

(2) Acts 10: 38—"How God anointed Jesus of Nazareth with the Holy Ghost and with power: who went about doing good, and healing all that were oppressed of the devil; for God was with him." (Compare Luke 3: 22 and Luke 4: 1, 14, 17, 18—"And the Holy Ghost *descended in a bodily shape like a dove upon him*, and a voice came from heaven, which said, Thou art my beloved Son; in thee I am well pleased. . . . And Jesus *being full of the Holy Ghost* returned from Jordan, and was led by the Spirit into the wilderness. . . . And Jesus returned *in the power of the Spirit* into Galilee: and there went out a fame of him through all the region round about. . . . And there was delivered unto him the book of the prophet Esaias. And when he had opened the book, he found the place where it was written, *The Spirit of the Lord is upon me*, because he hath anointed me to preach the gospel to the poor; he hath sent me to heal the broken-hearted, to preach deliverance to the captive, and recovering of sight to the blind, to set at liberty them that are bruised."

SECOND PROPOSITION: Jesus Christ Himself, though the only begotten Son of God, did not enter upon His ministry until the Spirit of God had come upon Him, and He had thus been "anointed with the Holy Ghost and power."

(3) Acts 8: 14-16—"Now when the apostles which were at Jerusa-lem heard that Samaria had received the word of God they sent unto them Peter and John: who, when they were come down, *prayed for them, that they might receive the Holy Ghost:* for as yet he was fallen upon none of them: only they were baptized in the name of the Lord Jesus."

Acts 19: 1, 2—"And it came to pass, that, while Apollos was at Corinth, Paul having passed through the upper coasts came to Ephesus; and finding certain disciples, he said unto them, *Have ye received the Holy Ghost* since ye believed? And they said unto him, We have not so much as heard whether there be any Holy Ghost."

✴ *THIRD PROPOSITION: When the apostles found believers in Christ they at once demanded whether they had received the Holy Ghost, and, if not, they at once saw to it that they did.*

✴ *GENERAL PROPOSITION: The Baptism with the Holy Spirit is absolutely necessary in every Christian for the service that Christ demands and expects of him.*

IV. Possibility of the Baptism with the Holy Spirit, or for whom is the Baptism with the Holy Spirit?

Acts 2: 38, 39—"Then Peter said unto them, Repent, and be bap-tized every one of you in the name of Jesus Christ for the remission of sins, and *ye shall receive the gift of the Holy Ghost. For the promise is unto you, and to your children, and to all that are afar off, even as many as the Lord our God shall call.*"

(The promise of these verses is "the Baptism with the Holy Spirit" or "gift of the Holy Spirit." Compare Acts 1: 4; 2: 33, and also context.)

FIRST PROPOSITION: The Baptism with the Holy Spirit was not merely for the apostles, nor merely for those of the apostolic age, but for "all that are afar off, even as many as the Lord our God shall call" as well, i. e., it is for every believer in every age of the Church's history. If any believer in any age does not have the Baptism with the Holy Spirit, it is solely because he does not claim his privilege in Christ.

V. The Refilling with the Holy Spirit.

Acts 2: 4—"And they were *all filled* with the Holy Ghost, and began to speak with other tongues, as the Spirit gave them utter-ance."

Acts 4: 8, 31—"Then *Peter, filled* with the Holy Ghost, said unto them, Ye rulers of the people, and elders of Israel. . . And when they had prayed, the place was shaken where they were assembled together; and they were *all filled* with the Holy Ghost, and they spake the word of God with boldness."

FIRST PROPOSITION: The same disciple (Peter) is said to have been "filled with the Holy Spirit" on three different occasions.

It is not enough that one be filled with the Holy Spirit once. We need a new filling of the Holy Spirit for each new emergency of Christian service.

VI.   The Conditions upon which the Baptism with the Holy Spirit is given.

(1)   Acts 2: 38, R.V.—"*Repent* ye, and *be baptized* every one of you *in the name of Jesus Christ* unto the remission of your sins, and ye shall receive the gift of the Holy Ghost."

Acts 10: 44—"While Peter yet spake these words, the Holy Ghost fell *on all them which heard* the word.   Compare Acts 15: 8, 9—"And God which knoweth the hearts, bare them witness, giving them the Holy Ghost even as he did unto us, and put no difference between us and them, purifying their hearts *by faith.*"

Gal. 3: 2—"Received ye the Spirit by the works of the law, or *by the hearing of faith*"?

FIRST PROPOSITION: The fundamental conditions upon which the gift (or Baptism with the Holy Spirit) is bestowed are: Repentance, faith in Jesus Christ as an all-sufficient Saviour (apart from works of the law), and baptism in the name of Jesus Christ unto the remission of sins.

(2)   Acts 19: 2, 6, R.V.—"He said unto them, Did ye receive the Holy Ghost when ye believed? And they said unto him, Nay, *we did not so much as hear whether the Holy Ghost was given.*" (Compare v. 6.)

SECOND PROPOSITION: For those who believe on Jesus Christ the experimental reception of the Baptism with the Holy Spirit is sometimes conditioned on the believer's knowing that there is such a blessing and that it is for him now.

(3)   Acts 5: 32 (last part)—"The Holy Ghost, whom God hath given *to them that obey him.*"

THIRD PROPOSITION: God gives the Holy Ghost to them that obey Him.

Obedience means *absolute surrender*. This is really involved in true repentance and faith in Jesus Christ. It is one of the most fundamental conditions of entering into this blessing. It is the point at which thousands fail of it to-day.

(4) Acts 8: 15, 16—"Who, when they were come down, *prayed* for them that they might receive the Holy Ghost; for as yet he was fallen on none of them," etc. (See, also, v. 17.)

FOURTH PROPOSITION: The Baptism with the Holy Spirit is given to those who have already believed on Christ and been baptized with water (v. 12) in answer to definite prayer. (Compare Luke 11: 13.) *But there may be much earnest praying and still the Holy Spirit not come because the prayer is not in faith.* (Jas. 1: 6, 7.) *The faith that receives this, as every other blessing at once, is the faith that counts it as its own.* (Mark, 11: 24, R.V.; 1 Jno. 5: 14, 15.)*

----

*This whole subject is discussed at length in the author's book entitled " The Baptism with the Holy Spirit."

CHAPTER VIII.

THE WORK OF THE HOLY SPIRIT IN PROPHETS AND APOSTLES.

I. The Distinctive Character of the Work of the Holy Spirit in Prophets and Apostles.

(1) 1 Cor. 12: 4, 8-11, 28, 29—"Now, there are diversities of gifts, but the same Spirit. . . . For to one is given by the Spirit the word of wisdom; to another the word of knowledge by the same Spirit; to another faith by the same Spirit; to another the gifts of healing by the same Spirit; to another the working of miracles; *to another prophecy*; to another discerning of spirits; to another divers kinds of tongues; to another the interpretation of tongues: But all these worketh that one and the selfsame Spirit, dividing to every man severally as he will. . . . And God hath set some in the church, *first apostles, secondly prophets*, thirdly teachers, after that miracles, then gifts of healing, helps, governments, diversities of tongues. *Are all apostles? are all prophets?* are all teachers? are all workers of miracles ?"

FIRST PROPOSITION: The work of the Holy Spirit in Apostles and Prophets differs from His work in other believers. He imparts to Apostles and Prophets an especial gift for an especial purpose.

The doctrine which is becoming so common and so popular in our day, that the work of the Holy Spirit in preachers and teachers and in ordinary believers, illuminating them and guiding them into the truth and into the understanding of the Word of God, is the same in kind and differs only in degree from the work of the Holy Spirit in Prophets and Apostles, is thoroughly unscriptural and untrue. It overlooks the clearly stated and carefully elucidated fact that while there is "the same Spirit," "there are diversities of gifts," "diversities of ministrations," "diversities of workings " (1 Cor. 12: 4-6, R.V.), and that not all are prophets or apostles. (1 Cor. 12: 29.)

NOTE.—Those who desire to minimize the difference between the work of the Holy Spirit in Apostles and Prophets, and his work in other men, often refer to the fact that the Bible says that Bezaleel was to be "filled with the Spirit of God" to devise the work of the Tabernacle (Ex. 31: 1-11), as a proof that the inspiration of the prophet does not differ from the inspiration of the artist or architect; but they are ignorant of the fact, or forget it, that the Tabernacle was to be built after the pattern shown to Moses in the Mount (Ex. 25: 9, 40), and that, therefore, it was itself a prophecy, and an exposition of the truth of God. It was the word of God done into wood, gold, silver, brass, cloth, skin, etc. There is much reasoning about inspiration to-day that appears at first sight very learned, but that will not bear much rigid scrutiny or candid comparison with the word of God. There is nothing in the Bible more inspired than the Tabernacle, and if the higher critics would study it more they would give up their ingenious but untenable theories.

II. Results of the Work of the Holy Spirit in Prophets and Apostles.

(1) Eph. 3: 5, R.V.—"Which in other generations was not made known unto the sons of men, *as it hath now been revealed unto his holy apostles and prophets in the Spirit.*"

FIRST PROPOSITION: Truth hidden from men for ages, and which they had not discovered, and could not discover by the unaided processes of human reasoning, has been revealed to Apostles and to Prophets in the Spirit.

The Bible contains truth that men never had discovered, and never would have discovered if left to themselves, but which the Father in great grace has revealed to his children through His servants, the Prophets and the Apostles. We see here the folly of testing the statements of Scripture by the conclusions of human reasoning or "the Christian Consciousness." The revelation of God transcends human reasoning, and a consciousness that is truly and fully Christian is the product of the study and absorption of Bible truth. If our consciousness differs from the statements of this book, it is not yet fully Christian, and the thing to do is not to try to pull God's revelation down to the level of our consciousness, but to tone our consciousness up to the level of God's Word.

(2) 1 Pet. 1: 10, 11, 12—"Of which salvation the prophets have inquired and searched diligently, who prophesied of the grace that should come unto you: *Searching what, or what manner of time the Spirit of Christ which was in them did signify*, when it testified beforehand the sufferings of Christ, and the glory that should follow. Unto whom it was revealed, that not unto themselves but unto us they did minister

the things which are now reported unto you by them that have preached the gospel unto you with the Holy Ghost sent down from heaven; which things the angels desire to look into."

SECOND PROPOSITION: The Revelation made to the Prophets was independent of their own thinking; it was made to them by the Spirit of Christ which was in them—and was a subject of inquiry to their own mind as to its meaning. It was not their thought, but His.

(3) 2 Pet. 1: 21, R.V.—"For no prophecy ever came by the will of man: but men spake from God, being moved by the Holy Ghost."

THIRD PROPOSITION: No prophetic utterance was of the Prophets' own will, but they spake from God, and the Prophet was carried along in it by the Holy Spirit.

(4) Heb. 3: 7—"Wherefore *as the Holy Ghost saith*, To-day, if ye will hear his voice."

10: 15, 16—"Whereof *the Holy Ghost also is a witness* to us: for after that *he had said* before, This is the covenant that I will make with them after those days, saith the Lord; I will put my laws into their hearts, and in their minds will I write them."

Acts. 28: 25—"And when they agreed not among themselves, they departed, after that Paul had spoken one word. *Well spake the Holy Ghost* by Esaias the prophet unto our fathers."

2 Sam. 23: 2, R.V.—"*The Spirit of the* LORD *spake by me, and his word was in my tongue.*"

FOURTH PROPOSITION: It was the Holy Spirit who spoke in the prophetic utterance; it was His word that was upon the Prophet's tongue.

The prophet was simply the mouth by which the Holy Spirit spake. As a man, except as the Spirit taught him and used him, the prophet was fallible as other men are, but when the Spirit was upon him, and he was taken up and borne along by the Holy Spirit, he was infallible in his teachings. The teaching, indeed, was not his, but the Holy Spirit's. God was speaking, not the prophet. For example, Paul doubtless had many mistaken notions, but when he taught as an apostle, under the Spirit's power, he was infallible—or rather the Spirit who taught through him, and the consequent teaching, were infallible—as infallible as God. We do well to carefully distinguish what Paul may have thought as a man, and what he actually did teach as an apostle.

In the Bible we have the record of what he taught as an apostle, with the possible exception of 1 Cor. 7: 6, 25—"But I speak this by *permission*, and not of commandment. . . . Now concerning virgins I have no commandment of the Lord: yet I give my judgment, as one that hath obtained mercy of the Lord to be faithful," and the context. Here he does not seem to have been sure that he had the word of the Lord and is careful to note the fact, thus giving additional certainty to all other passages.

It is sometimes said that Paul taught in his early epistles that the Lord would return during his lifetime, and in this was of course mistaken. But Paul never taught anywhere that the Lord would return during his lifetime. In 1 Thess. 4: 17 ("Then *we which are alive and remain* shall be caught up together with them in the clouds, to meet the Lord in the air: and so shall we be ever with the Lord"), as he was still alive, he naturally did not include himself with those who were fallen asleep in speaking of the Lord's return. Quite probably he did believe that he might be alive, and the attitude of expectancy is the true attitude in all ages for every believer. Paul probably rather believed he would live to the coming of the Lord, but he did not so teach. The Holy Spirit kept him from this as all other errors in his teachings.

(5) 1 Cor. 2: 13—"Which things also we speak, not *in the words* which man's wisdom teacheth, but which the Holy Ghost teacheth; comparing spiritual things with spiritual." (See Am. Ap. to R.V.)

FIFTH PROPOSITION: The Holy Spirit in the Apostle taught not only the thought (or "concept") but the words in which the thought was to be expressed.

This is not only a necessary inference from the fact that thought is conveyed from mind to mind by words, and if the words were imperfect the thought expressed in those words would necessarily be imperfect, but it is distinctly so stated. Nothing could be plainer than Paul's statement "IN WORDS, which the Spirit teacheth." The Holy Spirit has Himself anticipated all these modern ingenious but unbiblical and false theories regarding His own work in the apostles.

The more carefully and minutely one studies the *wording* of the statements of this wonderful book, the more he will become convinced of the marvelous accuracy of the words used to express the thought. To a superficial student the doctrine of verbal inspiration may appear questionable or even absurd, but any regenerated and Spirit-taught man who *ponders the words* of the Scripture day after day and year after year will become convinced that the wisdom of God is in the very words, as well as in the thought which is expressed in the words. It is an impressive fact that our difficulties with the Bible rapidly disappear as we note the precise language used. The change of a word or letter, of a tense, case, or number would land us in contradiction or untruth, but taking the *words* just as written, difficulties disappear and truth shines forth.

The Divine origin of nature shines forth clearly under the use of the microscope as we see the perfection of form and adaptation of the minutest particles of matter. So likewise the Divine origin of the Bible shines forth clearly under the microscope as we note the perfection with which the turn of a word reveals the absolute thought of God.

QUESTION: If the Holy Spirit is the author of the words of Scripture, how do we account for variations in style and diction?—that, for example, Paul always uses Pauline language, and John, Johannean, etc.

ANSWER: If we could not account at all for this fact it would have little weight against the explicit statement of God's Word, with anyone who is humble and wise enough to recognize that there are a great many things which he can not account for at all, which could be easily accounted for if he knew more. But these variations are easily accounted for. The Holy Spirit is quite wise enough and has quite enough facility in the use of language in revealing truth to and through any individual, to use words, phrases and forms of expression in that person's vocabulary and forms of thought, and to make use of that person's peculiar individuality. It is a mark of the Divine wisdom of this book that the same Divine truth is expressed with absolute accuracy in such widely variant forms of expression.

(6) Mark 7:13—"Making *the word of God* of none effect through your traditions, which ye have delivered: and many such like things do ye."

2 Sam. 23:2—"The Spirit of the LORD spake by me, and *his word* was in my tongue."

1 Thess. 2: 13—" For this cause also thank we God without ceasing, because, when ye received *the word of God, which ye heard* of us, ye received it not as the word of men, but, as *it is in truth the word of God,* which effectually worketh also in you that believe."

SIXTH PROPOSITION: The utterances of the Apostles and the Prophets were the Word of God.   When we read these words we are not listening to the voice of man but to the voice of God.

CHAPTER IX.

THE WORK OF THE HOLY SPIRIT IN JESUS CHRIST.

I. How the Holy Spirit Worked in Jesus Christ.

(1) Luke 1:35—"And the angel answered and said unto her, *The Holy Ghost shall come upon thee*, and the power of the highest shall overshadow thee: therefore also that holy thing which shall be born of thee shall be called the Son of God."

FIRST PROPOSITION: Jesus Christ was begotten of the Holy Spirit.

In regeneration the believer is begotten of God; Jesus Christ was begotten of God in generation. He is the only begotten Son of God. (Jno. 3: 16—"For God so loved the world, that he gave his *only begotten* Son, that whosoever believeth in him should not perish but have everlasting life.") The regenerated man has the carnal nature received from his earthly father and the new nature imparted by God. Jesus Christ had only the new holy nature. He was, however, real man as he had a human mother.

(2) Heb. 9: 14—"How much more shall the blood of Christ, who *through the eternal Spirit offered himself without spot* to God, purge your conscience from dead works to serve the living God."

SECOND PROPOSITION: Jesus Christ led a holy, spotless life, and offered Himself to God, through the working of the Holy Spirit.

(3) Acts 10: 38—"How God anointed Jesus of Nazareth *with the Holy Ghost and with power*: who went about doing good, and healing all that were oppressed of the devil; for God was with him."

Is. 61: 1—"The *Spirit of the* LORD *God is upon me;* because the LORD hath anointed me to preach good tidings unto the meek; he hath sent me to bind up the brokenhearted, to proclaim liberty to the captive, and the opening of the prison to them that are bound."

Luke 4: 14, 18—"And Jesus returned *in the power of the Spirit* into Galilee: and there went out a fame of him through all the region round about. . . *The Spirit of the Lord is upon me*, because he hath anointed me to preach the gospel to the poor; he hath sent me to heal the brokenhearted, to preach deliverance to the captives, and recovering of sight to the blind, to set at liberty them that are bruised."

THIRD PROPOSITION: Jesus Christ was anointed for service by the Holy Spirit.

(Compare Luke 3: 21, 22—" Now when all the people were baptized, it came to pass, that Jesus also being baptized, and praying, the heaven was opened, and the Holy Ghost descended in a bodily shape like a dove upon him, and a voice came from heaven, which said, Thou art my beloved Son; in thee I am well pleased," and Luke 4: 1, 14—" And Jesus *being full of the Holy Ghost* returned from Jordan, and was led by the Spirit into the wilderness. . . . And Jesus *returned in the power of the Spirit* into Galilee: and there went out a fame of him through all the region round about.")

(4) Luke 4: 1—"And Jesus being full of the Holy Ghost returned from Jordan, and *was led by the Spirit* into the wilderness."

FOURTH PROPOSITION: Jesus Christ was led by the Holy Spirit in His movements.

(5) Is. 11: 2—"And the Spirit of the LORD shall rest upon him, the spirit of wisdom and understanding, the spirit of counsel and might, the spirit of knowledge and of the fear of the LORD."

(Compare Matt. 12: 17, 18—" That it might be fulfilled which was spoken by Esaias the prophet, saying, behold my servant whom I have chosen; my beloved, in whom my soul is well pleased: I will put my Spirit upon him, and he shall shew judgment to the Gentiles.")

FIFTH PROPOSITION: Jesus Christ was taught by the Spirit who rested upon Him. The Spirit of God was the source of His wisdom in the days of His flesh.

NOTE.—Jno. 1: 33—"And I knew him not: but he that sent me to baptize with water, the same said unto me, Upon whom thou shalt see the Spirit descending, *and remaining on him*, the same is he which baptizeth with the Holy Ghost."

(6) Jno. 3: 34, R.V.—"For he whom God hath sent *speaketh the words* of God: for he giveth not the Spirit by measure."

SIXTH PROPOSITION: The Holy Spirit abode upon Him in fulness and the words He spoke were the words of God.

(7) Acts 1: 2—"Until the day in which he was taken up, after that he through the Holy Ghost had given commandments unto the apostles whom he had chosen."

SEVENTH PROPOSITION: Jesus Christ gave commandment to His apostles whom he had chosen, through the Holy Spirit.

(8) Matt. 12: 28—"But if I cast out devils by the Spirit of God, then the kingdom of God is come unto you."

EIGHTH PROPOSITION: Jesus Christ wrought His miracles in the power of the Holy Spirit.

Compare 1 Cor. 12: 9, 10—"To another faith by the same Spirit; to another the gift of healing by the same Spirit; to another the working of miracles," etc., etc.

(9) Rom. 8: 11—"But if *the Spirit of Him that raised up Jesus* from the dead dwell in you, he that raised up Christ from the dead shall also quicken your mortal bodies by his Spirit that dwelleth in you."

NINTH PROPOSITION: Jesus Christ was raised from the dead by the power of the Holy Spirit.

II. Practical Inferences from the Work of the Holy Spirit in Jesus Christ.

Several things are evident from the study of the work of the Holy Spirit in Jesus Christ.

(1.) *The completeness of His humanity.* He lived, thought, worked, taught, conquered sin and won victories for God in the power of that same Spirit whom we may all have.

(2.) *Our dependence upon the Holy Spirit.* If it was in the power of the Holy Spirit that Jesus Christ, the only begotten Son of God, lived, worked and triumphed, how much more are we dependent upon Him at every turn of life, service and conflict with Satan and sin !

(3.) *The wondrous world of privilege, blessing, victory and conquest that is open to us.* The same Spirit by which Jesus was begotten is at our disposal for us to be begotten of Him. The same Spirit by which Jesus Christ offered Himself without spot to God is at our disposal for us to offer ourselves without spot, the same Spirit by which Jesus was anointed for service is at our disposal for us to be anointed for service, and so on through all the points given above.

Jesus Christ is our pattern (1 Jno. 2: 6), the firstborn among many brethren. Whatever he realized through the Holy Spirit is there for us to realize also.

BOOK IV.

—

WHAT THE BIBLE TEACHES ABOUT MAN.

CHAPTER L

HIS ORIGINAL CONDITION.

I. Man Created in the Image of God.

(1) Gen. 1: 26, 27—"And God said, Let us make man *in our image after our likeness:* and let them have dominion over the fish of the sea, and over the fowl of the air, and over the cattle, and over all the earth, and over every creeping thing that creepeth upon the earth. So God created man in his own image, in the image of God created he him; male and female created he them."

Gen. 9: 6—"Whoso sheddeth man's blood, by man shall his blood be shed: for *in the image of God made he man.*"

FIRST PROPOSITION: God created man in His own image, after His own likeness.

QUESTION: To what do this "image" and "likeness" refer?

ANSWER:

(*a*) Eph. 4: 23, 24—"And be renewed in the spirit of your mind; and that ye put on the new man, *which after God is created in right eousness and true holiness.*"

Col. 3: 10—"And have put on the new man, which is *renewed in knowledge after the image* of him that created him."

Rom. 8: 29—"For whom he did foreknow, he also did predestinate to be conformed to the image of his Son, that he might be the first-born among many brethren."

2 Cor. 3: 18—"But we all, with open face beholding as in a glass the glory of the Lord, are changed into the same image from glory to glory, even as the Spirit of the Lord."

Col. 1: 15—"Who is the *image of the invisible God*, the firstborn of every creature."

The image and likeness plainly have reference to the intellectual and moral nature of man.

(*b*) Ps. 17: 15, R.V. (Marg. in part)—"As for me, I shall behold thy face in righteousness: I shall be satisfied, when I awake, with thy form." (The Hebrew word used here clearly means a visible form. Compare Num. 12: 8, R.V.—"With him will I speak mouth to mouth, even manifestly, and not in dark speeches; and the *the form of the* LORD *shall he behold:* wherefore then were ye not afraid to speak against my servant, against Moses?")

The image and likeness would seem also to have some reference to the visible likeness. It is true God is essentially spirit
(Jno. 4: 24), and invisible (Col. 1: 15), but God has a form in
which he manifests Himself to the eye (Is. 6: 1; Acts 7: 56;
Phil. 2: 6 [See Thayer's Greek-English Lex. of the N. T. or
the word translated "form" in this last passage], and man
seems to have been created not only in the intellectual and moral,
but also the visible likeness of God. (Compare Gen. 5: 1, 3—
"This is the book of the generations of Adam. In the day that
God created man, in the likeness of God made he him. . . .
And Adam lived a hundred and thirty years, and begat a son in
his own likeness, after his image; and called his name Seth.")

It is perhaps impossible to say how much of this visible likeness was lost by the Fall, but in the regeneration man is not only
recreated intellectually and morally in the likeness of God (Eph.
4: 23, 24; Col. 3: 10), but when the regeneration is complete in
the outward, visible likeness as well. (Compare Phil. 3: 21—
" Who shall change *our vile body*, that it may be fashioned *like
unto his glorious body*, according to the working whereby he is
able even to subdue all things unto himself.")

But from Jno. 17: 5 ("And now, O Father, glorify thou
me with thine own self with the glory which I had with thee before the world was"), compared with Phil. 2: 6 ("Who, being
in the form of God, thought it not robbery to be equal with
God"), we see that "the form" of Christ was the form of God.

II. The Original Intellectual and Moral Condition of Man.

(1) Gen. 2: 19—"And out of the ground the LORD God formed
every beast of the field, and every fowl of the air; and brought them
unto Adam *to see what he would call them;* and *whatsoever Adam
called every living creature, that was the name* thereof."

Gen. 1: 28—"And God blessed them, and God said unto them, Be
fruitful, and multiply, and replenish the earth, and *subdue it;* and
have dominion over the fish of the sea, and over the fowl of the air,
and over every living thing that moveth upon the earth."

*FIRST PROPOSITION: Man was created with sufficient in-
tellectual capacity to give names to all living creatures and to have
dominion over them.*

Man was not created an ignoramus nor a savage, but a being
with lofty intellectual powers. Whatever truth there may be in

the doctrine of evolution as applied within limits to the animal world, it breaks down when applied to man. It contradicts not only Scripture, but the known facts of history. The development of man from an originally low order of intellectual beings closely resembling the ape, is a figment of unbridled imagination falsely dubbed science. There is absolutely not one fact to sustain it. The first view we get of man is of a being of splendid intellectual powers.

(2) Gen. 3: 1-6—"Now the serpent was more subtil than any beast of the field which the LORD God had made. And he said unto the woman, Yea, hath God said, Ye shall not eat of every tree of the garden? And the woman said unto the serpent, We may eat of the fruit of the trees of the garden: but of the fruit of the tree which is in the midst of the garden, God hath said, Ye shall not eat of it, neither shall ye touch it, lest ye die. And the serpent said unto the woman, Ye shall ·not surely die: For God doth know that in the day ye eat thereof, ·then your eyes shall be opened, and ye shall be as gods, knowing good and evil. And when the woman saw that the tree was good for food, and that it was pleasant to the eyes, and a tree to be desired to make one wise, she took of the fruit thereof, and did eat, and gave also unto her husband with her; and he did eat."

Rom. 5: 12, 14—" Wherefore, as *by one man sin entered into the world*, and death by sin; and so death passed upon all men, for that all have sinned: . . . Nevertheless death reigned from Adam to Moses, even over them that had not sinned after the similitude of Adam's transgression, who is the figure of him that was to come." (Eccl. 7: 29.)

SECOND PROPOSITION: Man was not created a sinner, but sin entered into the world through man, by his conscious and voluntary choice.

CHAPTER II.

THE FALL.

I. The Fact of the Fall.

(1) Gen. 3: 1-6—"Now the serpent was more subtil than any beast of the field which the LORD God had made. And he said unto the woman, Yea, hath God said, Ye shall not eat of every tree of the garden? And the woman said unto the serpent, We may eat of the fruit of the trees of the garden: but of the fruit of the tree which is in the midst of the garden, God hath said, Ye shall not eat of it, neither shall ye touch it, lest ye die. And the serpent said unto the woman, Ye shall not surely die: For God doth know that in the day ye eat thereof, then your eyes shall be opened, and ye shall be as gods, knowing good and evil. And when the woman saw that the tree was good for food, and that it was pleasant to the eyes, and a tree to be desired to make one wise, she took of the fruit thereof, and did eat, and gave also unto her husband with her; and he did eat."

PROPOSITION: The first man fell

The steps in the Fall were:
(1) Listening to slanders against God.
(2) Doubting God's word and His love.
(3) Looking at what God had forbidden.
(4) Lusting for what God had prohibited. (The lust of the flesh, the lust of the eye and the vainglory of life, v. 6. Compare 1 Jno. 2: 16.)
(5) Disobeying God's commandments.

The woman was the first in this deception and transgression. (V. 1, etc.)

(Compare 1 Tim. 2: 14—"And Adam was not deceived, but the woman being deceived was in the transgression.")

II. Result of the Fall.

(1) Rom. 5: 19, R.V.—"For as through the one man's disobedience the many were made sinners, even so through the obedience of the one shall many be made righteous."

PROPOSITION: Through the one man's disobedience the many were made (or constituted) sinners.

Adam stood as the representative of the race; indeed, he was the race, and all coming generations were in him. (Compare Heb. 7: 9, 10.) In his fall the race fell. "All sinned." Rom. 5: 12, R.V.—"Therefore, as through one man sin entered into the world, and death through sin; and so death passed unto all men, *for that all sinned.*"

Many thoughtless infidels say: "I would rather stand for myself." If you had stood for yourself you would have fallen as Adam did. God's plan, when we see the whole of it, is far more gracious than this. As the first Adam fell for us, so we all would have done for ourselves; so the second Adam obeyed for us, as none of us would have done if left to stand for ourselves.

CHAPTER III.

THE PRESENT STANDING BEFORE GOD AND CONDITION OF MEN OUTSIDE OF THE REDEMPTION THAT IS IN CHRIST JESUS.

I.   The Present Standing before God of men outside of the Redemption that is in Christ Jesus.

(1)   Rom. 3: 9, 10, 22 (l. cl.), 23—"What then ? are we better than they ?   No, in no wise: for we have before proved both Jews and Gentiles, that they are all under sin; As it is written, There is none righteous, no, not one; . . .   for there is no difference: for all have sinned, and come short of the glory of God."

Ps. 14: 2, 3—"The LORD looked down from heaven upon the children of men, to see if there were any that did understand, and seek God.   They are all gone aside, they are all together become filthy: there is none that doeth good, no, not one."

Is. 53: 6—"*All we* like sheep have gone astray; we have turned every one to his own way; and the LORD hath laid on him the iniquity of us all."

1 Jno. 1: 8, 10—"If we say that we have no sin, we deceive ourselves, and the truth is not in us. . . .   If we say that we have not sinned, we make him a liar, and his word is not in us."

FIRST PROPOSITION: Outside of the Redemption in Christ Jesus there is no difference in the standing of men before God: for all have sinned and come short of the glory of God; there is none righteous, no, not one.

(2)   Rom. 3: 19, R.V.—"Now we know that what things soever the law saith, it speaketh to them that are under the law; that every mouth may be stopped, and all the world may be brought under the judgment of God."

SECOND PROPOSITION: Every mouth is stopped and all the world brought under the judgment of God.

(Compare Ps. 130: 3—"If thou, LORD, shouldest mark iniquity, O LORD, who shall stand ?"   Ps. 143: 2—"And enter not into judgment with thy servant: for in thy sight shall no man living be justified.")

(3) Gal. 3: 10 (note context vv. 13, 14)—"For **as many as are of** the works of the law are under the curse: for it is written, Cursed is every one that continueth not in all things which are written in the book of the law to do them."

Rom. 2: 12—"For as many as have sinned without law shall also perish without law; and as many as have sinned in the law shall be judged by the law."

THIRD PROPOSITION: All who are of the deeds of the law (i. e., outside of the grace of God in Jesus Christ) *are under a curse.*

(4) 1 Jno. 3: 8–10—"He that committeth sin is of the devil; for the devil sinneth from the beginning. For this purpose the Son of God was manifested, that he might destroy the works of the devil. Whosoever is born of God doth not commit sin; for his seed remaineth in him; and he cannot sin, because he is born of God. In this the children of God are manifest, and the children of the devil; whosoever doeth not righteousness is not of God, neither he that loveth not his brother."

FOURTH PROPOSITION: All who have not been born of God (i. e., all outside of the Redemption in Christ Jesus) *are children of the Devil.*

The doctrine of the universal Fatherhood of God is utterly unscriptural and untrue. It is true all men are his offspring, or stock, or race, or nation (Acts 17:28, γένος not τέκνα, see usage in Greek concordance), in the sense of being His creatures, having our being in Him, and made in His likeness. (See context vv. 28, 29.) But we become His "sons" or "children" by faith in Christ Jesus. (Gal. 3: 26, R.V.; Jno. 1:12, R.V.)

II. The Present Condition of men outside of the Redemption that is in Christ Jesus.

(1) Eph. 4:18, R.V.—"Being *darkened in their understanding, alienated from the life of God* because of the ignorance that is in them, because of the *hardening* of their hearts."

FIRST PROPOSITION: They are darkened in their understanding, alienated from the life of God through the ignorance that is in them, hardened in heart.

(2) 1 Cor. 2:14—"But the natural man receiveth not the things of the Spirit of God: for they are foolishness unto him: neither can he know them, because they are spiritually discerned."

SECOND PROPOSITION: *The natural man receiveth not the things of the Spirit of God, neither can he know them.*

(3) Jer. 17:9, R.V.—" The heart is deceitful above all things, and it is desperately sick: who can know it ?"

THIRD PROPOSITION: *The natural heart is deceitful above all things and desperately sick.*

(4) Gen. 6:5, 12—"And God saw that the wickedness of man was great in the earth, and that *every imagination of the thoughts of his heart was only evil continually.* . . . And God looked upon the earth, and behold it was corrupt; for all flesh had corrupted his way upon the earth."

Gen. 8:21—"And the LORD smelled a sweet savour; and the LORD said in his heart, I will not again curse the ground any more for man's sake; for *the imagination of man's heart is evil from his youth:* neither will I again smite any more every thing living, as I have done."

Ps. 94:11—"The LORD knoweth the thoughts of man, that they are vanity."

FOURTH PROPOSITION: *The entire moral and intellectual nature of unredeemed man is corrupted by sin.*

(5) Tit. 3:3—"For we ourselves also were sometimes foolish, disobedient, deceived, serving divers lusts and pleasures; living in malice and envy, hateful, and hating one another."

Eph. 2:3, R.V.—"Among whom we also once lived in the lusts of our flesh, doing the desires of the flesh and of the mind."

Col. 3:5, 7—"Mortify therefore your members which are upon the earth; fornication, uncleanness, inordinate affection, evil concupiscence, and covetousness, which is idolatry: . . . In the which ye also walked sometime, when ye lived in them."

FIFTH PROPOSITION: *The outward life of unredeemed men is vile and detestable.*

(6) Rom. 7:5, 8, 14, 15, 19, 23, 24—"For when we were in the flesh, the motions of sin, which were by the law, did work in our members to bring forth fruit unto death. . . . But sin, taking occasion by the commandment, wrought in me all manner of concupiscence. For without the law sin is dead. . . . For we know that the law is spiritual: for I am carnal, sold under sin. For that which I do, I allow not: for what I would, that do I not; but what I hate, that do I. . . . For the good that I would, I do not: but the evil which I would not, that I do. . . . But I see another law in my members, warring against the law of my mind, and bringing me into captivity to the law of sin which is in my members. O wretched man that I am, who shall

deliver me from the body of this death ? " (Compare 8: 2—" For the law of the Spirit of life in Christ Jesus hath made me free from the law of sin and death," and Rom. 6: 17, R.V.—"Ye were servants [Marg. bondservants, Greek slaves] of sin, etc.")

SIXTH PROPOSITION: Men unsaved by Christ are the slaves of sin, in helpless and hopeless captivity to the law of sin and death.

(7) Eph. 2: 2—"Wherein in time past ye walked according to the course of this world, according to the prince of the power of the **air**, *the spirit that now worketh in the children of disobedience."*

SEVENTH PROPOSITION: Outside of redemption in Christ men are under the control of the Prince of the power of the air.

(8) Eph. 2: 3—"And were by nature the children of wrath, even as others."

EIGHTH PROPOSITION: They are by nature children of wrath.

(9) Rom. 8: 7, 8, R.V.—"Because the mind of the flesh is enmity against God; for it is not subject to the law of God neither indeed can be; and they that are in the flesh cannot please God."

NINTH PROPOSITION: The mind of the flesh is enmity against God: it is not subject to the law of God, neither indeed can be: and they that are in the flesh cannot please God.

(10) Eph. 2: 1—"And you hath he quickened, who were dead in trespasses and sins."

TENTH PROPOSITION: Men outside of Christ's saving power are dead through their trespasses and sins.

(11) 1 Jno. 5: 19, R.V.—"We know that we are of God, and the whole world lieth in the evil one."

ELEVENTH PROPOSITION: " The whole world," the whole mass of men who have not received Christ, " lieth in the evil one "—rest in his arms, in his power, in himself.

CONCLUSION.—The present standing or condition of men out of Christ as pictured in the Bible is dark and hopeless. One word will express it—*lost*, utterly lost. This is very different from the conception of man that is popular in novels, on the lecture-platform, and in many pulpits to-day. But it is accord-ant with the facts. The more one has to do with men and women, and the more one comes to know the depths of his own heart, the more convinced he becomes of the truthfulness and accuracy in every line of this hideous and repulsive picture. The nearer one gets to God, the more fully he sees the truth of this picture; the fact that one has an exalted opinion of human nature, and his own nature, does not show that he is living near God, but far from God. Compare Isaiah's, Job's and the Psalmist's conception of self and man when they were brought face to face with God:

Is. 6: 1, 5—" In the year that King Uzziah died I saw also the LORD sitting upon a throne, high and lifted up, and his train filled the temple. . . . Then said I, Woe is me ! for I am undone; because I am a man of unclean lips, and I dwell in the midst of a people of unclean lips: for mine eyes have seen the King, the LORD of Hosts."

Job 42: 5, 6—" I have heard of thee by the hearing of the ear; but now mine eye seeth thee: Wherefore I abhor myself, and repent in dust and ashes."

Ps. 14: 2-3—" The fool hath said in his heart, There is no God. They are corrupt, they have done abominable works, there is none that doeth good. The LORD looked down from heaven upon the children of men, to see if there were any that did understand, and seek God. They are all gone aside, they are all together become filthy: there is none that doeth good, no, not one."

Evidently those who live nearest God and see things most nearly from His standpoint have the poorest opinion of self and human nature.

CHAPTER IV.

THE FUTURE DESTINY OF THOSE WHO REJECT THE RE-DEMPTION THAT IS IN JESUS CHRIST.

I. The Future Destiny of those who do not believe that Jesus is the Son of God.

Jno. 8: 24—"I said therefore unto you, that ye shall die in your sins: for if ye believe not that I am he, ye shall die in your sins." (Note context, verse 21.)

PROPOSITION: Those who believe not that Jesus is the Messiah and Son of God shall die in their sins; whither He goes they cannot come.

NOTE.—The faith here spoken of is not a mere opinion, but a faith that governs the life. (Compare John's use of faith everywhere; *e. g.,* 1 Jno. 5: 1, 4, 5.)

II. The Future Destiny of those who have done ill.

Jno. 5: 28, 29, R.V.—"Marvel not at this: for the hour cometh in which all that are in the tombs shall hear his voice, and shall come forth, they that have done good, unto the resurrection of life; and they that have done ill, unto the resurrection of judgment."

PROPOSITION: All men shall be raised again from the dead, those who reject Christ as well as those who accept Him, but to the one it will be a resurrection unto life, to the other a resurrection unto judgment.

(Compare 1 Cor. 15: 22—"For as in Adam all die, even so in Christ shall *all* be made alive.")

III. The Future Destiny of the factious and disobedient.

Rom. 2: 5, 6, 8, 9, R.V.—"But after thy hardness and impenitent heart treasurest up for thyself wrath in the day of wrath and revelation of the righteous judgment of God; who will render to every man according to his works: . . . but unto them that are factious, and obey not the truth, but obey unrighteousness, shall be wrath and indignation, tribulation and anguish upon every soul of man that worketh evil, of the Jew first, and also of the Greek."

PROPOSITION: Unto them that are factious, and obey not the truth (Compare Jno. 14: 6; 3: 18, 19), *but obey unrighteousness, shall be wrath and indignation, tribulation and anguish, upon every soul of man that worketh evil.*

IV. The Future Destiny of those who know not God and obey not the Gospel.

2 Thess. 1: 8, 9, R.V.—"In flaming fire, rendering vengeance to them that know not God, and to them that obey not the gospel of our Lord Jesus: who shall suffer punishment, even eternal destruction from the face of the Lord and from the glory of his might, when he shall come to be glorified in his saints."

PROPOSITION: Those who know not God and that obey not the gospel of our Lord Jesus, shall suffer punishment, even eternal destruction from the face of the Lord and from the glory of his might, when He shall come to be glorified in His saints.

NOTE.—What "destruction" means we shall see later.

V. The Future Destiny of those who are not found written in the book of life.

Rev. 20: 15, R.V—"And if any was not found written in the book of life, he was cast into the lake of fire."

PROPOSITION: If anyone at the judgment of the great white throne is not found written in the book of life, he shall be cast into the lake of fire.

VI. The Future Destiny of those who neglect Christ by neglecting His brethren.

Matt. 25: 41, 46, R.V.—"Then shall he say unto them on the left hand, Depart from me, ye cursed, into the eternal fire which is prepared for the devil and his angels: . . . And these shall go away into eternal punishment: but the righteous into eternal life."

PROPOSITION: When Christ comes to judge the nations He shall say to those on His left hand (i. e., those who have neglected Him, by neglecting their duty to His hungry, thirsty, lonely, naked, imprisoned brethren), *"Depart from me, ye cursed, into the eternal fire which is prepared for the Devil and his angels, and these shall go away into eternal punishment."*

VII. The Future Destiny of the fearful, unbelieving, etc.

Rev. 21: 8—"But the fearful, and unbelieving, and the abom-inable, and murderers, and whoremongers, and sorcerers, and idola-ters, and all liars, shall have their part in the lake which burneth with fire and brimstone: which is the second death."

PROPOSITION: The fearful, and unbelieving, and the abomina-ble, and murderers, and whoremongers, and sorcerers, and idolaters, and all liars, shall have their part in the lake which burneth with fire and brimstone.

VIII. Questions answered.

FIRST QUESTION: Is the fire spoken of as the future penalty of sin literal fire?

ANSWER: (1) Note the frequency with which the word fire and synonymous expressions are used:

Matt. 7: 19—"Every tree that bringeth not forth good fruit is hewn down, and cast *into the fire.*"

Jno. 15: 6—"If a man abide not in me, he is cast forth as a branch, and is withered; and men gather them, and cast them *into the fire,* and they are burned."

Is. 66: 24—"And they shall go forth, and look upon the carcasses of the men that have transgressed against me: for their worm shall not die, *neither shall their fire be quenched;* and they shall be an abhorring unto all flesh."

Heb. 6: 8—"But that which beareth thorns and briers is rejected, and is nigh unto cursing; whose end is *to be burned.*"

Heb. 10: 26, 27, R.V.—"For if we sin willfully after that we have received the knowledge of the truth, there remaineth no more sacrifice for sins, but a certain fearful expectation of judgment, and a *fierceness of fire* which shall devour the adversaries."

Rev. 20: 15—"And whosoever was not found written in the book of life was cast into *the lake of fire.*"

Rev. 21: 8—"But the fearful, and unbelieving, and the abominable, and murderers, and whoremongers, and sorcerers, and idolaters, and all liars, shall have their part in the lake which *burneth with fire* and brimstone: which is the second death."

(2) Matt. 13: 30, 41, 42—"Let both grow together until the har-vest: and in the time of harvest I will say to the reapers, Gather ye together first the tares, and bind them in bundles to burn them: but gather the wheat into my barn. . . . The Son of man shall send forth his angels, and they shall gather out of his kingdom all things that offend, and them which do iniquity; and shall cast them into a *furnace of fire:* there shall be wailing and gnashing of teeth."

In a parable we expect figures, but in the explanation of the parable we expect the figures to be explained by the literal facts which they are intended to represent. But in the parable of the tares every item of the parable is explained except the fire, but that remains fire in the interpretation of the parable as well as in the parable itself. (Compare also Matt. 13: 47–50.)

SECOND QUESTION: Is the Lake of Fire a place of con-tinued conscious torment, or is it a place of annihilation of being, or is it a place of non-conscious existence?

ANSWER: The punishment of the wicked is spoken of as "death" and "destruction." What do these words mean in Biblical usage?

" DEATH."

(1) 1 Tim. 5: 6—" But she that liveth in pleasure is *dead while she liveth.*"

Eph. 2: 1—"And you hath he quickened, *who were dead* in tres-passes and sins."

FIRST PROPOSITION: The word "death" is applied to sinners while still existing, but existing in a wrong way—while they have life in the sense of existence, but not true life, real life, in the sense of right existence. (Compare 1 Tim. 6: 19, A.V. and R.V.)

(2) Rev. 21: 8—"But the fearful, and unbelieving, and the abominable, and murderers, and whoremongers, and sorcerers, and idolaters, and all liars, shall have their part in the lake which burneth with fire and brimstone: *which is the second death.*"

SECOND PROPOSITION: The death which is the final out-come of a life of sin and unbelief is defined in the Bible as a portion in the place of torment.

(3) Jno. 17: 3—"AND THIS is life eternal, that they might know thee the only true God, and Jesus Christ, whom thou hast sent."

1 Jno. 1: 2—"For the life was manifested, and *we have seen* it, and bear witness, and show unto you that eternal life, which was with the Father, and was manifested unto us."

THIRD PROPOSITION: Life is defined in the Bible not merely as existence but as right existence, knowing the true God, the life manifested in Jesus Christ. Death, then, is not mere non-existence, but wrong, wretched, debased, devilish existence.

"DESTRUCTION."

(1)   The general use of the word.

Matt. 9: 17—" Neither do men put new wine into old bottles: else the bottles break, and the wine runneth out, and the bottles *perish:* but they put new wine into new bottles, and both are preserved."

FIRST PROPOSITION: When anything is said " to perish " (the verb from which the noun commonly translated "destruction" and "perdition" is derived) *it is not meant that it ceases to be, but that it is so ruined that it no longer subserves the use for which it was designed.*   (See Thayer's Greek-English Lexicon of New Testament.)

Compare also Matt. 26: 8—" But when his disciples saw it, they had indignation, saying, to what purpose is this *waste?* "   (Same word elsewhere translated "destruction" and "perdition.")

(2)   The specific use of the word as applied to the doom of the wicked.

Rev. 17: 8, 11—" The beast that thou sawest was, and is not; and shall ascend out of the bottomless pit, and go into *perdition:* and they that dwell on the earth shall wonder, whose names were not written in the book of life from the foundation of the world, when they behold the beast that was, and is not, and yet is. . . . And the beast that was, and is not, even he is the eighth, and is of the seven, and goeth into perdition."

(Note the Greek word here translated " perdition " is the word translated " destruction " in 2 Pet. 3: 16, A.V. and R.V.; Phil. 3: 19, A.V.; 2 Pet. 3: 7, R.V.   Now if we can find what the beast " goeth "into, we shall know what " destruction " or " perdition " means.   Turn to Rev. 19: 20—" And the beast was taken, and with him the false prophet that wrought miracles before him, with which he deceived them that had received the mark of the beast, and them that worshipped his image. *These both were cast alive into a lake of fire burning with brimstone.* "   Turn again to Rev. 20: 10—" And the devil that deceived them was cast into the lake of fire and brimstone, *where the beast and the false prophet are,* and shall be tormented day and night forever and ever." Here we find the beast still in the lake of fire and being tormented after a thousand years have passed away.)

SECOND PROPOSITION: " Destruction " is clearly defined in the New Testament as the condition of beings in a place of conscious and unending torment.

That "destruction" does not mean annihilation is also evident from Luke 19: 10—"For the Son of man is come to seek and
to save that which was lost." (Greek.)

(3) Rev. 14: 10, 11—"The same shall drink of the wine of the wrath
of God, which is poured out without mixture into the cup of his indignation; and he shall be tormented with fire and brimstone in the presence of the holy angels, and in the presence of the Lamb: And the
smoke of their torment ascendeth up forever and ever; and they have
no rest day nor night, who worship the beast and his image, and whosoever receiveth the mark of his name.

*THIRD PROPOSITION: The ultimate condition of those who
receive the mark of the beast is described as a condition of unending, unresting, conscious torment.*

OBJECTION: "This passage does not refer to the eternal
state as it speaks of 'day and night.'"

ANSWER:—

(1) Compare Rev. 4: 8—"And the four beasts had each of them
six wings about him; and they were full of eyes within; and they
rested not *day and night*, saying, Holy, holy, holy, Lord God Almighty,
which was, and is, and is to come."

Rev. 7: 14, 15—"And I said unto him, Sir, thou knowest. And he
said to me, These are they which came out of great tribulation, and
have washed their robes, and made them white in the blood of the
Lamb. Therefore are they before the throne of God, and serve him
day and night in his temple; and he that sitteth on the throne shall
dwell among them."

Rev. 20: 10—"And the devil that deceived them was cast into the
lake of fire and brimstone, where the beast and the false prophets are,
and shall be tormented *day and night* FOREVER AND EVER."

(2) Rev. 19: 20—"And the beast was taken, and with him the false
prophet that wrought miracles before him, with which he deceived
them that had received the mark of the beast, and them that worshipped
his image. These both were cast alive into a lake of fire burning
with brimstone." Compare with Rev. 20: 10—"And the devil that
deceived them was cast into the lake of fire and brimstone, where the
beast and the false prophet are, and shall be tormented day and night
for ever and ever," shows us the beast and false prophet still in the
lake of fire at the end of *the thousand years*, and still *being tormented.*

THIRD QUESTION: Is this condition of torment endless ?

ANSWER:—

Matt. 25: 41—"Then shall he say unto them on the left hand,
Depart from me, ye cursed, into *everlasting* fire, *prepared for the devil
and his angels.*" (Compare Rev. 20: 10—"And the devil that deceived

them was cast into the lake of fire and brimstone, where the beast and the false prophet are, and shall be tormented day and night for ever and ever.")

Rev. 14: 11—"And the smoke of their torment ascended up *for ever and ever:* and they have *no rest day nor night,* who worship the beast and his image, and whosoever receiveth the mark of his name."

Compare 2 Thess. 1: 9, 10—"Who shall be punished with *everlasting destruction* from the presence of the Lord, and from the glory of his power; when he shall come to be glorified in his saints, and to be admired in all them that believe (because our testimony among you was believed) in that day."

PROPOSITION: They are tormented day and night for ever and ever, and they have no rest day nor night.

What does "for ever and ever" mean?

Literally, "Unto the ages of the ages." The expression occurs twelve times in the Book of Revelation.

Rev. 1: 6—"And hath made us kings and priests unto God and his Father; to him be glory and dominion for ever and ever. Amen."

4: 9, 10—"And when those beasts give glory and honor and thanks to him that sat on the throne, who liveth for ever and ever, the four and twenty elders fall down before him that sat on the throne, and worship him that liveth for ever and ever, and cast their crowns before the throne, saying."

5: 13—"And every creature which is in heaven, and on the earth, and under the earth, and such as are in the sea, and all that are in them, heard I saying, Blessing, and honor, and glory, and power, be unto him that sitteth upon the throne, and unto the Lamb for ever and ever."

7: 12—"Saying, Amen: Blessing, and glory, and wisdom, and thanksgiving, and honor, and power, and might, be unto God for ever and ever. Amen."

10: 6—"And sware by him that liveth for ever and ever, who created heaven, and the things that therein are, and the earth, and the things that therein are, and the sea, and the things which are therein, that there should be time no longer."

11: 15—"And the seventh angel sounded; and there were great voices in heaven, saying, the kingdoms of this world are become the kingdoms of our Lord, and of his Christ; and he shall reign for ever and ever." (See also Rev. 14: 11.)

15: 7—"And one of the four beasts gave unto the seven angels seven golden vials full of the wrath of God, who liveth for ever and ever." (Also, 19: 2, 3; 20: 10.)

22: 5—"And there shall be no night there; and they need no candle, neither light of the sun; for the Lord God giveth them light: and they shall reign for ever and ever."

Eight times it refers to the duration of the existence or reign or glory of God and Christ. Once to the duration of the blessed reign of the righteous, and in the three remaining instances to the duration of the torment of the Devil, Beast, False Prophet, and the wicked.

The word frequently translated "eternal" or "everlasting" means "age-long," and may be used of a limited period; but the expression "for ever and ever" means "unto the ages of the ages" (Rev. 19: 3; 20: 10—See R.V. Marg. and Greek), or "unto ages of ages" (Rev. 14: 11, R.V. Marg. and Greek); *i. e.*, not merely throughout an age, but throughout all ages. It is a picture not merely of years tumbling upon years, but of ages tumbling upon ages in endless succession. It is never in a single instance used of a limited period. Nothing could more plainly or graphically picture absolute endlessness.

FOURTH QUESTION: When are the issues of eternity settled?

(1) Jno. 8: 21—"Then said Jesus again unto them, I go my way, and ye shall seek me, and shall die in your sins: whither I go, ye cannot come."

FIRST PROPOSITION: Those who die in their sins cannot go where Jesus is.

(2) Heb. 9: 27, R.V.—"And inasmuch as it is appointed unto men once to die, and after this cometh judgment."

SECOND PROPOSITION: It is appointed unto men once to die, and after this judgment.

(3) Jno. 5: 28, 29—"Marvel not at this: for the hour is coming, in which all that are in the graves shall hear his voice, and shall come forth; they that have done good, unto the resurrection of life; and they that have done evil, unto the resurrection of damnation."

THIRD PROPOSITION: All who are in their graves who have done evil shall be raised unto a resurrection of judgment.

(4) Luke 16: 26—"And beside all this, between us and you there is a great gulf fixed: so that they which would pass from hence to you cannot; neither can they pass to us, that would come from thence."

FOURTH PROPOSITION: Between those who pass out of this world lost and those who pass out accepted of God, there is a great gulf fixed and no passing from the one side to the other. The destinies of eternity are settled in the life that now is.

FIFTH QUESTION: May not those who have never heard of Christ in this world have another opportunity ?

ANSWER: (*a*) There is not a line of Scripture upon which to build such a hope. (*b*) All men have sufficient light to condemn them if they do not obey it.

> Rom. 2: 12, 16—"For as many as have sinned without law shall also perish without law; and as many as have sinned in the law shall be judged by the law; (For not the hearers of the law are just before God, but the doers of the law shall be justified. For when the Gentiles, which have not the law, do by nature the things contained in the law, these, having not the law, are a law unto themselves: Which show the work of the law written in their hearts, their conscience also bearing witness, and their thoughts the meanwhile accusing or else excusing one another;) In the day that God shall judge the secrets of men by Jesus Christ according to my gospel."

> NOTE.—The passage here quoted was not given to show, as some strangely imagine, how men are saved by the light of nature, but how the Gentile is under condemnation by the law written in his heart, just as the Jew is under condemnation by the law of Moses. The conclusion of the whole matter is found in Rom. 3: 19, 20, 21, 22—"Now we know that what things soever the law saith, it saith to them who are under the law: that every mouth may be stopped, and all the world may become guilty before God. Therefore by the deeds of the law there shall no flesh be justified in his sight: for by the law is the knowledge of sin. But now the righteousness of God without the law is manifested, being witnessed by the law and the prophets; even the righteousness of God which is by faith of Jesus Christ unto all and upon all them that believe; for there is no difference."

GENERAL CONCLUSION: The future state of those who reject the redemption offered to them in Christ is plainly declared to be a state of conscious, unutterable, endless torment and anguish. This conception is an awful and appalling one. It is, however, the Scriptural conception and also a reasonable one when we come to see the appalling nature of sin, and especially the appalling nature of the sin of trampling under foot God's mercy toward sinners, and rejecting God's glorious Son, whom His love has provided as a Saviour.

Shallow views of sin and of God's holiness, and of the glory of Jesus Christ and His claims upon us, lie at the bottom of weak theories of the doom of the impenitent. *When we see sin in all its hideousness and enormity, the Holiness of God in all its perfection, and the glory of Jesus Christ in all its infinity, nothing but a doctrine that those who persist in the choice of sin, who love darkness rather than light, and who persist in the rejection of the Son of God, shall endure everlasting anguish, will satisfy the demands of our own moral intuitions.* Nothing but the fact that we dread suffering more than we loathe sin, and more than we love the glory of Jesus Christ, makes us repudiate the thought that beings who eternally choose sin should eternally suffer, or that men who despise God's mercy and spurn His Son should be given over to endless anguish.

SIXTH QUESTION. What about our impenitent friends and loved ones?

ANSWER: (a) It is better to recognize facts, no matter how unwelcome, and try to save these friends from the doom to which they are certainly hurrying than to quarrel with facts and seek to remove them by shutting our eyes to them. You cannot avert a hurricane by merely refusing to believe it is coming. (b.) If we love Christ supremely, as we should love Him, and realize His glory and His claims upon men, as we should realize them, we will say if the dearest friend we have on earth *persists in trampling Christ under foot* he ought to be tormented forever and ever.

Suppose one you greatly love should commit some hideous wrong against one you love more, and persist in it eternally, would you not consent to his eternal punishment?

If, after men have sinned and God still offers them mercy, and makes the tremendous sacrifice of His Son to save them—if they still despise that mercy and trample God's Son under foot, if then they are consigned to everlasting torment, I say: "Amen! Hallelujah! True and righteous are thy judgments, O Lord!"

At all events the doctrine of conscious, eternal torment for impenitent men is clearly revealed in the Word of God, and whether we can defend it on philosophic grounds or not, it is our business to believe it; and leave it to the clearer light of Eternity to explain what we cannot now understand, realizing that God may have infinitely wise reasons for doing things for which we in our ignorance can see no sufficient reason at all. It is the most ludicrous conceit for beings so limited and foolish as the wisest of men are, to attempt to dogmatize how a God of infinite wisdom must act. All we know as to how God will act is what God has seen fit to tell us.

In conclusion, two things are certain.   First, the more closely men walk with God and the more devoted they become to His service, the more likely they are to believe this doctrine.   Many men tell us they love their fellow men too much to believe this doctrine; but the men who show their love in more practical ways than sentimental protestations about it, the men who show their love for their fellow men as Jesus Christ showed His, by laying down their lives for them, *they* believe it, even as Jesus Christ Himself believed it.

As Christians become worldly and easy-going they grow loose in their doctrine concerning the doom of the impenitent. The fact that loose doctrines are spreading so rapidly and widely in our day is nothing for them, but against them, for worldliness is also spreading in the Church. (1 Tim. 4:1; 2 Tim. 3:1; 4:2, 3.) Increasing laxity of life and increasing laxity of doctrine go arm in arm. A church that dances and frequents theatres and lives in self-indulgence during the week, enjoys a doctrine on the Lord's Day that makes the punishment of the wicked not so awful after all.

Second, men who accept a loose doctrine regarding the ultimate penalty of sin (Restorationism or Universalism or Annihilationism) lose their power for God. They may be very clever at argument and zealous in proselyting, but they are poor at soul-saving. They are seldom found beseeching men to be reconciled to God. They are more likely to be found trying to upset the faith of those already won by the efforts of others, than winning men who have no faith at all. If you really believe the doctrine of the endless, conscious torment of the impenitent, and the doctrine really gets hold of you, you will work as you never worked before for the salvation of the lost. If you in any wise abate the doctrine, it will abate your zeal. Time and again the author has come up to this awful doctrine and tried to find some way of escape from it, but when he has failed, as he always has at last, when he was honest with the Bible and with himself, he has returned to his work with an increased burden for souls and an intensified determination to spend and be spent for their salvation.

Finally : Do not believe this doctrine in a cold, intellectual, merely argumentative way. If you do, and try to teach it, you will repel men from it. But meditate upon it in its practical.

personal bearings, until your heart is burdened by the awful peril of the wicked and you rush out to spend the last dollar, if need be, and the last ounce of strength you have, in saving those imperiled men from the certain, awful hell of conscious agony and shame to which they are fast hurrying.

CHAPTER V.

JUSTIFICATION.

I. What does Justify mean?

Note.—The way to decide this is by an examination of the Biblical use of the word and the words derived from it.   The question is not, What is the etymological significance of the word? for words are frequently used in a meaning widely different from their etymological significance.   The question is, What is the significance of the word as determined by its usage in the Bible?   The way to determine this is by taking a Concordance and Bible, and looking up every passage in which the word is used. The following passages are sufficient to illustrate the Biblical usage. In the passages taken from the O.T., the LXX uses the same Greek verb that is translated "justify" in the N.T.

Deut. 25: 1—"If there be a controversy between men, and they come unto judgment, that the judges may judge them; then they shall justify the righteous, and condemn the wicked."

Ex. 23: 7—"Keep thee far from a false matter: and the innocent and righteous slay thou not: for I will not justify the wicked."

Is. 5: 23—"Which justify the wicked for reward, and take away the righteousness of the righteous from him!"

Luke 16: 15—"And he said unto them, Ye are they which justify yourselves before men; but God knoweth your hearts: for that which is highly esteemed among men is abomination in the sight of God."

Rom. 2: 13—"For not the hearers of the law are just before God, but the doers of the law shall be justified."

Rom. 3: 23, 24—"For all have sinned, and come short of the glory of God; being justified freely by his grace through the redemption that is in Christ Jesus. "

Luke 18: 14—" I tell you this man went down to his house justified rather than the other: for every one that exalteth himself shall be abased; and he that humbleth himself shall be exalted."

See, also, Rom. 4: 2–8, R.V.—"For if Abraham was justified by works, he hath whereof to glory; but not toward God.   For what saith the scripture ?   And Abraham believed God, and it was *reckoned unto him* for righteousness.   Now to him that worketh, the reward is not reckoned as of grace, but as of debt.   But to him that worketh not, but believeth on him that justifieth the ungodly, his *faith is reckoned for righteousness.*   Even as David also pronounceth blessing upon the man, unto whom God reckoned righteousness apart from works, saying:

" Blessed are they whose iniquities are forgiven,

" And whose sins are covered.

" Blessed is the man to whom the Lord will not reckon sin."

To "justify," in Biblical usage, signifies not "to make righteous," but to "reckon," "declare," or "show to be righteous." A man is justified before God when God reckons him righteous.

NOTE.—Etymologically the word translated "justify" means "to make righteous," but Thayer, in his Greek-English Lexicon of the New Testament, says: "This meaning is extremely rare, if not altogether doubtful." (See, also, Liddell & Scott.) It certainly is not the New Testament usage of the word.

II. How Are Men Justified ?

(1) Rom. 3: 20—" Therefore *by the deeds of the law there shall no flesh be justified* in his sight: for by the law is the knowledge of sin."

Gal. 2: 16—" Knowing that *a man is not justified by the works of the law*, but by the faith of Jesus Christ, even we have believed in Jesus Christ, that we might be justified by the faith of Christ, and not by the works of the law; for *by the works of the law shall no flesh be justified.*"

FIRST PROPOSITION: *Men are not justified by works of the law. No man is justified by works of the law.*

QUESTION: Why not ?

ANSWER:—

Gal. 3: 10—" For as many as are of the works of the law are under the curse: for it is written, Cursed is every one that continueth not in all things which are written in the book of the law to do them." Rom. 3: 23—" For all have sinned, and come short of the glory of God."

Because in order to be justified by works of the law we must continue *in all things* which are written in the book of the law to do them. This no man has done, but all men have sinned. The moment the law is broken at any point, justification by works of the law becomes impossible. So those who are of works of the law are under the curse. God did not give men the law with the intention of justifying men thereby, but to produce conviction of sin, to stop men's mouths, and to lead them to Christ.

Rom. 3: 19, 20—" Now we know that what things soever the law saith, it saith to them who are under the law: that every mouth may be stopped, and all the world may become guilty before God. Therefore by the deeds of the law there shall no flesh be justified in his sight: for by the law is the knowledge of sin." Gal. 3: 24—" Wherefore the law was our schoolmaster to bring us unto Christ, that we might be justified by faith."

Yet strangely enough there are many to-day preaching the law as the way of salvation.

(2) Rom. 3: 24—"Being justified freely by his grace through the redemption that is in Christ Jesus."

SECOND PROPOSITION: *Men are justified as a free gift by God s grace through the redemption that is in Christ Jesus.*

Justification is not on the ground of any desert there is in us. It is a gift God bestows without pay. The channel through which it is bestowed is the redemption that is in Christ Jesus.

(3) Rom. 5: 9 (Note R.V. Marg.)—"Much more then, being now justified by (in) his blood, we shall be saved from wrath through him."

THIRD PROPOSITION: *Men are justified or counted righteous in Christ's blood—i. e., on the ground of Christ's propitiatory death.*

(Compare Gal. 3: 13—"Christ hath redeemed us from the curse of the law, being made a curse for us: for it is written, Cursed is every one that hangeth on a tree." 1 Pet. 2: 24—"Who his own self bare our sins in his own body on the tree, that we, being dead to sins, should live unto righteousness: by whose stripes ye were healed." Is. 53: 6—"All we like sheep have gone astray; we have turned every one to his own way; and the LORD hath laid on him the iniquity of us all." 2 Cor. 5: 21—"For he hath made him to be sin for us, who knew no sin; *that we might be made the righteousness of God in him.*")

The ground of justification is the shed blood of Christ.

(4) Rom. 3: 26—"To declare, I say, at this time his righteousness: that he might be just, and the justifier *of him that believeth* in Jesus." —Rom. 4: 5—"But to him that worketh not, but believeth on him that justifieth the ungodly, *his faith is counted for righteousness.*" —Rom. 5: 1—"Therefore being *justified by faith*, we have peace with God through our Lord Jesus Christ."

Acts 13: 39—"And by him *all that believe are justified* from all things, from which ye could not be justified by the law of Moses."

FOURTH PROPOSITION: *Men are justified on condition of faith in Jesus.*

Faith makes ours the shed-blood, which is the ground of justification, and we are justified when we believe in Him who shed the blood. Provision is made for our justification by the shedding of the blood; we are actually justified when we believe.

(5) Rom. 3: 28, R.V.—"We reckon therefore that a man is justified by faith *apart from the works of the law.*"

Rom. 4: 5, R.V.—"But to *him that worketh not*, but believeth on him that justifieth the ungodly, his faith is reckoned for righteousness."

FIFTH PROPOSITION: A man is justified by faith apart from works of the law—i. e., *he is justified on condition that he believes even though he has no works to offer as a ground upon which he might claim justification.*

When he ceases to work for justification and simply believes on Him who justifieth the ungodly, that faith is reckoned for righteousness, and he, the believer, is counted righteous.

The question is not, have you any works to offer, but do you believe on Him who justifies the ungodly? Works have nothing to do with justification except to hinder it when we trust in them. [The blood of Christ secures it, faith in Christ appro- priates it. We are justified, not by our works, but by His work. We are justified upon the simple and single ground of His blood, and upon the simple and single condition of our faith. It is exceedingly difficult to hold men to this doctrine of justification on faith apart from works of the law. They are constantly seek ing to bring in works somewhere.

(6) Rom. 10: 9, 10—"That if thou shalt confess with thy mouth the Lord Jesus, and shalt believe in thine heart that God hath raised him from the dead, thou shalt be saved. For with the heart man believeth unto righteousness; and with the mouth confession is made unto sal- vation."

SIXTH PROPOSITION: The faith that leads to justification is a faith "with the heart."

The heart in the Bible stands for the entire inner man, thought, feeling and purpose. To believe "with the heart," is to believe with the whole man. It involves the surrender of the thought, the feelings and the will to the truth believed. A heart faith is more than mere opinion. It is a conviction that governs the whole inner man and consequently shapes the outward life.

(7) Jas. 2: 14, 18–24, R.V.—"What doth it profit, my brethren, if a man say he hath faith, but have not works? can that faith save him? . . . Yea, a man will say, Thou hast faith, and I have works: shew me thy faith apart from thy works, and I by my works will shew thee my faith. Thou believest that God is one; thou doest well: the devils also believe, and shudder. But wilt thou know, O vain man, that faith apart

from works is barren ?   Was not Abraham our father justified by works, in that he offered up Isaac his son upon the altar ?   Thou seest that faith wrought with his works, and by works was faith made perfect; and the scripture was fulfilled which saith, And Abraham believed God, and it was reckoned unto him for righteousness; and he was called the friend of God.   Ye see that by works a man is justified, and not by faith.''

SEVENTH PROPOSITION: The faith that one says he has, but which does not manifest itself in action along the line of the faith professed, will not justify.   The faith that justifies is the real faith that leads to action accordant with the truth professed.

We are justified simply upon faith, but it must be a real faith.   '' We are justified by faith without works, but we are not justified by a faith that is without works.''   The faith which God sees and upon which He justifies, leads inevitably to works which man can see.   God saw the faith of Abraham and counted it to him for righteousness, but the faith God saw was real and led Abraham to works that all could see and which proved his faith. The proof to us of the faith is the works, and we know that he that does not work has not justifying faith.

We must not lose sight of the truth which Paul emphasizes against legalism on the one side—that we are justified on the simple condition of a real faith in Christ.   We must not lose sight of the truth which James emphasizes against antinomian-ism on the other side—that it is only the faith that proves its genuineness by works, that justifies.   To the legalist, who is seeking to *do* something to merit justification, we must say ''stop working and believe on Him that justifieth the ungodly.''   (Rom. 4:5.)   To the antinomian, who is boasting that he has faith and is justified by it, but who does not show his faith by his works, we must say '' what doth it profit, if a man *say* he hath faith, but have not works ?   Can *that* faith save him.   (Jas. 2:14, R.V.)   We are justified by faith alone, but we are justified by that faith alone that works.

(8)   Rom. 4:25—''Who was delivered for our offences, and was raised again for (because of) our justification.''

EIGHTH PROPOSITION: Jesus was raised because of our justification.

This does not mean that Jesus was raised in order that we might be justified.   We were already justified by His death.   Because we were thus reckoned righteous God raised Jesus from the dead and thus declared us justified. The resurrection of Jesus Christ is the proof that God has accepted the sacrifice for us which He made. Jesus rose as our representative. In raising Him God declared Him accepted and us accepted in Him.

(9) 1 Cor. 6: 11, R.V.—"And such were some of you: but ye were washed, but ye were sanctified, but ye were *justified in the name of the Lord Jesus Christ*, and *in the Spirit of our God*."

NINTH PROPOSITION: We are justified in the name of the Lord Jesus Christ and in the Spirit of our God—i. e., on the ground of what Jesus is and did, and on the condition of our union with Him, and also on the condition of our union with the Spirit of God.

III. The Extent of Justification.

(1) Acts 13: 39, R.V.—"And by him (Greek: in him) *every one that believeth* is justified *from all things*, from which ye could not be justified by the law of Moses."

FIRST PROPOSITION: In Christ every one that believeth is justified from all things.

The whole account against the believer is wiped out.

God has absolutely nothing which He reckons against the believer in Jesus Christ.

(Compare Rom. 8: 1, 33, 34, R.V.—"There is therefore now *no condemnation to them which are in Christ Jesus. . . . Who shall lay anything* to the charge of God's elect? It is God that justifieth; who is he that shall condemn? It is Christ that died, yea rather, that was raised from the dead, who is at the right hand of God, who also maketh intercession for us.")

(2) 2 Cor. 5: 21—"For he hath made him to be sin for us, who knew no sin; that *we might be made the righteousness of God in him.*"

Phil. 3: 9, R.V.—"That I may gain Christ, and be found in him, not having a righteousness of mine own, even that which is of the law, but that which is through faith in Christ, the righteousness which is of God by (upon) faith."

SECOND PROPOSITION: The believer is made the righteousness of God in Christ. He has a righteousness not of his own, but a "righteousness which is of God upon faith."

(Compare Rom. 3: 21, 22—" But now the righteousness of God without the law is manifested, being witnessed by the law and the prophets, even the righteousness of God which is by faith of Jesus Christ unto all and upon all them that believe; for there is no difference.")

There has been an absolute interchange of positions between Christ and the justified believer. Christ took our place, the place of the curse (Gal. 3: 13). He was made sin (2 Cor. 5: 21). God reckoned Him a sinner and dealt with Him as a sinner (Is. 53: 6; Matt. 27; 46). And when we are justified we step into His place—the place of acceptance. We are made the righteousness of God in Him.

To be justified is more than to be forgiven. Forgiveness is negative, the putting away of sin. Justification is positive, the reckoning of positive and perfect righteousness to one. Jesus Christ is so united to the believer that God reckons our sins to Him. The believer is so united to Christ that God reckons His righteousness to us. God sees us in Him and reckons us as righteous as He is. When Christ's work in us is completed we will be in actual fact what we are already in God's reckoning.

i Jno. 3: 2—"Beloved, now are we the sons of God, and it doth not yet appear what we shall be: but we know that, when he shall appear, we shall be like him; for we shall see him as he is."

But our present standing before God is absolutely perfect, though our present state may be far below this.

Jno. 17: 23—"I in them, and thou in me, that they may be made perfect in one; and that the world may know that thou hast sent me, and *hast loved them, as thou hast loved me.*"

"Near, so very near to God,
Nearer I cannot be.
For in the person of His Son
I'm just as near as He.

"Dear, so very dear to God,
Dearer, I cannot be;
For in the person of His Son
I'm just as dear as He."

IV. The Time of Justification.

Acts 13: 39, R.V.—"And by him every one that believeth is justified from all things, from which ye could not be justified by the law of Moses."

PROPOSITION: In Christ every believer is justified from all things.

The moment a man believes in Christ, that moment he becomes united to Christ, and God reckons the righteousness of God to Him.

V. The Results of Justification.

(1) Rom. 5: 1 (See R.V. and Am. Ap.)—"Therefore being justified by faith, *we have peace* with God through our Lord Jesus Christ."

FIRST PROPOSITION: Being justified by faith, we have peace with God through our Lord Jesus Christ.

The enmity between the sinner and God is put away by the cross (Eph 2: 14–17; Col. 1: 20–22), and the moment the sinner believes in Christ he is justified and has peace with God through our Lord Jesus Christ. He may not yet know he has "peace with God," and so will not have "the peace of God." "Peace with God" has to do with our standing; "the peace of God" has to do with our state.

(2) Rom. 8: 33, 34—"Who shall lay anything to the charge of God's elect ? It is God that justifieth. Who is he that condemneth ? It is Christ that died, yea rather, that is risen again, who is even at the right hand of God, who also maketh intercession for us."

SECOND PROPOSITION: No one can lay anything to the charge of the justified man. It is God, the great Judge, who justifies; no one can condemn.

(Compare Rom. 8: 1, R.V.—"There is therefore now no condemnation to them who are in Christ Jesus.")

The believer in Christ is made secure against all condemnation by the death, resurrection, ascension and intercession of Christ. When the death of Christ ceases to satisfy God regarding sin, and when the intercession of Christ ceases to prevail with God, then the justified man can be condemned and not till then.

(3) Tit. 3: 7, R.V.—"That, being justified by his grace, we might be made heirs according to the hope of eternal life."

THIRD PROPOSITION: Being justified by God's grace, we are made heirs according to the hope of eternal life.

(4) Rom. 5: 9, R.V., Marg.—"Much more then, being now justified in his blood, shall we be saved from the wrath of God through him."

FOURTH PROPOSITION: Being justified in Christ's blood we shall be saved from the coming wrath of God.

All who are justified through faith in Jesus Christ will have no part in that long-restrained wrath of God that is soon to burst upon an apostate world.

(Compare Jno. 5: 24, R.V.—"Verily, verily, I say unto you, He that heareth my word, and believeth on him that sent me, hath eternal life, and *cometh* NOT *into judgment*, but *hath passed out of death into life*.")

Judgment regarding sin is past for the believer. His sin has been already judged and punished in the death of Christ.

1 Pet. 2: 24—"Who his own self bare our sins in his own body on the tree, that we, being dead to sins, should live unto righteousness: by whose stripes ye were healed."

Gal. 3: 13—"Christ hath redeemed us from the curse of the law, being made a curse for us: for it is written, Cursed is every one that hangeth on a tree."

The only judgment that awaits the believer is a judgment for rewards according as his works have been good or worthless. (2 Cor. 5: 10; 1 Cor. 3: 11–15.)

(5) Rom. 8: 30—"Moreover, whom he did predestinate, them he also called: and whom he called, them he also justified: and whom he justified, them he also glorified."

FIFTH PROPOSITION: The one God justifies He will also glorify. God has already glorified in His own thought and purpose those whom He has justified.

(6) Rom. 5: 16, 17, R. V.—"And not as through one that sinned, so is the gift: for the judgment came of one unto condemnation, but the free gift came of many trespasses unto justification. For if, by the trespass of the one, death reigned through the one; much more shall they that receive the abundance of grace and of the gift of righteousness reign in life through the one, even Jesus Christ."

SIXTH PROPOSITION: Those who are justified shall reign in life through the one, even Jesus Christ.

CHAPTER VI.

THE NEW BIRTH.

I. What Is the New Birth?

(1) 2 Cor. 5: 17—"Therefore if any man be in Christ, he is *a new creature:* old things are passed away; behold, all things are become new."

Gal. 6: 15—"For in Christ Jesus neither circumcision availeth any thing, nor uncircumcision, but *a new creature.*"

FIRST PROPOSITION: The New Birth is a new creation.

(2) 1 Jno. 3: 14, R.V.—"We know that we have. *passed out of death into life,* because we love the brethren. He that loveth not abideth in death."

Eph. 2: 1, 4, 5, R.V.—"And *you did he quicken, when ye were dead* through your trespasses and sins. . . . But God being rich in mercy, for his great love wherewith he loved us, even when we were dead through our trespasses, quickened us together with Christ (by grace have ye been saved)."

SECOND PROPOSITION: The New Birth is a passing out of death into life, the impartation of life to men dead through trespasses and sins.

Note 1.—It is evident that Baptism is not the New Birth. The language used above does not fit baptism. One of the passages given (Gal. 6: 15) expressly contrasts the New Birth with an outward ceremonial.

The same thing is evident from 1 Cor. 4: 15—"For though ye have ten thousand instructors in Christ, yet have ye not many fathers: for in Christ Jesus I have begotten you through the gospel." Here Paul tells the saints in Corinth that he had begotten them again. If Baptism were the New Birth this must mean that Paul had baptized them. But in 1 Cor. 1: 14, 17 ("I thank God that I baptized none of you, but Crispus and Gaius: . . . For Christ sent me not to baptize, but to preach the gospel: not with wisdom of words, lest the cross of Christ should be made of none effect "), Paul says he had not baptized them. Clearly the New Birth is not Baptism.

That Baptism is not the New Birth is clear also from Acts 8: 13, 20–23—"Then Simon himself believed also: and when he *was baptized,* he continued with Philip, and wondered, beholding the miracles and signs which were done. . . . But Peter said unto him, Thy money perish with thee, because thou hast thought that the gift of God may be purchased with money. Thou hast neither part nor lot in this matter: for *thy heart is not right in the sight of God.* Repent therefore of this thy wickedness, and pray God, if perhaps the thought of thine heart may be forgiven thee. For I perceive that *thou art in the gall of bitterness, and in the bond of iniquity.*" In this passage we are told that Simon was "baptized," but that he was "in the gall of bitterness and bond of iniquity," and bound for perdition. Compare also Luke 23: 43—"And Jesus said unto him, Verily I say unto thee, To-day shalt thou be with me in paradise," with Jno. 3: 3, 5—"Jesus answered and said unto him, Verily, verily, I say unto thee, Except a man be born again, he cannot see the kingdom of God. . . . Jesus answered, Verily, verily, I say unto thee, Except a man be born of water and of the Spirit, he cannot enter into the kingdom of God."

QUESTION: If Baptism is not the New Birth, to what does the word water in Jno. 3: 5 refer?

ANSWER: Let us look elsewhere and see what are the agents and instruments by which the work of regeneration is wrought:

1 Pet. 1: 23—"Being born again, not of corruptible seed, but of incorruptible, *by the word of God,* which liveth and abideth for ever."

Jas. 1: 18—"Of his own will begat he us *with the word of truth,* that we should be a kind of first fruits of his creatures."

1 Cor. 4: 15—"For though ye have ten thousand instructors in Christ, yet have ye not many fathers: for in Christ Jesus I have begotten you *through the gospel.*"

Tit. 3: 5—"Not by works of righteousness which ye have done, but according to his mercy he saved us, by the washing of regeneration, and renewing of the Holy Ghost."

In these passages we see that regeneration is wrought by the word of God and Spirit of God. We are born again by the word of God and the Spirit of God. Now in Jno. 3: 5 ("Jesus answered, Verily, verily, I say unto thee, Except a man be born *of water* and *of the Spirit,* he cannot enter into the kingdom of God"), we have the Spirit. Can the "water" be taken to mean "the word" without forcing the language? Compare Eph. 5: 25, 26—"Husbands, love your wives, even as Christ also loved the Church, and gave himself for it; that he might sanctify and cleanse it with the *washing of water by the word.*" It has been said that the Greek word translated "word" here in Ephesians, is a different word from the word translated "word" when the Word of God is spoken of. But see 1 Pet. 1: 25. Here the same

Greek word that is translated "word" in Eph. 5: 26, is used twice of "the Word of God," and that, too, in direct connection with regeneration by the Word. See also Jno. 15: 3— "Now ye are *clean through the word* which I have spoken unto you." See also Jno. 17: 17—"*Sanctify* them through thy truth: *thy word* is truth." ———

But some may ask why did not Jesus say plainly, without a figure, "Except a man be born of the word and the Spirit"? The answer to this is very simple. The whole passage is highly figurative. The word translated "the Spirit" is itself figurative: means literally "wind" and is without the definite article. Literally translated the passage would read, "Except any one be begotten out of water and wind." In this the wind symbolizes the vivifying element, the Holy Spirit. (Compare Ezek. 37: 9, 10.) Naturally, therefore, "the water" symbolizes the cleansing element, the "word." (Compare Jno. 15: 3.) The passage thus reduced to unfigurative language would read, "Except any man be born of the word of God and the Spirit of God." Thus we would have Jesus teaching the doctrine afterwards taught by Paul and James and Peter. (1 Cor. 4: 15; Tit. 3: 5; Jas. 1: 18; 1 Pet. 1: 23.)

Another interpretation is suggested. This takes both water and wind as symbols of the Spirit, the one setting forth His cleansing work, the other His quickening work. It matters very little, so far as Bible doctrine is concerned, which interpretation we accept: for whether or not the doctrine that men are begotten again by the Word is found here, it certainly is found elsewhere. (Jas. 1: 18; 1 Pet. 1: 23; 1 Cor. 4: 15.) And, if the cleansing work of the Spirit is not found here, it is found elsewhere. Indeed, whatever work you find attributed to the Holy Spirit in the Bible, you will also find attributed to the Word. This is due to the fact that the Spirit works through the Word. The Word is the Sword of the Spirit. (Eph. 6: 17.)

If it is still insisted that the water here refers to Baptism, it is still evident that mere water Baptism is not regeneration, for the passage says, "Except a man be born of water AND THE SPIRIT."

In any case, it is clear that Baptism is not the New Birth.

NOTE 2.—It is also evident that the New Birth is not a mere outward change of conduct. The language used above does not fit this.

(3) Rom. 12: 2.—"And be not conformed to this world: but *be ye transformed* by *the renewing* of your mind, that ye may prove what *is* that good, and acceptable, and perfect will of God." Compare Tit. 3: 5—"Not by works of righteousness which we have done, but according to his mercy he saved us, by the washing of regeneration, and *renewing* of the Holy Ghost."

THIRD PROPOSITION: The New Birth is a making anew of the mind.

The word for mind here includes thoughts, feelings and purposes.

(4) 2 Pet. 1: 4, R.V.—"Whereby he hath granted unto us his precious and exceeding great promises; that through these ye may become partakers of the divine nature, having escaped from the corrupt that that is in the world by lust."

FOURTH PROPOSITION: The New Birth is the impartation of a new nature, even God's own nature, to the one who is begotten again.

The natural or unregenerate man is intellectually blind to the truth, "the things of the Spirit" (1 Cor. 2: 14), corrupt in his affections (Gal. 5: 19, 20, 21), perverse in his will (Rom. 8: 7). This is the condition of every unregenerate man, no matter how cultured, refined or outwardly moral he may be. (See Chapter on Present Standing before God and Condition of Men outside of the Redemption that is in Christ Jesus.) In the New Birth God imparts to us His own wise and holy nature, a nature that thinks as God thinks (Col. 3: 10), feels as God feels, wills as God wills. (1 Jno. 3: 14; 4: 7, 8.) "Old things are passed away, behold they are become new." (2 Cor. 5: 17, R.V.) Compare Ezek. 36: 26, 27: "A new heart also will I give you, and a new spirit will I put within you: and I will take away the stony heart out of your flesh, and I will give you a heart of flesh. And I will put my Spirit within you, and cause you to walk in my statutes, and ye shall keep my judgments, and do them."

The New Birth is a most desirable and glorious experience. Just to think that the All Holy God comes to men sunken in sin, dead through trespasses and sins, the vilest of sinners, blind, corrupt, perverse, and imparts to them His own wise, holy and glorious nature. The doctrine of the New Birth is one of the most precious and inspiring in the Word of God.

II. The Results of the New Birth.

(1) 1 Cor. 3: 16—"Know ye not that ye are the temple of God, and that the Spirit of God dwelleth in you?"

1 Cor. 6: 19—"What! know ye not that your body is the temple of the Holy Ghost which is in you, which ye have of God, and ye are not your own?"

FIRST PROPOSITION: The Regenerated Man is a temple of God; the Spirit of God dwelleth in him.

When anyone submits himself to the regenerating work of the Holy Spirit, the Holy Spirit takes up His abode in Him.

(2) Rom. 8: 9—"But ye are not in the flesh, but in the Spirit, if so be that the Spirit of God dwell in you. Now if any man have not the Spirit of Christ, he is none of his."

SECOND PROPOSITION: The Regenerated Man is not in the flesh, but in the Spirit—i. e., the flesh is not the sphere in which he thinks, feels, lives and acts; on the other hand, the Spirit is the sphere in which he thinks, feels, lives and acts.

NOTE.—While the regenerated man is not in the flesh, he still has the flesh. Gal. 5: 16, 17—"This I say then, Walk in the Spirit, and ye shall not fulfill the lust of the flesh. For the flesh lusteth against the Spirit, and the Spirit against the flesh: and these are contrary the one to the other; so that ye cannot do the things that ye would." The new nature received in regeneration does not expel, destroy nor eradicate the old nature. The two exist side by side. The old nature is present, but its deeds are to be put to death through the Spirit. Rom. 8: 13—"For if ye live after the flesh, ye shall die: but if ye through the Spirit do mortify the deeds of the body, ye shall live." The flesh is present but we are not under its dominion. It is said by some that "Gal. 5: 17 represents a lower experience, but in Rom. 8 we get a higher experience when the carnal nature is eradicated." But in Rom. 8: 12, 13, we see the flesh still present but triumphed over.

(3) Rom. 8: 2—"For the law of the Spirit of life in Christ Jesus hath made me free from the law of sin and death."

THIRD PROPOSITION: The Regenerated Man is made free from the law of sin and death.

What the law of sin and death is we see in Rom. 7: 14–24:

"For we know that the law is spiritual: but I am carnal, sold under sin. For that which I do, I allow not: for what I would, that do I not; but what I hate, that do I. If then I do that which I would not, I consent unto the law that it is good. Now then it is no more I that do it, but sin that dwelleth in me. For I know that in me (that is, in my flesh), dwelleth no good thing: for to will is present with me; but how to perform that which is good I find not. For the good that I would, I do not: but the evil which I would not, that I do. Now if I do that I would not, it is no more I that do it, but sin that dwelleth in me. I find then a law, that, when I would do good, evil is present with me. For I delight in the law of God after the inward man: But I see another law in my members, warring against the law of my mind, and bringing me into captivity to the law of sin which is my members. O wretched man that I am! who shall deliver me from the body of this death?"

After regeneration the law still works, but the higher "law of the Spirit of Life" comes in and sets us free from its power. Whereas in man merely awakened by law, the "law of sin and death" gets a perpetual victory, in the regenerate man the law of "the Spirit of life in Christ Jesus" gets the perpetual victory.

(4) Rom. 12: 2, R.V.—"And be not fashioned according to this world: but be ye transformed by the renewing of your mind, that ye may prove what is the good and acceptable and perfect will of God."

FOURTH PROPOSITION: The Regenerated Man is outwardly transformed by the inward renewing of his mind so that he is no longer fashioned according to this world.

NOTE.—The regenerated man, however, does not at once manifest perfectly that of which he has the germ in himself. He begins as a babe and must grow: 1 Pet. 2: 2—"As newborn babes, desire the sincere milk of the word, that ye may grow thereby." Eph. 4: 13-15—"Till we all come in the unity of the faith, and of the knowledge of the Son of God, unto a perfect man, unto the measure of the stature of the fulness of Christ: That we henceforth be no more children, tossed to and fro, and carried about with every wind of doctrine, by the sleight of men, and cunning craftiness, whereby they lie in wait to deceive; but speaking the truth in love, may grow up into him in all things, which is the head, even Christ." The new life must be fed and developed.

(5) Col. 3: 10, R.V.—"And have put on the new man, which is being renewed unto knowledge after the image of him that created him."

FIFTH PROPOSITION: The Regenerated Man is being made anew into the likeness of his Creator in knowledge.

This result of the new birth is a progressive process. The mind of the believer is brought day by day into conformity with that of God.

(6) Rom. 8: 5—"For they that are after the flesh do mind the things of the flesh; but they that are after the Spirit the things of the Spirit."

SIXTH PROPOSITION: The Regenerated Man minds the things of the Spirit—i. e., *he directs his mind toward the things of the Spirit; sets his thoughts, affections and purposes upon them.*

(7) 1 Jno. 5: 1—"Whosoever believeth that Jesus is the Christ is born of God: and every one that loveth him that begat loveth him also that is begotten of him."

SEVENTH PROPOSITION: The Regenerated Man believes that Jesus is the Christ.

Of course the faith that John here speaks of is a faith that is real—*i. e.*, a faith that enthrones Jesus as Christ in the heart.

Compare Matt. 16: 16, 17—"And Simon Peter answered and said, thou art the Christ, the Son of the living God. And Jesus answered and said unto him, Blessed art thou, Simon Bar-jona: for flesh and blood hath not revealed it unto thee, but my Father which is in heaven." Jno. 1: 12, 13—"But as many as received him, to them gave he power to become the sons of God, even to them that believe on his name: which were born, not of blood, nor of the will of the flesh, nor of the will of man, but of God."

(8) 1 Jno. 5: 4, R.V.—"For whatsoever is begotten of God *overcometh the world:* and this is the victory that hath overcome the world, even our faith."

EIGHTH PROPOSITION: The Regenerated Man overcomes the world.

The world is at variance with God, it lieth in the evil one (1 Jno. 5: 19), and it is constantly exercising a power to draw the believer into disobedience to God (See context, 1 Jno. 5: 3), but the one born of God by the power of faith gets the victory over the world.

(9) 1 Jno. 3: 9, R.V. (see Greek)—"Whosoever is begotten of God doeth no (is not doing) sin; for his seed remaineth in him: and he cannot sin (be sinning), because he is born of God."

NINTH PROPOSITION: In the one born of God the seed of God remains, and therefore the one born of God does not practice sin.

Note 1.—What is meant here by sin? Sin here is manifestly something done. What kind of a something done is defined in v. 4,

"Transgression of the law" or "lawlessness." (R.V.), *i. e.*, such acts as reveal disregard for the will of God as revealed in His word. Sin then is here, a conscious intentional violation of the law of God. The regenerate man will not be doing that which he knows to be contrary to the will of God. He may do that which is contrary to God's will, but which he does not know to be contrary to God's will. It is not therefore lawlessness. Perhaps he ought to have known that it was contrary to God's will, and when he is led to see it he will confess his guilt to God. Taking sin in a broader sense than John here takes it, it is sin.

NOTE 2.—The tense of the verb here used is the present, which denotes progressive or continued action. The literal translation of the passage would be "Every one begotten out of God, sin is not doing, because his seed in him is remaining; and he cannot be sinning, because out of God he is begotten." It is not taught that he never sins in a single act, but it is taught that he is not going on sinning, making a practice of sin. What his practice is will appear under the next head.

The one begotten of God cannot be sinning, because he is begotten of God. The new nature imparted in regeneration renders the continuous practice of sin impossible.

(10) 1 Jno. 2: 29, R.V.—"If ye know that he is righteous, ye know that every one also that *doeth righteousness* is begotten of him."

TENTH PROPOSITION: He that is begotten of God practices righteousness.

Here again we have the present tense (the present participle) denoting continuous action. It is evident here that the thought is not that he does righteousness in a single case, but that he makes a practice of it. By righteousness is meant the performance of such acts as are conformed to the straight line of God's will revealed in His word. Righteousness is the habitual practice of the one who is begotten of God. He may do individual acts which are unrighteous, but he is a doer of righteousness; "righteousness" is his practice.

NOTE.—The force of the present tense as indicating continuous action is very evident in this verse. If we took it as referring to a single act the verse would teach that everyone who does a single righteous act is begotten of God. Of course this is not meant. It does not refer to a single act of righteousness, and evidently the contrasted passage (Chap. 3: 9) cannot refer to a single act of lawlessness.

(11) 1 Jno. 3: 14, R.V.—"We know that we have passed out of death into life, because we *love the brethren.* He that loveth not abideth in death."

1 Jno. 4: 7, R.V.—"Beloved, let us love one another: for love is of God; and *every one that loveth* is begotten of God, and knoweth God."

ELEVENTH PROPOSITION: *He that is begotten of God loveth the brethren.*

QUESTION: Who are meant by the brethren ?

ANSWER: (1 Jno. 5: 1—"Whosoever believeth that Jesus is the Christ is begotten of God: and whosoever loveth him that begat loveth *him* also *that is begotten of him.*") Those who are begotten of God. The one who is begotten of God loveth every other one who is begotten of God. The other may be an American, or Englishman, or Negro, or Chinaman; he may be educated or uneducated, but he is a child of God and a brother, and as such an object of love.

QUESTION: What is meant by love ?

ANSWER: The following verses (1 Jno. 3: 16–18) define what John means by love. It is not mere emotion or sentiment, but that genuine desire for another's good that leads to sacrifice for him—even the sacrifice of our own life if necessary. This love is the supreme result, evidence and test of the New Birth.

(12) 2 Cor. 5: 17, R.V.—"Wherefore if any man is in Christ he is a new creature: the *old things are passed away;* behold they are become new."

TWELFTH PROPOSITION: *In the Regenerated Man old things are passed away; they are become new.*

In the place of the old ideas, old affections, old purposes, old choices, are new ideas, new affections, new purposes, new choices.

(13) Tit. 3: 5—"Not by works of righteousness which we have done, but according to his mercy he saved us, by the washing of regeneration, and renewing of the Holy Ghost."

THIRTEENTH PROPOSITION: *Through the bath of regeneration and renewing of the Holy Spirit the regenerated man is already saved.*

GENERAL NOTE.—These results of regeneration are also its evidence and tests, especially 7, 8, 9, 10, 11. If anyone would know whether he has indeed been begotten again let him inquire, "Are the facts stated under 7, 8, 9, 10, 11, true of me?"

III. The Necessity of the New Birth.

(1) Jno. 3: 3—"Jesus answered and said unto him, Verily, verily, I say unto thee, *Except a man be born again, he cannot see the kingdom of God.*"

FIRST PROPOSITION: No man can see the Kingdom of God except he be born again. The necessity is universal.

(2) Jno. 3: 7—"Marvel not that I said unto thee, ye *must* be born again."

SECOND PROPOSITION: Men not only may but must be born again. The necessity is absolute and imperative.

Nothing else will take the place of the New Birth. Education, morality, religion, orthodoxy, baptism, reform—none of these nor all of them together are sufficient.

Gal. 6: 15—"For in Christ Jesus neither circumcision availeth anything, nor uncircumcision, but a new creature." "Ye must be born again."

(3) Jno. 3: 5, 6—"Jesus answered, Verily, verily, I say unto thee, Except a man be born of water and of the Spirit, he cannot enter into the kingdom of God. That which is born of the flesh is flesh; and that which is born of the Spirit is spirit."

THIRD PROPOSITION: The reason why men must be born again is because all one gets by natural generation is "flesh."

What the character of the flesh is we learn from Paul:

Gal. 5: 19-21—"Now, the works of the flesh are manifest, which are these, adultery, fornication, uncleanness, lasciviousness, idolatry, witchcraft, hatred, variance, emulations, wrath, strife, sedition, heresies, envyings, murders, drunkenness, revellings, and such like; of the which I tell you before, as I have also told you in time past, that they which do such things shall not inherit the kingdom of God." Rom. 8: 7, R.V.—"Because the mind of the flesh is enmity against God; for it is not subject to the law of God, neither indeed can be."

"The flesh" is radically and essentially bad. They that are in the flesh "cannot please God," nor "inherit the kingdom of God." The flesh is incapable of improvement. (Jer. 13: 23.) What man needs is not to cultivate nor to improve the old nature, but to get a new one.

Matt. 12: 33—"Either make the tree good, and his fruit good; or else make the tree corrupt, and his fruit corrupt: for the tree is known by his fruit."

IV. The Manner of the New Birth, or How Men are Born Again.

(1) Jno. 1: 13—"Which were born, not of blood, nor of the will of the flesh, nor of the will of man, but of God."

FIRST PROPOSITION: Believers are begotten again—not of blood, nor of the will of the flesh, nor of the will of man, but of God. The New Birth is God's work, having its origin entirely in God s will.

(2) Tit. 3: 4, 5—"But after that the kindness and love of God our Saviour toward man appeared, not by works of righteousness which we have done, but according to his mercy HE saved us, by the washing of regeneration, and renewing of the Holy Ghost."

Jno. 3: 5, 6—"Jesus answered, Verily, verily, I say unto thee, Except a man be born of water and of the Spirit, he cannot enter into the kingdom of God. That which is born of the flesh is flesh; and that which is born of the Spirit is spirit."

SECOND PROPOSITION: God begets men anew through the cleansing, quickening, renewing work of the Holy Spirit.

(3) Jas. 1: 18—"Of his own will begat he us *with the word of truth*, that we should be a kind of firstfruits of his creatures." (Compare Col. 1: 5—"For the hope which is laid up for you in heaven, whereof ye heard before in the word of the truth of the gospel. ")

1 Pet. 1: 23, 25—"Being born again, not of corruptible seed, but of incorruptible, *by the word of God*, which liveth and abideth forever. . . . But the word of God endureth for ever. And this is the word which by the gospel is preached unto you."

THIRD PROPOSITION: " The word of Truth " or " The word of God "—(i. e., the word which is preached by the gospel)—is the instrument the Holy Spirit uses in regeneration.

(4) 1 Cor. 4: 15—"For though ye have ten thousand instructors in Christ, yet have ye not many fathers: for in Christ Jesus I have begotten you through the gospel."

FOURTH PROPOSITION: Men, by the preaching of the gospel, are used of God for the regeneration of believers.

(5) Gal. 3: 26—"For ye are all the children of God *by faith in Christ Jesus.*"

Jno. 1: 12, 13—"But *as many as received him*, to them gave he power to become the sons of God, *even to them that believe on his name:* which were born, not of blood, nor of the will of the flesh, nor of the will of man, but of God."

FIFTH PROPOSITION: We become children of God through believing in or receiving Jesus Christ.

This same thought is illustrated by Jesus in Jno. 3: 14, 15 by a reference to the brazen serpent. These words are an answer to the question of Nicodemus "How can these things be?" (v. 9.) As the dying Israelite, with the poison of the fiery serpents coursing through his veins, was saved by looking at the brazen serpent on the pole, and had new life coursing through his veins as soon as he looked, so we dying men, with the poison of sin coursing through our veins, are saved by looking at Christ "made in the likeness of sinful flesh," lifted up on the cross, and have new life coursing through our veins as soon as we look. All we have to do with our regeneration is to receive Christ. (Compare 2 Cor. 5: 17—"Therefore if any man be in Christ, he is a new creature: old things are passed away; behold all things are become new.")

In the New Birth the Word of God is the seed; the human heart is the soil; the preacher of the Word is the sower, and drops the seed into the soil; God by His Spirit opens the heart to receive the seed (Acts 16: 14); the hearer believes; the Spirit quickens the seed into life in the receptive heart; the new Divine Nature springs up out of the Divine Word; the believer is born again, created anew, made alive, passed out of death into life.

CHAPTER VII

ADOPTION.

I. What is Adoption?

(1) Etymologically the word translated "adoption" means "the placing a son."

(2) In Greek usage outside of the Bible from Pindar and Herodotus down the two words from which the word translated "adoption" is derived mean "an adopted son."

(3) Scriptural usage:

Rom. 9: 4—"Who are Israelites; to whom pertaineth *the adoption*, and the glory, and the covenants, and the giving of the law, and the service of God, and the promises."

(Compare Ex. 4: 22, 23; Deut. 14: 1; Is. 43: 6; Jer. 31: 9; Hos. 11: 1.)

Rom. 8: 15, 23—"For ye have not received the spirit of bondage again to fear; but ye have received *the Spirit of adoption whereby we cry, Abba, Father.* . . . And not only they, but ourselves also, which have the firstfruits of the Spirit, even we ourselves groan within ourselves, *waiting for the adoption*, to wit, the redemption of our body."

Eph. 1: 5—"Having predestinated us unto the adoption of children by Jesus Christ to himself, according to the good pleasure of his will."

Gal. 4: 5—"To redeem them that were under the law, that ye might receive the adoption of sons."

These are all the passages in which the word is found. Here the word means the "placing" or "adoption" as sons. In regeneration we receive the nature of sons of God; in adoption we receive the position of sons of God. Regeneration is a change of nature. Adoption is a change of position or relation.

II. The Origin and Ground of Adoption.

Eph. 1: 3–6, R.V.—"Blessed be the God and Father of our Lord Jesus Christ, who hath blessed us with every spiritual blessing in the heavenly places in Christ: even as he chose us in him before the foundation of the world, that we should be holy and without blemish before him in love: *having foreordained us unto adoption* as sons through Jesus Christ unto himself, according to the good pleasure of his will, to the praise of the glory of his grace, which he freely bestowed on us in the Beloved."

(1) Adoption originates in the eternal, sovereign, unmerited grace of God. Not because of any merit seen or foreseen in us, but because of His own loving, gracious choice, He foreordained us to adoption as sons. He did not foreordain us to adoption as sons because we were fit for the place; but, having foreordained us to adoption as sons, He makes us fit for the place to which He has graciously foreordained us.

(2) Adoption is through Jesus Christ—*i. e.*, on the ground of what He is and does. Because of what His only begotten Son is and does, He adopts many to be sons.

III. The Recipients of Adoption, or who receive the Grace of Adoption.

(1) Gal. 3: 25, 26—"But after that faith is come, *we* are no longer under a schoolmaster, but *ye* are all the children of God *by faith in Christ Jesus.*"

Gal. 4: 4–7—"But when the fulness of the time was come, God sent forth his Son, made of a woman, made under the law, to redeem them that were under the law, that *we* might receive the adoption of sons. And because ye are sons, God hath sent forth the Spirit of his Son into your hearts, crying, Abba, Father. Wherefore thou art no more a servant, but a son; and if a son, then an heir of God through Christ."

Jno. 1: 12, R.V—"But as many as received him, to them gave he the right to become children of God, *even to them that believe on his name.*"

PROPOSITION: All those who believe in, or receive Christ Jesus, receive the adoption of sons—i. e., they obtain a place or right as sons in the family of God.

IV. The Time of Adoption, or when the Believer receives his place as a Son.

(1) Gal. 3: 25, 26—"But after that faith is come, we are no longer under a schoolmaster. For ye are all the children of God by faith in Christ Jesus."

4: 6—"And because *ye are sons*, God hath sent forth the Spirit of his Son into your hearts, crying Abba, Father."

1 Jno. 3: 1, 2, R.V.—"Behold what manner of love the Father hath bestowed upon us, that we should be called children of God: and *such we are.* For this cause the world knoweth us not, because it knew him not. Beloved, now are we children of God, and it is not yet made manifest what we shall be. We know that, if he shall be manifested, we shall be like him; for we shall see him even as he is."

FIRST PROPOSITION: The Believer has already received his place as a son in the family of God.

We now have the rights of sons; we are not under tutors, governors nor law. All things in the house are ours.

(2) Rom. 8: 23—"And not only they, but ourselves also, which have the firstfruits of the Spirit, even we ourselves groan within ourselves, *waiting for the adoption*, to wit, the redemption of our body."

SECOND PROPOSITION: The full working out and manifestation of our position as sons—the completion of our placing as sons, our manifestation to the world as sons of God—lies in the future, and will not be realized until the body as well as the Spirit is redeemed.

Col. 3: 4, R.V.—"When Christ, who is our life, shall be manifested, *then* shall ye also with him be manifested in glory."

V. The Proof of our Adoption, or How we know that we have the Place of Sons in the Family of God.

(1) Gal. 3: 23-26, R.V.—"For before faith came, we were kept in ward under the law, shut up unto the faith which should afterwards be revealed. So that the law hath been our tutor to bring us unto Christ, that we might be justified by faith. But now that faith is come, we are no longer under a tutor. For ye are all sons of God, through faith in Christ Jesus."

FIRST PROPOSITION: We know by the explicit statement of God's Word that we are no longer under the tutor, law, but have a place as sons in the family of God.

(2) Gal. 4: 6—"And because ye are sons, *God hath sent forth the Spirit of his Son into your hearts, crying, Abba Father.*"
Rom. 8: 15, 16, R.V.—"For ye received not the spirit of bondage again unto fear; but ye received the spirit of adoption, whereby we cry, *Abba*, Father. The Spirit himself beareth witness with our spirit, that we are children of God."

SECOND PROPOSITION: Because we are sons, God has sent the Spirit of His Son into our hearts. This Spirit of Christ bears witness together with our spirit that we are children of God, crying, Abba Father.

VI. The Results of Adoption.

(1) Gal. 4: 6—"And because ye are sons, God hath sent forth the Spirit of his son into our hearts, crying, Abba, Father."

FIRST PROPOSITION: *God sends the Spirit of His Son into our hearts, crying, Abba, Father.*

(2) Rom. 8: 15—"For ye have not received the spirit of bondage again to fear; but ye have received the spirit of adoption, whereby we cry, Abba, Father."

SECOND PROPOSITION: *We are delivered from bondage and fear, and brought into filial trust in God.*

(3) Gal. 4: 4-6: "But when the fulness of the time was come, God sent forth his Son, made of a woman, made under the law, to redeem them that were under the law, that we might receive the adoption of sons. And because ye are sons, God hath sent forth the Spirit of his Son into your hearts, crying, Abba, Father."

Gal. 3: 25, 26—"But after that faith is come, we are no longer under a schoolmaster, for ye are all the children of God by faith in Christ Jesus."

THIRD PROPOSITION: *We are delivered from the bondage under the law to serve in the liberty of sons.*

(4) Rom. 8: 17—"And if children, then heirs; heirs of God, and joint heirs with Christ; if so be that we suffer with him, that we may be also glorified together."

FOURTH PROPOSITION: *Having received a place as children we are made heirs of God and joint heirs with Jesus Christ. We are made heirs of all God is and all God has.*

CHAPTER VIII.

SANCTIFICATION.

I. What does Sanctification mean ?

FIRST MEANING:

Lev. 27: 14, 16—" And when a man shall *sanctify his house to be holy unto the* LORD, then the priest shall estimate it, whether it be good or bad: as the priest shall esteem it, so shall it stand. . . . And if a man shall *sanctify unto the* LORD some part of a field of his possession, then *thy* estimation shall be according to the seed thereof; a homer of barley seed shall be valued at fifty shekels of silver."

Num. 8: 17—" For all the firstborn of the children of Israel are mine, both man and beast: on the day that I smote every firstborn in the land of Egypt I *sanctified them for myself.*"

2 Chron. 7: 16—" For now have I chosen and *sanctified this house, that my name may be there* forever: and mine eyes and my heart shall be there perpetually."

Jer. 1: 5—" Before I formed thee in the belly I knew thee; and before thou camest forth out of the womb I sanctified thee, and I ordained thee a prophet unto the nations."

Matt. 23: 17—" Ye fools and blind: for whether is greater, the gold, or the temple that *sanctifieth the gold ?*

Jno. 10: 36—" Say ye of him, whom the Father hath *sanctified*, and sent into the world, thou blasphemest; because I said, I am the Son of God ?

FIRST PROPOSITION: To sanctify means to separate or set apart for God.   Sanctification is the process of setting apart or state of being set apart for God.   This is the primary meaning of the word.

SECOND MEANING:

2 Chron. 29: 5, 15-18—" And said unto them, Hear me, ye Levites; *sanctify now yourselves*, and *sanctify the house* of the LORD God of your Fathers, *and carry forth the filthiness out of the holy places.* . . . And they gathered their brethren, and sanctified themselves, and came, according to the commandment of the king, by the words of the LORD, *to cleanse the house* of the LORD. And the priests went into the inner

part of the house of the LORD, to *cleanse* it, and *brought out all the uncleanness* that they found in the temple of the LORD into the court of the house of the LORD. And the Levites took it, to carry it out abroad into the brook Kidron. Now they began of the first day of the first month *to sanctify*, and on the eighth day of the month came they to the porch of the LORD: *so they sanctified the house* of the LORD in eight days; and in the sixteenth day of the first month they made an end. Then they went in to Hezekiah the king, and said, *We have cleansed* all the house of the LORD, and the altar of burnt offering, with all the vessels thereof, and the shew-bread table, with all the vessels thereof."

Lev. 11: 44—"For I am the LORD your God: ye shall therefore *sanctify yourselves, and ye shall be holy;* for I am holy: *neither shall ye defile yourselves* with any manner of creeping things that creepeth upon the earth."

Lev. 20: 7—"*Sanctify* yourselves therefore, *and be ye holy:* for I am the LORD your God."

1 Chron. 15: 12, 14—"And said unto them, Ye are the chief of the fathers of the Levites; *sanctify yourselves*, both ye and your brethren, that ye may bring up the ark of the LORD God of Israel unto the place that I have prepared for it. . . . *So the priests and the Levites sanctified themselves* to bring up the ark of the LORD God of Israel."

Ex. 19: 20-22—"And the LORD came down upon mount Sinai, on the top of the mount: and the LORD called Moses up to the top of the mount; and Moses went up. And the LORD said unto Moses, Go down, charge the people, lest they break through unto the LORD to gaze, and many of them perish. And let the priests also, which come near to the LORD, *sanctify themselves*, lest the LORD break forth upon them."

1 Thess. 5: 22, 23—"Abstain from all appearance of evil. And the very God of peace *sanctify you wholly;* and I pray God your whole spirit and soul and body be *preserved blameless* unto the coming of our Lord Jesus Christ."

Heb. 9: 13—"For if the blood of bulls and of goats, and the ashes of a heifer sprinkling the unclean, *sanctifieth to the purifying of the flesh*."

1 Thess. 4: 7, R.V.—"For God called us *not for uncleanness, but in sanctification*."

1 Thess. 4: 3—"For this is the will of God, even your *sanctification, that ye should abstain from fornication*."

SECOND PROPOSITION: To sanctify means to separate from ceremonial or moral defilement, to cleanse. Sanctification is the process of separating, or state of being separated, from ceremonial or moral defilement.

The two meanings of the word are closely allied. One cannot be truly separated to God without being separated from sin.

THIRD MEANING:

Ezek. 20: 41—"I will accept you with your sweet savour, when I bring you out from the people, and gather you out of the countries wherein ye have been scattered; and I will be sanctified in you before the heathen."

Ezek. 28: 22—"And I say, Thus saith the LORD God; Behold, I am against thee, O Zidon; and I will be glorified in the midst of thee: and they shall know that I am the LORD, when I shall have executed judgments in her, and shall be sanctified in her."

Ezek. 36: 23—"And I will sanctify my great name, which was profaned among the heathen, which ye have profaned in the midst of them; and the heathen shall know that I am the LORD, saith the LORD God, when I shall be sanctified in you before their eyes."

Ezek. 38: 16—"And thou shalt come up against my people of Israel, as a cloud to cover the land; it shall be in the latter days, and I will bring thee against my land, that the heathen may know me, when I shall be sanctified in thee, O Gog, before their eyes."

Ezek. 39: 27—"When I have brought them again from the people, and gathered them out of their enemies' hands, and am sanctified in them in the sight of many nations."

THIRD PROPOSITION: God is spoken of as being sanctified by the revelation of His own character, not that He is made holy but shown to be Holy.

II. How are men sanctified?

(1) 1 Thess. 5: 23—"And the very *God* of peace *sanctify you* wholly; and I pray God your whole spirit and soul and body be preserved blameless unto the coming of our Lord Jesus Christ."

Jno. 17: 17—"Sanctify them through thy truth: thy word is truth."

FIRST PROPOSITION: God sanctifies men.

Sanctification—the separation of men from sin and separating them unto God—is God's own work.

As it was God who in the Old Dispensation set apart the firstborn unto Himself, so it is God who in the New Dispensation sets apart the believer unto Himself and separates him from sin.

(2) Eph. 5: 25, 26, R.V.—"Husbands, love your wives, even as Christ also loved the church, and gave himself up for it; *that he might sanctify it,* having cleansed it by the washing of water with the word."

SECOND PROPOSITION: Christ sanctifies the Church. Sanctification is Christ's work.

By the giving up or sacrifice of Himself, Christ sets the Church apart for God. The sacrifice of Christ puts a difference between the Church and the world, just as the blood of the Passover Lamb put a difference between Israel and the Egyptians. (Ex. 11: 7; 12: 12, 13.)   Heb. 10: 10, R. V.—"By which will we have been sanctified through the offering of the body of Jesus Christ once for all."   By the offering of His own body Jesus Christ has forever set the believer apart for God.   The cross stands between the believer and the world.   He belongs to God.

(3)   2 Thess. 2: 13—"But we are bound to give thanks always to God for you, brethren beloved of the Lord, because God hath from the beginning chosen you to salvation through *sanctification of the Spirit* and belief of the truth."

1 Pet. 1: 2—"Elect according to the foreknowledge of God the Father, through *sanctification of the Spirit,* unto obedience and sprinkling of the blood of Jesus Christ: Grace unto you, and peace, be multiplied."

THIRD PROPOSITION: The Holy Spirit sanctifies the believer. Sanctification is the Holy Spirit's work.

Just as in the Old Testament type, tabernacle, altar and priest were set apart for God by the anointing oil (Lev. 8: 10–12), so in the New Testament anti-type the believer, who is both tabernacle and priest, is set apart for God by the anointing of the Holy Spirit. It is also the Holy Spirit's working in the heart that overcomes the flesh and its defilements, and thus separates the believer from sin and clothes him with Divine graces of character, and makes him fit to be God's own.

Gal. 5: 16–23—"This I say then, Walk in the Spirit, and ye shall not fulfil the lust of the flesh. For the flesh lusteth against the Spirit, and the Spirit against the flesh; and these are contrary the one to the other; so that ye cannot do the things ye would. But if ye be led of the Spirit, ye are not under the law. Now the works of the flesh are manifest, which are these, adultery, fornication, uncleanness, lasciviousness, idolatry, witchcraft, hatred, variance, emulation, wrath, strife, sedition, heresies, envyings, murders, drunkenness, revellings, and such like: of the which I tell you before, as I have also told you in time past, that they which do such things shall not inherit the kingdom of God. But the fruit of the Spirit is love, joy, peace, long-suffering, gentleness, goodness, faith, meekness, temperance; against such there is no law."

(4) Heb. 13: 12, R.V.—"Wherefore Jesus also, that he might *sanctify the people through his own blood,* suffered without the gate."

FOURTH PROPOSITION: *Believers are sanctified through the blood.*

The blood cleanses us from *all the guilt* of sin and thus separates us from the mass of men under the curse of the law, and sets us apart for God. (Compare 1 Jno. 1: 7, 9—"But if we walk in the light, as he is in the light, we have the fellowship one with another, and the blood of Jesus Christ his son *cleanseth us from all sin.* . . . If we confess our sins, he is faithful and just to forgive us our sins, and to cleanse us from all unrighteousness.")

In the Old Testament the blood of the sacrifice cleansed the Israelites from the *guilt* of ceremonial offenses and set them apart for God; in the New Testament the blood of Christ cleanses the believer from *guilt* of moral offenses and sets him apart for God.

(5) Jno. 17: 17, R.V.—"Sanctify them in the truth: thy word is truth."

FIFTH PROPOSITION: *We are sanctified in the truth, the Word of God.*

The Word cleanses from the presence of sin, separates us from it, and sets us apart for God. (Ps. 119: 9, 11.)

Jno. 15: 3—"Now are ye *clean through the word* which I have spoken unto you."

As we bring our lives into daily contact with the Word, the sins and imperfections of our lives and hearts are disclosed and put away, and we are more and more separated from sin unto God. (Jno. 13: 10—"Jesus saith to him, He that is washed needeth not *save to wash his feet*, but is clean every whit: and ye are clean, but not all.")

(6) 1 Cor. 1: 30, R.V.—"But of him are ye in *Christ Jesus*, who *was made unto us* wisdom from God, and righteousness and *sanctification*, and redemption."

SIXTH PROPOSITION: *Jesus Christ was made unto us from God sanctification.*

Separation from sin and separation to God was provided for us in Christ. By the appropriation of Christ we obtain this sanctification thus provided. The more completely we appropriate Christ, the more completely are we sanctified. But perfect sanctification is provided in Him, just as perfect wisdom is provided in Him. (Col. 2: 3.) We appropriate each in ever-increasing measure. Through the indwelling Christ, presented to us by the Spirit in the Word, we are made Christ-like and bear fruit.

Jno. 15: 1-7—"I am the true vine, and my Father is the husbandman. Every branch in me that beareth not fruit he taketh away: and every branch that beareth fruit, he purgeth it, that it may bring forth more fruit. Now ye are clean through the word which I have spoken unto you. Abide in me, and I in you. As the branch cannot bear fruit of itself, except it abide in the vine; no more can ye, except ye abide in me. I am the vine, ye are the branches. He that abideth in me, and I in him, the same bringeth forth much fruit; for without me ye can do nothing. If a man abide not in me, he is cast forth as a branch, and is withered; and men gather them, and cast them into the fire, and they are burned. If ye abide in me, and my words abide in you, ye shall ask what ye will, and it shall be done unto you."

As Christ takes continually more and more complete possession of every corner of our being we are more and more completely sanctified.

(7) Heb. 12: 10, 11 (Note v. 14.)—"For they verily for a few days chastened us after their own pleasure; but he for our profit, that we might be partakers of his holiness. Now no chastening for the present seemeth to be joyous but grievous: nevertheless, afterward it yieldeth the peaceable fruit of righteousness unto them which are exercised thereby."

SEVENTH PROPOSITION: We become partakers of God's holiness through the administration of chastisement by our Heavenly Father.

NOTE.—The word "holiness" in this passage is not precisely the same word as the one translated "sanctification" in other passages, but it is from precisely the same root, and in v. 14, precisely the same word is used, and it is translated "sanctification" in the Revised Version.

(8) Heb. 12: 14, R.V.—"Follow after peace with all men, and the sanctification without which no man shall see the Lord."

EIGHTH PROPOSITION: Sanctification is something that we must pursue, or seek earnestly, if we are to obtain it. While it is God's work we have our part in it; viz.: to make it the object of our earnest desire and pursuit.

(9) Rom. 6: 19 (last half), 22, R.V.—"For as ye presented your members as servants to uncleanness and to iniquity unto iniquity, even so now *present your members as servants to righteousness* unto sanctifi-

cation. But now being made free from sin, and *become servants to God*, ye have your fruit unto sanctification, and the end eternal life."

NINTH PROPOSITION: We attain unto sanctification through presenting our members as servants (literally "slaves ") *to righteousness and becoming ourselves bondservants unto God.*

(10) 2 Cor. 6: 17; 7: 1—"Wherefore come out from among them, and be ye separate, saith the Lord, and touch not the unclean thing; and I will receive you. Having therefore these promises, dearly beloved, *let us cleanse ourselves from all filthiness* of the flesh and spirit, *perfecting holiness* in the fear of God."

TENTH PROPOSITION: We perfect holiness by cleansing ourselves from all defilement of flesh and spirit. To this end we are to come out from among unbelievers, refusing all alliances with them and touching no unclean thing.

It is, of course, under the guidance and in the power of the Holy Spirit that we do this, but it is *we* that do it.

(11) Col. 1: 21–23, R.V.—"And you, being in time past alienated and enemies in your mind in your evil works, yet now hath he reconciled in the body of his flesh through death, *to present you holy and without blemish and unreproveable* before him: *if so be that ye continue in the faith, grounded and steadfast*, and not moved away from the hope of the gospel which ye heard, which was preached in all creation under heaven; whereof I Paul was made a minister."

*ELEVENTH PROPOSITION: The completion by Christ of the work of sanctification in us—*i. e., *our presentation before God, holy, without blemish and unreproveable—is conditioned upon our continuance in the faith, grounded and steadfast.*

NOTE.—If we have a genuine faith we will so continue. Heb 10: 39—"But we are not of them who draw back unto perdition; but of them that believe to the saving of the soul."

(12) Acts 26: 18—"To open their eyes, and to turn them from darkness to light, and from the power of Satan unto God, that they may receive forgiveness of sins, and inheritance among them which are *sanctified by faith* that is in me."

TWELFTH PROPOSITION: We are sanctified by faith in Christ.

Sanctification, just as Justification, Regeneration and Adoption, is conditioned upon faith. Faith is the hand that appropriates this as all other blessings of God.

III. When does Sanctification take Place ?

(1) 1 Cor. 1: 2, R.V.—"Paul, called to be an apostle of Jesus Christ through the will of God, and Sosthenes our brother, unto the church of God which is at Corinth, *even them that* ARE *sanctified* in Christ Jesus, called to be saints, with all that call upon the name of our Lord Jesus Christ in every place, their Lord and ours."

1 Cor. 6: 11, R.V.—"And such were some of you; but ye were washed, but *ye were sanctified*, but ye were justified in the name of the Lord Jesus Christ, and in the Spirit of our God."

FIRST PROPOSITION: All members of the Church of God already are sanctified in Christ Jesus.

The moment anyone becomes a member of the Church of God by faith in Christ Jesus, that moment he is sanctified.

QUESTION: In what sense are we already sanctified?

ANSWER:

(a) Heb. 10: 10, 14—"By the which will we are sanctified *through the offering of the body of Jesus Christ* once for all. . . . For by one offering he hath perfected forever them that are sanctified." (Compare v. 1.)

By the offering of the body of Jesus Christ once for all we are cleansed forever from all the guilt of sin, we are "perfected forever" as far as our standing before God is concerned. The sacrifice does not need to be repeated as the Jewish sacrifices (v. 1). The work is done once for all, sin is put away (Heb. 9: 26. Compare Gal. 3: 13) forever, and we are set apart forever as God's peculiar and eternal possession. (b) There is another sense in which every believer may be already sanctified. (Rom. 12: 1—"I beseech you, brethren, by the mercies of God, that ye present your bodies a living sacrifice, holy, acceptable unto God, which is your reasonable service.") It is the believer's present and blessed privilege, and immediate and solemn duty, to present his body to God a living sacrifice—not some part or parts of the body, but the whole body with its every member and every faculty. Such an offering is "well pleasing to God." (R. V. Marg.) As God in the Old Testament showed His pleasure in an offering by sending down fire to take it to Himself, so when the whole body is thus offered to God He still sends down fire, the fire of the Holy Ghost, and takes to Himself what is thus presented. The believer, then, so far as the will, the governing purpose of his life, the centre of his being, is concerned, is wholly God's or perfectly sanctified. He may and will daily discover, as he studies the Word of God and is illumined by the Holy Spirit, acts of his, habits of life, forms of feeling, speech and action that are not in conformity with this central purpose of his life. These must be confessed to God as blameworthy, and be put away, and this department of his being and life brought by God's Spirit and the indwelling Christ into conformity with God's will as revealed in His Word.

The victory in this newly discovered and unclaimed territory can be instantaneous. For example, I discover in myself an irritability of temper that is manifestly displeasing to God. I can go to God and confess it, renounce it and then instantly, not by my own strength, but by looking to Jesus and claiming his patience and gentleness, overcome it and never have another failure in that direction. And so with everything in my life that I am brought to see is displeasing to God.

(2) 1 Thess. 3: 12—"And the Lord make you to *increase and abound* in love one toward another, and toward all men, even as we do toward you."

4: 1, 10, R.V.—"Finally then, brethren, we beseech and exhort you in the Lord Jesus, that, as ye received of us how ye ought to walk and to please God, even as ye do walk—that ye *abound more and more* . . . for indeed ye do it toward all the brethren which are in Macedonia. But we exhort you, brethren, that ye *abound more and more*."

2 Pet. 3: 18, R.V.—"But *grow* in the grace and knowledge of our Lord and Saviour Jesus Christ. To him be the glory both now and forever. Amen."

2 Cor. 3: 18, R.V —"But we all, with unveiled face reflecting as a mirror the glory of the Lord, are transformed into the same image *from glory to glory*, even as from the Lord the Spirit."

Eph. 4: 11-15—"And he gave some, apostles; and some, prophets; and some, evangelists; and some, pastors and teachers; For the perfecting of the saints, for the work of the ministry, for the edifying of the body of Christ: Till we all come in the unity of the faith, and of the knowledge of the Son of God, unto a perfect man, unto the measure of the stature of the fulness of Christ: that we henceforth be no more children, tossed to and fro, and carried about with every wind of doctrine, by the sleight of men, and cunning craftiness, whereby they lie in wait to deceive; but speaking the truth in love, *may grow* up into him in all things, which is the head, even Christ."

SECOND PROPOSITION: There is a progressive work of sanctification; an increasing in love; an abounding more and more in a godly walk and in pleasing God; a growing in the grace and the knowledge of our Lord and Saviour Jesus Christ; a being transformed into the image of our Lord Jesus from glory unto glory, each new gaze at Him making us more like Him; a growing up into Christ in all things, until we attain unto a full-grown man, unto the measure of the stature of the fulness of Christ.

(3) 1 Thess. 5: 23, R.V.—"And the God of peace himself *sanctify you wholly;* and may your spirit and soul and body be preserved entire without blame *at the coming of our Lord Jesus Christ.*"

1 Thess. 3: 12, 13—"And the Lord make you to increase and abound in love one toward another, and toward all men, even as we do toward you: to the end he may *establish your hearts unblamable in holiness* before God, even our Father, *at the coming of our Lord Jesus Christ with all his saints.*"

THIRD PROPOSITION: The complete sanctification of believers is something to be sought for in prayer, to be accomplished by God in the future.

It is at the coming of our Lord Jesus with all his saints that He is to establish our hearts unblamable in holiness before our God and Father, and that our spirit and soul and body are to be preserved entire without blame. (Compare 1 Jno. 3: 2.) It is through our Lord making us to increase and abound in love unto one another and unto all men that this is accomplished. It is not in the life that now is, nor is it at death, but at the coming of Christ that we are entirely sanctified in this sense.

IV. The Results of Sanctification.

(1) Heb. 10: 14—"For by one offering he hath perfected forever them that are sanctified."

FIRST PROPOSITION: By the one offering, the sacrifice of Himself for sins, Christ hath perfected forever those who are sanctified.

Their standing before God as guiltless is already forever secured for the sanctified. The sanctification here spoken of is the separation from the guilt of sin and unto God secured by the shed blood.

(2) Heb. 2: 11—"For both he that sanctifieth and they who are sanctified are all of one: for which cause he is not ashamed to call them brethren."

SECOND PROPOSITION: Those whom Jesus sanctifies are of one with Him, and He is not ashamed to call them brethren.

(3) 2 Thess. 2: 13—"But we are bound to give thanks always to God for you, brethren beloved of the Lord, because God hath from the beginning chosen you to *salvation through sanctification* of the Spirit and belief of the truth."

THIRD PROPOSITION: We are saved through sanctification.

Sanctification results in salvation. The sanctification here spoken of is the sanctification which the Holy Spirit works; and the salvation here spoken of is not salvation in the mere sense of the forgiveness of sins, but salvation in the fullest sense of deliverance from sin's dominion and presence.

(4) Heb. 12: 14, R.V—"Follow after peace with all men, and the sanctification without which no man shall see the Lord."

FOURTH PROPOSITION: Sanctification results in seeing the Lord.

The sanctification here spoken of is sanctification in the sense of separation from sin, the sanctification which is the outcome of our eager desire for it and God's chastening. (Compare vv. 10, 11.) Without this cleansing from sin it will be impossible to know the blessed vision of the Lord that awaits those who are purified. The purity that leads to this blessed vision of God is not merely outward purity but heart purity. (Matt. 5: 8— "Blessed are the pure in heart: for they shall see God.") Even in the life that now is, the more completely we are sanctified the clearer is our perception of God.

(5) Acts 20: 32—"And now, brethren, I commend you to God, and to the word of his grace, which is able to build you up, and to give you *an inheritance among all them which are sanctified.*"

Acts 26: 18—"To open their eyes, and to turn them from darkness to light, and from the power of Satan unto God, that they may receive forgiveness of sins, and *inheritance among them which are sanctified* by faith that is in me."

FIFTH PROPOSITION: Sanctification secures an inheritance.

Sanctification by God's Spirit makes us joint heirs with God's Son.

Rom. 8: 2, 3, 4, 5, 6, 12, 13, 14, 16-18—"For the law of the Spirit of life in Christ Jesus hath made me free from the law of sin and death. For what the law could not do, in that it was weak through the flesh, God sending his own Son in the likeness of sinful flesh, and for sin, condemned sin in the flesh: That the righteousness of the law might be fulfilled in us, who walk not after the flesh, but after the Spirit. For they that are after the flesh do mind the things of the flesh; but they that are after the Spirit, the things of the Spirit. For to be carnally minded is death; but to be spiritually minded is life and peace. . . . There-fore, brethren, we are debtors, not to the flesh, to live after the flesh, for if ye live after the flesh, ye shall die: but if ye through the Spirit do mortify the deeds of the body, ye shall live. For as many as are led by the Spirit of God, they are the Sons of God. . . . The Spirit itself beareth witness with our spirit, that we are the children of God: And if children, then heirs; heirs of God, and joint heirs with Christ; if so be that we suffer with him, that we may be also glorified together. For I reckon that the sufferings of this present time are not worthy to be compared with the glory which shall be revealed in us."

CHAPTER IX.

REPENTANCE.

I. The Importance of the Subject.

(1) Matt. 3: 2—"And saying, REPENT ye: for the kingdom of heaven is at hand."

4: 17—"From that time Jesus began to preach, and to say, REPENT: for the kingdom of heaven is at hand."

Mark 6: 12—"And they went out and preached that men should REPENT."

Acts 2: 38—"Then Peter said unto them, REPENT, and be baptized every one of you in the name of Jesus Christ for the remission of sins, and ye shall receive the gift of the Holy Ghost."

FIRST PROPOSITION: The keynote of the preaching of John the Baptist, Jesus, the Disciples on their first missionary tour and Peter at Pentecost, was " Repent."

(2) Acts 20: 21—"Testifying both to the Jews, and also to the Greeks, *repentance* toward God, and faith toward our Lord Jesus Christ."

26: 20—"But shewed first unto them of Damascus, and at Jerusalem, and throughout all the coasts of Judea, and then to the Gentiles, that they should *repent* and turn to God, and do works meet for repentance."

SECOND PROPOSITION: The sum and substance of Paul's testimony to Jew and to Gentile was repentance toward God and faith toward our Lord Jesus Christ.

(3) Luke 24: 47, R.V.—"And that *repentance* and remission of sins should be preached in his name unto all the nations, beginning from Jerusalem."

THIRD PROPOSITION: The heart of Christ's parting commission to the twelve was that " Repentance and Remission of Sins " should be preached unto all the nations.

(4) 2 Pet. 3: 9, R.V.—"The Lord is not slack concerning his promise, as some count slackness; but is longsuffering to you-ward, not

wishing that any should perish, but that all should *come to repentance.*"

FOURTH PROPOSITION: *The Lord s supreme desire concerning all men is that they should come to repentance.*

(5) Acts 17: 30—"And the times of this ignorance God winked at; but now commandeth all men everywhere to repent."

FIFTH PROPOSITION: *God s one command to all men everywhere is " Repent."*

(6) Luke 13: 3, 5—"I tell you, Nay: but, *except ye repent*, ye shall all likewise perish. . . . I tell you, Nay: but except ye repent, ye shall all likewise perish."

SIXTH PROPOSITION: *The only door of escape from perdition for any man is repentance.*

NOTE.—The universal call of Old Testament prophets was repent. There surely is not the emphasis laid upon repentance in modern preaching that there is in the Bible.

II. What Is Repentance ?

(1) THE ETYMOLOGY OF THE WORDS USED:

The primary thought of the Hebrew word translated "repent" in the Old Testament is, to pant, to sigh, to groan, and so to lament, to grieve, to grieve about one's doing. This Hebrew word occurs frequently in the Old Testament in the active form in the sense to comfort—*e. g.*, Ps. 23: 4—"Yea, though I walk through the valley of the shadow of death, I will fear no evil: for thou art with me; thy rod and thy staff they comfort me." The Greek word in the New Testament translated "repent" means "to change one's mind."

The same Greek word is used in the LXX for the Hebrew word mentioned above. So its New Testament meaning is to be determined by this Old Testament usage. There is another Greek word used in the New Testament five times and translated "repent." This word means "it is a care to one afterwards,"—*i. e.*, it "repents one." This word is also used in the LXX to translate the Hebrew word mentioned above. The thought of both sorrow and change of purpose is in the words.

(2) USAGE OF THE WORDS IN THE BIBLE:

Jer. 8: 6—"I hearkened and heard, but they spake not aright: no man repented him of his wickedness, saying, What have I done? every one turned to his course, as the horse rusheth into the battle."

Jer. 18: 8—"If that nation, against whom I have pronounced, turn from their evil, I will repent of the evil that I thought to do unto them."

Jer. 26: 3—"If so be they will hearken, and turn every man from his evil way, that I may repent me of the evil, which I proposed to do unto them because of the evil of their doings."

Jer. 42: 10—"If ye will still abide in this land, then will I build you, and not pull you down; and I will plant you, and not pluck you up: for I repent me of the evil that I have done unto you."

Ezek. 24: 14—"I the LORD have spoken it: it shall come to pass, and I will do it; I will not go back, neither will I spare, neither will I repent; according to thy ways, and according to thy doings, shall they judge thee, saith the LORD God."

Joel 2: 13, 14—"And rend your heart, and not your garments, and turn unto the LORD your God: for he is gracious and merciful, slow to anger, and of great kindness, and repenteth him of the evil."

Am. 7: 1-3, 4-6—"Thus hath the Lord GOD shewed unto me; and behold, he formed grasshoppers in the beginning of the shooting up of the latter growth after the king's mowings. And it came to pass, that when they had made an end of eating the grass of the land, then I said, O Lord GOD, forgive I beseech thee: by whom shall Jacob arise? for he is small. *The* LORD *repented for this: It shall not be, saith the* LORD. Thus hath the Lord GOD shewed unto me: and, behold, the LORD God called to contend by fire, and it devoured the great deep, and did eat up a part. Then said I, O Lord GOD, cease, I beseech thee: by whom shall Jacob arise? for he is small. The LORD repented for this: This also shall not be, saith the Lord GOD."

Jonah 3: 9, 10—"Who can tell if God will turn and *repent, and turn away* from his fierce anger, that we perish not? And God saw their works, that they turned from their evil way; and *God repented* of the evil, that he had said that he would do unto them; and *he did it not.*"

Matt. 12: 41—"The men of Nineveh shall rise in judgment with this generation, and shall condemn it: because *they repented* at the preaching of Jonas; and, behold, a greater than Jonas is here." (Compare Jon. 3: 8-10—"But let man and beast *be covered with sackcloth,* and cry mightily unto God: yea, let them *turn every one from his evil way,* and from the violence that is in their hands. Who can tell if God will turn and *repent, and turn away* from his fierce anger, that we perish not? And God saw their works, that *they turned from their evil ways;* and God repented of the evil, that he had said that he would do unto them; and he did it not.")

In the usage of the words the thought of regret, and the thought of change of purpose and action, are both found; but the emphasis is upon the change of purpose and action, especially in the first New Testament word mentioned above. In our day there is danger of underestimating the importance of sorrow for sin. Sorrow for sin is not repentance, but it is an element in repentance. What the repentance or change of mind is about must always be determined by the context. Repentance of sin is such a sorrow for sin or abhorrence of sin, such a change of mind about it, as leads the sinner to turn away from it with all his heart.

III. How Repentance Is Manifested.

(1) Luke 10: 13—"Woe unto thee Chorazin! woe unto thee, Bethsaida! for if the mighty works had been done in Tyre and Sidon, which have been done in you, they had a great while ago repented *sitting in sackcloth and ashes.*"

Joel 2: 12, 13—"Therefore also now, saith the LORD, turn ye even to me with all your heart, and *with fasting*, and *with weeping*, and *with mourning:* And *rend your heart*, and not your garments, and turn unto the LORD your God: for he is gracious and merciful, slow to anger, and of great kindness, and repenteth him of the evil."

Job 42: 5, 6—"I have heard of thee by the hearing of the ear; but now mine eye seeth thee: Wherefore *I abhor myself and repent in dust and ashes.*"

FIRST PROPOSITION: *Repentance is manifested in deep sorrow for sin and in self-humiliation and in self-abhorrence.*

(Compare Luke 18: 13—"And the publican, standing afar off, would not lift up so much as his eyes unto heaven, but *smote upon his breast*, saying, God be merciful to me a sinner.")

There is not enough made of this manifestation of Repentance in these days.

(2) Hosea 14: 1, 2—"O Israel, return unto the LORD thy God; for thou hast fallen by thine iniquity. *Take with you words*, and turn to the LORD: say unto him, *Take away all iniquity*, and receive us graciously: so will we render the calves of our lips."

Luke 18: 13, 14—"And the publican, standing afar off, would not lift up so much as his eyes unto heaven, but smote upon his breast, saying, *God be merciful to me a sinner.* I tell you this man went down to his house justified rather than the other: for every one that exalteth himself shall be abased; and he that humbleth himself shall be exalted."

SECOND PROPOSITION: Repentance is manifested in confession of sin and prayer to God for mercy.

(3) Matt. 12: 41—"The men of Nineveh shall rise in judgment with this generation, and shall condemn it: because *they repented* at the preaching of Jonas; and, behold, a greater than Jonas is here."

(Compare Jon. 3: 5-8—"So the people of Nineveh believed God, and proclaimed a fast, and put on sackcloth, from the greatest of them even to the least of them. For the word came unto the king of Nineveh, and he arose from his throne, and he laid his robe from him, and covered him with sackcloth, and sat in ashes. And he caused it to be proclaimed and published through Nineveh by the decree of the king and his nobles, saying, Let neither man nor beast, herd nor flock, taste any thing: let them not feed nor drink water: but let man and beast be covered with sackcloth, and cry mightily unto God: Yea, *let them turn every one from his evil way and from the violence that is in their hands.*

Ezek. 18: 30—"Therefore I will judge you, O house of Israel, every one according to his ways, saith the Lord GOD. Repent *and turn yourselves from all your transgressions;* so iniquity shall not be your ruin."

14: 6—"Therefore say unto the house of Israel, thus saith the Lord GOD; Repent, and *turn yourselves from your idols;* and *turn away your faces from all your abominations.*"

Is. 55: 7—"Let the wicked *forsake his way and the unrighteous man his thoughts:* and let him return unto the LORD, and he will have mercy upon him; and to our God, for he will abundantly pardon."

THIRD PROPOSITION: Repentance is manifested by the sinner turning away from his evil way—from all his transgressions, his idols and his abominations and his thoughts.

This is the most important and decisive manifestation of repentance, the one upon which the Bible lays the most emphasis. Note the frequency and urgency of the use of the word "turn" in the Bible. See also Acts 3: 19, R. V —"Repent ye therefore, and turn again, that your sins may be blotted out, that so there may come seasons of refreshing from the presence of the Lord." Conversion is the outward proof of the inward Repentance. (Compare 1 Thess. 1: 9.)

(4) Acts 26: 20, R.V.—"But declare both to them of Damascus first, and at Jerusalem, and throughout all the country of Judæa, and also to the Gentiles, that they should repent and *turn to God, doing works worthy of repentance.*"

1 Sam. 7: 3—"And Samuel spake unto all the house of Israel, saying, If ye do return unto the LORD with all your hearts, *then put away the strange gods and Ashtaroth from among you,* and *prepare your*

hearts unto the Lord, and serve him only: and he will deliver you out of the hand of the Philistines."

Matt. 3: 8, R.V.—"Bring forth therefore fruit worthy of repent- ance."

FOURTH PROPOSITION: Repentance is manifested by:

(a) *Turning to God to trust and serve Him.*

There are two sides to Repentance—turning from and turn- ing to. 1 Thess. 1: 9—"For they themselves shew of us what manner of entering in we had unto you, and how ye turned to God from idols to serve the living and true God."

(b) *By bringing forth fruit, or doing works, worthy of re- pentance.*

Not merely abstinence from evil, but performance of good. Compare Luke 3: 10–14—"And the people asked him, saying, What shall we do then? He answereth and saith unto them, He that hath two coats, let him impart to him that hath none; and he that hath meat, let him do likewise. Then came also publicans to be baptized, and said unto him, Master, what shall we do? And he said unto them, Exact no more than that which is appointed you. And the soldiers. likewise demanded of him, saying, And what shall we do? And he said unto them, Do vio- lence to no man, neither accuse any falsely; and be content with your wages."

(5) Mark 1: 4—"John did baptize in the wilderness, and preach *the baptism of repentance* for the remission of sins."

Acts 13: 24—"When John had first preached before his coming the *baptism of repentance* to all the people of Israel."

Acts 2: 38—"Then Peter said unto them, Repent, *and be baptized* every one of you in the name of Jesus Christ for the remission of sins, and ye shall receive the gift of the Holy Ghost."

FIFTH PROPOSITION: Repentance is manifested by baptism.

This is God's appointed and deeply significant way of pub- licly professing our repentance. What right have we to substi- tute some other ?

IV. The Results of Repentance.

(1) Luke 15: 7, 10—"I say unto you, that likewise *joy shall be in heaven* over one sinner that repenteth more than over ninety and nine just persons, which need no repentance. . . . Likewise, I say unto you, there is *joy in the presence of the angels of God* over one sinner that repenteth."

FIRST PROPOSITION: There is joy in heaven, in the presence of the Angels of God, over one sinner that repenteth.

This is the supreme result of repentance. We should work for the repentance of sinners more because of the joy it brings to God and Christ than because of the blessings it brings to men.

(2) Is. 55: 7—"Let the wicked forsake his way, and the unrighteous man his thoughts: and let him return unto the LORD, and *he will have mercy upon him;* and to our God, for *he will abundantly pardon.*"

Luke 24: 47—"And that repentance *and remission of sins* should be preached in his name among all nations, beginning at Jerusalem."

Mark 1: 4, R.V.—"John came, who baptized in the wilderness and preached the baptism of repentance *unto remission of sins.*"

Acts 2: 38, R.V.—"And Peter said unto them, Repent ye, and be baptized every one of you in the name of Jesus Christ *unto the remission of your sins;* and ye shall receive the gift of the Holy Ghost."

Acts 3: 19 (first clause)—"Repent ye therefore, and be converted, that your sins may be blotted out."

SECOND PROPOSITION: Repentance results in pardon, remission of sins, the blotting out of sins.

This remission is "in the name of Jesus Christ"—*i. e.,* on the ground of His work. Repentance is the condition upon which the remission secured by the death of Jesus Christ is made our own.

(3) Acts 2: 38, R.V.—"And Peter said unto them, *Repent* ye, and be baptized every one of you in the name of Jesus Christ unto the remission of your sins; *and ye shall receive the gift of the Holy Ghost.*"

THIRD PROPOSITION: Repentance is one of the primary conditions for receiving the gift of the Holy Ghost.

The gift of the Holy Ghost is for all those who repent and are baptized in the name of Jesus Christ unto the remission of sins. It is for them to "take" (the exact force of the word rendered "receive").

(4) Acts 3: 19, 20, 21, R.V.—"Repent ye therefore, and turn again, that your sins may be blotted out, *that so there may come seasons of refreshing* from the presence of the Lord; *and that he may send the Christ* who hath been appointed for you, even Jesus: whom the heaven must receive until the times of restoration of all things, whereof God spake by the mouth of his holy prophets which have been since the world began."

FOURTH PROPOSITION: The Repentance of God's people will result in times of refreshing from the presence of the Lord and the sending of the Messiah.

These words were spoken to the Israelites and the implication is that the repentance of Israel will result in the coming of the Christ who has been appointed for them, even Jesus.

V.   How Repentance Is Effected.

(1) Acts 11: 18—"When they heard these things, they held their peace, and glorified God, saying, Then hath *God* also to the Gentiles *granted* repentance unto life."

(The word rendered "granted" in this verse is the word ordinarily translated "given.")

FIRST PROPOSITION: Repentance unto life is God's gift.

(2) Acts 5: 30, 31, R.V.—" The God of our fathers raised up Jesus, whom ye slew, hanging him on a tree.   Him did God exalt with his right hand to be a Prince and a Saviour, for *to give repentance to Israel,* and remission of sins."   See also 3: 26—"Unto you first God, having raised up his servant, sent him to bless you, in turning away every one of you from your iniquities."

SECOND PROPOSITION: Jesus, once crucified but now exalted, gives repentance.

(3) Acts 2: 37, 38, 41—"Now *when they heard this*, they were pricked in their heart, and said unto Peter and to the rest of the apostles, Men and brethren, what shall we do?   Then Peter said unto them, Repent, and be baptized every one of you in the name of Jesus Christ for the remission of sins, and ye shall receive the gift of the Holy Ghost. . . .   Then they that gladly received his word were baptized: and the same day there were added unto them about three thousand souls."

By the verses that precede we see that what they heard was the word of God, preached by men "filled with the Holy Ghost."

THIRD PROPOSITION: Repentance is effected through the preaching of the Word by men filled with the Holy Ghost.

(Compare 1 Thess. 1: 5, 6, 9, 10—"For our gospel came not unto you in word only, *but also in power, and in the Holy Ghost,* and in much assurance; as ye know what manner of men we were among you for your sake. . . .   For they themselves shew of us what manner of entering in we had unto you, and *how ye turned* to God from idols to serve the living and true God; and to wait for his son from heaven, whom he raised from the dead, even Jesus, which delivered us from the wrath to come."

The Word of God is the means used for the bestowal of the gift of repentance.

(4) Jonah 3: 5-10—"So the people of Nineveh *believed God*, and proclaimed a fast, and put on sackcloth, from the greatest of them even to the least of them. For word came unto the king of Nineveh, and he arose from his throne, and he laid his robe from him, and covered him with sackcloth, and sat in ashes. And he caused it to be proclaimed and published through Nineveh by the decree of the king and his nobles, saying, Let neither man nor beast, herd nor flock, taste any thing: let them not feed, nor drink water: But let man and beast be covered with sackcloth, and cry mightily unto God: yea, let them turn every one from his evil way, and from the violence that is in their hands. Who can tell if God will turn and repent, and turn away from his fierce anger, that we perish not ? And God saw their works, that they turned from their evil way: and God repented of the evil, that he had said that he would do unto them; and he did it not."

FOURTH PROPOSITION: Repentance results when men believe God's Word.

(5) Rom. 2: 4—"Or despisest thou the riches of his goodness and forbearance and longsuffering; not knowing that *the goodness of God leadeth thee to repentance ?*"

FIFTH PROPOSITION: The goodness of God leadeth men to Repentance.

The word here rendered "goodness" is an adjective meaning ordinarily in the New Testament usage "kind" (Luke 6: 35; Eph. 4: 32), or "gracious" (1 Pet. 2: 3). It is the kindness and patience and forbearance of God that leads men to repentance.

(Compare 2 Pet. 3: 9—"The Lord is not slack concerning his promises, as some men count slackness; but is longsuffering to usward, not willing that any should perish, but that all should come to repentance.")

(6) Rev. 3: 19—"As many as I love, *I rebuke and chasten:* be zealous therefore, and repent."

Heb. 12: 6, 10, 11—"For whom the Lord loveth he chasteneth, and scourgeth every son whom he receiveth. . . . For they verily for a few days chastened us after their own pleasure; but he for our profit, that we might be partakers of his holiness. Now no chastening for the present seemeth to be joyous, but grievous: nevertheless, afterward it yieldeth the peaceable fruit of righteousness unto them which are exercised thereby."

SIXTH PROPOSITION: Repentance is effected through God's loving reproof and chastisement.

(Compare Ps. 119: 67—"Before I was afflicted I went astray: but now have I kept thy word.")

(7) 2 Tim. 2: 24, 25, R.V.—"And the Lord's servant must not strive, but be gentle towards all, apt to teach, forbearing, *in meekness correcting them that oppose themselves;* if peradventure God may give them repentance unto the knowledge of the truth."

SEVENTH PROPOSITION: Repentance is effected through the meek and gentle correction administered by the servant of the Lord.

(8) 2 Cor. 7: 8-11, R.V.—"For though I made you sorry with my epistle, I do not regret it, though I did regret; for I see that that epistle made you sorry, though but for a season. Now I rejoice, not that ye were made sorry, but that ye were made sorry unto repentance: for ye were made sorry after a godly sort, that ye might suffer loss by us in nothing. For *godly sorrow worketh repentance* unto salvation, a repentance which bringeth no regret: but the sorrow of the world worketh death. For behold, this selfsame thing, that ye were made sorry after a godly sort, what earnest care it wrought in you, yea, what cleansing of yourselves, yea, what indignation, yea, what fear, yea, what longing, yea, what zeal, yea, what avenging! In everything ye approved yourselves to be pure in the matter."

EIGHTH PROPOSITION: Godly sorrow worketh repentance.

The godly sorrow in this case was itself wrought by the correction administered by the Lord's servant.

(9) Job 42: 5, 6—"I have heard of thee by the hearing of the ear; but now *mine eye seeth thee: Wherefore I abhor myself and repent* in dust and ashes."

NINTH PROPOSITION: The sight of God causes repentance.

Nothing is so calculated to impress sinful man with a hatred of sin, and abhorrence of self as a sinner, as a real view of God. If then we wish to bring men to repentance, let us bring them face to face with God. This can be effected by showing them God as revealed in His Word. But it must be done in the power of the Holy Spirit.

CHAPTER X.

FAITH.

I. What is Faith?

(1) MEANING OF FAITH IN GENERAL.

Heb. 11: 1, R.V.—"Now faith is the assurance of things hoped for, the proving of things not seen." And Am. Ap., "Now faith is assurance of things hoped for, a conviction of things not seen."

(Compare vv. 7, 11, 17-19, 22, 30—"By faith Noah, *being warned of God* concerning things not seen as yet, moved with godly fear, prepared an ark to the saving of his house; through which he condemned the world, and became heir of the righteousness which is according to faith. . . . By faith even Sarah herself received power to conceive seed when she was past age, since she *counted him faithful who had promised:* . . . By faith Abraham, being tried, offered up Isaac: yea, he that had gladly received the promises was offering up his only begotten son; even he to whom it was said, In Isaac shall thy seed be called: accounting that God is able to raise up, even from the dead; from whence he did also in a parable receive him back. . . . By faith Joseph, when his end was nigh, made mention of the departure of the children of Israel: and gave commandment concerning his bones.")

Faith is the assurance of things hoped for, a conviction (or proving, putting to the test) of things not seen. The foundation upon which this assurance of things hoped for, this conviction of things not seen, rests, is God's Word.

(2) MEANING OF "FAITH" WHEN USED IN CONNECTION WITH PRAYER.

Jas. 1: 5-7, R.V.—"But if any of you lacketh wisdom, let him ask of God, who giveth to all liberally and upbraideth not; and it shall be given him. But let him ask in faith, *nothing doubting:* for he that doubteth is like the surge of the sea driven by the wind and tossed. For let not that man think that he shall receive anything of the Lord."

Mark 11: 24, R.V.—"Therefore I say unto you, All things whatsoever ye pray and ask for, *believe that ye have received* them, and ye shall have them."

Faith, in prayer, is the firm expectation or assurance, free from all doubts, of getting the thing asked.

The prayer of faith reckons the thing asked as already really
its own, because God has heard the request and granted the thing
asked, and what God has granted is as really ours as if we had it
already in our possession experimentally.

Compare 1 Jno. 5: 14, 15—"And this is the confidence that we have
in him, that, if we ask anything according to his will, he heareth us:
and if we know that he hear us, whatsoever we ask, *we know that we
have the petitions that we desire of him*," and 1 Cor. 3: 21—"Therefore let no man glory in men: for all things are yours."

(3) MEANING OF "FAITH" WHEN USED IN CONNECTION WITH
GOD.

(a) 1 Jno. 5: 10, R. V.—"He that believeth on the Son of God hath
the witness in him: he that believeth not God hath made him a
liar; because he hath not believed in the witness that God hath borne
concerning His Son."

Jno. 5: 24, R.V.—"Verily, verily, I say unto you, He that heareth
my word, and *believeth him* that sent me, hath eternal life, and cometh not into judgment, but hath passed out of death into life."

Acts 27: 22-25—"And now I exhort you to be of good cheer: for
there shall be no loss of any man's life among you, but of the ship.
For there stood by me this night the angel of God, whose I am, and
whom I serve, saying, Fear not, Paul; thou must be brought before
Caesar: and, lo, God hath given thee all them that sail with thee.
Wherefore, sirs, be of good cheer: for *I believe God*, that it shall be
even as it was told me."

Rom. 4: 3—"For thus saith the Scriptures? Abraham *believed God*
and it was counted unto him for righteousness." (Compare Gen. 15:
4-6—"And, behold, the word of the LORD came unto him, saying,
This shall not be thine heir; but he that shall come forth out of thine own
bowels shall be thine heir.   And he brought him forth abroad, and said,
Look now toward heaven, and tell the stars, if thou be able to number
them: and he said unto him, So shall thy seed be. *And he believed in
the* LORD; and he counted it to him for righteousness.")

Rom. 4: 19-21, R.V.—"And without being weakened in faith he
considered his own body now as good as dead (he being about a hundred years old), and the deadness of Sarah's womb: yea, *looking unto
the promise of God, he wavered not through unbelief*, but waxed strong
through faith, giving glory to God, and *being fully assured that, what
he had promised, he was able also to perform*."

*To believe God is to rely upon or have unhesitating assur-
ance of the truth of God's testimony, even though it is unsup-
ported by any other evidence, and to rely upon or have unfaltering
assurance of the fulfillment of his promises, even though everything
seen seems against fulfillment.*

It is "taking God at his word." Faith is not belief without evidence. It is belief on the very best of evidence, the word of Him who cannot lie. (Tit. 1:2.) Faith is so rational that it asks no other evidence than this all-sufficient evidence. To ask other evidence than the word of Him "who cannot lie" is not "rationalism," but consummate irrationalism.

(*b*) 2 Chron. 20:20—"And they rose early in the morning, and went forth into the wilderness of Tekoa: and as they went forth, Jehoshaphat stood and said, Hear me, O Judah, and ye inhabitants of Jerusalem; *Believe in the* LORD your God, so shall ye be established; believe his prophets, so shall ye prosper."

Jno. 14, 1: R.V., Am. Ap.—"Let not your heart be troubled; ye *believe in God*, believe also in me."

To believe in God is to rely upon, or put confidence in **God** *Himself*. When we believe God we trust His word; when we believe in God we trust Himself. When we believe God we fix our eyes on what He has said (Rom. 4:20); when we believe in God we fix our eyes upon what He is, upon His person, upon Himself.

NOTE.—There are two Hebrew words for "trust" and "faith." The first, translated "believe" and "trust," means primarily, in the transitive, "to prop," "to stay," "to support"; in the intransitive, "to stay oneself." The second word, translated "trust," seems to mean "to cast oneself upon." When we believe God we stay ourselves upon His word: When we believe in God we stay ourselves upon Himself.

(4) MEANING OF "FAITH" WHEN USED IN CONNECTION WITH JESUS CHRIST.

Jno. 14:1—"Let not your heart be troubled: ye believe in God, believe also in me."

Matt. 9:21, 22—"For she said within herself, If I may but touch his garment, I shall be whole. But Jesus turned him about, and when he saw her, he said, Daughter, be of good comfort; *thy faith* hath made thee whole. And the woman was made whole from that hour."

Matt. 9:29—"Then touched he their eyes, saying, *According to thy faith* be it unto you."

Matt. 15:25, 28—"Then came she and worshipped him, saying, Lord help me. . . . Then Jesus answered and said unto her, O woman, great is thy faith; be it unto thee even as thou wilt. And her daughter was made whole from that very hour."

Matt. 8:8-10—"The centurion answered and said, Lord, I am not worthy that thou shouldest come under my roof: but speak the word only, and my servant shall be healed. For I am a man under authority, having soldiers under me: and I say to this man, Go, and he goeth; and to another, Come, and he cometh; and to my servant, do this, and he doeth it. When Jesus heard it, he marvelled, and said to them that followed, Verily, I say unto you, *I have not found so great faith*, no, not in Israel."

Luke 7:48-50—"And he said unto her, Thy sins are forgiven. And they that sat at meat with him began to say within themselves, Who is this that forgiveth sins also? And he said to the woman, *Thy faith* hath saved thee; go in peace."

Jno. 14:12—"Verily, verily, I say unto you, He that believeth on me, the works that I do shall he do also; and greater works than **these** shall he do; because I go unto my Father."

Faith in Jesus Christ is relying upon, or putting confidence in Jesus Christ. It is the assurance that he will do the things sought of him or take care of the matters intrusted to him. (2 Tim. 1:12.) *It is simply relying upon him for these things.* What Jesus Christ is relied upon for varies in different cases. (In the several cases cited above it was for care, healing, sight, help, the healing of another, pardon, power.) What he is relied upon for, that will he do.

Matt. 9:29—"Then touched he their eyes, saying, According to your faith be it unto you."

Relying upon Christ for healing brings healing, relying upon Christ for help brings help, relying upon Christ for pardon brings pardon, relying upon Christ for power brings power, relying upon Christ for victory brings victory. What we have a right to rely upon him for is determined by his character and his definite promises.

II. Saving Faith.

(1) THE CHARACTER OF SAVING FAITH, OR HOW WE MUST BELIEVE IN ORDER TO BE SAVED.

(1) Rom. 10:9, 10—"That if thou shalt confess with thy mouth the Lord Jesus, and shalt believe *in thine heart* that God hath raised him from the dead, thou shalt be saved. For *with the heart* man believeth unto righteousness; and with the mouth confession is **made** unto salvation."

FIRST PROPOSITION: Saving Faith is believing with the heart.

In order to be saved we must believe with the heart. In the Bible the heart stands for the thought, feelings and will. A heart-faith, then, is a faith that rules the thought, the feelings and

the will.   The manifestation of heart-faith is action in the direction of that which is believed.

Compare Heb. 11: 7, 8, 17, 19, 20, 22, 24-26, 28—"By faith Noah
being warned of God of things not seen as yet, moved with fear, *prepared an ark* to the saving of his house; by the which he condemned
the world, and became heir of the righteousness which is by faith.
By faith Abraham, when he was called to go out into a place which he
should after receive for an inheritance, obeyed; and *he went out*, not
knowing whither he went. . . .   By faith Abraham, when he was
tried, *offered up Isaac:* and he that had received the promises offered
up his only begotten son. . . .   *Accounting that God was able to
raise him up*, even from the dead; from whence also he received him
in a figure.   By faith Isaac *blessed Jacob and Esau concerning things
to come.* . . .   By faith Joseph, when he died, *made mention of the
departing of the children of Israel;* and *gave commandment concerning
his bones.* . . .   By faith Moses, when he was come to years, *refused to be called the son of Pharaoh's daughter;* Choosing rather to
suffer affliction with the people of God, than to enjoy the pleasures of
sin for a season; Esteeming the reproach of Christ greater riches than
the treasures in Egypt: for he had respect unto the recompense of the
reward. . . .   Through faith *he kept the passover*, and the sprinkling of blood, lest he that destroyed the firstborn should touch them,"
and Rom. 4: 18-21, R.V.—"Who in hope believed against hope, to the
end that he might become a father of many nations, according to that
which had been spoken, So shall thy seed be.   And without being
weakened in faith he considered his own body now as good as dead
(he being about a hundred years old) and the deadness of Sarah's
womb: yea, looking unto the promise of God, *he wavered not* through
unbelief, but *waxed strong* through faith, *giving glory to God*, and
being fully assured that, what he had promised, he was able also to
perform."

(2) Jas. 2: 14, 21, 22, 25, R.V.—"What doth it profit, my brethren,
if a man say he hath faith, but have not works? . . .   Was not
Abraham our father justified by works, in that he offered up Isaac his
son upon the altar?   Thou seest that faith wrought with his works,
and by works was faith made perfect; . . .   And in like manner
was not also Rahab the harlot justified by works, in that she received
the messengers, and sent them out another way?"

*SECOND PROPOSITION: Saving Faith is a faith that works
by doing that which the one who is believed in bids us do.*

(3) Gal. 5: 6—"For in Jesus Christ neither circumcision availeth
anything, nor uncircumcision; but faith *which worketh by love.*"

*THIRD PROPOSITION: Saving Faith is the faith which works
by love.*

(4) Jno. 1: 12—" But as many as received him, to them gave he power to become the sons of God, even to them that believe on his name."

FOURTH PROPOSITION: Saving Faith is the faith which receives Jesus Christ as He comes to us, and for all that He offers Himself to be.

He offers Himself as our sin-bearer. Saving Faith accepts Him as such and rests all its hope for pardon on His atoning blood. He offers Himself as our deliverer from sin's power (Jno. 8: 34, 36). Saving Faith accepts Him as such and relies utterly upon Him and expects Him to give such deliverance. He offers Himself as our Teacher and Lord (Jno. 13: 13). Saving Faith accepts Him as such and surrenders the mind unreservedly to His teaching and the life to His absolute control.

(5) 2 Tim. 1: 12—" For the which cause I also suffer these things: nevertheless I am not ashamed; for I know whom I have believed, and am persuaded that he is able to keep that which I have committed unto him against that day."

FIFTH PROPOSITION: Saving Faith in Jesus Christ is the faith that commits to Jesus Christ.

(6) Rom. 10: 13, 14—" For whosoever shall call upon the name of the Lord shall be saved. How then shall they call on him in whom they have not believed ?" etc.

SIXTH PROPOSITION: Saving Faith is a faith that calls upon the name of the Lord.

Note.—The context plainly shows that the Lord here is the Lord Jesus Christ (v. 9, R.V.). To call upon His name implies: First, a deep recognition of our need of salvation. Second, an earnest desire to be saved. Third, an utter casting away of hope in any other way of salvation. Fourth, a hope that He will save. The faith that recognizes our own lost condition, that earnestly desires salvation, that casts away all hope in any one or any thing but the Lord Jesus, and that hopes (or has the assurance) that He will save, and puts Him to the test by crying to Him, is the faith that saves.

(7) Rom. 10: 9, R.V.—"Because if thou shalt *confess with thy mouth Jesus as Lord*, and shalt believe in thy heart that God raised him from the dead, thou shalt be saved."

SEVENTH PROPOSITION: Saving Faith is the faith that confesses Jesus as Lord.

(8) Heb. 10: 38, 39, R.V.—"But my righteous one shall live by faith: And *if he shrink back*, my soul hath no pleasure in him. But we are *not of them that shrink back unto perdition; but of them that have faith* unto the saving of the soul." (See context vv. 32–37.)

EIGHTH PROPOSITION: Saving Faith is the faith that does not shrink back from the confession and service of Christ Jesus in danger and trial.

(2) THE CONTENTS OF SAVING FAITH, OR WHAT WE MUST BELIEVE IN ORDER TO BE SAVED.

(1) Jno. 20: 31—"But these are written, that ye might believe *that Jesus is the Christ, the Son of God;* and that believing ye might have life through his name."

FIRST PROPOSITION: In order that we may have life we must believe that Jesus is the Christ, the Son of God. (Compare 1 Jno. 5: 1.)

Of course this must be a heart-faith, a faith that leads to action along the line of that which is believed, as seen above. Not merely a theological opinion that Jesus is the Christ, the Son of God, but such an assurance or conviction that He is as leads us to put our trust in him, and to submit our thoughts and feelings and purposes and lives to His control.

(2) Rom. 1: 16—"For I am not ashamed of the gospel of Christ: for it is the power of God unto salvation to every one that believeth; to the Jew first, and also to the Greek."

SECOND PROPOSITION: In order to be saved we must believe the gospel.

QUESTION: What is the gospel?

ANSWER:

1 Cor. 15: 1–4—"Moreover, brethren, I declare unto you the gospel which I preached unto you, which also ye have received, and wherein ye stand; By which also ye are saved, if ye keep in memory what I preached unto you, unless ye have believed in vain. For I delivered unto you first of all that which I also received, how that *Christ died for our sins* according to the Scriptures; and that he *was buried*, and that he *rose again the third day* according to the Scriptures." (See also Rom. 1: 17–25.)

The gospel is, that "Christ died for our sins according to the Scriptures . . . was buried . . . and rose again." This we must believe in order to be saved. This involves faith in Him as the Christ the Son of God. (Rom. 1: 4—"And declared to be the Son of God with power, according to the Spirit of holiness, *by the resurrection from the dead.*")

Faith that He died for our sins brings pardon; faith that he rose again brings deliverance from sin's power. Of course, this also must be a heart-faith.

(3) Rom. 10: 9—"That if thou shalt confess with thy mouth the Lord Jesus, and shalt believe in thine heart *that God hath raised him from the dead*, thou shalt be saved."

THIRD PROPOSITION: In order to be saved we must believe that God hath raised the Lord Jesus from the dead.

This involves faith in His Divinity (Rom. 1:4), in His propitiatory death and God's acceptance of it (Rom. 4: 25), and in His intercession for us (Heb. 7: 25), and His power to deliver us from sin.

(4) Luke 7: 48–50—"And he said unto her, Thy sins are forgiven. And they that sat at meat with him began to say within themselves, Who is this that forgiveth sins also? And he said to the woman, Thy faith hath saved thee; go in peace."

FOURTH PROPOSITION: In order to be saved we must believe that Jesus can and will forgive our sin.

This faith involves faith in the Divinity of Jesus, for God alone can forgive sin.

III. How Faith is Manifested.

(1) Mark 2: 3–5—"And they came unto him, bringing one sick of the palsy, which was borne of four. And when they could not come nigh unto him for the press, they uncovered the roof where he was: and when they had broken it up, they let down the bed wherein the sick of the palsy lay. When Jesus saw their faith, he said unto the sick of the palsy, Son, thy sins be forgiven thee."

FIRST PROPOSITION: Faith in Jesus is manifested by our bringing to Him our need and surmounting all the obstacles that lie between us and him.

(2) Matt. 15: 22–28—"And, behold, a woman of Canaan came out of the same coasts, and cried unto him, saying, have mercy on me, O Lord, thou Son of David; my daughter is grievously vexed with a devil. But he answered her not a word. And his disciples came and besought him, saying, Send her away; for she crieth after us. But he

answered and said, I am not sent but unto the lost sheep of the
house of Israel. Then came she and worshipped him, saying, Lord,
help me. But he answered and said, It is not meet to take the children's bread, and cast it to dogs. And she said, Truth, Lord: yet
the dogs eat of the crumbs which fall from their master's table. Then
Jesus answered and said unto her, O woman, great is thy faith: be it
unto thee even as thou wilt. And her daughter was made whole from
that very hour."

*SECOND PROPOSITION: Faith in Jesus is manifested by our
holding on to Jesus for the desired blessing in the face of dis-
couragement, even in the face of His apparent refusal to bestow it.*

(3) Acts 11: 19, 21, R.V.—"They therefore that were scattered
abroad upon the tribulation that arose about Stephen travelled as far
as Phœnicia, and Cyprus, and Antioch, speaking the word to none save
only Jews. . . . And the hand of the Lord was with them: and a
great number that believed *turned unto the Lord.*"

*THIRD PROPOSITION: Faith in God's Word is manifested by
men turning to the Lord.*

(4) Heb. 11: 8, 17—" By faith Abraham, when he was called to go
out into a place which he should after receive for an inheritance,
obeyed; and he went out, not knowing whither he went. . . . By
faith Abraham, when he was tried, offered up Isaac: and he that had
received the promises offered up his only begotten son."

*FOURTH PROPOSITION: Faith is manifested by prompt
and exact obedience to the commandments of Him who is believed in, simply because He commands, though we know not the
purpose of His command, nor the outcome of our obedience*

(5) Heb. ·11: 17-19—"By faith Abraham, when he was tried,
offered up Isaac: and he that had received the promise offered up his
only begotten son of whom it was said, That in Isaac shall thy
seed be called: Accounting that God was able to raise him up, even
from the dead; from whence also he received him in a figure."
Rom. 4: 18-21, R.V.—"Who in hope believed against hope, to the
end that he might become a father of many nations, according to that
which had been spoken, So shall thy seed be. And without being
weakened in faith he considered his own body now as good as dead (he
being about a hundred years old), and the deadness of Sarah's womb:
yea, looking unto the promise of God, he wavered not through unbelief, but waxed strong through faith, giving glory to God, and being
fully assured that, what he had promised, he was able also to perform."

FIFTH PROPOSITION: Faith is manifested by a disregard for the difficulties that lie in the way of the fulfillment of God's promises. (Compare Num. 13: 31–33; 14: 6–9.)

Difficulties are nothing to one who believes in God and His Word: God is mightier than all obstacles, and His Word sure in face of all apparent impossibility of fulfillment.

(6) Heb. 11: 27—"By faith he forsook Egypt, not fearing the wrath of the king: for he endured, as seeing him who is invisible."

SIXTH PROPOSITION: Faith is manifested by steadfastness (see Greek) *in the path God points out in face of obstacles, peril and apparent loss.*

(7) Heb. 11: 24–26—"By faith Moses, when he was come to years, refused to be called the son of Pharaoh's daughter; choosing rather to suffer affliction with the people of God, than to enjoy the pleasures of sin for a season; Esteeming the reproach of Christ greater riches than the treasures in Egypt: for he had respect unto the recompense of the reward.

SEVENTH PROPOSITION: Faith is manifested by the sacrifice of the present seen, but transient advantage, for the sake of the future unseen, but permanent advantage.

(8) Heb. 11: 20, 21—"By faith Isaac blessed Jacob and Esau concerning things to come. By faith Jacob, when he was a dying, blessed both the sons of Joseph; and worshipped, leaning upon the top of his staff."

(Comp. Gen. 27: 27–29—"And he came near, and kissed him: and he smelled the smell of his raiment, and blessed him, and said, See, the smell of my son is as the smell of a field which the LORD hath blessed: Therefore God give thee of the dew of heaven, and the fatness of the earth, and plenty of corn and wine: let people serve thee, and nations bow down to thee: be lord over thy brother, and let thy mother's sons bow down to thee: cursed be every one that curseth thee, and blessed be he that blesseth thee. . . . And Esau said unto his father, Hast thou but one blessing, my father? bless me, even me also, O my father. And Esau lifted up his voice, and wept. And Isaac his father answered and said unto him, Behold, thy dwelling shall be the fatness of the earth, and of the dew of heaven from above; and by thy sword shalt thou live, and shalt serve thy brother; and it shall come to pass when thou shalt have the dominion, that thou shalt break his yoke from off thy neck," and Gen. 48: 5–20—"And now thy two sons, Ephraim and Manasseh, which were born unto thee in the land of Egypt, before I came unto thee into Egypt, are mine: as Reuben and Simeon, they shall be mine. And thy issue, which thou begettest after them, shall be thine, and shall be called after the name of their brethren in their inheritance: and as for me, when I came from Padan, Rachel died by me in the land of Canaan in the way when yet there was but a little way to come unto Ephrath: and I buried her there in the way of Ephrath; the same is Beth-lehem. And Israel beheld Joseph's sons, and said, Who are these? And Joseph said unto his father, They are my sons, whom God hath given me in this place. And he said, Bring them, I pray thee, unto me, and I will bless them. Now the eyes of Israel were dim for age, so that he could not see. And he brought them near unto him; and he kissed them, and embraced them. And Israel said unto Joseph, I had not thought to see thy face: and, lo, God hath shewed me also thy seed. And Joseph brought them out from between his knees, and he bowed himself with his face to the earth. And Joseph took them both, Ephraim in his right hand toward Israel's left hand, and Manasseh in his left hand toward Israel's right hand, and brought them near unto him. And Israel stretched out his right hand, and laid it upon Ephraim's head, who was the younger, and his left hand upon Manasseh's head, guiding his hands wittingly; for Manasseh was the first born. And he blessed Joseph, and said, God, before whom my fathers Abraham and Isaac did walk, the God which fed me all my life long unto this day, the Angel which redeemed me from all evil, bless the lads; and let my name be named on them, and the name of my fathers Abraham and Isaac; and let them grow into a multitude in the midst of the earth. And when Joseph saw that his father laid his right hand upon the head of Ephraim, it displeased him: and he held up his father's hand, to remove it from Ephraim's head unto Manasseh's head. And Joseph said unto his father, Not so, my father: for this is the firstborn; put thy right hand upon his head. And his father refused, and said, I know it, my son, I know it: he also shall become a people, and he also shall be great: but truly his younger brother shall be greater than he, and his seed shall become a multitude of nations. And he blessed them that day, saying, In thee shall Israel bless, saying, God make thee as Ephraim and as Manasseh: and he set Ephraim before Manasseh.''

EIGHTH PROPOSITION: Faith is manifested by large expectations based upon God's large promises, even though as yet nothing may be seen.

IV. The Results of Faith.

(1) Eph. 2: 8—'' For by grace are ye saved through faith; and that not of yourselves: it is the gift of God.''

FIRST PROPOSITION: We are saved through faith.

Salvation is God's free gift; faith appropriates to itself this gift freely offered to all. Rom. 1:16—"For I am not ashamed of the gospel of Christ: for it is the power of God unto salvation to every one that believeth; to the Jew first, and also to the Greek." The gospel has power to save, but that power is displayed only in those who believe. See, also, 1 Tim. 4:10—"For therefore we both labour and suffer reproach, because we trust in the living God, who is the Saviour of all men, specially of those that believe."

Salvation is a manifold process, but every factor in it is dependent upon faith.

(a) Acts 10:43—"To him give all the prophets witness, that through his name whosoever believeth in him shall receive remission of sins."

We receive remission of sins through faith. God offers forgiveness to all men on the ground of the shed blood of Christ. The one who believes appropriates to himself individually this universal offer of salvation.

(b) Rom. 5:1—"Therefore being justified by faith, we have peace with God through our Lord Jesus Christ."

We are justified by faith.

Gal. 3:13—"Christ hath redeemed us from the curse of the law, being made a curse for us: for it is written, Cursed is every one that hangeth on a tree."

On the ground of Christ's having been made a curse for us God offers justification to us. This offer is appropriated by faith.

(c) Jno. 20:31—"But these are written, that ye might believe that Jesus is the Christ, the Son of God; and that believing ye might have life through his name."

We receive eternal life through believing. Belief in Him who is the life (Jno. 14:6) makes that life ours. Life is in Him (1 Jno. 5:11); by our believing in Him this life enters into us.

(d) Jno. 1:12, R.V.—"But as many as received him, to them gave he the right to become children of God, even to them that believe on his name."

Gal. 3:26—"For ye are all the children of God by faith in Christ Jesus."

We receive the right to become sons of God by faith. In His only begotten Son God makes to man the offer of adoption into

His family.   We appropriate this offer to ourselves by believing
in His name.

(*e*) 2 Pet. 1: 4 (see context vs. 5)—"Whereby are given unto us
exceeding great and precious promises; that by these ye might be partakers of the divine nature, having escaped the corruption that is in
the world through lust."

We become partakers of the Divine Nature through faith in
the exceeding great and precious promises of God.

(*f*) Acts 26: 18—"To open their eyes, and to turn them from
darkness to light, and from the power of Satan unto God, that they
may receive forgiveness of sins, and inheritance among them which are
sanctified by faith that is in me."

We are sanctified by faith.   God offers to us in His word
sanctifying grace.   By faith we appropriate this sanctifying grace
to ourselves.

(*g*) Acts 15: 9—"And put no difference between us and them
purifying their hearts by faith."

Our hearts are cleansed by faith.   There is heart-cleansing
power in the Word of God.   Upon faith in that Word it exercises
its heart-cleansing power in us.

(Compare Ps. 119: 9, 11—"Wherewithal shall a young man cleanse
his way ? by taking heed thereto according to thy word. . . . Thy
word have I hid in mine heart, that I might not sin against thee.")

(*h*) Eph. 3: 17, R.V.—"That Christ may dwell in your hearts
through faith, etc."

Christ dwells in our hearts through faith.   God presents
Christ to us by His Spirit through the Word.   Faith lays hold
upon Christ thus presented and he comes to dwell in the heart
and work all His glorious work within.

(*i*) 1 Pet. 1: 5—"Who are kept by the power of God through faith
unto salvation ready to be revealed in the last time."

We are kept through faith by the power of God unto a salvation ready to be revealed in the last time.   God provides keeping, His own almighty power to keep.   Faith simply lays hold of
the almighty power divinely provided.

(*j*) 2 Cor. 1: 24—"Not for that we have dominion over your faith,
but are helpers of your joy: for by faith ye stand."

We stand by faith.   By faith we enter into or appropriate to
ourselves the grace of God wherein we stand.

Rom. 5: 2—"By whom also we have access by faith into this grace wherein we stand, and rejoice in hope of the glory of God."

(*k*) 1 Jno. 5: 4, 5—"For whatsoever is born of God overcometh the world: and this is the victory that overcometh the world, even our faith. Who is he that overcometh the world, but he that believeth that Jesus is the Son of God?"

Eph. 6: 16, R.V.—"Withal taking up the shield of faith, wherewith ye shall be able to quench all the fiery darts of the evil one."

By faith we get the victory over the world and over the evil one. God freely provides for us and offers to us overcoming grace in Jesus Christ. By faith we appropriate this overcoming grace to ourselves.

(*l*) Heb. 4: 1–3—"Let us therefore fear, lest, a promise being left us of entering into his rest, any of you should seem to come short of it. For unto you was the gospel preached, as well as unto them: but the word preached did not profit them, not being mixed with faith in them that heard it. For we which have believed do enter into rest, as he said, As I have sworn in my wrath, if they shall enter into my rest: although the works were finished from the foundation of the world."

We enter into rest by faith. From beginning to end, at every step, salvation is by faith. God freely offers to us in Jesus Christ a manifold salvation; forgiveness, justification, eternal life, the right to be His sons, participation in His own nature, sanctification, heart-cleansing, an indwelling Christ, keeping unto a salvation ready to be revealed in the last time, power to stand, victory over the world and the evil one, rest. We appropriate to ourselves every item in this salvation by faith. By grace are we saved through faith from first to last.

(2) Matt. 9: 22, 29—"But Jesus turned him about, and when he saw her, he said, Daughter, be of good comfort; thy faith hath made thee whole. And the woman was made whole from that hour. . . . Then touched he their eyes, saying, According to your faith be it unto you."

Jas. 5: 14, 15—"Is any sick among you? let him call for the elders of the church; and let them pray over him, anointing him with oil in the name of the Lord. And the prayer of faith shall save the sick, and the Lord shall raise him up; and if he have committed sins, they shall be forgiven him."

SECOND PROPOSITION: We receive physical healing through faith.

God has provided for us and offers to us physical healing and strength in Jesus Christ. Matt. 8: 16, 17—"When the even was come, they brought unto him many that were possessed with devils: and he cast out the spirits with his word, and healed all that were sick: that it might be fulfilled which was spoken by Esaias the prophet, saying, Himself took our infirmities, and bare our sicknesses." We appropriate it to ourselves by faith. We miss it by our unbelief. Mark 6: 5, 6—"And he could there do no mighty work, save that he laid his hand on a few sick folk, and healed them. And he marvelled because of their unbelief. And he went round about the villages, teaching."

(3) Jno. 12: 46—"I am come a light into the world, that whosoever believeth on me should not abide in darkness."

THIRD PROPOSITION: We pass out of spiritual darkness into light by faith in Christ.

By nature we are all in darkness and children of darkness. God sends Jesus into the world to be "the light of the world." (Jno. 8: 12.) The light there is in Him, the light He Himself is, streams into our hearts when we believe in Him. (Jno. 12: 36.) Faith opens the window and lets the light in.

(4) Jno. 14: 1, R.V., Am. App.—"Let not your heart be troubled: believe in God, believe also in me."

FOURTH PROPOSITION: We are delivered from all anxiety of heart by faith, faith in God and Jesus Christ. (Compare Is. 26: 3.)

(5) Jno. 6: 35—"And Jesus said unto them, I am the bread of life: he that cometh to me shall never hunger; and he that believeth on me shall never thirst."

FIFTH PROPOSITION: We are fully and forever satisfied through faith in Jesus.

God has provided for us and offers to us full satisfaction for every desire of our spirits in Jesus; by faith we appropriate this satisfaction to ourselves.

(6) 1 Pet. 1: 8, R.V.—"Whom not having seen ye love; on whom, though now ye see him not, yet believing, ye rejoice greatly with joy unspeakable and full of glory."

SIXTH PROPOSITION: Through believing on Jesus Christ we rejoice greatly with joy unspeakable and full of glory.

In no other way can we get such joy.

(7) Jno. 7: 38, 39—"He that believeth on me, as the Scripture hath said, out of his belly shall flow rivers of living water. (But this spake he of the Spirit, which they that believe on him should receive: for the Holy Ghost was not yet given; because that Jesus was not yet glorified.)"

SEVENTH PROPOSITION: Through believing on Jesus Christ we become fountains from which rivers of living water flow out.

This is through the Holy Spirit who is given to those who believe on Jesus Christ. God has given to the crucified, risen and glorified Jesus His Spirit for His body, the Church. (Jno. 7: 39; 14: 12; Acts. 2: 33.) We appropriate this promise of God by faith. The Spirit comes upon us and makes us fountains of living water.

(8) Matt. 21: 22—"And all things, whatsoever ye shall ask in prayer, believing, ye shall receive."

Jas. 1: 5-7—"If any of you lack wisdom, let him ask of God, that giveth to all men liberally, and upbraideth not; and it shall be given him. But let him ask in faith, nothing wavering: for he that wavereth is like a wave of the sea driven with the wind and tossed. For let not that man think that he shall receive anything of the Lord."

Mark 11: 24, R.V.—"Therefore I say unto you, All things whatsoever ye pray and ask for, believe that ye have received them, and ye shall have them."

EIGHTH PROPOSITION: We receive the answer to our prayers when we believe we have received.

God is willing to answer prayer; yes, is anxious to answer prayer. But He demands, as a condition of answering, that we shall believe His naked promise and believe the prayer is heard, and that the thing asked, is ours.

(9) Matt. 21: 21—"Jesus answered and said unto them, Verily I say unto you, if ye have faith, and doubt not, ye shall not only do this which is done to the fig tree, but also if ye shall say unto this mountain, Be thou removed, and be thou cast into the sea; it shall be done."

Jno. 14: 12—"Verily, verily, I say unto you, He that believeth on me, the works that I do shall he do also; and greater works than these shall he do; because I go unto my Father."

Heb. 11: 32-34—"And what shall I more say? For the time would fail me to tell of Gideon, and of Barak, and of Samson, and of Jephthah; of David also, and of Samuel, and of the prophets: who through faith subdued kingdoms, wrought righteousness, obtained promises, stopped the mouths of lions, quenched the violence of fire, escaped the edge of the sword, out of weakness were made strong, waxed valiant in fight, turned to flight the armies of the aliens."

NINTH PROPOSITION: *We receive power to work wonders through faith in God and Jesus Christ.*

"Power belongeth unto God."   (Ps. 62: 11.)   But the power that belongeth unto God is at the disposal of His children. We lay hold of it by faith.   God's power is the reservoir, our faith is the supply pipe; therefore, according to our faith is our experimental possession of God's power. (Matt. 9: 29.) Unbelief limits our power, or rather the inflow of God's power into us.

Matt. 17: 19, 20—"Then came the disciples to Jesus apart, and said, Why could not we cast him out? And Jesus said unto them, *Because of your unbelief:* for verily I say unto you, If ye have faith as a grain of mustard seed, ye shall say unto this mountain, Remove hence to yonder place; and it shall remove: and nothing shall be impossible unto you." Jno. 11: 40—"Jesus saith unto her, Said I not unto thee, that, if thou wouldest believe, thou shouldest see the glory of God?"

If we believe, we shall see the glory of God. It is our wretched unbelief that is shutting many of us out of seeing it in our own lives.

(10) Heb. 6: 12—"That ye be not slothful, but followers of them who through faith and patience inherit the promises."

Luke 1: 45, R.V.—"And blessed is she that believed; for there shall be a fulfillment of the things which have been spoken to her from the Lord."

TENTH PROPOSITION: *Through faith we receive the fulfillment of God's promises.*

The actual enjoyment of God's promises is conditioned upon our belief of them.   No matter how explicit a promise may be, the thing promised becomes ours only upon condition of our believing the promise.

Jas. 1: 5-7—"If any of you lack wisdom, let him ask of God, that giveth to all men liberally, and upbraideth not; and *it shall be given him. But let him ask in faith*, nothing wavering: for he that wavereth is like a wave of the sea driven with the wind and tossed. For let not that man think that he shall receive any thing of the Lord."

The promises are for us; they are all yea and amen in Christ (2 Cor. 1: 20), but they become actually and experimentally ours only as we reach out the hand of faith and appropriate them to ourselves. As far as we believe we receive. (Mark 11: 24, R.V.) We get what we believe for. Heb. 4: 1, 2—"Let us therefore fear, lest, a promise being left us of entering into his rest, any of you should seem to come short of it. For unto us was the gospel preached, as well as unto them: but the word preached did not profit them, not being mixed with faith in them that heard it." (See R.V., Am. Ap.) The fulness of God's blessing is for those who claim it and in so far as they claim it. Josh. 1: 3—"Every place *that the sole of your foot shall tread upon,* THAT have I given unto you, as I said unto Moses."

(11) Mark 9: 23—"Jesus said unto him, If thou canst believe, all things are possible to him that believeth."

ELEVENTH PROPOSITION: All things are possible to him that believeth.

By faith we lay hold of God and His almightiness. Faith can do anything God can do.

V. How to get Faith.

(1) Rom. 12: 3—"For I say, through the grace given unto me, to every man that is among you, not to think of himself more highly than he ought to think; but to think soberly, according *as God hath dealt to every man the measure of faith."*

1 Cor. 12: 4, 8, 9—"Now there are diversities of gifts, but the same Spirit. . . . For *to one is given* by the Spirit the word of wisdom; to another the word of knowledge by the same Spirit; To another *faith by the same Spirit;* to another the gifts of healing by the same Spirit."

1 Cor. 2: 4, 5—"And my speech and my preaching was not with enticing words of man's wisdom, but in demonstration of the Spirit and of power: That your faith should not stand in the wisdom of men, but *in the power of God."*

FIRST PROPOSITION: Faith is God's gift.

Like all of God's gifts it is at the disposal of all who wish it, for there is no respect of persons with Him. We shall see directly that it is given through a certain instrument that is within reach of all, and upon certain conditions that any of us can fulfill.

(2) Rom. 10: 17—"So then faith cometh by hearing, and hearing by the word of God."

Acts 4: 4—"Howbeit many of them *which heard the word* believed; and the number of the men was about five thousand."

SECOND PROPOSITION: The Word of God is the instrument God has appointed for, and that he uses in, imparting faith.

This is true of Saving Faith. When Paul and Silas told the Philippian jailer to believe on the Lord Jesus Christ and he would be saved, they immediately proceeded to speak the word of the Lord unto him. (Acts 16: 31, 32.)

It is true of the faith that prevails in prayer. If we wish to believe that our prayer is heard we should search the promises of God and just rest our faith upon them. Feeding upon the Word makes a mighty man of prayer.

It is true of faith in all its aspects. Faith comes through the Word and grows by feeding upon the Word. If we wish others to have faith we should give them the Word of God. If we wish faith ourselves we should feed on the Word of God. (2 Tim. 3: 15; Jas. 1: 21; Jno. 20: 31.) No amount of praying for faith will bring it if we neglect faith's proper nourishment, the Word of God, any more than praying for physical health and strength will bring it if we neglect wholesome food and live on mince pie and candy.

(3) Gal. 5: 22—"But the *fruit of the Spirit* is love, joy, peace, long suffering, gentleness, goodness, faith."

THIRD PROPOSITION: Faith is the work of the Holy Spirit.

It is part of the fruit of the Spirit. The Word is the instrument by which it is produced, but it is the Word carried home, and made a living thing in the heart by the Holy Spirit's power.

(4) Heb. 12: 2—"Looking unto Jesus, the author and finisher of our faith; who for the joy that was set before him endured the cross, despised the shame, and is set down at the right hand of the throne of God."

FOURTH PROPOSITION: Jesus is the author and finisher of our faith.

OUR PART.

(5) Rom. 4: 19, 20, R.V.—"And without being weakened in faith he considered his own body now as good as dead (he being about a hundred years old), and the deadness of Sarah's womb: yea, *looking unto the promises of God*, he wavered not through unbelief, but waxed strong through faith, giving glory to God."

FIFTH PROPOSITION: *If we would have faith we must fix our eyes upon the promise of God.*

(If we wish another to have faith we must hold up the promise of God before him, and hold his attention to it.)

(6) Luke 11: 9, 11, 13—"And I say unto you, Ask, and it shall be given you; seek, and ye shall find; knock, and it shall be opened unto you. . . . If a son shall ask bread of any of you that is a father, will he give him a stone? or if he ask a fish, will he for a fish give him a serpent? . . . If ye then, being evil, know how to give good gifts unto your children; how much more shall your heavenly Father give the Holy Spirit *to them that ask him ?* "

Mark 9: 24—"And straightway the father of the child cried out, and said with tears, Lord, I believe; help thou mine unbelief." (The context shows that Christ at once answered that prayer.)

Luke 22, 32—"But I *have prayed for thee;* that thy faith fail not: and when thou art converted, strengthen thy brethren."

SIXTH PROPOSITION: *We should pray for Faith.*

As already seen, faith is God's gift. He bestows His gifts in answer to prayer. It is the Holy Spirit's work, and the Holy Spirit is given in answer to prayer. Prayer is an expression of our helplessness and dependence upon God.

(7) Matt. 25: 29 (Note preceding context vv. 14–28)—"For unto every one that hath shall be given, and he shall have abundance: but from him that hath not shall be taken away even that which he hath."

SEVENTH PROPOSITION: *If we wish more faith we should use the faith we have.*

(8) Jno. 5: 44, R.V.—"How can ye believe, which receive glory one of another, and the glory that cometh from the only God ye seek not ? "

EIGHTH PROPOSITION: *A great hindrance to faith is seeking glory from men and not the glory that cometh from God only.*

This and all hindrances must be put away if we would have faith.

(9) Heb. 12: 2—"Looking unto Jesus the author and finisher of our faith; who for the joy that was set before him endured the cross, despising the shame, and is set down at the right hand of the throne of God."

NINTH PROPOSITION: *If we would have faith we must look unto Jesus.*

Peter's faith failed when he took his eyes off from Jesus and began to look at the wind and waves.

Matt. 14: 30, 31—"But *when he saw the wind* boisterous, he was afraid; and beginning to sink, he cried, saying, Lord, save me. And immediately Jesus stretched forth his hand, and caught him, and said unto him, O thou of little faith, wherefore didst thou doubt ?"

(10) Jno. 8: 12—"Then spake Jesus again unto them, saying, I am the light of the world; he that followeth me shall not walk in darkness, but shall have the light of life."

TENTH PROPOSITION: If we are to have faith we must follow Jesus.

The more closely we follow Him the more our faith will grow. Those who follow most closely in the footsteps of Christ have the most faith. When Peter began to follow Christ " afar off " his faith failed rapidly. The more of Christlike denial of self and of true cross-bearing and humility there is in our lives the more our faith will grow. Faith cannot flourish in an atmosphere of self-indulgence, self-will and pride. Selfishness and faith cannot walk together. They are not agreed.

VI. The Relation of Faith and Repentance to each other.

(1) Acts 11: 19, 21—"Now they which were scattered abroad upon the persecution that arose about Stephen, traveled as far as Phenice, and Cyprus, and Antioch, preaching the word to none but unto the Jews only. And the hand of the Lord was with them: and a great number *believed, and turned unto the Lord.*"

Matt. 3: 2, 6—" And saying, Repent ye: for the kingdom of heaven is at hand. . . . And were baptized of him in Jordan confessing their sins."

Acts 2: 37, 41—" Now *when they heard this*, they were pricked in their heart, and said unto Peter and the rest of the apostles, Men and brethren, what shall we do? . . . Then *they that gladly received his word* were baptized: and the same day there were added unto them about three thousand souls."

FIRST PROPOSITION: Believing the Word of God leads to repentance.

(2) Acts 2: 36, 37, 38—" Therefore let all the house of Israel know assuredly, that God hath made that same Jesus, whom ye have cruci-fied, both Lord and Christ. Now when they heard this, they were pricked in their heart, and said unto Peter and to the rest of the apostles, Men and brethren, what shall we do ? Then Peter said unto

them, *Repent, and be baptized every one of you in the name of Jesus* Christ for the remission of sins, and ye shall receive the gift of the Holy Ghost."

SECOND PROPOSITION: The principal element in evangelical repentance is a change of mind about Christ; a change from an unbelieving and rejecting attitude to a believing and accepting attitude.

(3) Jno. 5: 44, R.V.—"How can ye believe, which receive glory one of another, and the glory that cometh from the only God ye seek not ?"

THIRD PROPOSITION: There must be a repentance from the attitude of mind that seeks the glory that comes from man, to the attitude that seeks the glory that comes from God, in order to believe in Christ.

(4) Acts 19: 18, 19—"And *many that believed* came, and *confessed, and showed their deeds.* Many of them also which used curious arts brought their books together, and burned them before all men: and they counted the price of them, and found it fifty thousand pieces of silver."

FOURTH PROPOSITION: True Faith in Christ involves the confession and forsaking of sin.

GENERAL PROPOSITION: True Repentance and Faith are inseparable. They are mutually dependent upon each other.

CHAPTER XI.

LOVE TO GOD.

I. Its Importance.

Matt. 22: 37, 38—"Jesus said unto him, thou shalt love the Lord thy God with all thy heart, and with all thy soul, and with all thy mind. This is the first and great commandment."

Mark 12: 29-34—"And Jesus answered him, The first of all the commandments is, Hear, O Israel; the Lord thy God is one Lord: and thou shalt love the Lord thy God with all thy heart, and with all thy soul, and with all thy mind, and with all thy strength: this is the first commandment. And the second is like, namely this: Thou shalt love thy neighbour as thyself. There is none other commandment greater than these. And the scribe said unto him, Well, Master, thou hast said the truth: for there is one God; and there is none other but he: And to love him with all the heart, and with all the understanding, and with all the soul, and with all the strength, and to love his neighbor as himself, is more than all whole burnt offerings and sacrifices. And when Jesus saw that he answered discreetly, he said unto him, Thou art not far from the kingdom of God. And no man after that durst ask him any question."

Deut. 10: 12—"And now, Israel, what doth the Lord thy God require of thee, but to fear the Lord thy God, to walk in all his ways, and to love him, and to serve the Lord thy God with all thy heart, and with all thy soul."

PROPOSITION: *To love God with all the heart and with all the soul, and all the mind is the first and great commandment.*

(It includes all else.)

II. How Love to God Is Manifested.

(1) Ex. 20: 6—"And shewing mercy unto thousands of them that love me, *and keep my commandments.*"

2 Jno. 6—"And this is love, *that we walk after his commandments.* This is the commandment, That, as ye have heard from the beginning, ye should walk in it. '

1 Jno. 5: 3—"For this is the love of God, *that we keep his commandments:* and his commandments are not grievous."

FIRST PROPOSITION: The supreme manifestation of love to God is keeping His commandments.

This *is* love to God. *Keeping* God's commandments is more than merely obeying God's commandments. The word translated ' keep," expresses watchful care. It means to "attend to carefully," "take care of," "guard." So also the Old Testament word.

(2) Deut. 10: 12—"And now, Israel, what doth the LORD thy God require of thee, but to fear the LORD thy God, to walk in all his ways, and to love him, *and to serve the* LORD thy God with all thy heart and with all thy soul."

SECOND PROPOSITION: Love to God is manifested by serving Him with all the heart and all the soul.

Paul in writing to the Thessalonians speaks of their "*labor of love.*" The word for "labor" denotes "intense" labor, "toil." The one who loves God will labor intensely for Him. An easy-going Christian life proves an absence of love for God.

(3) Ps. 97: 10—"Ye that love the LORD hate evil."

THIRD PROPOSITION: Love to God manifests itself in a hatred of evil.

The man who loves God cannot regard sin with favor or indifference. He hates it. All sin. There is no small sin to him.

(4) 1 Jno. 2: 15—"Love not the world, neither the things that are in the world. If any man love the world, the love of the Father is not in him."

FOURTH PROPOSITION: Love to God manifests itself in not loving the world.

The man who loves God cannot set his affections upon the world with its gain and its honor, and its pleasure, and its gratifications. All that is in the world is not of the Father, it draws away from Him, and a lover of God cannot love it.

(5) 1 Jno. 4: 20, 21—"If a man say, I love God, and hateth his brother, he is a liar: for he that loveth not his brother whom he hath seen, how can he love God whom he hath not seen? And this commandment have we from him, that he who loveth God love his brother also."

FIFTH PROPOSITION: Love to God is manifested by a love to God s children, our brethren.

III. Results of Love to God.

(1) UNDER THE OLD COVENANT.

Deut. 5: 10—"And *shewing mercy unto thousands of them that love me* and keep my commandments."

7: 9—"Know therefore that the LORD thy God, he is God, the faithful God, which keepeth covenant and mercy with them that love him and keep his commandments, to a thousand generations."

Ex. 20: 6—"And shewing mercy unto thousands of them that love me, and keep my commandments.

Ps. 69: 36—"The seed also of his servants shall inherit it: and they that love his name shall dwell therein."

Ps. 91: 14—"Because he hath set his love upon me, therefore will I deliver him: I will set him on high, because he hath known my name."

145: 20—"The LORD preserveth all them that love him: but all the wicked will he destroy."

Is. 56: 6, 7—"Also the sons of the stranger, that join themselves to the LORD, to serve him, and to love the name of the LORD, to be his servants, every one that keepeth the Sabbath from polluting it, and taketh hold of my covenant; Even them will I bring to my holy mountain, and make them joyful in my house of prayer: their burnt offerings and their sacrifices shall be accepted upon mine altar; for mine house shall be called a house of prayer for all people.

PROPOSITION: The blessings and promises under the Old Covenant were for those who loved God.

(2) UNDER THE NEW COVENANT.

(1) 1 Cor. 8: 3—"But if any man love God, the same is known of him."

FIRST PROPOSITION: He that loveth God is known by God.

(2) Jas. 1: 12—"Blessed is the man that endureth temptation; for when he is tried, he shall receive the crown of life, which the Lord hath promised to them that love him."

SECOND PROPOSITION: The Crown of Life is for those who love God.

(3) Jas. 2: 5—"Hearken, my beloved brethren, Hath not God chosen the poor of this world rich in faith, and heirs of the kingdom, which he hath promised to them that love him?"

THIRD PROPOSITION: The Kingdom is promised to those who love God.

(4) 1 Cor. 2: 9—"But it is written, Eye hath not seen, nor ear heard, neither have entered into the heart of man, the things which God hath prepared for them that love him."

FOURTH PROPOSITION: God hath prepared for those who love Him things beyond those which eye hath seen or ear heard, and those which have entered into the heart of man; deep things which the Spirit alone searches and reveals. (See context.)

(5) Rom 8: 28—"And we know that all things work together for good to them that love God, to them who are called according to his purpose."

FIFTH PROPOSITION: All things work together for good for those who love God.

(6) Rom. 8: 28, 29, 30, R.V.—"And we know that to them that love God all things work together for good, even to them that are called according to his purpose. For whom he foreknew, he also fore-ordained to be conformed to the image of his Son, that he might be the firstborn among many brethren: and whom he foreordained, them he also called: and whom he called them he also justified: and whom he justified, them he also glorified."

SIXTH PROPOSITION: Those who love God are "the called according to his purpose," "foreknown," "foreordained to be conformed to the image of His Son," "justified," "glorified."

IV. How to Get Love to God.

(1) 1 Jno. 4: 7—" Beloved, let us love one another: for love is of God; and every one that loveth is *born of God*, and knoweth God."

FIRST PROPOSITION: We get love to God by being born of God.

We are not saved *by* loving God, we are saved *to* loving God.

(2) 1 Jno. 4: 19—"We love him, because he first loved us."

SECOND PROPOSITION: We get love to God by believing in and meditating upon His love to us.

(3) 2 Thess. 3: 5—"And the Lord direct your hearts into the love of God, and into the patient waiting for Christ."

THIRD PROPOSITION: God, in answer to prayer, directs our hearts into the Love of God.

CHAPTER XII.

LOVE TO CHRIST.

I. Its Importance.

(1) Matt. 10:35-38—"For I am come to set a man at variance against his father, and the daughter against her mother, and the daughter-in-law against her mother-in-law. And a man's foes shall be they of his own household. He that loveth father or mother more than me is not worthy of me: and he that loveth son or daughter more than me is not worthy of me. And he that taketh not his cross, and followeth after me, is not worthy of me."

Luke 14: 26—"If any man come to me, and hate not his father, and mother, and wife, and children, and brethren, and sisters, yea, and his own life also, he cannot be my disciple."

FIRST PROPOSITION: Supreme love to Christ is the condition of Christian discipleship.

Christ in the New Testament claims the same supreme love for Himself that Jehovah in the Old Testament claims for Himself. Here is undoubted proof of the Divinity of Christ. Unless Christ has a place in our hearts above father, mother, wife, children, brothers, sisters, yea, and his own life, we cannot be his disciples.

(2) 1 Pet. 1:8—"Whom having not seen, ye love."

(Compare v. 2, as to whom the "ye" of v. 8 are—"Elect according to the foreknowledge of God the Father, through sanctification of the Spirit, unto obedience and sprinkling of the blood of Jesus Christ: Grace unto you, and peace, be multiplied.")

SECOND PROPOSITION: Love to Christ (though we see Him not) is an unfailing mark of the elect.

(3) Jno. 8: 42—"Jesus said unto them, If God were your Father, ye would love me: for I proceeded forth and came from God; neither came I of myself, but he sent me."

THIRD PROPOSITION: If we are children of God we will love Christ.

Absence of love to Christ is decisive proof that one is not a child of God.

(4) 1 Cor. 16: 22—"If any man love not the Lord Jesus Christ, let him be Anathema Maran-atha."

FOURTH PROPOSITION: Any one who does not love Christ will be Anathema (i. e., "Devoted without hope of being redeemed," "doomed to destruction ") at the coming of Christ.

II. How Love to Christ Is Manifested.

(1) Jno. 14: 15, 21, 23, R.V.—"If ye love me, *ye will keep my commandments. . . .* He that hath my commandments, and keepeth them, he it is that loveth me: and he that loveth me shall be loved of my Father, and I will love him, and will manifest myself unto him. . . . Jesus answered and said unto him, If a man love me, he will keep my word: and my Father will love him, and we will come unto him, and make our abode with him."

FIRST PROPOSITION: Love to Christ is manifested by keeping His words and commandments. (The same thing that is said elsewhere of love to God.)

(2) 2 Cor. 5: 14, 15, R.V.—"For the love of Christ constraineth us; because we thus judge, that one died for all, therefore all died; and he died for all, that they which live should no longer live unto themselves, but unto him who for their sakes died and rose again."

SECOND PROPOSITION: Love to Christ is manifested by our not living unto ourselves, but unto Him who for our sakes died and rose again.

(3) Jno. 21: 15-17, R.V.—"So when they had broken their fast, Jesus saith to Simon Peter, Simon, son of John, lovest thou me more than these? He saith unto him, Yea, Lord; thou knowest that I love thee. He saith unto him, Feed my lambs. He saith to him again a second time, Simon, son of John, lovest thou me? He saith unto him, Yea, Lord; thou knowest that I love thee. He saith unto him, Tend my sheep. He saith unto him the third time, Simon, son of John, lovest thou me? Peter was grieved because he said unto him the third time, Lovest thou me? And he said unto him, Lord, thou knowest all things; thou knowest that I love thee. Jesus saith unto him, Feed my sheep."

THIRD PROPOSITION: Love to Christ is manifested by feeding His lambs and shepherding His sheep.

(4) Luke 7:44-47—"And he turned to the woman, and said unto Simon, Seest thou this woman? I entered into thine house, thou gavest me no water for my feet: but she hath washed my feet with tears, and wiped them with the hairs of her head. Thou gavest me no kiss: but this woman, since the time I came in, hath not ceased to kiss my feet. My head with oil thou didst not anoint: but this woman hath anointed my feet with ointment. Wherefore I say unto thee, Her sins, which are many, are forgiven; for she loved much: but to whom little is forgiven, the same loveth little."

FOURTH PROPOSITION: Love to Christ is manifested by ministering to Him.

How can we? Matt. 25: 40—"And the king shall answer and say unto them, Verily I say unto you, Inasmuch as ye have done it unto one of the least of these my brethren, ye have done it unto me."

(5) Phil. 3: 7, 8—"But what things were gain to me, those I counted loss for Christ. Yea doubtless, and I count all things but loss for the excellency of the knowledge of Christ Jesus my Lord: for whom I have suffered the loss of all things, and do count them but dung, that I may win Christ."

FIFTH PROPOSITION: Love to Christ is manifested by counting all things but loss and gladly sacrificing them for His sake.

(6) Acts 21: 13—"Then Paul answered, what mean ye to weep and to break mine heart? for I am ready not to be bound only, but also to die at Jerusalem for the name of the Lord Jesus."

SIXTH PROPOSITION: Love to Christ is manifested by a willingness to suffer and to die for His name.

(7) 2 Cor. 5: 8—"We are confident, I say, and willing rather to be absent from the body, and to be present with the Lord."
Phil. 1: 23, R.V.—"But I am in a strait betwixt the two, having the desire to depart and be with Christ; for it is very far better."

SEVENTH PROPOSITION: Love to Christ manifests itself in a desire to be with Christ.

(8) 2 Tim. 4: 8—"Henceforth there is laid up for me a crown of righteousness, which the Lord, the righteous judge, shall give me at that day: and not to me only, but unto all of them also that love his appearing."
Rev. 22: 20—"He which testifieth these things saith, Surely I come quickly: Amen. Even so, come, Lord Jesus."

EIGHTH PROPOSITION: *Love to Christ manifests itself in a longing for His appearing.*

III. Results of Love to Christ.

(1) Eph. 6: 24—"Grace be with all them that love our Lord Jesus Christ in sincerity. Amen."

FIRST PROPOSITION: *There is grace for all who love Jesus Christ in sincerity.*

(2) Jno. 14: 21-23—"He that hath my commandments, and keepeth them, he it is that loveth me: and he that loveth me shall be loved of my Father, and I will love him, and will manifest myself to him. Judas saith unto him, not Iscariot, Lord, how is it that thou wilt manifest thyself unto us, and not unto the world? Jesus answered and said unto him, if a man love me, he will keep my words: and my Father will love him, and we will come unto him, and make our abode with him."

SECOND PROPOSITION: (a) *Those who love Christ are loved of the Father.*

God loves all men, but he has a peculiar love for those who love His Son. (Compare Ch. 17: 23, R.V.—"I in them, and thou in me, that they may be perfected into one; that the world may know that thou didst send me, and *lovedst them, even as thou lovedst me.*")

SECOND PROPOSITION: (b) *Those who love Christ are loved of Christ.*

SECOND PROPOSITION: (c) *Christ manifests Himself unto those who love Him.*

How ? (vv. 15, 16, 23, and Ch. 16: 14.)

SECOND PROPOSITION: (d) *The Father and Christ make their abode with the one who loves Christ.*

(3) Jno. 14: 15-17, R.V.—"If ye love me ye will keep my commandments. And I will pray the Father, and he shall give you another comforter, that he may be with you for ever, even the Spirit of truth: whom the world cannot receive; for it beholdeth him not, neither knoweth him: ye know him; for he abideth with you, and shall be in you."

THIRD PROPOSITION: *The Father's gift of the Holy Spirit, as the Paraclete to abide with and be in us, is for those who love Christ.*

(4) 2 Tim. 4: 8—"Henceforth there is laid up for me a crown of righteousness, which the Lord, the righteous judge, shall give me at that day: and not to me only, but unto all them also that love his appearing."

FOURTH PROPOSITION: At His coming the Lord will give a crown of righteousness to all who love His appearing.

IV. How Can We Attain unto Love to Christ?

(1) Luke 7: 47–50—"Wherefore I say unto thee, Her sins, which are many, are forgiven; for she loved much: but to whom little is forgiven, the same loveth little. . . . And he said to the woman, Thy faith hath saved thee; go in peace."

FIRST PROPOSITION: Love to Christ arises from a realization of our sin and from faith in the wondrous pardoning love of Christ.

This is finely illustrated in Paul: 1 Tim. 1: 12–15—"And I thank Christ Jesus our Lord, who hath enabled me, for that he counted me faithful, putting me into the ministry; who was before a blasphemer, and a persecutor, and injurious: but I obtained mercy, because I did it ignorantly in unbelief. And the grace of our Lord was exceeding abundant with faith and love which is in Christ Jesus. This is a faithful saying, and worthy of all acceptation, that Christ Jesus came into the world to save sinners; of whom I am chief." Gal. 2: 20—"I am crucified with Christ: nevertheless I live; yet not I, but Christ liveth in me: and the life which I now live in the flesh I live by the faith of the Son of God, who loved me, and gave himself for me." And in John: 1 Jno. 4: 10—"Herein is love, not that we loved God, but that he loved us, and sent his Son to be the propitiation for our sins."

CHAPTER XIII.

LOVE TO MAN.

I. What is Love?

(1) Matt. 5:43-47—"Ye have heard that it hath been said, thou shalt love thy neighbor, and hate thine enemy. But I say unto you, Love your enemies, bless them that curse you, do good to them that hate you, and pray for them which despitefully use you, and persecute you: That ye may be the children of your Father which is in heaven: for he *maketh his sun to rise on the evil and on the good, and sendeth rain on the just and on the unjust.* For if ye love them which love you, what reward have ye ? do not even the publicans the same ? And if ye salute your brethren only, what do ye more than others ? do not even the publicans so ? "

1 Jno. 3: 14, 16, 17—"We know that we have passed from death unto life, because we love the brethren. He that loveth not his brother abideth in death. . . . Hereby perceive we the love of God, *because he laid down his life for us:* and we ought to lay down our lives for the brethren. But whoso hath this world's good, and seeth his brother have need, and shutteth up his bowels of compassion from him, how dwelleth the love of God in him ? "

Love for another is a desire for and delight in their good. Love is not mere fondness for another nor pleasure in their society. The character of another may be hateful to me, and his society disagreeable, but still a real desire for his welfare is love.

II. The Objects of Christian Love.

(1) 1 Pet. 2: 17—"Honor all men. *Love the brotherhood.* Fear God. Honor the king."

Eph. 1: 15—"Wherefore I also, after I heard of your faith in the Lord Jesus, and *love unto all the saints.*"

FIRST PROPOSITION: We should love the brethren, those born of God, all saints.

While, as we shall see, a Christian should love all men, he should and will have a peculiar love for God's children. (Compare Gal. 6: 10—"As we have therefore opportunity, let us do good unto all men, especially unto them who are of the household of faith.")

(2) Matt. 19: 19—" Honor thy father and thy mother: and, Thou shalt love thy neighbor as thyself." Matt. 22: 39—"And the second is like unto it, Thou shalt love thy neighbor as thyself."

SECOND PROPOSITION:　We should love our neighbor.

Who is that ?　Luke 10: 29–37—" But he, willing to justify himself, said unto Jesus, And who is my neighbor ?　And Jesus answering said, A certain man went down from Jerusalem to Jericho, and fell among thieves, which stripped him of his raimet, and wounded him, and departed, leaving him half dead. And by chance there came down a certain priest that way; and when he saw him, he passed by on the other side, and likewise a Levite, when he was at the place, came and looked on him, and passed by on the other side.　But a certain Samaritan, as he journeyed, came where he was; and when he saw him, he had compassion on him, and went to him, and bound up his wounds, pouring in oil and wine, and set him on his own beast, and brought him to an inn, and took care of him.　And on the morrow when he departed, he took out two pence, and gave them to the host: and said unto him, Take care of him: and whatsoever thou spendest more, when I come again, I will repay thee. Which now of these three, thinkest thou, was neighbour unto him that fell among the thieves ?　And he said, He that shewed mercy on him.　Then said Jesus unto him, Go, and do thou likewise."

(3) 1 Thess. 3: 12—" And the Lord make you to increase and abound in love one toward another; *and toward all men*, even as we do toward you."

THIRD PROPOSITION:　We should love all men.

(4) Matt. 5: 44—" But I say unto you, Love your enemies, bless them that curse you, do good to them that hate you, and pray for them that despitefully use you, and persecute you."

FOURTH PROPOSITION:　We should love our enemies.

Enemies are specialized because they are the ones whom we would be least likely to love.

How shall we show our love to our enemies ?   The remainder of the verse shows.   See, also, Rom. 12. 20—"Be not overcome of evil, but overcome evil with good."

(5) Eph. 5: 25—"Husbands, love your wives, even as Christ also loved the church and gave himself for it."

FIFTH PROPOSITION: Husbands should love their wives.

The husband has an especial duty of love toward his wife. The doctrine that a husband should have no more interest in the welfare of his wife than in that of any other woman is totally unscriptural.   While Christ has a love for all men, He has an altogether especial and peculiar love for the Church, and so the Christian husband should love all, but have an altogether special and peculiar love for his wife.

(6) Tit. 2: 4—"That they may teach the young women to be sober, to love their husbands, to love their children."

SIXTH PROPOSITION: Wives should love their husbands.

III. How Love?

(1) 1 Cor. 16: 24—"My love be with you all in Christ Jesus. Amen."

FIRST PROPOSITION: We should love in Christ Jesus.

Christ Jesus is the author of our love.   It is for His sake we love.   Our special love to the brethren is because of their special relation to Him.

(2) Rom. 12: 9 (first part), R.V.—"Let love be without hypocrisy."

SECOND PROPOSITION: We should love without hypocrisy. Our love should be genuine, unfeigned.

Much professed love is a mere pretense.   Much calling of one another "brother" is the hollowest formalism and sham.

(3) 1 Jno. 3: 18—"My little children, let us not love in word, neither in tongue; but in deed and in truth."

THIRD PROPOSITION: We should not love merely in word, neither in tongue, but in deed and in truth; not in saying, but in doing; not in profession, but in practice.

(4) 1 Pet. 4: 8—"And above all things have fervent charity among yourselves; for charity shall cover the multitude of sins."

1 Pet. 1: 22, R.V.—"Seeing ye have purified your souls in your obedience to the truth unto unfeigned love of the brethren, love one another from the heart fervently."

FOURTH PROPOSITION: We should love from the heart, fervently—rather, "intensely."

(5) Phil. 1: 9—"And this I pray, that your love may abound yet more and more in knowledge and in all judgment."

1 Thess. 3:12—"And the Lord make you to increase and abound in love one toward another, and toward all men, even as we do toward you:"

FIFTH PROPOSITION: We should love aboundingly.

No mean, niggardly outgoings of love.

(6) Matt. 19: 19—"Honor thy father and thy mother: and thou shalt love thy neighbour as thyself."

Rom. 13: 8, 9—"Owe no man anything, but to love one another: for he that loveth another hath fulfilled the law. For this, thou shalt not commit adultery, thou shalt not kill, thou shalt not steal, thou shalt not bear false witness, thou shalt not covet; and if there be any other commandment, it is briefly comprehended in this saying, namely, Thou shalt love thy neighbour as thyself."

Gal. 5: 14—"For all the law is fulfilled in one word, even in this; Thou shalt love thy neighbor as thyself."

SIXTH PROPOSITION: We should love our neighbor as ourself.

(7) Jno. 13: 34, R.V.—"A new commandment I give unto you, that ye love one another; even as I have loved you, that ye also love one another."

Jno. 15: 12, R.V.—"This is my commandment, that ye love one another, even as I have loved you."

SEVENTH PROPOSITION: We should love the brethren even as Christ loved us.

How much was that? Jno. 15:13—"Greater love hath no man than this, that a man lay down his life for his friends." 1 Jno. 3: 16—"Hereby perceive we the love of God, because he *laid down his life for* us: and we ought to lay down our lives for the brethren."

IV. How Love Is Manifested.

(1) Rom. 13: 10—"Love worketh no ill to his neighbor; therefore love is the fulfilling of the law."

FIRST PROPOSITION: Love is manifested by abstaining from everything that would injure another.

"Love worketh no ill." There is much here for reflection. The applications are countless.

(2) Gal. 6: 10—"As we have therefore opportunity, let us do good unto all men, especially unto them ·who are of the household of faith."

SECOND PROPOSITION: Love is manifested by doing good as we have opportunity.

It is not merely negative—abstaining from doing injury, it is positive, doing positive good.

(3) Gal. 5: 13, R.V.—"For ye, brethren, were called for freedom; only use not your freedom for an occasion to the flesh, but through love be servants one to another."

THIRD PROPOSITION: Love is manifested by becoming a servant to others.

This is illustrated in Jesus Christ. Jno. 13: 1, 2, 3, 4, 5— "Now before the feast of the passover, when Jesus knew that the hour was come that he should depart out of this world unto the Father, having loved his own which were in the world, he loved them unto the end. And supper being ended, the devil having now put into the heart of Judas Iscariot, Simon's son, to betray him; Jesus knowing that the Father had given all things into his hands, and that he was come from God, and went to God; he riseth from supper, and laid aside his garments; and took a towel, and girded himself. After that he poureth water into a basin, and began to wash the disciples' feet, and to wipe them with the towel wherewith he was girded." Phil. 2: 4–7—"Look not every man on his own things, but every man also on the things of others. Let this mind be in you, which was also in Christ Jesus: Who being in the form of God, thought it not robbery to be equal with God: But made himself of no reputation, and took upon him the form of a servant, and was made in the likeness of men." The man who wishes to be served but will not serve does not love. Love seeks lowly places of service.

(4) 1 Cor. 10: 24, R.V.—"Let no man seek his own, but each his neighbour's good."

FOURTH PROPOSITION: Love is manifested by our not seeking our own, but our neighbor's good.

(5) Phil. 2: 4, R.V.—"Not looking each of you to his own things, but each of you also to the things of others."

FIFTH PROPOSITION: Love is manifested by our not looking to (or caring for, having a regard to) our own things, but to the things of others. (e. g., We are not to be concerned about our glory and honor, but the honor of others. See context in vv. 5–8.)

(6) Gal. 6: 2—"Bear ye one another's burdens, and so fulfill the law of Christ."

SIXTH PROPOSITION: Love is manifested by our bearing one another's burdens.

(7) Rom. 15: 1–3, R.V.—"Now we that are strong ought to bear the infirmities of the weak, and not to please ourselves. Let each one of us please his neighbor for that which is good, unto edifying. For Christ also pleased not himself; but, as it is written, The reproaches of them that reproached thee fell upon me."

SEVENTH PROPOSITION: Love is manifested (a) by our bearing the infirmities of the weak (see context); (b) not pleasing ourselves; (c) pleasing others for that which is good unto edifying.

Christ the great example here also.

(8) 2 Cor. 2: 7, 8—"So that contrariwise ye ought rather to forgive him, and comfort him, lest perhaps such a one should be swallowed up with overmuch sorrow."

EIGHTH PROPOSITION: Love is manifested by forgiving and comforting the wayward.

In this particular instance the man had gone deeply into sin, the vilest sin.

(9) Gal. 6: 1, R.V.—"Brethren, even if a man be overtaken in any trespass, ye which are spiritual, restore such a one in a spirit of meekness; looking to thyself, lest thou also be tempted."

NINTH PROPOSITION: Love is manifested by restoring in a spirit of meekness the one overtaken in any trespass.

(10) 1 Thess. 5: 14, R.V.—"And we exhort you, brethren, admonish the disorderly, encourage the fainthearted, support the weak, be longsuffering toward all." (Note context.)

TENTH PROPOSITION: Love is manifested by (a) admonishing the disorderly; (b) encouraging the faint-hearted; (c) supporting the weak; (d) being long-suffering toward all.

(11) Rom. 14: 15, 21, R.V.—"For if because of meat thy brother is grieved, thou walkest no longer in love. Destroy not with thy meat him for whom Christ died. . . . It is good not to eat flesh, nor to drink wine, nor do anything whereby thy brother stumbleth."

ELEVENTH PROPOSITION: Love is manifested by avoiding that by which a brother stumbleth.

(12) Rom. 14: 19—"Let us therefore follow after the things which make for peace, and things wherewith one may edify another."

TWELFTH PROPOSITION: Love is manifested by following after the things which make for peace and things whereby one may edify another.

(13) Rom. 12: 15—"Rejoice with them that do rejoice, and weep with them that weep."

THIRTEENTH PROPOSITION: Love is manifested by rejoicing with them that do rejoice and weeping with them that weep.

(14) Luke 6: 35, and R.V.—"But love ye your enemies, and do good, and lend, *hoping for nothing again;* and your reward shall be great, and ye shall be the children of the highest: for he is kind unto the unthankful and to the evil." R.V.—"But love your enemies, and do them good, and lend, *never despairing;* and your reward shall be great, and ye shall be sons of the Most High: for he is kind toward the unthankful and evil."

FOURTEENTH PROPOSITION: Love is manifested by lending, never despairing (or despairing of no man).

Lend and keep on lending, hoping against hope.

(15) Eph. 4: 2—"With all lowliness and meekness, with long-suffering, forbearing one another in love."

FIFTEENTH PROPOSITION: *Love is manifested by forbear-ing one another*—i. e., *suffering wrong and ill without venge-fulness and retaliation; overcoming evil with good.*

(16)   Eph. 4, 32, R.V.—"And be ye kind one to another, tender-hearted, forgiving each other, even as God also in Christ forgave you."

SIXTEENTH PROPOSITION: *Love is manifested* (a) *by be-ing kind;* (b) *by being tender-hearted:* (c) *by forgiving one an-other even as also God in Christ forgave us.*

(17)   2 Cor. 8: 24—"Wherefore shew ye to them, and before the churches, the proof of your love, and of our boasting on your behalf." (See context.)

1 Jno. 3: 17—"But whoso hath this world's goods, and seeth his brother have need, and shutteth up his bowels of compassion from him, how dwelleth the love of God in him?"

SEVENTEENTH PROPOSITION: *Love is manifested by giv-ing of our means to meet another's need.*

(18)   Rom. 12: 10—"Be kindly affectionate one to another with brotherly love; in honor preferring one another."

EIGHTEENTH PROPOSITION: *Love is manifested* (a) *by be-ing kindly affectionate one toward another;* (b) *by in honor pre-ferring one another*—i. e., *by seeking the higher place for some one else, the lower place for oneself.*

It is easy to do this in little conventionalities, as *e. g.*, in the matter of passing through a door first; but do we do it in the really important affairs of life?

(19)   1 Cor. 13: 4–7, R.V.—"Love suffereth long, and is kind; love envieth not; love vaunteth not itself, is not puffed up, doth not behave itself unseemly, seeketh not its own, is not provoked, taketh not ac-count of evil; rejoiceth not in unrighteousness, but rejoiceth with the truth; beareth all things, believeth all things, hopeth all things, en-dureth all things."

NINETEENTH PROPOSITION: *Love is manifested* (a) *by suffering long;* (b) *by being kind* [Had this already in 16]; (c) *by envying not;* (d) *by vaunting not oneself;* (e) *by not be-ing puffed up;* [Conceit is a mark of selfishness. If we love others as we do ourselves we will not think ourselves better than they.] (f) *by not behaving unseemly;* [Rude, ungentlemanly, unladylike, inconsiderate conduct, bad manners, reveal a disregard for the sensibilities of others—it is a form of self-ishness]; (g) *by not seeking our own;* (h) *by not being provoked* (Compare A. V.); (i) *by not taking account of evil* (See A. V.); (j) *by not rejoicing in unrighteousness;* (k) *by rejoicing with the truth;* (l) *by bearing all things;* (m) *by believing all things;* (n) *by hoping all things;* (o) *by enduring all things.*

(20)   Lev. 19: 17—"Thou shalt not hate thy brother in thine heart: thou shalt in any wise rebuke thy neighbor, and not suffer sin upon him."

Prov. 27: 5—"Open rebuke is better than secret love."

Eph. 5: 11—"And have no fellowship with the unfruitful works of darkness, but rather reprove them."

TWENTIETH PROPOSITION: Love to those who do wrong is manifested by rebuking them.

How? (*a*)   Matt. 18: 15-17—"Moreover if thy brother shall trespass against thee, go and tell him his fault between thee and him alone: if he shall hear thee, thou hast gained thy brother. But if he will not hear thee, then take with thee one or two more, that in the mouth of two or three witnesses every word may be established.   And if he shall neglect to hear them, tell it unto the church: but if he neglect to hear the church, let him be unto thee as a heathen man and a publican."   Personal wrong, first privately, then before one or two witnesses, then before the church. (*b*) 1 Tim. 5: 20, R. V.—"Them that sin reprove in the sight of all, that the rest also may be in fear."   Public offenses, in the sight of all.   (N. B.—This public reproof is by an elder.) (*c*) Tit. 1: 12, 13, R. V.—"One of themselves, a prophet of their own, said, Cretans are always liars, evil beasts, idle gluttons. This testimony is true.   For which cause reprove them sharply, that they may be sound in the faith."   Sharply, when necessary.

(21)   Matt. 5: 44, R.V.—"But I say unto you, Love your enemies, and pray for them that persecute you."

TWENTY-FIRST PROPOSITION: Love for others is manifested by praying for them.   There is no way in which we can do more for them.

(22) 1 Jno. 5: 2, R.V.—"Hereby we know that we love the children of God, when we love God, and do his commandments.

TWENTY-SECOND PROPOSITION: Love to the children of God is manifested by loving God Himself and doing His commandments.

(23) Jno. 15: 13—"Greater love hath no man than this, that a man lay down his life for his friends."

1 Jno. 3: 16, R.V.—"Hereby know we love, because he laid down his life for us: and we ought to lay down our lives for the brethren."

TWENTY-THIRD PROPOSITION: Love to the brethren is manifested by our laying down our lives for them.

The manifestations of love specifically and definitely mentioned in the Bible are very numerous. As one goes over them he begins to see how love covers every duty to every class of men, and how true it is, as Paul says, that "Love is the fulfillment of the law." (Rom. 13: 10, R.V.)

V. The Importance of Love to Man.

(1) 1 Cor. 13: 1-3, R.V.—"If I speak with the tongues of men and of angels, but have not love, I am become sounding brass, or a clanging cymbal. And if I have the gift of prophecy, and know all mysteries and all knowledge; and if I have all faith, so as to remove mountains, but have not love, I am nothing. And if I bestow all my goods to feed the poor, and if I give my body to be burned, but have not love, it profiteth me nothing."

FIRST PROPOSITION: Love is absolutely indispensable.

Eloquence and the gift of prophecy and knowledge and faith and sacrifice of possessions and martyrdom are of no value if love be wanting.

(2) 1 Cor. 13: 13, R.V.—"But now abideth faith, hope, love, these three; and the greatest of these is love."

SECOND PROPOSITION: Love is greater than faith and hope.

(3) 1 Cor. 13: 8, R.V.—"Love never faileth: but whether there be prophecies, they shall be done away; whether there be tongues, they shall cease; whether there be knowledge, it shall be done away."

THIRD PROPOSITION: Love never faileth.

(4) Rom. 13: 8, 10, R.V.—"Owe no man anything, save to love one another: for he that loveth his neighbour hath fulfilled the law. . . . Love worketh no ill to his neighbour: love therefore is the fulfillment of the law."

FOURTH PROPOSITION: Love is the fulfillment of the law. All individual precepts are but applications of this law.

(Compare 1 Tim. 1: 5—"Now the end of the commandment is charity out of a pure heart, and of a good conscience, and of faith unfeigned:" Jno. 15: 17—"These things I command you, that ye love one another.")

(5) 1 Jno. 3: 23, 11—"And this is his commandment, That we should believe on the name of his Son Jesus Christ, and love one another, as he gave us commandment. . . . For this is the message that ye heard from the beginning, that we should love one another."

Jno. 13: 34—"A new commandment I give unto you, That ye love one another; as I have loved you, that ye also love one another."

FIFTH PROPOSITION: Love to one another is the sum of God's commandment, the original and fundamental message of Christianity, Christ's new and all-inclusive commandment.

(6) Jas. 2: 8—"If ye fulfil the royal law according to the Scripture, Thou shalt love thy neighbour as thyself, ye do well.

SIXTH PROPOSITION: Love is the royal law.

(7) Col. 3: 14, R.V.—"And above all these things put on love, which is the bond of perfectness."

SEVENTH PROPOSITION: Love is the bond that unites all the virtues together into a perfect whole.

(Note the figure used in context, vv. 12: 13: "*Put on* therefore, as God's elect, holy and beloved, a heart of compassion, kindness, humility, meekness, longsuffering; forbearing one another, and forgiving each other, if any man have a complaint against any; even as the Lord forgave you, so also do ye."

(8) Jno. 13: 35—"By this shall all men know that ye are my disciples, if ye have love one to another."

EIGHTH PROPOSITION: Love is the supreme and decisive test of discipleship.

(9) 1 Jno. 4: 8—"He that loveth not, knoweth not God; for God is love."

NINTH PROPOSITION: (a) *Love is the supreme and decisive test of our knowing God;* (b) *Love is the one Divine thing.*

(10) 1 Jno. 4: 7—"Beloved, let us love one another: for love is of God; and every one that loveth is born of God, and knoweth God."

3: 10—"In this the children of God are manifest, and the children of the devil: whosoever doeth not righteousness is not of God, neither he that loveth not his brother."

TENTH PROPOSITION: Love is the supreme test of our being born of God, and being children of God.

(Compare Eph. 5: 1, 2—"Be ye therefore *followers of God, as dear children; and walk in love,* as Christ also hath loved us, and hath given himself for us an offering and a sacrifice to God for a sweet smelling savour.")

(11) 1 Jno. 3: 14, R.V.—"We know that we have passed out of death into life, *because we love the brethren.* He that loveth not abideth in death."

ELEVENTH PROPOSITION: Love is the supreme test of our having passed out of death into life.

(12) 1 Jno. 4: 12, 16—"No man hath beheld God at any time; if we love one another, God abideth in us, and his love is perfected in us: . . . And we know and have believed the love which God hath in us. God is love; and he that abideth in love abideth in God, and God abideth in him."

TWELFTH PROPOSITION: Love is the supreme test of our abiding in God and God abiding in us.

(13) 1 Jno. 4: 20—"If a man say, I love God, and hateth his brother, he is a liar: for he that loveth not his brother whom he hath seen, can not love God whom he hath not seen."

THIRTEENTH PROPOSITION: Love to brethren is the supreme test of love to God.

(14) 1 Pet. 4: 8, R.V.—"*Above all things* being fervent in your love among yourselves; for love covereth a multitude of sins."

FOURTEENTH PROPOSITION: Love is the one thing above all things which we are to seek to have.

Paul, John, James, Peter and Jesus, with one voice proclaim the supremacy of love.

VI. The Blessings that Result from Love to Men.

(1) 1 Pet. 4: 8—"Above all things being fervent in your love among yourselves; for love covereth a multitude of sins."

FIRST PROPOSITION: Love covereth a multitude of sins.

(2) 1 Cor. 8: 1, R.V.—"Now concerning things sacrificed to idols: We know that we all have knowledge. Knowledge puffeth up, but love edifieth."

SECOND PROPOSITION: Love buildeth up.

(3) Col. 2: 2—"That their hearts might be comforted, being *knit together in love*, and unto all riches of the full assurance of understanding, to the acknowledgment of the mystery of God, and of the Father, and of Christ."

THIRD PROPOSITION: Love knits together.

(4) 1 Jno. 2: 10—"He that loveth his brother abideth in the light, and there is none occasion of stumbling in him."

FOURTH PROPOSITION: He that loveth his brother abideth in the light and there is none occasion of stumbling in him.

(5) 1 Jno. 3: 22, 23—"And whatsoever we ask, we receive of him, because we keep his commandments, and do those things that are pleasing in his sight. And this is his commandment, That we should believe on the name of His Son Jesus Christ, and love one another, as He gave us commandment.

FIFTH PROPOSITION: Love to brethren gives prevailing power to prayer.

VII. How Love to Men Is Obtained.

(1) 1 Jno. 4: 7—"Beloved, let us love one another: for love is of God; and every one that loveth is born of God, and knoweth God."

FIRST PROPOSITION: Love is of God, and to love we must be born of God.

(2) 1 Jno. 4: 19, R.V.—"We love because he first loved us."

SECOND PROPOSITION: We love because God first loved us.

His love *to us* awakens love *in* us: first to Him and then to man. If we would learn to love we must believe in and meditate upon His love to us.

(3) Gal. 5: 6—"For in Jesus Christ neither circumcision availeth any thing, nor uncircumcision; but faith which worketh by love."

THIRD PROPOSITION: Faith works by love. Love is the outcome of faith. (Compare 1 Jno. 3: 23.)

Love is greater than faith, but faith is the root of love. Faith is the root of which love is the fruit.   To say "it is better to have love even without faith than it is to have faith without love," is much like saying it is better to have a crop of apples without having roots to your apple trees, than it is to have roots without apples.   Rootless trees do not bear fruit and faithless lives do not bring forth love.

(4) Gal. 5: 22—"But the fruit of the Spirit is love, joy, peace, long-suffering, gentleness, goodness, faith."

Rom. 5: 5—"And hope maketh not ashamed; because the love of God is shed abroad in our hearts by the Holy Ghost which is given unto us."

FOURTH PROPOSITION: Love is the fruit of the Spirit.

If you wish love let the Spirit work in your heart and bear His fruit in your life.   You will never attain unto love by any mere effort of your own.   Love is not a fruit that is native to the soil of the human heart.

(5) 1 Cor. 14: 1, a, R.V.—"Follow after love; yet desire earnestly spiritual gifts, but rather that ye may prophesy."

1 Tim. 6: 11—"But thou, O man of God, flee these things; and follow after righteousness, godliness, faith, love, patience, meekness."

2 Tim. 2: 22, R.V.—"But flee youthful lusts, and follow after righteousness, faith, love, peace, with them that call on the Lord out of a pure heart."

FIFTH PROPOSITION: We should follow after Love.

While love is the Holy Spirit's work it should be the object of our desire and pursuit.

(6) Heb. 10: 24—"And let us consider one another to provoke unto love and to good works."

SIXTH PROPOSITION: We should provoke (spur on) one another to love.

(7) 1 Thess. 4: 9—"But as touching brotherly love ye need not that I write unto you: for ye yourselves are taught of God to love one another."

SEVENTH PROPOSITION: God teaches us to love one another.

(8) Phil. 1: 9—"And this I pray, that your love may abound yet more and more in knowledge and in all judgment."

EIGHTH PROPOSITION: God imparts increasing love in answer to prayer.

(9) Gal. 2: 20—"I am crucified with Christ: nevertheless I live; yet not I, but Christ liveth in me: and the life which I now live in the flesh I live by the faith of the Son of God, who loved me, and gave himself for me."

NINTH PROPOSITION: If you would learn to love let Christ in to live His life in your heart. Renounce self, renounce the flesh, crucify it, put it in the place of the curse and let Christ live his life in you.

CHAPTER XIV.

PRAYER.

1. Who Can Pray so that God Will Hear?

(1) Ps. 66: 18—"If I regard iniquity in my heart, the LORD will not hear me."

FIRST PROPOSITION: The one who regards iniquity in his heart cannot pray so that God will hear.

The word translated "regard" means primarily to "see" or to "look." Then it comes to mean to "look at with favor," to "respect," "approve," "regard." God will not hear the man who in his heart looks upon sin with any favor or allowance. God looks at sin with abhorrence. He is of "purer eyes than to behold evil." (Hab. 1: 13—"Thou art of purer eyes than to behold evil, and canst not look on iniquity," etc.) The Hebrew verb here is the same as that translated "regard" above. We must have the same attitude toward sin that He has to be heard of Him. If we regard sin, He will not regard us when we pray. Herein lies the very simple explanation why many of us pray and are not heard.

(2) Prov. 28: 9—"He that turneth away his ear from hearing the law, even his prayer shall be abomination."

SECOND PROPOSITION: He that turneth away his ear from hearing the law, his prayer is an abomination. He cannot pray so that God will hear.

If we turn our ears away from what God says to us in His law, He will turn His ears away from what we say to Him in our prayers. We have an illustration of this in Zech. 7: 11–13:

"But they refused to hearken, and pulled away the shoulder, and stopped their ears, that they should not hear. Yea, they made their hearts as an adamant stone, lest they should hear the law, and the words which the LORD of hosts hath sent in his Spirit by the former prophets: therefore came a great wrath from the LORD of hosts. Therefore it came to pass, that as he cried, and they would not hear; so they cried, and I would not hear, saith the LORD of hosts."

Many are saying, "The promises of God are not true. God does not hear my prayers." Has God ever promised to hear *your* prayers? God very plainly describes the class whose prayers He hears. Do you belong to that class? Are you listening to His words? If not, He has distinctly said He will not listen to your prayers, and in not listening to you, He is simply keeping His word.

(Compare Prov. 1: 24, 25, 28, R.V.—"Because I have called, and you refused; I have stretched out my hand, and no man regarded; But ye have set at nought all my counsel, and would none of my reproof. . . . Then shall they call upon me, but I will not answer; They shall seek me diligently, but they shall not find me."

(3) Prov. 21: 13—"Whoso stoppeth his ears at the cry of the poor, he also shall cry, but shall not be heard."

THIRD PROPOSITION: Whoever stoppeth his ears at the cry of the poor cannot pray so that God will hear.

If we will not listen to the poor when they cry unto us in their need, God will not listen unto us when we cry unto Him in our need. The world's maxim is, "The Lord helps those who help themselves." The truth is, The Lord helps those who help others.

(4) Luke 18: 13, 14—"And the publican, standing afar off, would not lift up so much as his eyes unto heaven, but smote upon his breast, saying, God be merciful to me a sinner. I tell you, this man went down to his house justified rather than the other: for every one that exalteth himself shall be abased; and he that humbleth himself shall be exalted."

FOURTH PROPOSITION: The great sinner, who is sorry for and humbled by his sin, and who desires pardon, can pray so that God will hear.

The question is often asked, "Shall we get unconverted people to pray?" What do you mean by unconverted people? If a man is sorry for his sin, and wishes to forsake it and find mercy, and is willing to humble himself before God and ask for pardon, he is taking the very steps by which a man turns around, or is "converted." To tell a man he must not pray under such circumstances, is to tell him that he must not be converted until he is converted; that he must not turn until he is turned round. To get him to pray is just the thing to do, "For whosoever shall call upon the name of the Lord shall be saved." (Rom. 10: 13.)

But how, some one may ask, can he pray until he has faith? The answer is very simple. This prayer itself is the first act of faith. The first and most natural and most proper thing for one who honestly wishes to turn from sin and to believe on Christ and to be saved to do, is to pray. The Lord Jesus looked on with delight when he could say to Ananias of the stubborn rebel, Saul of Tarsus, "Behold, he prayeth." (Acts 9: 11 —"And the Lord said unto him, Arise, and go into the street which is called Straight, and inquire in the house of Judas for one called Saul of Tarsus: for, behold, he prayeth.") We should be sure, however, that the sinner really is sorry for sin and really wishes to forsake it before we tell him to pray for pardon. You can get him on his knees even before this, and so get him to realize that he is in God's presence, so that his rebellious heart may be humbled, but do not have him pray until he really does wish to turn from sin.

(5) 1 Jno. 5: 13-15, R.V.—"These things have I written unto you, that ye may know that ye have eternal life, *even unto you that believe on the name of the Son of God.* And this is the boldness which *we* have toward him, that, *if we ask* anything according to his will, he heareth us: and if we know that he heareth us whatsoever we ask, we know that we have the petitions which we have asked of him."

FIFTH PROPOSITION: Those that believe on the name of the Son of God can pray so that God will hear.

The promises of the New Testament cannot be applied indiscriminately to all men. A great mistake is often made by taking promises made to the believer and applying them as if they referred to all classes of men; or, by taking promises made to those that have surrendered absolutely to the will of God, and applying them as if they referred to all professed believers. When we find promises with "we" and "ye" in them, we should study the context and find out who the "we's" and "ye's" are, and whether we belong to that class.

(6) Ps. 34: 15, 17—"The eyes of the LORD are upon *the righteous,* and his ears are open to their cry . . . *The righteous* cry, and the LORD heareth, and delivereth them out of all their troubles."

Prov. 15: 29—"The LORD is far from the wicked; but he heareth the prayer of the *righteous.*"

Prov. 15: 8—" The sacrifice of the wicked is an abomination to the LORD: but the prayer of *the upright* is his delight."

SIXTH PROPOSITION: The righteous and the upright can pray so that God will hear.

NOTE.—The words translated righteous and upright have practically the same significance. They both mean primarily "right" or "straight." (The latter may mean also "level" or "even.")

(7) Ps. 32: 6—"For this shall *every one that is godly* pray unto thee in a time when though mayest be found; surely in the floods of great waters they shall not come nigh unto him."

SEVENTH PROPOSITION: The godly (or merciful) can pray so that God will hear.

The word translated "godly" in this passage is so translated three times in the Authorized Version (four times in R.V.) But its primary significance is "kind," or "merciful." It could be so translated in at least almost every passage where used. It is frequently translated "saints."

(8) Ps. 145: 19—"He will fulfil the desire of them that fear him: he also will hear their cry, and will save them."

EIGHTH PROPOSITION: Those that fear God can pray so that God will hear.

To fear God means to have that reverent regard for God that is due him and that manifests itself in glad obedience to His will. (Heb. 12: 28, 29; 1 Pet. 2: 17; Rev. 14: 7; 2 Cor. 7: 1; 2 Sam. 23: 3; Prov. 8: 13; 16: 6; Is. 11: 2, 3; Ps. 2: 11; 25: 14; 33: 18; 34: 7, 9; Rev. 19: 5; Ps. 115: 11; 118: 4.)

(9) 1 Jno. 3: 22—"And whatsoever we ask, we receive of him because we keep his commandments, and do those things that are pleasing to his sight."

NINTH PROPOSITION: Those that keep God's commandments and do those things which are pleasing in His sight can pray so that God will hear.

Here we find one of the greatest secrets of prevailing prayer. If we listen to God's commandments God will listen to our prayers. If we do as He bids us in His word, He will do as we ask him in our prayers. If we do what pleases Him, He will do what pleases us. This is the converse of (2) above. The one who turns away his ear from hearing God's law cannot pray so that God will hear; the one who turns his ear to listen attentively to God's Word can pray so that God will hear. This explains why some men's prayers are heard and some men's are not. To keep His commandments means more than merely yield obedience to them; it means to guard them as a precious possession, to treasure them. It is the opposite of the spirit of those "critics" who are trying to pare down the Word of God to the smallest possible dimensions. The more they can give away of God's Word the more they seem delighted. They cannot pray so God will hear. If they have so little regard for God's Word, God will have very little regard for theirs.

(10) Jno. 15: 7, R.V.—"If ye abide in me, and my words abide in you, ask whatsoever ye will, and it shall be done unto you."

TENTH PROPOSITION. Those who abide in Christ, and Christ's words abide in them, can pray so that God will hear. They can ask whatsoever they will and it will be done unto them.

This is the other great secret of prevailing prayer. It is closely related to the preceding. What is it to abide in Christ? It is to continue in living union with Him. To bear the same relation to Him that the living healthy branch, the continuously fruit-bearing branch, does to the vine. This branch has no independent life of its own. Its sap and vigor all come from the vine. Its leaves, buds, blossoms, fruit are all the product of the life of the vine in it. So we abide in Christ in so far as we have no independent life of our own. In so far as we do not seek to have any thoughts, plans, feelings, purposes, works, fruit of our own, but let Christ think his thoughts, feel His feelings, purpose His purposes, work His works, bear His fruit, in us. When we do this, and in so far as we do this, we may ask whatsoever we will and it shall be done.

It may be asked: "But what if we ask something contrary to God's will?" We cannot in so far as we abide in Christ; our prayers themselves will be the outcome of the Christ-life in us. The Father heareth Him always and will hear Him when He prays through us. Note that He says also, "And my words abide in you." It is through His words, and only through His words, that Christ imparts His life to us and lives His life in us. The words of Christ are the vehicle of the life of Christ. It is vain, then, to talk or think of abiding in Christ if we neglect His words. We must let His words sink deep into our souls and form us, mould our thoughts, our feelings, our purposes, our plans, our actions. "If ye abide in me, *and my words* abide in you, ask whatsoever ye will, and it shall be done unto you" is the way the promise reads.

(11) Ps. 91: 1, 14, 15—"He that dwelleth in the secret place of the most high shall abide under the shadow of the Almighty. . . . Be. cause he hath set his love upon me, therefore will I deliver him: I will set him on high, because he hath known my name. He shall call upon me, and I will answer him: I will be with him in trouble; I will deliver him, and honor him."

ELEVENTH PROPOSITION: The one who dwells in the secret place of the Most High, who sets his love upon God and knows His name, can pray so that God will hear.

What is it to dwell in the secret place of the Most High ? The word translated "secret place," means primarily "a covering," then "hiding-place," "protection." It is translated "protection" once, and "hiding-place" a number of times. To dwell in the secret place of the Most High, means, then, to put oneself and keep oneself under the protection of the Most High, to be covered and hid from all harm by Him. It means to leave all our welfare absolutely to Him, and to look to Him and to trust Him to take care of it.

To know His name, means to know Him as he has revealed Himself to us. That is only possible through the study of the Word.

(12) Ps. 37: 4—"Delight thyself also in the LORD; and he shall give thee the desires of thine heart."

TWELFTH PROPOSITION: He that delighteth himself in the Lord can pray so that the Lord will hear.

If our delight is in Him, our great prayer will be for Him- self, and He is always willing to give Himself. With Himself He will grant every other desire of our hearts. If our delight is in Him, it will be His delight to give us what we ask. Do you de- light in the Lord ? Remember that "delight" is a very strong word.

(13) Ps. 37: 5—" Commit thy way unto the LORD; trust also in him; and he shall bring it to pass."

THIRTEENTH PROPOSITION: He that committeth his way unto the Lord and trusteth in Him can pray so that God will hear.

The word here translated " commit " means literally " roll." (See Marg. A.V. and R.V.) To commit our way unto the Lord is to roll it upon Him, leave its direction and protection entirely to Him. Have you done this ? Put the entire guidance and out-come of your life in His hands, and your way will always be so near His that He can hear your faintest whisper when you call unto Him.

(14) Ps. 9: 12—" When he maketh inquisition for blood he remem-bereth them: he forgetteth not the cry of the humble."
Ps. 10: 17—" LORD thou hast heard the desire of the humble: thou wilt prepare their heart, thou wilt cause thine ear to hear."

FOURTEENTH PROPOSITION: The humble can pray so that God will hear.

The Revised Version translates the words differently in these two passages. In Ps. 9: 12, it translates it " poor." In 10: 17, it translates it "meek." The two words so translated are closely related, almost identical, and are from the same root. . . . (According to one reading they are precisely the same.) The thought of the words is " the afflicted " who bear their afflic-tion with meekness and humility. This latter thought is espe-cially true of the word used in Ps. 10: 17. (See also Zeph. 2: 3— "Seek ye the LORD, all ye meek of the earth, which have wrought his judgment; seek righteousness, seek meekness: it may be ye shall be hid in the day of the LORD's anger.")

(15) Ps. 69: 33, R.V.—"For the LORD heareth the needy; and de-spiseth not his prisoners."
Ps. 102: 17—" He will regard the prayer of the destitute, and not despise their prayer."

FIFTEENTH PROPOSITION: The needy and the destitute can pray so that God will hear.

The word translated " destitute " is a very strong word, meaning primarily "naked." Those to whom man does not listen are just the ones to whom God does listen. "The hungry he hath filled with good things; and the rich he hath sent empty away." (Luke 1: 53, R.V.) The poor cannot get a hearing down here, but they can up there. The more a man has, the more attentively the world listens to him; the more a man needs, the more attentively God listens to him.

(16) Jas. 5: 13, R.V. (first half)—"Is any among you suffering ? let him pray."

SIXTEENTH PROPOSITION: The suffering ones among God's people can pray so that God will hear.

Men ofttimes hesitate to pray to God because their afflictions are so many. These afflictions are a warrant for praying, and a guarantee that God will hear you. (Compare Matt. 11: 28.) Many are saying, "My troubles and sorrows are so many, what shall I do ?" Pray. "Is any among you suffering let him pray."

(17) Is. 19: 20—"And it shall be for a sign and for a witness unto the LORD of hosts in the land of Egypt: for they shall cry unto the LORD because of the oppressors, and he shall send them a saviour, and a great one, and he shall deliver them."

Jas. 5: 4—"Behold, the hire of the laborers who have reaped down your fields, which is of you kept back by fraud, crieth: and the cries of them which have reaped are entered into the ears of the Lord of Sabaoth."

SEVENTEENTH PROPOSITION: The oppressed can pray so that God will hear.

The oppressed cry for justice down here, but only get greater oppression; but God will hear if they cry to Him, and will deliver and avenge them. Israel cried to Pharaoh and were only sent to more bitter bondage, to make bricks without straw. Israel cried to Jehovah, and He brought them forth with a mighty hand and an outstretched arm. So will He do again when the oppressed cry to Him and not to human governments.

(18) Ex. 22: 22, 23—"Ye shall not afflict any widow, or fatherless child. If thou afflict them in any wise, and they cry at all unto me, I will surely hear their cry."

EIGHTEENTH PROPOSITION: Widows and fatherless children can pray unto God in their oppression so that God will hear.

(19) Jas. 1: 5—"If any of you lack wisdom, let him ask of God, that giveth to all men liberally, and upbraideth not; and it shall be given him."

NINETEENTH PROPOSITION: *The child of God who lacks wisdom can pray so that God will hear.*

If we lack human wisdom we can have God's wisdom. If we are full of our own wisdom we can not have His.

(20) Acts. 10: 24, 31, 32—"And the morrow after they entered into Cesarea. And Cornelius waited for them, and had called together his kinsman and near friends. . . . And said, Cornelius, *thy prayer is heard*, and thine alms are had in remembrance in the sight of God. Send therefore to Joppa, and call hither Simon, whose surname is Peter; he is lodged in the house of one Simon a tanner by the sea side: who, when he cometh, shall speak unto thee."

(Compare Acts 11: 14—"Who shall tell thee words, whereby thou and all thy house *shall be saved.*")

TWENTIETH PROPOSITION: *The man who is sincerely seeking the truth, and obeying the truth as fast as he finds it, even though he does not yet know the truth as it is in Jesus, and so is not as yet saved, can pray so that God will hear.*

II. To Whom to Pray.

(1) Acts 12: 5—"Peter therefore was kept in prison: but prayer was made without ceasing of the church *unto God* for him."

FIRST PROPOSITION: *We should pray to God.*

Much so-called prayer is not to God. There is very little thought of God in it. We think of the audience; we think, it may be, of our need; but there is not a clear, deep sense that we have come into the presence of the all holy, almighty, all-loving One, and are laying hold upon Him for His help. This is one of the most frequent causes of failure in prayer. We do not really pray to God. The first thing to do when we pray is to actually come into God's presence, to dismiss from our minds, so far as possible, all thought of our surroundings and look to the Spirit to present God to our minds and make Him real to us. It is possible by the Holy Spirit's aid to have God so really present that it almost seems as if we could see and touch Him. Indeed, we do see Him with the spirit's eyes, and touch Him with the hand of faith.

(2) Matt. 6: 9—"After this manner therefore pray ye: *Our Father* which art in heaven, Hallowed be thy name."

Luke 11: 13—"If ye then, being evil, know how to give good gifts unto your children; how much more shall *your heavenly Father* give the Holy Spirit to them that ask him ?"

Jno. 16: 23—"And in that day ye shall ask me nothing. Verily, verily, I say unto you, Whatsoever ye shall ask *the Father* in my name, he will give it you."

SECOND PROPOSITION: *We should pray to the Father.*

Various modes of address to him are found in the prayers recorded in the Bible. Father. (Jno. 17: 1.) Holy Father. (Jno. 17: 11.) Righteous Father. (Jno. 17: 25.) Our Father which art in Heaven. (Matt. 6: 9.) "Lord, thou art God, which has made heaven, and earth, and sea, and all that in them is." (Acts 4: 24.) "God of our Lord Jesus Christ, the Father of Glory." (Eph. 1: 17.) "Father of our Lord Jesus Christ." (Eph. 3: 14.) "Our God and Father." (1 Thess. 3: 11, R. V.)

(3) Acts 7: 59, R.V.—"And they stoned Stephen, calling upon the Lord, and saying, *Lord Jesus*, receive my spirit."

2 Cor. 12: 8, 9—"For this thing I besought *the Lord* thrice, that it might depart from me. And he said unto me, My grace is sufficient for thee: for my strength is made perfect in weakness. Most gladly therefore will I rather glory in my infirmities, that the power of *Christ* may rest upon me."

Acts. 9: 9, 10, 13, 14, 17, 20, 21—"And he was three days without sight, and neither did eat nor drink. And there was a certain disciple at Damascus, named Ananias; and to him said the Lord in a vision, Ananias. And he said, Behold, I am here, Lord. . . . Then Ananias answered, Lord, I have heard by many of this man, how much evil he hath done to thy saints at Jerusalem: And here he hath authority from the chief priests to bind all that call on thy name. . . . And Ananias went his way, and entered into the house; and putting his hands on him said, Brother Saul, *the Lord, even Jesus*, that appeared unto thee in the way as thou camest, hath sent me, that thou mightest receive thy sight, and be filled with the Holy Ghost. . . . And straightway he preached Christ in the synagogues, that he is the Son of God. But all that heard him were amazed, and said; Is not this he that destroyed them which *called on this name* in Jerusalem, and came hither for that intent, that he might bring them bound unto the chief priests ?"

2 Tim. 2: 22—"Flee also youthful lusts: but follow righteousness, faith, charity, peace, with them that *call on the Lord* out of a pure heart." (Compare 4:8—"Henceforth there is laid up for me a crown of

righteousness, which the Lord, the righteous judge, shall give me at
that day: and not to me only, but unto all them also that love his
appearing.")

1 Cor. 1: 2—"Unto the church of God which is at Corinth, to them
which are sanctified in Christ Jesus, called to be saints, with all that
in every place *call upon the name of Jesus Christ* our Lord, both theirs
and ours: "

Rom. 10: 12, 13—"For there is no difference between the Jew and
the Greek: for *the same Lord* over all is rich unto all that *call upon*
him.   For whosoever shall call upon the name of the Lord shall be
saved."   (Compare v. 9—"That if thou shalt confess with thy mouth
the Lord Jesus, and shalt believe in thine heart that God hath raised
him from the dead, thou shalt be saved.")

THIRD PROPOSITION: *We should pray to the Lord Jesus Christ.*

One of the most distinctive characteristics of Christians is
that they pray to Jesus Christ.   They were spoken of in apostolic
days as those who called on the name of Jesus.   (Acts 9: 14, 21.)
Paul described them as those "that call upon the name of our
Lord Jesus Christ."   (1 Cor. 1: 2, R. V.)

QUESTION: Ought we to pray to the Holy Spirit?

ANSWER: There is no recorded prayer in the Bible to the
Holy Spirit, but the communion of the Holy Spirit is spoken of.
This may imply prayer, but it may mean the partaking of the
Holy Spirit.   (Compare 1 Cor. 10: 16.)   We are dependent upon
the Holy Spirit for everything, and so must look to Him, which
implies prayer.   Yet it is the Father and the Son who give the
Holy Spirit.   (Jno. 14: 16, 17; 15: 26; Acts 2: 33.)   It would
seem then that if we wished Him, instead of praying directly to
Him, we should pray to the Father or Son for Him.

III.   For Whom to Pray.

(1)   1 Chron. 4: 10—"And Jabez called on the God of Israel, saying,
Oh that thou wouldst *bless me* indeed, and enlarge my coast, and that
thine hand might be with me, and that thou wouldst keep me from
evil, that it may not grieve me !   And God granted him that which he
requested."

Ps. 106: 4, 5—"Remember *me*, O LORD, with the favor that thou
bearest unto thy people: O visit me with thy salvation; That I may
see the good of thy chosen, that I may rejoice in the gladness of thy
nation, that I may glory with thine inheritance."

2 Cor. 12: 7, 8—"And lest I should be exalted above measure through the abundance of the revelations, there was given to me a thorn in the flesh, the messenger of Satan to buffet me, lest I should be exalted above measure. For this thing I besought the LORD thrice, that it might depart *from me.*"

Heb. 5: 7—" Who in the days of his flesh, when he had offered up prayers and supplications with strong crying and tears unto him that was able to save him from death, and was heard in that he feared."

Jno. 17: 1—"These words spake Jesus, and lifted up his eyes to heaven, and said, Father, the hour is come; glorify thy Son, that thy Son also may glorify the."

FIRST PROPOSITION: We should pray for ourselves.

A prayer for self is not by any means necessarily a selfish prayer. We may pray for something for ourselves in order that God may be glorified by our receiving it. (Jno. 17: 1; Ps. 50: 15.) If we would pray more for ourselves, God would be more glorified in us, and we would be a greater blessing to others. It was well for the world that Jesus spent so much time in prayer for Himself. If we would be fit to pray for others we must spend much time in prayer for ourselves. It is a bad sign when one is always praying for others and never for himself. He is not like his Master.

(2) Jas. 5: 16—" Confess your faults one to another, and *pray one for another,* that ye may be healed. The effectual fervent prayer of a righteous man availeth much."

Rom. 1: 9—" For God is my witness, whom I serve in my spirit in the gospel of his Son, that without ceasing I make mention of you always in my prayers."

SECOND PROPOSITION: We should pray for one another— i. e., *believers should pray for fellow-believers.*

(3) Eph. 6: 19, 20—"*And for me,* that utterance may be given unto me, that I may open my mouth boldly, to make known the mystery of the gospel. For which I am *an ambassador* in bonds; that therein I may speak boldly, as I ought to speak."

Col. 4: 3—" Withal praying also for us, that God would open unto us a door of utterance, to speak the mystery of Christ, for which I am also in bonds."

2 Thess. 3: 1, 2—" Finally, brethren, pray for us, that the word of the Lord may have free course, and be glorified, even as it is with you: And that we may be delivered from unreasonable and wicked men: for all men have not faith."

Acts 13: 2, 3—" As they ministered to the Lord, and fasted, the Holy Ghost said, Separate me Barnabas and Saul for the work whereunto I have called them. And when they had fasted and prayed, and laid their hands on them, they sent them away."

Matt. 9: 38—"Pray ye therefore the Lord of the harvest, that he will send forth *labourers* into his harvest."

THIRD PROPOSITION: *We should pray for Ministers of the Word.*

Those whom God has called to devote their lives to the ministry of the Word should be the especial objects of the prayers of God's people. The neglect of prayer on the part of God's people accounts very largely for the absence of power on the part of God's ministers.

(4) 1 Thess. 3: 9–13—"For what thanks can we render to God again for you, for all the joy wherewith we joy for your sakes before our God; Night and day praying exceedingly that we might see your face, and might perfect that which is lacking in your faith? Now God himself and ·our Father, and our Lord Jesus Christ, direct our way unto you. And *the Lord make you to increase* and abound in love one toward another, and toward all men, even as we do toward you: To the end he may stablish your hearts unblameable in holiness before God, even our Father, at the coming of our Lord Jesus Christ with all his saints."

FOURTH PROPOSITION: *We should pray for those who have been converted through our ministry.*

It is remarkable how often Paul writes to his converts about his praying for them. We find Jesus also praying for His converts in Jno. 17: 9–26:

"I *pray for them:* I pray not for the world, but for them which thou hast given me; for they are thine. And all mine are thine, and thine are mine; and I am glorified in them. And now I am no more in the world, but these are in the world, and I come to thee. Holy Father, keep through thine own name those whom thou hast given me, that they may be one, as we are. While I was with them in the world, I kept them in thy name: those that thou gavest me, I have kept, and none of them is lost, but the son of perdition; that the Scriptures might be fulfilled. And now come I to thee; and these things I speak in the world, that they might have my joy fulfilled in themselves. I have given them thy word; and the world hath hated them, because they are not of the world, even as I am not of the world. I pray not that thou shouldest take them out of the world, but that thou shouldest keep them from the evil. They are not of the world, even as I am not of the world. Sanctify them through thy truth, thy word is truth. As thou hast sent

me into the world, even so have I also sent them into the world. And
for their sakes I sanctify myself, that they also might be sanctified
through the truth. Neither pray I for these alone, but for them also
which shall believe on me through their word; that they may be one; as
thou, Father, art in me, and I in thee, that they also may be one in us: that
the world may believe that thou hast sent me. And the glory which
thou gavest me I have given them; that they may be one, even as we
are one: I in them, and thou in me, that they may be made perfect in
one; and that the world may know that thou hast sent me, and hast
loved them, as thou hast loved me. Father, I will that they also,
whom thou hast given me, be with me where I am; that they may behold my glory, which thou hast given me: for thou lovedst me before
the foundation of the world. O righteous Father, the world hath not
known thee: but I have known thee, and these have known that thou
hast sent me. And I have declared unto them thy name, and will declare it; that the love wherewith thou hast loved me may be in them,
and I in them."

It is to be feared that few modern ministers pray for their
converts with the frequency and intensity that Paul did for his.
" Night and day praying exceedingly " he writes in one place.

(5) Jas. 5: 14, 16—" Is any sick among you? let him call for the elders of the church; and let them pray over him, anointing him with
oil in the name of the Lord: . . . Confess your faults one to another, and pray one for another, that ye may be healed. The effectual fervent prayer of a righteous man availeth much."

FIFTH PROPOSITION: *We should pray for sick brethren.*

(6) 1 Jno. 5, 16—" If any man see his brother sin a sin which is not
unto death, he shall ask, and he shall give him life for them that sin
not unto death. There is a sin unto death; I do not say that he shall
pray for it."

SIXTH PROPOSITION: *We should pray for any brother we see sinning a sin not unto death.*

(7) Eph. 6: 18, R.V—" With all prayer and supplication praying at
all seasons in the Spirit, and watching thereunto in all perseverance and
supplication for all the saints."

SEVENTH PROPOSITION: *We should pray for all the saints.*

Christ's prayer took in all believers in all ages. (Jno.
17: 9, 20.) Our sympathies, and consequently our prayers, should
take in the whole Church of Christ. It is astounding how
narrow is the circle taken in by the prayers of the average

Christian. Every child of God is my brother, and should be re-membered in my prayers. Let us give our prayers a wider sweep. (Compare Ps. 36:10—"O continue thy loving kindness unto them that know thee; and thy righteousness to the upright in heart.")

(8) 1 Chron. 29: 19—"And give unto *Solomon my son* a perfect heart, to keep thy commandments, thy testimonies and thy statutes, and to do all these things, and to build the palace, for the which I have made provision."

EIGHTH PROPOSITION: We should pray for our children.

(9) 1 Tim. 2: 2, 3—"For kings, and for all that are in authority; that we may lead a quiet and peaceable life in all godliness and hon-esty. For this is good and acceptable in the sight of God our Sa-viour."

NITNH PROPOSITION: We should pray for our rulers.

It is to be feared that most Christians to-day are grievously disobedient to God at this point. The present fashion is to rail at our rulers. This is in direct disobedience to God's Word. (Jude 8: 9, R.V.; 2 Pet. 2: 10, 11; 1 Pet. 2: 17.) Christians can ac-complish far more for "good government" by praying for than by railing at the powers that be.

(10) Jer. 29: 7—"And seek the peace of the city whither I have caused you to be carried away captives, and pray unto the LORD for it: for in the peace thereof shall ye have peace."

TENTH PROPOSITION: We should pray for the city where we live.

A Christian should be interested in all lands and in all places. But we have an especial responsibility and duty in prayer, as well as service, toward the place where God puts us.

(11) Rom. 10: 1—"Brethren, my heart's desire and prayer to God for Israel is, that they might be saved."

Joel 2: 17—"Let the priests, the ministers of the LORD, weep be-tween the porch and the altar, and let them say, Spare thy people, O LORD, and give not thine heritage to reproach, that the heathen should rule over them: wherefore should they say among the people, where is their God?"

Is. 62: 6, 7—"I have set watchmen upon thy walls, O Jerusalem, which shall never hold their peace day nor night: ye that make mention of the LORD, keep not silence, and give him no rest, till he establish, and till he make Jerusalem a praise in the earth."

ELEVENTH PROPOSITION: *We should pray for Israel.*

It is a sin not to. 1 Sam. 12:23—"Moreover as for me, God forbid that I should sin against the LORD in ceasing to pray for you: but I will teach you the good and the right way."

An especial blessing is pronounced upon those who pray for Jerusalem. Ps. 122:6, 7—"Pray for the peace of Jerusalem· *they shall prosper* that love thee. Peace be within thy walls, and prosperity within thy palaces." Jerusalem is very dear to God. 1 Kg. 11:13—"Howbeit I will not rend away all the king-dom; but will give one tribe to thy son for David my servant's sake, and 'for Jerusalem's sake which I have chosen." Zech. 2:7, 8, 10–12—"Deliver thyself, O Zion, that dwellest with the daughter of Babylon. For thus saith the LORD of hosts: After the glory hath he sent me unto the nations which spoiled you: he that toucheth you, toucheth the apple of his eye. . . . Sing and rejoice, O daughter of Zion: for, lo, I come, and I will dwell in the midst of thee, saith the LORD. And many nations shall be joined to the LORD in that day, and shall be my people: and I will dwell in the midst of thee, and thou shalt know that the LORD of hosts hath sent me unto thee. And the LORD shall inherit Judah, his portion in the holy land, and shall choose Jeru-salem again. Be silent, O all flesh, before the LORD: for he is raised up out of his holy habitation."

(12) Luke 6:28—"Bless them that curse you, and pray for them which despitefully use you."

Matt. 5:44, R.V.—"But I say unto you, Love your enemies, and pray for them that persecute you."

TWELFTH PROPOSITION: *We should pray for them that despitefully use us and persecute us.*

(Compare Luke 23:34; Acts 7:60.) We have an especial obligation of prayer toward those who do us wrong.

(13) 1 Tim. 2:1—"I exhort therefore, that, first of all, supplications, prayers, intercessions, and giving of thanks, be made for all men."

We should pray for all men. The love of God takes in the world. (Jno. 3:16.) So should our prayers: but there are cer-tain classes, as seen above, toward whom we have an especial obligation of prayer.

IV. When to Pray.

(1) Dan. 6: 10—"Now when Daniel knew that the writing was signed, he went into his house; and, his windows being open in his chamber toward Jerusalem, he kneeled upon his knees *three times a day*, and prayed, and gave thanks before his God, as he did aforetime."

Ps. 55: 16, 17—"As for me, I will call upon God; and the Lord shall save me. *Evening and morning, and at noon*, will I pray, and cry aloud: and he shall hear my voice."

Acts 10: 9, 30—"On the morrow, as they went on their journey, and drew nigh unto the city, Peter went up upon the housetop to pray about *the sixth hour:* . . . And Cornelius said, Four days ago I was fasting until this hour; and *at the ninth* hour I prayed in my house, and, behold, a man stood before me in bright clothing." (See also Acts 2: 1, 15—"The third hour.")

FIRST PROPOSITION: The holy men of the Bible prayed three times a day, evening, morning and at noon.

(2) Ps. 119: 146, 147—"I cried unto thee; save me, and I shall keep thy testimonies. I prevented the dawning of the morning, and cried: I hoped in thy word."

Mark 1: 35—"And *in the morning*, rising up *a great while before day*, he went out, and departed into a solitary place, and there prayed."

SECOND PROPOSITION: We should pray very early in the morning, before dawn.

(3) Luke 6: 12—"And it came to pass in those days, that he went out into a mountain to pray, and continued *all night* in prayer to God."

THIRD PROPOSITION: Our Master and Example "continued all night in prayer to God."

This was on the eve of a decisive step in His life, the choice of the twelve. A similar thing occurred at a great crisis in His life, when the multitude wished to take Him and make Him king. (Jno. 6: 15. Compare Mark 6: 46–48.) It is a good example to follow. There are some who strangely object to whole nights spent in prayer. They say that faith takes at once what it asks. Had not the Saviour faith? (Compare also Is. 40: 31.) Nights of prayer to God are followed by days of power with men. It is recorded of John Livingston that he spent a night in prayer and religious intercourse with a company like minded, and that the next day he preached with such power in the kirk of Shotts that 500 people dated their conversion or some definite advance in their spiritual life from that sermon. Of course, one can keep a night of prayer in a false and legal way.

(4) Ps. 88: 1—"O Lord God of my salvation, I have cried day and night before thee."

FOURTH PROPOSITION: *We should pray day and night.*

At all times our heart should be looking up to God, and this upward look of the heart will be frequently uttering itself in a cry to Him.

(5) Matt. 14: 19—"And he commanded the multitude to sit down on the grass, and took the five loaves, and the two fishes, and looking up to heaven, he blessed and brake, and gave the loaves to his disciples, and the disciples to the multitude."

Acts 27: 35—"And when he had thus spoken, he took bread, and gave thanks to God in presence of them all; and when he had broken it, he began to eat."

1 Tim. 4: 4, 5—"For every creature of God is good, and nothing to be refused, if it be received with thanksgiving: For it is sanctified by the word of God *and prayer.*"

FIFTH PROPOSITION: *We should pray at every meal.*

(6) Ps. 50: 15—"And call upon me in the day of trouble: I will deliver thee, and thou shalt glorify me."

Ps. 81: 7—"Thou calledst in trouble, and I delivered thee; I answered thee in the secret place of thunder: I proved thee at the waters of Meribah."

Ps. 77: 1, 2—"I cried unto God with my voice, even unto God with my voice; and he gave ear unto me. *In the day of my trouble* I sought the Lord: my sore ran in the night, and ceased not: my soul refused to be comforted."

Ps. 86: 7—"In the day of my trouble I will call upon thee: for thou wilt answer me."

SIXTH PROPOSITION: *We should pray to God in the day of trouble.*

(Compare Ps. 18: 6; 120: 1; 118: 5—Here two different Hebrew words are used, but both are from the same root as the words used in passages given above.)

(7) Ps. 3: 1, 2—"Lord, how are they increased that trouble me! many are they that rise up against me. Many there be which say of my soul, There is no help for him in God. Selah."

SEVENTH PROPOSITION: We should pray to God when those increase who trouble us and many rise up against us.

When enemies increase we should not despair but cry to God. Then we can lie down without fear to sleep. We need not fear though ten thousands of people set themselves against us round about. (Compare vv. 5, 6.)

(8) 1 Chron. 5: 20—"And they were helped against them, and the Hagarites were delivered into their hand, and all that were with them: for they cried to God in the battle, and he was entreated of them; because they put their trust in him."

EIGHTH PROPOSITION: We should pray to God in the day of battle.

Victory is of the Lord (Prov. 21:31, R.V.), therefore, in every battle we should cry to Him.

(9) 2 Chron. 14:8, 9, 11—"And Asa had an army of men that bare targets and spears, out of Judah three hundred thousand; and out of Benjamin, that bare shields and drew bows, two hundred and fourscore thousand: all these were mighty men of valor. And there came out against them Zerah the Ethiopian with a host of a thousand thousand, and three hundred chariots; and came unto Mareshah. . . . And Asa cried unto the LORD his God, and said, LORD, it is nothing with thee to help, whether with many, or with them that have no power: help us, O LORD our God; for we rest on thee, and in thy name we go against this multitude. O LORD, thou art our God; let no man prevail against thee."

20: 1–4, 12—"It came to pass after this also, that the children of Moab, and the children of Ammon, and with them others besides the Ammonites, came against Jehoshaphat to battle. Then there came some that told Jehoshaphat, saying, There cometh a great multitude against thee from beyond the sea on this side Syria; and, behold, they be in Hazazon-tamar, which is En-gedi. And Jehoshaphat feared, and set himself to seek the LORD, and proclaimed a fast throughout all Judah. And Judah gathered themselves together, to ask help of the LORD: even out of all the cities of Judah they came to seek the LORD. . . . O our God, wilt thou not judge them ? for we have no might against this great company that cometh against us; neither know we what to do: but our eyes are upon thee."

NINTH PROPOSITION: We should pray to God when outnumbered by enemies and when we have no might against them, and know not what to do.

When there is nothing else left to do, there is one thing that always remains—pray to God.

(10) 2 Chron. 13: 13-16—"But Jeroboam caused an ambushment to come about behind them: so they were before Judah, and the ambushment was behind them. And when Judah looked back, behold, a battle was before and behind: and they cried unto the Lord, and the priests sounded with the trumpets. Then the men of Judah gave a shout and as the men of Judah shouted, it came to pass, that God smote Jeroboam and all Israel before Abijah and Judah. And the children of Israel fled before Judah: and God delivered them into their hands."

TENTH PROPOSITION: We should pray to God when in great extremities.

(11) Ps. 60: 11—"Give us help from trouble: for vain is the help of man."

ELEVENTH PROPOSITION: We should pray to God when all human help fails.

(12) Jonah 2: 7—"When my soul fainted within me I remembered the Lord: and my prayer came in unto thee, into thine holy temple."

TWELFTH PROPOSITION: We should pray to God when our soul faints within us.

(13) Ps. 61: 2—"From the end of the earth will I cry unto thee, when my heart is overwhelmed: lead me to the rock that is higher than I."

THIRTEENTH PROPOSITION: We should pray to God when our heart is overwhelmed.

(14) Ps. 130: 1—"Out of the depths have I cried unto thee, O Lord."

FOURTEENTH PROPOSITION: We should pray unto God when in the depths.

(15) Deut. 4: 25-29—"When thou shalt beget children, and children's children, and ye shall have remained long in the land, and shall corrupt yourselves, and make a graven image, or the likeness of any thing, and shall do evil in the sight of the Lord thy God, to provoke him to anger; I shall call heaven and earth to witness against you this day, that ye shall soon utterly perish from off the land whereunto ye go over Jordan to possess it: ye shall not prolong your days upon it, but shall utterly be destroyed. And the Lord shall scatter you among

the nations, and ye shall be left few in number among the heathen, whither the LORD shall lead you. And there ye shall serve gods, the work of men's hands, wood and stone, which neither see, nor hear, nor eat, nor smell. But if from thence thou shalt seek the LORD thy God, thou shalt find him, if thou seek him with all thy heart and with all thy soul."

FIFTEENTH PROPOSITION: We should pray to God in the day when we are being chastened for sin, when we are in a far country and desiring to come back to God.

The chastisements of God are a call to prayer.

(16) Is. 55: 6—"Seek ye the LORD while he may be found, call ye upon him while he is near."

SIXTEENTH PROPOSITION: We should call upon God while He is near and may be found

(17) Ps. 116: 1, 2—"I love the LORD, because he hath heard my voice and my supplications. Because he hath inclined his ear unto me, therefore will I call upon him as long as I live."

SEVENTEENTH PROPOSITION: We should pray to God as long as we live.

The last utterances of Christ were prayers. The last words of the Bible are prayers.

(18) Luke 18: 1—"And he spake a parable unto them to this end, that men ought always to pray, and not to faint."

Eph. 6: 18, R.V.—"With all prayer and supplication praying *at all seasons* in the Spirit, and watching thereunto in all perseverance and supplication for all the saints."

1 Thess, 5: 17—"Pray without ceasing."

EIGHTEENTH PROPOSITION: We should pray always and not faint, at all seasons, without ceasing.

A Christian should breathe an atmosphere of prayer. Faith in God has always an upward look. True trust in God is constantly crystallizing into definite prayer to God.

V. Where to Pray.

(1) Matt. 6: 6, R.V.—"But thou, when thou prayest, enter into thine inner chamber, and having shut thy door, pray to thy Father which is in secret, and thy Father which seeth in secret shall recompense thee."

FIRST PROPOSITION: *We should pray in secret, in our inner chamber.*

Shut in alone with God, the world shut out. There is a temptation when prayer is offered in presence of others to think of what observers are thinking of us. True prayer is taken up with God, not with men. The especial form of this danger which Christ is guarding against in this passage is that of ostentatious piety, hypocrisy, praying to be seen of men. The Heavenly Father is "thy Father which is *in secret,*" "Thy Father which seeth in secret." Every one should have a secret place to meet God, a place in which he is absolutely alone with God.

(2) Matt. 14: 23—"And when he had sent the multitudes away, he went up into a mountain apart to pray: and when the evening was come, he was there alone." (Luke 6: 12; 9: 28.)

SECOND PROPOSITION: *Jesus was wont to go apart into the mountains to pray.*

The primary purpose of His seeking this place to pray seems to have been that He might be alone with God. The mountains were His "secret" place. Further than this the mountains, in their majesty, seem to bring God wonderfully near to us and us wonderfully near to God

(3) Mark 1: 35—"And in the morning, rising up a great while before day, he went out, and departed into a solitary place, and there prayed."

THIRD PROPOSITION: *Jesus went into a solitary place to pray.*

The purpose of this is essentially the same as in (1) and (2.)

(4) Acts 16: 25—"And at midnight Paul and Silas prayed, and sang praises unto God: and the prisoners heard them."

FOURTH PROPOSITION: *The prisoner should pray in prison.*

Doubtless some of the most acceptable and effective prayers that God has ever heard have ascended to Him from prison-cells. Prayer transforms a prison-cell into a portal of heaven.

(5) Jonah 2: 2, R.V. Marg.—"I called by reason of mine affliction unto the LORD; And he answered me; Out of the belly of Sheol cried I, and thou heardest my voice."

FIFTH PROPOSITION: We may pray to God in the very jaws of death.

(6) Jno. 17: 1—"These words spake Jesus, and lifted up his eyes to heaven, and said, Father, the hour is come; glorify thy Son, that thy Son also may glorify thee."   (See context.)

SIXTH PROPOSITION: We should pray to God in the assembly of believers.

(7) Acts 27: 35—"And when he had thus spoken, he took bread, and gave thanks to God in *presence of them all;* and when he had broken it, he began to eat."   (See context.)

SEVENTH PROPOSITION: We should pray to God in the presence of the unsaved.

In doing so we must ever be on guard against praying to be seen and heard of men.   By far the greater part of our praying should be in secret.   But there should be public acknowledgment of our sense of dependence upon God.

(8) 1 Tim. 2: 8, R.V.—"I desire therefore that the men pray in every place, lifting up holy hands, without wrath and disputing."

EIGHTH PROPOSITION: We should pray in every place.

VI. For What to Pray.
A. PRAYERS RELATING TO GOD.

(1)   Matt. 6: 9—"After this manner therefore pray ye: Our Father which art in heaven, Hallowed be thy name."

FIRST PROPOSITION: We should pray for the hallowing of God's name.

The supreme desire of every believer's heart should be that God be duly honored and reverenced.   This should be the highest motive in all our prayers.   The chief purpose of all our prayers should be that God may be glorified in granting our petitions. (Compare Jno. 17: 1; 12: 27, 28.)   How deep and intense is your desire that God's name may be hallowed, and how often do you really pray for this?   To what extent is this the ruling motive of your prayers?

(2) Matt. 6: 10 (a)—"Thy kingdom come.

SECOND PROPOSITION: We should pray for the coming of God's kingdom.

God's kingdom will surely come anyway, but our prayers will hasten the coming of that kingdom. Little do most of us realize how far our prayers go in hastening the coming of God's kingdom, and how far our neglect of prayer goes in retarding the coming of that kingdom. The coming of God's kingdom is one of the intensest desires of the true believer's heart. Yet this prayer is often uttered thoughtlessly and mechanically.

(3) Rev. 22: 20—"He that testifieth these things saith, Surely I come quickly: Amen. Even so, come, Lord Jesus.

THIRD PROPOSITION: We should pray for the coming of God's king, Jesus.

The kingdom will never come until the King comes. Yet there are many who have prayed often that the kingdom of God would come, who have never prayed once that the King would come. This prayer stands as the climax of Christian aspiration. It is the final prayer of the Bible. The whole revelation of the Book leads up to this. How often have you prayed for this?

(4) Matt. 6: 10 (b), R. V. ——"Thy will be done as in heaven, so on earth."

FOURTH PROPOSITION: We should pray that God's will be done on earth as in heaven.

God's will is the most desirable thing in the universe to the true child of God. (Compare Jno. 4: 34.) He wishes it done in himself, but not only in himself, but everywhere and in every person and thing. No other prayer rings out quite so heartily from an understanding soul as this, "Thy will be done."

(5) Hab. 3: 2—"O LORD, I have heard thy speech, and was afraid: O LORD, revive thy work in the midst of the years, in the midst of the years make known; in wrath remember mercy."
Ps. 85: 6.

FIFTH PROPOSITION: We should pray for the reviving of God's work and God's people.

There is much prayer for revival in these days, but how much of that prayer is governed by the thought that it is *God's* work and *God's* people that must be revived ? How much of our concern is, because it is *God's* work that is languishing and *God's* people that are fainting ?   Far too often, it is only the interests of men that are to be subserved by a revival, that we have in view in our prayers and efforts for revival.   Prayer for the reviving of *God's* work and *God's* people is a prayer that God is especially pleased to answer.   All through the centuries of Israel's history, and of the Church's history, God has granted His reviving grace in answer to prayer.   Prayer has been the most prominent human element in great revivals.   It has been back of everything else.   There have been extraordinary revivals without extraordinary preaching; there have never been extraordinary revivals without extraordinary praying.

B.   PRAYERS RELATING TO MINISTERS OF THE WORD.

(6)   Matt. 9: 38—" Pray ye therefore the Lord of the harvest, that He will send forth laborers into His harvest."

SIXTH PROPOSITION: We should pray the Lord of the harvest that He send forth laborers into His harvest.

How often and how earnestly have you prayed this prayer ? Christ has given us a very urgent command to do so.   Have you obeyed it ?   There was never a time when there was a greater need for laborers than to-day.   The fields are white and open to the harvesters as perhaps never before in the history of the Church and the world.   The way to get the right sort of laborers is to pray for them.   There are a great many professed laborers in the Lord's harvest in these days whom He surely never sent.   The way to get the right laborers for any particular field is to pray for them.   (Compare Acts 1: 24.)   If Paul and Barnabas had taken to God in prayer the matter of whether Mark was God's man to take with them on their second missionary journey, instead of trying to settle it themselves, it is quite certain there would have never been occasion to write one of the saddest verses in the Bible.   (Acts. 15: 39.)   Many another bitter separation among brethren over ministers could have been avoided in the same way.

(7)   Col. 4: 3—" Withal praying also for us, that God would open unto us a door of utterance, to speak the mystery of Christ, for which I am also in bonds."

SEVENTH PROPOSITION: We should pray for a door of utterance to be opened for those who preach the Word.

That is the way to get open doors, ask for them. There are few more pitiable sights than men who believe God has called them to preach who can find no open door. True prayer to God to open a door, and a willingness to enter the door God opens, would solve the difficulty. If there is any place where the Gospel ought to be preached, but where there is no open door, pray for it. Paul was in a most unlikely place to find an open door when he made this request. He was in prison, but God heard the prayer and Paul entered a door to an audience to whom he is still preaching Many a door in heathen lands seemingly closed and barred against the Gospel, has been opened in the same way. Prayer to God will open more doors than appeals to human governments.

(8) Eph. 6: 19, 20, R.V.—"That utterance may be given unto me in opening my mouth, to make known with boldness the mystery of the Gospel, for which I am ambassador in chains; that in it I may speak boldly as I ought to speak."

EIGHTH PROPOSITION: We should pray for utterance to be given to ministers of the Word in opening their mouths, to make known with boldness the mystery of the Gospel, that in it they may speak boldly, as they ought to speak.

Not only open doors are needed, but open mouths to enter the opened doors. Ministers of the Word greatly need boldness in this time-serving and compromising age, and in all ages, and God's children should be in constant prayer that ministers of the Word may have this needed boldness. If even fearless Paul felt the need of prayer along this line, how much more do ordinary men need it. There are plenty to-day to criticise the timidity of preachers of the Word; how many are there who are in constant and earnest prayer that they may be given utterance, to make known with boldness the mystery of the gospel? Praying will accomplish far more along this line than grumbling and criticising. (See Acts 4: 29, 31.)

(9) 2 Thess. 3: 1, R.V.—"Finally, brethren, pray for us, that the word of the Lord may run and be glorified, even as also it is with you."

NINTH PROPOSITION: We should pray for ministers of the Word, that the Word of the Lord may run and be glorified.

We complain of the slow progress of the Word. Are we praying that it may run ?

(10) Ps. 132:9 (a)—"Let thy priests be clothed with righteousness."

TENTH PROPOSITION: We should pray that God's ministers may be clothed with righteousness.

The text applies primarily to priests, and the preacher of the Word is, strictly speaking, no more a priest than any other believer; but he does in a peculiar way represent God, and God's honor is involved in his walk. We may then quite legitimately apply to him this petition for the Old Testament representative of God. We should desire and pray for the righteous walk of those who represent God. This is sadly needed in this day when so many of them are falling into sin, and when the enemies of the Lord are so glorying in their downfall. We live in a perilous time, and we do well to pray for all saints, but especially for those in whose steadfast righteousness God is peculiarly honored, and in whose fall God is peculiarly dishonored. Let us often and earnestly pray that God's ministers be clothed with righteousness.

C. Prayers for Spiritual Blessings.

(11) Matt. 6: 12—"And forgive us our debts, as we forgive our debtors."

Ps. 25: 11—"For thy name's sake, O Lord, pardon mine iniquity; for it is great."

Ps. 51: 1—"Have mercy upon me, O God, according to thy loving-kindness: according unto the multitude of thy tender mercies blot out my transgressions."

Luke 18: 13—"And the publican, standing afar off, would not lift up so much as his eyes unto heaven, but smote upon his breast, saying, God be merciful to me a sinner."

Hos. 14: 2—"Take with you words, and turn to the Lord: say unto him, Take away all iniquity, and receive us graciously: so will we render the calves of our lips."

Ex. 34: 9—"And he said, if now I have found grace in thy sight, O Lord, let my Lord, I pray thee, go among us; for it is a stiffnecked people; and pardon our iniquity and our sin, and take us for thine inheritance."

Ex. 32: 31, 32—"And Moses returned unto the Lord, and said, Oh, this people have sinned a great sin, and have made them gods of gold.

Yet now, if thou wilt forgive their sin—and if not, blot me I pray thee, out of thy book which thou hast written."

1 Kg. 8: 47-50—"Yet if they shall bethink themselves in the land whither they were carried captives, and repent, and make supplication unto thee in the land of them that carried them captive saying, We have sinned, and have done perversely, we have committed wickedness; And so return unto thee with all their heart, and with all their soul, in the land of their enemies, which led them away captive, and pray unto thee toward their land, which thou gavest unto their fathers, the city which thou hast chosen, and the house which I have built for thy name: Then hear thou their prayer and their supplication in heaven thy dwelling place, and maintain their cause, and forgive thy people that have sinned against thee, and all their transgressions wherein they have transgressed against thee, and give them compas· sion before them who carried them captive, that they may have com· passion on them."

Acts. 8: 22—"Repent therefore of this thy wickedness, and pray God, if perhaps the thought of thine heart may be forgiven thee."

ELEVENTH PROPOSITION: *We should pray for forgiveness of our sins.*

It is sometimes said that believers ought not to pray for forgiveness of sin, but simply to confess their sins. That comes from forcing 1 Jno. 1: 9 ("If we confess our sins, he is faithful and just to forgive us our sins, and to cleanse us from all unrighteousness") beyond what it says, and contradicts the plain teachings of the Word elsewhere. It is true that God has provided pardon for all the believer's sins on the ground of the all-sufficing atoning blood of Christ, but what God has thus provided we appropriate to ourselves by confession of sin and prayer for pardon. Prayer for pardon is a proper acknowledgment to God of our guiltiness. Prayers for pardon are more frequent in the Bible than prayers for almost anything else. Of course, we ought not to pray again and again for the forgiveness of some sin that we have already laid before God, and that has thus been put away forever.

(12) Ps. 139: 23, 24—"Search me, O God, and know my heart: try me, and know my thoughts: And see if there be any wicked way in me, and lead me in the way everlasting."

TWELFTH PROPOSITION: *We should pray the Lord to search us and try us.*

The true child of God will desire that every evil way in him be searched out and brought to light. This work can never be thoroughly and satisfactorily done by any process of personal self examination. God must do it, and He does it in answer to prayer. It needs to be done frequently. Sin and selfishness and carnality and worldliness surround us as the very atmosphere we breathe, and are constantly creeping into our hearts and lives unawares. Each day should close by our going into God's presence and laying our inmost lives and outward walk before him, and asking Him to search them through and through, and to lay bare to us whatever in them is hateful to Him. This will be to us a painful, but a salutary process.

(13) Ps. 51: 7—"Purge me with hyssop, and I shall be clean: wash me, and I shall be whiter than snow."

Ps. 19: 12—"Who can understand his error? cleanse thou me from secret faults."

THIRTEENTH PROPOSITION: We should pray for cleansing from sin.

The Hebrew verb translated "cleanse" in both of these passages means to "clear" or "acquit." (See R.V. of Ps. 19: 12.) This prayer is a prayer for pardon—cleansing from guilt—rather than for cleansing from the presence of sin.

(14) Ps. 51: 10—"Create in me a clean heart, O God; and renew a right spirit within me."

FOURTEENTH PROPOSITION: We should pray God to create in us a clean heart.

It is vain for us to try to cleanse our own heart. A clean heart requires a creative act that God alone can perform. He will do it in answer to prayer. He will create in us a heart that loves righteousness and hates sin.

(15) Ps. 119: 117—"Hold thou me up, and I shall be safe: and I will have respect unto thy statutes continually."

FIFTEENTH PROPOSITION: We should pray God to hold us up.

If God holds us up we "shall be safe." We are never safe unless God does holds us up. It is a hopeless task to try to stand alone. The way is too slippery, and not one of us is sure footed.

He "that thinketh he standeth" needs to "take heed lest he fall." (1 Cor. 10: 12.) The only sure way of taking heed is by humble, honest and earnest prayer. God is abundantly able and willing to hold us up. (1 Cor. 10: 13.)

(16) Ps. 19: 13—"Keep back thy servant also from presumptuous sins; let them not have dominion over me: then shall I be upright, and I shall be innocent from the great transgression."

SIXTEENTH PROPOSITION: We should pray to be kept back from, and delivered from the dominion of, presumptuous sins.

The word here translated presumptuous, means primarily boiling, then swelling, insolent, arrogant, proud. Pride and arrogance are common to us all. God alone can keep us back from them.

(17) Ps. 119: 10—"With my whole heart have I sought thee: O let me not wander from thy commandments."

SEVENTEENTH PROPOSITION: We should pray that God will not let us wander from His commandments.

"Prone to wander" is what every child of Adam is. Unless we are constantly looking to God to keep us from wandering we are sure to go astray from the straight path of His Word. But He is very ready to keep us from wandering if we look to Him to do it.

(18) Matt. 6: 13, R.V. (a)—"And bring us not into temptation."
Mark 14: 38, R.V.—"Watch and pray, that ye enter not into temptation: the spirit indeed is willing, but the flesh is weak."

EIGHTEENTH PROPOSITION: We should pray that we be not brought, nor enter, into temptation.

This is the prayer that springs from a true knowledge of self. If we have true humility we will recognize our own weakness and this petition will be often upon our lips. No man who has any true knowledge of himself will court temptation. He will flee from it and pray God not to bring him into it. Many a man who has made seemingly great attainments in the spiritual life, has fallen because he has lost the spirit of this prayer. It is one of the most suggestive petitions of the wonderful prayer which Jesus taught His disciples.

(19) Matt. 6: 13 (b), R.V.—"But deliver us from the evil one."

NINETEENTH PROPOSITION: We should pray to be de-livered from the Evil One.

Anyone who carefully and candidly studies the New Testa-ment and human history must be convinced of the existence and awful power, cunning and malignity of the Evil One.   We must realize that our only security against his wiles and his power is in constant prayer to God.

(20)   Ps. 141: 3—"Set a watch, O LORD, before my mouth; keep the door of my lips."

TWENTIETH PROPOSITION: We should pray that the door of our lips be kept.

This is the only way in which our speech can be governed. "The tongue can no man tame: it is a restless evil" (Jas. 3: 8, R.V.), but God can govern it and will in answer to prayer

Under the immediately preceding heads (17, 18, 19, 20), we have a fourfold keeping: our lips kept from uttering what they ought not, our feet kept from wandering where they ought not, and we ourselves kept from doing what we ought not and from all the power of the enemy.

(21)   Ps. 86: 11 (a)—"Teach me thy way, O LORD; I will walk in thy truth: unite my heart to fear thy name."

Ps. 119: 33 (a)—"Teach me, O LORD, the way of thy statutes; and I will keep it unto the end."

25: 4—"Shew me thy ways, O LORD; teach me thy paths."

143: 10 (*a*)—"Teach me to do thy will; for thou art my God: thy Spirit is good; lead me into the land of uprightness."

TWENTY-FIRST PROPOSITION: We should pray Jehovah to teach us His way, the way of His statutes, His path, to do His will.

We will never know His way nor how to do His will until He Himself teaches us, and He will not teach us unless we ask Him to.   We can, however, ask Him with absolute confidence that He will teach us.

(22)   Ps. 90: 12, R.V.—"So teach us to number our days, that we may get us an heart of wisdom."

TWENTY-SECOND PROPOSITION: We should pray the Lord to so teach us to number our days that we may get us a heart of wisdom.

(23) Luke 11: 1—"And it came to pass, as he was praying in a cer
tain place, when he ceased, one of his disciples said unto him, Lord,
teach us to pray, as John also taught his disciples."

TWENTY-THIRD PROPOSITION: *We should pray to be taught
to pray.*

"We know not how to pray as we ought," but the Lord is
just as ready to teach us to-day by His Spirit (Rom. 8: 26, R. V.),
and by His Word, as He was to teach His disciples when here, by
word of mouth.

(24) Ps. 119: 18—"Open thou mine eyes, that I may behold wondrous things out of thy law."

TWENTY-FOURTH PROPOSITION: *We should pray the Lord
to open our eyes to behold wondrous things out of His own Word.*

We shall never see nor appreciate the wondrous things of
God's Word until God Himself opens our eyes to behold them.
This He does in answer to prayer. Prayer gives a keenness of
perception to spiritual beauty of which the prayerless man never
dreams. No amount of study of Hebrew or Greek, or mere intellectual study of any sort, will open spiritual eyes blinded by sin.
The prayerless eye can no more see the spiritual beauty of God's
truth revealed in the pages of the Bible, through the spectacles of
linguistic knowledge, than the blind natural eye can see the
beauties of the natural world through any spectacles no matter
how scientifically constructed. There must be natural sight to
discern natural beauty. There must be spiritual sight to discern
spiritual beauty. A man who has sight can see more beauty
without spectacles, than a sightless man can with the best glasses
ever constructed. So the man who has spiritual sight can see
more beauty in the Word of God without the aid of scholarship,
than the spiritually sightless man can with all the aids of the most
recent and most approved scholarship. There is many a modern
Bartimeus occupying a theological professorship who needs to cry:
"Lord, that I might receive my sight." (Mark 10: 51.) But they
go on, the blind leading the blind, and both are falling into the
ditch of destructive criticism. Only prayer will open our eyes to
a real appreciation of the Bible. One can see more of its beauty
and learn more of its truth in an hour at the feet of Jesus, than
in four years at the feet of men, who, professing themselves to be

wise, are become fools. (Rom. 1: 22.) Every minister and every
believer needs to take a course in that Seminary in which one
matriculates by prayer. The most ignorant and most learned
child of God will find that the Bible opens up wonderfully by
prayer. One ought never to open his Bible, even for a few
moments' study, without at least breathing to God the substance
of the Psalmist's prayer.

(25) Ps. 31: 3—"For thou art my rock and my fortress: therefore
for thy name's sake lead me, and guide me."

Ps. 27: 11—"Teach me thy way, O LORD, and lead me in a plain
path, because of mine enemies."

Ps. 139: 24—"And see if there be any wicked way in me, and lead
me in the way everlasting."

TWENTY-FIFTH PROPOSITION: We should pray to be led and guided.

Who knows the way he ought to take? Perils are on every
hand, but there is ever an unerring hand within reach to lead us
safely on. We grasp that hand by prayer. We need God's guidance at every step of the way. We cannot altogether trust the
wisest human guides. We do not need to. It is our privilege
not only to ask God to lead us, but to lead us "in a plain path."
(Ps. 27: 11.) He is ready to lead us in the way everlasting.

(26) Eph. 1: 16–19, R.V.—"Cease not to give thanks for you, making mention of you in my prayers; that the God of our Lord Jesus
Christ, the Father of glory, may give unto you a spirit of wisdom and
revelation in the knowledge of him; having the eyes of your heart enlightened that ye may know what in the hope of his calling, what the
riches of the glory of his inheritance in the saints, and what the exceeding greatness of his power to us-ward who believe, according to that
working of the strength of his might which he wrought in Christ."

TWENTY-SIXTH PROPOSITION: We should pray for a spirit of wisdom and revelation in the knowledge of our Lord Jesus Christ.

The only way to really know Christ is through that spirit of
wisdom which God gives in anwer to prayer. No amount of unaided searching will ever find Him out.

The result of receiving this "spirit of wisdom and revelation
in the knowledge of Him" will be, that we shall have the eyes of
our hearts enlightened so that we shall know what is the hope oŗ

His calling, what are the riches of the glory of His inheritance in the saints, and what is the exceeding greatness of His power to us-ward who believe.

(27) Col. 1: 9, 10, R.V.—"For this cause we also, since the day we heard it, do not cease to pray and make request for you, that ye may be filled with the knowledge of his will in all spiritual wisdom and understanding, to walk worthily of the Lord unto all pleasing, bearing fruit in every good work, and increasing in the knowledge of God."

TWENTY-SEVENTH PROPOSITION: We should pray to be filled with the knowledge of His will in all spiritual wisdom and understanding, to walk worthily of the Lord unto all pleasing, bearing fruit in every good work, and increasing in the knowledge of the Lord.

This prayer is worthy of deep and careful meditation.

(28) Eph. 3: 14, 15, R.V.—"For this cause I bow my knees unto the Father . . . that he would grant you, according to the riches of His glory, that ye may be strengthened with power through his Spirit in the inward man."

TWENTY-EIGHTH PROPOSITION: We should pray God the Father that He would grant us according to the riches of His glory, that we may be strengthened with power through the Spirit in the inner man.

The result of the inward strengthening thus granted will be: First, that Christ will dwell in our hearts through faith; second, that we, being rooted and grounded in love, shall be made strong to apprehend together with all the saints what is the breadth and length and height and depth, and to know the love of Christ which passeth knowledge; third, that we shall be filled unto all the fulness of God. (vv. 17–19.)

Surely that is a glorious and inexhaustible prayer.

(29) 1 Thess. 3: 12—"And the Lord make you to increase and abound in love one toward another, and toward all men, even as we do toward you."

TWENTY-NINTH PROPOSITION: We should pray the Lord to make us to increase and abound in love one toward another, and toward all men.

Many of us bewail our lack of love. This verse indicates

the way to get it.　Ask for it.　In this way He will establish our hearts unblamable in holiness before our God and Father, at the coming of our Lord Jesus Christ.　(V. 13.)

(30) 1 Thess. 5: 23, R.V.—"And the God of peace himself sanctify you wholly; and may your spirit and soul and body be preserved entire, without blame at the coming of our Lord Jesus Christ."

THIRTIETH PROPOSITION:　We should pray the God of peace to sanctify us wholly, and that our spirit and soul and body be preserved entire, without blame at the coming of our Lord Jesus Christ.

The word for " wholly " in this passage is an extremely strong word; it is a double word, and means "perfect in every respect," absolutely perfect.　Nothing short of absolute perfection will satisfy the true child of God.　We may have already attained a relative perfection, a condition of maturity (Phil. 3: 15; 1 Cor. 2: 6; 2 Cor. 13: 11), but we pray for absolute perfection, and in answer to our prayers it shall be ours at the coming of our Lord Jesus Christ.

(31) Ps. 27: 4, R.V.—"One thing have I asked of the LORD, that will I seek after; that I may dwell in the house of the LORD all the days of my life to behold the beauty of the LORD and to inquire in his temple."

THIRTY-FIRST PROPOSITION:　We should pray for personal nearness to and communion with God and the glad contemplation of His beauty.

This was the Psalmist's supreme request.　He longed not so much for Jehovah's gifts as for Jehovah Himself.

(32) Luke 11: 13—"If ye then, being evil, know how to give good gifts unto your children; how much more shall your heavenly Father give the Holy Spirit to them that ask him."
Acts 8: 15—"Who, when they were come down, prayed for them that they might receive the Holy Ghost."
(Compare Jno. 4: 10.　Compare 7: 37-39.)

THIRTY-SECOND PROPOSITION:　We should pray for the gift of the Holy Spirit.

(33) Ps. 51: 12 (a)—"Restore unto me the joy of thy salvation."

THIRTY-THIRD PROPOSITION: When the joy of the salvation of the Lord has been lost, we should pray for its restoration.

D. PRAYERS FOR TEMPORAL BLESSINGS.

(34) Jas. 1: 5—"If any of you lack wisdom, let him ask of God, that giveth to all men liberally, and upbraideth not; and it shall be given him."

THIRTY-FOURTH PROPOSITION: We should pray for wisdom.

This is not altogether a temporal blessing, but this promise covers wisdom in temporal matters as well as in spiritual. We have a right to ask God for wisdom in all the affairs of life (Compare Prov. 3: 6.)

(35) Matt. 6: 11—"Give us this day our daily bread."

THIRTY-FIFTH PROPOSITION: We should pray for our daily bread.

The exact meaning of the word translated "daily" is hard to determine, as it is used nowhere else, except in the parallel passage Luke 11: 3. Various translations have been suggested, such as "sufficient bread," "bread proper for our sustenance," "needful bread," "bread for the coming day." They amount to about the same thing. In any case the thought is that we are to depend upon God from day to day to supply our physical need as it arises. The petition does not give us any warrant to ask God for stores for future need, but it does invite us to ask God for sufficient supplies for each day's need as it arises. In the Old Testament (Gen. 27: 28; 1 Chron. 4: 10) we find prayers for large earthly prosperity which were answered. (Compare also Gen. 28: 3.)

(36) Jas. 5: 14-16—"Is any sick among you? let him call for the elders of the church; and let them pray over him, anointing him with oil in the name of the Lord: And the prayer of faith shall save the sick, and the Lord shall raise him up; and if he hath committed sins, they shall be forgiven him. Confess your faults one to another, and pray one for another, that ye may be healed. The effectual fervent prayer of a righteous man availeth much."

THIRTY-SIXTH PROPOSITION: We should pray to the Lord for healing in physical weakness. (Compare Ps. 103: 3.)

In Judges 16: 28, we find Samson praying for extraordinary physical strength for an extraordinary emergency. The strength was granted, and God to-day gives men extraordinary strength for extraordinary emergencies. This fact gives us no warrant for tempting God by overwork.

(37) Ps. 17: 8, 9, R.V.—"Keep me as the apple of the eye; Hide me under the shadow of thy wings, from the wicked that spoil me, my deadly enemies, that compass me about."

THIRTY-SEVENTH PROPOSITION: We may pray to God for keeping from the wicked who spoil us and the deadly enemies who compass us about.

This will afford us surer protection in a lawless city or in the perils of the foreign field than carrying firearms for self-defense. (Compare also Is. 19: 20, R.V.; Ps. 59: 1; 2 Thess. 3: 2.)

(38) Ps. 122: 6—"Pray for the peace of Jerusalem: they shall prosper that love thee."

THIRTY-EIGHTH PROPOSITION: We should pray for the peace of Jerusalem. (Compare Is. 62: 6; Ps. 51: 18.)

(39) Jer. 29: 7—"And seek the peace of the city whither I have caused you to be carried away captives, and pray unto the LORD for it; for in the peace thereof shall ye have peace."

THIRTY-NINTH PROPOSITION: We should pray for the peace of the city in which God has placed us.

It is doubtful if we can accomplish much in some cities by our votes, but there is no city in which we cannot accomplish much by our prayers. There is a place where the influence of a child of God counts more than at the polling-booth or the caucus— that is at the throne of grace. There are many to-day urging Christians to vote as they pray. The average nineteenth century Christian needs more to be urged to pray as he votes. If he were to vote as he prayed he would not vote at all. Prayer needs to be made a power which it is not in municipal affairs.

(40) 1 Jno. 5: 14—"And this is the confidence that we have in him, that, if we ask any thing according to his will, he heareth us."

FORTIETH PROPOSITION: We should pray for anything which is according to the will of God.

The question arises, How are we to know what is according to the will of God? The answer is simple: By the promises of His Word, and by the leadings of His Holy Spirit. Whenever I find God promising anything in His Word I know it is His will to give it. Whenever the Holy Spirit leads my heart to pray for anything, I know that this also is according to the will of God. (Rom. 8: 26, 27.)

(41) Phil. 4: 6, 19, R.V.—"In nothing be anxious; but in everything by prayer and supplication with thanksgiving let your requests be made known unto God. . . . And my God shall fulfill every need of yours according to his riches in glory in Christ Jesus."

FORTY-FIRST PROPOSITION: We should pray for everything we need.

It is our privilege to live a life absolutely free from anxious thought. This is only possible by taking every need, great and small, to the Father in trustful prayer. Then "the peace of God which passeth all understanding shall guard our hearts and thoughts in Christ Jesus." (V. 7.)

VII. How to Pray.

(1) Jno. 14: 13, 14—"And whatsoever ye shall ask *in my name*, that will I do, that the Father may be glorified in the Son. If ye shall ask anything in my name, I will do it."

Jno. 15: 16—"Ye have not chosen me, but I have chosen you, and ordained you, that ye should go and bring forth fruit, and that your fruit should remain; that whatsoever ye shall ask of the Father in my name, he may give it you."

FIRST PROPOSITION: We should pray in the name of Jesus Christ.

QUESTION: What does it mean to pray in the name of Christ?

ANSWER:

See Luke 24: 47—"And that repentance and remission of sins should be preached *in his name* among all nations, beginning at Jerusalem." (Compare Acts 10: 43.)

Matt. 7: 22—"Many will say to me in that day, Lord, Lord, have we not prophesied *in thy name?* and *in thy name* have cast out devils? and *in thy name* done many wonderful works?

Mark 9: 38, 39—"And John answered him, saying, Master, we saw one casting out devils *in thy name*, and he followed not us: and we forbade him, because he followed not us. But Jesus said, Forbid him not; for there is no man which shall do a miracle *in my name*, that can lightly speak evil of me."

Acts 3: 6—"Then Peter said, Silver and gold have I none; but such as I have give I thee: *In the name of Jesus Christ* of Nazareth rise up and walk."

1 Cor. 6: 11—"And such were some of you: but ye are washed, but ye are sanctified, but ye are justified *in the name of the Lord Jesus*, and by the Spirit of our God."

Eph. 5: 20—"Giving thanks always for all things unto God and the Father *in the name of our Lord Jesus Christ.*"

Col. 3: 17—"And whatsoever ye do in word or deed, do all *in the name of the Lord Jesus*, giving thanks to God and the Father by him."

Jas. 5: 14—"Is any sick among you? let him call for the elders of the church; and let them pray over him, anointing him with oil *in the name of the Lord.*"

Jno. 16: 23, R.V.—"And in that day ye shall ask me nothing. Verily, verily, I say unto you, If ye shall ask anything of the Father, *he will give it you in my name.*

To pray in the name of Christ is to pray relying upon what Christ is and has done, to pray on the ground of Jesus Christ's acceptability with the Father. When I go to a bank with my own name on the check I ask money in my own name, and if I have that much money there I get what I ask. When I go to a bank with another man's name on the check, I ask in his name, and it matters nothing whether I have money in the bank or not. If he has I get it. Jesus Christ has given to believers in Him the right to put His name upon their checks. We have nothing in the bank of Heaven, no claim upon it. He has unlimited credit there. If we ask God in our own name, on the ground of any claim we have upon Him, we will get nothing. But if we come renouncing any claim of our own and simply trusting in the claims of Christ, we will get "whatsoever we ask."

The distinctive characteristic of Christian prayer is, that it is prayer in the name of Christ. It is that which radically distinguishes Christian prayer from pagan prayer.

(2) Ps. 145: 18—"The LORD is nigh unto all them that call upon him, to all that call upon him in truth."

SECOND PROPOSITION: We should call upon the Lord "in truth."

QUESTION: What is it to call "in truth?"

ANSWER: The primary meaning of the word translated "truth" is "firmness," then "faithfulness," then "truth as opposed to falsehood," "good faith," "sincerity as opposed to hypocrisy." This latter is evidently the meaning here. (Compare Josh. 24: 14; 1 Sam. 12: 24; 1 Kg. 2: 4; Is. 10: 20.) To call upon the Lord in truth is to ask Him for that which we really desire and to really depend upon Him to give it. There is much prayer that is not in truth. People constantly ask God for things which they do not really desire. They also constantly ask Him for things which they do not expect Him to give, and for which they are not depending upon Him at all. Before asking God for anything we should ask ourselves, Do I really desire this? and then, Do I really expect God to give it? and Am I depending upon Him for it? . . . There is very much that is called prayer that is really profanity, taking the sacred and awful name of God in vain.

(3) Jer. 29: 12, 13—"Then shall ye call upon me, and ye shall go and pray unto me, and I will hearken unto you. And ye shall seek me, and find me, when ye shall search for me with all your heart."

Deut. 4: 29—"But if from thence thou shalt seek the LORD thy God, thou shalt find him, if thou seek him with all thy heart and with all thy soul."

THIRD PROPOSITION: *We should pray unto the Lord with all our heart and all our soul.*

Many prayers are sincere so far as they go, but the whole heart is not in them. We must not expect such prayers to have much power with God. When our whole heart is in the asking, His whole heart will be in the giving.

(4) Acts 12: 5, R.V.—"Peter therefore was kept in the prison: but prayer was made *earnestly* of the church unto God for him."

FOURTH PROPOSITION: *We should pray earnestly—intensely.*

The word translated "earnestly" in this passage is a very strong word. It means, literally, "stretched-out-ly." It is a pictorial word. It pictures the mind stretched out in intensity of desire. The same word is used of our Lord's praying in Luke 22: 44, where, in the intensity of His agony, "His sweat became as it were great drops of blood falling down upon the ground." It is the prayer into which the whole soul goes in an intensity of desire that lays hold upon God. These indifferent, heartless, bloodless prayers, that we offer, and soon forget what we ask for, count little with Him. Paul called upon the believers in Rome to "strive

together " with him in their prayers to God. (Rom. 15: 30.)
The word for "strive" means, literally, "to enter a contest,"
"to struggle," "to contend," "to endeavor with strenuous zeal."
It is the word from which our word "agonize" is derived. There
seems to be little praying of this sort in our day. Some fancy it
is a mark of faith to take things easy in prayer as well as elsewhere. They call it "the rest of faith." This is evidently a
form of faith the Lord Jesus had not learned. Heb. 5: 7—"Who
in the days of his flesh, when he had offered up prayers and supplications with strong crying and tears unto Him that was able to
save Him from death, and was heard in that He feared." If this
kind of praying is rare, it has power to-day when it is found, even
as it had in the olden time. (Compare Gen. 32: 26.)

(5) Rom. 12: 12, R.V.—"Rejoicing in hope; patient in tribulation;
continuing steadfastly in prayer."

Col. 4:2, R.V.—" *Continue steadfastly* in prayer, watching therein
with thanksgiving."

Luke 18: 1-8—"And he spake a parable unto them to this end, that
men ought always to pray, and *not to faint;* saying, There was in a
city a judge, which feared not God, neither regarded man: And there
was a widow in that city; and she came unto him, saying, Avenge me
of mine adversary. And he would not for a while: but afterward he
said within himself, Though I fear not God, nor regard man: yet because this woman troubleth me, I will avenge her, lest by her contin-
ual coming she weary me. And the Lord said, Hear what the unjust
judge saith. And shall not God avenge his own elect, which cry day
and night unto him, though he bear long with them? I tell you that he
will avenge them speedily. Nevertheless, when the Son of man
cometh, shall he find faith on the earth?"

*FIFTH PROPOSITION: We should pray with steadfast contin-
uance—perseverance.*

The true and earnest prayer will not give up because his
petition is not heard the first time. It is a form of spiritual laziness that tries to palm itself off as submission to the will of
God, that concludes because we do not get a thing the first time
we ask for it that it is not the will of God to give it. God often
tests our faith and our earnestness. (Compare Matt. 20: 31;
15·23-28.) Of course there are times when we can count the
thing we have asked for as already ours (Jno. 11:4; 1 Jno.
5:14, 15; Mark 11:24; R.V.), so need not continue praying.

Some say it indicates a lack of faith to ask anything a second time, and not take it by simple faith upon the first asking. But Jesus prayed three times for the same thing. (Matt. 26: 44.)

(6) Matt. 6: 7—"But when ye pray use not vain repetitions, as the heathen do: for they think that they shall be heard for their much speaking."

SIXTH PROPOSITION: We should not use vain repetitions when we pray.

The word here translated "use vain repetitions" means, literally, "to stammer or stutter," and thus to repeat the same thing over and over. The thought is, as the rest of the verse clearly shows, that we are not to keep repeating the same request over and over in the same prayer, as if God saw some merit in each time it was offered, and thus multiplied merit in the frequency with which it was repeated. It applies directly to the Roman Catholic practice of rattling off so many "Pater Nosters" or other prayers. There is repetition that comes from intense earnestness. (Contrast the 26th and 37th verses of 1 Kg. 18.)

7) Dan. 9: 3—"And I set my face unto the LORD God, to seek by prayer and supplications, *with fasting*, and sackcloth, and ashes."

Acts 14: 23—"And when they had ordained them elders in every church, and had prayed *with fasting*, they commended them to the Lord, on whom they believed."

Acts 13: 2, 3—"As they ministered to the Lord, *and fasted*, the Holy Ghost said, Separate me Barnabas and Saul for the work whereunto I have called them. And when they *had fasted and prayed*, and laid their hands on them, they sent them away."

SEVENTH PROPOSITION: We should pray with fasting.

This, of course, does not mean that we should fast every time we pray. But there are times of emergency or of special crisis in work, or in our individual lives, when men of downright earnestness will withdraw themselves from even the gratification of natural appetites, that would be perfectly proper under other circumstances, that they may give themselves up wholly to prayer. There is peculiar power in such prayer. Every great crisis in life and work should be met in that way. On the appropriateness of fasting in the present dispensation see also Matt. 9: 15—"And Jesus said unto them, can the children of the bride-chamber mourn, as long as the bridegroom is with them? But the days will come, when the bridegroom shall be taken from them, and then shall they fast."

(8) 2 Chron. 7: 14—"If my people, which are called by my name, shall humble themselves, and pray, and seek my face, and turn from their wicked ways; then will I hear from heaven, and will forgive their sin, and will heal their land."

EIGHTH PROPOSITION: In times when we have wandered from God we should pray with humiliation of self and renunciation of sin.

(9) Phil. 4: 6—"Be careful for nothing; but in every thing by prayer and supplication *with thanksgiving* let your requests be made known unto God."

Col. 4: 2—"Continue in prayer, and watch in the same *with thanksgiving.*"

NINTH PROPOSITION: We should pray with thanksgiving.

In approaching God to ask for new blessings we should not neglect to return thanks for blessings already granted.   Doubtless one reason why so many of our prayers lack power is because we have neglected to return thanks for blessings already received.   God is deeply grieved by this thoughtlessness and ingratitude of which so many of us are guilty.   (See Luke 17: 17, 18, R. V.)

(10) Matt. 18: 19, 20—"Again I say unto you, That if two of you shall agree on earth as touching anything that they shall ask, it shall be done for them of my Father which is in heaven.   For where two or three are gathered together in my name, there am I in the midst of them."

TENTH PROPOSITION: We should pray in union with others.

God everywhere emphasizes and blesses the unity of believers and there is especial power in united prayer.   Note that the two must not merely agree together to ask, they must agree *concerning the thing* that they ask—*i. e.*, there must be real unity of desire concerning this specific thing.   It is very easy to get some one to unite with me in asking some thing I desire, but still there may be no unity of desire.   The other asks it simply because I wish it.   But when the Holy Spirit leads two believing hearts to beat as one concerning some coveted blessing, then there is power,—when, for example, two persons in a community have a common desire for the outpouring of the Spirit in that community. Whenever you can find another whose heart the Holy Spirit is drawing out in the same direction He does yours, you can approach God with great confidence of obtaining this thing.

(11) Matt. 21: 22—"And all things, whatsoever ye shall ask in prayer, believing, ye shall receive."

ELEVENTH PROPOSITION: We should pray believing.

Believing in this place does not mean a general trust in God, but the unwavering expectation of getting the thing we ask. (See Jas. 1: 5, 6.) Indeed, faith goes beyond expecting and reckons the thing asked as already ours. What we thus reckon ours becomes ours in actual experimental possession. (Mark 11: 24, R.V.) God delights to honor the faith that counts on Him.

QUESTION: How can we have such faith?

ANSWER: (a) By the Word of God. (Rom. 10:17; compare Rom. 4:20, 21, R.V.) (b) By the Holy Spirit's teaching. Rom. 8:26, 27, R.V.—"And in like manner the Spirit also helpeth our infirmity: for we know not how to pray as we ought; but the Spirit himself maketh intercession for us with groanings which cannot be uttered; and he that searcheth the hearts knoweth what is in the mind of the Spirit, because he maketh intercession for the saints according to the will of God."

(12) Eph. 6: 18, R.V.—"With all prayer and supplication praying at all seasons *in the Spirit*, and watching thereunto in all perseverance and supplication for all the saints, and on my behalf."

Jude 20, R.V.—"But ye, beloved, building up yourselves on your most holy faith, praying *in the Holy Spirit*."

TWELFTH PROPOSITION: We should pray in the Holy Spirit.

All approach to God should be in the Holy Spirit's power. The true believer has no confidence in the flesh. (Phil. 3: 3, R.V.) The flesh may prompt me to pray for many things. That is no reason for asking them. I should no more follow the promptings of the flesh in praying than in sinning. I should submit every desire to the Holy Spirit, and seek His guidance in prayer. Very much prayer of many excellent people is in the flesh, and is, of course, not answered. Many a minister's longing for a revival, many a wife's longing for the conversion of her husband, is thoroughly carnal. We should pray in the Holy Spirit, under His prompting and guidance. As the disciples said to Jesus during His earthly life, "teach us to pray," so we should look constantly to the "other Paraclete" (Jno. 14: 16; 16: 7) to teach us to pray, and He will. This thought disposes of all the objections against prayer from the standpoint of its "subjecting the infinite wisdom of God to the foolish whims of finite creatures." Those who thus talk are ignorant of the Bible doctrine of prayer. It disposes also of most of the other objections that the spiritually superficial and ignorant urge against prevailing prayer.

VIII. Hindrances to Prayer; or, Why Many Prayers Are not Answered.

(1) Jas. 4: 3, R.V.—"Ye ask, and receive not, because ye ask amiss, that ye may spend it in your pleasures.'

FIRST PROPOSITION: Prayer is often unanswered because it is offered from a selfish purpose.

The chief purpose in prayer should be that God may be glorified in the answer. If we ask merely that we may receive for use in our pleasures, or for our own gratification in one way or another, we "ask amiss," and need not expect to receive what we ask. This explains why many prayers remain unanswered.

(2) Is. 59: 1, 2—"Behold the Lord's hand is not shortened, that it cannot save; neither his ear heavy, that it cannot hear: But *your iniquities* have separated between you and your God, and *your sins* have hid his face from you, that he will not hear."

SECOND PROPOSITION: Prayer is unanswered because sin separates between the one who prays and the God to whom he prays. (Compare Deut. 1: 43–45.)

If we ask God for anything and do not get it, we should not conclude necessarily that it is not God's will to give the thing we have asked. We should rather ask if there is any sin in our outward or inward lives that is separating us from God and closing His ear to our cry. So long as we hold on to sin or have any controversy with God, we cannot expect Him to heed our prayers.

(3) Ezek. 14: 3, R.V.—"Saying, Son of man, these men have *taken their idols into their heart*, and put the stumbling block of their iniquity before their face: should I be inquired of at all by them ?"

THIRD PROPOSITION: Prayer is unanswered when the one who prays takes idols into his heart.

Many professedly Christian men and women have idols in their hearts as truly as the ancient Israelites. They do not recognize these things as idols, but they are. Anything upon which we have set our heart, and would not give up for Christ's sake, is an idol and hinders prayer. God often calls our attention to the fact that we have an idol by not answering our prayer, and thus leading us to ask why our prayer is not answered. Thus we discover the idol, put it away and God hears our prayer.

(4) Mark 11: 25, 26—"And when ye stand praying, forgive, if ye have aught against any; that your Father also which is in heaven may forgive you your trespasses. But if ye do not forgive neither will your Father which is in heaven forgive your trespasses."

FOURTH PROPOSITION: Prayer is unanswered because we do not forgive those against whom we have something.

This is one of the commonest hindrances to prayer. Far more common than we think. Prayer is answered on the basis that our sins are forgiven, but God cannot deal with us on the basis of forgiveness while we are harboring ill-will against those who have wronged us. Anyone who is harboring a grudge against another has fast closed the ear of God against his own cry.

(5) Jas. 1: 5-7, R.V.—"But if any of you lacketh wisdom, let him ask of God, who giveth to all liberally and upbraideth not; and it shall be given him. But let him ask in faith, nothing doubting: for he that doubteth is like the surge of the sea driven by the wind and tossed. For let not that man think that he shall receive anything of the Lord."

FIFTH PROPOSITION: Prayers are unanswered because of our unbelief—i. e., because we question whether we shall receive that which God has promised.

God demands that we shall believe His Word absolutely To question it is to make Him a liar. Many do this when they plead his promises, and it is no wonder that their prayers are not answered.

(6) 1 Pet. 3: 6, 7—"Even as Sarah obeyed Abraham, calling him Lord; whose daughters ye are, as long as ye do well, and are not afraid with any amazement, likewise, ye husbands, dwell with them ac-

cording to knowledge, giving honor unto the wife, as unto the weaker vessel, and as being heirs together of the grace of life; that your prayers be not hindered.

SIXTH PROPOSITION: The prayers of husbands are hindered because they do not render to their wives that considerate regard which is their due.

It is doubtless also true that the prayers of wives are hindered because of their failure in duty toward their husbands. If husbands and wives should seek diligently for the cause of their unanswered prayers, they would often find it in their relations to one another and actions toward one another as husband and wife.

IX. The Results of Prayer.

(1) Jas. 5: 16, R.V.—"Confess therefore your sins one to another, and pray one for another, that ye may be healed. The supplication of a righteous man availeth much in its working."

FIRST PROPOSITION: Prayer availeth much in its working.

How much?

Vv. 17: 18—"Elijah was a man of like passions with us, and he prayed fervently that it might not rain; and it rained not on the earth for three years and six months. And he prayed again; and the heaven gave rain, and the earth brought forth her fruit."

1 Kg. 18: 37, 38—"Hear me, O Lord, hear me, that this people may know that thou, Lord, art God, and that thou hast turned their heart back again. Then the fire of the Lord fell, and consumed the burnt offering, and the wood, and the stones, and the dust, and licked up the water that was in the trench." (See also passages under Section VI.)

The great secret of the poverty and powerlessness of the average believer and average church is found in Jas. 4: 2—"Ye have not because ye ask not."

(2) Jno. 14: 13, 14—"And whatsoever ye shall ask in my name, that will I do, that the Father may be glorified in the Son. If ye ask anything in my name, I will do it."

SECOND PROPOSITION: Prayer secures the very thing asked.

(3) 1 Jno. 3: 22—"And whatsoever we ask, we receive of him, because we keep his commandments, and do those things that are pleasing in his sight.

THIRD PROPOSITION: Whatsoever we ask from God we receive when we keep His commandments and do the things that are pleasing in his sight.

(4) 1 Jno. 5: 14, 15—"And this is the confidence that we have in him, that, if we ask anything according to his will, he heareth us: And if we know that he hear us, whatsoever we ask, we know that we have the petitions that we desired of him."

FOURTH PROPOSITION: If we ask anything according to His will He hears us, and when our prayer is heard the thing asked is ours.

CHAPTER XV.

THANKSGIVING.

The importance of this subject will be manifest to anyone who will note the space occupied in the Bible by thanksgiving and praise.

I. The Duty.

(1) Ps. 92: 1, 2, 4—"It is a good thing to give thanks unto the LORD, and to sing praises unto thy name, O Most High: To shew forth thy loving kindness in the morning, and thy faithfulness every night, . . . For thou, LORD, hast made me glad through thy work: I will triumph in the works of thy hands."

FIRST PROPOSITION: It is a good thing to give thanks unto the Lord.

The Lord's dealings with us make thanksgiving and praise on our part the only fitting thing. In the 107th Psalm the Psalmist burst out four times into the cry: "Oh that men would praise the LORD for his goodness, and for his wonderful works to the children of men." As we reflect to-day upon the wondrous goodness of God to men on the one hand, and, on the other hand, upon the little thought and strength and time not only men, but even the average Christian, gives to thanksgiving, we may well utter the same cry.

(2) Ps. 100: 4—"Enter into his gates with thanksgiving, and into his courts with praise: be thankful unto him and bless his name."

Eph. 5: 4—"Neither filthiness, nor foolish talking, nor jesting, which are not convenient: but rather giving of thanks."

Col. 3: 15, 17—"And let the peace of God rule in your hearts, to the which also ye are called in one body; and be ye thankful."

1 Thess. 5: 18—"In everything give thanks: for this is the will of God in Christ Jesus concerning you."

SECOND PROPOSITION: We are commanded again and again to give thanks.

The failure to return thanks unto God " who daily loadeth us with benefits " is just as distinct and definite disobedience to God's commands as to steal or to murder.

(3) Ps. 69: 30, 31—" I will praise the name of God with a song, and will magnify him with thanksgiving. This also shall please the LORD better than an ox or bullock that hath horns and hoofs."

THIRD PROPOSITION: The rendering of thanks unto God is more acceptable to Him than costly sacrifices.

We cannot all bring expensive offerings to God, but we can all bring the more pleasing offering of true and hearty thanksgiving.

(4) Luke 24: 52, 53—"And they worshipped him, and returned to Jerusalem with great joy: and were continually in the temple, praising and blessing God. Amen."

Acts 2: 46, 47—" And they, continuing daily with one accord in the temple, and breaking bread from house to house, did eat their meat with gladness and singleness of heart, praising God, and having favor with all the people. And the LORD added to the church daily such as should be saved."

FOURTH PROPOSITION: The early Christians gave themselves continually to praise and thanksgiving.

Thanksgiving and praise were among the most noticeable and notable characteristics of their lives. The same thing is true of the holy men and women of the Old Testament. I can not think of a good person, mentioned at all prominently in the Bible, of whom it is not definitely recorded that he thanked God for some act of his goodness.   The Bible is very largely taken up with praise and thanksgiving.   (Look up the words " thank," " praise " and " bless " and synonymous words.   Note the Epistles of Paul.)

(5) Jno. 11: 41—"Then they took away the stone from the place where the dead was laid. And Jesus lifted up his eyes, and said, Father I thank Thee that Thou hast heard me."

Matt. 11: 25—" At that time Jesus answered and said, I thank thee, O Father, Lord of heaven and earth, because thou hast hid these things from the wise and prudent, and hast revealed them unto babes."

FIFTH PROPOSITION: The Lord Jesus Christ returned thanks.

These are only specimen passages, but again and again do we get glimpses into the life of Christ that show us that it was a

life of abounding thankfulness to God. Christ's manner of returning thanks at the simplest meal was so noticeable that two of His
disciples recognized Him by this after His resurrection. (Luke
24: 30, 31, 35.)

(6) Col. 1: 9, 12—"For this cause we also, since the day we heard
it, do not cease to pray for you, and to desire that ye might be filled
with the knowledge of his will in all wisdom and spiritual understanding. . . . Giving thanks unto the Father, which hath made us meet
to be partakers of the inheritance of the saints in light."

SIXTH PROPOSITION: *Giving thanks unto the Father is one
of the inevitable results of being "filled with the knowledge of
His will in all wisdom and spiritual understanding."*

(7) Eph. 5: 18–20—"And be not drunk with wine, wherein is excess; but be filled with the Spirit; Speaking to yourselves in psalms
and hymns and spiritual songs, singing and making melody in your
heart to the Lord; giving thanks always for all things unto God and
the Father in the name of our Lord Jesus Christ."

SEVENTH PROPOSITION: *Giving thanks is one of the inevitable results of being filled with the Spirit.*

(8) 2 Cor. 9: 12—"For the administration of this service not only
supplieth the want of the saints, but is abundant also by many thanks-
givings unto God."

2 Cor. 4: 15, R.V.—"For all things are for your sakes, that the
grace, being multiplied through the many, may cause the thanksgiving
to abound unto the glory of God."

EIGHTH PROPOSITION: *The rendering of thanks brings glory
to God.*

(9) Jno. 11: 41, 42—"Then they took away the stone from the place
where the dead was laid. And Jesus lifted up his eyes, and said,
Father, I thank thee that thou hast heard me. And I knew that thou
hearest me always: but because of the people which stand by I said it,
that they may believe that thou hast sent me."

NINTH PROPOSITION: *The rendering of thanks leads other
men to believe.*

(10) Luke 17: 15–18—"And one of them, when he saw that he was
healed, turned back, and with a loud voice glorified God. And fell
down on his face at his feet, giving him thanks; and he was a Samaritan. And Jesus answering said, Were there not ten cleansed? But

where are the nine? There are not found that returned to give glory to God save this stranger. And he said unto him, Arise, go thy way: thy faith hath made thee whole."

TENTH PROPOSITION: *The failure to return thanks for definite blessings received is a manifestation of ingratitude that surprises and grieves Jesus Christ.*

(11) Rom. 1: 18, 21, R.V. (Note also following vv. 24, 26)—"For the wrath of God is revealed from heaven against all ungodliness and unrighteousness of men, who hold down the truth in unrighteousness. . . . Because that, knowing God, they glorified him not as God, *neither gave thanks;* but became vain in their reasonings, and their senseless heart was darkened."

ELEVENTH PROPOSITION: *The failure to return thanks is one of the principal reasons for the revelation of the wrath of God from heaven, and for giving men up to a reprobate mind.*

(12) Phil. 4: 6—"Be careful for nothing; but in everything by prayer and supplication with thanksgiving let your requests be made known to God."

TWELFTH PROPOSITION: *Thanksgiving is a necessary accompaniment of prevailing prayer.*

II. To Whom to Give Thanks.

(1) Ps. 75: 1—"Unto thee, O God, do we give thanks, unto thee do we give thanks: for that thy name is near thy wonderous works declare."

1 Cor. 15: 57—"But thanks be to God, which giveth us the victory through our Lord Jesus Christ."

FIRST PROPOSITION: *Thanks should be given to God.*

(2) Col. 1: 12—"Giving thanks unto the Father, which hath made us meet to be partakers of the inheritance of the saints in light."
Eph. 5: 20, R.V.—"Giving thanks always for all things in the name of our Lord Jesus Christ to God, even the Father."

SECOND PROPOSITION: *Thanks should be given to God, even the Father.*

(3) Eph. 1: 3—"Blessed be the God and Father of our Lord Jesus Christ, who hath blessed us with all spiritual blessings in heavenly places in Christ."

THIRD PROPOSITION: Thanks should be given to the God and Father of our Lord Jesus Christ.

(4) 1 Tim. 1: 12, R.V.—"I thank him that enabled me, even Christ Jesus our Lord, for that he counted me faithful, appointing me to his service."

FOURTH PROPOSITION: Thanks should be rendered to Christ Jesus our Lord.

In the overwhelming majority of instances, however, in the New Testament, to say nothing of the Old, the offering of thanks is to God the Father. It is through Jesus Christ. The reason for this seems to be that God the Father is the original source of all our blessings. Even Jesus is His gift. (Jno. 3: 16; Rom. 5, 8.) While all the Father's love is manifested to us in Christ, still it is the Father's love. We need to recognize the Father back of Christ as the source of all. The conception of God as only brought to love us because of what Christ did, is utterly foreign to the thought and life of the New Testament. It is true that God, being holy, can deal with sinners in mercy only on the ground of the propitiatory work of Christ, but it is God Himself who furnishes the propitiation: 1 Jno. 4: 10—"Herein is love, not that we loved God, but that he loved us, and sent his son to be the propitiation for our sins." The Son came, as He so often said, to do the Father's will.

III. Who Can Render Acceptable Thanks.

(1) Ps. 107: 1, 2—"O give thanks unto the LORD, for he is good: for his mercy endureth for ever. Let the redeemed of the LORD say so, whom he hath redeemed from the hand of the enemy."

FIRST PROPOSITION: The redeemed of the Lord can render acceptable thanks.

(2) 1 Tim. 4: 3—"Forbidding to marry, and commanding to abstain from meats, which God hath created to be received with thanksgiving *of them which believe and know the truth.*"

SECOND PROPOSITION: Those who believe and know the truth can render acceptable thanks

The body of believers "a spiritual house, an holy priest-hood" exists for this purpose, "to offer up spiritual sacrifices acceptable to God through Jesus Christ." (1 Pet. 2: 5, R.V. Compare Heb. 13: 15, R. V.)

(3) Prov. 15: 8—"The sacrifice of the wicked is an abomination to the Lord: but the prayer of the upright is his delight."

(Compare Heb. 13: 15—"By him therefore let us offer the sacrifice of praise to God continually, that is, the fruit of our lips, giving thanks to his name.")

THIRD PROPOSITION: The wicked cannot render to God acceptable thanksgiving. Their sacrifice is an abomination to the Lord.

IV. For What to Render Thanks.

(1) Luke 2: 27, 28—"And he came by the Spirit into the temple: and when the parents brought in the child Jesus, to do for him after the custom of the law, then took he him up in his arms, and blessed God, and said."

Luke 2: 36–38—"And there was one Anna, a prophetess, the daughter of Phanuel, of the tribe of Aser: she was of a great age, and had lived with a husband seven years from her virginity; and she was a widow of about fourscore and four years, which departed not from the temple, but served God with fastings and prayers night and day. And she coming in that instant gave thanks likewise unto the Lord, and spake of him to all them that looked for redemption in Jerusalem."

FIRST PROPOSITION: We should render thanks for Jesus Christ.

As all our blessings center in Him and come through Him, our thanks to God will be for Him.

(2) Ps. 103: 1, 3—"Bless the Lord, O my soul: and all that is within me, bless his holy name. . . . Who forgiveth all thine iniquities."

SECOND PROPOSITION: We should render thanks for forgiveness of iniquities.

(3) Rom. 7: 24, 25—"O wretched man that I am! who shall deliver me from the body of this death? I thank God through Jesus Christ our Lord." (See context.)

THIRD PROPOSITION: We should render thanks for deliverance from the power of the law of sin and death.

(4) Ps. 103: 3—"Who healeth all thy diseases."

FOURTH PROPOSITION: We should render thanks for the healing of our diseases. (Compare the lepers Luke 17: 15–18.)

(5) 1 Cor. 15: 57 (see context)—"But thanks be to God, which giveth us the victory through our Lord Jesus Christ."

FIFTH PROPOSITION: We should render thanks for victory through our Lord Jesus Christ over sin and death and the grave.

(6) 1 Pet. 1: 3, R.V.—"Blessed be the God and Father of our Lord Jesus Christ, who according to his great mercy begat us again unto a lively hope by the resurrection of Jesus Christ from the dead."

SIXTH PROPOSITION: We should render thanks for a new birth unto a living hope by the resurrection of Christ.

(7) Col. 1: 12—"Giving thanks unto the Father, which hath made us meet to be partakers of the inheritance of the saints in light."

SEVENTH PROPOSITION: We should render thanks for being made meet to be partakers of the inheritance of the saints in light.

(8) 2 Cor. 1: 3, 4—"Blessed be God, even the Father of our Lord Jesus Christ, the Father of mercies, and the God of all comfort; who comforteth us in all our tribulation, that we may be able to comfort them which are in trouble, by the comfort wherewith we ourselves are comforted of God."

EIGHTH PROPOSITION: We should render thanks for comfort in all our tribulations.

(9) Jno. 11: 41—"Then they took away the stone from the place where the dead was laid. And Jesus lifted up his eyes and said, Father, I thank thee that thou hast heard me.'

NINTH PROPOSITION: We should render thanks for answered prayer.

Every answered prayer should be met by definite thanksgiving to God. We never forget to thank anyone but God for granted requests.

(10) Dan. 2: 23—"I thank thee, and praise thee, O thou God of my fathers, who hast given me wisdom and might, and hast made known unto me now what we desired of thee: for thou hast now made known unto us the king's matter."

TENTH PROPOSITION: We should render thanks for wisdom and might.

(11) 1 Tim. 1: 12—"And I thank Christ Jesus our Lord, who hath enabled me, for that he counted me faithful, putting me into the ministry."

ELEVENTH PROPOSITION: We should render thanks for enabling or empowering for service.

(12) 1 Tim. 4: 3—"Forbidding to marry, and commanding to abstain from meats, which God hath created to be received with thanksgiving of them which believe and know the truth."

TWELFTH PROPOSITION: We should render thanks for food.

It is remarkable how frequent are the references in the New Testament to thanksgiving for food. Over and over again attention is called, in the brief record of the life of Christ, to His returning thanks for food—even when it consisted of five cheap barley loaves and two small fishes for a great company. (Jno. 6: 23.)

(13) 1 Cor. 14: 18—"I thank my God, I speak with tongues more than ye all."

THIRTEENTH PROPOSITION: We should render thanks for spiritual gifts.

(14) Acts 28: 15—"And from thence, when the brethren heard of us, they came to meet us as far as Appii Forum, and the three Taverns; whom when Paul saw, he thanked God and took courage."

FOURTEENTH PROPOSITION: We should render thanks for Christian companions and fellowship.

(15) Rom. 6: 17—"But God be thanked, that ye were the servants of sin, but ye have obeyed from the heart that form of doctrine which was delivered you."

FIFTEENTH PROPOSITION: We should render thanks for the conversion of others.

(16) 2 Thess. 2: 13—"But we are bound to give thanks always to God for you, brethren beloved of the Lord, because God hath from the beginning chosen you to salvation through sanctification of the Spirit and belief of the truth."

SIXTEENTH PROPOSITION: We should render thanks for the elect and their salvation.

(17) 1 Cor. 1: 4 (see context)—"I thank my God always on your behalf, for the grace of God which is given you by Jesus Christ."

SEVENTEENTH PROPOSITION: We should render thanks for the grace bestowed upon others.

(18) Rom. 1: 8—" First I thank my God through Jesus Christ for you all, that your faith is spoken of throughout the whole world."

Eph. 1: 15, 16—"Wherefore I also, after I heard of your faith in the Lord Jesus, and love unto all the saints, cease not to give thanks for you, making mention of you in my prayers."

Col. 1: 3, 4—"We give thanks to God and the Father of our Lord Jesus Christ, praying always for you, since we heard of your faith in Christ Jesus and the love which ye have to all the saints."

1 Thess. 1: 2, 3—" We give thanks to God for you all, making mention of you in our prayers; remembering without ceasing your work of faith and labor of love, and patience of hope in our Lord Jesus Christ in the sight of God and our Father."

2 Thess. 1: 3, R.V.—"We are bound to give thanks to God always for you, brethren, even as it is meet, for that your faith groweth exceedingly, and the love of each one of you all toward one another aboundeth."

Philemon 4: 5—"I thank my God, making mention of thee always in my prayers, hearing of thy love and faith, which thou hast toward the Lord Jesus, and toward all saints."

EIGHTEENTH PROPOSITION: We should render thanks for the faith and love (and patience of hope) of others.

This seems to have been one of the most frequent occasions of thanksgiving with Paul.   Whenever he heard of the faith and love of an individual or church, his heart seems to have gone out at once in thanksgiving to God

(19) 1 Thess. 3: 8, 9—"For now we live, if ye stand fast in the Lord.   For what thanks can we render to God again for you, for all the joy wherewith we joy for your sakes before our God."

NINETEENTH PROPOSITION: We should render thanks for the steadfastness of the love of others.

(20) 1 Thess. 2: 13—"For this cause also thank we God without ceasing, because, when ye received the word of God which ye heard of us, ye received it not as the word of men, but, as it is in truth, the word of God, which effectually worketh also in you that believe."

TWENTIETH PROPOSITION: We should render thanks for the reception on the part of believers of God's Word as the word of God.

(21) 1 Tim. 2: 1—"I exhort therefore, that, first of all, supplications, prayers, intercessions, and giving of thanks, be made for all men."

TWENTY-FIRST PROPOSITION: We should render thanks for all men.

(22) Phil. 4: 6—"Be careful for nothing: but *in everything* by prayer and supplication with thanksgiving let your requests be made known unto God."

1 Thess. 5: 18—"*In everything* give thanks: for this is the will of God in Christ Jesus concerning you."

Eph. 5: 20—"Giving thanks always *for all things* unto God and the Father in the name of our Lord Jesus Christ."

TWENTY-SECOND PROPOSITION: We should render thanks in everything and for all things.

How can we?

Rom. 8: 28—"And we know that all things work together for good to them that love God, to them that are called according to his purpose."

There is no greater, nor more simple secret of a life of uninterrupted and ever-increasing joyfulness, than rendering thanks for all things. Our disappointments become "His appointments," our sorrows become joys, and our tears become rainbows.

V. When to Give Thanks.

(1) Ps. 92: 1, 2—"It is a good thing to give thanks unto the LORD, and to sing praises unto thy name, O Most High: to show forth thy loving-kindness in the morning, and thy faithfulness every night."

FIRST PROPOSITION: We should give thanks in the morning and every night.

Each day should be begun and closed with thanksgiving to God. The thought of God's goodness to us should rule our lives. With this thought we should arise every morning to work and lie down every night to sleep.

(2) Ps. 119: 62—"At midnight I will rise to give thanks unto thee because of thy righteous judgments."

SECOND PROPOSITION: We should give thanks at midnight.

The judgments here spoken of are the judgments of God's word. (Compare vv. 7, 13, 30, 39, 43, 53, 75, 102, 106, 108, 120, 137, 149, 156, 160, 164, 175, eighteen times, and all in this Psalm.) We should be so taken up with the excellence of God's Word that we awake in the night to thank Him for it.

(3) 1 **Tim.** 4: 4, 5—"For every creature of God is good, and noth‑ ing to be refused, if it be received with thanksgiving: For it is sancti‑ fied by the word of God and prayer."

Rom. 14: 6—"He that eateth, eateth to the Lord, for he giveth God thanks; and he that eateth not, to the Lord he eateth not, and giveth God thanks." (Compare Acts 27: 35.)

THIRD PROPOSITION: We should give thanks every time we eat.

(4) Phil. 4: 6—"Be careful for nothing; but in every thing by prayer and supplication with thanksgiving let your requests be made known unto God."

Col. 4: 2—"Continue in prayer, and watch in the same with thanksgiving."

FOURTH PROPOSITION: We should give thanks every time we pray.

Thanksgiving for prayers answered and blessings granted in the past, can alone prepare for new answers and new blessings. Furthermore, definite thanks for blessings already received will strengthen our faith to appropriate larger blessings.

(5) Col. 3: 17—"And whatsoever ye do in word or deed, do all in the name of the Lord Jesus, giving thanks to God and the Father by him."

FIFTH PROPOSITION: We should give thanks in all our do‑ ing in word or in deed.

As all the doing of a Christian is in Christ's name and in Christ's strength, it should all be done with thanksgiving to Him who gives us the name and strength in which to do it. This ap‑ plies to all our activities, and not to those alone which we ordi‑ narily call Christian work. All work of one abiding in Christ is Christian work, the work of the man digging a ditch or of the woman at the washtub, and it should all be done in Christ's name and with thanksgiving to God. There is no drudgery in a life thus lived. The whole of life becomes a song, a psalm of praise.

(6) 1 Thess. 5: 18—"In every thing give thanks: for this is the will of God in Christ Jesus concerning you."

SIXTH PROPOSITION: We should return thanks in everything.

(7) Eph. 5: 20—"Giving thanks always for all things unto God and the Father in the name of our Lord Jesus Christ."

SEVENTH PROPOSITION: *We should give thanks always.*

As we are to pray without ceasing, so are we to return thanks always. There cannot, of course, always be the word of thanks on our lips, but there can always be the heart going up toward God in gratitude and praise. Thanksgiving and prayer should be the atmosphere in which we live, the air we breathe, and just as a man keeps right on breathing while doing a thousand other things without ever stopping to think how he does it, so we can keep on praising and thanking, and praying while doing a thousand other things without ever stopping to think how we do it. For example, a man can be preaching in the power of the Holy Spirit, and throwing all the energy of his soul and body into his preaching, and all the time be thanking God for the power in which he is preaching. This does not hinder but increases the inflow of the power. There must, of course, be times in which we give ourselves up exclusively to prayer and thanksgiving, by which this perpetual atmosphere of prayer and thanksgiving are maintained. There should be ejaculatory thanks as well as ejaculatory prayer. But we should bless God at all times: His praise should be continually in our mouths. (Ps. 32: 1.)

(8) Ps. 89: 1—"I will sing of the mercies of the LORD forever: with my mouth will I make known thy faithfulness to all generations."

EIGHTH PROPOSITION: *We should give thanks forever.*

Thanksiving and praise will be a large part of the occupation of Heaven. Rev. 5: 8–14:

"And when he had taken the book, the four beasts and four and twenty elders fell down before the Lamb, having every one of them harps, and golden vials full of odours, which are the prayers of saints. And they sung a new song saying, Thou art worthy to take the book, and to open the seals thereof: for thou wast slain, and hast redeemed us to God by thy blood out of every kindred, and tongue, and people, and nation: And hast made us unto our God kings and priests, and we shall reign on the earth. And I beheld, and I heard the voice of many angels round about the throne, and the beasts, and the elders: and the number of them was ten thousand times ten thousand, and thousands of thousands; saying with a loud voice, Worthy is the Lamb that was slain to receive power, and riches, and wisdom, and strength, and honor, and glory, and blessing. And every creature which is in heaven, and on the earth, and under the earth, and such as are in the sea, and all that are in them, heard I saying, Blessing, and honor, and glory,

and power, be unto him that sitteth upon the throne, and unto the
Lamb for ever and ever. And the four beasts said, Amen. And the
four and twenty elders fell down and worshipped him that liveth for
ever and ever."

Rev. 7: 11-17—"And all the angels stood round about the throne,
and about the elders and the four beasts, and fell before the throne on
their faces, and worshipped God, Saying, Amen: Blessing, and glory,
and wisdom, and thanksgiving, and honor, and power, and might, be
unto our God for ever and ever. Amen. And one of the elders
answered, saying unto me, What are these which are arrayed in white
robes? and whence came they? And I said unto him, Sir, thou
knowest. And he said to me, These are they which came out of great
tribulation, and have washed their robes, and made them white in the
blood of the Lamb. Therefore are they before the throne of God, and
serve him day and night in his temple: and he that sitteth on the
throne shall dwell among them. They shall hunger no more, neither
thirst any more; neither shall the sun light on them, nor any heat.
For the Lamb which is in the midst of the throne shall feed them, and
shall lead them unto living fountains of water: and God shall wipe
away all tears from their eyes."

Heavenly life will be a perpetual jubilee. We can have an
unceasing year of jubilee down here in which to prepare for the
year of jubilee that never ends.

VI. How to Return Thanks.

(1) Eph. 5: 20—"Giving thanks always for all things unto God
and the Father *in the name of our Lord Jesus Christ*."

Rom. 1: 8—"First, I thank my God *through Jesus Christ* for you
all, that your faith is spoken of throughout the whole world."

Col. 3: 17; R.V.—"And whatsoever ye do, in word or in deed, do
all *in the name of the Lord Jesus*, giving thanks to God the Father
through him.

*FIRST PROPOSITION: We should render our thanks to God
in the name of Christ, or through Christ.*

Christ is man's only way of approach to God. (Jno. 14: 6.)
As there was no way of approach to God in the Old Testament
except on the ground of the shed blood, so there is no way of
approach to the real holy of holies except by the way of the rent
vail of Christ's flesh and his outpoured blood. (Heb. 10: 19, 20.)
Christ has access to God, and we only in His name and through
Him. God receives no offering of thanks from men except that
offered in Christ's name. The man who has been the vilest sinner
can offer up thanks to God in Jesus' name that are the sweetest

incense to Him the man whose life has been most exemplary can offer no acceptable thanks except in the same name and way. This shows the utter impossibility of a union thanksgiving service between an intelligent believer in Christ and a Jew or a Unitarian. There is no common way of approach to God.

(2) Eph. 5: 18–20—"And be not drunk with wine, wherein is excess; but *be filled with the Spirit;* speaking to yourselves in psalms and hymns and spiritual songs, singing and making melody in your heart to the Lord; giving thanks always for all things unto God and the Father in the name of our Lord Jesus Christ."

SECOND PROPOSITION: We should render our thanks to God in the Spirit's power.

The Holy Spirit alone can lead to acceptable thanks. It is the thanks that God the Spirit inspires, that are offered through God the Son; that God the Father accepts. No strange fire must be brought before God. We should cast ourselves upon the Holy Spirit to teach us to return thanks aright.

(3) 1 Kg. 8: 15, 20, 22–24—"And he said, Blessed be the LORD God of Israel, which spake with his mouth unto David my father, and hath with his hand fulfilled it, saying. . . . And the LORD hath performed his word that he spake, and I am risen up in the room of David my father, and sit on the throne of Israel, as the LORD promised, and have built an house for the name of the LORD God of Israel. . . . And Solomon stood before the altar of the LORD in the presence of all the congregation of Israel, and spread forth his hands toward heaven: And he said, LORD God of Israel, there is no God like thee, in heaven above, or on earth beneath, who keepest covenant and mercy with thy servants that walk before thee with all their heart: who has kept with thy servant David my father that thou promisedst him: thou spakest also with thy mouth, and hast fulfilled it with thine hand, as it is this day."

Jno. 11: 41—"Then they took away the stone from the place where the dead was laid. And Jesus lifted up his eyes, and said, Father, I thank thee that thou hast heard me."

THIRD PROPOSITION: We should give thanks definitely.

Definite acknowledgment of definite blessings received. (The above are only illustrative instances. Such instances abound in the Bible.)

(4) Col. 2: 6, 7—"As ye have therefore received Christ Jesus the Lord, so walk ye in him: Rooted and built up in him, and stablished

in the faith, as ye have been taught, abounding therein with thanks-giving."

FOURTH PROPOSITION: We should render thanks abound-ingly. No mean, niggardly, grudging rendering of thanks.

(5) 1 Thess. 2: 13—"For this cause also thank we God *without ceasing*, because when ye received the word of God which ye heard of us, ye received it not as the word of men, but, as it is in truth, the word of God, which effectually worketh also in you that believe."

FIFTH PROPOSITION: We should render thanks without ceas-ing.

CHAPTER XVI.

WORSHIP.

L. What Is Worship?

Ex. 4: 31—"And the people believed: and when they heard that the LORD had visited the children of Israel, and that he had looked upon their afflictions, then *they bowed their heads and worshipped.*"

Ex. 24: 1—"And the LORD said unto Moses, Come up unto the LORD, thou, and Aaron, Nadab, and Abihu, and seventy of the elders of Israel; and worship ye afar off."

Ex. 33: 10—"And all the people saw the cloudy pillar stand at the tabernacle door; and all the people rose up and worshipped, every man in his tent door."

Ex. 34: 5-8—"And the LORD descended in the cloud, and stood with him there, and proclaimed the name of the LORD. And the LORD passed by before him, and proclaimed, The LORD, The LORD God, merciful and gracious, longsuffering and abundant in goodness and truth, keeping mercy for thousands, forgiving iniquity and transgression and sin, and that will by no means clear the guilty; visiting the iniquity of the fathers upon the children, and upon the children's children, unto the third and to the fourth generation. And Moses made haste, and *bowed his head toward the earth and worshipped.*"

Josh. 5: 13, 14—"And it came to pass, when Joshua was by Jericho, that he lifted up his eyes and looked, and, behold, there stood a man over against him with his sword drawn in his hand: and Joshua went unto him, and said unto him, Art thou for us, or for our adversaries? And he said, Nay; but as captain of the host of the LORD am I now come. *And Joshua fell on his face to the earth, and did worship*, and said unto him, What saith my LORD unto his servant?"

2 Chron. 7: 3—"And when all the children of Israel saw how the fire came down, and the glory of the LORD upon the house, *they bowed themselves with their faces to the ground upon the pavement, and worshipped*, and praised the LORD, saying, For he is good; for his mercy endureth for ever."

2 Chron. 20: 18—"And Jehoshaphat bowed his head with his face to the ground: and all Judah and the inhabitants of Jerusalem *fell before the* LORD, *worshipping the* LORD."

2 Chron. 29: 29—"And when they had made an end of offering, the king and all that were present with him *bowed themselves and worshipped.*"

Neh. 8: 6—"And Ezra blessed the LORD, the great God. And all the people answered, Amen, Amen, with lifting up their hands: and *they bowed their heads and worshipped* the LORD with their faces to the ground."

PROPOSITION: Worship is the soul bowing itself in adoring contemplation before the object worshiped. To worship God is to bow before God in adoring contemplation of Himself.

The word worship is commonly used in a very loose and unscriptural manner—*e. g.*, we speak of the whole service of Lord's Day morning and evening as "public worship," but there is a great deal in it that is not worship. Reading the Bible and meditating upon it is not worship. It may lead to worship but it is not worship. Listening to a sermon is not worship. Praying is not worship. It may be, and should be, accompanied by worship; but it is not worship. Singing is not necessarily nor generally worship. There are hymns which, if sung intelligently and in the proper spirit, would be worship, but they are comparatively few in the hymnology of the day. Worship is a definite act of a character very clearly defined in the Bible. It is, as said, the soul bowing before God in adoring contemplation of Himself. The root of the Hebrew word translated "worship" in the Old Testament means "to bow down." It has been well said "in prayer we are occupied with our needs, in thanksgiving we are occupied with our blessings, in worship we are occupied with Himself."

II. Whom to Worship.

(1) Matt. 4: 10—"Then saith Jesus unto him, Get thee hence, Satan: for it is written, *Thou shalt worship the Lord thy God*, and him only shalt thou serve."

FIRST PROPOSITION: We should worship the Lord our God and Him alone.

We may admire men, we must worship God alone. No holy man, saint, nor angel should be worshiped.

Acts 10: 25, 26, R.V.—"And when it came to pass that Peter entered, Cornelius met him, and fell down at his feet, and worshipped him. But Peter raised him up, saying, Stand up; I myself also am a man."

Rev. 22: 8, 9, R.V.—"And I John am he that heard and saw these things. And when I heard and saw, I fell down to worship before the feet of the angel which shewed me these things. And he saith unto me, See thou do it not: I am a fellow servant with thee and with thy brethren the prophets, and with them which keep the words of this book: worship God."

(2) Jno. 4: 23--"But the hour cometh, and now is, when the true worshippers shall *worship the Father* in spirit and in truth: for the Father seeketh such to worship him."

SECOND PROPOSITION: We should worship the Father.

(3) Heb. 1: 6—"And again, when he bringeth in *the firstbegotten* into the world, he saith, And *let all the angels of God worship him*."

Phil. 2: 10, 11—"That at (R.V. and Greek, "in") the name of Jesus every knee should bow, of things in heaven, and things in earth, and things under the earth; and that every tongue should confess that Jesus Christ is Lord, to the glory of God the Father."

Rev. 5: 8-13—"And when he had taken the book, the four beasts and four and twenty elders fell down *before the Lamb*, having every one of them harps, and golden vials full of odours, which are the prayers of saints. And they sung a new song, saying, Thou art worthy to take the book, and to open the seals thereof: for thou wast slain, and hast redeemed us to God by thy blood out of every kindred and tongue, and people, and nation; and hast made us unto our God kings and priests: and we shall reign on the earth. And I beheld, and I heard the voice of many angels round about the throne, and the beasts, and the elders; and the number of them was ten thousand times ten thousand and thousands of thousands; saying with a loud voice, Worthy is the Lamb that was slain to receive power, and riches, and wisdom, and strength, and honour, and glory, and blessing. And every crea·ture which is in heaven, and on the earth, and under the earth, and such as are in the sea, and all that are in them, heard I saying, Blessing, and honour, and glory, and power, be unto him that sitteth upon the throne, and unto the Lamb for ever and ever."

THIRD PROPOSITION: We should worship Jesus Christ.

QUESTION: How reconcile this with proposition 1 ?

ANSWER: Jno. 20: 28—"And Thomas answered and said unto Him, My Lord and my God." Jesus Christ is the Lord our God.

III. The Duty of Worship.

(1) Matt. 4: 10—"Then saith Jesus unto him, Get thee hence, Satan: for it is written, Thou shalt worship the Lord thy God, and him only shalt thou serve."

Heb. 1: 6—"And again when he bringeth in the firstbegotten into the world, he saith, And let all the angels of God worship him."

FIRST PROPOSITION: Worship of God and of Christ is commanded.

We owe worship to God. It is His due. We owe (love) to man, (obedience) to parents, (worship) to God. It is our first duty toward Him. He is the All holy, All wise, Almighty, The Infinite, All Perfect One, and our rightful attitude toward Him is that of bowing before Him, or prostrating ourselves before Him, in adoring contemplation of His infinite loveliness and glory, of His attributes, of Himself. If we do not worship God we are robbing Him of what is His due. It is not enough that we obey Him, that we pray to Him, that we return thanks to Him, that we seek to serve Him and do His will. We must worship. Have you ever *worshiped* God? How much time do you spend daily in worshiping Him—in pure and simple worship, in bowing before Him in silent and adoring contemplation of Himself?

(2) Jno. 4: 23, R.V.—"But the hour cometh, and now is, when the true worshippers shall worship the Father in spirit and truth: for such doth the Father seek to be his worshippers."

SECOND PROPOSITION: God is seeking true worshipers.

The one thing above all else that God desires of men is worship. God desires obedience of men, He desires service, He desires prayer, He desires praise and thanksgiving, but His supreme desire from men is worship. He is *seeking* "worshipers."

It has been said that "we are saved that we may serve." This is true, but still more profoundly true is it that we are saved that we may worship. The whole work of redemption finds its culmination and completion in a body of men and women being found and fitted to worship God.

Rev. 7: 9–15—"After this I beheld, and lo, a great multitude, which no man could number, of all nations, and kindreds, and people, and tongues, stood before the throne, and before the Lamb, clothed with white robes, and palms in their hands; and cried with a loud voice, saying, Salvation to our God which sitteth upon the throne and unto the Lamb. And all the angels stood round about the throne, and about the elders and the four beasts, and fell before the throne on their faces, and worshipped God, saying, Amen: Blessing, and glory, and wisdom, and thanksgiving, and honour, and power, and might, be unto

God for ever and ever. Amen. And one of the elders answered, say-ing unto me, What are these which are arrayed in white robes? and whence come they? And I said unto him, Sir, thou knowest. And he said to me, These are they which came out of great tribulation, and have washed their robes, and made them white in the blood of the Lamb. Therefore are they before the throne of God, and serve him day and night in his temple: and he that sitteth on the throne shall dwell among them."

(The word translated "serve" here, is the same word trans-lated "worship" in Phil. 3: 3.)

IV. Where to Worship.

Jno. 4: 19-23—"The woman saith unto him, Sir, I perceive that thou art a prophet. Our fathers worshipped in this mountain; and ye say, that in Jerusalem is the place where men ought to worship. Jesus saith unto her, Woman, believe me, the hour cometh, when ye shall neither in this mountain, nor yet at Jerusalem, worship the Father. Ye worship ye know not what: we know what we worship; for salvation is of the Jews. But the hour cometh, and now is, when the true worshippers shall worship the Father in spirit and in truth: for the Father seeketh such to worship him."

PROPOSITION: The place is not important.

V. How to Worship.

(1) Heb. 9: 7, 14—"But into the second went the high priest alone once every year, not without blood, which he offered for himself, and for the errors of the people: . . . How much more shall the blood of Christ, who through the eternal spirit offered himself without spot to God, purge your conscience from dead works to serve the living God?"

Heb. 10: 19—"Having therefore, brethren, boldness to enter into the holiest by the blood of Jesus."

FIRST PROPOSITION: We should worship on the ground of the shed blood of Jesus.

There is no approach to God except on the ground of shed blood.

(2) Phil. 3: 3, R.V.—"For we are the circumcision, who worship *by the Spirit of God*, and glory in Christ Jesus, and have no confidence in the flesh." (Compare Jno. 4: 24—"God is a Spirit: and they that worship him must worship him *in spirit and in truth*.")

SECOND PROPOSITION: We should worship by the Spirit of God.

The only true worship, worship which is acceptable to God, is the worship which the Spirit inspires. Not all worship of God is "in the Spirit." Very much is of man himself, in the power of his own will. It is of the flesh. The flesh seeks to intrude into every sphere of life, even the highest and most sacred. The flesh has its worship. Men seek to do the things that please God, and win credit for themselves, of their own motion and in their own strength. But this worship is not acceptable. Men may be very earnest in this worship, very sincere in it, but it is not acceptable. It is not what God is seeking. God is seeking worshipers who worship in the Spirit, and who have "no confidence in the flesh." To worship aright we must recognize the utter inability of the flesh—*i. e.*, ourselves untaught, unprompted and ungoverned by God's Spirit—to worship acceptably. We must realize the danger there is that the flesh intrude itself into our worship. In utter self-abnegation we must cast ourselves upon the Holy Spirit to lead us in our worship. The first thing we should do when we would worship, is, with a realization of our own utter helplessness, to look up to the Holy Spirit to teach us and enable us to worship aright. He must present God to our mind for our contemplation. He must subdue and awe our hearts before Him in true adoration. The only living that is acceptable to God is living in the Spirit, the only walk that is acceptable to God is walk in the Spirit, the only service that is acceptable to God is service in the Spirit, the only prayer that is acceptable to God is prayer in the Spirit, the only thanks that are acceptable to God, are thanks in the Spirit, and the only worship that is acceptable to God is worship in the Spirit. Would we worship aright our hearts must look up and cry, "Teach me, Holy Spirit, to worship"; and He will do it.

(3) Jno. 4: 24—"God is a Spirit: and they that worship him must worship him in spirit and in truth."

THIRD PROPOSITION: We should worship "in truth."

QUESTION: What does it mean to "worship in truth"?

ANSWER: 1 Jno. 3: 18—"My little children, let us not love in word, neither in tongue; but in deed and in truth." Phil. 1:18—"What then? notwithstanding, every way, whether in pretense, or in truth, Christ is preached; and I therein do rejoice, yea, and will rejoice." Not in mere form or profession or pretense, but in reality. There is much worship that is not real. The head bows, the body is prostrated, but the soul does not bow in true adoration before God. The Spirit alone leads to worship in truth.

VI. The Results of True Worship.

(1) Jno. 4: 23—"But the hour cometh, and now is, when the true worshippers shall worship the Father in spirit and in truth: for the Father seeketh such to worship him."

FIRST PROPOSITION: When there is true worship the Father is satisfied.   He has found what he seeks.

(2) Ps. 27: 4—"One thing have I desired of the LORD, that will I seek after: that I may dwell in the house of the LORD all the days of my life, to behold the beauty of the LORD, and to inquire in his temple."

SECOND PROPOSITION: The worshiper is satisfied.   His highest joy is found.

There is no higher, no deeper, no purer joy than that which springs from the adoring contemplation of God. I have walked miles, and climbed through underbrush and briers and over crags and precipice, just to get some beautiful view, and as I have looked out upon it, and feasted upon the never-to-be-forgotten vision of mountain and valley, forest and river, village and hamlet, cloud and sunshine, I have felt well repaid for the trial and suffering and weariness. I have sat by the hour before a great painting in joyous beholding of its beauty. Earth has few purer joys than these, but they are nothing to the profound and holy joy that fills the soul as we bow before God in worship, asking nothing, seeking nothing from Him, occupied with and satisfied with Himself. Was the Psalmist thinking only of the future, or of what he had enjoyed in the present, when he wrote: "In thy presence is fulness of joy"? (Ps. 16: 11.) One of the highest privileges of heaven will be that we shall see His face.

(3) 2 Cor. 3: 18, and R.V.—"But we all, with open face beholding as in a glass the glory of the Lord, are changed into the same image from glory to glory, even as by the Spirit of the Lord."

R.V.—"But we all, with unveiled face reflecting as a mirror the glory of the Lord, are transformed into the same image from glory to glory, even as from the Lord the Spirit."

THIRD PROPOSITION: The worshiper is transformed into God's likeness from glory to glory.

Beholding God and worshiping God we become like God. (Moses, Ex. 34:29.) Our complete transformation into His likeness will come through the complete and undimmed vision of Himself.

> 1 Jno. 3: 2—"Beloved, now are we the sons of God, and it doth not yet appear what we shall be: but we know that, when he shall appear, we shall be like him; for we shall see him as he is."
> (4) Is. 6: 5—"Then said I, Woe is me! for I am undone; because I am a man of unclean lips, and I dwell in the midst of a people of unclean lips: for mine eyes have seen the king, the LORD of hosts."
> Job 42: 5, 6—"I have heard of thee by the hearing of the ear; but now mine eye seeth thee: wherefore I abhor myself, and repent in dust and ashes."

FOURTH PROPOSITION: Worship empties us of pride, and reveals our weakness and vileness.

Is. 40:31—"But they that wait upon the LORD shall renew their strength; they shall mount up with wings as eagles; they shall run, and not be weary; and they shall walk, and not faint." It is true that power comes in answer to definite prayer, but not only in answer to prayer. Power belongeth unto God, and the coming into contact and remaining in contact with God in worship fills our souls with power. Spiritual power has many points of similarity to electric force, and just as a receptive body can be charged with electricity by being insulated and brought into contact with some source of electric energy, so we can be charged with the energy of God by the insulation from the world and contact with Himself that is found in worship. As we worship God His power flows into us. Nights spent in contact with God, on our faces before Him in worship, are followed by days of power in contact with men. One great secret of the lack of power in service to-day is the absence of worship in our relations to God Himself.

FIRST PROPOSITION: We may know that we have eternal life through what is written—through the testimony of God Himself in the Bible, especially in the First Epistle of John.

The testimony of Scripture is the testimony of God. This is widely questioned to-day, even by professing Christians. It is none the less true. Many of us know it to be true; all may know it to be true. What do the Scriptures say about the believer's having salvation and eternal life?

Jno 3: 36—"He that believeth on the Son *hath eternal life;* but he that believeth not the Son, shall not see life, but the wrath of God abideth on him."

5: 24—"Verily, verily, I say unto you, He that heareth my word, and believeth on him that sent me HATH *everlasting life*, and shall not come into condemnation; but is passed from death unto life."

6: 47—"Verily, verily, I say unto you, He that believeth on me HATH everlasting life."

Acts 10: 43—"To him give all the prophets witness, that through his name whosoever believeth in him shall receive remission of sins."

Acts 13: 38, 39—"Be it known unto you, therefore, men and brethren, that through this man is preached unto you the forgiveness of sins: And by him *all that believe* ARE *justified* from all things, from which ye could not be justified by the law of Moses."

Jno. 1: 12—"But as many as received him, to them gave he power to become the sons of God, even to them that believe on his name."

Now we know whether we believe or not, whether we have that real faith in Christ that leads us to receive Him. If we have this faith in Christ we have God's own written testimony that we have eternal life, that our sins are forgiven, that we are children of God. The word "know" (a translation of two different Greek words) is found twenty-seven times in the First Epistle of John.

NOTE.—1 Jno. 5: 10-12, R.V.—"He that believeth on the Son of God hath the witness in him: he that believeth not God hath made him a liar; because he hath not believed in the witness that God hath borne concerning his Son. And the witness is this, that God gave unto us eternal life, and this life is in his Son. He that hath the Son hath the life; he that hath not the Son of God hath not the life." Anyone who believes not God's testimony that He has given to us eternal life, and that this life is in His Son, and that he that hath the Son hath the life, makes God a liar. It is sometimes said, "It is presumption for anyone to say he knows he is saved, or to say he knows he has eternal life." Is it presumption to believe God? Is it not rather presumption not to believe God, to "make God a liar?" When Jesus said to the one who was a sinner "Thy sins are forgiven" (Luke 7: 48), was it presumption for her to go out and say "I know my

CHAPTER XVII.

THE BELIEVER'S ASSURANCE OF SALVATION AND ETERNAL LIFE.

I. The Believer's Privilege of Having Assurance, or Knowing that He Has Eternal Life.

(1) 1 Jno. 5: 13, R.V.—"These things have I written unto you, that ye may know that ye have eternal life, even unto you that believe on the name of the Son of God."

FIRST PROPOSITION: John wrote his first Epistle to those who believe on the name of the Son of God, for the express purpose that they may know that they have eternal life. Anyone who believes on the name of the Son of God may know that he has eternal life.

To deny the possibility of the believer's knowing that he has eternal life, is to say that the First Epistle of John was written in vain, and is to insult the Holy Spirit, who is its real author.

(2) Acts 13: 39—"And by him all that believe are justified from all things, from which ye could not be justified by the law of Moses."

SECOND PROPOSITION: The believer may know that he is justified from all things; for the Word of God says so.

(3) Jno. 1: 12, R.V.—"But as many as received him to them gave he the right to become children of God, even to them that believe on his name."

THIRD PROPOSITION: The believer may know that he is a child of God; for the Word of God asserts that he is.

II. How We may Know that We have Eternal Life.

(1) 1 Jno. 5: 13, R.V.—"These things *have I written* unto you, that ye may know that ye have eternal life, even unto you that believe on the name of the Son of God."

sins are all forgiven ? " Is it any more presumption for a believer to-day to say " My sins are all forgiven, I have eternal life," when God says in His permanent, written testimony to " every one that believeth," " you are justified from all things " (Acts 13: 39, R.V.), "you have eternal life?" (Jno. 3: 36; 1 Jno. 5: 13.) It is the blood of Christ that makes us safe, it is the word of God that makes us sure. (Ex. 12: 13.)

(2) 1 Jno. 3: 14, R.V.—" We know that we have passed out of death into life, *because we love the brethren.* He that loveth not abideth in death."

SECOND PROPOSITION: We know that we have passed out of death into life from the testimony of the life itself.

A man who is physically alive knows it from the conscious-ness of the life itself that is coursing through his veins. Men may try to convince him that he is dead but he knows he is alive. Just so spiritually. The life of love is the life of God, is eternal life. (1 Jno. 4: 7, 16.) Selfishness is death. He therefore that really loves his brethren, knows that he has passed " out of death into life." He knows it by the testimony of the life itself.

NOTE.—It is important to notice, however, what God's tests of love are. They are given in the immediately following verses (16–18): "Hereby know we love, *because he laid down his life* for us: and we ought to lay down our lives for the brethren. But whoso hath the world's goods, and beholdeth his brother in need, and shutteth up his compassion from him, how doth the love of God abide in him ? My little children, let us not love in word, neither with the tongue; but in deed and truth." The laying down our life for those we love is the supreme test. This may be done by actually dying in their stead when there is call for that, as there often is. It may also be done by putting our life at their disposal and using it for them. There is always call for this. The every-day test of love is, giving what you have of this world's good to meet the known need of others. The one who knows a brother who hath need while he himself has that which will meet this need, and does not give it; such a one can-not say he has love for the brethren, and cannot know that he has passed out of death into life by the evidence of the life itself. How much more practical and searching are the Bible tests of love of the brethren than those we hear so much in modern prayer meetings—*e. g.*, "I love the brethren, I love to meet with them and hear their testimony. No place is so precious to me as the gathering together of God's people." Are you laying down your life for the brethren ? Are you giving what you have to meet the need of others ?

(3) Rom. 8: 16, R.V.—" The Spirit himself beareth witness with our spirit, that we are children of God."

THIRD PROPOSITION: We know that we are the children of God because the Spirit Himself beareth witness together with our spirit that we are.

QUESTION: What is the testimony of the Spirit ?

ANSWER: Gal. 4: 6—"And because ye are sons, God hath sent forth the Spirit of his Son into your hearts, crying, Abba, Father." When we have accepted Christ and come out from under the bondage of the law into sonsnip, and thus become sons, God sends the Spirit of His Son into our hearts as a personal presence, and this Spirit of the Son in our hearts cries, Abba, Father. He thus bears witness along with our spirit to our sonship. This comes after faith, resting upon the bare word of God. Many are looking for the testimony of the Spirit before they will accept the testimony of God's written word. This is the inversion of God's order. (See also Eph. 1: 13, 14.)

We have, then, a threefold ground of assurance: the testimony of God in the written Word, the testimony of the life itself, the testimony of the Spirit. The testimony of the Word alone is sufficient, and we must accept the testimony of the bare Word to start with. Then we get also the testimony of the life and, to crown all, the testimony of the Spirit. With this threefold ground of assurance, is it presumption to say "I know I am a child of God, I know I have eternal life? "

III. How to Obtain Assurance.

(1) 1 Jno. 5: 13, R.V.—" These things *have I written* unto you; that ye may know that ye have eternal life, *even unto you that believe on the name of the Son of God.*"

FIRST PROPOSITION: (a) *In order to have well-grounded assurance of eternal life we must " believe on the name of the Son of God."*

There are doubtless many who say they know they have eternal life who do not really believe on the name of the Son of God. This is not true assurance. It has no sure foundation in the word of Him who cannot lie. If we wish to get assurance of salvation we must first get saved. The reason why many have not assurance that they are saved is because they are not saved. They ought not to have assurance. What they need first is salvation. Many workers in dealing with others make the great mistake of trying to press them to the point of saying they know they are saved before it is clear that they are saved.

(b) *We obtain assurance of eternal life through what is " written,"* therefore in order to obtain assurance we should study the Word. The assurance that rests upon our states of feeling will come and go as those states vary. But the assurance that rests upon the unchanging Word of God will be intelligent and steadfast. Ignorance of the Word of God is one of the greatest sources of the lack of assurance.

(2) 1 Jno. 5: 10-12--" He that believeth on the Son of God hath the witness in himself: he that believeth not God hath made him a liar; because he believeth not the record that God gave of his Son. And this is the record, that God hath given to us eternal life, and this life is in his Son. He that hath the Son hath life; and he that hath not the Son of God hath not life."

SECOND PROPOSITION: We obtain assurance by believing God's testimony.

Merely studying the word will not bring assurance. We must believe it as well as study it.

(3) 1 Jno. 3: 14-19—" We know that we have passed from death unto life, because we love the brethren. He that loveth not his brother abideth in death. Whosoever hateth his brother is a murderer: and ye know that no murderer hath eternal life abiding in him. Hereby perceive we the love of God, because he laid down his life for us: and we ought to lay down our lives for the brethren. But whoso hath this world's good, and seeth his brother have need, and shutteth up his bowels of compassion from him, how dwelleth the love of God in him ? My little children, let us not love in word, neither in tongue: but in deed and in truth. And *hereby we know that we are of the truth*, and shall assure our hearts before him."

THIRD PROPOSITION: In order to have assurance we should live out a life of love; love not merely in word and in tongue, but in deed and in truth. (Compare Jno. 8: 12.)

(4) Rom. 8: 14-16, R.V.—" For as many as are led by the Spirit of God, these are the sons of God. For ye received not the spirit of bondage again unto fear; but ye received the spirit of adoption, whereby we cry, Abba, Father. The Spirit himself beareth witness with our spirit, that we are children of God."

FOURTH PROPOSITION: In order to obtain the witness of the Spirit together with that of our spirit we should give ourselves up to be led by the Spirit.

Verse 16 in Romans viii is clearly dependent upon verse 14, and it is only those who know verse 14 as a personal experience who can expect to know verse 16 as a personal experience. It is also clearly implied by the connection with verse 17, that it is in suffering together with Christ that we especially enjoy the assurance of sonship by the Spirit's testimony and the assurance that we shall be glorified together with Him.

CHAPTER XVIII.

THE FUTURE DESTINY OF BELIEVERS.

I. 1 Jno. 2:17—"And the world passeth away and the lust thereof: but he that doeth the will of God abideth forever."

FIRST PROPOSITION: He that doeth the will of God abideth forever. The world and all it contains passeth, he continues.

II. Jno. 11: 25, 26—"Jesus said unto her, I am the resurrection, and the life: he that believeth in me, though he were dead, yet shall he live: And whosoever liveth and believeth in me shall never die. Believest thou this ? "

Jno. 8: 51, R.V.—"Verily, verily, I say unto you, if a man keep my word, he shall never see death."

SECOND PROPOSITION: He that believeth on Jesus Christ shall never die. He that keepeth the word of Jesus Christ shall never see death.

Believers in Christ fall asleep, they never die. (Compare Acts 7: 60.)

III. 1 Thess. 4: 13, 14,15—"But ·I would not have you to be ignorant brethren, concerning *them which are asleep*, that ye sorrow not, even as others which have no hope. For if we believe that Jesus died and rose again, even so them also which *sleep in Jesus* will God bring with him. For this we say unto you by the word of the Lord, that we which are alive and remain unto the coming of the Lord shall not prevent them which are *asleep*."

THIRD PROPOSITION: Until the coming of Christ believers in Christ who have departed from this life sleep.

QUESTION: What is meant by sleep? Does it refer to a state of unconsciousness? Is this state called sleep to distinguish it from being awake, or is it called sleep to distinguish it from death?

The full answer to this question will be found under the next proposition. But note this, that sleep is not necessarily a state of unconsciousness, but oftentimes of highest consciousness and mental activity.   Sleep is, however, usually a condition in which one is largely shut out of intercourse with the outside world and shut up to himself and God and His angels, or the Devil and his angels.

IV.   Phil. 1: 23, 24, R.V—"For I am in a strait betwixt the two, having the desire to depart and be with Christ; for it is very far better: yet to abide in the flesh is more needful for your sake."

2 Cor. 5: 6, 8, R.V.—"Being therefore always of good courage, and knowing that, whilst we are at home in the body, we are absent from the Lord. . . . We are of good courage, I say, and are willing rather to be absent from the body, and to be at home with the Lord."

FOURTH PROPOSITION: When the believer gets out of the flesh (the body) he departs to be with Christ; when he is absent from the body he is at home with the Lord.   (Compare 2 Cor. 12: 2–4.)

QUESTION: What is the precise and definite character of our existence when "absent from the body" and "at home with the Lord," up to the time of the coming of the Lord and our being "clothed upon with our habitation which is from heaven?"   (2 Cor. 5: 8, 2, 4, R.V.)

ANSWER: The Bible seems to give but little explicit and detailed information on this point.   It does say, however, that this state "is very far better" than our present state.   (Phil. 1: 23.)   This leaves no room for purgatorial tortures, nor for a state of unconsciousness.   It is evidently a state of conscious bliss. It evidently is not the highest state to which the believer shall attain.   "For we know that, if our earthly house of this tabernacle were dissolved, we have a building of God, a house not made with hands, eternal in the heavens.   For in this we groan, earnestly desiring to be clothed upon with our house which is from heaven: If so be that being clothed we shall not be found naked.   For we that are in this tabernacle do groan, being burdened: *not for that we would be unclothed,* but clothed upon, that mortality might be swallowed up of life.   . . .   We are confident, I say, and willing rather to be absent from the body, and to be present with the Lord."   (2 Cor. 5: 1, 2, 3, 4, 8.)

V.   1 Thess. 4: 16—"For the Lord himself shall descend from heaven with a shout, with the voice of the archangel, and with the trump of God: and the dead in Christ shall rise first."

1 Cor. 15: 12, 13, 20–23, 35–38—"Now if Christ be preached that he rose from the dead, how say some among you that there is no resur‑rection of the dead ?   But if there be no resurrection of the dead, then is Christ not risen: . . .   But now is Christ risen from the dead, and become the ·firstfruits of them that slept.   For since by man came death, by man came also the resurrection of the dead.   For as in Adam all die, even so in Christ shall all be made alive.   But every man in his own order: Christ the firstfruits; afterward they that are Christ's at his coming.   . . .   But some man will say, How are the dead raised up ? and with what body do they come ?   Thou fool, that which thou sowest is not quickened, except it die; and that which thou sowest, thou sowest not that body that shall be, but bare grain, it may chance of wheat, or of some other grain: But God giveth it a body as it hath pleased him, and to every seed his own body."

FIFTH PROPOSITION: At the coming of Jesus Christ the bodies of those who sleep in Christ shall be raised from the dead.   Not, however, precisely the same bodies, even as the grain that grows is not precisely the same as the grain that was sown.

The grain that was sown disintegrates and many of its con‑stituent elements go, no one can say whither.   But the formative principle takes to itself many new elements, no one can fully say whence.   So it is in the resurrection.

VI.   2 Cor. 5: 1, 2, 4, R.V.—" For we know that if the earthly house of our tabernacle be dissolved, we have a building from God, a house not made with hands, eternal in the heavens.   For verily in this we groan, longing to be clothed upon with our habitation which is from heaven; . . .   For indeed we that are in this tabernacle do groan, being burdened; not for that we would be unclothed, but that we would be clothed upon, that what is mortal may be swallowed up of life."

SIXTH PROPOSITION: At the resurrection we shall be given in place of "the earthly house of our tabernacle,"—i. e., our pres‑ent physical frame—"a building from God, a house not made with hands, eternal in the heavens"—i. e., the resurrection body. Mortality shall be swallowed up of life.

VII.   Phil. 3: 20, 21, R.V.—" For our citizenship is in heaven; from whence also we wait for a Saviour, the Lord Jesus Christ: who shall fashion anew the body of our humiliation, that it may be conformed to the body of his glory, according to the working whereby he is able even to subject all things unto himself."

SEVENTH PROPOSITION: At His coming our Saviour, the Lord Jesus Christ, "shall fashion anew the body of our humiliation, that it may be conformed to the body of His glory.'

THE CHARACTERISTICS OF THE RESURRECTION BODY.

(1)   I Cor. 15: 35-38—"But some man will say, How are the dead raised up ? and with what body do they come ? Thou fool, that which thou sowest is not quickened, except it die: And that which thou sowest, thou sowest not that body that shall be, but bare grain, it may chance of wheat, or of some other grain: But God giveth it a body as it hath pleased him, and to every seed his own body."

It will not be the same body that is laid in the grave.

(2)   I Cor. 15: 50, 51—"Now this I say, brethren, that *flesh and blood cannot inherit the kingdom of God;* neither doth corruption inherit incorruption.   Behold, I shew you a mystery; We shall not all sleep, but we shall all be changed."

It will not be flesh and blood.

(3)   Luke 24: 39—"Behold my hands and my feet, that it is I myself: handle me, and see; for a spirit hath not flesh and bones, as ye see me have." (Compare Phil. 3: 21.)

It will not be pure spirit, but have flesh and bones.

(4)   I Cor. 15: 42—"So also is the resurrection of the dead.   It is sown in corruption, it is raised in incorruption."

It will be incorruptible—not subject to decay, imperishable.

(5)   I Cor. 15: 43 (a)—"It is sown in dishonor, it is raised in glory."

It will be glorious.   (Compare Rev. 1: 13-17.)

(6)   I Cor. 15: 43 (b)—"It is sown in weakness, it is raised in power."

It will be powerful.   The days of weariness and weakness will be forever at an end.   The body will be able to accomplish all the Spirit purposes.

(7)   I Cor. 15: 47-49—"The first man is of the earth, earthy: the second man is the Lord from heaven.   As is the earthy, such are they also that are earthy: and as is the heavenly, such are they also that are heavenly.   And as we have borne the image of the earthy, we shall also bear the image of the heavenly."

It will be heavenly.

(8)   Matt. 13: 43—"*Then shall the righteous shine forth as the sun* in the kingdom of their Father.   Who hath ears to hear, let him hear."

Dan. 12: 3—"And *they that be wise shall shine* as the brightness of the firmament; and they that turn many to righteousness, *as the stars* for ever and ever."

Compare Matt. 17: 2—"And was transfigured before them: and *his face did shine as the sun,* and his raiment was white as the light."

Luke 9: 29—"And as he prayed, the fashion of his countenance was altered, and his raiment was white and glistering."

It will be luminous, shining, dazzling, bright like the sun.

NOTE.—It has been conjectured that the bodies of Adam and Eve were so before they sinned, and that this glory served as a covering which departed when they sinned. So "they knew that they were naked." (Gen. 3: 7.)

(9) Matt. 22: 30—"For in the resurrection they neither marry, nor are given in marriage, but are as the angels of God in heaven."

Luke 20: 35, 36—"For they which shall be accounted worthy to obtain that world, and the resurrection from the dead, neither marry nor are given in marriage: Neither can they die any more: for they are equal unto the angels; and are the children of God, being the children of the resurrection."

They will be "like the angels." *(a)* They do not marry. *(b)* They cannot die any more.

(10) 1 Cor. 15: 41, 42 (a)—"There is one glory of the sun, and another glory of the moon, and another glory of the stars; for one star differeth from another star in glory. So also in the resurrection of the dead."

Resurrection bodies differ from one another.

(11) Rom. 8: 23—"And not only they, but ourselves also, which have the firstfruits of the Spirit, even we ourselves, groan within ourselves, waiting for the adoption, to wit, the redemption of our body."

The Resurrection Body will be the consummation of the adoption, our placing as sons. In the Resurrection Body it will be outwardly manifest that we are sons of God. Before His incarnation Christ was "in the form of God" (Phil. 2: 6), *i. e.*, in the visible appearance of God. So shall we be in the resurrection. (Compare Col. 3: 4, R. V.; 1 Jno. 3: 2, R. V.)

VIII. 1 Thess. 4: 17 (a)—"Then we which are alive and remain shall be caught up together with them in the clouds, to meet the Lord in the air."

EIGHTH PROPOSITION: At the coming of Christ and the resurrection of those who sleep in Jesus, believers who have remained alive until that time, and those who are raised, shall be caught up together to meet the Lord in the air.

IX. Jno. 14: 3—"And if I go and prepare a place for you, I will come again, and receive you unto myself; that where I am, there ye may be also."

1 Thess. 4: 17 (b)—"And so shall we ever be with the Lord."

Jno. 12: 26—"If any man serve me, let him follow me; and where I am, there shall also my servant be: if any man serve me, him will my father honour."

NINTH PROPOSITION: After the coming of Christ and our being caught up to meet Him, we shall ever be with the Lord; there shall be no more separation from Him.

WHERE BELIEVERS SHALL BE.

(1) Jno. 14: 2—"In my Father's house are many mansions: if it were not so, I would have told you. I go to prepare a place for you."

We shall be in a prepared place. A place that Jesus himself has gone for the express purpose of preparing for us. We shall be a prepared people in a prepared place. This place that Jesus is preparing He speaks of as "abodes" or "abiding places" (translated "mansions").

(2) Heb. 11: 10, 16—"For he looked for a city which hath foundations, whose builder and maker is God. . . . But now they desire a better country, that is a heavenly: wherefore God is not ashamed to be called their God: for he hath prepared for them a city."

We shall be in a city which hath foundations whose builder and maker is God, a better country than this, a heavenly country; a city prepared of God for us.

CHARACTERISTICS OF THAT CITY.

(1) Heb. 13: 14—"For here we have no continuing city, but we seek one to come."

It will be an abiding city.

(2) Rev. 21: 22, R.V.—"And I saw no temple therein: for the Lord God the Almighty, and the Lamb, are the temple thereof."

The Lord God, the Almighty, and the Lamb are the temple thereof. We will not go to some building to worship, but right to themselves.

(3) Rev. 21: 23, R.V.—"And the city hath no need of the sun, neither of the moon, to shine upon it: for the glory of God did lighten it, and the lamp thereof is the Lamb."

That city has no need of the sun, neither of the moon, to shine upon it: for the glory of God lightens it, and the Lamb himself is the lamp thereof. Paul got a hint of the dazzling brilliance of that light on the Damascus Road. Our resurrection eyes will be able to endure and enjoy the glory that blinded him. There will be no dark days.

(4) Rev. 21: 25—" And the gates of it shall not be shut at all by day: for there shall be no night there."

The gates shall never be shut and there shall be no night. Perfect security and no darkness.

(5) Rev. 21: 27, R.V.—" And there shall in no wise enter into it anything unclean, or he that maketh an abomination and a lie: but only they which are written in the Lamb's book of life."

There will be there nothing unclean, nothing abominable, nothing false, untrue, nor unreal.   No saloons, no filth, no shams.

(6) Rev. 22: 1, 2, R.V.—" And he shewed me a river of water of life, bright as crystal, proceeding out of the throne of God and of the Lamb, in the midst of the street thereof.   And on this side of the river and on that was the tree of life, bearing twelve manner of fruits, yielding its fruit every month: and the leaves of the tree were for the healing of the nations."

There shall be a river of water of life, bright as crystal, proceeding out of the throne of God and of the Lamb, in the midst of the street thereof, and on both sides of the river shall be the tree of life, bearing twelve fruits, yielding its fruit every month; and the leaves of the tree for the healing of the nations.

X.   2 Thess. 1: 7—" And to you who are troubled rest with us, when the Lord Jesus shall be revealed from heaven with his mighty angels."

Heb. 4: 9—" There remaineth therefore a rest to the people of God."

TENTH PROPOSITION: When the Lord shall be revealed from heaven we shall be given rest.

Now we have conflict and tribulation.   Then we shall have rest and glory.

XI. Jno. 17: 24—" Father, I will that they also, whom thou hast given me, be with me where I am; that they may behold my glory, which thou hast given me: for thou lovedst me before the foundation of the world."

ELEVENTH PROPOSITION: We shall behold the glory of our Lord, the glory which the Father has given Him.

The word translated "behold," is a strong word.   It means to gaze at with interest and intentness.   We shall put our whole being into rapturous and adoring contemplation of the revealed glory of Him who on earth suffered shame for us.

XII. 1 Jno. 3: 2—"Beloved, now are we the sons of God, and it doth not yet appear what we shall be: but we know that, when he shall appear, *we shall be like him:* for we shall see him as he is."

TWELFTH PROPOSITION: We shall be like Him.

QUESTION: Does the Him here refer to Christ or the Father ?

ANSWER: It matters not; for if we are like the one, we shall be also like the other: Heb. 1: 3—"Who being the brightness of his glory, and the express image of his person, and upholding all things by the word of his power, when he had by himself purged our sins, sat down on the right hand of the Majesty on high." Jno. 14: 9—"Jesus saith unto him, Have I been so long time with you, and yet hast thou not known me, Philip: he that hath seen me hath seen the Father; and how sayest thou then, Show us the Father?" Phil 2: 6—"Who being in the form of God, thought it not robbery to be equal with God."

XIII. Col. 3: 4, R.V.—"When Christ, who is our life, shall be manifested, then shall ye also with him be manifested in glory.

THIRTEENTH PROPOSITION: We shall with Him be mani fested in glory.

We shall not only behold His glory, but reflect it in ourselves. Our life is now a hidden one, hid with Christ in God (Col. 3: 3), but when He is manifested in glory we shall be too.

NOTES.—(1) Rom. 8: 18—"For I reckon that the sufferings of this present time are not worthy to be compared with the glory which shall be revealed in us."

The sufferings of this present time are not worthy to be compared with the glory which shall be revealed to usward.

(2) 2 Cor. 4: 17, R.V.—"For our light affliction, which is for the moment, worketh for us more and more exceedingly an eternal weight of glory."

This eternal weight of glory is being worked out for us more and more exceedingly by our present momentary light affliction.

(3) Jno. 17: 22—"And the glory which thou gavest me I have given them; that they may be one, even as we are one."

2 Thess. 2: 14—"Whereunto he called you by our gospel, to the obtaining of the glory of our Lord Jesus Christ."

The glory that God hath given to Jesus shall be ours.

(4) 1 Thess. 2: 12, R.V.—"That ye would walk worthy of God, who calleth you into his own kingdom and glory.

We shall be sharers in God's own glory and kingdom. In a word, we shall be heirs of God and joint heirs with Jesus Christ, glorified together with Him. (Rom. 8: 17.)

XIV. Matt. 25: 20–23—"And so he that had received five talents came and brought other five talents, saying, Lord, thou deliveredst unto me five talents; behold, I have gained beside them five talents more. His lord said unto him, Well done, thou good and faithful servant: thou hast been faithful over a few things, I will make thee ruler over many things: enter thou into the joy of thy lord. He also that had received two talents came and said, Lord, thou deliveredst unto me two talents; behold, I have gained two other talents beside them. His lord said unto him, Well done, good and faithful servant; thou hast been faithful over a few things, I will make thee ruler over many things: enter thou into the joy of thy lord."

FOURTEENTH PROPOSITION: At the coming of Christ and His reckoning with His servants, His faithful servants will be commended by Him and enter into the joy of their Lord.

Leighton says, "Here a few drops of joy enter into us, there we enter into joy as vessels put into a sea of happiness."

(15) Luke 19: 12, 13, 15–19—"He said therefore, A certain nobleman went into a far country to receive for himself a kingdom, and to return. And he called his ten servants, and delivered them ten pounds, and said unto them, Occupy till I come. . . . And it came to pass, that when he was returned, having received the kingdom, then he commanded these servants to be called unto him, to whom he had given the money, that he might know how much every man had gained by trading. Then came the first, saying, Lord, thy pound hath gained ten pounds. And he said unto him, Well, thou good servant: because thou hast been faithful in a very little, have thou authority *over ten cities*. And the second came, saying, Lord, thy pound hath gained five pounds. And he said likewise to him, Be thou also *over five cities*."

FIFTEENTH PROPOSITION: Rewards will vary in proportion to fidelity in service.

We are saved by faith but rewarded according to our own works. (Compare Matt. 6:20; 1 Cor. 3:11–15.)

XV. Rev. 7: 9, 10, 13–17, R.V.—"After these things I saw, and behold, a great multitude, which no man could number, out of every nation, and of all tribes and peoples and tongues, standing before the throne and before the Lamb, arrayed in white robes, and palms in their hands; and they cry with a great voice, saying, Salvation unto

our God which sitteth on the throne, and unto the Lamb. . .
And one of the elders answered, saying unto me, These which are arrayed in the white robes, who are they, and whence came they? And
I say unto him, My lord, thou knowest, and he said to me, These are
they which come out of the great tribulation, and they washed their
robes, and made them white in the blood of the Lamb. Therefore
are they before the throne of God; and they serve him day and night
in his temple: and he that sitteth on the throne shall spread his tabernacle over them. They shall hunger no more, neither thirst any more;
neither shall the sun strike upon them, nor any heat: for the Lamb
which is in the midst of the throne shall be their shepherd, and shall
guide them unto fountains of waters of life: and God shall wipe away
every tear from their eyes."

*FIFTEENTH PROPOSITION: Those who come out of the
great tribulation, having washed their robes and made them
white in the blood of the Lamb, shall stand before the throne
and before the Lamb, arrayed in white robes, and palms in their
hands.* (Purity, victory and festal joy.) *They shall serve
God day and night in His temple. He that sitteth on the throne
shall spread His tabernacle over them. They shall hunger no
more, neither thirst any more; neither shall the sun strike upon
them, nor any heat, for the Lamb which is in the midst of the
throne shall be their shepherd, and shall guide them unto fountains of waters of life, and God shall wipe away every tear from
their eyes.*

XVI. Jas. 1:12, R.V.—"Blessed is the man that endureth temptation: for when he hath been approved, he shall receive the crown of
life, which the Lord promised to them that love him."

*SIXTEENTH PROPOSITION: Those who endure temptation
shall receive the crown of life which the Lord hath promised to
them that love Him.*

The word translated "endure" means not merely to suffer,
but to continue or persevere under, to stand fast. This is the
proof of true love to Christ, that we stand true to him under
trial, and this wins the crown of life.

XVII. 2 Tim. 4:8, R.V.—"I have kept the faith: henceforth there
is laid up for me the crown of righteousness, which the Lord, the
righteous judge, shall give to me at that day; and not only to me, but
also to all them that have loved his appearing."

SEVENTEENTH PROPOSITION: "*At that day,*" *the Lord, the righteous judge, shall give the crown of righteousness to all those who have loved His appearing.*

XVIII. 1 Pet. 5: 1-4, R.V.—"The elders therefore among you I exhort, who am a fellow-elder, and a witness of the sufferings of Christ, who am also a partaker of the glory that shall be revealed: Tend the flock of God which is among you, exercising the oversight, not of constraint, but willingly, according unto God; nor yet for filthy lucre, but of a ready mind; neither as lording it over the charge al-lotted to you, but making yourselves examples to the flock. And when the chief Shepherd shall be manifested, ye shall receive the crown of glory that fadeth not away."

EIGHTEENTH PROPOSITION: *When the chief Shepherd shall be manifested, He shall give the crown of glory that fadeth not away to the undershepherds who have tended the flock of God, exercising the oversight, not of constraint, but willingly, accord-ing unto God; not for money, but with eager readiness; not lord-ing it over the charge allotted to them, but making themselves examples unto the flock.*

Note the three crowns—"The Crown of Life," "the Crown of Righteousness," and "the Crown of Glory"—and who is to re-ceive each.

XIX. Jas. 2: 5—"Hearken, my beloved brethren, Hath not God chosen the poor of this world rich in faith, and heirs of the kingdom which he hath promised to them that love him?"

Luke 22: 28, 29—"Ye are they which have continued with me in my temptations. And I appoint unto you a kingdom, as my Father hath appointed unto me."

Luke 12: 32—"Fear not, little flock; for it is your Father's good pleasure to give you the kingdom."

NINETEENTH PROPOSITION: *God hath promised, Christ hath appointed, and it is the Father's good pleasure to give a kingdom unto them that love God and continue with Christ in His temptations.*

NOTES ABOUT THE KINGDOM.

(1) Rev. 20: 6—"Blessed and holy is he that hath part in the first resurrection: on such the second death hath no power, but they shall be priests of God and of Christ, and shall reign with him a thousand years."

In this kingdom we shall reign with Christ as priests of God and of Christ.

(2) Matt. 25: 34—"Then shall the king say unto them on his right hand, Come ye blessed of my Father, inherit the kingdom prepared for you from the foundation of the world."

This kingdom was prepared for us from the foundation of the world.

(3) Heb. 12: 28, R.V.—"Wherefore, receiving a kingdom that can-not be shaken, let us have grace, whereby we may offer service well pleasing to God with reverence and awe."

This kingdom cannot be shaken.

XX. Promises to Him that Overcometh (or carries off the victory).

(1) Rev. 2: 7, R.V.—"He that hath an ear, let him hear what the Spirit saith to the churches. To him that overcometh, to him will I give to eat of the tree of life, which is in the Paradise of God."

To him that overcometh Christ will give to eat of the tree of life which is in the Paradise of God.

(2) Rev. 2: 11—"He that hath an ear, let him hear what the Spirit saith to the churches. He that overcometh shall not be hurt of the second death."

He that overcometh shall not be hurt of the second death.

(3) Rev. 2: 17, R.V.—"He that hath an ear let him hear what the Spirit saith to the churches. To him that overcometh, to him will I give of the hidden manna, and I will give him a white stone, and upon the stone a new name written, which no one knoweth but he that re-ceiveth it."

To him that overcometh Christ will give of the hidden manna, a white stone, and upon the stone a new name written, which no one knoweth but he that receiveth it.

(4) Rev. 2: 26, 27, R.V.—"And he that overcometh, and he that keepeth my works unto the end, to him will I give authority over the nations: and he shall rule them with a rod of iron, as the vessels of the potter are broken to shivers; as I also have received of my Father."

Christ will give to him that overcometh and that keepeth His works unto the end, authority over the nations; and he shall rule them with a rod of iron, as the vessels of the potter are broken to shivers; and Christ will give him the morning star. (v. 28.)

(5) Rev. 3: 4, 5, R.V.—"But thou hast a few names in Sardis which did not defile their garments: and they shall walk with me in white; for they are worthy. He that overcometh shall thus be arrayed

in white garments; and I will in no wise blot his name out of the book of life, and I will confess his name before my Father, and before his angels."

He that overcometh shall be arrayed in white garments: and Christ will in no wise blot his name out of the book of life; and Christ will confess his name before His Father and before the angels of the Father, and he shall walk in Christ in white.

(6) Rev. 3: 12, R.V.—" He that overcometh, I will make him a pillar in the temple of my God, and he shall go out hence no more: and I will write upon him the name of my God, and the name of the city of my God, the New Jerusalem, which cometh down out of heaven from my God, and mine own new name."

He that overcometh, him will Christ make a pillar in the temple of his God, and he shall go out thence no more; and Christ will write upon him the name of His God, and the name of the city of His God, the New Jerusalem, which cometh down out of heaven from God, and His own new name.

(7) Rev. 3: 21, R.V.—" He that overcometh, I will give to him to sit down with me in my throne, as I also overcame, and sat down with my Father in his throne."

He that overcometh, to him will Christ give to sit down with Himself in His throne.

XXI. Rev. 21: 4, R.V.—"And he shall wipe away every tear from their eyes; and death shall be no more; neither shall there be mourning, nor crying, nor pain, any more: the first things are passed away."

TWENTY-FIRST PROPOSITION: God shall wipe away every tear from the eyes of His people. Death shall be no more; neither shall there be mourning, nor crying, nor pain any more. (See also, v. 3.)

XXII. 1 Cor. 13: 12, R.V.—" For now we see in a mirror, darkly; but then face to face: now I know in part; but then shall I know even as also I have been known."

TWENTY-SECOND PROPOSITION: We shall see no longer in a mirror, in a riddle, but face to face. We shall know no longer in part, but we shall know God and all things in that perfect way in which He already knows us.

XXIII. 1 Cor. 1: 8, R.V.—" Who shall also confirm you unto the end, that ye be unreproveable in the day of our Lord Jesus Christ."

TWENTY-THIRD PROPOSITION: In the day of our Lord Jesus Christ we shall be unreprovable. We will so perfect us that there will be absolutely nothing in us that even He can find fault with or be displeased with. (Compare Jude 24.)

XXIV. Eph. 5: 27, R.V.—"That he might present the church to himself a glorious church, not having spot or wrinkle or any such thing; but that it should be holy and without blemish."

TWENTY-FOURTH PROPOSITION: Christ will present the Church to Himself, a glorious Church, not having spot nor wrinkle, nor any such thing; but holy and without blemish."

XXV. 1 Pet. 1: 4, 5, R.V.—"Unto an inheritance incorruptible, and undefiled, and that fadeth not away, reserved in heaven for you, who by the power of God are guarded through faith unto a salvation to be revealed in the last time."

TWENTY-FIFTH PROPOSITION: We who are guarded by God's power, through faith, unto a salvation ready to be revealed in the last time, shall receive an inheritance, incorruptible, and undefiled, and that fadeth not away, reserved in heaven for us.

BOOK V.

—

WHAT THE BIBLE TEACHES ABOUT ANGELS.

CHAPTER I.

ANGELS: THEIR NATURE, POSITION, NUMBER AND ABODE.

I. Their Nature and Position.

(1) Col. 1:16, R.V.—"For in him were all things created, in the heavens and upon the earth, things visible and things invisible, whether thrones or dominions or principalities or powers; all things have been created through him, and unto him."

FIRST PROPOSITION: Angels are created beings—created by ("in," Greek), through and unto the Son of God.

(2) 2 Pet. 2:11—"Whereas angels, which are greater in power and might, bring not railing accusation against them before the Lord."

SECOND PROPOSITION: Angels are greater than man in power and might. (Compare Ps. 8:4, 5.)

(3) 2 Thess. 1:7—"And to you who are troubled, rest with us, when the Lord Jesus shall be revealed from heaven with his mighty angels."

THIRD PROPOSITION: Angels are mighty—have great power.

E. g., Acts 5:19, R.V.—"But an angel of the Lord by night opened the prison doors, and brought them out." 12:7, 23, R.V.—"And behold, an angel of the Lord stood by him, and a light shined in the cell: and he smote Peter on the side, and awoke him, saying, Rise up quickly. And his chains fell off from his hands."

(4) Matt. 22:30—"For in the resurrection they neither marry, nor are given in marriage, but are as the angels of God in heaven."

Luke 20:35, 36—"But they which shall be accounted worthy to obtain that world, and the resurrection from the dead, neither marry, nor are given in marriage: Neither can they die any more: for they are equal unto the angels: and are the children of God, being the children of the resurrection."

FOURTH PROPOSITION: Angels neither marry nor die.

(5) Mark 13:32, R.V.—"But of that day or that hour knoweth no one, not even the angels in heaven, neither the Son, but the Father."

FIFTH PROPOSITION: *Angels have great knowledge, but are not omniscient.*   (Compare Eph. 3: 10, 11; 1 Pet. 1: 12.)

(6) Rev. 22: 8, 9, R.V.—"And I John am he that heard and saw these things. And when I heard and saw, I fell down to worship before the feet of the angel which shewed me these things. And he saith unto me, See thou do it not: I am a fellow servant with thee and with thy brethren the prophets, and with them which keep the words of this book: worship God."

SIXTH PROPOSITION: *Angels are not proper objects of worship.*

Here is a clear and broad line of distinction between Jesus and the angels.

(7) Jude 9—"Yet Michael *the archangel*, when contending with the devil he disputed about the body of Moses, durst not bring against him a railing accusation, but said, The LORD rebuke thee."

1 Thess. 4: 16—"For the Lord himself shall descend from heaven with a shout, with the voice *of the archangel*, and with the trump of God: and the dead in Christ shall rise first."

1 Pet. 3: 22—"Who is gone into heaven, and is on the right hand of God; *angels* and *authorities* and *powers* being made subject unto him."

SEVENTH PROPOSITION: (a) *There are ranks or orders of angels.*   (b) *All ranks of angels have been made subject unto Jesus Christ.*

(8) Heb. 1: 6—"And again, when he bringeth in the firstbegotten into the world, he saith, And let all the angels of God worship him."

EIGHTH PROPOSITION: *All the angels of God are bidden to worship Jesus the Son of God.*

(9) Luke 9: 26—"For whosoever shall be ashamed of me and my words, of him shall the Son of man be ashamed, when he shall come in his own glory, and in his Father's, and of the holy angels."

NINTH PROPOSITION: *The angels are glorious beings.*

(Compare Matt. 28: 2, 3, R.V.—"And behold, there was a great earthquake; for an angel of the Lord descended from heaven, and came and rolled away the stone, and sat upon it. His appearance was as lightning, and his raiment white as snow." Rev. 10: 1, R.V.—"And I saw another strong angel coming down out of heaven, arrayed with a cloud; and the rainbow was upon his head, and his face was as the sun, and his feet as pillars of fire." Dan. 10: 6—"His body also was like the beryl, and his face as the appearance of lightning, and his eyes as lamps of fire, and his arms and his feet like in color to polished brass, and the voice of his words like the voice of a multitude.")

(10) 2 Pet. 2: 4, R.V.—"And if God spared not angels when they sinned, but cast them down to hell, and committed them to pits of darkness, to be reserved unto judgment."

TENTH PROPOSITION. Some of the angels sinned, and God cast them down to hell and committed them to pits of darkness, to be reserved unto judgment.

It has been suggested that they were the earlier inhabitants of the earth, and that the earth became " without form and void " (Gen. 1: 2) as a judgment upon their sins, just as, after it was reorganized for man's abode, it was cursed because of man's fall.

(Compare Is. 34: 10, 11—"It shall not be quenched night nor day; the smoke thereof shall go up forever: from generation to generation it shall lie *waste;* none shall pass through it for ever and ever. But the cormorant and the bittern shall possess it; the owl also and the raven shall dwell in it: and he shall stretch out upon it the line of *confusion,* and the stones of emptiness.")

Here we read the land was made "waste" because of sin, and the line of "confusion" (same Hebrew as " without form ") and plummet of "emptiness" (same Hebrew as "void") stretched over it. Also Jer. 4: 23–27:

"I beheld the earth, and lo, it was *without form, and void;* and the heavens, and they had no light. And I beheld the mountains, and lo, they trembled, and all the hills moved lightly. And I beheld, and lo, there was no man, and all the birds of the heavens were fled. I beheld, and lo, the fruitful place was a wilderness, and all the cities thereof were broken down at the presence of the LORD, and by his fierce anger. For thus hath the LORD said, The whole land shall be desolate; yet will I not make a full end."

Is. 45: 18, R.V.—" For thus saith the LORD that created the heavens; he is God; that formed the earth and made it; he established it, *he created it not a waste,* he formed it to be inhabited: I am the LORD; and there is none else."

In this last verse we are told God did not create the earth a "waste." (Same Hebrew word as that translated "without form" in Gen. 1: 2.) It seems clear, then, that it must have become so by *someone's* sin before man's creation. Gen. 1: 2 should then be translated, "And the earth *became* without form, and void" (or "waste and void"). The first verse of the chapter would then describe the creation; the second verse, the desolation visited upon the earth because of the sin of pre-Adamite inhabitants; the latter part of verse 2 and following verses, the rehabilitation of the earth to be a habitation for the new Adamite race.

(11) 1 Cor. 6: 3—"Know ye not that we shall judge angels ? how much more things that pertain to this life ?"

ELEVENTH PROPOSITION: Angels shall be judged by believers.

This may refer only to the angels who fell.

(12) Luke 2: 9, 13, R.V.—"And an angel of the Lord stood by them, and the glory of the Lord shone round about them: and they were sore afraid."

Jno. 20: 12—"And seeth two angels in white sitting, the one at the head, and the other at the feet, where the body of Jesus had lain."

Gen. 32: 1, 2—"And Jacob went on his way, and the angels of God met him. And when Jacob saw them, he said, This is God's host: and he called the name of that place Mahanaim."

TWELFTH PROPOSITION: Angels have sometimes been seen by men.

(13) Ps. 78: 25—"Men did eat angels' food: he sent them meat to the full."

THIRTEENTH PROPOSITION: Angels eat.

But see, R.V.—"Man did eat the bread of the mighty: He sent them meat to the full."

II. Number of the Angels.

(1) Heb. 12: 22, R.V.—"But ye are come unto Mount Zion, and unto the city of the living God, the heavenly Jerusalem, and to innumerable hosts of angels."

PROPOSITION: There are innumerable hosts of angels—literally myriads of angels. (See R.V. Marg.)

(Compare 2 Kg. 6: 17—"And Elisha prayed, and said, LORD, I pray thee, open his eyes, that he may see. And the LORD opened the eyes of the young man; and he saw: and, behold, the mountain was full of horses and chariots of fire round about Elisha," and Matt. 26: 53— "Thinkest thou that I cannot now pray to my Father, and he shall presently give me more than twelve legions of angels? ")

III. The Abode of the Angels.

(1) Matt. 22: 30—"For, in the resurrection they neither marry, nor are given in marriage, but are as the angels of God *in heaven.*"

Eph. 3: 10—"To the intent that now unto the principalities and powers *in heavenly places* might be known by the church the manifold wisdom of God."

Jno. 1: 51—"And he saith unto him, Verily, verily, I say unto you, Hereafter ye shall see heaven open, and the angels of God ascending and descending upon the Son of man."

Luke 2: 13, 15—"And suddenly there was with the angel a multitude of the *heavenly host* praising God, and saying."

PROPOSITION: The present abode of the angels is heaven.

CHAPTER II.

THE WORK OF ANGELS.

I. Their Work in behalf of the Heirs of Salvation.

Heb. 1: 13, 14, R.V.—"But of which of the angels hath he said at any time, Sit thou on my right hand till I make thine enemies the footstool of thy feet? Are they not all ministering spirits, sent forth to do service for the sake of them that shall inherit salvation?"

PROPOSITION: Angels are ministering spirits sent forth to do service for the sake of them that shall inherit salvation.

(1) 1 Kg. 19: 5-8—"And as he lay and slept under a juniper tree, behold, then an angel touched him, and said unto him, Arise and eat. And he looked, and, behold, there was a cake baken on the coals and a cruse of water at his head. And he did eat and drink, and laid him down again. And the Angel of the Lord came again the second time and touched him, and said, Arise and eat: because the journey is too great for thee. And he arose, and did eat and drink, and went in the strength of that meat forty days and forty nights unto Horeb the mount of God."

Matt. 4: 11—"Then the devil leaveth him, and, behold, angels came and ministered unto him."

Luke 22: 43—"And there appeared an angel unto him from heaven, strengthening him."

The angels minister to the physical needs of God's children.

(2) Ps. 91: 11, 12—"For he shall give his angels charge over thee, to keep thee in all thy ways. They shall bear thee up in their hands, lest thou dash thy foot against a stone."

The angels have charge to keep in all his ways the one who abides in the secret place of the Most High and makes the Most high his habitation. (See context.) They preserve him from accident and harm.

(3) 2 Kg. 6: 15-17—"And when the servant of the man of God was risen early, and gone forth, behold a host compassed the city both with horses and chariots. And his servant said unto him, Alas, my master! how shall we do? And he answered, Fear not: for they that be with us are more than they that be with them."

Matt. 26: 53—"Thinkest thou that I cannot now pray to my Father, and he will presently give me more than twelve legions of angels?"

The angels protect God's servants from their enemies. (Comp. Gen. 19: 11; 2 Kg. 6: 18.)

God works largely through second causes. Much that God does for His children He does through their fellow-men. Other things He does through the angels.

NOTE.—It is thought by some, and not altogether without reason, that each child of God has an angel assigned to protect him: (See Matt. 18: 10.)

(4) Acts 5: 19, R.V.—"But an angel of the Lord by night opened the prison doors, and brought them out."

Acts. 12: 8–11—"And the angel said unto him, Gird thyself, and bind on thy sandals. And he did so. And he saith unto him, Cast thy garment about thee, and follow me. And he went out, and followed: and he wist not that it was true which was done by the angel, but thought he saw a vision. And when they were past the first and second ward, they came unto the iron gate that leadeth into the city; which opened to them of its own accord: and they went out, and passed through one street; and straightway the angel departed from him. And when Peter was come to himself, he said, Now I know of a truth, that the Lord hath sent forth his angel and delivered me out of the hand of Herod, and from all the expectations of the people of the Jews."

Dan. 6: 22—"My God hath sent his angel, and hath shut the lions' mouths, that they have not hurt me: forasmuch as before him innocency was found in me; and also before thee, O king, have I done no hurt."

The angels deliver God's servants from peril and evil.

(5) Acts 27: 23, 24, R.V.—"For there stood by me this night an angel of the God whose I am, whom also I serve, saying, Fear not, Paul; thou must stand before Cæsar: and lo, God hath granted thee all them that sail with thee."

The angels cheer God's servants in hardship and seeming danger.

(6) Luke 1: 11–13, 19—"And there appeared unto him an angel of the Lord standing on the right side of the altar of incense. And when Zacharias saw him, he was troubled, and fear fell upon him. But the angel said unto him, Fear not, Zacharias; for thy prayer is heard; and thy wife Elizabeth shall bear thee a son, and thou shalt call his name John. . . . And the angel answering said unto him, I am Gabriel, that stand in the presence of God; and am sent to speak unto thee, and to show thee these glad tidings."

The angels reveal God's purposes unto His servants.

(7) **Matt. 2: 13, 19, 20, R.V.**—"Now when they were departed, behold, an angel of the Lord appeared to Joseph in a dream, saying, Arise and take the young child and his mother, and flee into Egypt, and be thou there until I tell thee: for Herod will seek the young child to destroy him. . . . But when Herod was dead, behold, an angel of the Lord appeareth in a dream to Joseph in Egypt, saying."

Matt. 1: 20—"But when he thought on these things, behold, an angel of the Lord appeared unto him in a dream, saying, Joseph, thou son of David, fear not to take unto thee Mary thy wife: for that which is conceived in her is of the Holy Ghost."

Acts. 8: 26—"But an angel of the Lord spake unto Philip, saying, Arise, and go toward the south unto the way that goeth down from Jerusalem unto Gaza: the same is desert."

Acts. 10: 3–6—"He saw in a vision, as it were about the ninth hour of the day, an angel of God coming in unto him, and saying unto him, Cornelius. And he, fastening his eyes upon him, and being affrighted, said, What is it, Lord? And he said unto him, Thy prayers and thine alms are gone up for a memorial before God. And now send men to Joppa, and fetch one Simon, who is surnamed Peter: he lodgeth with one Simon a tanner, whose house is by the sea side."

The angels show God's servants what to do.

(8) **Luke 16: 22**—"And it came to pass, that the beggar died, and was carried by the angels into Abraham's bosom: the rich man also died and was buried."

The angels take God's servants at their death to a place of blessedness.

(9) **Matt. 24: 31**—"And he shall send his angels with a great sound of a trumpet, and they shall gather together his elect from the four winds, from one end of heaven to the other."

At the coming of the Son of man He shall send His angels and they shall gather together His elect from the four winds, from one end of heaven to the other.

II. The Law Given through Angels.

Heb. 2: 2, R.V.—"For if the word spoken through angels proved steadfast, and every transgression and disobedience received a just recompense of reward."

Gal. 3: 19, R.V.—"What then is the law? It was added because of transgressions, till the seed should come to whom the promise hath been made; and it was ordained through angels by the hand of a mediator."

Acts 7: 53—"Who have received the law by the disposition of angels, and have not kept it."

PROPOSITION: The law was given through the angels.

III. Their Presence with the Lord Jesus at His Coming.

Matt. 25: 31, 32—"When the Son of man shall come in his glory, and all the holy angels with him, then shall he sit upon the throne of his glory: And before him shall be gathered all nations: and he shall separate them one from another, as a shepherd ·divideth his sheep from the goats."

2 Thess. 1: 7, 8—"And to you who are troubled, rest with us; when the Lord Jesus shall be revealed from heaven with his mighty angels, in flaming fire taking vengeance on them that know not God, and that obey not the gospel of our Lord Jesus Christ."

PROPOSITION: The angels will come with the Son of man when He comes to judge the nations and to execute wrath upon them that know not God and obey not the gospel of our Lord Jesus Christ.

IV. The Executioners of God's Wrath toward the Wicked.

Matt. 13 (24–30) 39–42, R.V.—"And the enemy that sowed them is the devil: and the harvest is the end of the world; and the reapers are angels. As therefore the tares are gathered up and burned with fire; so shall it be in the end of the world. The Son of man shall send forth his angels, and they shall gather out of his kingdom all things that cause stumbling, and them that do iniquity, and shall cast them into the furnace of fire: there shall be the weeping and gnashing of teeth."

Matt. 13: 47–50, R.V.—"Again the kingdom of heaven is like unto a net, that was cast into the sea, and gathered of every kind: which, when it was filled, they drew up on the beach; and they sat down, and gathered the good into vessels, but the bad they cast away. So shall it be in the end of the world: the angels shall come forth, and sever the wicked from among the righteous, and shall cast them into the furnace of fire: there shall be the weeping and gnashing of teeth."

PROPOSITION: In the end of the age the angels shall gather out of the kingdom of the Son of man all things that cause stumbling, and those persons who do iniquity, and shall cast them into the furnace of fire. They shall sever the wicked out of the midst of the righteous, and shall cast them into the furnace of fire.

The angels are the executioners of God's wrath toward the wicked as well as His mercy toward the righteous. In this also are they not doing service for the sake of them that shall inherit salvation?

BOOK VI.

—

WHAT THE BIBLE TEACHES ABOUT THE DEVIL, OR SATAN.

CHAPTER I.

THE DEVIL; HIS EXISTENCE, NATURE, POSITION AND CHARACTER.

PRELIMINARY NOTE.—Distinguish carefully between the Devil and Demons. This distinction is quite overlooked in the Authorized Version, and even in the Revised Version, though the Revised Version notes it in the margin. The Devil and Demons are two entirely distinct orders of beings. The Bible doctrine regarding Satan is a very practical doctrine. There are certainly few doctrines that will go further than this in teaching us our utter dependence upon God and in driving us to prayer.

I. The Existence of the Devil, or Satan.

Matt. 13: 19, 39—"When any one heareth the word of the kingdom, and understandeth it not, *then cometh the wicked one*, and catcheth away that which was sown in his heart. This is he that receiveth seed by the way-side. . . . *The enemy that sowed them is the devil;* the harvest is the end of the world; and the reapers are the angels." (Is this a mere figure of speech? In parables the figures always occur in the parables themselves. In the interpretation of the parables the figures are explained, and we have the realities which the figures represent. The verses above are not taken from the parable but from Christ's own interpretation of it.)

Jno. 13: 2—"And supper being ended, *the devil* having now put into the heart of Judas Iscariot, Simon's son, to betray him."

Acts 5: 3—"But Peter said, Ananias, why hath *Satan* filled thine heart to lie to the Holy Ghost, and to keep back part of the price of the land?"

I Pet. 5: 8—"Be sober, be vigilant; because your adversary *the devil*, as a roaring lion, walketh about, seeking whom he may devour."

Eph. 6: 11, 12—"Put on the whole armour of God, that ye may be able to stand against the wiles *of the devil*. For we wrestle not against flesh and blood, but against principalities, against powers, against the rulers of the darkness of this world, against spiritual wickedness in high places." (Also many other passages.)

PROPOSITION: There is a personal devil.

His personality will come out more clearly as we study his nature.

II. The Position and Nature of Satan.

(1) Jude: 8, 9, R. V.—"Yet in like manner these also in their dream-ings defile the flesh, and set at naught dominion and rail at *dignities*. But Michael the archangel, when contending with the devil he disputed about the body of Moses, *durst not bring against him a railing judgment*, but said, The Lord rebuke thee."

FIRST PROPOSITION: The position of the Devil was so exalted that even Michael, the archangel, did not dare to bring a railing judgment against him.

The context might seem to imply that the position of the Devil was more exalted than that of Michael himself. Further on other passages will be considered that seem to confirm this idea. Light, contemptuous speech about the Devil is entirely unwarranted.

(2) Eph. 2: 2—"Wherein in time past ye walked according to the course of this world, according to *the prince of the power of the air*, the spirit that now worketh in the children of disobedience."

SECOND PROPOSITION: The Devil is the Prince of the Power of the Air.

(3) Jno. 12: 31—"Now is the judgment of this world: now shall the *prince of this world* be cast out."

Jno. 14: 30—"Hereafter I will not talk much with you: for *the prince of this world* cometh, and hath nothing in me."

Jno. 16: 11—"Of judgment, because *the prince of this world* is judged."

THIRD PROPOSITION: The Devil is the Prince of this World.

QUESTION: When did he become so? Did he become so through Adam and Eve listening to him in Eden, or was this world a department assigned to him of God as separate kingdoms have been assigned to different celestial potentates? (Dan. 10: 12, 13.) And did he drag his dominion down with him in his own fall? These are questions which the Bible does not seem to answer very clearly, and we ought not to try to be wise above what is written. (Deut. 29: 29.) But this much is clear: he is now "the Prince of this World." This is clear also from a study of the social and commercial life of the day.

(4) 2 Cor. 4: 4—"In whom *the god of this world* hath blinded the minds of them which believe not, lest the light of the glorious gospel of Christ, who is the image of God, should shine unto them."

FOURTH PROPOSITION: The Devil is the god of this Age.

(The word translated "world" in this passage, both A.V. and R.V., is not the same word translated "world" in passages under the preceding proposition. It should be translated "age," as in Marg. R.V.)

III. The Devil's Power.

(1) Eph. 6: 11, 12, R.V.—"Put on the whole armour of God, that ye may be able to stand against the wiles of the devil. For our wrestling is not against flesh and blood, but against the principalities, against the powers, against the world-rulers of this darkness, against the spiritual hosts of wickedness in the heavenly places."

FIRST PROPOSITION: The Devil has far greater power than men—flesh and blood.

He has under him beings so great in power and dignity as to be spoken of as "the Principalities, the Powers, the World-rulers, Spiritual Hosts (spiritual beings) of wickedness in the heavenly places." The conflict we have on hand is terrific. Let us not underestimate it.

(2) Luke 11: 14-18—"And he was casting out a devil, and it was dumb. And it came to pass, when the devil was gone out the dumb spake; and the people wondered. But some of them said, He casteth out devils through Beelzebub the chief of the devils. And others, tempting him, sought of him a sign from heaven. But he, knowing their thoughts, said unto them, Every kingdom divided against itself is brought to desolation; and a house divided against a house falleth. If Satan also be divided against himself, how shall his kingdom stand? because ye say, that I cast out devils through Beelzebub."

SECOND PROPOSITION: Satan is king over the realm of demons.

(3) Dan. 10: 5, 6, 12, 13—"Then I lifted up mine eyes, and looked, and behold a certain man clothed in linen, whose loins were girded with fine gold of Uphaz: His body also was like the beryl, and his face as the appearance of lightning, and his eyes as lamps of fire, and his arms and his feet like in colour to polished brass, and the voice of his words like the voice of a multitude. . . . Then said he unto me, fear not, Daniel: for from the first day that thou didst set thine heart

to understand, and to chasten thyself before thy God, thy words were heard, and I am come for thy words. But the prince of the kingdom of Persia withstood me one and twenty days: but, lo, Michael, one of the chief princes, came to help me; and I remained there with the kings of Persia."

THIRD PROPOSITION: The Devil, or one of his subordinates, has power to resist and retard a glorious angel many days.

(4) Acts 26: 18—"To open their eyes, and to turn them from darkness to light, and from the power of Satan unto God, that they may receive forgiveness of sins, and inheritance among them which are sanctified by faith that is in me."

FOURTH PROPOSITION: The whole mass of unsaved men are in Satan's power.

(5) 1 Jno. 5: 19, R.V.—"We know that we are of God, and the whole world lieth in the evil one."

FIFTH PROPOSITION: The whole world—i. e., the entire mass of men, except those who have been called out, the Church —lieth in the Evil One. They rest supinely in his embrace.

(6) Job. 1: 10–12—"Hast not thou made a hedge about him, and about his house, and about all that he hath on every side? thou hast blessed the work of his hands, and his substance is increased in the land. But put forth thine hand now, and touch all that he hath, and he will curse thee to thy face. And the LORD said unto Satan, Behold, all that he hath is in thy power; only upon himself put not forth thine hand. So Satan went forth from the presence of the Lord."

SIXTH PROPOSITION: Satan can exert his vast power only so far as Jehovah suffers him to do so.

IV. The Devil's Cunning.

(1) 2 Cor. 2: 11—"Lest Satan should get an advantage of us: for we are not ignorant of his devices."

FIRST PROPOSITION: The Devil has many and subtle devices.

(2) Eph. 6: 11, 12, R.V.—"Put on the whole armour of God, that ye may be able to stand against the wiles of the devil. For our wrestling is not against flesh and blood, but against the principalities, against the powers, against the world-rulers of this darkness, against the spiritual hosts of wickedness in the heavenly places."

SECOND PROPOSITION: The Devil has so many and such cunning wiles that we need to put on the whole armor of God to stand against them.

The Devil doubtless gets the mastery of many, through his wiles and devices, that he could not overcome by an open exercise of his power. We have an illustration of his wiles in the temptation of Eve and of Christ. The "old serpent" is more dangerous than the "roaring lion."

(3) 2 Thess. 2: 9, 10, R.V.—"Even he, whose coming is according to the working of Satan with all power and signs and lying wonders, and with all deceit of unrighteousness for them that are perishing: because they received not the love of the truth, that they might be saved."

THIRD PROPOSITION: Satan displays such power and signs and wonders of falsehood as utterly deceive those who receive not the love of the truth.

(Comp. Matt. 24: 24—"For there shall arise false Christs, and false prophets, and shall shew great signs and wonders; insomuch that, if it were possible, they shall deceive the very elect.")

Some have said, "The Devil is God's Ape"—*i. e.*, he imitates God's work.

(4) 2 Cor. 11: 14—"And no marvel; for Satan himself is transformed into an angel of light."

FOURTH PROPOSITION: Satan fashioneth himself into an angel of light.

The Devil is never more dangerous than when he does this. When Satan gets into the pulpit, or the theological chair, and pretends to teach Christianity, when in reality he is corrupting it; pretends to be teaching Christian evidences when in reality he is undermining the very foundations of faith; pretends to be teaching Biblical Introduction, when in reality he is making the Bible out to be a book that is not worthy of being introduced—then look out for him; he is at his most dangerous work. There was never a science more really godless and subversive of true Christian faith than that which Satan is now exploiting under the pseudonym, "*Christian* Science." Happy is the man in these days who is not ignorant of the devices of the Devil, and realizes that he frequently masquerades as an angel of light.

V. The Devil's Wickedness.

(1) 1 Jno. 5: 19, R.V.—"We know that we are of God, and the whole word lieth in *the evil one*."

Matt. 5: 37, R.V.—"But let your speech be, Yea, yea; Nay, nay: and whatsoever is more than these is of *the evil one.*"

6: 13, R.V.—"And bring us not into temptation, but deliver us from *the evil one.*"

FIRST PROPOSITION: The Devil is the Evil One. He is the impersonation of evil and the source of it in others.

(2) 1 Jno. 3: 8—"He that committeth sin is of the devil; for the devil sinneth from the beginning. For this purpose the Son of God was manifested, that he might destroy the works of the devil."

SECOND PROPOSITION: The Devil sinneth from the beginning.

QUESTION: What beginning is here referred to? Does this mean that the Devil sinned from the very origin of all things, and that he was created sinful? We shall see later that Ezek. 28:15 refers to Satan, and that the Devil was created upright. The verse means, then, that Satan is the original sinner. The expression "from the beginning" is characteristic of this epistle, and does not necessarily mean from the origin of things. (See *e. g.*, the 11th verse.)

(3) Jno. 8: 44—"Ye are of your father the devil, and the lusts of your father ye will do: he was a murderer from the beginning, and abode not in the truth, because there is no truth in him. When he speaketh a lie, he speaketh of his own; for he is a liar and the father of it."

THIRD PROPOSITION: The Devil was a murderer from the beginning. He is a liar and the father of it. There is absolutely no truth in him.

VI. The Malignity of the Devil.

(1) Jno. 8: 44—"Ye are of your father the devil, and the lusts of your father ye will do: he was a murderer from the beginning, and abode not in the truth, because there is no truth in him. When he speaketh a lie, he speaketh of his own: for he is a liar, and the father of it."

FIRST PROPOSITION: The Devil was a murderer from the beginning.

(2) 2 Cor. 4: 4, R.V.—"In whom the god of this world hath blinded the minds of the unbelieving, that the light of the gospel of the glory of Christ, who is the image of God, should not dawn upon them."

SECOND PROPOSITION: *The Devil blinds the minds of men to the end that the light of the gospel of the glory of Christ, who is the image of God, may not dawn upon them.*

What marvelous, incredible malignity is that!

(3) Luke 8:12—"Those by the wayside are they that hear; then cometh the devil, and taketh away the word out of their hearts, lest they should believe and be saved."

THIRD PROPOSITION: *The Devil comes and takes away the saving Word of God out of the hearts of men where it has been sown, in order to keep them from believing and being saved.*

We will have further evidence and illustration of his malignity under his work.

VII. His Cowardice.

Jas. 4:7—"Submit yourselves therefore to God. Resist the devil, and he will flee from you."

PROPOSITION: *When the Devil is resisted he flees.*

CHAPTER II.

EZEKIEL XXVIII.

Ezek. 28:1-19, R.V.—"The word of the LORD came again unto me, saying, Son of man, say unto the prince of Tyre, Thus saith the LORD God: Because thine heart is lifted up, and thou hast said, I am a god, I sit in the seat of God, in the midst of the seas; yet thou art man, and not God, though thou didst set thine heart as the heart of God: behold, thou art wiser than Daniel; there is no secret that they can hide from thee: by thy wisdom and by thine understanding thou hast gotten thee riches, and hast gotten gold and silver into thy treasures: by thy great wisdom and by thy traffic hast thou increased thy riches, and thine heart is lifted up because of thy riches: therefore thus saith the Lord God: Because thou hast set thine heart as the heart of God; therefore behold, I will bring strangers upon thee, the terrible of the nations: and they shall draw their swords against the beauty of thy wisdom, and they shall defile thy brightness. They shall bring thee down to the pit; and thou shalt die the death of them that are slain, in the heart of the seas. Wilt thou yet say before him that slayest thee, I am God? but thou art man, and not God, in the hand of him that woundeth thee. Thou shalt die the deaths of the uncircumcised by the hand of strangers: for I have spoken it, saith the LORD God. Moreover the word of the LORD came unto me, saying, Son of man, take up a lamentation for the King of Tyre, and say unto him, Thus saith the LORD God: *Thou sealest up the sum, full of* wisdom, and perfect in beauty. Thou *wast in Eden the garden of God:* every precious stone was thy covering, the sardius, the topaz, and the diamond, the beryl, the onyx, and the jasper, the sapphire, the emerald, and the carbuncle, and gold: the workmanship of thy tabrets and of thy pipes was in thee; in the day that thou wast created they were prepared. Thou wast *the anointed cherub that covereth:* and I set thee, so that thou *wast upon the holy mountain of God;* thou hast walked up and down *in the midst of the stones of fire.* Thou wast perfect in thy ways from the day that thou wast created, till unrighteousness was found in thee. By the multitude of thy traffic they filled the midst of thee with violence, and thou hast sinned: therefore have I cast thee as profane out of the mountain of God; and I have destroyed thee, O covering cherub, from the midst of the stones of fire. Thine heart was lifted up because of thy beauty, thou hast corrupted thy wisdom by reason of thy brightness: I have cast thee to the ground, I have laid thee before kings, that they may behold thee. By the multitude of thine ini-

quities, in the unrighteousness of thy traffic, thou hast profaned thy
sanctuaries; therefore have I brought forth a fire from the midst of
thee, it hath devoured thee, and I have turned thee to ashes upon the
earth in the sight of all them that behold thee. All they that know
thee among the peoples shall be astonished at thee: thou art become a
terror, and thou shalt never be any more."

To whom does this remarkable passage refer ?

Vv. 1–10 refer at least primarily to the prince of Tyre, then
reigning (Ittiobalus by name, according to Josephus). They
were fulfilled in the seige of Tyre by Nebuchadnezzar.

Vv. 11–19 have expressions which it is difficult, if not
impossible, to refer to any mere man—e. g., vv. 12, 13, 14. There
are, however, other verses that seem to indicate an earthly kingdom—e. g., 16, 18.

What is the explanation of this enigma ?

We frequently find in prophecy that the prophet is borne
on from speaking of a contemporaneous event to some event of
the last times, of which the contemporaneus event is in some respects a type. For example, in Matt. 24: 15–21, Christ speaks of
the destruction of Jerusalem, which was in a very true sense a
Day of the Lord, and from that he passes on to speak of the great
Day of the Lord yet to come in vv. 22–31. So swift is the tran-
sition from the one to the other that it is difficult to mark exactly
where it takes place. So in Ezekiel's prophecy. Ittiobalus was
in important respects a type of "the man of sin." (Vv. 2, 5, 6.
Compare 2 Thess, 2: 3, 4. Also v. 2 with Dan. 11: 41–45. Note
"The heart of the seas " and " between the seas.")

But there are some things in vv. 11–19 (the king of Tyre)
that seem to apply to a supernatural and some to an earthly
king. This earthly king is to have enormous commerce. Compare the great development of commerce in the last days.

Rev. 13: 16, 17—" And he caused all, both small and great, rich and
poor, free and bond, to receive a mark in their right hand, or in their
foreheads: and that no man might buy or sell, save he that had the
mark, or the name of the beast, or the number of his name."

Rev. 18: 3, 9–19—" For all nations have drunk of the wine of the
wrath of her fornication, and the kings of the earth have committed
fornication with her, and the merchants of the earth are waxed rich
through the abundance of her delicacies. . . . And the kings of
the earth, who have committed fornication and lived deliciously with
her, shall bewail her, and lament for her, when they shall see the

smoke of her burning, standing afar off for the fear of her torment, saying, Alas, alas, that great city, that was clothed in fine linen, and purple, and scarlet, and decked with gold, and precious stones, and pearls ! For in one hour so great riches is come to nought. And every shipmaster, and all the company in ships, and sailors, and as many as trade by sea, stood afar off. And cried when they saw the smoke of her burning; saying, What city is like unto this great city ! And they cast dust on their heads, and cried, weeping and wailing, saying, Alas, alas, that great city, wherein were made rich all that had ships in the sea by reason of her costliness! For in one hour is she made desolate."

The simplest explanation of all this is that the King of Tyre represents the Anti-Christ (as the Prince of Tyre was the type of the Anti-Christ) and that he is to be an incarnation of Satan as the true Christ was an incarnation of God.

(Comp. 2 Thess. 2: 8, 9, R.V.—"When shall be revealed the law-less one . . . whose coming is according to the working of Satan with all power, etc.")

If this is the true solution, this passage teaches us much about Satan.

(1) V. 12—"Son of man, take up a lamentation upon the king of Tyrus, and say unto him, thus saith the Lord God; Thou sealest up the sum, full of wisdom, and perfect in beauty."

FIRST PROPOSITION: Satan was full of wisdom and perfect in beauty, sealing up the sum of created perfection.

(2) V. 13—"Thou hast been in Eden the garden of God; every precious stone was thy covering, the sardius, topaz, and the diamond, the beryl, the onyx, and the jasper, the sapphire, the emerald, and the carbuncle, and gold; the workmanship of thy tabrets and of thy pipes was prepared in thee in the day that thou wast created."

SECOND PROPOSITION: He was in Eden, the garden of God.

This does not appear to have been the Adamic Eden, but an earlier one. The Adamic Eden was remarkable for its vegetable glory. (Gen. 2: 9.) This early Eden for its mineral glory. Compare the New Jerusalem which is to be.

Rev. 21: 10–21—"And he carried me away in the spirit to a great and high mountain, and shewed me that great city, the holy Jerusalem, descending out of heaven from God. Having the glory of God: and her light was *like unto a stone most precious*, even *like a jasper stone*, clear as crystal; and had a wall great and high, and had twelve gates, and at the gates twelve angels, and names written thereon, which are the names of the twelve tribes of the children of Israel: On the east

three gates; on the north three gates; on the south three gates; and on
the west three gates. And the wall of the city had twelve foundations,
and in them the names of the twelve apostles of the Lamb. And he
that talked with me had a golden reed to measure the city, and the
gates thereof, and the wall thereof. And the city lieth foursquare,
and the length is as large as the breadth; and he measured the city
with the reed, twelve thousand furlongs. The length and the breadth
and the height of it are equal. And he measured the wall thereof, a
hundred and forty and four cubits, according to the measure of a man,
that is, of the angel. And the building of the wall of it was *of jasper:*
and the city was pure gold, like unto clear glass, and the foundations
of the wall of the city were garnished with all manner of precious
stones. The first foundation was *jasper;* the second, *sapphire;* the
third, a *chalcedony;* the fourth an *emerald;* the fifth, *sardonyx;* the
sixth, *sardius;* the seventh, chrysolite: the eighth, beryl; the ninth
a topaz; the tenth, a chrysoprasus; the eleventh, a jacinth; the twelfth
an amethyst. And the twelve gates were twelve pearls; every several
gate was of one pearl; and the street of the city was pure gold, as it
were transparent glass."

In the Adamic Eden Satan was present not as here, as a
minister of God, but as an apostate spirit and a tempter. The
glory of this early Eden seems to have been specially prepared
for Satan. (R.V., last clause v. 13.) There was also the pomp
of royalty, tabrets and pipes.

(3) V. 14 (a)—"Thou wast the anointed cherub that covereth."

*THIRD PROPOSITION: Satan was the anointed cherub that
covereth.*

(*a*) Anointed and set apart as the priest of God. (Lev.
8:12.) (*b*) A Cherub, a high, or it may be the highest, rank
in the angelic world. Compare the living creatures leading the
worship of the universe in Rev. 4:9, 10, R.V.:

"And when the living creatures shall give glory and honour and
thanks to him that sitteth on the throne, to him that liveth for ever
and ever, the four and twenty elders shall fall down before him that
sitteth on the throne, and shall worship him that liveth for ever and
ever, and shall cast their crowns before the throne, saying." Rev.
5: 14, R.V.—"And the four living creatures said, Amen. And the
elders fell down and worshipped."

(*c*) He was not *a* cherub, but "*the* cherub"; (*d*) the
cherub "*that covereth.*" There may be an allusion to this in the
covering cherubim.

Ex. 37: 9—"And the cherubim spread out their wings on high, and *covered with their wings over the mercy seat,* with their faces one to another; even to the mercy seatward were the faces of the cherubim."

It seems to be hinted that Satan was the one who led the worship of the universe. If so, he tried to direct to himself what properly belonged to God. This is a danger with all priests and ministers.

(4) V. 14 (b)—"And I set thee, so that thou wast upon the holy mountain of God."

FOURTH PROPOSITION: The Devil was "upon the holy mountain of God"—i. e., the place where God visibly manifested His glory.

(5) V. 14 (c)—"Thou hast walked up and down in the midst of the stones of fire."

FIFTH PROPOSITION: The Devil "walked up and down in the midst of the stones of fire."

The living creatures of Ezek. 1: 15, 22, 25, 26, R. V., were just beneath a "firmament, like the colour of the terrible crystal." "And above the firmament was the likeness of a throne, as the *appearance of a sapphire stone."* In Ex. 24: 10, R. V., when the seventy elders "saw the God of Israel," "there was under his feet as it were a paved work of sapphire stone, and as it were the very heaven for clearness." In the seventeenth verse "the appearance of the glory of the LORD was like devouring fire on the top of the mount in the eyes of the children of Israel." This may give us an idea of what "the stones of fire" were. Satan seems to have been very near God.

(6) V. 15—"Thou wast perfect in thy ways from the day that thou wast created, till unrighteousness was found in thee."

SIXTH PROPOSITION: Satan was perfect in his ways from the day that he was created until unrighteousness was found in him. He is evidently a created being.

(7) V. 16—"By the multitude of thy traffic they filled the midst of thee with violence, and thou hast sinned."

This seems to refer in part to Satan's manifestation in the Anti-Christ. It has been suggested that the word translated "traffic" comes from a root which means to travel either for merchandise or for slander, and the word should have been translated "slander," and that the Devil means "the slanderer." (Compare Rev. 12:10; Job 1:9.) This is not likely. There is a closely related word, from the same root, which is translated in the several passages where used "slander," "carry tales," "tale-bearer," but the precise word found in our passage is used four times (Ezek. 28:5; Ezek. 28:18; Ezek. 26:12; Ezek. 28:16), and is translated either "traffic" or "merchandise." All these passages are in Ezekiel, and some of them it would be impossible to translate by "slander." The word from which it is immediately derived is used twice (Song of Solomon 3:6; Ezek. 27:20) and is translated "merchant" (R.V. of Ezek. 27:20, "trafficker").

(8) V. 17 (a,b)—"Thine heart was lifted up because of thy beauty, thou hast corrupted thy wisdom by reason of thy brightness."

SEVENTH PROPOSITION: Satan's heart was lifted up because of his beauty; he corrupted his wisdom because of his brightness. (Compare 1 Tim. 3:6, R.V. Marg.)

(9) V. 16—"Therefore have I cast thee as profane out of the mountain of God; and I have destroyed thee, O covering cherub, from the midst of the stones of fire."

EIGHTH PROPOSITION: Satan shall be (or is) cast out of the mountain of God and destroyed from the midst of the stones of fire.

(10) V. 17 (c)—"I have cast thee to the ground, I have laid thee before kings, that they may behold thee."

NINTH PROPOSITION: He shall be cast to the earth and made a spectacle, and "turned to ashes" before kings and all that behold. (V. 18.) (Compare Rev. 12:9, 10; 2 Thess. 2:8; Rev. 19:20.)

CHAPTER III.

THE ABODE AND WORK OF SATAN.

1. The Abode of Satan.

(1) Eph. 6: 11, 12, R.V.—"Put on the whole armour of God, that ye may be able to stand against the wiles of the devil. For our wrestling is not against flesh and blood, but against the principalities, against the powers, against the world-rulers of this darkness, against the spiritual hosts of wickedness *in the heavenly places.*"

FIRST PROPOSITION: Satan and the principalities, the powers, the world-rulers of this darkness, the spiritual hosts of wickedness are in the heavenly places, or heavenlies.

(Compare Job. 1: 6—"Now there was a day when the sons of God came to present themselves before the LORD, and Satan came also among them." Rev. 12:9—"And the great dragon was cast out, that old serpent, called the Devil, and Satan, which deceived the whole world: he was cast out into the earth, and his angels were cast out with him.")

The prophecy of this latter verse seems to refer to a time yet to come.

On the other hand we are told "God spared not angels when they sinned, but cast them down to hell, etc." (2 Pet. 2: 4, R.V.) However, it does not say, as in the Authorized Version "the angels that sinned," which might imply all of them, but simply "angels sinning," without specifying whether some or all.

(2) Job. 1:7—"And the LORD said unto Satan, Whence comest thou? Then Satan answered the LORD, and said, *From going to and fro in the earth,* and from walking up and down in it."

SECOND PROPOSITION: Satan goes to and fro in the earth and walks up and down in it.

(Compare 1 Pet. 5: 8—"Be sober, be vigilant; because your adversary the devil, as a roaring lion walketh about, seeking whom he may devour.")

The earth seems to be the especial field of his activity. As in the coming day, Christ and His Church, though heavenly beings, will rule an earthly kingdom, so now Satan and his hosts, heavenly beings, exercise their activity among an earthly people.

II. The Work of Satan.

(1) Gen. 3: 1–6—"Now the serpent was more subtle than any beast of the field which the LORD God had made. And he said unto the woman, Yea, hath God said, Ye shall not eat of every tree of the garden? And the woman said unto the serpent, We may eat of the fruit of the trees of the garden: but of the fruit of the tree which is in the midst of the garden, God hath said, Ye shall not eat of it, neither shall ye touch it, lest ye die. And the serpent said unto the woman, Ye shall not surely die: for God doth know that in the day ye eat thereof, then your eyes shall be opened, and ye shall be as gods, know-ing good and evil. And when the woman saw that the tree was good for food, and that it was pleasant to the eyes, and a tree to be desired to make one wise, she took of the fruit thereof, and did eat, and gave also unto her husband with her; and he did eat." (Compare Rev. 12: 9.)

FIRST PROPOSITION: Satan is the author of sin in this world.

(2) Acts 10: 38—"How God anointed Jesus of Nazareth with the Holy Ghost and with power: who went about doing good, and *healing* all that were *oppressed of the devil;* for God was with him."

Luke 13: 16—"And ought not this woman, being a daughter of Abraham, *whom Satan hath bound,* lo, these eighteen years, be loosed from this bond on the Sabbath day"?

SECOND PROPOSITION: Satan is the author of sickness.

(3) Heb. 2: 14—"Forasmuch then as the children are partakers of flesh and blood, he also himself likewise took part of the same; that through death he might destroy him that had the power of death, that is, the devil."

THIRD PROPOSITION: Satan has the power of death.

He is its author. Every cemetery and every funeral, and every separation by death, owes its existence to the Devil.

(4) 1 Chron. 21: 1, R.V.—"And Satan stood up against Israel, and moved David to number Israel."

Matt. 4: 1, 3, 5, 6, 8, 9—"Then was Jesus led up of the Spirit into the wilderness to be *tempted* of the devil. . . . And when *the tempter* came to him, he said, If thou be the Son of God, command that these stones be made bread. . . . Then the devil taketh him up into the holy city, and setteth him on a pinnacle of the temple, and saith unto him, If thou be the Son of God, cast thyself down: for it is written, He shall give his angels charge concerning thee: and in their hands they shall bear thee up, lest at any time thou dash thy foot against a stone. . . . Again the devil taketh him up into an exceeding high mountain, and sheweth him all the kingdoms of the world, and the glory of them; and saith unto him, All these things will I give thee, if thou wilt fall down and worship me."

FOURTH PROPOSITION; The Devil tempts men to sin. He is the "tempter." (Compare 1 Thess. 3: 5.)

(5) 1 Tim. 3: 7—"Moreover he must have a good report of them which are without; lest he fall into reproach and the snare of the devil."

2 Tim. 2: 26—"And that they may recover themselves out of the snare of the devil, who are taken captive by him at his will."

FIFTH PROPOSITION: The Devil lays snares for men.

(6) Acts 5: 3—"But Peter said, Ananias, why hath Satan filled thine heart, to keep back part of the price of the land?"

Jno. 13: 2—"And supper being ended, the devil having now put into the heart of Judas Iscariot, Simon's son, to betray him."

SIXTH PROPOSITION: The Devil puts wicked purposes into the hearts of men.

This is, of course, by their consent, or when they leave an opening.

Eph. 4: 27—"Neither give place to the devil." Jas. 4: 7—"Submit yourselves therefore to God. Resist the devil, and he will flee from you."

(7) Jno. 13: 27—"And after the sop Satan entered into him. Then said Jesus unto him, That thou doest, do quickly."

SEVENTH PROPOSITION: The Devil personally enters into men.

He caricatures God's work. (Jno. 14: 23. Compare also Eph. 2: 2 with Phil. 2: 13.)

(8) 2 Cor. 4: 4, R.V.—"In whom the god of this world hath blinded the minds of the unbelieving, that the light of the gospel of the glory of Christ, who is the image of God, should not dawn upon them."

EIGHTH PROPOSITION: Satan blinds the minds of the unbelieving that the light of the gospel of the glory of Christ, who is the image of God, may not dawn upon them.

It is the work of the Holy Spirit to illuminate the minds of men—especially believers—and reveal Jesus. It is the work of the Evil One to blind the minds of men—especially unbelievers—so that they cannot see the glory that is in Jesus. It is for each individual to say to the work of which he will surrender himself. The awful, almost incredible blindness of men who are intelligent on other subjects to the simplest and plainest truth about Christ is due to this blinding work of Satan.

(9)   Mark 4: 15—"And these are they by the way side, where the word is sown; but when they have heard, Satan cometh immediately, and taketh away the word that was sown in their hearts."

NINTH PROPOSITION: Satan taketh away the word out of the hearts of those who hear it but do not understand and hold it fast. (See Matt. 13: 19.)

Wherever the word is preached Satan is present, either in person or through his agents, to snatch away the seed sown.   It is needful for us to pray God to keep guard over the seed sown.   It is also needful to hold fast to the truth we have heard lest Satan snatch it away. (Luke 8: 15, R.V.) It is the work of the Spirit to "bring to remembrance" what Christ has spoken. (Jno. 14: 26.) It is the work of Satan to make men forget it.   The world and the flesh are quite ready to co-operate with the Devil in this work.

(10)   Matt. 13: 39—"The enemy that sowed them is the devil; the harvest is the end of the world; and the reapers are the angels."

TENTH PROPOSITION: The Devil sows tares in God's field.

The field here is the world (v. 38). Satan mixes his children up with God's. He does this also in the visible Church. Satan is ever busy corrupting the Church and its doctrine. He gets the woman to mix the leaven in the children's meal, and the rotten stuff goes on putrefying, and all is fermented. (Compare Matt. 13: 33 and 1 Cor. 5: 6, 7.)

(11)   2 Thess. 2: 9, 10, R.V—" Even he, whose coming is according to the working of Satan with all power and signs and lying wonders, and with all deceit of unrighteousness for them that are perishing; because they received not the love of the truth, that they might be saved."

ELEVENTH PROPOSITION: Satan will give power to the lawless one to utterly deceive the perishing, those who receive not the love of truth.

Men can have truth or lies, whichever they prefer. If they will to do God's will, He will give them truth (Jno. 7: 17, R.V.), and the Spirit will guide them ultimately into all the truth. (Jno. 16: 13, R.V.) But if men will not have truth Satan will lead them step by step into all manner of delusion and falsehood.

(12) 2 Cor. 11: 14, 15—"And no marvel; for Satan himself is transformed into an angel of light. Therefore it is no great thing if *his ministers* also be transformed as the ministers of righteousness; whose end shall be according to their works."

Rev. 3: 9—"Behold, I will make them of *the synagogue of Satan*, which say they are Jews, and are not, but do lie; behold, I will make them to come and worship before thy feet, and to know that I have loved thee."

TWELFTH PROPOSITION: Satan has his ministers and his churches to carry on his work.

(13) 2 Cor. 12: 7—"And lest I should be exalted above measure through the abundance of the revelations, there was given to me a thorn in the flesh, the messenger of Satan to buffet me, lest I should be exalted above measure."

THIRTEENTH PROPOSITION: Satan, by his messengers, buffets Gods servants.

This, however, results in good to them. It keeps them humble and drives them to prayer. (Compare v. 8.)

(14) Zech. 3: 1—"And he shewed me Joshua the high priest standing before the angel of the LORD, and Satan standing at his right hand to resist him."

Dan. 10: 13—"But the prince of the kingdom of Persia withstood me one and twenty days: but, lo, Michael, one of the chief princes, came to help me; and I remained there with the kings of Persia."

FOURTEENTH PROPOSITION: Satan resists the servants of God in the prosecution of their work.

(15) 1 Thess. 2 18, R.V.—"Because we would fain have come unto you, I Paul once and again; and Satan hindered us."

FIFTEENTH PROPOSITION: Satan hinders Christ's servants in the carrying out of their desires.

But good may come of that. This hindering of Paul going to Thessalonica gave to the saints there, and to coming generations, this precious epistle.

(16) Luke 22:31—"And the Lord said, Simon, Simon, behold, Satan hath desired to have you, that he may sift you as wheat."

SIXTEENTH PROPOSITION: Satan shakes Christ's disciples up and sifts them.

Only good comes of this in the end. Simon came out of Satan's merciless sieve purer wheat than he was before. Satan simply succeeded in sifting some of the chaff out of him. (Rom. 8:28.)

(17) Rev. 12:9, 10—"And the great dragon was cast out, that old serpent, called the Devil, and Satan, which deceiveth the whole world: he was cast out into the earth, and his angels were cast out with him. And I heard a loud voice saying in heaven, Now is come salvation, and strength, and the kingdom of our God, and the power of his Christ: for the accuser of our brethren is cast down, which accused them before our God day and night.

SEVENTEENTH PROPOSITION: Satan accuses the brethren before God day and night.

The Greek word for "devil" means "traducer," "accuser," "slanderer." (Comp. Job. 1:6–9; 2:3–5.)

(18) Rev. 2:10—"Fear none of those things which thou shalt suffer: behold, the devil shall cast some of you into prison, that ye may be tried; and ye shall have tribulation ten days: be thou faithful unto death, and I will give thee a crown of life."

EIGHTEENTH PROPOSITION: The Devil casts Christ's servants into prison.

Only good need come of that. They are thus tried and purified and obtain the crown of life.

CHAPTER IV.

OUR DUTY REGARDING THE DEVIL, AND HIS DESTINY.

I. Our Duty Regarding the Devil.

(1) 1 Pet. 5: 8, R.V.—"Be sober, be watchful: your adversary the devil, as a roaring lion, walketh about seeking whom he may devour."

FIRST PROPOSITION: The fact of the Devil's existence, activity and power should make us circumspect and watchful.

Carelessness and heedlessness are out of the question when such an enemy is abroad.

(2) Eph. 4: 27—"Neither give place to the devil."

SECOND PROPOSITION: We must give no place to the Devil.

He is ever seeking an opening. We should see to it that he gets none. The context (v. 26) suggests how such an opening is often given—viz., by being angry and continuing in wrath. This door into the heart is a favorite one with the Devil.

(3) Jas. 4: 7—"Submit yourselves therefore to God. Resist the devil and he will flee from you."

THIRD PROPOSITION: We should resist the Devil.

Though the Devil is strong it is ours in God's strength, and by the power of the Word, to withstand him. (1 Jno. 2: 14.)

(4) Eph. 6: 11—"Put on the whole armour of God, that ye may be able to stand against the wiles of the devil."

FOURTH PROPOSITION: We should put on the whole armor of God that we may be able to stand against the wiles of the Devil.

What that armor is, is fully described in vv. 14-18: "Stand therefore, having your loins girt about with truth, and having on the breast-plate of righteousness; and your feet shod with the preparation of the gospel of peace; above all taking the shield of faith, wherewith ye shall be able to quench all the fiery darts of the wicked.   And take the helmet of salvation, and the sword of the Spirit, which is the word of God: Praying always with all prayer and supplication in the Spirit, and watching thereunto with all perseverance and supplication for all saints."

NOTE.—1 Jno. 5: 18, R.V.—"We know that whosoever is begotten of God sinneth not; but he that was begotten of God keepeth him, and the evil one toucheth him not." Col. 1: 13—"Who hath delivered us from the power of darkness, and hath translated us into the kingdom of his dear Son."

Christ guardeth and delivereth God's children from the Devil's power.   (Compare also Jno. 10: 28, 29.)

II. The Devil's Destiny.

(1) Gen. 3: 14—"And the LORD God said unto the serpent, because thou hast done this, thou art cursed above all cattle, and above every beast of the field; upon thy belly shalt thou go, and dust shalt thou eat all the days of thy life."

FIRST PROPOSITION: Ever since he tempted man, Satan has been under an especial curse.

The serpent does not share in the coming redemption of the animal world.   He shall still eat dust.   (Is. 65: 25.)

(2) Matt. 25: 41, R.V.—"Then shall he say also unto them on the left hand, Depart from me, ye cursed, into the eternal fire which is prepared for the devil and his angels."

SECOND PROPOSITION: The eternal fire is prepared for the Devil and his angels.

(3) 1 Jno. 3: 8—"He that committeth sin is of the devil; for the devil sinneth from the beginning. For this purpose the Son of God was manifested, that he might destroy the works of the devil."

THIRD PROPOSITION: The Son of God was manifested that he might destroy the works of the Devil.   Utter failure, disappointment and torment awaits him on every hand.

(4) Heb. 2: 14, R.V.—"Since then the children are sharers in flesh and blood, he also himself in like manner partook of the same; that through death he might bring to nought him that had the power of death, that is, the devil."

FOURTH PROPOSITION: Jesus Christ has already brought him to naught (or made him utterly ineffective) through His death.

Satan's power was utterly undermined and doomed by the death of Christ.

(5) Col. 2: 15, R.V.—"Having put off from himself the principalities and the powers, he made a show of them openly, triumphing over them in it."

FIFTH PROPOSITION: Christ made an open show of Satan's hosts and triumphed over them in the cross.

(6) Jno. 12: 31—"Now is the judgment of this world: now shall the prince of this world be cast out."

SIXTH PROPOSITION: By Christ's death Satan, as the prince of this world, was cast out.

His dominion received its death blow at Calvary. The actual casting out thus secured may be in the future, but the death of Christ secured it and it is now assured. Potentially Satan is already cast out. He is an already conquered enemy: Luke 10: 18—"And he said unto them, I beheld Satan as lightning fall from heaven." He may bother us still, but he has got to go.

(8) Rom. 16: 20—"And the God of peace shall bruise Satan under your feet shortly."

SEVENTH PROPOSITION: The God of peace shall bruise Satan under our feet shortly.

The word translated "bruise" is a very strong word, meaning to "break" or "break in pieces."

(8) Rev. 20: 1-3, R.V.—"And I saw an angel coming down out of heaven, having the key of the abyss and a great chain in his hand. And he laid hold on the dragon, the old serpent, which is the Devil and Satan, and bound him for a thousand years, and cast him into the abyss, and shut it, and sealed it over him: that he should deceive the nations no more, until the thousand years should be finished: after this he must be loosed for a little time."

EIGHTH PROPOSITION: At the coming of Christ Satan shall be bound with a great chain and cast into the abyss for a thousand years.

(9) Rev. 20: 7, 8—"And when the thousand years are finished, Satan shall be loosed out of his prison, and shall come forth to deceive the nations which are in the four corners of the earth, Gog and Magog, to gather them together to the war: the number of whom is as the sand of the sea."

NINTH PROPOSITION: At the end of the thousand years Satan shall for a little season be loosed out of his prison and come forth to deceive the nations.

(10)   Rev. 20: 10, R.V.—"And the devil that deceived them was cast into the lake of fire and brimstone, where are also the beast and the false prophet; and they shall be tormented day and night for ever and ever."

TENTH PROPOSITION: Finally the Devil shall be cast into the lake of fire and brimstone, and shall be tormented day and night for ever and ever.

INDEX.